Lecture Notes in Computer Science 12180

More information about this series at http://www.springer.com/series/7408

Andreas Blass · Patrick Cégielski ·
Nachum Dershowitz · Manfred Droste ·
Bernd Finkbeiner (Eds.)

Fields of Logic and Computation III

Essays Dedicated to Yuri Gurevich
on the Occasion of His 80th Birthday

 Springer

Editors
Andreas Blass
Department of Mathematics
University of Michigan
Ann Arbor, MI, USA

Nachum Dershowitz
School of Computer Science
Tel Aviv University
Tel Aviv, Israel

Bernd Finkbeiner
Reactive Systems Group
Universität des Saarlandes
Saarbrücken, Germany

Patrick Cégielski
Université Paris Est Créteil
Fontainebleau, France

Manfred Droste
Fakultät für Mathematik und Informatik
Universität Leipzig
Leipzig, Germany

ISSN 0302-9743   ISSN 1611-3349 (electronic)
Lecture Notes in Computer Science
ISBN 978-3-030-48005-9   ISBN 978-3-030-48006-6 (eBook)
https://doi.org/10.1007/978-3-030-48006-6

LNCS Sublibrary: SL2 – Programming and Software Engineering

Cover illustration: The cover illustration is from a decorative platter for the Hebrew month in which Purim occurs, created by Maurice Ascalon's Pal-Bell Company in the 1940s.
The Hebrew legend is from the Talmud: "When Adar begins, one increases rejoicing." Image courtesy Village Gallery, Israel. Used with permission.

This Springer imprint is published by the registered company Springer Nature Switzerland AG
The registered company address is: Gewerbestrasse 11, 6330 Cham, Switzerland

Yuri Gurevich (b. 1940)

Dedicated to

Yuri Gurevich

*in honor of his 80th birthday
with deep admiration, gratitude and affection.*

היתה אורה ושמחה וששן ויקר
There was light and gladness and joy and honor
(Esther 8:16)

Wishing him many years filled with joy.

Preface

May 7, 2020, was Yuri Gurevich's 80th birthday. To celebrate this event and to honor Yuri and his work, a conference and a Festschrift were planned. The conference, Yurifest 2020, was to be combined with the 39th Journées sur les Arithmétiques Faibles also celebrating Yuri's 80th birthday and was to take place May 18–20 in Fontainebleau, France. Unfortunately, the coronavirus crisis forced postponement of Yurifest 2020. The Festschrift, on the other hand, was produced as planned; it is the present book.

This volume is a collection of articles contributed by some of Yuri's many friends; all articles were reviewed as usual. They address a very wide variety of topics, but by no means all of the fields of logic and computation in which Yuri has made important progress. Yuri's work stretches from highly theoretical (e.g., structure of abelian ordered groups) to very applied (e.g., file-transfer protocols) and from classical problems (e.g., decision problems for prefix-classes in first-order logic) to the newest frontiers (e.g., quantum computing).

Yuri retired from Microsoft Research in 2018. This was his second retirement; he retired from the University of Michigan in 2000 (after moving to Microsoft in 1998 and being on leave from Michigan for the next two years). Despite being doubly retired, Yuri remains very active scientifically; see his annotated bibliography at https://web.eecs.umich.edu/~gurevich/annotated.htm for details. He also remains very active physically, taking long (by other people's standards) walks near his homes in Michigan (during the summers) and Florida (during the winters). We wish him many more years of enjoyable activity, of both sorts.

We thank all those who wrote articles for this volume, all those who anonymously refereed the articles, all those who were scheduled to speak at the conference in Fontainebleau before the postponement, and all those who will speak at the rescheduled conference after the coronavirus crisis ends. We also thank Springer for enabling us to continue the *Fields of Logic and Computation* series (LNCS 6300 and 9300) in honor of Yuri with the present volume.

Spring 2020

Andreas Blass
Patrick Cégielski
Nachum Dershowitz
Manfred Droste
Bernd Finkbeiner

Contents

x   Contents

On Yuri Gurevich

To Yuri at 80 and More than 40 Years of Friendship

Johann A. Makowsky[✉]

Department of Computer Science, Technion-IIT, Haifa, Israel
janos@cs.technion.ac.il

Abstract. An after-dinner speech for Yuri Gurevich's 80th birthday.

Dear Yuri!

Our paths crossed several times, geographically and scientifically. We met first in 1976 in Jerusalem, we worked in parallel on the book *Model Theoretic Logics*, we explored together in many conversations, but without a single joint publication, the role of Logic (not only Computability) in the theoretical foundations of Computer Science, we founded together the *European Association of Computer Science Logic*. We shared our curiosity and encountered repeatedly, but not simultaneously, similar questions. We were not competing but occasionally inspiring each other, for over 44 years. There are others who shared your journey more than me. Andreas Blass, your most frequent coauthor, and Saharon Shelah, of course. However, we share the not always easy experience of geographic, cultural and scientific migration. We met when we were new to an Israel very different from today's. It was still during the *Cold War*, and we were coming from very different socio-cultural backgrounds. We shared the transition from mathematical logic to theoretical computer science while still being interested in foundational questions. The years 1976–1982 included both the Logic Year in 1980 in Jerusalem, and the recognition of *Logic in Computer Science* by the IEEE.

So let me sketch a few stations of our interlacing paths.

First Meeting

I first arrived in Israel in February 1976. I was a Lady Davis Fellow at the Hebrew University in Jerusalem, invited by Saharon Shelah. At the time I was a junior faculty at the Free University in West-Berlin. To save money I took a flight with TAROM, the Romanian Airline, from East-Berlin, via Bucharest, to Tel Aviv. Saharon personally met me at the airport. He greeted me warmly and helped finding a shared taxi. Finally we sat in a car with five oversized ultra-religious fellow Jews, squeezed between one of them and his big box for an extra hat, and the car moved in direction of Jerusalem. "Well", Saharon resumed our earlier conversation, "did you think about what I wrote to you in my letter?". It was my first visit to Israel. It was still daylight, and I asked Saharon to let me enjoy the view.

© Springer Nature Switzerland AG 2020
A. Blass et al. (Eds.): Gurevich Festschrift, LNCS 12180, pp. 3–6, 2020.
https://doi.org/10.1007/978-3-030-48006-6_1

Thirty minutes later it was dark. "Well", Saharon repeated his question. "It's dark already, can we talk mathematics, now?".......

A few days later I was introduced by Saharon to the participants of the Logic Seminar: Azriel Levy, Haim Gaifman, Menachem Magidor, Jonathan Stavi, Mati Rubin, Ami Litman, Shai Ben-David, and Yuri Gurevich. Yuri, you were curious about me, even inquisitive. You were a recent immigrant, not even two years in Israel, with a Soviet past and full of Zionist hopes. You must have heard about my political past and my infection with "Communism's Children Disease" (as Lenin called Leftism). I felt that you perceived me as a constant provocation.

For you Israel was full of unexpected provocations. You wanted to wear a hat to protect your baldness from the sun. Soon you learned that choosing a hat in Israel was always a political statement. Either it showed a religious affiliation with or without political undertones, or it was a statement of class struggle with or without secular or laicist undertones. Whatever hat you chose, people immediately ask questions.

From Nikolayev to Beer-Sheva

Yuri, you went a long way. Born on May 7, 1940 in Nikolayev, in Southern Ukraine, you left your hometown to study from 1962–1968 in Yekaterinburg (Sverdlovsk, Russia) at the Ural University, where you also worked as a programmer. From 1971 on you were a Professor and Chairman of the Computer Science Department at the Kuban University in Krasnodar (Russia). On your way to emigration to Israel you spent 1972–73 as a senior science fellow at the computing center of the Georgian Academy Sciences in Tbilisi (Georgia). Finally, you arrived in Israel in 1974 to become an Associate Professor of mathematics at the Ben-Gurion University in Beer-Sheva, Israel. Your early research was on decidability and undecidability questions for First Order and some fragments of Second Order Logic for algebraic systems, in particular Ordered Abelian Groups, and the Decision Problem of Predicate Calculus and some of its variations. Your early work in Israel continued some of these lines of research which naturally merged with some of the interests of Saharon Shelah.

From Budapest to Berlin

I was born on March 12, 1948 in Budapest (Hungary). Due to the political developments in 1948–1949, my parents divorced and my mother emigrated with me in June 1949 to Zurich, Switzerland. I studied at the Swiss Federal Institute of Technology in Zurich from 1967–1974. My early research was first in classical, and later in abstract Model theory. My first work with Saharon Shelah and Jonathan Stavi was an extension of my PhD-thesis. Saharon invited me to join him in Jerusalem to continue working with him and Jonathan Stavi. My visit in 1976 in Jerusalem had a lasting effect. In 1980 joined the Computer Science Department of the Technion - Israel Institute of Technology.

Logic in Computer Science

When we first met we both worked with Saharon Shelah. You were an established researcher in the *Algebra i Logika* tradition and I was a young model theorist with a past in stability theory and a future in abstract model theory. Our contributions in the book *Model Theoretic Logics* reflect this. You wrote the chapter on Monadic Second Order Logic, and I wrote three chapters, one of them the beginning of Saharon's theory of Abstract Elementary Classes (then called Abstract Embedding Relations). But we both developed an interest in theoretical computer science. Starting in 1978 I happened to discuss problems in relational databases with Catriel Beeri in Jerusalem. Quite a few topics of our discussions found their way into M. Vardi's PhD thesis. I, and independently A. Chandra and H. Lewis, proved the undecidability of the consequence problem for embedded database dependencies. You and M. Vardi refined this undecidability result.

In 1982 I was an invited speaker at the Logic Colloquium in Florence giving a lecture on *Model theoretic issues in theoretical computer science*, dealing with relational data bases and abstract data types. In the same year you visited me in Haifa to learn from me what my talk had been about. Some of our conversations influenced your paper on *Logic and the challenge of Computer Science*. Descriptive complexity theory was in the making. A. Chandra and D. Harel produced their landmark papers on computable queries in databases. Inspired by papers by R. Fagin, A. Selman and N. Jones, N. Immerman and M. Vardi characterized polynomial time and logarithmic space for ordered structures. Descriptive complexity theory would remain a recurrent topic in your career, and also in mine.

One of the topics we also discussed in 1982 was how to extend the work of A. Chandra and D. Harel to describe computable transformation of structures rather than just querying them. You developed from this your Abstract State Machines, a topic which would finally bring you to work at Microsoft. I worked with Y. Stavi, and later with E. Dahlhaus, on extending query languages to hierarchical databases. But my own work in this direction was slowed down by Y. Stavi's progressive withdrawal from publishing research, and by my struggle to find my way in computer science. I helped laying the logical foundations of the Entity-Relationship model in databases, I dabbled in logic programming, examined the meaning of normal forms in database, specification of abstract data types, and explored why Horn formulas matter in computer science. Yuri, we could have worked together much more.

Another Emigration

You left Israel shortly after our long conversations. There were various reasons for that. You found a new scientific home in Ann Arbor. You found new collaborators, E. Boerger, E. Graedel, and foremost, Andreas Blass. You continued to visit Jerusalem to work with Saharon. Your vast productivity encompassed many aspects of computer science. Let me quote from your own description of your research.

Your general direction is from pure mathematics to applications: to computer science, software engineering, privacy and security, quantum computing: You worked first on ordered Abelian groups and the classical decision problem. Your magnum opus is your book with E. Boerger and E. Graedel on this topic. You explored monadic second-order theories and games, in collaboration with S. Shelah and L. Harrington. You worked in finite model theory and database theory, and in average case complexity. This is where our mutual work interests met most. You kept questioning what is an algorithm, looking for evidence for the so called Church Turing thesis. And finally, you had a great impact on the foundations of software engineering with your abstract state machines, which even found applications to access control, other security issues, and privacy. In the last years at Microsoft you got interested in quantum computing, when you invited me to learn about my only paper in that field.

Happy Birthday

Dear Yuri!

We all wish you a happy birthday, with many years to come. May you be healthy and enjoy your family, your friends, and your unrelenting scientific curiosity.

Ad Mea VeEsrim.

Technical Papers

State of the Art in Logics for Verification of Resource-Bounded Multi-Agent Systems

Natasha Alechina[1](✉) and Brian Logan[2]

[1] Utrecht University, Utrecht, The Netherlands
`n.a.alechina@uu.nl`
[2] University of Nottingham, Nottingham, UK
`bsl@cs.nott.ac.uk`

Abstract. Approaches to the verification of multi-agent systems are typically based on games or transition systems defined in terms of states and actions. However such approaches often ignore a key aspect of multi-agent systems, namely that the agents' actions require (and sometimes produce) resources. We survey previous work on the verification of multi-agent systems that takes resources into account, extending substantially a survey from 2016 [9].

1 Introduction

A multi-agent system (MAS) is a system that is composed of multiple interacting agents. An agent is an *autonomous* entity that has the ability to collect information, reason about it, and perform actions in pursuit of its goals or on behalf of others. Examples of agents are controllers for satellites, non-driver transport systems such as UAVs, smart manufacturing cells, smart energy grids, and nodes in sensor networks.

Many distributed hardware and software systems can be naturally modelled as multi-agent systems. Such systems are often extremely complex, and the interaction between the components and their environment can lead to undesired behaviours that are difficult to predict in advance. With the increasing use of autonomous agents in safety critical systems, there is a growing need to *verify* that their behaviour conforms to the desired system specification, and over the last decade verification of multi-agent systems has become a thriving research area [35].

A key approach to the verification of MAS is *model checking*. Model checking involves checking whether a model of the system satisfies a temporal logic formula corresponding to some aspect of the system specification. In a model-checking approach to the verification of multi-agent systems, a MAS is represented by a finite state transition system.[1] A state transition system consists of a set of

---

[1] There is work on model-checking infinite state transition systems, see, for example, [18], but in this paper we concentrate on the finite case.

© Springer Nature Switzerland AG 2020
A. Blass et al. (Eds.): Gurevich Festschrift, LNCS 12180, pp. 9–29, 2020.
https://doi.org/10.1007/978-3-030-48006-6_2

states and transitions between them. Intuitively, each state of a MAS corresponds to a tuple of states of the agents and of the environment, and each transition corresponds to actions performed by the agents. Each state is labelled with atomic propositions that are true in that state. A standard assumption is that each state in the system has at least one outgoing transition (if a state is a deadlock state in the original MAS, we can model this by adding a transition to itself by some null action and labelling it with a 'deadlock' proposition). Properties of the system to be verified are expressed in an appropriate temporal logic L. The *model-checking problem for L* is, given a state transition system M (and possibly a state s) and an L formula ϕ, check whether ϕ is true in M (at state s, or on all paths from s, etc.). For example, Linear Time Temporal Logic (LTL) can express properties of infinite runs through the system using a unary operator 'in the next state' $\bigcirc$ ($\bigcirc\phi$ means that on this path, the next state satisfies ϕ) and a binary operator 'until' $\mathcal{U}$ ($\phi\mathcal{U}\psi$ means that on this path, ψ holds after finitely many steps, and before that, ϕ holds in every state). Using these operators, one can define operators such as $\Diamond$ (in some state on this path) and $\Box$ (in every state on this path) and specify properties of interest of the system, such as deadlock never happens ($\Box\neg d$) and every request is eventually answered ($\Box(r \rightarrow \Diamond a)$). In model checking MAS, such temporal logics are often extended with additional modalities capturing the knowledge of agents, or the strategic ability of groups of agents. Model checking has the advantage that it is a fully automated technique, which facilitates its use in the MAS development process.[2] A wide range of approaches to model-checking MAS have been proposed in the literature, ranging from the adaptation of standard model-checking tools, e.g., [20,21] to the development of special-purpose model checkers for multi-agent systems, e.g., [33,41].

In many multi-agent systems, agents are *resource-bounded*, in the sense that they require resources in order to act. Actions require time to complete and typically require additional resources depending on the application domain, for example energy or money. For many applications, the availability or otherwise of resources is critical to the properties to be verified: a multi-agent system may have very different behaviours depending on the resource endowment of the agents that comprise it. For example, an agent with insufficient energy may be unable to complete a task in the time assumed by a team plan if it has to recharge its battery before performing the task.

In this paper we survey state of the art in the emerging field of logics for verification of resource-bounded agents, and highlight a number of challenges that must be overcome to allow practical verification of resource-bounded MAS. We argue that recent work on the complexity of model-checking for logics of strategic ability with resources offers the possibility of significant progress in the field, new verification approaches and tools, and the ability to verify the properties of a large, important class of autonomous system that were previously out of reach.

---

[2] Another strand of work focusses on theorem proving, e.g., [44], but such approaches typically require user interaction to guide the search for a proof.

The remainder of the paper is organised as follows. In Sect. 2, we introduce some necessary background material on weighted games. Reachability in weighted games can be seen as a verification technique in its own right; however, it is included here as a source of technical results relevant for strategic resource logics. In this section, we also introduce the syntax and semantics of strategy logics (without resources) that are the underlying formalism for resource logics. In Sect. 3 we briefly survey recent work in resource logics and study two logics, RB ± ATL and RB ± ATL*, in greater detail. We conclude in Sect. 4 with a summary of results and open problems.

2   Background

In this section, we recall relevant definitions and results for energy games, vector addition systems with states, and the logics of strategic ability ATL and ATL*.

We first introduce some notational conventions. In what follows, we use the usual point-wise notation for vector comparison and addition. In particular, $(b_1, \ldots, b_n) \leq (d_1, \ldots, d_n)$ iff $b_i \leq d_i \ \forall i \in \{1, \ldots, n\}$, $(b_1, \ldots, b_n) = (d_1, \ldots, d_n)$ iff $b_i = d_i \ \forall i \in \{1, \ldots, n\}$, and $(b_1, \ldots, b_n) + (d_1, \ldots, d_n) = (b_1 + d_1, \ldots, b_n + d_n)$ and $(b_1, \ldots, b_n) - (d_1, \ldots, d_n) = (b_1 - d_1, \ldots, b_n - d_n)$. We define $(b_1, \ldots, b_n) < (d_1, \ldots, d_n)$ as $(b_1, \ldots, b_n) \leq (d_1, \ldots, d_n)$ and $(b_1, \ldots, b_n) \neq (d_1, \ldots, d_n)$. Given a function f returning a vector, we denote by f_i the function that returns the i-th component of the vector returned by f. We use bold letters to denote vectors.

Given a set S, the set of finite sequences of elements from S is denoted by S^+. For a sequence $\lambda = s_1 \ldots s_k \in S^+$, we use the notation $\lambda[i] = s_i$ for $i \leq k$, $\lambda[i, j] = s_i \ldots s_j \ \forall \ 1 \leq i \leq j \leq k$, and $|\lambda| = k$ for the length of λ.

2.1   Energy Games and Vector Addition Systems with States

Distributed systems that produce and consume resources have been modelled using a variety of approaches, including Petri nets, energy games and vector addition systems with states. In this section, we briefly recall some results from these areas relevant to resource logics and model checking resource-bounded MAS. We will first briefly introduce a version of *energy games* before introducing a variant of *alternating vector addition systems with states (AVASS)*. We focus on the reachability and non-termination problems for AVASS, as these are the most relevant for the results on resource logics in Sect. 3.

Energy Games. *Energy games* [28] are games between two players, played on *multi-weighted game graphs*.

Definition 1. *A multi-weighted game graph of dimension r is a tuple (S, r, R) where S is the set of vertices, $R \subseteq S \times \mathbb{Z}^r \times S$ is a finite set of edges labelled by a vector of integers of length r called a weight. Each vertex has at least one outgoing edge. The set of vertices is partitioned into two sets, Player 1 vertices S_1 and Player 2 vertices S_2.*

The dimension is the number of resource types, where resource types can be, e.g., energy, memory or some other kind of capacity, time, money, etc. The vertices can be thought of as states, and edges as transitions between states with associated costs and rewards for each resource type. The weight of an edge describes how the corresponding transition affects the resource amounts. Note that, in the graph, there are no resource vectors associated with the vertices, so that the structure can be finitely represented. However we can talk about *configurations* which are pairs $(s, \mathbf{v})$ where s is a vertex and $\mathbf{v}$ a vector of resources: intuitively, $\mathbf{v}$ is the resource amounts available in s in this configuration. A *path* is a finite sequence of configurations $(s_1, \mathbf{v}_1), \ldots, (s_n, \mathbf{v}_n)$, such that for each j with $1 \leq j \leq n$ there is an edge $(s_j, \mathbf{v}_{j+1} - \mathbf{v}_j, s_{j+1})$. A *play from vertex* s is an infinite sequence of configurations $\rho = (s, \mathbf{v}), \ldots$, such that every finite prefix is a path. A *strategy* for a player i is a function F_i taking as input a path $\rho \cdot (s, \mathbf{v})$ ending in Player i vertex s and returning an edge $F_i(\rho \cdot (s, \mathbf{v}))$ of the form $(s, \mathbf{u}, s')$ from E. A play $\rho = (s_1, \mathbf{v}_1), \ldots, (s_j, \mathbf{v}_j) \ldots$ is *consistent* with a strategy F_p for Player p if whenever s_j is in S_p, then $F_p(\rho[1, j]) = (s_j, \mathbf{v}_{j+1} - \mathbf{v}_j, s_{j+1})$.

Definition 2. *Given a multi-weighted graph* (S, r, R), *an initial vertex* s, *and a vector* $\mathbf{b} \in \mathbb{N}^r$, *a play* ρ *from* s *is* winning *for Player 1 in the energy game on* (S, r, R) *with initial credit* $\mathbf{b}$ *if for all configurations* $\rho[j] = (s_j, \mathbf{v}_j)$, $\mathbf{v}_j \geq \mathbf{0}$. *Otherwise, Player 2 wins the play. Player 1 wins the energy game on* (S, r, R) *from* s *with initial credit* $\mathbf{b}$ *if there exists a winning strategy* F_1 *for Player 1, that is, a strategy such that for all strategies* F_2 *of Player 2, the play consistent with both strategies is winning for Player 1.*

Intuitively, starting in state s with initial credit (resource allocation) $\mathbf{b}$, Player 1 can play forever without any resource amount dropping below 0. Clearly, the higher the initial credit, the better for Player 1; if Player 1 has a winning strategy for $(s, \mathbf{b})$, and $\mathbf{b} \leq \mathbf{b}'$, then Player 1 has a winning strategy from $(s, \mathbf{b}')$.

Definition 3. *The following problem is the existence of a winning strategy for Player 1 with known initial credit.*

Input: *A multi-weighted graph* (S, R, r), *an initial state* $s \in S$ *and an initial credit* $\mathbf{b}$.

Question: *Does Player 1 have a winning strategy in the corresponding energy game?*

An *energy game with unknown initial credit* starting in s is won by Player 1 iff for *some* initial credit, Player 1 has a winning strategy.

Definition 4. *The following problem is the existence of a winning strategy for Player 1 with unknown initial credit.*

Input: *A multi-weighted graph* (S, R, r) *and an initial state* $s \in S$.

Question: *Does Player 1 have a winning strategy in the corresponding energy game for some initial credit* $\mathbf{b}$?

Both problems (existence of a winning strategy for known and unknown initial credit) were first shown to be decidable in [22]. In [37] both problems were shown to be decidable in 2EXPTIME (polynomial in the size of the graph, double exponential in the dimension r). In [37] it was also shown that the set of all Pareto optimal (non-dominated) initial credits for which Player 1 has a winning strategy is computable in time doubly exponential in the dimension and pseudo-polynomial in the number of states and edges.

There are many versions of energy games: with only unit costs, with only one resource type, with imperfect information. A version with finite strategies was studied in [28] and shown to be decidable and in coNP.

Alternating Vector Addition Systems with State. An *alternating vector addition system with state* (AVASS) can be used as a setting for various two player games. There are many different versions of AVASS and decision problems for them. The game semantics for AVASS presented below was introduced in [38].

Definition 5. *An* alternating vector addition system with states *(AVASS) is a tuple* $A = (S, r, R_1, R_2)$, *where* S *is a finite set of states,* r *is the dimension (number of resource types),* $R_1 \subseteq S \times \mathbb{Z}^r \times S$ *and* $R_2 \subseteq S^3$.

Intuitively, R_1 edges correspond to Player 1 moves, and R_2 triples (s, s_1, s_2) correspond to Player 2 choices of where to move from the state s, to s_1 or to s_2. Note that unlike in energy games, the setting is *asymmetric* in that only Player 1 moves change resource amounts. A path of configurations is defined the same way as for energy games: in a configuration $(s, \mathbf{b})$, if the next move is $(s, \mathbf{v}, s') \in R_1$, then the next configuration is $(s', \mathbf{b} + \mathbf{v})$; if the next move is $(s, s_1, s_2) \in R_2$, then, depending on the choice made by Player 2, the next configuration is either $(s_1, \mathbf{b})$ or $(s_2, \mathbf{b})$.

The following problem is essentially the same as the existence of a winning strategy for Player 1 in an energy game with known initial credit:

Definition 6. *The following problem is the* known initial credit *non-termination problem for AVASS:*

Input: *An AVASS* $A = (S, r, R_1, R_2)$, *an initial state* $s \in S$ *and an initial credit* **b**.

Question: *Does Player 1 have a strategy such that every play consistent with this strategy is infinite and all resource amounts in configurations on the path are non-negative?*

This problem was shown to be decidable and in $(r - 1)$-EXPTIME in [22], 2EXPTIME hard in [30], and in 2EXPTIME in [37]. The unknown initial credit version of the problem is also 2EXPTIME-complete [37]. The set of all Pareto optimal initial credits for which Player 1 has a winning strategy can be computed in 2EXPTIME [37].

Another problem which has been studied in the AVASS literature is state reachability. The state reachability problem is whether Player 1 has a strategy to reach a particular state while ensuring resource amounts remain non-negative (as opposed to reachability of a particular configuration $(s', \mathbf{v})$, which is undecidable, [40]). The state reachability problem for energy games is undecidable [2].

Definition 7. *The following problem is the known initial credit state reachability problem for AVASS:*

Input: *An AVASS $A = (S, r, R_1, R_2)$, an initial state $s \in S$, an initial credit $\mathbf{b}$ and state $s' \in S$.*

Question: *Does Player 1 have a strategy such that every path generated by this strategy eventually reaches a configuration where the state is s', and until that configuration, all resource amounts on the path are non-negative?*

This problem was shown to be decidable in [43], and to be 2EXPTIME-complete in [30]. In the same paper, the state reachability problem with unknown initial credit was also shown to be 2EXPTIME-complete. The set of all Pareto optimal initial credits for which Player 1 has a winning strategy can be computed in 2EXPTIME [37].

Parity Games on AVASS. Another kind of games on AVASS is *parity games*. Let $A = (S, r, R_1, R_2)$ be an AVASS. A colouring *col* is defined as a map $S \rightarrow \{0, \dots, k\}$ for some $k \geq 1$.

Definition 8. *The* parity game problem for AVASS *is as follows:*

Input: *An AVASS A, an initial state $s \in A$, an initial credit $\mathbf{b} \in \mathbb{N}^r$ and a colouring $col : S \rightarrow \{0, \dots, k\}$*

Question: *Does Player 1 have a strategy in $(s, \mathbf{b})$ such that every play consistent with this strategy is infinite, resource amounts in configurations on the path are non-negative, and on every play the maximal colour that appears infinitely often is even?*

The parity game problem for alternating VASS is decidable. This was shown in [5] to be a consequence of Corollary 2 in [1] which states the decidability of parity games for single-sided VASS. A single-sided VASS is an AVASS where the set of states is partitioned into S_1 and S_2, R_1 transitions start from states in S_1, R_2 transitions start from states in S_2, and there is at most one R_2 transition from each S_2 state.

2.2 Strategy Logics

In this section, we briefly recall some key results for the strategy logics Alternating Time Temporal Logic (ATL) [16] and the more expressive ATL* that are the underlying formalisms for many of the resource logics discussed in Sect. 3.

Alternating Time Temporal Logic. ATL generalises other temporal logics such as Computation Tree Logic (CTL) [29] (which can be seen as a one-agent ATL) by introducing a notion of strategic ability. ATL allows us to express properties relating to the strategic abilities of a coalition or set of agents regardless of what the other agents in the system do.

ATL is interpreted over concurrent game structures. A concurrent game structure is a transition system in which edges correspond to a tuple of actions performed simultaneously by all the agents (see below and Fig. 1 for an example).

Definition 9. *A concurrent game structure (CGS) is a tuple* $M = (Agt, S, \Pi, \pi, Act, d, \delta)$ *where:*

- *Agt is a non-empty finite set of n agents,*
- *S is a non-empty finite set of states;*
- *Π is a finite set of propositional variables and $\pi : \Pi \to \wp(S)$ is a truth assignment which associates each proposition in Π with a subset of states where it is true;*
- *Act is a non-empty set of actions*
- *$d : S \times Agt \to \wp(Act) \setminus \{\emptyset\}$ is a function which assigns to each $s \in S$ a non-empty set of actions available to each agent $a \in Agt$. We denote joint actions by all agents in Agt available at s by $D(s) = d(s, a_1) \times \cdots \times d(s, a_n)$;*
- *$\delta : S \times Act^{|Agt|} \to S$ is a partial function that maps every $s \in S$ and joint action $\sigma \in D(s)$ to a state resulting from executing σ in s.*

Given a CGS M and a state $s \in S$, a *joint action by a coalition* $A \subseteq Agt$ is a tuple $\sigma = (\sigma_a)_{a \in A}$ (where σ_a is the action that agent a executes as part of σ, the ath component of σ) such that $\sigma_a \in d(s, a)$. The set of all joint actions for A at state s is denoted by $D_A(s)$.

Given a joint action by Agt $\sigma \in D(s)$, σ_A (a projection of σ on A) denotes the joint action executed by A as part of σ: $\sigma_A = (\sigma_a)_{a \in A}$. The set of all possible outcomes of a joint action $\sigma \in D_A(s)$ at state s is:

$$out(s, \sigma) = \{s' \in S \mid \exists \sigma' \in D(s) : \sigma = \sigma'_A \land s' = \delta(s, \sigma')\}$$

Depending on the variant of ATL, a strategy is a choice of actions which either only depends on the current state (memoryless strategy) or on the finite history of the current state (perfect recall strategy). In this survey, we concentrate mainly on perfect recall strategies. A *strategy for a coalition* $A \subseteq Agt$ in a CGS M is a mapping $F_A : S^+ \to Act^{|A|}$ such that, for every $\lambda \in S^+$, $F_A(\lambda) \in D_A(\lambda[|\lambda|])$. A computation (infinite path) λ is consistent with a strategy F_A iff, for all i, $\lambda[i+1] \in out(\lambda[i], F_A(\lambda[1, i]))$. We denote by $out(s, F_A)$ the set of all computations λ starting from s that are consistent with F_A.

The language of ATL contains atomic propositions, boolean connectives $\neg, \land$, etc. and modalities $\langle\!\langle A \rangle\!\rangle \bigcirc$, $\langle\!\langle A \rangle\!\rangle \square$ and $\langle\!\langle A \rangle\!\rangle \mathcal{U}$ for each subset A of the set of all agents Agt (or coalition, in ATL terms), which express the strategic ability of the coalition A. $\langle\!\langle A \rangle\!\rangle \bigcirc \phi$ means that the coalition of agents A has a choice of actions such that, regardless of what the other agents in the system do, ϕ will hold in the next state. $\langle\langle A\rangle\rangle\Box\phi$ means that coalition A has a strategy to keep ϕ true forever, regardless of what the other agents do. Finally, $\langle\langle A\rangle\rangle\phi\,\mathcal{U}\,\psi$ means that A has a strategy to ensure that after finitely many steps ψ holds, and in all the states before that, ϕ holds.

Given a CGS M and a state s of M, the truth of an ATL formula ϕ with respect to M and s is defined inductively on the structure of ϕ as follows:

- $M, s \models p$ iff $s \in \pi(p)$;
- $M, s \models \neg\phi$ iff $M, s \not\models \phi$;
- $M, s \models \phi \vee \psi$ iff $M, s \models \phi$ or $M, s \models \psi$;
- $M, s \models \langle\langle A\rangle\rangle\bigcirc\phi$ iff $\exists$ strategy F_A such that for all $\lambda \in out(s, F_A)$, $M, \lambda[2] \models \phi$;
- $M, s \models \langle\langle A\rangle\rangle\phi\,\mathcal{U}\,\psi$ iff $\exists$ strategy F_A such that for all $\lambda \in out(s, F_A)$, $\exists i$ such that $M, \lambda[i] \models \psi$ and $M, \lambda[j] \models \phi$ for all $j \in \{1, \ldots, i-1\}$;
- $M, s \models \langle\langle A\rangle\rangle\Box\phi$ iff $\exists$ strategy F_A such that for all $\lambda \in out(s, F_A)$, for all i, $M, \lambda[i] \models \phi$.

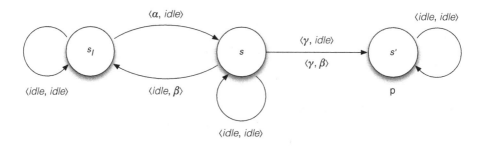

Fig. 1. Example of a state transition system.

Example. Figure 1 illustrates a simple ATL model of a system with two agents, 1 and 2, and actions α, β, γ and *idle*. Action tuples on the edges show the actions of each agent, for example, in the transition from state s_I to s, agent 1 performs action α and agent 2 performs *idle*. In this system, in state s_I, agent 1 has a (memoryless) strategy to enforce that p holds eventually in the future no matter what agent 2 does, which can be expressed in ATL as $\langle\langle\{1\}\rangle\rangle\top\,\mathcal{U}\,p$. Similarly, in s_I agent 1 has a memoryless strategy to keep $\neg p$ true forever, so $\langle\langle\{1\}\rangle\rangle\Box\neg p$ holds in s_I.

Definition 10. *The following problem is the model checking problem for ATL:*

Input: *A CGS M, a formula ϕ of ATL, and a state $s \in M$.*
Question: *Does it hold that $M, s \models \phi$?*

The model-checking problem for ATL can be solved in time polynomial in the size of the transition system and the property [16], and there exist model-checking tools for ATL, for example, MOCHA [17] and MCMAS [41].

ATL*. ATL* is strictly more expressive than ATL in allowing arbitrary combinations of temporal modalities and booleans after the coalition modalities. The syntax of ATL* includes two kinds of formulas, state formulas ϕ and path formulas γ. Formulas of ATL* are defined by the following syntax:

$$\phi ::= p \mid \neg\phi \mid \phi \vee \phi \mid \langle\langle A \rangle\rangle \gamma$$

$$\gamma ::= \phi \mid \neg\gamma \mid \gamma \vee \gamma \mid \bigcirc\gamma \mid \gamma\,\mathcal{U}\,\gamma \mid \square\gamma$$

where $p \in \Pi$ is a proposition and $A \subseteq Agt$.

The language of ATL* is interpreted on the same CGS as ATL. However, there are two satisfaction relations, $\models_s$ for state formulas, and $\models_p$ for path formulas:

- $M, s \models_s p$ iff $s \in \pi(p)$;
- $M, s \models_s \neg\phi$ iff $M, s \not\models_s \phi$;
- $M, s \models_s \phi \vee \psi$ iff $M, s \models_s \phi$ or $M, s \models_s \psi$;
- $M, s \models_s \langle\langle A^b \rangle\rangle \gamma$ iff exists a strategy F_A such that for all $\lambda \in out(s, F_A)$, $M, \lambda \models_p \gamma$; $M, \lambda \models_p \phi$ iff $M, \lambda[1] \models_s \phi$ (for state formulas ϕ)
- $M, \lambda \models_p \bigcirc\gamma$ iff $M, \lambda[2, \infty) \models_p \gamma$
- $M, \lambda \models_p \gamma_1\mathcal{U}\gamma_2$ iff $\exists k$ such that $M, \lambda[k, \infty) \models \gamma_2$ and $M, \lambda[j, \infty) \models \gamma_1$ for all $j \in \{1, \ldots, k-1\}$.
- $M, \lambda \models_p \square\gamma$ iff for all $jM, \lambda[j, \infty) \models_p \gamma$.

Definition 11. *The following problem is the model checking problem for ATL*:*

Input: *A CGS M, a state formula ϕ of ATL*, and a state s in M.*
Question: *Does it hold that $M, s \models_s \phi$?*

The complexity of the model checking problem for ATL* is 2EXPTIME-complete [16].

3   Resource Logics

In order to model multi-agent systems where the actions of agents produce and consume resources, it is necessary to modify strategy logics in two ways. The first modification is to add resource annotations to the actions in the transition system: for each individual action and each resource type, we need to specify how many units of this resource type the action produces or consumes. For example, suppose that there are two resource types, r_1 and r_2 (e.g., energy and money). Then we can specify that action α in Fig. 1 produces two units of r_1 and consumes one unit of r_2, action β consumes one unit of r_1 and produces one unit of r_2, action γ consumes five units of r_1, and action *idle* does not produce or consume any resources. Clearly, this makes the transition system of a CGS resemble multi-weighted graphs or AVASS introduced in Sect. 2.1.

The second modification is to extend the logical language so that we can express properties related to resources. For example, we may want to express a property that a group of agents A can eventually reach a state satisfying ϕ or can maintain the truth of ψ forever, provided that they have available n_1 units of resource type r_1 and n_2 units of resource type r_2. Such statements about coalitional ability under resource bounds can be expressed in an extension of ATL where coalitional modalities are annotated with a resource bound on the strategies available to the coalition. We call logics where every action is associated the resources it produces and/or consumes and where the syntax allows the resource requirements of agents to be expressed, *resource logics*.

To illustrate the properties resource logics allow us to express, consider the model in Fig. 1 with the production and consumption of resources by actions specified above. In this setting, we can verify if agent 1 can eventually enforce p provided that it has one unit of r_2 in state s_I, or whether the coalition of agents $\{1, 2\}$ can achieve p under this resource bound by working together. There are surprisingly many different ways of measuring costs of strategies and deciding which actions are executable by the agents given the resources available to them, but under at least one possible semantics, the answer to the first question is no and to the second one yes, but the latter requires a perfect recall strategy (the two agents should loop between states s_I and s until they produce a sufficient amount of resource r_1, and then execute actions corresponding to the $\langle \gamma, idle \rangle$ transition from s to s').

Clearly, the model-checking problem for temporal logics is a special case of the model-checking problem for the corresponding resource logics. The question is, how much harder does the model-checking problem become when resources are added?

3.1   Overview of Resource Logics

In this section, we briefly review the historical development of resource logics, and introduce some resource logics in more detail. We focus on expressiveness and model-checking complexity, as these features determine the suitability of a particular logic for practical verification.

Consumption of Resources. Early work on resource logics considered only consumption of resources (i.e., no action produces resources), and initial results were encouraging.

One of the first logics capable of expressing resource requirements of agents was a version of Coalition Logic (CL),[3] called Resource-Bounded Coalition Logic (RBCL), where actions only consume (and don't produce) resources. RBCL was introduced in [3] with the primary motivation of modelling systems of resource-bounded reasoners (with three resource types: time, space, and communication

---

[3] CL is a fragment of ATL with only the next time $\langle\langle A \rangle\rangle \bigcirc$ modality.

cost), however the framework is sufficiently general to model any kind of action. The model-checking problem for this logic was shown to be decidable in [11] in polynomial time in the transition system and the property, and exponential in the number of resource types.

A resource-bounded version of ATL, RB-ATL, where again actions only consume (and not produce) resources was introduced in [4]. It was also shown that the model-checking problem for this logic is decidable in time polynomial in the size of the transition system and exponential in the number of resource types. (For a single resource type, e.g., energy, the model-checking problem is no harder than for ATL.) Its syntax is the same as $RB \pm ATL$ given in Sect. 3.2 below, but in the semantics no actions produce resources. Probabilistic RB-ATL was introduced in [42] and its model checking problem shown to be decidable in EXPTIME.

Practical work on model-checking standard computer science transition systems (not multi-agent systems) with resources also falls in the category of consumption-only systems, for example the probabilistic model-checking of systems with numerical resources in the PRISM model-checker [39] assumes costs monotonically increasing with time.

Bounded Production and Undecidability in the Unbounded Setting. However, when resource production is considered in addition to consumption, the situation changes. In a separate strand of work, a range of different formalisms for reasoning about resources was introduced in [23, 25]. In those formalisms, both consumption and production of resources was considered. In [24] it was shown that the problem of halting on empty input for two-counter automata [36] can be reduced to the model-checking problem for several of their resource logics. Since the halting problem for two-counter automata is undecidable, the model-checking problem for a variety of resource logic with production of resources is undecidable. The reduction uses two resource types (to represent the values of the two counters) and either one or two agents depending on the version of the logic (whether the agents have perfect recall, whether the formula talking about coalition A can also specify resource availability for remaining agents, and whether nested operators 'remember' initial allocation of resources or can be evaluated independently of such initial allocation).

The only decidable cases considered in [23] are an extension of CTL with resources (essentially one-agent ATL) and a version where on every path only a fixed finite amount of resources can be produced. In [23], the models satisfying this property are called bounded, and the authors note that RBCL and RB-ATL are logics over a special kind of bounded models (where no resources are produced at all). Other decidability results for bounded resource logics have also been reported in the literature. For example, [31] define a decidable logic, PRB-ATL (Priced Resource-Bounded ATL), where the total amount of resources in the system has a fixed bound. The model-checking algorithm for PRB-ATL requires time polynomial in the size of the model and exponential in the number of resource types and the resource bound on the system. In [32] an EXPTIME lower bound in the number of resource types for the PRB-ATL model-checking problem is shown.

A general logic over systems with numerical constraints called QATL* was introduced in [26]. In that paper, more undecidability results for the model-checking problem of QATL* and its fragments were shown. For example, QATL (Quantitative ATL) is undecidable even if no nestings of coalition modalities is allowed. The main proposals for restoring decidability to the model-checking problem for QATL in [26] are removing negative payoffs (similar to removing resource production) and also introducing memoryless strategies. Shared resources were considered in [27]; most of the cases considered there have undecidable model-checking (apart from the case of a single shared resource, which has decidable model-checking).

In summary, one approach to decidable model checking in the presence of resource production is to bound the amount of resources produced globally in the model. For some systems of resource-bounded agents, this is a reasonable restriction. For example, agents that need energy to function and are able to charge their battery, can never 'produce' more energy than the capacity of their battery. This is a typical bounded system. A special case of bounded systems, where model checking is even more tractable, are systems where one of the resources is always consumed by any action. A typical example of such a resource is time. Several resource logics with *diminishing resource* were investigated in [10] and shown to have a PSPACE or EXPSPACE model checking procedure (while the corresponding logic without diminishing resource sometimes has undecidable model checking).

In the next couple of sections, we report results for resource logics with unbounded production of resources and a decidable model checking problem.

3.2   RB ± ATL

In [12] a version of ATL, RB ± ATL, was introduced where actions both produce and consume resources. The models of the logic do not impose bounds on the overall production of resources, and the agents have perfect recall. The syntax of RB ± ATL is very similar to that of ATL, but coalition modalities have superscripts which represent resource allocation to agents. Instead of stating the existence of *some* strategy, they state the existence of a strategy such that every computation generated by following this strategy consumes at most the given amount of resources. Coming back to the example, the property that agent 1 can eventually enforce p provided that it has one unit of r_2 can be expressed as $\langle\!\langle \{1\}^{(0,1)} \rangle\!\rangle \top \mathcal{U} p$. Here, $(0, 1)$ is the allocation of 0 units of r_1 and 1 unit of r_2 to coalition $\{1\}$. In RB ± ATL, resource allocation is only shown for the proponent agents, $\{1\}$ in this case. Versions of resource logic where opponents are also resource-bounded all have an undecidable model-checking problem, see [23]. It is also possible to consider individual allocations of resources to agents in the proponent coalition, which would affect complexity results below for one resource type.

Formally, the syntax of RB ± ATL is defined relative to the following sets: $Agt = \{a_1, \ldots, a_n\}$ is a set of n agents, $Res = \{res_1, \ldots, res_r\}$ is a set of

r resource types, Π is a set of propositions, and $\mathcal{B} = \mathbb{N}^r$ is a set of resource bounds. Formulas of RB $\pm$ ATL are defined by the following syntax:

$$\phi, \psi ::= p \mid \neg\phi \mid \phi \vee \psi \mid \langle\!\langle A^b \rangle\!\rangle \bigcirc \phi \mid \langle\!\langle A^b \rangle\!\rangle \phi \,\mathcal{U}\, \psi \mid \langle\!\langle A^b \rangle\!\rangle \square \phi$$

where $p \in \Pi$ is a proposition, $A \subseteq Agt$, and $b \in \mathcal{B}$ is a resource bound. Here, $\langle\!\langle A^b \rangle\!\rangle \bigcirc \phi$ means that a coalition A can ensure that the next state satisfies ϕ under resource bound b. $\langle\!\langle A^b \rangle\!\rangle \phi \,\mathcal{U}\, \psi$ means that A has a strategy to enforce ψ while maintaining the truth of ϕ, and the cost of this strategy is at most b. Finally, $\langle\!\langle A^b \rangle\!\rangle \square \phi$ means that A has a strategy to maintain ψ forever, and the cost of this strategy is at most b.

The language is interpreted on resource-bounded concurrent game structures.

Definition 12. *A resource-bounded concurrent game structure (RB-CGS) is a tuple* $M = (Agt, Res, S, \Pi, \pi, Act, d, c, \delta)$ *where:*

- *$Agt, S, \Pi, \pi, Act, d, \delta$ are as in Definition 9;*
- *Res is a non-empty finite set of r resource types,*
- *$c : S \times Act \to \mathbb{Z}^r$ is a partial function which maps a state s and an action σ to a vector of integers, where the integer in position i indicates consumption or production of resource r_i by the action (here, we assume negative value for consumption and positive value for production for consistency with AVASS, unlike in [12]).*

A strategy for a set of agents A is a function $F_A : S^+ \to Act^A$ such that $F_A(\lambda) \in D_A([\lambda[|\lambda|]])$. Given a bound $b \in \mathcal{B}$, a computation $\lambda \in out(s, F_A)$ is *b-consistent* iff for every i,

$$b + \Sigma^i c(F_A(\lambda[1, i])) \geq 0$$

In other words, if agents start with allocation b, the amount of resources any of the agents have on the computation is never negative for any resource type.

A strategy F_A is *b-consistent* in s, if all computations in $out(s, F_A)$ are b-consistent.

Given a RB-CGS M and a state s of M, the truth of an RB $\pm$ ATL formula ϕ with respect to M and s is defined inductively on the structure of ϕ as follows:

- $M, s \models p$ iff $s \in \pi(p)$;
- $M, s \models \neg\phi$ iff $M, s \not\models \phi$;
- $M, s \models \phi \vee \psi$ iff $M, s \models \phi$ or $M, s \models \psi$;
- $M, s \models \langle\!\langle A^b \rangle\!\rangle \bigcirc \phi$ iff $\exists\, b$-consistent strategy F_A such that for all $\lambda \in out(s, F_A)$, $M, \lambda[2] \models \phi$;
- $M, s \models \langle\!\langle A^b \rangle\!\rangle \phi \,\mathcal{U}\, \psi$ iff $\exists\, b$-consistent strategy F_A such that for all $\lambda \in out(s, F_A)$, $\exists i$ such that $M, \lambda[i] \models \psi$ and $M, \lambda[j] \models \phi$ for all $j \in \{1, \ldots, i-1\}$.
- $M, s \models \langle\!\langle A^b \rangle\!\rangle \square \phi$ iff $\exists\, b$-conststent strategy F_A such that for all $\lambda \in out(s, F_A)$, for all $i, M, \lambda[i] \models \phi$.

Definition 13. *The following problem is the model checking problem for RB $\pm$ ATL:*

Input: *A RB-CGS M, a formula ϕ of $RB \pm ATL$, and a state $s \in M$.*
Question: *Does it hold that $M, s \models \phi$?*

The model-checking problem for $RB \pm ATL$ is decidable. The existence of a decidable resource logic with unbounded production was surprising, as it was the first indication that it is possible to automatically verify properties of this important class of resource-bounded multi-agent systems. In [12], decidability of the model-checking problem was shown by producing a direct model checking algorithm and arguing that it terminates due to the fact that in any sequence of elements from $\mathbb{N}^r$, eventually two elements are comparable in $\leq$ (well-quasi ordering of $\mathbb{N}^r$).

3.3 Correspondence Between Games on AVASS and RB $\pm$ ATL Semantics

There are clear similarities between $RB \pm ATL$ semantics and decidable problems for AVASS and energy games. In [5] these similarities were made precise, and the model checking problem for $RB \pm ATL$ was shown to be polynomial in the size of the model and the formula, and double exponential in the number of resource types, by reducing the model checking to decision problems on AVASS. We will briefly recapitulate the correspondence here.

For the purposes of making the correspondence easier to state, the definitions of AVASS and the state reachability problem were generalised as follows, without affecting the complexity of decision problems ([5], Lemma 7):

- instead of $R_2 \subseteq S^3$, elements in R_2 can be tuples of any length $n \geq 2$ (but R_2 is finite);
- the input to the reachability problem is a set of goal states $S' \subseteq S$ (instead of a singleton set $\{s'\}$).

This generalisation of AVASS makes it easier to transfer complexity results from AVASS to resource logics, since the transition systems that form the models of resource logics may have more than binary branching, and reachability refers to properties (sets of states) rather singleton states. Here, we will refer to this generalisation as *generalised AVASS*.

Next we briefly elaborate on the concrete reduction of $RB \pm ATL$ model-checking problem to decision problems on generalised AVASS. Assume that we are designing a state labelling model checking algorithm for $RB \pm ATL$, where given a formula ϕ and a model, we label each state with subformulas of ϕ true in that state, in the increasing order of complexity of subformulas. Clearly, there is no problem with doing this for propositional variables and for boolean combinations of earlier encountered formulas, and in fact also for the next state operators. The only difficulty is formulas of the form $\langle\!\langle A^b \rangle\!\rangle \psi_1 \, \mathcal{U} \, \psi_2$ or $\langle\!\langle A^b \rangle\!\rangle \Box \psi$. Intuitively, we need to build a different AVASS for every state in the model and every subformula of this form, and then solve a reachability or non-termination problem for them. We describe next how we build this generalised AVASS.

Given an RB-CGS $M = (Agt, Res, S, \Pi, \pi, Act, d, c, \delta)$, a distinguished state s^* (where we want to evaluate the formula) and a coalition $A \subseteq Agt$ (from the main coalition modality in the formula), the corresponding generalised AVASS $G = (S^G, r^G, R_1^G, R_2^G)$ is constructed as follows. The set of states of G is defined as follows:

$$S^G = \{s^*\} \cup \{(s', \alpha) \mid s' \in S, \alpha \in D_A(s')\} \cup \{(\sigma, s'') \mid s'' \in S, \sigma \in D(s'')\}.$$

Obviously, $r^G = Res$. Transitions are defined as follows:

$$R_1^G = \{(s^*, cost(s^*, \alpha), (s^*, \alpha)) \mid \alpha \in D_A(s^*)\} \cup \{((\sigma, s'), cost_A(s', \sigma),$$
$$(s', \alpha)) \mid (\sigma, s') \in S^G, \alpha \in D_A(s')\}$$
$$R_2^G = \{((s', \alpha), (\sigma^1, s^1), \ldots, (\sigma^k, s^k)) \mid \sigma^i \in D(s'), \alpha = \sigma_A^i, s^i = \delta(s', \sigma^i)\}$$

Note that the size of G is polynomial in M. When evaluating a subformula of the form $\langle\!\langle A^b \rangle\!\rangle \square \psi$, the strategy witnessing the truth of the formula has to visit only states satisfying ψ. Since the complexity of ψ is less than the complexity of $\langle\!\langle A^b \rangle\!\rangle \square \psi$, we can assume that we know which states in M satisfy ψ. To compute the generalised AVASS where a winning strategy for non-termination exists iff $\langle\!\langle A^b \rangle\!\rangle \square \psi$ is true, we remove from S^G all states where the state component of the pair does not satisfy ψ. We denote the resulting generalised AVASS G_ψ. Similarly, to make sure that a strategy to reach a ψ_2 state always goes only through ψ_1 states before reaching ψ_2, we remove from G all states that satisfy neither ψ_1 nor ψ_2. We denote the resulting generalised AVASS G_{ψ_1, ψ_2}.

In [5], Lemmas 2–6 and Theorem 1 demonstrate that $M, s^* \models \langle\!\langle A^b \rangle\!\rangle \psi_1 \, \mathcal{U} \, \psi_2$ if, and only if, there is a winning strategy for Player 1 in a reachability game in the corresponding generalised AVASS G_{ψ_1, ψ_2} with initial credit b and target the set of ψ_2 states, and $M, s^* \models \langle\!\langle A^b \rangle\!\rangle \square \psi$ if, and only if, there is a winning strategy for Player 1 in a non-termination game in the corresponding generalised AVASS G_ψ with initial credit b.

3.4   RB ± ATL*

RB ± ATL* is a more expressive logic than RB ± ATL, and was introduced in [5].

As is the case with ATL*, the syntax of RB ± ATL* includes state formulas ϕ and path formulas γ. Formulas of RB ± ATL* are defined by the following syntax

$$\phi ::= p \mid \neg\phi \mid \phi \vee \phi \mid \langle\!\langle A^b \rangle\!\rangle \gamma$$

$$\gamma ::= \phi \mid \neg\gamma \mid \gamma \vee \gamma \mid \bigcirc\gamma \mid \gamma \, \mathcal{U} \, \gamma \mid \square\gamma \mid$$

where $p \in \Pi$ is a proposition, $A \subseteq Agt$, and $b \in \mathcal{B}$ is a resource bound.

The language of RB ± ATL* is interpreted on the same RB-CGS as RB ± ATL. The truth definition is identical to that of ATL*, apart from the following clause:

- $M, s \models_s \langle\!\langle A^b \rangle\!\rangle \gamma$ iff $\exists \, b$-consistent strategy F_A such that for all $\lambda \in out(s, F_A)$, $M, \lambda \models_p \gamma$;

Definition 14. *The following problem is the model checking problem for* $RB \pm ATL^*$:

Input: *A RB-CGS M, a state formula* ϕ *of* $RB \pm ATL^*$, *and a state* $s \in M$.
Question: *Does it hold that* $M, s \models_s \phi$?

Surprisingly, even without idle actions, which seem to make the difference between decidable and undecidable model-checking for some resource logics (see Sect. 3.2), the model checking problem for $RB \pm ATL^*$ is decidable [5] by reduction to parity games on single sided VASS [1]. Moreover, it is decidable in 2EXP-TIME, that is, has the same complexity as $RB \pm ATL$.

In [19], several fragments of $RB \pm ATL$ and $RB \pm ATL^*$ of the form $RB \pm ATL$ (n, r) and $RB \pm ATL^*$ (n, r), where the logic is parameterised by the number n of agents and the number r of resource types were studied.[4] In particular, $RB \pm ATL$ $(1, 1)$ was shown to be PTIME-complete, and $RB \pm ATL^*$ $(1, 1)$ PSPACE-complete (see Table 1).

3.5 Other Resource Logics with Decidable Model-Checking

RAL is a very expressive resource logic with undecidable model-checking problem introduced in [23]. In [6], a new syntactic fragment FRAL of RAL with a decidable model-checking problem was identified. FRAL restricts the occurrences of coalitional modalities on the left of Until formulas. On the other hand, it allows nested modalities to refer to resource allocation at the time of evaluation, rather than always considering a fresh resource allocation, as in $RB \pm ATL$. For example, the formula $\langle\!\langle A^b \rangle\!\rangle \phi \, \mathcal{U} \, \langle\!\langle A^\downarrow \rangle\!\rangle \psi_1 \, \mathcal{U} \, \psi_2$ says that, given resource allocation b, coalition A can always reach a state (maintaining ϕ) where, with the remaining resources, it can reach ψ_2 while maintaining ψ_1. In [6] the boundary between decidability and undecidability was also investigated, and the availability of an 'idle' action (i.e., if the semantics requires that in every state each agent has an action that does not produce or consume resources) was shown to be critical: model checking FRAL is decidable in the presence of idle actions, and is not decidable otherwise.

Although model-checking of ATL with perfect recall and uniform strategies is undecidable, if uniformity is replaced with a weaker notion, for example, if it is defined in terms of distributed knowledge, model checking becomes decidable [34]. A similar result hold for $RB \pm ATSEL$, a version of $RB \pm ATL$ with syntactic epistemic knowledge and a weaker notion of uniformity [8].

4 Summary and Future Challenges

In Table 1 we summarise the complexity results for the resource logics with a decidable model checking problem discussed in Sect. 3. In the table, the 'Idle' column indicates whether the semantics for a logic requires that in every state

---

[4] Note that $RB \pm ATL$ $(n, 1)$ was referred to in [14] as 1-$RB \pm ATL$.

each agent has an action that produces and consumes no resources. New results not appearing in the previous survey [9] are highlighted in bold.

Table 1. Resource logics with decidable model-checking problem

Logic	Resource production	Idle	Complexity of model-checking
RBCL	no	yes	in EXPTIME (PTIME in model) [3]
RB-ATL	no	yes	in EXPTIME (PTIME in model) [4]
PRB-ATL	bounded	yes	EXPTIME-c [32]
RB $\pm$ ATL	yes	yes	**2EXPTIME-c** [5]
RB $\pm$ ATL $(n, 1)$	yes	yes	in PSPACE [14]
RB $\pm$ ATL $(1, 1)$	yes	yes	**PTIME-c** [19]
FRAL	yes	yes	?
RB $\pm$ ATSEL	yes	yes	?
RB $\pm$ ATL*	yes	no	**2EXPTIME-c** [5]
RB $\pm$ ATL* $(n, 1)$	yes	no	**EXPSPACE-c** [5]
RB $\pm$ ATL* $(1, 1)$	yes	yes	**PSPACE-c** [5,19]

The results for (fragments of) RB $\pm$ ATL and RB $\pm$ ATL* offer the possibility of significant progress in the verification of resource-bounded multi-agent systems. However many challenges remain for future research. Below we list three of the most important.

Understanding the Sources of Undecidability. Developing a better understanding of the sources of decidability and undecidability (beyond boundedness) will be critical to future progress. As observed in [23], subtle differences in truth conditions for resource logics result in the difference between decidability and undecidability of the model checking problem. Some work in this direction is reported in [5–7].

Logics with Lower Complexity. It is useful to discover sources of undecidability and how to construct expressive logics for which the model-checking problem is decidable. However, it is even more important to be able to develop logics, or fragments of existing logics such as RB $\pm$ ATL, that are sufficiently expressive for practical problems, and where the model-checking problem has tractable complexity. Only then will we be able to implement practical model-checking tools for systems of resource-bounded agents.

Practical Tools. Although model checking algorithms have been proposed for several of the logics surveyed, work on implementation is only beginning. We aim to develop practical model-checking tools for verifying resource-bounded MAS by extending the MCMAS model checker [41] to allow the modelling of multi-agent systems in which agents can both consume and produce resources. Work on symbolic encoding of RB-ATL model-checking is reported in [15] and work on symbolic encoding of RB $\pm$ ATL model-checking is reported in [13].

Addressing these challenges will allow practical model-checking of resource logics and significant advances in multi-agent system verification.

Acknowledgements. The authors thank Stéphane Demri for helpful discussions.

References

1. Abdulla, P.A., Mayr, R., Sangnier, A., Sproston, J.: Solving parity games on integer vectors. In: D'Argenio, P.R., Melgratti, H. (eds.) CONCUR 2013. LNCS, vol. 8052, pp. 106–120. Springer, Heidelberg (2013). https://doi.org/10.1007/978-3-642-40184-8_9
2. Abdulla, P.A., Bouajjani, A., d'Orso, J.: Deciding monotonic games. In: Baaz, M., Makowsky, J.A. (eds.) CSL 2003. LNCS, vol. 2803, pp. 1–14. Springer, Heidelberg (2003). https://doi.org/10.1007/978-3-540-45220-1_1
3. Alechina, N., Logan, B., Nguyen, H.N., Rakib, A.: A logic for coalitions with bounded resources. In: Proceedings of the 21st International Joint Conference on Artificial Intelligence, IJCAI 2009, vol. 2, pp. 659–664. IJCAI/AAAI, AAAI Press (2009)
4. Alechina, N., Logan, B., Nguyen, H.N., Rakib, A.: Resource-bounded alternating-time temporal logic. In: Proceedings of the 9th International Conference on Autonomous Agents and Multiagent Systems, AAMAS 2010, pp. 481–488. IFAAMAS (2010)
5. Alechina, N., Bulling, N., Demri, S., Logan, B.: On the complexity of resource-bounded logics. Theor. Comput. Sci. **750**, 69–100 (2018). https://doi.org/10.1016/j.tcs.2018.01.019
6. Alechina, N., Bulling, N., Logan, B., Nguyen, H.N.: On the boundary of (un)decidability: decidable model-checking for a fragment of resource agent logic. In: Yang, Q. (ed.) Proceedings of the 24th International Joint Conference on Artificial Intelligence, IJCAI 2015. IJCAI, AAAI Press, Buenos Aires, Argentina, July 2015
7. Alechina, N., Bulling, N., Logan, B., Nguyen, H.N.: The virtues of idleness: a decidable fragment of resource agent logic. Artif. Intell. **245**, 56–85 (2017). https://doi.org/10.1016/j.artint.2016.12.005
8. Alechina, N., Dastani, M., Logan, B.: Verifying existence of resource-bounded coalition uniform strategies. In: Rossi, F. (ed.) IJCAI 2016, Proceedings of the 25th International Joint Conference on Artificial Intelligence. IJCAI/AAAI (2016)
9. Alechina, N., Logan, B.: Verifying systems of resource-bounded agents. In: Beckmann, A., Bienvenu, L., Jonoska, N. (eds.) CiE 2016. LNCS, vol. 9709, pp. 3–12. Springer, Cham (2016). https://doi.org/10.1007/978-3-319-40189-8_1
10. Alechina, N., Logan, B.: Resource logics with a diminishing resource (extended abstract). In: Dastani, M., Sukthankar, G., Andre, E., Koenig, S. (eds.) Proceedings of the 17th International Conference on Autonomous Agents and Multiagent Systems, AAMAS 2018, pp. 1847–1849. IFAAMAS (2018)
11. Alechina, N., Logan, B., Nga, N.H., Rakib, A.: Logic for coalitions with bounded resources. J. Logic Comput. **21**(6), 907–937 (2011)

12. Alechina, N., Logan, B., Nguyen, H.N., Raimondi, F.: Decidable model-checking for a resource logic with production of resources. In: Proceedings of the 21st European Conference on Artificial Intelligence, ECAI-2014, pp. 9–14. ECCAI, IOS Press, Prague, Czech Republic, August 2014
13. Alechina, N., Logan, B., Nguyen, H.N., Raimondi, F.: Symbolic model-checking for one-resource RB+-ATL. In: Yang, Q. (ed.) Proceedings of the 24th International Joint Conference on Artificial Intelligence, IJCAI 2015. IJCAI, AAAI Press, Buenos Aires, Argentina, July 2015
14. Alechina, N., Logan, B., Nguyen, H.N., Raimondi, F.: Model-checking for resource-bounded ATL with production and consumption of resources. J. Comput. Syst. Sci. **88**, 126–144 (2017)
15. Alechina, N., Logan, B., Nguyen, H.N., Raimondi, F., Mostarda, L.: Symbolic model-checking for resource-bounded ATL. In: Proceedings of the 2015 International Conference on Autonomous Agents and Multiagent Systems, AAMAS 2015, pp. 1809–1810. ACM (2015)
16. Alur, R., Henzinger, T., Kupferman, O.: Alternating-time temporal logic. J. ACM **49**(5), 672–713 (2002)
17. Alur, R., Henzinger, T.A., Mang, F.Y.C., Qadeer, S., Rajamani, S.K., Tasiran, S.: MOCHA: modularity in model checking. In: Hu, A.J., Vardi, M.Y. (eds.) CAV 1998. LNCS, vol. 1427, pp. 521–525. Springer, Heidelberg (1998). https://doi.org/10.1007/BFb0028774
18. Belardinelli, F.: Verification of non-uniform and unbounded artifact-centric systems: decidability through abstraction. In: Bazzan, A.L.C., Huhns, M.N., Lomuscio, A., Scerri, P. (eds.) International Conference on Autonomous Agents and Multi-Agent Systems, AAMAS 2014, pp. 717–724. IFAAMAS/ACM (2014)
19. Belardinelli, F., Demri, S.: Resource-bounded ATL: the quest for tractable fragments. In: Elkind, E., Veloso, M., Agmon, N., Taylor, M.E. (eds.) Proceedings of the 18th International Conference on Autonomous Agents and MultiAgent Systems, AAMAS 2019, pp. 206–214. International Foundation for Autonomous Agents and MultiAgent Systems (2019)
20. Bordini, R.H., Fisher, M., Visser, W., Wooldridge, M.: Model checking rational agents. IEEE Intell. Syst. **19**(5), 46–52 (2004)
21. Bordini, R.H., Fisher, M., Visser, W., Wooldridge, M.: Verifying multi-agent programs by model checking. J. Auton. Agents Multi-Agent Syst. **12**(2), 239–256 (2006). http://dro.dur.ac.uk/622/
22. Brázdil, T., Jančar, P., Kučera, A.: Reachability games on extended vector addition systems with states. In: Abramsky, S., Gavoille, C., Kirchner, C., Meyer auf der Heide, F., Spirakis, P.G. (eds.) ICALP 2010. LNCS, vol. 6199, pp. 478–489. Springer, Heidelberg (2010). https://doi.org/10.1007/978-3-642-14162-1_40
23. Bulling, N., Farwer, B.: On the (un-)decidability of model checking resource-bounded agents. In: Proceedings of the 19th European Conference on Artificial Intelligence, ECAI 2010. Frontiers in Artificial Intelligence and Applications, vol. 215, pp. 567–572. IOS Press (2010)
24. Bulling, N., Farwer, B.: On the (un-)decidability of model checking resource-bounded agents. Technical report Ifl-10-05. Clausthal University of Technology (2010)
25. Bulling, N., Farwer, B.: Expressing properties of resource-bounded systems: the logics RTL* and RTL. In: Dix, J., Fisher, M., Novák, P. (eds.) CLIMA 2009. LNCS (LNAI), vol. 6214, pp. 22–45. Springer, Heidelberg (2010). https://doi.org/10.1007/978-3-642-16867-3_2

26. Bulling, N., Goranko, V.: How to be both rich and happy: combining quantitative and qualitative strategic reasoning about multi-player games (extended abstract). In: Mogavero, F., Murano, A., Vardi, M.Y. (eds.) Proceedings 1st International Workshop on Strategic Reasoning, SR 2013. EPTCS, vol. 112, pp. 33–41 (2013)

27. Bulling, N., Nguyen, H.N.: Model checking resource bounded systems with shared resources via alternating Büchi pushdown systems. In: Chen, Q., Torroni, P., Villata, S., Hsu, J., Omicini, A. (eds.) PRIMA 2015. LNCS (LNAI), vol. 9387, pp. 640–649. Springer, Cham (2015). https://doi.org/10.1007/978-3-319-25524-8_47

28. Chatterjee, K., Doyen, L., Henzinger, T.A., Raskin, J.: Generalized mean-payoff and energy games. In: Lodaya, K., Mahajan, M. (eds.) IARCS Annual Conference on Foundations of Software Technology and Theoretical Computer Science, FSTTCS 2010, 15–18 December 2010, Chennai, India. LIPIcs, vol. 8, pp. 505–516. Schloss Dagstuhl - Leibniz-Zentrum fuer Informatik (2010)

29. Clarke, E.M., Emerson, E.A., Sistla, A.P.: Automatic verification of finite-state concurrent systems using temporal logic specifications. ACM Trans. Program. Lang. Syst. **8**(2), 244–263 (1986)

30. Courtois, J.-B., Schmitz, S.: Alternating vector addition systems with states. In: Csuhaj-Varjú, E., Dietzfelbinger, M., Ésik, Z. (eds.) MFCS 2014. LNCS, vol. 8634, pp. 220–231. Springer, Heidelberg (2014). https://doi.org/10.1007/978-3-662-44522-8_19

31. Della Monica, D., Napoli, M., Parente, M.: On a logic for coalitional games with priced-resource agents. Electron. Notes Theor. Comput. Sci. **278**, 215–228 (2011)

32. Della Monica, D., Napoli, M., Parente, M.: Model checking coalitional games in shortage resource scenarios. In: Proceedings of the 4th International Symposium on Games, Automata, Logics and Formal Verification, GandALF 2013. EPTCS, vol. 119, pp. 240–255 (2013)

33. Dennis, L.A., Fisher, M., Webster, M.P., Bordini, R.H.: Model checking agent programming languages. Autom. Softw. Eng. **19**(1), 5–63 (2012)

34. Dima, C., Tiplea, F.L.: Model-checking ATL under imperfect information and perfect recall semantics is undecidable. CoRR abs/1102.4225 (2011). http://arxiv.org/abs/1102.4225

35. Fisher, M., Dennis, L.A., Webster, M.P.: Verifying autonomous systems. Commun. ACM **56**(9), 84–93 (2013)

36. Hopcroft, J.E., Ullman, J.D.: Introduction to Automata Theory, Languages and Computation. Addison-Wesley, Boston (1979)

37. Jurdziński, M., Lazić, R., Schmitz, S.: Fixed-dimensional energy games are in pseudo-polynomial time. In: Halldórsson, M.M., Iwama, K., Kobayashi, N., Speckmann, B. (eds.) ICALP 2015. LNCS, vol. 9135, pp. 260–272. Springer, Heidelberg (2015). https://doi.org/10.1007/978-3-662-47666-6_21

38. Kanovich, M.I.: Petri nets, horn programs, linear logic and vector games. Ann. Pure Appl. Logic **75**(1–2), 107–135 (1995)

39. Kwiatkowska, M., Norman, G., Parker, D.: PRISM 4.0: verification of probabilistic real-time systems. In: Gopalakrishnan, G., Qadeer, S. (eds.) CAV 2011. LNCS, vol. 6806, pp. 585–591. Springer, Heidelberg (2011). https://doi.org/10.1007/978-3-642-22110-1_47

40. Lincoln, P., Mitchell, J.C., Scedrov, A., Shankar, N.: Decision problems for propositional linear logic. Ann. Pure Appl. Logic **56**(1–3), 239–311 (1992)

41. Lomuscio, A., Qu, H., Raimondi, F.: MCMAS: a model checker for the verification of multi-agent systems. In: Bouajjani, A., Maler, O. (eds.) CAV 2009. LNCS, vol. 5643, pp. 682–688. Springer, Heidelberg (2009). https://doi.org/10.1007/978-3-642-02658-4_55

42. Nguyen, H.N., Rakib, A.: A probabilistic logic for resource-bounded multi-agent systems. In: Kraus, S. (ed.) Proceedings of the Twenty-Eighth International Joint Conference on Artificial Intelligence, IJCAI 2019, Macao, China, 10–16 August 2019, pp. 521–527. ijcai.org (2019)
43. Raskin, J., Samuelides, M., Begin, L.V.: Games for counting abstractions. Electron. Notes Theor. Comput. Sci. **128**(6), 69–85 (2005)
44. Shapiro, S., Lespérance, Y., Levesque, H.J.: The cognitive agents specification language and verification environment for multiagent systems. In: Proceedings of the First International Joint Conference on Autonomous Agents and Multiagent Systems, AAMAS 2002, pp. 19–26. ACM Press, New York (2002)

Why Predicative Sets?

Arnon Avron[(✉)]

School of Computer Science, Tel Aviv University, Tel Aviv, Israel
aa@cs.tau.ac.il

Abstract. The predicativist program for the foundations of mathematics, initiated by Poincaré and first developed by Weyl, seeks to establish certainty in mathematics without revolutionizing it. The program was later extensively pursued by Feferman, who developed proofs systems for predicative mathematics, and showed that a very large part of classical analysis can be developed within them. Both Weyl and Feferman worked within type-theoretic frameworks. In contrast, set theory is almost universally accepted now as the foundational theory in which the whole of mathematics can and should be developed. We explain how to reconstruct Weyl's ideas and system within the set-theoretical framework, and indicate the advantages that this approach to predicativity and to set theory has from both the foundational as well as the computational points of views.

1 Why Predicativism?

In [24] the basic problem of the research in foundations of mathematics is formulated as follows:

> How to reconstruct mathematics on a secure basis, one maximally immune to rational doubts.

Now Shapiro's formulates this problem in order to *attack* it. He acknowledged that this was the historic problem of FOM (Foundations Of Mathematics), but according to him, its time has passed. As far as I was able to see, he gave no reason why he thinks that this problem is not important anymore - except that it is not fashionable nowadays to work on it. That he is right at least about *that* is reflected in the discussion in Sect. 2 of [7] about the value of foundations in mathematics. Two related questions raised and answered there are: "Why do we need foundations at all?", and whether it is true that "the problem of foundations for mathematics is completely solved; in other words, the study of foundations of mathematics is dead." The answer given there to the first question provides three practical advantages of having a uniform general axiomatic framework (like set theory) for mathematics, none of them related to the basic problem mentioned above. The reply to the second is that the present accepted foundations (i.e. ZFC) is not sufficiently strong, since "There are things in ordinary mathematics that 'stick out' of the set-theoretic foundation" (e.g. category theory). Again: no worry at all about trusting the content of current mathematics.

© Springer Nature Switzerland AG 2020
A. Blass et al. (Eds.): Gurevich Festschrift, LNCS 12180, pp. 30–45, 2020.
https://doi.org/10.1007/978-3-030-48006-6_3

In complete opposition to the views described above and to the tendency of most working mathematicians (and following them—many philosophers of mathematics) not to care about the basic problem of foundations, stand people who do not think that mathematics is just the game of mathematicians. For them the basic problem is still, and will remain (until solved satisfactorily) the main big challenge of FOM. As H. Friedman once wrote:[1]

> The question "is mathematics certain?" is of far greater interest to almost anybody outside of mathematics than any topic in normal mathematics. And of far greater interest to almost anybody outside of mathematical logic than any topic in mathematical logic.[2]
>
> ...
>
> The first point about "is mathematics certain?" is that it would appear that some mathematics may be certain and other mathematics not certain. Or even that some mathematics is more certain than other mathematics.

The predicativist program ([16]) has been one of the attempts to solve the basic problem of FOM. It seeks to establish certainty in mathematics in a constructive way, but without revolutionizing it (as the intuitionistic program does). The program was initiated by Poincaré [22], in his follow up on [23]. Its viability was demonstrated by Hermann Weyl, who seriously developed it for the first time in his famous small book "Das Kontinuum" ([27], English translation in [28]). After Weyl, the predicativist program was extensively pursued by Feferman, who in a series of papers (see e.g. [13–16]) developed proof systems for predicative mathematics. Weyl and Feferman have shown that a very large part of classical analysis can be developed within their systems. Feferman further argued that predicative mathematics in fact suffices for developing all the mathematics that is actually indispensable to present-day natural sciences. Hence the predicativist program has been successful in solving the basic problem of FOM. (In my opinion it is the only one about which this can truly be said.)[3]

Note 1. As noted in [16], there are a number of ideas of predicativity that have been considered in the literature. In this paper we reserve the name to the main one: Poincaré-Weyl-Feferman predicativity, which is sometimes called 'predicativity given the natural numbers'.

---

[1] See https://cs.nyu.edu/pipermail/fom/1998-September/002156.html.

[2] Let me add to this observation of Friedman that I believe that this question has recently become more important and pressing than perhaps anytime before, since we live in an era of "alternative facts", in which not only politicians, but also many respectable people in the academy deny the existence of anything absolute, claiming that there is no absolute truth, and there are no absolute moral values. It is very fashionable therefore to deny the existence of certainty even in Mathematics.

[3] There is a price to pay, of course, for this success. There are parts of current mathematics which cannot be justified predicatively. However, as Weyl and Feferman have shown, the most important parts do.

2   What Is Predicativism?

A Predicativist is first of all a mathematician who finds as vague and possibly meaningless the notion of an 'arbitrary subset of S' in case S is an infinite collection. The use of this notion means commitment to the "existence" in a mysterious way of objects we (as humane beings) cannot even describe, refer to, or comprehend. Thus most subsets of $\mathbf{N}$ (say) are mystic objects that only an infinite mind (whatever this means) can identify, and belief in their existence is exactly this: a sort of religious belief. Now beliefs of this sort may be true of course. God may exist. Angels may exist. Spirits (good and bad) may exist. One may conduct one's life according to such beliefs. But pure mathematics, to the extent it is expected to provide certain knowledge, immune to rational doubts, cannot be based on beliefs of this sort. (This does *not* mean that *all* of useful or interesting mathematics should be absolutely certain. Thus I see no reason why the mathematics which is used in some scientific theory should be more certain than other parts of that theory).

On the other hand a predicativist finds as crystal clear finite mathematical objects that are (at least potentially) fully describable, have concrete finite representations, and can be identified, distinguished from one another and manipulated in precise ways by any finite mind given enough (finite) time and (finite) space. Examples are the natural numbers, finite strings of symbols from some finite alphabet, hereditarily finite sets, etc. Moreover: predicativists take as meaningful and self-evident the use of classical first-order logic at least when the intended domain of discourse is a constructively defined collection of such objects, as long as it is finite or *potentially infinite*. This means that the objects of the collection can be obtained one by one by an effective process that can be continued indefinitely. Both Poincare and Weyl took this to be an absolute minimum needed not only for mathematical thinking, but for thinking in general, including thinking *about* mathematics. Thus our notions of a '(formal) proposition' and a '(formal) proof' are completely based on this minimum.

The main difficulty of the predicativists is that the "real" numbers, so central to modern mathematics and science, are not objects of the crystal clear type described above. Accordingly, their main problem is how to reconstruct the theory of real numbers (or at least the most significant parts of it) and (the most significant parts of) modern analysis "on a secure basis, immune to rational doubts". The border between predicativists and platonists passed therefore somewhere between $\mathbf{N}$ and its powerset $P(\mathbf{N})$, between the rational(s) and the (arbitrary) irrational(s), between the potential infinite and the actual infinite. On the other hand the main difference between predicativists and constructivists is that predicativists acknowledge the fact that there are, or at least can be, meaningful propositions with determined truth-value, without us knowing this value or being capable of finding it.

Now there are of course infinite higher order constructs, like certain sets of natural numbers, or certain sets of functions, which are *not* arbitrary, and *can* safely be used. These constructs are acceptable only when introduced through *legitimate definitions* that fully determine them. Such definitions cannot of course be circular, and one can only refer in them to constructs which were introduced by previous definitions.

As a concrete example of the way mathematics can be developed according to predicatively accepted line, we describe in the next section the work done by Weyl in [27]. The reason for this choice (in addition to its obvious historical significance) is that for reasons explained below, in our opinion Weyl's system is *superior* to its more modern counterparts (like Feferman's various systems or those system which are predicatively acceptable among those investigated in [25]) for the task of serving as a basis of a predicatively justified, natural and comprehensive development of classical analysis.

3   Weyl's "Das Kontinuum"

3.1   Weyl's Basic Ideas and Principles

As said above, Weyl totally rejected as meaningless the modern notions of an *arbitrary* set, and of a function as an arbitrary set of pairs. He insisted that only sets and functions which have legitimate definitions can be admitted. He also maintained that the practice of the standard foundations of analysis involves the sin of *vicious circularity*. This is due to its use of impredicative definitions of objects, where a definition is impredicative for Weyl if it tries to select an object from an 'open into infinity' collection. In more details: Weyl divides all collections into three sorts:

(I) The 'extensionally determinate' collections, i.e. those that remain invariant under extensions of the universe. (An example for Weyl is the collection **N** of the natural numbers.)

(II) Collections which may not be extensionally determinate (and so are open), but are definite in the sense that the question whether a given object belongs to them has a definite answer. (For Weyl, an example of such a collection is provided by $\mathbb{R}$, the set of real numbers.)

(III) Collections that are not even definite. (For Weyl an example is provided here by the collection of continuous functions over $\mathbb{R}$.)

Only a collection of sort (I) or (II) can be an object in Weyl's universe, and only one of sort(I) can be treated as closed, so definitions which include quantification over it are allowed.

At this point a natural question arises: given a definition of a collection, how can we decide whether it is predicative, in the sense that the defined collection is extensionally determinate? Most of the first chapter (out of two) of [27] is devoted to this question, that is: to providing a list of effective rules for producing predicative definitions, which is sufficiently strong (though not necessarily complete) for a safe development of analysis.

Here are some of the basic principles that underlie Weyl's universe:

P1 Every object, as well as each place in a relation, is affiliated with a definite type (or 'category').

P2 A few of the types are taken as *basic*. These types should be extension-ally determinate and well-understood. Associated with each of them are few, particularly simple *primitive relations*. One of these relations should be the identity relation.

P3 One of the basic types is that of the natural numbers, equipped with just two binary relations: identity and "successor of".[4] In Weyl's system for analysis this is the *sole* basic type.

P4 On top of the basic types there is an *infinite hierarchy of 'ideal' types*. The objects of the ideal types are sets and functions.[5]

P5 Existence can be attributed only to a set (or a function) which has a (legit-imate) *definition*.

P6 Sets are introduced genetically: they are derived by adequate, "logical" means from some small collection of basic types and relations.

From **P4** it follows that all types are derived from the basic types by repeated use of two operations: one for introducing types of terms for sets, the other for introducing types of terms for functions. As for the former, the idea is that if $\tau_1, \ldots, \tau_n$ are n arbitrary types, then $S(\tau_1 \times, \ldots, \times \tau_n)$ is the type of terms for n-dimensional subsets of $\tau_1 \times, \ldots, \times \tau_n$. In addition, the list of basic predicates of the language includes the equality predicate $=$ between terms of the same type, and the relation $\in$ between tuples of objects and sets of such tuples.

It should be emphasized that *formulas have two different roles in Weyl's system*. One is the usual one, of expressing propositions. Their other role, for which only 'delimited' (i.e. predicative) formulas can be used, is as the main tool for defining (and by this creating) those objects that Weyl calls "ideal", that is: sets and functions.

3.2   Weyl's Notion of a Function

We turn to the nature of the third sort of objects in Weyl's universes: functions. Weyl chose to allow only functions whose range is a type of sets, and to make functions as a sort of a generalization of sets. Hence types of functions have the form $(\sigma_1 \times \cdots \times \sigma_k) \to S(\tau_1 \times \cdots \times \tau_n)$, and the *canonical* form of terms of such a type is (in modern notation) $\lambda y_1, \ldots, y_k.\{(x_1, \ldots, x_n) \mid \psi\}$, where ψ is predicative, and $\{x_1, \ldots, x_n\} \cap \{y_1, \ldots, y_k\} = \emptyset$. Concerning this notion of a function, Weyl remarked that "[O]nce we become aware of it, we also immediately grasp its significance". He gave no further explanations about this significance. However, the same notion of a function was independently used in [4] in order to provide a unified theory of constructions and operations as they are used in different branches of mathematics and computer science, including set theory,

---

[4] In particular, addition and multiplication are *not* primitive in Weyl's system.

[5] Feferman's direct formalization of Weyl's system in [14] is just second-order. As was already demonstrated in [1], his formalization was not faithful to Weyl.

computability theory, and database theory. It is based on the following two basic principles (which I believe are essentially what Weyl had in mind):[6]

– From an abstract logical point of view, the focus of a general theory of computations should be on functions of the form:

$$\lambda y_1, \ldots, y_k.\{\langle x_1, \ldots, x_n \rangle \in S^n \mid S \models \varphi(x_1, \ldots, x_n, y_1, \ldots, y_k)\}$$

where S is a structure for some first-order signature σ, φ is some formula of σ, and $\{\{x_1, \ldots, x_n\}, \{y_1, \ldots, y_k\}\}$ is a partition of the set of the free variables of φ. Here φ is used to define a *query* with parameters $y_1, \ldots, y_k$. Accordingly, the tuple $\langle y_1, \ldots, y_k \rangle$ provides here the input, while the output is the set of answers to the resulting specific query.
Note that usual functions to S^n can be identified with functions of the above form in which the output is a singleton.
– An allowable query should be *stable* in the sense that the answer to it does not depend on the exact domain of S, but only on the values of the parameters $\{y_1, \ldots, y_k\}$ and the part of S which is relevant to them and to the query (under certain conditions concerning the language and the relevant structures).

We refer the reader to [4] for further explanations of these two principles, including their use for characterizing Church Thesis.

The principles of Weyl that we have described so far are not even sufficient for defining addition or multiplication of natural numbers. To be able to develop analysis in a reasonable way nevertheless, Weyl added to his system the crucial *principle of iteration*. Given a function $F : \sigma \to \sigma$, this principle (in its most basic form) allows to construct a function $IT(F) : \mathbf{N} \times \sigma \to \sigma$ by letting $IT(F)(n, x) = F^n(x)$ for $n : \mathbf{N}$ and $x : \sigma$. In Weyl's view, this principle is justified by the same intuition that justifies taking the natural numbers as a basic type. What is more, according to Weyl its acceptance is what makes it possible to avoid the ramification (that is made in [13,29]) of the elements of types of the form $S(\sigma)$ into levels (something that Weyl rejected as artificial and impractical), sticking instead to a collection of first level sets, which should be made as extensive as possible.[7]

3.3 Axioms, Logic, and Semantics of Weyl's System

Next we turn to the axioms and logic which (implicitly and in some cases explicitly) Weyl employs. The axioms are rather standard: comprehension and

---

[6] Some examples of the usefulness and universality in mathematics of Weyl's notion of a function: construction problems in Euclidean geometry; procedures for solving various systems of equations and inequalities; queries in logic programming and queries in relational databases.

[7] In [14] Feferman claimed to spot an incoherence in Weyl's principles, since the principle of iteration makes it possible to go beyond the first level by constructing non-arithmetical subsets of $\mathbf{N}$. However, the incoherence here is only between Weyl's views and Feferman's unjustified identification of the first-level subsets of $\mathbf{N}$ with the arithmetical ones.

extensionality axioms for both sets and functions (where by comprehension for functions we mean β-reduction); the axioms that characterize the successor relation in $\mathbf{N}$, including induction in the form of an *axiom schema*[8]; and an axiom schema which describes the effect of the iteration operator IT. The logic is rather standard too: it is *classical* many-sorted first-order logic, with equality in all sorts/types, and with *variable binding term operators*. It is important to emphasize here that in "Das Kontinuum" Weyl still used classical logic freely, without expressing any intuitionist tendencies (as he did later).

The last claim seems to raise the following difficulty: if most of the collections that are referred to in Weyl systems (like the real numbers) are *open*, how come Weyl is using classical quantification over them in the propositions he proves? The answer is that Weyl treated his system as an *axiomatic theory*, designed to be able to prove only *absolutely true* propositions, where (exactly like in set theory) for Weyl a proposition is 'absolute', if its truth value remains unchanged in the passage from one universe to an expansion of it. Note that in general, propositions may of course have different truth value in different universes (i.e. models of Weyl's system). Thus Weyl writes[9]:

> If we regard the principles of definition as an *"open"* system, i.e., if we reserve the right to extend them when necessary by making additions, then in general the question of whether a given function is continuous must also remain *open* (though we may attempt to resolve any *delimited* question). For a function which, within our current system, is continuous can lose this property if our principles of definition are expanded and, accordingly, the real numbers "presently" available are joined by others in whose construction the newly added principles of definition play a role.

On the other hand, in each model each proposition does have a definite truth value. In particular, $\neg\varphi \vee \varphi$ always has the truth value true, and so is absolute, even in case φ itself is not. This explains and *fully justifies* the use of *classical logic* in Weyl's system!

For the reader convenience, a full formalization WA of Weyl's system for Analysis in [27] (in modern notations and terminology) is presented in Appendix 1 to this paper.

3.4   Developing Analysis in Weyl's System

In this Section we briefly outline the way Weyl developed the fundamentals of classical analysis in his system.

The real numbers are introduced in [27] as Dedekind cuts in $\mathbb{Q}$. Since elements of the latter are essentially represented in [27] by quadruples of natural numbers (where $\langle k, l, m, n \rangle$ represents $k/l - m/n$), a real number is in Weyl's system an object of type $S(\mathbf{N}^4)$. It follows that $\mathbb{R}$ (the set of all real numbers)

---

[8] Unlike what Feferman wrote in [14], the restricted second-order axiom of induction is not sufficient for some of the proofs given in [27].

[9] See P. 87 of [28].

is a set of sets, and so quantifications over $\mathbb{R}$ is not allowed in *definitions of sets and functions*. As a result, the LUB principle fails in Weyl's system. Instead Weyl proved and used Cauchy's convergence principle, and the *sequential* LUB principle: Every bounded *sequence* of real numbers has an LUB and a GLB. Weyl showed that these principle suffice for proving the basic properties of continuous functions, like that a continuous function assumes all intermediate values, and that a continuous function on a closed interval is uniformly continuous there, and has a maximum and minimum. After that, Weyl notes that the theory can be extended to continuous functions of several real arguments, and that the fundamental theorem of algebra also holds in his version of analysis. Finally, Weyl remarked that "In the realm of continuous functions, differentiation and integration serve as function-generating processes just as they do in contemporary analysis: no change in the foundations is required."

The fragment of analysis developed here by Weyl is very similar to that with is developed within the second-order system $\mathbf{ACA_0}$ in [25]. There is a great difference, though. Unlike in $\mathbf{ACA_0}$ or in Feferman's predicative systems, *Weyl is using no coding in developing analysis* (once the real number and sequences of them have been introduced). All the definitions and theorems are formulated almost exactly as in ordinary mathematical books. Thus his definition of the continuity of a function f in a point a is the usual ϵ-δ definition (with ϵ and δ limited to rational numbers—an insignificant constraint from the classical point of view as well as his). The proofs of the theorems can be made rather standard too. Therefore working in Weyl's system can be done in a rather natural way—something that cannot be said about the more modern systems, like $\mathbf{ACA_0}$.

4   Limitations of Weyl's System

Although WA has (in our opinion) great advantages over systems like $\mathbf{ACA_0}$ or Feferman's system $\mathbf{W}$ ([14]), it has the following serious drawbacks as well:

1. There are terms in the language of WA for all three sorts of collections (I-III) that were described in Sect. 3.1, even though collections of sort III (like the universal element of $S(S(S(\mathbf{N})))$ intuitively is) are not really objects according to predicative views in general, and those of Weyl in particular. Even worse is the fact that beyond the types of the form $S(\mathbf{N}^n)$, there is no effective criterion for distinguishing between, e.g., terms that denote extensionally determinate collections, and those which do not. Thus no method is provided by Weyl that can allow us to distinguish between the very different nature of the following two terms of type $S(S(\mathbf{N}))$, where $\mathcal{N} = \{n : \mathbf{N} \mid n = n\}$:
   (a) $\{\{n\} \mid n \in \mathcal{N}\} = \{X : S(\mathbf{N}) \mid \exists n : \mathbf{N}.\forall k : \mathbf{N}.k \in X \leftrightarrow k = n\}$
   (b) $\mathcal{P}(\mathcal{N}) - \{\emptyset\} = \{X : S(\mathbf{N}) \mid \exists n : \mathbf{N}.n \in X\}$
2. While $\{X : S(\mathbf{N}) \mid \forall n : \mathbf{N}.n \in X\}$ is a term of type $S(S(\mathbf{N}))$ that denotes the singleton $\{\mathcal{N}\}$, there is no term of type $S(S(S(\mathbf{N})))$ that denotes the singleton of this set (i.e. $\{\{\mathcal{N}\}\}$), even though this collection is obviously extensionally determinate.

3. The language of WA makes many duplications and artificial distinctions. For example, While **N** is the *type* of the natural numbers, $\mathcal{N}$ is a *term* of type $S(\mathbf{N})$, denoting the *set* of these numbers. Hence **N** and $\mathcal{N}$ are two completely different things, although their intuitive interpretations are the same. Similarly, if $\mathcal{P}(\mathcal{N}) = \{X : S(\mathbf{N}) \mid \forall n : \mathbf{N}.n \in X \rightarrow n = n\}$, then while $S(\mathbf{N})$ is the *type* of sets of natural numbers, $\mathcal{P}(\mathcal{N})$ is a term of type $S(S(\mathbf{N}))$, denoting the *set* of sets of natural numbers. Hence again $S(\mathbf{N})$ and $\mathcal{P}(\mathcal{N})$ are two completely different things, even though practically they denote the same collection.

4. Following Hölder in [17], it seems strange to (practically) allow quantification over any subset of $\mathcal{N}$, but not over any other extensionally determinate set.

5 Predicative Set Theory - Why and How?

The problems described in the previous sections are mainly due to the type-theoretic framework within which Weyl's system has been developed. They would disappear if the rest of his ideas would instead be implemented within the framework of set theory. The latter has anyway the great practical advantage of being the one which the great majority of the mathematicians in the world know and prefer. Thus the basic notions of set theory are nowadays used in any branch and textbook of modern mathematics. Moreover, as acknowledged in [7], set theory is almost universally accepted as the foundational theory in which mathematics should be developed.

Can the type-theoretical framework of WA be replaced by a set-theoretical one? To answer this question, observe that types are mainly used by Weyl in order to secure that the terms of his theory define "extensionally determinate" objects. In [5,6] it is shown that the same goal can be achieved (and in a much better way) using a predicative pure set theory called PZF, which is at least as strong as WA, but does not suffer the problematic aspects of the latter which were described above. On the other hand, PZF adheres to most of the ideas on which WA is based. This includes:

1. The natural numbers sequence is a well understood mathematical concept, and as a totality it constitutes a set.
2. The idea of iterating an operation or a relation a finite number of times is accepted as fundamental.
3. Induction on the natural numbers is accepted as a method of proof in its full generality, that is: as an (open) scheme.
4. Higher order objects, such as sets or functions, are acceptable only when introduced through legitimate definitions.
5. A definition of an object should determine it in a unique, absolute way.
6. Objects should be introduced genetically, and be derived by adequate, *logical* means from few objects and relations that are taken as basic.
7. The relations of elementhood ($\in$) and equality ($=$) are basic.

8. The use of quantification over a collection of objects should be allowed *in definitions of objects* only if that collection forms an object, and is (in Weyl's terminology) extensionally determinate, that is: it is introduced by a stable and invariant definition.
9. Sets are extensional: sets that have the same elements are identical.
10. Using ramification in definitions, and classifying sets of natural numbers according to "levels", are artificial, and should be avoided.
11. The use of classical logic is justified.
12. The possibility of introducing new methods of defining sets is taken into account. Therefore PZF has no single 'intended universe'.
13. Set terms of of the form $\{(x_1, \ldots, x_n) \mid \psi\}$, and operations of the form $\lambda y_1, \ldots, y_k.\{(x_1, \ldots, x_n) \mid \psi\}$, have a particularly central role.

Unsurprisingly, some of these common principles are implemented differently in PZF and in WA.

– The most important difference is with respect to the fifth principle in the above list. Recall that Weyl tried to implement this principle using two means: imposing type restrictions on variables, and allowing to use in definitions of objects only delimited formulas. The first of these means is not available in PZF, and even with its help the second one would not be sufficient. Therefore the use of these two independent constraints, one connected with a *property* of variables and the other with a *property* of formulas, is replaced in PZF by a constraint which is connected with a single *relation* $\succ$ between formulas and set of variables.[10] The intuitive meaning of '$\varphi(x_1, \ldots, x_n, y_1, \ldots, y_k) \succ \{x_1, \ldots, x_n\}$' is that the formula φ is "extensionally determinate" (that is: universe independent) with respect to the set of variables $\{x_1, \ldots, x_n\}$ for all values of the parameters $y_1, \ldots, y_k$. Note that this is a semantic notion. Like in WA, in order to base a proof system on it, it is imposed in PZF syntactically (and genetically), using adequate logical rules.
– The ZF-like framework of PZF causes apparent problems with implementing the first three principles in the list above. (Those that are connected with the natural numbers.) This is solved by using ancestral logic $\mathcal{AL}$ ([3,8,20,21,24]) as the underlying logic, rather than first-order logic. In fact, in [3] it was argued that the ability to form the transitive closure of a given relation (like forming the notion of an ancestor from the notion of a parent) should be taken as a major ingredient of our logical abilities (even prior to our understanding of the natural numbers), and that this concept is the key for understanding iteration, as well as inductive reasoning.

In Appendix 2 we present a version of the system PZF from [5], which has been designed according to the principles described above. An (incomplete) investigation of its power can be found in [6].

---

[10] Following the terminology of database theory ([26]), we call $\succ$ 'the safety relation of PZF'. (On the theory of safety relations in general, their use, and their connections with database theory and computability theory, see [2,4].).

6   The Computational Significance of Predicative Sets

We end this paper by a brief discussion of the importance of predicative set theory in general, and PZF in particular, to Computer Science.

As is emphasized and demonstrated in [9,10] and in [7], set theory has not only a great pragmatic advantage as a basic language for mathematical discourse, but it also has a great computational potential as a basis for specification languages, declarative programming, proof verifiers, and many other applications in computer science. However, in order to be used for such tasks, it is necessary to overcome the following serious gaps that exist between the "official" formulations of set theory (as given e.g. by ZFC) and actual mathematical practice:

- ZFC treats all the mathematical objects on a par, and so hid the computational significance of many of them. Thus although certain functions are first-class citizens in many programming languages, in set theory they are just "infinite sets", and ZFC in its usual presentation is an extremely poor framework for computing with such sets.
- The languages used in official formalizations of ZFC are very remote from real mathematical practice. In those languages variables (and perhaps a couple of constants) are the only terms which are directly provided. This feature makes these formalizations almost useless from a computational point of view. In contrast, *all* modern texts in all areas of mathematics (including set theory itself) employ much richer and more convenient languages. In particular: they make extensive use of terms for denoting sets, like abstractions terms of the form $\{x \mid \varphi\}$.
- Full ZFC is far too strong for core mathematics, which practically deals only with a small fraction of the set-theoretical "universe". It is obvious that much weaker systems, corresponding to universes which are smaller, *more effective*, and better suited for computations , would do (presumably, such weaker systems will also be easier to mechanize).

Obviously, PZF, with its extensive use of abstract set terms and operations, is free from the first two drawbacks. As for the third—not only it does not have it, but the universe it most naturally defines provides its main computational significance. Next we explain what this universe is, and what is its significance.

Let $\mathcal{T}$ be some set theory. From the platonist point of view the set $\mathcal{D}(\mathcal{T})$ of its closed terms induces some subset $\mathcal{S}(\mathcal{T})$ of the universe V of sets. In predicative theories like PZF, the identity of $\mathcal{S}(\mathcal{T})$ depends only on the *language* of $\mathcal{T}$ and on the interpretations of the symbols (if such exist) that its signature has in addition to $\in$ and $=$. It does not depend on its axioms. In addition, for any transitive model $\mathcal{M}$ of $\mathcal{T}$, $\mathcal{D}(\mathcal{T})$ determines some subset $\mathcal{M}(\mathcal{T})$ of $\mathcal{M}$ (which might not be an element of $\mathcal{M}$). Now a theory $\mathcal{T}$ is computationally interesting if the set $\mathcal{S}(\mathcal{T})$ it induces is a "universe" in the sense that it is a transitive model of $\mathcal{T}$. Moreover, $\mathcal{T}$ and $\mathcal{S}(\mathcal{T})$ have a special significance from a computational point of view if in addition the identity of $\mathcal{S}(\mathcal{T})$ is *absolute* in the sense that $\mathcal{M}(\mathcal{T}) = \mathcal{S}(\mathcal{T})$ for any transitive model $\mathcal{M}$ of $\mathcal{T}$ (implying that $\mathcal{S}(\mathcal{T})$ is actually a *minimal* transitive model of $\mathcal{T}$). In such a case computing with the elements of the abstract minimal model of $\mathcal{T}$ reduces to computing with the terms that denote these elements. Hence what we need to deal with is a collection of terms equipped with some equality relation (determined by the theory we use). As usual, a computation here would basically be a reduction of one term to another one, which should be equal to it, but has a certain "normal form".

From results in [5] it follows that PZF has both of the properties described above. In fact, $S(\text{PZF})$ is a well-known set: it is L_{ω^ω} in Gödel's hierarchy, which is identical to J_{ω^ω} in Jensen's hierarchy. (See [11,18].) This universe is rich enough for implementing every data structure one may needs.

Appendix 1. WA: Weyl's System in [27]

We use σ and τ as metavariables for types, t,s as metavariables for terms, and φ,ψ as metavariables for formulas. We also employ x,y,z,w as general variables for objects, n,k,m as variables for objects of type $\mathbf{N}$, f,g as variables for objects of types of functions, X,Y,Z for objects of types of sets. We let $\overline{\sigma} = \sigma_1 \times \cdots \times \sigma_k$, $\overline{\tau} = \tau_1 \times \cdots \times \tau_n$, $\boldsymbol{x} = x_1,\ldots,x_n$, $\boldsymbol{w} = w_1,\ldots,w_n$, $\boldsymbol{y} = y_1,\ldots,y_k$, $\boldsymbol{z} = z_1,\ldots,z_k$, $\boldsymbol{f} = f_1,\ldots,f_m$, $\boldsymbol{X} = X_1,\ldots,X_m$, $\forall x \ldots = \neg\exists x\neg\ldots$, $\exists x : \sigma \ldots = \exists x^\sigma \ldots$, $\forall \boldsymbol{z} : \overline{\sigma} \ldots = \forall z_1 : \sigma_1 \cdots \forall z_k : \sigma_k \ldots$.

A.1   Language

Types
1. $\mathbf{N}$ is a basic type.
2. If $\sigma_1,\ldots,\sigma_k$ and $\tau_1,\ldots,\tau_n$ are types, where $k \geq 0$ and $n \geq 1$, then $(\sigma_1 \times \cdots \times \sigma_k) \to S(\tau_1 \times \cdots \times \tau_n)$ is a type.

Terms and their type(s)
1. $x^\sigma : \sigma$ whenever x^σ is a variable of type σ.[11] (We assume an infinite supply of variables x^σ for each type σ.)
2. $f(t_1,\ldots,t_k) : S(\overline{\tau})$ in case $f : \overline{\sigma} \to S(\overline{\tau})$ and $t_i : \sigma_i$ for $1 \leq i \leq k$.
3. $\{(x_1,\ldots,x_n) \mid \psi\} : S(\overline{\tau})$ whenever $n \geq 1$, $x_i : \tau_i$ for $1 \leq i \leq n$, and ψ is a *delimited* formula.
4. $\lambda y_1,\ldots,y_k.t : \overline{\sigma} \to S(\overline{\tau})$ in case $t : S(\overline{\tau})$, and $y_i : \sigma_i$ for $1 \leq i \leq k$.
5. $IT^i_m(f_1,\ldots,f_m) : \mathbf{N}\times\overline{\sigma}\times S(\overline{\tau})^m \to S(\overline{\tau})$ in case $m > 0$, and for $1 \leq i \leq m$, either $f_i : \overline{\sigma} \times S(\overline{\tau}) \to S(\overline{\tau})$ or $f_i : \mathbf{N} \times \overline{\sigma} \times S(\overline{\tau}) \to S(\overline{\tau})$.

Delimited Formulas (d.f.)
1. If $t : \mathbf{N}$ and $s : \mathbf{N}$, then $Succ(t,s)$ is a delimited formula.
2. If $t : \mathbf{N}$ and $s : \mathbf{N}$, then $t = s$ is a delimited formula.
3. If $t_1,\ldots,t_n$ are terms of types $\tau_1,\ldots,\tau_n$ respectively, and $s : S(\overline{\tau})$, then $(t_1,\ldots,t_n) \in s$ is a delimited formula.
4. If φ and ψ are s. f. then so are $\neg\varphi$, $(\varphi \wedge \psi)$ and $(\varphi \vee \psi)$.
5. If x is a variable *of type* $\mathbf{N}$, and φ is a d. f. then so is $\exists x\varphi$.

---

[11] We shall usually omit the superscript, writing just $x : \sigma$.

Formulas

1. If $t : \mathbf{N}$ and $s : \mathbf{N}$, then $Succ(t, s)$ is a formula.
2. If t and s are terms *of the same type* then $t = s$ is a formula.
3. If $t_1, \ldots, t_n$ are terms of types $\tau_1, \ldots, \tau_n$ respectively, and $s : S(\overline{\tau})$, then $(t_1, \ldots, t_n) \in s$ is a formula.
4. If φ and ψ are formulas then so are $\neg\varphi$, $(\varphi \wedge \psi)$ and $(\varphi \vee \psi)$.
5. If x is a variable and φ is a formula, then $\exists x \varphi$ is a formula.

A.2   Proof System

Logic: Many-sorted first order logic with variable-binding terms operators, and with equality in *all* sorts (i.e. types).

Axioms:

Comprehension Axioms

- $\forall \boldsymbol{w}.(\boldsymbol{w}) \in \{(\boldsymbol{x}) \mid \psi\} \leftrightarrow \psi[\boldsymbol{w}/\boldsymbol{x}]$
- $\forall \boldsymbol{z}.(\lambda \boldsymbol{y}.t)(\boldsymbol{z}) = t[\boldsymbol{z}/\boldsymbol{y}]\}$

Extensionality Schema

- $\forall X : S(\overline{\tau}) \forall Y : S(\overline{\tau}).X = Y \leftrightarrow \forall \boldsymbol{w} : \overline{\tau}.\boldsymbol{w} \in X \leftrightarrow \boldsymbol{w} \in Y$
- $\forall f : \overline{\sigma} \to S(\overline{\tau}) \forall g : \overline{\sigma} \to S(\overline{\tau}).f = g \leftrightarrow \forall \boldsymbol{z} : \overline{\sigma}.f(\boldsymbol{z}) = g(\boldsymbol{z})$

The standard axioms for *Succ*

- $\exists! n \forall k. \neg Succ(k, n)$
- $\forall k \exists! n. Succ(k, n)$
- $\forall k \forall m \forall n. Succ(k, n) \wedge Succ(m, n) \to k = m$

Induction Schema

$\psi\{0/n\} \wedge (\forall n \forall k. Succ(n, k) \wedge \psi \to \psi\{k/n\}) \to \forall n \psi$

Axioms Schemas for iteration

For each $1 \le i \le m$:

- $\forall \boldsymbol{z} \forall \boldsymbol{f} \forall \boldsymbol{X}.IT_m^i(\boldsymbol{f})(1, \boldsymbol{z}, \boldsymbol{X}) = f_i([1,]\boldsymbol{z}, \boldsymbol{X})$
- $\forall n \forall k \forall \boldsymbol{z} \forall \boldsymbol{f} \forall \boldsymbol{X}.Succ(n, k) \to IT_m^i(\boldsymbol{f})(k, \boldsymbol{z}, \boldsymbol{X}) =$
  $\qquad IT_m^i(\boldsymbol{f})(n, \boldsymbol{z}, f_1([k,]\boldsymbol{z}, \boldsymbol{X}), \ldots, f_m([k,]\boldsymbol{z}, \boldsymbol{X}))$
  Where depending on the type of f_i , $f_i([k,]\boldsymbol{z}, \boldsymbol{X})$ means either $f_i(\boldsymbol{z}, \boldsymbol{X})$ or $f_i(k, \boldsymbol{z}, \boldsymbol{X})$, and similarly with $f_i([1,]\boldsymbol{z}, \boldsymbol{X})$.

Appendix 2: The Formal System PZF

Language

The language $\mathcal{L}_{PZF}$ of PZF is defined by a simultaneous recursion.

Predicates and Operations

- $=$ and $\in$ are binary predicates.
- If φ is a formula such that $\varphi \succ_{PZF} \emptyset$, and $Fv(\varphi) = \{x_1, \ldots, x_n\}$ where $n > 0$, then $[(x_1, \ldots, x_n) \mid \varphi]$ is an n-ary predicate.
- If t is a term such that $Fv(t) = \{y_1, \ldots, y_k\}$, then $\lambda y_1, \ldots, y_k.t$ is a k-ary operation.

Terms:
- Every variable is a term.
- If $\varphi \succ_{PZF} \{x\}$, then $\{x \mid \varphi\}$ is a term.
- If F is a k-ary operation, and $t_1, \ldots, t_k$ are terms, then $F(t_1, \ldots, t_k)$ is a term.

Formulas:
- If P is an n-ary predicate, then $P(t_1, \ldots, t_n)$ is an *atomic* formula whenever $t_1, \ldots, t_n$ are terms.
- If φ and ψ are formulas, and x is a variable, then $\neg\varphi$, $(\varphi \wedge \psi)$, $(\varphi \vee \psi)$, and $\exists x \varphi$ are formulas. ($\forall x \varphi$ and $\varphi \to \psi$ are taken as abbreviations for $\neg \exists x \neg \varphi$ and $\neg(\varphi \wedge \neg\psi)$, respectively.)
- If φ is a formula, t and s are terms, and x and y are distinct variables, then $(TC_{x,y}\varphi)(t, s)$ is a formula, and

$$Fv((TC_{x,y}\varphi)(t, s)) = (Fv(\varphi) - \{x, y\}) \cup Fv(t) \cup Fv(s)$$

The Safety Relation $\succ_{PZF}$:

($\in$) $x \in t \succ_{PZF} \{x\}$ if $x \notin Fv(t)$.
(**At**) $\varphi \succ_{PZF} \emptyset$ if φ is atomic.
(=)] $\varphi \succ_{PZF} \{x\}$ if $\varphi \in \{x \neq x, x = t, t = x\}$, and $x \notin Fv(t)$.
($\neg$) $\neg\varphi \succ_{PZF} \emptyset$ if $\varphi \succ_{PZF} \emptyset$.
($\vee$) $\varphi \vee \psi \succ_{PZF} X$ if $\varphi \succ_{PZF} X$ and $\psi \succ_{PZF} X$.
($\wedge$) $\varphi \wedge \psi \succ_{PZF} X \cup Y$ if $\varphi \succ_{PZF} X$, $\psi \succ_{PZF} Y$, and $Y \cap Fv(\varphi) = \emptyset$.
($\exists$) $\exists y \varphi \succ_{PZF} X - \{y\}$ if $y \in X$ and $\varphi \succ_{PZF} X$.
(TC) $(TC_{x,y}\varphi)(x, y) \succ_{PZF} X$ if $\varphi \succ_{PZF} X \cup \{x\}$, or $\varphi \succ_{PZF} X \cup \{y\}$.

Logic and Axioms

Logic: Classical $\mathcal{AL}$ with variable-binding terms operators, and equality.
Axioms:

Extensionality: $\forall z(z \in x \leftrightarrow z \in y) \to x = y$
Comprehension: The universal closures of formulas of the forms:
- $x \in \{x \mid \varphi\} \leftrightarrow \varphi$
- $[(x_1, \ldots, x_n) \mid \varphi](t_1, \ldots, t_n) \leftrightarrow \varphi\{t_1/x_1, \ldots, t_n/x_n\}$
- $(\lambda y_1, \ldots, y_k.t)(s_1, \ldots, s_k) = t\{s_1/y_1, \ldots, s_k/y_k\}$

$\in$-**induction:** $(\forall x(\forall y(y \in x \to \varphi\{y/x\}) \to \varphi)) \to \forall x \varphi$

References

1. Adams, R., Luo, Z.: Weyl's predicative classical mathematics as a logic-enriched type theory. ACM Trans. Comput. Log. **11**, 1–29 (2010)
2. Avron, A., Lev, S., Levy, N.: Safety, absoluteness, and computability. In: Ghica, D., Jung, A. (eds.) Proceedings of 27th EACSL Annual Conference on Computer Science Logic (CSL 2018), Leibniz International Proceedings in Informatics (LIPIcs), vol. 119, pp. 8:1–8:17 (2018)

3. Avron, A.: Transitive closure and the mechanization of mathematics. In: Kamareddine, F. (ed.) Thirty Five Years of Automating Mathematics, pp. 149–171. Kluwer Academic Publishers (2003)

4. Avron, A.: Constructibility and decidability versus domain independence and absoluteness. Theor. Comput. Sci. **394**, 144–158 (2008)

5. Avron, A.: A new approach to predicative set theory. In: Schindler, R. (ed.) Ways of Proof Theory, Onto Series in Mathematical Logic, pp. 31–63. onto verlag (2010)

6. Avron, A., Cohen, L.: Formalizing scientifically applicable mathematics in a definitional framework. J. Formaliz. Reason. **9**, 53–70 (2016)

7. Blass, A., Gurevich, Y.: Why sets? In: Avron, A., Dershowitz, N., Rabinovich, A. (eds.) Pillars of Computer Science. LNCS, vol. 4800, pp. 179–198. Springer, Heidelberg (2008). https://doi.org/10.1007/978-3-540-78127-1_11

8. Cohen, L., Avron, A.: The middle ground-ancestral logic. Synthese **196**(7), 2671–2693 (2019). https://doi.org/10.1007/s11229-015-0784-3

9. Cantone, D., Ferro, A., Omodeo, E.: Computable Set Theory. Clarendon Press, Oxford (1989)

10. Cantone, D., Omodeo, E., Policriti, A.: Set Theory for Computing: From Decisions Procedures to Declarative Programming with Sets. Springer, New York (2001). https://doi.org/10.1007/978-1-4757-3452-2

11. Devlin, K.J.: Constructibility. Perspectives in Mathematical Logic. Springer-Verlag, Berlin (1984)

12. Ewald, W.: From Kant to Hilbert. Clarendon Press, London (1996)

13. Feferman, S.: Systems of predicative analysis I. J. Symb. Log. **29**, 1–30 (1964)

14. Feferman, S.: Weyl Vindicated: Das Kontinuum seventy years later. In: Celluci, C., Sambin, G. (eds.) Remi e prospettive della logica e della scienza contemporanee, vol. I. Cooperative Libraria Universitaria Editrice, Bologna (1988). Reprinted in [15]

15. Feferman, S.: In the Light of Logic. Oxford University Press, New York (1998)

16. Feferman, S.: Predicativity. In: Shapiro, S. (ed.) The Oxford Handbook of the Philosophy of Mathematics and Logic, pp. 590–624. Oxford University Press (2005)

17. Hölder O.: Der angebliche Circulus Vitiosus und die sogennante Grundlagenkrise in der Analysis, Sitzungsber. der Leipziger Akademie **78**, 243–250 (1926). English translation in [19], pp. 143–148

18. Jensen, R.B.: The fine structure of the constructible hierarchy. Ann. Math. Log. **4**, 229–308 (1971)

19. Mancosu, P. (ed.) From Brouwer to Hilbert: The Debate on the Foundations of Mathematics in 1920s. Oxford University Press (1998)

20. Martin, R.M.: A homogeneous system for formal logic. J. Symb. Log. **8**, 1–23 (1943)

21. Myhill, J.: A derivation of number theory from ancestral theory. J. Symb. Log. **17**, 192–297 (1952)

22. Poincaré, H.: Les Mathématiques et la Logique, II, III, Revue de Métaphysique et Morale 14, pp. 17–34, 294–317 (1906). Translated in [12]

23. Richard, J.: Les Principes des Mathematiques et les problémes des ensembles. Revue general des sciences pures et appliqués **16**, 541–543 (1905)

24. Shapiro, S.: Foundations Without Foundationalism: A Case for Second-Order Logic. Oxford University Press, Oxford (1991)

25. Simpson, S.G.: Subsystems of Second-Order Arithmetic. Springer-Verlag, Berlin (1999)

26. Ullman, J.D.: Principles of Database and Knowledge-base Systems. Computer Science Press, New York (1988)

27. Weyl, H.: Das Kontinuum: Kritische Untersuchungen über die Grundlagen der Analysis, Veit, Leipzig (1918). Translated to English in [29]

28. Weyl, H.: The Continuum: A Critical Examination of the Foundation of Analysis. Thomas Jefferson University Press, Kirksville (1987). Translated by Stephen Pollard and Thomas Bole

29. Whitehead A.N., Russell B.: Principia Mathematica, 3 vols. Cambridge University Press, 1910–1913. Second edition, 1925–1927

Functional Thesauri, Classifying Topoi, Unification, and Flatness

Andreas Blass[✉]

Mathematics Department, University of Michigan, Ann Arbor, MI 48109-1043, USA
ablass@umich.edu

For Yuri Gurevich on the occasion of his eightieth birthday

Abstract. We describe a part of the theory of classifying topoi and its connections with various topics from computer science, logic, and algebra.

Keywords: Classifying topoi · Thesauri · Flat functors · Unification

1 Introduction

The goal of this paper is to indicate how a branch of category theory, the branch dealing with classifying topoi, interacts with some topics in computer science and some related algebra. Few if any of the results here are new, but I hope that assembling and juxtaposing them will be of some value.

To avoid excessive repetition, we refer to [2] for a general introduction to the most relevant ideas from topos theory, and to Johnstone's book [8], especially Chapters 4 and 6, for a detailed treatment.

For simplicity, results here will be presented in terms of Grothendieck topoi, but suitable formulations of them (using the internal logic) hold for elementary topoi bounded over any base topos with a natural number object.

2 Geometric Formulas, Sequents, and Theories

In this section, we review the definitions and basic properties of some classes of formulas that play a role in the theory of classifying topoi. We work in the context of a fixed, possibly multi-sorted, first-order vocabulary, and we treat equality as a logical symbol. Terms and atomic formulas are defined as usual in first-order logic.

The class of *geometric formulas* is the closure of the atomic formulas under finite conjunctions (including the empty conjunction $\top$), arbitrary, possibly infinite disjunctions (including the empty disjunction $\bot$), and existential quantification. This class is thus included in the classical infinitary language $L_{\infty,\omega}$, but we shall need to consider it in the context of (formally) intuitionistic logic, because that is the internal logic of topoi.

© Springer Nature Switzerland AG 2020
A. Blass et al. (Eds.): Gurevich Festschrift, LNCS 12180, pp. 46–56, 2020.
https://doi.org/10.1007/978-3-030-48006-6_4

Despite the restriction to intuitionistic logic, we still have that finite conjunctions distribute over disjunctions (even infinite disjunctions), that existential quantifiers can be pulled out of finite conjunctions (with bound variables renamed if necessary to avoid clashes, as in the algorithm for converting first-order formulas to prenex form), and that existential quantifiers distribute over disjunctions. (In contrast, we cannot, in general, pull all of the existential quantifiers out of an infinite disjunction, because the number of quantifiers, though finite in each disjunct, might not be bounded, and then the prenex form would have an infinite quantifier prefix.)

These facts suffice to imply that every geometric formula is equivalent to one in *geometric normal form*: A disjunction of existential quantifications of finite conjunctions of atomic formulas.

A *geometric sequent* is a sentence of the form $\forall \mathbf{x} \, (\varphi \to \psi)$ where φ and ψ are geometric formulas all of whose free variables occur in the finite sequence $\mathbf{x}$. Note that universal quantification and implication are applied here only to geometric formulas; they cannot be iterated.

A *geometric theory* is a set of geometric sequents. These are the theories for which classifying topoi are available.

The axioms of a geometric theory can be put into a somewhat simpler form as follows. First, in each of the theory's axioms $\forall \mathbf{x} \, (\varphi \to \psi)$, put φ and ψ into geometric normal form. Second, if the antecedent φ is a non-trivial disjunction $\bigvee_{i \in I} \varphi_i$, then replace the axiom

$$\forall \mathbf{x} \left(\left(\bigvee_{i \in I} \varphi_i \right) \to \psi \right)$$

with the logically equivalent set of sequents, one for each $i \in I$,

$$\forall \mathbf{x} \, (\varphi_i \to \psi).$$

(This step applies, in particular, when $I = \varnothing$; it simply removes the always true and therefore redundant sequent $\forall \mathbf{x} \, (\bot \to \psi)$ from the set of axioms.) After this step, the antecedents in the axioms are merely existentially quantified finite conjunctions of atomic formulas. Third, pull the existential quantifiers from the antecedents out into the universal quantifier prefix, so $\forall \mathbf{x} \, ((\exists \mathbf{y} \, \theta) \to \psi)$ becomes $\forall \mathbf{x}, \mathbf{y} \, (\theta \to \psi)$.

Thus, we can always arrange that, in the axioms of a geometric theory, all the antecedents are merely conjunctions of atomic formulas. None of these simplifications affect the consequents, which remain general geometric formulas (in geometric normal form, if desired).

A geometric sequent is called a *strict Horn sequent* if its antecedent is (as above) a finite conjunction of atomic formulas and its consequent is a single atomic formula. It would make little difference if the consequent were a finite conjunction $\bigwedge_{i \in I} \psi_i$ of atomic formulas, because such a sequent could be replaced by a logically equivalent finite set of sentences, one for each i, having just a single ψ_i in the consequent. On the other hand, existential quantifiers and disjunctions in the consequent will, in general, make a big difference, definitely affecting the structure of classifying topoi.

An important property of strict Horn theories T (i.e., geometric theories axiomatized by strict Horn sequents) is that one can describe models (in classical logic) by means of generators and relations. That is, given a set G of generators and a set R of atomic sentences built from our fixed vocabulary and names for the generators, there is a model whose elements are essentially the terms built, again, from the vocabulary plus generators, whose functions act in the natural way on terms, and whose relations are defined by making all and only those atomic sentences true which are entailed by the axioms of the theory T plus the relations in R. The word "essentially" in the preceding sentence refers to the fact that the equality relation is to be treated like other relations: it is to hold between two terms if and only if this follows from T plus R. So, strictly speaking, the elements of this model are not simply terms but rather equivalence classes of terms with respect to this equality relation. We denote this model by $\langle G : R \rangle$. (The assumption that T is axiomatized by strict Horn sequents is used in proving that the structure so defined satisfies T. For more general geometric theories, one would need something like Skolemization to take care of existential quantifiers and completion to take care of disjunctions in the consequents of the axioms.) Note that the terms and the atomic sentences used in this construction do not involve variables.

Particularly important for our purposes will be the case where both G and R are finite. In this case, we speak of *finitely presented* models of T. When dealing with these, it will often be convenient to identify the generators with some variables; this will cause no notational conflict because of the observation at the end of the preceding paragraph.

3   Classifying Topoi for Strict Horn Theories

The classifying topos of a strict Horn theory T admits a simple description as a topos of presheaves, i.e., the category of set-valued functors on a certain category associated to T. In fact, there are two natural ways to view that category, both of which are useful, so we describe the situation here in some detail.

We write **Set** for the category whose objects are all of the sets and whose morphisms are all of the functions between them. For any category **C**, we write $\mathbf{C}^{\mathrm{op}}$ for the dual category and $[\mathbf{C}, \mathbf{Set}]$ for the functor category whose objects are the functors from **C** to **Set** and whose morphisms are the natural transformations between such functors. A *presheaf* on **C** is contravariant functor from **C** to **Set**, so the category of presheaves on **C** is $[\mathbf{C}^{\mathrm{op}}, \mathbf{Set}]$.

By the *classifying topos* of a theory T, one means a topos $\mathbf{B}T$ such that, for any topos **E**, the category of geometric morphisms[1] $\mathbf{E} \to \mathbf{B}T$ is equivalent

---

[1] We adopt the "logical" convention that a morphism in this category is a natural transformation between the left-adjoint parts f^* of two geometric morphisms. The "geometric" convention would use the right-adjoint parts instead and would result in a category dual to ours.

to the category of models of T in $\mathbf{E}$ (in the sense of the internal logic of $\mathbf{E}$). In other words, models of T in any topos are essentially the same thing as geometric morphisms from that topos to the classifying topos of T. It is known [8, Chapter 6] that all geometric theories have classifying topoi.

If T is a strict Horn theory, then its classifying topos is the category $\mathbf{B}T = [\mathbf{FP}T, \mathbf{Set}]$ of covariant set-valued functors on the category $\mathbf{FP}T$ of finitely presented models of T. This description of the classifying topos for strict Horn theories is well known; the reference I'm aware of is the 1981 doctoral thesis of Andrej Ščedrov (now Andre Scedrov), published in [10]. (The description is also in [5], which, though published earlier than [10], was written later.)

Thus, the classifying topos $\mathbf{B}T$ is the topos of presheaves on the dual category $\mathbf{FP}T^{\mathrm{op}}$. This dual category admits the following alternative description. Given a finitely presented model $\langle G : R \rangle$ of T, we may assume, by renaming the generators if necessary, that G consists of a finite list $\mathbf{x}$ of variables. (Technically, we should have adopted some such convention sooner, because a presheaf is supposed to be a set-valued functor on a small category.) Then R is a finite set of atomic formulas involving variables only from this list $\mathbf{x}$. The conjunction of R defines a set in any model M of T, namely the set $\{\mathbf{x} : \bigwedge R\}^M$; if the list $\mathbf{x}$ has length l then this is the set of those l-tuples from (the underlying set of) M that satisfy in M all the formulas of R. In fact, for any model M of T in any topos, we similarly get a subobject $\{\mathbf{x} : \bigwedge R\}^M$ of M^l. We think of $\{\mathbf{x} : \bigwedge R\}$ (without a superscript M) as a syntactic description of these sets or subobjects, admitting semantic interpretations in all models M of T. These "syntactic sets" will be the objects in our alternative description of $\mathbf{FP}T^{\mathrm{op}}$.

A morphism from $\{\mathbf{x} : R\}$ to $\{\mathbf{y} : S\}$ is given by a list $\mathbf{t}$ of terms, of the same length as $\mathbf{y}$, and built from our fixed vocabulary and the variables in $\mathbf{x}$, satisfying the following condition: If one replaces in S each variable from $\mathbf{y}$ by the corresponding term from $\mathbf{t}$, then the resulting (atomic) formulas are consequences of T and R. The intuition behind this definition is that the terms $\mathbf{t}$, interpreted in any model M of T, tell how to map $\{\mathbf{x} : R\}^M$ to $\{\mathbf{y} : S\}^M$ by sending any tuple of values for $\mathbf{x}$ to the resulting values (in M) of the terms $\mathbf{t}$ as values for $\mathbf{y}$. Two lists of terms are regarded as defining the same morphism if their equality is entailed by $T \cup R$.

Notice that a tuple $\mathbf{t}$ of terms as described above also provides a homomorphism of models from $\langle \mathbf{y} : S \rangle$ to $\langle \mathbf{x} : R \rangle$. Namely, given any element of $\langle \mathbf{y} : S \rangle$, a term built from our vocabulary and $\mathbf{y}$, substitute the terms $\mathbf{t}$ for $\mathbf{y}$ to get a term built from $\mathbf{x}$. It is routine to check that this construction is well-defined, commutes with the interpretations of our vocabulary's function symbols, and preserves, in the forward direction, the interpretation of our vocabulary's predicate symbols. That is, it is a homomorphism of models of T.

These two ways of interpreting a tuple $\mathbf{t}$ of terms provide the equivalence between $\mathbf{FP}T^{\mathrm{op}}$ and the category of syntactic sets, a category sometimes called the syntactic site in this context. (There is a more general notion of syntactic site in [8, Section 7.4], defined there for finitary geometric theories but generalizable to arbitrary geometric theories. It is more complicated than what we have done here, partly because morphisms are not given by terms in general and partly because one needs to deal with sheaves rather than presheaves.)

4   The Object Classifier

This section is devoted to the simplest of strict Horn theories, the single-sorted theory O in the empty vocabulary (so the only atomic formulas are equations between variables) with no axioms. So a model of O is just a set, and a model of O in a topos $\mathbf{E}$ is just an object of $\mathbf{E}$. (The symbol O for the theory refers to "object".)

Although a finitely presented model $\langle G : R \rangle$ of O is in general given by a finite set G of variables and a finite set R of relations, it is always isomorphic to one for which R is empty and the model is just G. A somewhat inefficient but usefully generalizable proof of this reduction of R to $\varnothing$ consists of two observations: If R contains a relation of the form $x = x$, then this can simply be deleted without changing $\langle G : R \rangle$. If R contains an equation $x = y$ with distinct x and y, then we can delete this relation from R, replace y by x in all other relations in R, and delete y from G; again, $\langle G : R \rangle$ is unchanged.

So the category $\mathbf{FP}O$ of finitely presented models of O is (equivalent to) the category of finite sets and all functions between them, often called $\mathbf{Fin}$. As indicated earlier, though, it is better to use a small category here, by limiting the elements of these finite sets to come from some fixed infinite set, and it is convenient to take that infinite set to be the set of variables. So our $\mathbf{Fin}$ is the category of finite sets of variables. The classifying topos $\mathbf{B}O = [\mathbf{Fin}, \mathbf{Set}]$ is called the *object classifier*.

An object in the object classifier topos is thus a covariant functor $X : \mathbf{Fin} \to \mathbf{Set}$. So it consists of, first, for each finite set v of variables, a set $X(v)$ and, second, for each function $f : v \to w$, a function $X(f) : X(v) \to X(w)$, subject to the requirements for a functor that it respect composition and identity maps.

This sort of structure is familiar in a quite different context. Consider a single-sorted vocabulary consisting of only function symbols (a signature in the sense of universal algebra), and let $X(v)$, for any finite set v of variables, denote the set of all simple terms over v, by which I mean terms consisting of a single function symbol applied to a list of variables from v. (There is no nesting of function symbols here.) For any $f : v \to w$, there is an obvious function, which we call $X(f)$ from $X(v)$ to $X(w)$, namely, given a simple term over v, replace each of those variables by its image under f to get a simple term over w. It is clear that this construction produces a functor as in the preceding paragraph, i.e., an object of $\mathbf{B}O$.

If we select, for each function symbol α in our vocabulary, one term formed by α followed by a list of distinct variables, then any simple term is obtained from one of these by applying some $X(f)$ to suitably rename the variables. In this sense, the functor X is generated by these selected terms. We can think of it as generated by the vocabulary, and we can even, by abuse of language, think of X as essentially being the vocabulary. A (single-sorted) functional vocabulary "is" an object of $\mathbf{B}O$.

The converse, however, is not true. An object of $\mathbf{B}O$ can have more structure than a mere vocabulary. To see the issue in the simplest case, consider an X arising as above from a functional vocabulary. Suppose $v = \{x, y\}$ where x and y are distinct variables, let α be a binary function symbol of our vocabulary, so $\alpha(x, y)$ is a simple term in $X(v)$, and let f be the non-trivial permutation of v. Then $X(f)$ maps $\alpha(x, y)$ to a different term $\alpha(y, x)$. More generally, for arbitrary finite sets v of variables and arbitrary maps $f : v \to v$, the only simple terms in $X(v)$ that are fixed by $X(f)$ are those in the image of $X(i)$, where i is the inclusion map into v of the set of fixed points of f. (More generally yet, any X arising from a functional vocabulary preserves equalizers.)

An arbitrary X in $\mathbf{B}O$ may have far more fixed points than this. As an example, consider a vocabulary with a single, binary function symbol α, and let $X(v)$ consist not of simple terms over v but of equivalence classes of these under the commutative law, i.e., $\alpha(x, y) = \alpha(y, x)$. With the obvious action $X(f)$ for functions f, this produces an object of $\mathbf{B}O$ that does not arise from a vocabulary.

One can obviously generalize this example by having function symbols with various numbers of arguments and various degrees of symmetry under permutations of their arguments. One could generalize the notion of vocabulary by allowing such symmetry considerations to be built into the vocabulary. For example, the commutative law $\alpha(x, y) = \alpha(y, x)$ would then not be an axiom but rather a syntactic identity; the two sides of the equation would be the same term.

This extension of the notion of "vocabulary" to incorporate symmetry is parallel to an extension that Yuri and I introduced in [3] (see also [4]) incorporating various sorts of symmetry for predicates. The result (with some additional modifications[2]) was what we called thesauri. It seems that the idea of incorporating symmetry into the functions, rather than predicates, of a vocabulary is sufficiently similar to deserve the name *functional thesauri*.

The amount of structure that can occur in objects X of $\mathbf{B}O$, however, goes beyond symmetry of this sort, because X works with arbitrary functions f, not just permutations. Thus, for example, if a vocabulary contains a ternary function symbol β, then $X(v)$ could consist of equivalence classes of simple terms under the equivalence relation that makes $\beta(x, x, y) = \beta(x, y, y)$. More generally, we can start with objects X of $\mathbf{B}O$ given by vocabularies and form all sorts of quotients by imposing various identities between simple terms.

The reader may wonder why I restricted attention to simple terms. What would go wrong if we allowed arbitrary terms instead? Nothing would go wrong, but arbitrary terms have additional structure—namely the possibility of substituting terms for variables in other terms—that does not appear at the level of

---

[2] The additional modifications involved a group action and a probability distribution on the set of "truth values" of the predicates, a set that was not required to contain only "true" and "false". In our present, functional situation, there are no truth values, and so those modifications are not applicable.

just objects of $\mathbf{B}O$. It does, however, appear when we take account more fully of the role of $\mathbf{B}O$ as the object classifier. That will be the topic of the next section.

Before treating nesting, however, we describe the geometric morphisms $\mathbf{E} \to \mathbf{B}O$ that correspond to objects of a topos $\mathbf{E}$. Suppose that A is an object of $\mathbf{E}$, that $f : \mathbf{E} \to \mathbf{B}O$ is the corresponding geometric morphism, and that X is an object of $\mathbf{B}O$. So X is a functor $\mathbf{Fin} \to \mathbf{Set}$ as above, and $f^*(X)$ is an object of E. One can calculate, following Diaconescu [7] (see also [8, Section 4.3]), that this object $f^*(X)$ admits the following description in the internal logic of $\mathbf{E}$. Its elements are equivalence classes of pairs $(x, \boldsymbol{a})$ where $x \in X(v)$ for some finite set v of variables and $\boldsymbol{a}$ is a v-indexed family (also called a v-tuple) of elements of A. The equivalence relation is generated by declaring that, for any map $q : w \to v$, any $y \in X(w)$, and any v-tuple $\boldsymbol{a}$ of elements of A, the pair $(X(q)(y), \boldsymbol{a})$ is equivalent to $(y, (\boldsymbol{a})q)$, where $(\boldsymbol{a})q$ is the w-tuple obtained by rearranging $\boldsymbol{a}$ according to q, i.e., the w-tuple whose i^{th} component is the $q(i)^{\text{th}}$ component of $\boldsymbol{a}$.

In the case when X arises from a functional vocabulary, or even from a functional thesaurus, one can view the element of $f^*(X)$ given by $(x, \boldsymbol{a})$ as the result of substituting the elements of $\boldsymbol{a}$ for the variables of v in the simple term x. That is, the elements of x of $X(v)$ not only transform like function symbols under the transformations $X(f)$ but are used as function symbols in $f^*(X)$. It seems worthwhile to view all objects X of $\mathbf{B}O$, not just those arising from functional thesauri, as some sort of generalized functional vocabularies.

5   Monoidal Structure and Monoids

Because $\mathbf{B}O$ is the classifying topos for the theory O of objects, we know that any topos $\mathbf{E}$ is equivalent to the category whose objects are the geometric morphisms from $\mathbf{E}$ to $\mathbf{B}O$ and whose morphisms are natural transformations between the left-adjoint parts of these geometric morphisms. In particular, $\mathbf{B}O$ is equivalent to the category of its own geometric endomorphisms.

The category of geometric endomorphisms of $\mathbf{B}O$ (or of any topos) has a monoidal structure given by composition of endofunctors. That induces a monoidal structure on the equivalent category $\mathbf{B}O$, and we can calculate this tensor-product operation on the objects of $\mathbf{B}O$ as follows. Let A and B be two objects of $\mathbf{B}O$, with classifying geometric endomorphisms α and β, respectively, of $\mathbf{B}O$. Then $A \otimes B$ is defined as the object of $\mathbf{B}O$ classified by the composite endomorphism $\alpha \circ \beta$, and this is easily computed to be just $\beta^*(A)$. Applying the description in the preceding section, we find the following description of this object $A \otimes B$. For any finite set v, the set $(A \otimes B)(v)$ consists of equivalence classes of pairs $(a, \boldsymbol{b})$ where $a \in A(w)$ for some finite set w and where $\boldsymbol{b}$ is a w-tuple of elements of $B(v)$; two such pairs are deemed equivalent if their first components are related by some rearrangement function $q : w \to w'$ and the tuples in the second components are correspondingly rearranged.

In terms of generalized vocabularies, this means that the function symbols in $A \otimes B$ can be viewed as the result of nesting function symbols of B inside those of A. The nesting has depth exactly 2; a function symbol from A is applied to simple terms from vocabulary B.

In particular, $A \otimes A$ has function symbols that amount to depth-2 nesting of function symbols from A. Similarly, products of k factors in this monoidal structure correspond to depth-k nesting of function symbols.

The identity object I for this monoidal structure is the inclusion functor **Fin** $\rightarrow$ **Set**, which sends each finite set v and each function between finite sets to itself. Each variable x in the set v thus becomes a v-place function symbol in the vocabulary I; it should be thought of as the projection to the xth component. Often, one does not introduce special symbols for these projections but instead just uses the variables themselves. With this convention, I can be viewed as describing depth-0 nesting of function symbols, which seems appropriate since it is a 0-fold iteration of $\otimes$.

Like any monoidal structure, that of $\mathbf{B}O$ determines a notion of monoid, an object A of $\mathbf{B}O$ equipped with a multiplication morphism $\mu : A \otimes A \rightarrow A$ and a unit "element" $\eta : I \rightarrow A$, subject to a category-theoretic formulation of the associative and unit laws. Using the descriptions of $\otimes$ and I above, and thinking of an object A as a generalized functional vocabulary, we find that a monoid structure on A provides a way to interpret depth-2 nested terms as simple (i.e., depth-1) terms via μ. It also provides, via η, simple terms that can be identified with the variables themselves, i.e., projection operations. Specifically, if x is one of the elements of a finite set v of variables, then the η-image in $A(v)$ of $x \in I(v)$ serves as the projection from v-tuples to their x^{th} components. It turns out that the monoid laws, of associativity and units, are exactly what one needs to make this set-up an abstract clone. To summarize: Monoids in the monoidal category $\mathbf{B}O$ are equivalent to abstract clones.

6   Flatness

In this section, we slightly enlarge the context of the preceding two sections; instead of working with the theory O that has empty vocabulary and no axioms, we work with an equational theory, i.e., a theory T whose vocabulary consists of function symbols, and whose axioms are just equations. Such axioms are strict Horn sentences whose antecedents are just the empty conjunction $\top$. So we are essentially doing universal algebra.

Lawvere [9] found an elegant category-theoretic description of the models of such a theory T. Let **FF**T be the category of finitely generated free models of T. It is the full subcategory of **FP**T consisting of the objects $\langle G : R \rangle$ for which R is empty. Then a model M of T amounts to a functor **FF**$T^{\text{op}} \rightarrow$ **Set** that preserves products.

The dual category mentioned here, **FF**T^{op} is a syntactic site, as described earlier, but restricted to objects of the form $\{\mathbf{x} : \top\}$. The semantics of such an object associates to each model M the power M^l, where l is the length of the sequence of variables $\mathbf{x}$.

Note that a morphism from $\langle v : \varnothing \rangle$ to $\langle w : \varnothing \rangle$ in **FF**T is given by a v-tuple of terms built from the vocabulary of T and variables from w (modulo T-provable equality). The morphisms of **FFT** thus amount to tuples of elements from the clone determined by T. Part of Lawvere's discovery was that the axioms for clones, when arranged in this context, become the familiar notion of preserving products.

What happens if we try to use the simpler category **FFT** instead of **FPT** to produce a classifying topos? Diaconescu's theorem ([7] or [8, Theorem 4.34]) tells us that [**FFT**, **Set**] is the classifying topos for *flat presheaves* on **FFT**. We refer to [8] for the general notion of a flat functor and confine ourselves here to the case where the domain category has finite products, since this covers our current situation where the domain is **FFT**^{op}.

Definition 1. *A functor F from a category* **C** *with finite products to* **Set** *is flat if it preserves products and, whenever $\gamma, \delta : A \to B$ in* **C** *and $a \in F(A)$ with $F(\gamma)(a) = F(\delta)(a)$, then there exist $\alpha : E \to A$ and $e \in F(E)$ such that $\gamma \circ \alpha = \delta \circ \alpha$ and $a = F(\alpha)(e)$.*

If **C** had not only finite products but also equalizers, then flatness would be equivalent to preserving finite limits. But **FFT**^{op} does not generally have equalizers.

The condition about a and e in the definition of flatness says intuitively that an equation $F(\gamma)(a) = F(\delta)(a)$ between elements in the image of F is "caused" by an equation $\gamma \circ \alpha = \delta \circ \alpha$ in **C** that is applicable to a because $a = F(\alpha)(e)$. It is analogous to one of the characterizations of flat modules in algebra that says any linear relation between elements of the module is "caused" by a linear relation in the ring.

A more abstract connection with module theory arises from the fact that one can define a tensor-product between covariant and contravariant set-valued functors on any small category; the tensor-product is just a set. It then turns out that a covariant functor is flat if and only if tensor product with it, as an operation from contravariant functors to sets, is left-exact. This matches the fact that a module is flat if and only if tensor product with it is left-exact.

Two special cases are worth mentioning. First, if **C** is a partially ordered set, considered as a category with at most one morphism between any two objects, then a flat functor on **C** amounts to just a filter F in that partially ordered set. The values of the functor are singletons or empty, and the places where it is a singleton are the filter F. Second, if **C** is a group, considered as a category with only one object, then a flat functor on **C** amounts to just a torsor under that group.

Flat functors on any **C** are models of a certain geometric theory. A particularly interesting case arises when **C** is **FFT** for a theory as above but with no axioms. So, in the language of universal algebra, models of T are arbitrary algebras for the signature of T. By Lawvere's work, these algebras are the product-preserving functors **FFT**$^{\mathrm{op}} \to$ **Set**. Which of them are flat? It turns out that they are characterized by the following geometric sequents, in which we omit the initial quantifiers; all free variables are to be understood as universally quantified over the whole sequent.

- $x = t \rightarrow \bot$ when x is a variable that occurs in the term t but is not the whole term t.
- $f(\mathbf{x}) = g(\mathbf{y}) \rightarrow \bot$ when f and g are distinct function symbols.
- $f(\mathbf{x}) = f(\mathbf{y}) \rightarrow x_i = y_i$ where x_i and y_i are corresponding components of $\mathbf{x}$ and $\mathbf{y}$.

These axioms are familiar from a quite different context: unification. They are the properties used to simplify unification problems, where one is given a list of equations between terms and one seeks the most general terms which, when substituted for the variables, make the given list of equations true (or to show that no such terms exist). The axioms above, together with general facts about equality (like substituting equals for equals) are used to simplify the given equations until the solution becomes trivial.

7   Conclusion

An exploration of a small part of the theory of classifying topoi has led to connections with thesauri (which first arose in connection with zero-one laws in finite model theory), with flatness (a useful technical tool in commutative algebra and a frequently used "good behavior" assumption in algebraic geometry), and with unification (an essential ingredient in logic programming).

There is much more to explore. We have looked here only at classifying topoi for strict Horn theories. A natural but small first step is to remove "strict", i.e., to allow the consequent in a sequent to be $\bot$ rather than an atomic formula. It turns out that one still gets a classifying topos of presheaves on a syntactic site, but not every presentation $\langle G : R \rangle$ defines a model, because R can be inconsistent with the axioms.

Having allowed the empty disjunction in the consequent, it is natural to allow more general disjunctions. Here, presheaves no longer suffice in general; one needs sheaves. Nevertheless, those sheaf topoi can often be simplified by means of the "Lemme de comparaison" of [1], and, in fortunate cases, the simplification can bring us back to a presheaf topos.

For example, consider the theory with one binary relation $\neq$ and axioms saying that it is the negation of equality. In the terminology of intuitionistic logic, the models of this theory are sets with decidable equality. In geometric form, the axioms are (again omitting universal quantifiers)

- $x \neq x \rightarrow \bot$.
- $\top \rightarrow (x = y \vee x \neq y)$.

Its classifying topos is the topos $[\mathbf{FI}, \mathbf{Set}]$ where $\mathbf{FI}$ is the category of finite sets and one-to-one maps, a category that has recently made multiple appearances in representation theory, beginning with [6].

References

1. Artin, M., Grothendieck, A., Verdier, J.-L.: Théorie des topos et cohomologie étale des schémas. Tome 1: Théorie des topos, Séminaire de Géométrie Algébrique du Bois-Marie 1963–1964 (SGA 4). Springer Lecture Notes in Mathematics, vol. 269. Springer, Heidelberg (1972). https://doi.org/10.1007/BFb0081551
2. Blass, A.: Topoi and computation. Bull. Europ. Assoc. Theor. Comp. Sci. **36**, 57–65 (1988)
3. Blass, A., Gurevich, Y.: Strong extension axioms and Shelah's zero-one law for choiceless polynomial time. J. Symb. Logic **68**, 65–131 (2003)
4. Blass, A., Gurevich, Y.: Zero-one laws: Thesauri and parametric conditions. Bull. Europ. Assoc. Theor. Comp. Sci. **91**, 125–144 (2007)
5. Blass, A., Ščedrov, A.: Classifying topoi and finite forcing. J. Pure Appl. Algebra **28**, 111–140 (1983)
6. Church, T., Ellenberg, J., Farb, B.: FI-modules and stability for representations of symmetric groups. Duke Math. J. **164**, 1833–1910 (2015). https://arxiv.org/abs/1204.4533
7. Diaconescu, R.: Change of base for toposes with generators. J. Pure Appl. Algebra **6**, 191–218 (1975)
8. Johnstone, P.T.: Topos Theory. Academic Press, Cambridge (1977)
9. Lawvere, W.F.: Functorial semantics of algebraic theories. Ph.D. thesis, Columbia University (1963). Reprinted with additional material from the author in Theory and Applications of Categories. http://tac.mta.ca/tac/reprints/articles/5/tr5.pdf
10. Ščedrov, A.: Forcing and classifying topoi, Mem. Amer. Math. Soc. **48** (1984). #295

Parameterized Parallel Computing
and First-Order Logic

Yijia Chen[1] and Jörg Flum[2(✉)]

[1] Fudan University, Shanghai, China
[2] Albert-Ludwigs-Universität, Freiburg im Breisgau, Germany
yijiachen@fudan.edu.cn, flum@uni-freiburg.de

Abstract. The relationship between the complexity class AC^0 and first-order logic transfers to the parameterized class para-AC^0, the parameterized analogue of AC^0. In the last years this relationship has turned out to be very fruitful. In this paper we survey some of the results obtained, mainly applications of logic to complexity theory. However the last section presents a strict hierarchy theorem for first-order logic obtained by a result of complexity theory.

1 Introduction

The complexity class AC^0 is seen as a model for effective parallel computing. It is one of the best understood classical complexity classes. Already in [1,16] it was shown that PARITY, the problem of deciding whether a binary string contains an even number of 1's, is not in AC^0. Since PARITY has a very low complexity, for many other problems, including VERTEX-COVER and CLIQUE, the AC^0-lower bound can be easily derived by reductions from PARITY.

Gurevich and Lewis [17] were the first to observe that AC^0 is intimately connected to first-order logic. The connection was further sharpened by Barrington et al. [6]. In fact, the problems decidable by dlogtime-uniform AC^0-circuits are precisely those definable in first-order logic FO with built-in arithmetic.

Based on the general guideline presented in [14] to define the parameterized analogue of a classical complexity class, in [13] Elberfeld et al. introduced and studied the parameterized class para-AC^0: A problem is in para-AC^0 if it can be computed by dlogtime-uniform AC^0-circuits after an (arbitrarily complex) *precomputation* on the parameter. Bannach et al. [3] showed that para-AC^0 contains the parameterized vertex cover problem, one of the archetypal fixed-parameter tractable problems. Rossman [20] proved that the parameterized clique problem is not in para-AC^0. Using some appropriate weak parameterized reductions, it is not hard to see that many other parameterized problems, including the dominating set problem [9], are not in para-AC^0.

The connection between AC^0 and first-order logic survives in the parameterized world: A parameterized problem is in para-AC^0 precisely if it is definable in FO with built-in arithmetic after a precomputation on the parameter. In [12] it was proven that for a parameterized problem Q this is equivalent to the fact that

© Springer Nature Switzerland AG 2020
A. Blass et al. (Eds.): Gurevich Festschrift, LNCS 12180, pp. 57–78, 2020.
https://doi.org/10.1007/978-3-030-48006-6_5

all slices of Q (i.e, all classes of positive instances of Q with the same parameter) are FO-definable with built-in arithmetic and bounded quantifier rank. Moreover in [12] it was shown with the color-coding method [2] that this is already the case if every slice is definable in the logic CFO with bounded quantifier rank. Here CFO, first-order logic with counting, denotes the logic obtained from FO by adding the quantifiers "there are at least k many x" for $k \in \mathbb{N}$ and specifying that each such quantifier adds only one to the quantifier rank. Note that for the class of all graphs without edges already the existence of at least k vertices cannot be expressed by an FO-sentence (without arithmetic) of quantifier rank $k - 1$, i.e., not by a sentence of quantifier rank independent of k.

Motivated by the preceding result, in [8] we analyzed what classes K of structures *have generalized quantifier elimination*. By this we mean that for K every FO-definable property can already be defined by an FO-formula with built-in arithmetic whose quantifier rank is bounded by a constant depending only on K. It turned out that a class K has generalized quantifier elimination if and only if the model-checking problem for FO on K parameterized by the length of the formula is in para-AC^0. Recently [10] we used this characterization to show that the model-checking problem for classes of graphs of bounded shrub-depth and FO (even for monadic second-order logic) is in para-AC^0.

To the best of our knowledge so far the color-coding method is the only nontrivial method to prove generalized quantifier elimination for a class of structures. There is a close relationship between parameterized model-checking problems and slicewise FO-definable parameterized problems [5,8]. Perhaps this explains why nearly all nontrivial proofs showing membership of a parameterized problem in para-AC^0 use the color-coding technique [3–5,9,10,12].

Content of this paper. In Sect. 2 we fix some notation. In Sect. 3 we present two results (proven in later sections), which we apply to various parameterized problems in order to show their membership in para-AC^0. In Sect. 4 we prove the following characterization of para-AC^0 in terms of FO: A parameterized problem is in para-AC^0 if and only if all its slices are definable in first-order logic with built-in arithmetic by sentences of bounded quantifier rank. The main tool to get this kind of slicewise FO-definability is the color-coding method. We explain this in Sect. 5. Using the characterization via slicewise FO-definability one can prove that the model-checking problem for a class K of structures and FO is in para-AC^0 just in case K has generalized quantifier elimination. This result is presented in Sect. 6. While so far all results can be viewed as applications of logic to complexity theory, in the last section we prove a result the other way round: We show that the hierarchy whose qth level is the class of FO-sentences of quantifier rank q is strict on the class of structures with built-in arithmetic.

2   Preliminaries

For $n \in \mathbb{N}$ we set $[n] := \{1, \ldots, n\}$ and $[0, n) := \{0, 1, \ldots, n - 1\}$.

A *vocabulary* τ is a finite set of relation symbols. Each relation symbol R has an *arity* denoted by ar(R). A *structure* $\mathcal{A}$ of vocabulary τ, or τ-*structure*, consists of a nonempty set A called the *universe* of $\mathcal{A}$, and of an interpretation $R^{\mathcal{A}} \subseteq A^r$ of each r-ary relation symbol $R \in \tau$. In this paper all structures have a finite universe. The letters $\tau, \tau', \ldots$ will always denote *relational* vocabularies. Let $\mathrm{STR}[\tau]$ denote the class of τ-structures.

Formulas φ of *first-order logic* FO of vocabulary τ are built up from *atomic formulas* $x_1 = x_2$ and $Rx_1 \ldots x_r$ (where $R \in \tau$ is of arity r and $x_1, x_2, \ldots, x_r$ are variables) using the boolean connectives $\neg$, $\wedge$, and $\vee$ and the universal $\forall$ and the existential $\exists$ quantifiers. The quantifier rank $\mathrm{qr}(\varphi)$ of an FO-formula is the maximum number of nested quantifiers in φ. By $\mathrm{FO}[\tau]$ (and $\mathrm{FO}_q[\tau]$ for $q \in \mathbb{N}$) we denote the class of FO-formulas (of quantifier rank $\leq q$) of vocabulary τ. By the notation $\varphi(\bar{x})$ with $\bar{x} = x_1, \ldots, x_e$ we indicate that the variables free in φ are among $x_1, \ldots, x_e$ and for a structure $\mathcal{A}$ and $\bar{a} = a_1, \ldots, a_e$ in A by $\mathcal{A} \models \varphi(\bar{a})$ we mean that $\bar{a}$ satisfies $\varphi(\bar{x})$ in $\mathcal{A}$.

3   Tools from Logic to Show Membership in para-AC^0

We already mentioned that para-AC^0 contains the parameterized problems that are in dlogtime-uniform AC^0 after a precomputation on the parameter. Before presenting precise definitions and a logical characterization of para-AC^0 in Sect. 4, we deal with two consequences of the results obtained in Sect. 5. They can be used as "black boxes" to derive membership of parameterized problems in para-AC^0. Indeed many results showing that a parameterized problem is in para-AC^0 have been obtained in this way more or less explicitly. First we recall the definition of parameterized problem in our logical framework.

Definition 1. A parameterized problem is a subclass Q of $\mathrm{STR}[\tau] \times \mathbb{N}$ for some vocabulary τ, where for each $k \in \mathbb{N}$ the class $Q_k := \{\mathcal{A} \mid (\mathcal{A}, k) \in Q\}$ is closed under isomorphisms. The class Q_k is the *kth slice* of Q.

Every pair $(\mathcal{A}, k) \in \mathrm{STR}[\tau] \times \mathbb{N}$ is an *instance* of Q, $\mathcal{A}$ its *input* and k its *parameter*.

In the following Q will always denote a parameterized problem and $Q \subseteq \mathrm{STR}[\tau] \times \mathbb{N}$ unless stated otherwise explicitly.

Let CFO be the extension of FO with counting quantifiers $\exists^{\geq k}$ for $k \in \mathbb{N}$ and specify that such a quantifier adds *one* to the quantifier rank. The meaning of a CFO-formula $\exists^{\geq k} x \varphi(x, \bar{y})$ is the same as that of

$$\exists x_1 \ldots \exists x_k \left(\bigwedge_{i,j \in [k],\ i<j} \neg x_i = x_j \ \wedge \ \bigwedge_{i \in [k]} \varphi(x_i, \bar{y}) \right).$$

If φ itself contains no further counting quantifiers, this is an FO-formula whose quantifier rank is $k + \mathrm{qr}(\varphi)$, i.e., depends on k. We view the quantifiers $\exists^{\leq k}, \exists^{=k}, \ldots$ in CFO-formulas as abbreviations; e.g., $\exists^{=k} x \varphi$ abbreviates $\exists^{\geq k} x \varphi \wedge \neg \exists^{\geq k+1} x \varphi$. Note that they all add one to the quantifier rank.

For $q \in \mathbb{N}$ let CFO$_q$ be the class of CFO-formulas of quantifier rank $\leq q$.

Definition 2. The parameterized problem Q is *eventually slicewise definable in CFO with bounded quantifier rank*, in short $Q \in_{evt} \text{CFO}_{qr}$, if there is a $q \in \mathbb{N}$, a computable function $k \mapsto \varphi_k$ with $\varphi_k \in \text{CFO}_q[\tau]$ and a computable function $evt : \mathbb{N} \to \mathbb{N}$ such that for all instances $(\mathcal{A}, k)$ with $|A| \geq evt(k)$,

$$(\mathcal{A}, k) \in Q \iff \mathcal{A} \models \varphi_k.$$

Here the first "logical" tool to show membership in **para-AC^0** (proven in Sect. 5).

Proposition 3. *Let Q be decidable. If $Q \in_{evt} \text{CFO}_{qr}$, then $Q \in$ para-AC^0.*

Let us see how we can apply this result. For $k \in \mathbb{N}$ consider the FO-sentences

$$\varphi_k := \exists x_1 \ldots \exists x_k \left(\bigwedge_{i,j \in [k],\ i<j} \neg x_i = x_j \wedge \forall y \bigwedge_{i \in [k]} E y x_i \right),$$

and

$$\psi_k := \exists x_1 \ldots \exists x_k \left(\bigwedge_{i,j \in [k],\ i<j} \neg x_i = x_j \wedge \bigwedge_{i,j \in [k],\ i<j} E x_i x_j \right).$$

The sentence φ_k can be written equivalently in the form $\exists^{\geq k} x \forall y E y x$ and thus the parameterized problem, whose kth slice is defined by φ_k, is slicewise definable by sentences in CFO_2 and hence, is in **para-AC^0** (by Proposition 3). For graphs the sentences ψ_k slicewise define the clique problem parameterized by the size of the clique. By a result of Rossman [20] the parameterized clique problem is not in **para-AC^0**. Hence the ψ_k's cannot be written equivalently in CFO with bounded quantifier rank.

Theorem 4. *The parameterized independent set problem p-deg-IS*

> *Instance:* A graph $\mathcal{G}$.
> *Parameter:* $k \in \mathbb{N}$.
> *Problem:* Is $k \geq \deg(\mathcal{G})$ and does $\mathcal{G}$ have an independent set of $k - \deg(\mathcal{G})$ elements?

is in **para-AC^0**.

Proof. An easy induction on $\ell := k - \deg(\mathcal{G})$ shows that every graph $\mathcal{G}$ with at least $(\deg(\mathcal{G}) + 1) \cdot \ell$ vertices has an independent set of size ℓ. Hence, for $(\mathcal{G}, k)$, where the graph $\mathcal{G}$ has at least $(k + 1) \cdot k$ vertices, we have

$$(\mathcal{G}, k) \in p\text{-}deg\text{-}IS \iff k \geq \deg(\mathcal{G}). \tag{1}$$

Let $d \in \mathbb{N}$. Then, for every vertex u of $\mathcal{G}$,

$$\mathcal{G} \models \exists^{\geq d} y E x y (u) \iff \text{the degree of } u \text{ in } \mathcal{G} \text{ is } \geq d.$$

Hence the degree of $\mathcal{G}$ is the unique d such that

$$\mathcal{G} \models \exists x \exists^{\geq d} y E x y \wedge \neg \exists x \exists^{\geq d+1} y E x y.$$

Thus, by (1), for $(\mathcal{G}, k)$ with $|G| \geq (k+1) \cdot k$,

$$(\mathcal{G}, k) \in p\text{-}deg\text{-}\mathrm{IS} \iff \mathcal{G} \models \bigvee_{d \leq k} \left(\exists x \exists^{\geq d} y\, Exy \wedge \neg \exists x \exists^{\geq d+1} y\, Exy \right).$$

Therefore, setting $evt(k) := (k+1) \cdot k$ we see that $p\text{-}deg\text{-}\mathrm{IS}$ is eventually slicewise definable by CFO_2-sentences and hence is in $\mathbf{para\text{-}AC^0}$ (by Proposition 3). $\square$

We present a further application of Proposition 3.

Theorem 5. *The parameterized weighted satisfiability problem $p\text{-}\mathrm{WSAT}(\Gamma_{1,1})$ for propositional formulas in $\Gamma_{1,1}$*

> *Instance:* A propositional formula γ of the form $\bigwedge_{i \in I} \lambda_i$
>   with literals λ_i.
> *Parameter:* $k \in \mathbb{N}$.
>   *Problem:* Does γ have a satisfying assignment setting
>   exactly k propositional variables to TRUE?

is in $\mathbf{para\text{-}AC^0}$.

Proof. For unary relation symbols P and N we view a $\Gamma_{1,1}$-formula $\gamma := \bigwedge_{i \in I} \lambda_i$ with variables $X_1, \ldots, X_s$ as the $\{P, N\}$-structure $\mathcal{A}(\gamma)$, where $A(\gamma) := \{X_1, \ldots, X_s\}$,

$$P^{\mathcal{A}(\gamma)} := \{X_j \mid \lambda_i = X_j \text{ for some } i \in I\} \quad N^{\mathcal{A}(\gamma)} := \{X_j \mid \lambda_i = \neg X_j \text{ for some } i \in I\}.$$

Clearly, for $k \in \mathbb{N}$,

$$(\gamma, k) \in p\text{-}\mathrm{WSAT} \iff P^{\mathcal{A}(\gamma)} \cap N^{\mathcal{A}(\gamma)} = \emptyset \text{ and } |P^{\mathcal{A}(\gamma)}| = k$$
$$\iff \mathcal{A}(\gamma) \models \neg \exists x (Px \wedge Nx) \wedge \exists^{=k} x\, Px.$$

Hence, $p\text{-}\mathrm{WSAT}(\Gamma_{1,1})$ is eventually slicewise definable by CFO_1-sentences and thus is in $\mathbf{para\text{-}AC^0}$ (we can take $evt(k) := 0$). $\square$

We come to the second tool. Recall that a *kernelization for Q* is a polynomial time computable function that assigns to every instance $(\mathcal{A}, k)$ of Q an instance $(\mathcal{A}', k')$ with

$$(\mathcal{A}, k) \in Q \iff (\mathcal{A}', k') \in Q \tag{2}$$

and with $|A'| \leq f_s(k)$ and $k' \leq f_p(k)$ for some computable functions f_s and f_p.

Definition 6. We use the notations for a kernelization of the preceding lines. The kernelization is *definable in CFO with bounded quantifier rank* if there is a $q \in \mathbb{N}$ and computable functions

$$k \mapsto \chi_{\mathrm{NO}}^k, \quad k \mapsto \Phi^k := \left(\varphi_{uni}^k(x), (\varphi_R^k(x_1, \ldots, x_{ar(R)}))_{R \in \tau} \right), \quad (k, \ell) \mapsto \psi_{k,\ell},$$

where all formulas are in $\mathrm{CFO}_q[\tau]$ and both (a) and (b) are satisfied for all instances $(\mathcal{A}, k)$ of Q.

(a) If $\mathcal{A} \models \chi^k_{\mathrm{NO}}$, then $(\mathcal{A}, k) \notin Q$.

(b) If $\mathcal{A} \models \neg\chi^k_{\mathrm{NO}}$, then "$\Phi^k$ defines $\mathcal{A}'$ in $\mathcal{A}$," that is,

$$A' := \{a \in A \mid \mathcal{A} \models \varphi^k_{uni}(a)\} \text{ and for } R \in \tau : \ R^{\mathcal{A}'} = \{\bar{a} \in (A')^{\mathrm{ar}(R)} \mid \mathcal{A} \models \varphi^k_R(\bar{a})\}.$$

(c) If $\mathcal{A} \models \neg\chi^k_{\mathrm{NO}}$, then k' is the unique $\ell \in \mathbb{N}$ such that $\mathcal{A} \models \psi_{k,\ell}$.

Our second tool reads as follows.

Proposition 7. *Assume that Q is decidable. If Q has a kernelization definable in* CFO *with bounded quantifier rank, then $Q \in$* para-AC^0.

Again let us see some examples. By [23] the parameterized matrix-dominating set problem is fixed-parameter tractable. We show:

Theorem 8. *The parameterized matrix-dominating set problem p-MAT-DOM-SET*

> *Instance:* A $\{0, 1\}$-matrix M and $k \in \mathbb{N}$.
> *Parameter:* k.
> *Problem:* Does M contain a set S of 1-entries of M such that each 1-entry lies in a row or a column that contains an element of S?

is in para-AC^0.

Proof. We fix a NO-instance (M_0, k_0) of p-MAT-DOM-SET[1]. In [23] it is shown that by applying to an instance (M, k) of p-MAT-DOM-SET once STEP 1 and STEP 2 we get a matrix M^* with the following properties:

$(M, k) \in p$-MAT-DOM-SET $\iff (M^*, k) \in p$-MAT-DOM-SET.

If $(M, k) \in p$-MAT-DOM-SET, then M^* has at most $2(k + 1)(2^k - 1)$ rows and columns.

STEP 1: Delete all rows and columns that contain only zeroes.

STEP 2: For all rows r, if there are at least $k + 2$ identical copies of r, then the rows can be reduced to $k + 1$ identical copies of r. Similarly for columns.

We set

$$(M', k') := \begin{cases} (M^*, k), & \text{if } M^* \text{ has at most } 2(k+1)(2^k - 1) \text{ rows and columns} \\ (M_0, k_0), & \text{otherwise.} \end{cases}$$

---

[1] The trivial NO-instance will be useful in the description of the kernelization function, though in our formulas we will use χ^k_{NO} to indicate the cases where the trivial NO-instance would have to be output (rather than presenting the cumbersome formula that outputs the trivial NO-instance).

Then $(M, k) \mapsto (M', k')$ is a kernelization of p-MAT-DOM-SET. We show that it is definable in CFO with bounded quantifier rank. We view the matrix M as the structure

$$\mathcal{M} := (R \cup C, R, C, <, \mathit{One}),$$

where R and C are the set of rows and the set of columns of M, respectively, $<$ is an arbitrary ordering of $R \cup C$, and One is given by

$$\mathit{One}\, r\, c \iff r \in R, c \in C, \text{ and the common element of } r \text{ and } c \text{ is a``1''}.$$

Let (M, k) be a YES-instance of p-MAT-DOM-SET. We may take as universe of M' the set of rows $r \in R$ and columns $c \in C$, which satisfy the following conditions:

- the row r does not contain only zeroes and there are at most k identical copies of r, which are $<$-smaller than r;
- the column c does not contain only zeroes and there are at most k identical copies of c, which are $<$-smaller than c.

We introduce the FO-formulas $copy\text{-}row(x, y)$ and $copy\text{-}column(x, y)$ expressing that x and y are identical rows and identical columns, respectively. E.g., we can take

$$copy\text{-}row(x, y) := Rx \wedge Ry \wedge \forall z \big(Cz \rightarrow (\mathit{One}\, xz \leftrightarrow \mathit{One}\, yz) \big).$$

The set M' is given by

$$\varphi^{k}_{uni}(x) := \exists z \big(\mathit{One}\, xz \vee \mathit{One}\, zx \big) \wedge \exists^{\leq k} y \big(y < x \wedge (copy\text{-}row(x, y) \vee copy\text{-}column(x, y)) \big).$$

The kernelization is definable in CFO with bounded quantifier rank. In fact, we can set:

- $\chi^{k}_{\text{NO}} := \exists^{> 2 \cdot (k+1) \cdot (2^{k} - 1)} x \varphi^{k}_{uni}(x)$;
- $\Phi_{k} := (\varphi^{k}_{uni}(x), Rx, Cx, x < y, \mathit{One}(x, y))$;
- $\psi_{k,k} := \forall x\, x = x$ and for $\ell \neq k$, $\psi_{k,\ell} := \neg \forall x\, x = x$.   □

Theorem 9. *The parameterized vertex cover problem* p-VERTEX-COVER

> *Instance:* A graph $\mathcal{G}$.
> *Parameter:* k.
> *Problem:* Does $\mathcal{G}$ have a vertex cover of size k?

is in para-AC^0.

Proof. Again fix a NO-instance $(\mathcal{G}_0, k_0)$ of p-VERTEX-COVER. To an instance $(\mathcal{G}, k)$ of p-VERTEX-COVER we apply once STEP 1 and STEP 2 (the main ingredients of Buss' kernelization):

STEP 1: If a vertex v has degree $\geq k + 1$ in $\mathcal{G}$, then v must be in every vertex cover of size k. Simultaneously remove all v of degree $\geq k + 1$ in $\mathcal{G}$, say m many, and set $k^* := k - m$.

STEP 2: Remove all isolated vertices.

Let $\mathcal{G}^+$ be the resulting induced subgraph of $\mathcal{G}$. If $k^* < 0$ or $\mathcal{G}^*$ has more than $k^* \cdot (k + 1)$ vertices, then $(\mathcal{G}^*, k^*)$, and hence also $(\mathcal{G}, k)$, is a NO-instance of p-VERTEX-COVER. We set

$$(\mathcal{G}', k') := \begin{cases} (\mathcal{G}^*, k^*), & \text{if } k^* \geq 0 \text{ and } \mathcal{G}^* \text{ has at most } k^* \cdot (k + 1) \text{ vertices} \\ (\mathcal{G}_0, k_0), & \text{otherwise.} \end{cases}$$

Then $(\mathcal{G}, k) \mapsto (\mathcal{G}', k')$ is a kernelization of p-VERTEX-COVER. We show that it is CFO-definable with bounded quantifier rank.

Let $(\mathcal{G}, k)$ be a YES-instance of p-VERTEX-COVER. Then we have

$$\mathcal{G} \models \varphi_{uni}^k(v) \iff v \text{ is a vertex of } \mathcal{G}'$$

for (compare STEP 1 and STEP 2)

$$\varphi_{uni}^k(x) := \neg \exists^{\geq k+1} y Exy \wedge \neg \forall y (Exy \to \exists^{\geq k+1} y Eyz).$$

The kernelization is definable in CFO with bounded quantifier rank. In fact, we can set:

- $\chi_{NO}^k := \exists^{\geq k+1} x \exists^{\geq k+1} y\, Exy \ \vee \ \exists^{>(k-m)\cdot(k+1)} x \varphi_{uni}^k(x);$
- $\Phi^k := (\varphi_{uni}^k(x), Exy);$
- $\psi_{k,\ell} := \exists^{=(k-\ell)} x \exists^{\geq k+1} y\, Exy$ if $\ell \leq k$ and $\psi_{k,\ell} := \neg \forall x x = x$, otherwise. $\qquad \square$

We kept our two tools as simple as possible; our goal was to present some applications. There are obvious extensions of our tools. We could consider the extension CFO* of CFO that for all $k, \ell \in \mathbb{N}$ contains the quantifiers $\exists_\ell^{\geq k}(x_1, \ldots, x_\ell)$ (adding ℓ to the quantifier rank) with the meaning "there are at least k many tuples $(x_1, \ldots, x_\ell)$." Proposition 3 would still be valid. In Definition 6 the tuple Φ^k defines an interpretation of τ-structures in τ-structures of width one. Proposition 7 would also hold if we allow interpretations of width greater than one.

4 First-Order Logic Characterization of para-AC^0

We present a characterization of para-AC^0 in terms of first-order logic. From it in the next section we will derive the tools we already used in the preceding section.

By the connection between (dlogtime-uniform) AC^0 and first-order logic with built-in arithmetic we also have to consider so-called *arithmetical vocabularies*, which we denote by $\alpha, \beta, \ldots$. Such an arithmetical vocabulary contains, besides relational symbols, the fixed relation symbols $<$ (binary) and $+$, $\times$ (both ternary). Furthermore, the unary function symbol S and the constant 0.

For an arithmetical vocabulary α we say that an α-structure $\mathcal{A}$ is *arithmetical* or *has built-in arithmetic* if the reduct $\mathcal{A} \upharpoonright \{<, +, \times, S, 0\}$ (that is, the reduct to the arithmetical symbols) is isomorphic to $\left([0, n), <^{[0,n)}, +^{[0,n)}, \times^{[0,n)}, S^{[0,n)}, 0\right)$. Here $n := |A|$, $[0, n) := \{0, 1, \ldots, n-1\}$, $<^{[0,n)}$ is the natural order on $[0, n)$, $+^{[0,n)}$ and $\times^{[0,n)}$ are the relations of addition and multiplication of $\mathbb{N}$ restricted to $[0, n)$; i.e., $+^{[0,n)} := \{(a, b, c) \mid a, b, c \in [0, n) \text{ with } c = a + b\}$ and $\times^{[0,n)} := \{(a, b, c) \mid a, b, c \in [0, n) \text{ with } c = a \cdot b\}$.

Furthermore, $S^{[0,n)}$ denotes the successor function on $[0, n)$ with the convention $S^{[0,n)}(n-1) := n-1$. By $\mathrm{ARI}[\alpha]$ we denote the class of arithmetical α-structures.

Atomic $\mathrm{FO}[\alpha]$-formulas may contain terms, i.e., variables or the constant 0 or terms obtained by applying to variables, to 0, or to terms the function symbol S. By $S^k(x)$ we abbreviate the term $S(S(\cdots S(x) \cdots))$ with k occurrences of S.

As the next lemma shows, every arithmetical structure $\mathcal{A}$ can be characterized by a quantifier-free sentence up to isomorphism since we can address each element of $\mathcal{A}$ using the successor function. For such a purpose the successor function was already used in [5, 14]. In previous papers we used constant symbols for an initial segment of the natural numbers instead of the successor function. The successor function allows a more readable and uniform presentation, not only here but also in further results.

We leave the proof of the next lemma to the reader (note that the sentence $S^m(0) = S^{m+1}(0)$ expresses that the universe has at most m elements in arithmetical structures).

Lemma 10. *For every $\mathcal{A} \in \mathrm{ARI}[\alpha]$ there is a quantifier-free $\mathrm{FO}[\alpha]$-sentence $\varphi_{\mathcal{A}}$ such that for all structures $\mathcal{B} \in \mathrm{ARI}[\alpha]$ we have $(\mathcal{B} \models \varphi_{\mathcal{A}} \iff \mathcal{A} \cong \mathcal{B})$.*

For a vocabulary τ (i.e., for a relational vocabulary without arithmetical symbols) we set $\alpha(\tau) := \tau \cup \{<, +, \times, S, 0\}$. Recall that Q always denotes a parameterized problem with $Q \subseteq \mathrm{STR}[\tau] \times \mathbb{N}$ unless stated otherwise explicitly.

Definition 11. Q *is slicewise definable in* FO *with bounded quantifier rank, in short $Q \in \mathrm{XFO}_{\mathrm{qr}}$, if there is a $q \in \mathbb{N}$ and a computable function $k \mapsto \varphi_k$ with $\varphi_k \in \mathrm{FO}_q[\alpha(\tau)]$ such that for all $(\mathcal{A}, k) \in \mathrm{ARI}[\alpha(\tau)] \times \mathbb{N}$,*

$$(\mathcal{A} \upharpoonright \tau, k) \in Q \iff \mathcal{A} \models \varphi_k.$$

We then say that Q *is slicewise definable in FO_q* and also write $Q \in \mathrm{XFO}_q$.

Using Lemma 10 we get the following simple but useful observation.

Proposition 12. *Let Q be decidable. Assume that Q is eventually slicewise definable in FO_q, that is, there is a computable function $k \mapsto \varphi_k$ with $\varphi_k \in \mathrm{FO}_q[\alpha(\tau)]$ and a computable function $g : \mathbb{N} \to \mathbb{N}$ such that for all $(\mathcal{A}, k) \in \mathrm{ARI}[\alpha] \times \mathbb{N}$ with $|A| \geq g(k)$,*

$$(\mathcal{A} \upharpoonright \tau, k) \in Q \iff \mathcal{A} \models \varphi_k.$$

Then Q is slicewise definable in FO_q.

Proof. Assume Q is eventually slicewise definable in FO_q and let φ_k and g be as above. The sentence ψ_k defining the kth slice of Q essentially says

$$\big(\text{the structure has at least } g(k) \text{ elements and satisfies } \varphi_k\big) \text{ or}$$
$$\big(\text{the structure has less than } g(k) \text{ elements and is in } Q\big).$$

Note that the sentence $S^{g(k)-1}(0) \neq S^{g(k)-2}(0)$ expresses that the universe has at least $g(k)$ elements. So we can set (compare Lemma 10)

$$\psi_k := \big(S^{g(k)-1}(0) \neq S^{g(k)-2}(0) \wedge \varphi_k\big) \vee \bigvee_{\substack{(\mathcal{A}\upharpoonright\tau,k)\in Q,\\ |A|<g(k)}} \varphi_{\mathcal{A}}.$$

As Q is decidable, the mapping $k \mapsto \psi_k$ is computable. $\square$

The importance of the class $\mathrm{XFO}_{\mathrm{qr}}$ from the point of view of complexity theory stems from the fact that it coincides with the class para-AC^0, the class of parameterized problems that are in dlogtime-uniform AC^0 after a precomputation (see Theorem 15). As dlogtime-uniform AC^0 contains precisely the class of problems definable in first-order logic with built-in arithmetic, the class para-AC^0 can be defined directly via first-order logic. For this purpose we need a notion of union of two arithmetical structures.

Definition 13. Assume $\mathcal{A} \in \mathrm{ARI}[\alpha]$ and $\mathcal{A}' \in \mathrm{ARI}[\alpha']$ satisfy $A \cap A' = \emptyset$ and $\alpha \cap \alpha' = \{<, +, \times, S, 0\}$. Let U be a new unary relation symbol. We set $\alpha \uplus \alpha' := \alpha \cup \alpha' \cup \{U\}$. Then $\mathcal{A} \uplus \mathcal{A}'$ is the structure $\mathcal{B} \in \mathrm{ARI}[\alpha \uplus \alpha']$ with

- $B := A \cup A'$;
- $U^{\mathcal{B}} := A$;
- $<^{\mathcal{B}} := <^{\mathcal{A}} \cup <^{\mathcal{A}'} \cup \{(a, a') \mid a \in A \text{ and } a' \in A'\}$, that is, the order $<^{\mathcal{B}}$ extends the orders $<^{\mathcal{A}}$ and $<^{\mathcal{A}'}$, and in $<^{\mathcal{B}}$ every element of A precedes every element of A';
- $R^{\mathcal{B}} := R^{\mathcal{A}}$ for $R \in \alpha$ and $R^{\mathcal{B}} := R^{\mathcal{A}'}$ for $R \in \alpha'$.

If $A \cap A' \neq \emptyset$, then we pass to isomorphic structures with disjoint universes before defining $\mathcal{A} \uplus \mathcal{A}'$.

A parameterized problem is in **para-AC^0** if it is in dlogtime-uniform AC^0 after a precomputation on the parameter, or, equivalently, if it is FO-definable after a precomputation on the parameter. This equivalence leads to the following definition.

Definition 14. Let Q be a parameterized problem. $Q \in$ para-AC^0 if for some vocabulary α' there is a computable function $pre : \mathbb{N} \to \mathrm{ARI}[\alpha']$, a *precomputation*, and a sentence $\varphi \in \mathrm{FO}\big[\alpha(\tau) \uplus \alpha'\big]$ such that for all $(\mathcal{A}, k) \in \mathrm{ARI}[\alpha(\tau)] \times \mathbb{N}$,

$$(\mathcal{A} \upharpoonright \tau, k) \in Q \iff \mathcal{A} \uplus pre(k) \models \varphi.$$

The main result of this section reads as follows. It is the modeltheoretic analogue of the equivalence between (i) and (ii) of [9, Proposition 3.5].

Theorem 15. para-AC^0 = XFO_{qr}.

Proof. $XFO_{qr} \subseteq$ para-AC^0: Assume that $Q \in XFO_{qr}$. Then there is a $q \in \mathbb{N}$ and a computable function $k \mapsto \varphi_k$ with $\varphi_k \in FO_q[\alpha(\tau)]$ such that

$$(A \restriction \tau, k) \in Q \iff A \models \varphi_k$$

for all $(A, k) \in \mathrm{ARI}[\alpha(\tau)] \times \mathbb{N}$. We have to find a precomputation $pre : \mathbb{N} \to \mathrm{ARI}[\alpha']$ and an $FO[\alpha(\tau) \uplus \alpha']$-sentence φ such that for all $(A, k) \in \mathrm{ARI}[\alpha(\tau)] \times \mathbb{N}$,

$$A \models \varphi_k \iff A \uplus pre(k) \models \varphi. \tag{3}$$

Essentially $pre(k)$ is the parse tree of φ_k and the sentence φ expresses that A satisfies the sentence given by this parse tree, that is, the sentence φ_k.

We can assume that all atomic subformulas in any φ_k containing the symbol S for the successor function have the form $z = S^m(0)$ for some $m \in \mathbb{N}$ and some variable z. In fact, if, say, R in $\alpha(\tau)$ is r-ary, then we can replace an atomic formula $RS^{m_1}(x_1) \ldots S^{m_r}(x_r)$ by $\exists y_1 \ldots \exists y_r (Ry_1 \ldots y_r \wedge \bigwedge_{i \in [r]} \exists y(y = S^{m_i}(0) \wedge x_i + y = y_i))$. Note that this process increases the quantifier rank of every φ_k at most by $1 + \mathrm{ar}(\alpha(\tau))$, where $\mathrm{ar}(\alpha(\tau))$ is the maximum of the arities of the relation symbols in $\alpha(\tau)$.

We can assume that sentences of quantifier rank $\leq q$ (hence, every φ_k) has the variables among $x_1, \ldots, x_q$ and negation symbols only occur in front of atomic formulas.

Let p_k be the number of nodes of the parse tree of φ_k and let m_k be the maximum m such that the term $S^m(0)$ occurs in φ_k. The structure $pre(k) \in \mathrm{ARI}[\alpha']$ has universe $[0, \max\{p_k, m_k + 1\})$ and the arithmetical symbols have their natural interpretation in this interval.

We now present the relation symbols of the vocabulary α'. The binary relation symbol E of α' is interpreted by the edge relation of the parse tree. Furthermore α' contains unary relation symbols *Forall*, *Exists*, $X_1, \ldots, X_q$, *And*, *Or*, and *Neg*. For every relational symbol in $\alpha(\tau)$ and for the equality symbol we need further relation symbols in α'. For $R \in \alpha(\tau)$ the vocabulary α' contains the unary relation symbols

$$At^R_\pi \quad \text{for } \pi : [\mathrm{ar}(R)] \to [q]$$

and for the equality symbol the unary relation symbols

$$At^=_\rho \quad \text{for } \rho : [2] \to [q]$$

and the binary relation symbol

$$At^{=,S}_j \quad \text{for } j \in [q].$$

For example, for a node u of $pre(k)$, for $\pi : [ar(R)] \to [q]$, $\rho : [2] \to [q]$, for $j \in [q]$, and $\ell \le m_k$ we have:

$$Exists^{pre(k)} \, u \iff \text{the node } u \text{ corresponds to an existentially quantified}$$
$$\text{variable}$$
$$X_j^{\,pre(k)} \, u \iff \text{the quantifier in } u \text{ binds the variable} x_j$$
$$Or^{pre(k)} \, u \iff u \text{ corresponds to a disjunction}$$
$$(At_\pi^R)^{pre(k)} \, u \iff u \text{ corresponds to the atomic formula } Rx_{\pi(1)} \ldots x_{\pi(ar(R))}$$
$$(At_\rho^=)^{pre(k)} \, u \iff u \text{ corresponds to the atomic formula } x_{\rho(1)} = x_{\rho(2)}$$
$$(At_j^{=,S})^{pre(k)} \, u \, \ell \iff u \text{ corresponds to the atomic formula } x_j = S^\ell(0).$$

On the left side of the last line $S^\ell(0)$ refers to the number ℓ element of the universe of $pre(k)$. We leave it to the reader to write down a sentence φ satisfying (3) but give a hint for the most involved part. Assume that φ_k contains a subformula of the form $x_j = S^\ell(0)$ (with $j \in [q]$ and $\ell \le m_k$). Recall that in $\mathcal{A} \uplus pre(k)$ the U-part is A. Hence if b in $\mathcal{A} \uplus pre(k)$ is the first element of $pre(k)$, then ℓ in the universe of $pre(k)$ is $b + \ell$ in $\mathcal{A} \uplus pre(k)$. Hence $x_j = S^\ell(0)$ is addressed by the following part of φ:

$$\Big(\exists x \big(\neg U\, x \wedge \forall y (y < x \to U\, y) \wedge \exists z \exists z' (x + z = z' \wedge At_j^{=,S} u\, z') \big) \to x_j = z \Big).$$

For simplicity here we did not take care of the case $\ell \ge |A|$.

para-AC$^0 \subseteq$ XFO$_{qr}$: Assume that $Q \in$ para-AC^0. Hence, for some vocabulary α' there is a computable function $pre : \mathbb{N} \to \text{ARI}[\alpha']$ and an FO$[\alpha(\tau) \uplus \alpha']$-sentence φ such that for all $(\mathcal{A}, k) \in \text{ARI}[\alpha(\tau)] \times \mathbb{N}$,

$$(\mathcal{A} \restriction \tau, k) \in Q \iff \mathcal{A} \uplus pre(k) \models \varphi.$$

Clearly, then Q is decidable. Therefore, by Proposition 12, it suffices to show that for some $q \in \mathbb{N}$ the problem Q is eventually slicewise definable in FO$_q$, that is, that there are a computable function $g : \mathbb{N} \to \mathbb{N}$ and a computable function $k \mapsto \psi_k \in \text{FO}_q[\alpha(\tau)]$ such that for all $(\mathcal{A}, k) \in \text{ARI}[\alpha(\tau)] \times \mathbb{N}$ with $|A| \ge g(k)$ we have

$$\mathcal{A} \uplus pre(k) \models \varphi \iff \mathcal{A} \models \psi_k. \tag{4}$$

The main idea: As pre is computable, for $(\mathcal{A}, k) \in \text{ARI}[\alpha(\tau)] \times \mathbb{N}$ with sufficiently large $|A|$ compared with $|pre(k)|$, we can FO-define $pre(k)$ in $\mathcal{A}$ using the built-in arithmetic. Furthermore, from $\mathcal{A}$ and from this FO-defined $pre(k)$ in $\mathcal{A}$, we get (an isomorphic copy of) $\mathcal{A} \uplus pre(k)$ in $\mathcal{A}$ by an FO-interpretation. Summing up, we can FO-interpret $\mathcal{A} \uplus pre(k)$ in $\mathcal{A}$. This FO-interpretation yields the desired ψ_k satisfying (4).

Some details: In the proof we shall need the following claim. Its proof uses the fact that every computable function may be defined on the natural numbers with built-in arithmetic by a Σ_1-sentence (that is, by an FO-sentence of the form $\exists x_1 \ldots \exists x_n \psi$ with quantifier-free ψ).

Claim. Let $f : \mathbb{N} \to \mathbb{N}$ be a computable function. Then there is an $\mathrm{FO}[\{<,+,\times,S,0\}]$-formula $\psi_f(x,y)$ and an increasing and computable function $g : \mathbb{N} \to \mathbb{N}$ with $g(m) > f(m)$ for $m \in \mathbb{N}$ such that for all $n, a \in \mathbb{N}$ with $n \geq g(a)$ and $b \in [0, n)$,

$$\left([0,n), <^{[0,n)}, +^{[0,n)}, \times^{[0,n)}, S^{[0,n)}, 0\right) \models \psi_f(a,b) \quad \Longleftrightarrow \quad f(a) = b.$$

The obvious generalization of this result to functions $f : \mathbb{N}^s \to \mathbb{N}$ for some $s \geq 1$ holds, too.   ⊣

Let α', the vocabulary of $pre(k)$, be the set $\{<,+,\times,S,0,R_1,\ldots,R_m\}$, where R_i is of arity r_i. As pre is computable, there is a computable function $f : \mathbb{N} \to \mathbb{N}$ with

$$f(k) = |pre(k)|.$$

We may assume that the universe of $pre(k)$ is $[0, f(k))$ and $<,+,\times,S,0$ have their natural interpretations in $pre(k)$. For easier presentation, let us assume that the same holds for $\mathcal{A}$; so, in particular, $[0,|A|)$ is the universe of $\mathcal{A}$.

For i with $i \in [m]$ let $h_i : \mathbb{N}^{1+r_i} \to \{0,1\}$ be the computable function with

$$h_i(k, b_1, \ldots, b_{r_i}) = 1 \quad \Longleftrightarrow \quad \left(b_1, \ldots, b_{r_i} < f(k) \quad \text{and} \quad R_i^{\,pre(k)} b_1, \ldots, b_{r_i}\right).$$

As f and $h_1, \ldots, h_m$ are computable, (we know that they are FO-definable in arithmetic and) by the claim, there is a computable and increasing function $g : \mathbb{N} \to \mathbb{N}$ with $g(k) > f(k)$ and there are FO-formulas $\psi_f(x,y)$ and $\psi_{h_i}(x, y_1, \ldots, y_{r_i})$ such that for the relevant arguments the formulas $\psi_f(x,y)$ and $\psi_{h_i}(x, y_1, \ldots, y_{r_i})$ correctly define f and h_i in models with built-in arithmetic of size at least $g(k)$. Clearly, once we have the values $f(k)$ and $h_i(k, b_1, \ldots, b_{r_i})$ for $i \in [m]$ and $b_1, \ldots, b_{r_i} < f(k)$, we can first-order define $pre(k)$, and hence $(\mathcal{A}, R_1^{\,pre(k)}, \ldots, R_m^{\,pre(k)})$, in $\mathcal{A}$, whenever $|A| \geq g(k)$.

By Proposition 16 (see below) there is an FO-interpretation yielding the structure $\mathcal{A} \uplus pre(k)$ from the structure $(\mathcal{A}, R_1^{\,pre(k)}, \ldots, R_m^{\,pre(k)})$. Putting these interpretations together, we obtain an FO-interpretation yielding $\mathcal{A} \uplus pre(k)$ in $\mathcal{A}$ assuming $|A| \geq g(k)$. Thus we obtain from φ an FO-sentence ψ_k satisfying the equivalence (4).   □

We already considered interpretations of width one in connection with kernelizations. In the previous proof we need a result on FO-interpretations of with s for some $s \in \mathbb{N}$. A part of such an FO-interpretation I is an FO-formula $\varphi_{uni}^I(x_1, \ldots, x_s)$ defining the universe of the defined structure. For example, if I is an interpretation of τ-structures in a class $K \subseteq \mathrm{ARI}[\alpha]$, then for every structure $\mathcal{A} \in K$ the set

$$(\varphi_{uni}^I)^{\mathcal{A}} := \{(a_1, \ldots, a_s) \in A^s \mid \mathcal{A} \models \varphi_{uni}^I(a_1, \ldots, a_s)\}$$

is the universe of the τ-structure $I(\mathcal{A})$ defined by I in $\mathcal{A}$.

In general, we cannot extend I to an interpretation J of $\alpha(\tau)$-structures in the class K of arithmetical structures such that

$$J(\mathcal{A}) = \left(I(\mathcal{A}), <^{J(\mathcal{A})}, +^{J(\mathcal{A})}, \times^{J(\mathcal{A})}, S^{J(\mathcal{A})}, 0^{J(\mathcal{A})}\right)$$

is in $\text{ARI}[\alpha(\tau)]$ (i.e., has built-in arithmetic). For example, for $\sigma = \{P\}$ with unary P let $K = \{\mathcal{A} \in \text{ARI}[\alpha(\sigma)] \mid P^{\mathcal{A}} \neq \emptyset\}$. Let τ be the empty vocabulary and I the interpretation of τ-structures in K with $\varphi^I_{uni}(x) := Px$; i.e., $I(\mathcal{A})$ is the τ-structure with $P^{\mathcal{A}}$ as universe. If for $\mathcal{A} \in K$ we could extend I to an interpretation J such that $J(\mathcal{A})$ has built-in arithmetic, then we could express in $J(\mathcal{A})$, and thus in $\mathcal{A}$, that "$P^{\mathcal{A}}$ is even", i.e., the problem PARITY, which is well known to be impossible.

The next result (proven in [6, Lemma 10.5], see also [19, Exercise 1.33]) shows that the situation is different if for $\varphi^I_{uni}(x_1, \ldots, x_s)$ we have $(\varphi^I_{uni})^{\mathcal{A}} = A^s$.

Proposition 16. *Let* $K \subseteq \text{ARI}[\alpha]$ *and let* I *be an* FO-*interpretation of* τ-*structures in* K *with* $\varphi^I_{uni} = \varphi^I_{uni}(x_1, \ldots, x_s)$. *If for all* $\mathcal{A} \in K$ *the set* $(\varphi^I_{uni})^{\mathcal{A}}$ *is an initial segment in the lexicographic order of* A^s *w.r.t.* $<^{\mathcal{A}}$, *then* I *can be extended to an* FO-*interpretation* J *of* $\alpha(\tau)$-*structures in* K *such that* $J(\mathcal{A}) \upharpoonright \tau = I(\mathcal{A})$ *and* $J(\mathcal{A}) \in \text{ARI}[\alpha(\tau)]$ *for all* $\mathcal{A} \in K$.

5 The Impact of Color-Coding on First-Order Logic

We show how in arithmetical structures CFO-formulas $\exists^{\geq k} x \varphi(x, \bar{y})$ with first-order φ can be expressed by an FO-formula of quantifier rank independent of k and then prove the tools used in Sect. 3.

For the first goal we use the color-coding technique of Alon et al. [2] essentially in the form presented in [15, p. 347]:

Lemma 17. *There is an* $n_0 \in \mathbb{N}$ *such that for all* $n \geq n_0$, *all* $k \leq n$ *and for every* k-*element subset* X *of* $[n]$, *there exist a prime* $p < k^2 \cdot \log_2 n$ *and a* $q < p$ *such that the function* $h_{p,q} : [n] \to \{0, \ldots, k^2 - 1\}$ *given by* $h_{p,q}(m) := (q \cdot m \bmod p) \bmod k^2$ *is injective on* X.

As already mentioned the following result allows to express the existence of k elements satisfying a first-order logic property by a bounded number of quantifiers.

Theorem 18. *Let* α *be an arithmetical vocabulary. There is an algorithm that assigns to every* $k \in \mathbb{N}$ *and every* FO$[\alpha]$-*formula* $\varphi(x, \bar{y})$ *an* FO$[\alpha]$-*formula* $\chi^k_\varphi(\bar{y})$ *such that for all* $\mathcal{A} \in \text{ARI}[\alpha]$ *with* $k^2 \leq |A|/\log|A|$ *and* $|A| \geq n_0$,

$$\mathcal{A} \models \forall \bar{y} \left(\exists^{\geq k} x \, \varphi(x, \bar{y}) \leftrightarrow \chi^k_\varphi(\bar{y}) \right) \tag{5}$$

and $\text{qr}(\chi^k_\varphi(\bar{x})) = \text{qr}(\varphi(x, \bar{y})) + O(1)$; *hence, there is a bound for* $\text{qr}(\chi^k_\varphi(\bar{x}))$ *independent of* k.

Note that the conditions "$k^2 \leq |A|/\log|A|$ *and* $|A| \geq n_0$*" on* $|A|$ *are fulfilled if* $|A| \geq \max\{2^{k^2}, n_0\}$ *(here* n_0 *is a natural number according to Lemma 17).*

Proof. We use $x = (y \bmod z)$ as an abbreviation for $\exists u(y = u \times z + x \wedge x < z)$. More precisely, as $+$ and $\times$ are relation symbols, an abbreviation for $x = (y \bmod z)$ is

$$\exists u \exists u'(u' = u \times z \wedge y = u' + x \wedge x < z).$$

By Lemma 17 we can set

$$\chi_\varphi^k(\bar{y}) := \exists p \exists q \Big(\bigvee_{0 \leq i_0 < \ldots < i_{k-1} < k^2} \bigwedge_{j \in [0,k)} \exists z \big(\text{``}h_{p,q}(z) = S^{i_j}(0)\text{''} \wedge \varphi(z, \bar{y}) \big) \Big),$$

where

$$\text{``}h_{p,q}(z) = S^{i_j}(0)\text{''} := (S^q(0) \times (z \mod S^p(0)) \mod S^p(0)) \mod S^{k^2}(0) = S^{i_j}(0).$$

We replaced $(q \times z \mod p)$ by $(q \times (z \mod p) \mod p)$, since $q \times z$ might exceed $|A|$. □

Writing down all the details of the formula $\chi_\varphi^k(\bar{y})$ one can show that $\text{qr}(\chi_\varphi^k(\bar{y})) = \max\{12, \text{qr}(\varphi(\bar{x}, y)) + 3\}$.

Now we can prove the tools introduced in Sect. 3. To get Proposition 3 assume that the parameterized problem Q is decidable and eventually slicewise definable in CFO with bounded quantifier rank. By Theorem 18, it is also eventually slicewise definable in FO with bounded quantifier rank. Hence, by Proposition 12 and Theorem 15, it is **para-AC^0**.

Proof of Proposition 7: Assume that $Q \subseteq \text{STR}[\tau] \times \mathbb{N}$ is decidable and has a kernelization $(\mathcal{A}, k) \mapsto (\mathcal{A}', k')$ with $|A'| \leq f_s(k)$ and $k' \leq f_p(k)$ for some computable f_s and f_p. Moreover, assume that this kernelization is definable by the computable functions

$$k \mapsto \chi_{\text{NO}}^k, \quad k \mapsto \Phi^k := \big(\varphi_{uni}^k(x), (\varphi_R^k(x_1, \ldots, x_{\text{ar}(R)}))_{R \in \tau}\big), \quad (k, \ell) \mapsto \psi_{k,\ell},$$

where all formulas are in CFO$_q$ (for some $q \in \mathbb{N}$) and satisfy (a)–(b) of Definition 6 for all instances $(\mathcal{A}, k)$ of Q. We show that $Q \in \text{XFO}_{\text{qr}}$. For $\mathcal{B} \in \text{ARI}[\alpha(\tau)]$ with $\mathcal{A} := \mathcal{B} \restriction \tau$ we have

$$(\mathcal{A}, k) \in Q \iff \mathcal{B} \models \neg\chi_{\text{NO}}^k \wedge \bigvee_{\ell \leq f_p(k)} \Big(\psi_{k,\ell} \wedge \bigvee_{j \in [f_s(k)]} (\exists^{=j} x \varphi_{uni}^k(x) \wedge \rho_{j,\ell}) \Big). \quad (6)$$

Here the sentence $\rho_{j,\ell}$, a sentence expressing (in $\mathcal{B}$ with an $\mathcal{A}'$ with exactly j elements) that $(\mathcal{A}', \ell) \in Q$, still has to be defined. We do that by saying that $\mathcal{A}'$ is isomorphic to one of the structures with j elements that together with the parameter ℓ is in Q. For this we have to be able to "define" an isomorphism. By the color-coding method we find p and q and $0 \leq i_0 < \cdots < i_{j-1} < j^2$ with

$$h_{p,q}(A') = \{S^{i_0}(0), \ldots, S^{i_{j-1}}(0)\}.$$

Then, we can speak of the first, the second, ... element of $\mathcal{A}'$. So if τ contains among others a binary relation symbol E, we can take as $\rho_{j,\ell}$ a sentence starting as follows:

$$\exists p \exists q \bigvee_{0 \le i_0 < ... < i_{j-1} < j^2} \Big(\bigwedge_{s \in [0,j)} \exists y \big(\varphi_{uni}^k(y) \wedge \text{``}h_{p,q}(y) = S^{i_s}(0)\text{''} \big) \wedge \bigvee_{\substack{(B,\ell) \in Q \\ B = [0,j)}}$$

$$\bigwedge_{\substack{s,t \in [0,j) \\ E^B st}} \exists y \exists z \big(\varphi_{uni}^k(y) \wedge \varphi_{uni}^k(z) \wedge \text{``}h_{p,q}(y) = S^{i_s}(0)\text{''} \wedge \text{``}h_{p,q}(y) = S^{i_t}(0)\text{''} \wedge \varphi_E^k(y,z) \big)$$

$$\dots \Big).$$

By the color-coding method (in the form of Theorem 18) it is clear that the sentence on the right hand side of (6) can be replaced by an FO-sentence whose quantifier rank has a bound independent of k.   □

Theorem 18 can be extended to formulas starting with a quantifier $\exists_\ell^{\ge k}(x_1, \dots, x_\ell)$ (see [11]). This allows us to prove the generalizations of our two tools of Sect. 3 indicated at the end of that section.

As already mentioned in the introduction (nearly) all nontrivial proofs showing membership in para-AC^0 use the color-coding method. In [4] repeated applications of this method have been used in order to show that the hitting set problem parameterized by the size of the hitting set plus the size of hyperedges is in para-AC^0. In [5] Bannach and Tantau "identify syntactic properties of first-order quantifiers that can be eliminated from formulas describing parameterized problems" (applying the color-coding method).

6   The Model-Checking Problem

We have seen that a parameterized problem is in para-AC^0 if and only if it is slice-wise FO-definable with bounded quantifier rank (using built-in arithmetic). This suggests that for a class K of structures the parameterized model-checking problem for FO-formulas parameterized by the length of the formula is in para-AC^0 if for some $q \in \mathbb{N}$ every FO-formula is equivalent in K to a formula of bounded quantifier rank (using built-in arithmetic). It turns out that this condition is not only sufficient but also necessary for the tractability of the model-checking problem in the sense of para-AC^0. In this section we introduce the exact concepts and state the precise result.

Definition 19. For a class K of τ-structures the *parameterized model-checking problem* p-$\mathrm{MC}(K,\mathrm{FO})$ *for* FO *on* K is the problem

---
p-$\mathrm{MC}(K, \Phi)$

   Instance: $\mathcal{A} \in K$, $\varphi(x_1, \dots, x_e) \in \Phi$, and $a_1, \dots, a_e \in A$.
   Parameter: $k \in \mathbb{N}$.
   Problem: Decide whether $|\varphi| = k$ and $\mathcal{A} \models \varphi(\bar{a})$.

We introduce the notion of generalized quantifier elimination.

Definition 20. Let K be a class of τ-structures. Then FO *has generalized quantifier elimination on* K if there is a $q \in \mathbb{N}$ such that for all FO$[\tau]$-formulas $\varphi(\bar{x})$ there is an FO$[\alpha(\tau)]$-formula $\varphi^*(\bar{x})$ of quantifier rank at most q such that for all $\mathcal{A} \in \text{Ari}[\alpha(\tau)]$ with $\mathcal{A} \upharpoonright \tau \in K$ and all $\bar{a}$ in $\mathcal{A}$,

$$\mathcal{A} \upharpoonright \tau \models \varphi(\bar{a}) \iff \mathcal{A} \models \varphi^*(\bar{a}),$$

or equivalently,

$$\mathcal{A} \models \forall \bar{x}\big(\varphi(\bar{x}) \leftrightarrow \varphi^*(\bar{x})\big). \tag{7}$$

If there is a computable mapping $\varphi \mapsto \varphi^*$, then FO *has an effective generalized quantifier elimination on* K.

Loosely speaking if FO has generalized quantifier elimination on K, then for some $q \in \mathbb{N}$ every FO-formula φ is equivalent in structures of K to an FO-formula of quantifier rank at most q if we use built-in arithmetic.

The following theorem of [8] contains a precise statement of the result indicated above.

Theorem 21. *For a class K of τ-structures the following are equivalent:*

(i) FO *has an effective generalized quantifier elimination on K.*
(ii) $p\text{-}\mathrm{MC}(K, \mathrm{FO}) \in \text{para-AC}^0$.

As the paper [8] contains a full proof of this theorem, we omit it here. Recently [10] we showed that $p\text{-}\mathrm{MC}(K, \mathrm{FO}) \in \text{para-AC}^0$ for every class K of graphs of bounded shrub-depth. Note that every class of graphs of bounded tree-depth has bounded shrub-depth. Moreover monadic second-order logic effectively collapses to first-order logic on classes of bounded shrub-depth (see [10]). Hence, also the model-checking problem for monadic second-order logic on these classes is in para-AC^0.

7   The Hierarchy $(\text{FO}_q)_{q \in \mathbb{N}}$ on arithmetical structures

For an arithmetical vocabulary α and $q \in \mathbb{N}$ by $\text{FO}_q[\alpha] \subsetneqq \text{FO}_{q+1}[\alpha]$ *on arithmetical structures* we mean that there is an $\text{FO}_{q+1}[\alpha]$-sentence which is not equivalent to any $\text{FO}_q[\alpha]$-sentence on all structures in $\text{Ari}[\alpha]$. We say that *the hierarchy* $\big(\text{FO}_q\big)_{q \in \mathbb{N}}$ *is strict on arithmetical structures* if there is an arithmetical vocabulary α such that $\text{FO}_q[\alpha] \subsetneqq \text{FO}_{q+1}[\alpha]$ on arithmetical structures for every $q \in \mathbb{N}$.

Theorem 22. *The hierarchy* $\big(\text{FO}_q\big)_{q \in \mathbb{N}}$ *is strict on arithmetical structures.*

First we derive from this result the corresponding hierarchy result for parameterized problems in para-AC^0.

Corollary 23. *Let $q \in \mathbb{N}$. Then there is a parameterized problem in* $\text{XFO}_{q+1} \setminus \text{XFO}_q$.

Proof. By Theorem 22 we know that there is an α and an $\mathrm{FO}_{q+1}[\alpha]$-sentence φ which is not equivalent to any $\mathrm{FO}_q[\alpha]$-sentences on $\mathrm{ARI}[\alpha]$. Then for $\tau := \alpha \setminus \{<, +, \times, S, 0\}$,

$$Q := \{(\mathcal{A} \restriction \tau, 0) \mid \mathcal{A} \in \mathrm{ARI}[\alpha] \text{ and } \mathcal{A} \models \varphi\}$$

is not in XFO_q (as the 0th slice is not definable by an FO_q-sentence). As $Q \in \mathrm{XFO}_{q+1}$, this gives the desired separation. □

Some preparations are necessary in order to prove Theorem 22. First, we recall how structures are represented by strings. Let τ be a (nonempty, relational) vocabulary and $n \in \mathbb{N}$. We encode a τ-structure $\mathcal{A}$ with $A = [0, n)$ by a binary string $\mathrm{enc}(\mathcal{A})$ of length

$$\ell_{\tau,n} := \sum_{R \in \tau} n^{\mathrm{ar}(R)}.$$

For instance, assume $\tau = \{E, P\}$ with binary E and unary P, then

$$\mathrm{enc}(A) = i_0 i_1 \cdots i_{n^2-1} \, j_0 j_1 \cdots j_{n-1},$$

where for every $a, b \in [0, n)$,

$$i_{a+b\cdot n} = 1 \iff (a, b) \in E^{\mathcal{A}},$$
$$j_a = 1 \iff a \in P^{\mathcal{A}}.$$

Let K be a class of τ-structures. A family of circuits $(\mathsf{C}_n)_{n \in \mathbb{N}}$ *decides* K if

- every C_n has $\ell_{\tau,n}$ inputs,
- $(\mathcal{A} \in K \iff \mathsf{C}_n(\mathrm{enc}(\mathcal{A})) = 1)$ for $n \in \mathbb{N}$ and every τ-structure $\mathcal{A}$ with $A = [0, n)$.

Recall that for $n \in \mathbb{N}$ the classes Σ_n and Π_n of formulas are defined as follows: Σ_0 and Π_0 are the class of quantifier-free formulas. The class Σ_{n+1} (the class Π_{n+1}) is the class of formulas of the form $\exists x_1 \ldots \exists x_k \varphi$ with $\varphi \in \Pi_n$ (of the form $\forall x_1 \ldots \forall x_k \varphi$ with $\varphi \in \Sigma_n$) and arbitrary $k \in \mathbb{N}$.

Lemma 24. *Every $\mathrm{FO}[\tau]$-formula of quantifier rank q is logically equivalent to a $\Sigma_{q+1}[\tau]$-formula and to a $\Pi_{q+1}[\tau]$-formula.*

Proof. The proof is by induction on q. For $q = 0$ the claim is trivial. The induction step follows from the facts:

- An FO-formula of quantifier rank $q + 1$ is a Boolean combination of formulas of the form $\exists x \psi$ and $\forall x \psi$, where ψ has quantifier rank $\leq q$. In formulas of the form $\exists x \psi$ we replace, using the induction hypothesis, the formula ψ by an equivalent Σ_{q+1}-formula, in formulas of the form $\forall x \psi$ we replace the formula ψ by an equivalent Π_{q+1}-formula.
- Boolean combinations of Σ_{q+1}-formulas and of Π_{q+1}-formulas are equivalent to both, a Σ_{q+2}-formula and to a Π_{q+2}-formula. □

Lemma 25. *Let $q \in \mathbb{N}$. Then for every sentence $\varphi \in \mathrm{FO}_q[\tau]$ there is a family of circuits $(C_n)_{n \in \mathbb{N}}$ of depth $\leq q + 2$ and size $n^{O(1)}$ which decides $\mathrm{Mod}(\varphi) = \{\mathcal{A} \mid \mathcal{A} \models \varphi\}$. Moreover, the output of C_n is an OR gate, and the bottom layer of gates in C_n has fan-in bounded by a constant which only depends on φ.*

Proof. To simplify the discussion, we assume $q = 3$. The other cases can be proved along the same lines. By Lemma 24 the sentence φ is equivalent to a Σ_4-sentence

$$\psi = \exists x_{1,1} \cdots \exists x_{1,i_1} \forall x_{2,1} \cdots \forall x_{2,i_2} \exists x_{3,1} \cdots \exists x_{3,i_3} \forall x_{4,1} \cdots \forall x_{4,i_4} \bigwedge_{p \in I_\wedge} \bigvee_{q \in I_\vee} \chi_{pq},$$

where $I_\wedge$ and $I_\vee$ are index sets and every χ_{pq} is a literal.

For $n \in \mathbb{N}$ we construct the desired circuit $C = C_n$ using the standard translation from FO-sentences to AC^0-circuits. That is, every existential (universal) quantifier corresponds to a $\bigvee$ ($\bigwedge$) gate with fan-in n; the conjunction is translated to a $\bigwedge$ gate with fan-in $|I_\wedge|$ and the disjunctions to $\bigvee$ gates with fan-in $|I_\vee|$. Next we merge consecutive layers of gates that are all $\bigwedge$, or that are all $\bigvee$. The resulting circuit C_n is of depth $q + 2$. It has an OR as output gate and bottom fan-in bounded by $|I_\vee|$. $\square$

Key to our proof of Theorem 22 are the following Boolean functions, also known as *Sipser functions*.

Definition 26 ([7,22]). *Let $d \geq 1$ nd $m_1, \ldots, m_d \in \mathbb{N}$. For every $i_1 \in [m_1]$, $i_2 \in [m_2]$, $\ldots$, $i_d \in [m_d]$ we introduce a Boolean variable $X_{i_1,\ldots,i_d}$. Define*

$$f_d^{m_1,\ldots,m_d} := \bigwedge_{i_1 \in [m_1]} \bigvee_{i_2 \in [m_2]} \cdots \bigodot_{i_d \in [m_d]} X_{i_1,\ldots,i_d}, \tag{8}$$

where $\bigodot$ is $\bigvee$ if d is even, and $\bigvee$ otherwise. For every $d \geq 2$ and $m \geq 1$ we set

$$\mathrm{Sipser}_d^m := f_d^{m_1,\ldots,m_d}$$

with $m_1 = \left\lceil \sqrt{m/\log m} \right\rceil$, $m_2 = \cdots m_{d-1} = m$, and $m_d = \left\lceil \sqrt{d/2 \cdot m \cdot \log m} \right\rceil$. Observe that the size of Sipser_d^m is bounded by $m^{O(d)}$.

The following lower bound for Sipser_d^m is proved in [18]. We use the version presented as Theorem 4.2 in [21].

Theorem 27. *Let $d \geq 2$. Then there exists a constant $\beta_d > 0$ so that if a depth $d+1$, bottom fan-in k circuit with an OR gate as the output and at most G gates in levels 1 through d computes Sipser_d^m, then either $G \geq 2^{m^{\beta_d}}$ or $k \geq m^{\beta_d}$.*

Proof of Theorem 22: $\mathrm{FO}_0 \subsetneq \mathrm{FO}_1$ is trivial by considering the sentence $\exists x \, Ux$ where U is a unary relation symbol. We still need to show that for an appropriate arithmetical vocabulary α it holds $\mathrm{FO}_q[\alpha] \subsetneq \mathrm{FO}_{q+1}[\alpha]$ on $\mathrm{ARI}[\alpha]$ for every $q \geq 1$.

Let $d, m \in \mathbb{N}$. We identify the function Sipser_d^m with the circuit in (8) which computes it. Let E be a binary relation symbol and U a unary relation symbol.

Then we view the underlying (directed) graph of Sipser_d^m as a $\{E, U\}$-structure $\mathcal{A}_{d,m}$ with

$$A_{d,m} := \{v_g \mid g \text{ a gate in } \mathrm{Sipser}_d^m\},$$
$$E^{\mathcal{A}_{d,m}} := \{(v_{g'}, v_g) \mid g' \text{ is an input to } g\},$$
$$U^{\mathcal{A}_{d,m}} := \{v_g \mid g \text{ is an input to the output gate}\}.$$

Let P be a unary relation symbol. Every assignment B of (truth values to the input nodes of) Sipser_d^m can be identified with

$$P^{\mathcal{A}_{d,m}} := \{g \mid g \text{ an input node assigned to TRUE by } B\} \tag{9}$$

For $\tau' := \{E, U, P\}$ we define an FO$[\tau']$-sentence φ_d such that for all m,

$$\mathrm{Sipser}_d^m(P^{\mathcal{A}_{d,m}}) = \mathrm{TRUE} \quad \Longleftrightarrow \quad (\mathcal{A}_{d,m}, P^{\mathcal{A}_{d,m}}) \models \varphi_d. \tag{10}$$

Fix $q \geq 1$. Assume q is even and set $d := q + 1$ (the case of odd q is treated similarly). We define inductively FO$[\tau']$-formulas $\psi_\ell(x)$ by

$$\psi_0(x) := Px, \quad \text{and} \quad \psi_{\ell+1}(x) := \begin{cases} \forall y(Eyx \rightarrow \psi_\ell(y)) & \text{if } \ell \text{ is even,} \\ \exists y(Eyx \wedge \psi_\ell(y)) & \text{if } \ell \text{ is odd.} \end{cases}$$

We set (recall the definition of $U^{\mathcal{A}_{d,m}}$)

$$\varphi_{q+1} := \forall x(Ux \rightarrow \psi_q(x)).$$

It is straightforward to verify that $\mathrm{qr}(\varphi_{q+1}) = q + 1$ and that φ_{q+1} satisfies (10) (for $d = q + 1$). We define

$$\mathrm{SIPSER}_{q+1} := \{\mathcal{A} \in \mathrm{ARI}[\alpha(\tau)] \mid \mathcal{A} \models \varphi_{q+1}\}.$$

By definition the class SIPSER_{q+1} is axiomatizable in FO$_{q+1}[\alpha(\tau)]$. We show that the class SIPSER_{q+1} is not axiomatizable in FO$_q[\alpha(\tau)]$. For a contradiction, assume that $\mathrm{SIPSER}_{q+1} = \mathrm{Mod}(\varphi)$ for some $\varphi \in \mathrm{FO}_q[\alpha(\tau)]$. Then by Lemma 25 there exists a family of circuits $(C_n)_{n \in \mathbb{N}}$ such that the following conditions are satisfied.

(C1) Every C_n has $\ell_{\tau,n}$ inputs nodes, depth $q + 2$, and size $\ell_{\tau,n}^{O(1)}$.
(C2) The output of C_n is an OR gate, and its bottom fan-in is bounded by a constant.
(C3) For every $n \in \mathbb{N}$ and every τ-structure $\mathcal{A}$ with $A = [0, n)$

$$\mathcal{A} \in \mathrm{SIPSER}_{q+1} \quad \Longleftrightarrow \quad C_n(\mathrm{enc}(\mathcal{A})) = 1.$$

Let $m \in \mathbb{N}$ and let n be the number of variables in Sipser_{q+1}^m, i.e.,

$$n = \left\lceil \sqrt{m/\log m} \right\rceil \cdot m^{q-1} \cdot \left\lceil \sqrt{(q+1)/2 \cdot m \cdot \log m} \right\rceil.$$

Consider the structure $\mathcal{A}_{q+1,m}$ associated with Sipser^m_{q+1} and expand it with $<$, $+, \times, S, 0$ to an arithmetical $\alpha(\tau)$-structure. Thus for any assignment of the n inputs, identified with the unary relation $P^{\mathcal{A}_{q+1,m}}$ (see (9)), we have

$$\mathrm{Sipser}^m_{q+1}(P^{\mathcal{A}_{q+1,m}}) = 1 \iff \left(\mathcal{A}_{q+1,m}, <, +, \times, S, 0, P^{\mathcal{A}_{q+1,m}}\right) \models \varphi$$

$$\iff C_n\left(\mathrm{enc}\left(\mathcal{A}_{q+1,m}, <, +, \times, S, 0, P^{\mathcal{A}_{q+1,m}}\right)\right) = 1.$$

Here is the crucial observation. In the string $\mathrm{enc}(\mathcal{A}_{q+1,m}, <, +, \times, S, 0, P^{\mathcal{A}_{q+1,m}})$ only the last n bits depend on the assignment, that is, on $P^{\mathcal{A}_{q+1,m}}$. These are precisely the n input bits for the Sipser^m_{q+1} function. Thus we can simplify the circuit C_n by fixing the values of the first $\ell_{\tau,n} - n$ inputs according to $(\mathcal{A}_{q+1,m}, <, +, \times, S, 0)$. Let C^*_n be the resulting circuit. We have

$$\mathrm{Sipser}^m_{q+1}(P^{\mathcal{A}_{q+1,m}}) = 1 \iff C^*_n(P^{\mathcal{A}_{q+1,m}}) = 1.$$

By (C1), C^*_n has depth $q + 2$ and size $n^{O(1)}$ (as $\ell_{\tau,n} = n^{O(1)}$). By (C2) its output is an OR gate, and its bottom fan-in is bounded by a constant. As $m \in \mathbb{N}$ is arbitrary, this clearly contradicts Theorem 27.   □

Acknowledgement. We thank an anonymous referee whose detailed review has improved the presentation considerably. The collaboration of the authors is funded by the Sino-German Center for Research Promotion (GZ 1518). Yijia Chen is also supported by National Natural Science Foundation of China (Project 61872092).

References

1. Ajtai, M.: Σ^1_1 formulae on finite structures. Ann. Pure Appl. Log. **24**(3), 1–48 (1983)
2. Alon, N., Yuster, R., Zwick, U.: Color-coding. J. ACM **42**(4), 844–856 (1995)
3. Bannach, M., Stockhusen, C., Tantau, T.: Fast parallel fixed-parameter algorithms via color coding. In: Proceedings of IPEC 2015, pp. 224–235 (2015)
4. Bannach, M., Tantau, T.: Computing hitting set kernels by AC^0-circuits. In: Proceedings of STACS 2018, pp. 9:1–9:14 (2018)
5. Bannach, M., Tantau, T.: On the descriptive complexity of color coding. In: Proceedings of STACS 2019, pp. 11:1–11:16 (2019)
6. Mix Barrington, D.A., Immerman, N., Straubing, H.: On uniformity within NC^1. J. Comput. Syst. Sci. **41**(3), 274–306 (1990)
7. Boppana, R.B., Sipser, M.: The complexity of finite functions. In: Handbook of Theoretical Computer Science, Volume A: Algorithms and Complexity (A), pp. 757–804 (1990)
8. Chen, Y., Flum, J.: Tree-depth, quantifier elimination, and quantifier rank. In: Proceedings of LICS 2018, pp. 225–234 (2018)
9. Chen, Y., Flum, J.: Some lower bounds in parameterized AC^0. Inf. Comput. **267**, 116–134 (2019)
10. Chen, Y., Flum, J.: FO-definability of shrub-depth. In: Proceeding of CSL 2020, pp. 15:1–15:16 (2020)
11. Chen, Y., Flum, J.: Understanding some graph parameters by infinite model theory (2020, to appear)

12. Chen, Y., Flum, J., Huang, X.: Slicewise definability in first-order logic with bounded quantifier rank. In: Proceedings of CSL 2017, pp. 19:1–19:16 (2017)
13. Elberfeld, M., Stockhusen, C., Tantau, T.: On the space and circuit complexity of parameterized problems: classes and completeness. Algorithmica **71**(3), 661–701 (2015)
14. Flum, J., Grohe, M.: Describing parameterized complexity classes. Inf. Comput. **187**(2), 291–319 (2003)
15. Flum, J., Grohe, M.: Parameterized Complexity Theory. Springer, Heidelberg (2006). https://doi.org/10.1007/3-540-29953-X
16. Furst, M.L., Saxe, J.B., Sipser, M.: Parity, circuits, and the polynomial-time hierarchy. Math. Syst. Theory **17**(1), 13–27 (1984)
17. Gurevich, Y., Lewis, H.R.: A logic for constant-depth circuits. Inf. Control **61**(1), 65–74 (1984)
18. Håstad, J.: Almost optimal lower bounds for small depth circuits. In: Randomness and Computation, pp. 6–20. JAI Press (1989)
19. Immerman, N.: Descriptive Complexity. Graduate Texts in Computer Science. Springer, Heidelberg (1999). https://doi.org/10.1007/978-1-4612-0539-5
20. Rossman, B.: On the constant-depth complexity of k-clique. In: Proceedings of STOC 2008, pp. 721–730 (2008)
21. Segerlind, N., Buss, S.R., Impagliazzo, R.: A switching lemma for small restrictions and lower bounds for k-DNF resolution. SIAM J. Comput. **33**(5), 1171–1200 (2004)
22. Sipser, M.: Borel sets and circuit complexity. In: Proceedings of STOC 1983, pp. 61–69 (1983)
23. Weston, M.: A fixed-parameter tractable algorithm for matrix domination. Inf. Process. Lett. **90**(5), 267–272 (2004)

Betweenness in Order-Theoretic Trees

Bruno Courcelle$^{(\boxtimes)}$

LaBRI, CNRS, 351 Cours de la Libération, 33405 Talence, France
courcell@labri.fr

Abstract. The ternary *betweenness relation* of a tree, $B(x, y, z)$, indicates that y is on the unique path between x and z. This notion can be extended to *order-theoretic trees* defined as partial orders such that the set of nodes greater than any node is linearly ordered. In such generalized trees, the unique "path" between two nodes can have infinitely many nodes.

We generalize some results obtained in a previous article for the betweenness of *join-trees*. Join-trees are order-theoretic trees such that any two nodes have a least upper-bound. The motivation was to define conveniently the rank-width of a countable graph. We have called *quasi-tree* the betweenness relation of a join-tree. We proved that quasi-trees are axiomatized by a first-order sentence.

Here, we obtain a monadic second-order axiomatization of betweenness in order-theoretic trees. We also define and compare several *induced betweenness relations*, *i.e.*, restrictions to sets of nodes of the betweenness relations in generalized trees of different kinds. We prove that induced betweenness in quasi-trees is characterized by a first-order sentence. The proof uses order-theoretic trees.

Keywords: Betweenness · Order-theoretic tree · Join-tree · First-order logic · Monadic second-order logic · Quasi-tree

Introduction

In order to define the rank-width of a countable graph in such a way that it be the least upper-bound of those of its finite induced subgraphs [8], we defined in [3] generalized undirected trees called *quasi-trees* such that the unique "path" (in a precise sense extending the usual notion) between any two nodes can have infinitely many nodes, in particular, can have the order-type of the interval $[0, 1]$ of rational numbers. A related notion is that of an *order-theoretic tree* defined as a partial order such that the set of nodes greater than any node is linearly ordered. It is a *join-tree* if any two nodes have a least upper-bound. It may have no root, *i.e.*, no largest element. Quasi-trees can be seen as undirected join-trees.

The *betweenness relation* of a usual tree is the ternary relation B, such that $B(x, y, z)$ holds if and only if x, y, z are distinct and y is on the unique path between x and z. This notion can be generalized to order-theoretic trees. A quasi-tree is the betweenness relation of a countable (which means possibly finite)

© Springer Nature Switzerland AG 2020
A. Blass et al. (Eds.): Gurevich Festschrift, LNCS 12180, pp. 79–94, 2020.
https://doi.org/10.1007/978-3-030-48006-6_6

join-tree, and quasi-trees are the countable structures (N, B) that satisfy (hence, are axiomatized by) a first-order sentence. We also obtained in [2, 3] an algebraic characterization of the join-trees and quasi-trees that are the unique countable models of monadic-second order sentences. This type of characterization will be extended to order-theoretic trees in a future work. In this article, we obtain a *monadic second-order axiomatization for betweenness in order-theoretic trees*.

We also define and study several *induced betweenness relations, i.e.*, the restrictions to sets of nodes of betweenness in generalized trees of different kinds. An induced betweenness in a quasi-tree need not be a quasi-tree. However, induced betweenness in quasi-trees is also characterized by a *single first-order sentence*, which does not follow immediately from the first-order characterization of quasi-trees by a general logical argument. The proof uses order-theoretic trees.

We obtain four types of betweenness and induced betweenness relations $S = (N, B)$. In each case, such a structure S is defined from an order-theoretic tree T. Except for the case of induced betweenness in order-theoretic trees, some defining tree T can be *described in S* by *monadic second-order formulas*. In technical words, T is defined from S by a *monadic second-order transduction* (see [6] for a thorough study).

In order to obtain a concrete view of our generalized trees, we embed them in *topological trees*, defined as connected unions of segments of straight lines in the plane that have no subset homeomorphic to a circle. Induced betweenness relations in topological trees and in quasi-trees are the same.

Other Works on Betweenness
Betweenness in partial orders of any cardinality is axiomatized by J. Lihova in [7] by an infinite set of universal first-order sentences. It is not stated whether this set can be replaced by a finite one, but presumably not. It can be by a monadic second-order sentence[1].

Motivated by the study of *convex geometries*, V. Chvatal studies in [1] *betweenness in finite triangulated graphs*. It is relative to induced paths : y is between x and z if it is an intermediate vertex on a chordless path between x and z. No axiomatization is provided.

Complete proofs for all stated results and counter-examples can be found in [5], which can be read on line at : https://hal.archives-ouvertes.fr/hal-02205829.

1 Definitions and Basic Facts

All sets, trees, graphs and logical structures are countable, which means, finite or countably infinite. If n is a positive integer, then $[n] := \{1, 2, ..., n\}$.

---

[1] *Betweenness in partial orders*, work in preparation.

1.1 Trees

A *tree* is a possibly empty, undirected graph that is connected and has no cycles. Hence, it has no loops and no two edges with same end vertices. The set of nodes of a tree T is N_T.

A *rooted tree* is a nonempty tree equipped with a distinguished node called its *root*. We define on N_T the partial order $\leq_T$ such that $x \leq_T y$ if and only if y is on the unique path between x and the root. The least upper-bound of x and y, denoted by $x \sqcup_T y$ is their least common ancestor, also called their *join*. The minimal elements are the *leaves*, and the root is the greatest node.

Fact 1: A partial order $(N, \leq)$ is $(N_T, \leq_T)$ for some rooted tree T if and only if it has a largest element and, for each $x \in N$, the set $L_\geq(x) := \{y \in N \mid x \leq y\}$ is finite and linearly ordered. These conditions imply that any two nodes have a join.

1.2 Order-Theoretic Forests and Trees

Definition 2: *O-forests and O-trees.*

In order to have a simple terminology, we will use the prefix O- to mean *order-theoretic* and to distinguish these generalized trees from those of [4].

(a) An *O-forest* is a pair $F = (N, \leq)$ such that:

1) N is a possibly empty set called the set of *nodes*,
2) $\leq$ is a partial order on N such that, for every node x, the set $L_\geq(x)$ is linearly ordered.
   It is an *O-tree* if furthermore:
3) every two nodes x and y have an upper-bound.
   An O-forest is thus the disjoint union of O-trees that are its connected components, with respect to its Gaifman graph[2]. Two nodes are in a same composing O-tree if and only if they have an upper-bound.
   The *leaves* are the minimal elements. If N has a largest element r ($x \leq r$ for all $x \in N$) then F is a *rooted* O-tree and r is its *root*.
(b) An O-tree T is a *join-tree*[3] if every two nodes x and y have a least upper-bound denoted by $x \sqcup_T y$ and called their *join* (cf. Subsect. 1.1). □

Examples and Remarks 3

(1) If T is a rooted tree, then $(N_T, \leq_T)$ is a join-tree. Every finite O-tree is a join-tree of this form.
(2) Every linear order is (trivially) a join-tree.

---

[2] Defined for a relational structure: two elements are adjacent if they belong to some tuple of some relation.

[3] An *ordered tree* is a rooted tree such that the set of sons of any node is linearly ordered. This notion is extended in [4] to join-trees. Ordered join-trees should not be confused with order-theoretic trees, that we call O-trees for simplicity.

(3) Let $S := \mathbb{N} \cup \{a, b, c\}$ be strictly ordered by $<_S$ such that $a <_S b, c <_S b$ and $b <_S i <_S j$ for all $i, j \in \mathbb{N}$ such that $j < i$, and a and c are incomparable. Then $(S, \leq_S)$ is a join-tree. In particular $a \sqcup_S c = b$. It is not the partial order associated with any rooted tree by Fact 1. If $S' := S - \{b\}$, we obtain an O-tree with set of nodes S'. It is not a join-tree because a and c have no join.

(4) We can consider $\mathbb{N} \cup \{a, b\}$ as forming a path[4] in the join-tree$(S, \leq_S)$ (of (3)) between a and 0, the largest element.

2   Quasi-trees and Betweenness in O-Trees

In this section, we will define a *betweenness relation* in O-trees, and compare it with the *betweenness relation induced* by sets of nodes of join-trees or O-trees. We generalize the notion of quasi-tree defined and studied in [3] and [4].

For a ternary relation B on a set N and $x, y \in N$, we define $[x, y]_B := \{x, y\} \cup \{z \in N \mid (x, z, y) \in B\}$. If $n > 2$, then the notation $\neq (x_1, x_2, ..., x_n)$ means that $x_1, x_2, ..., x_n$ are pairwise distinct.

2.1   Betweenness in Trees and Quasi-trees

Definition 4:   *Betweenness in linear orders and trees.*

(a) Let $L = (X, \leq)$ be a linear order[5]. Its *betweenness relation* B_L is the ternary relation on X defined by :

$$B_L(x, y, z) :\Longleftrightarrow x < y < z \text{ or } z < y < x.$$

(b) If T is a tree or a forest, its *betweenness relation* B_T is the ternary relation on N_T defined by :

$B_T(x, y, z) :\Longleftrightarrow x, y, z$ are pairwise distinct and y is on the unique path between x and z.

If R is a rooted tree, we define its *betweenness relation* B_R as $B_{Und(R)}$ where $Und(R)$ is the tree obtained from R by forgetting its root and its edge directions. We have :

$B_R(x, y, z) \Longleftrightarrow x, y, z$ are pairwise distinct, x and z have a join $x \sqcup_R z$ and $(x <_R y \leq_R x \sqcup_R z$ or $z <_R y \leq_R x \sqcup_R z)$.

(c) With a ternary relation B on a set X, we associate the ternary relation A, also on X :

$$A(x, y, z) :\Longleftrightarrow B(x, y, z) \vee B(x, z, y) \vee B(y, x, z).$$

---

[4] Formal definition in [5].

[5] This definition can be used in partial orders. The corresponding notion of betweenness is axiomatized in [7]. We will *not* use it for defining betweenness in order-theoretic trees, although these trees are defined as partial orders.

It is to be read : x, y, z are *aligned*.

If $n \geq 3$, then $B^+(x_1, x_2, ..., x_n)$ stands for the conjunction of the conditions $B(x_i, x_j, x_k)$ for all $1 \leq i < j < k \leq n$ and all $1 \leq k < j < i \leq n$.

Proposition 5 [Proposition 5.2 in [4]]: (a) The betweenness relation B of a linear order $(X, \leq)$ satisfies the following properties for all $x, y, z, u \in X$.

A1: $B(x, y, z) \Rightarrow \neq (x, y, z)$.
A2: $B(x, y, z) \Rightarrow B(z, y, x)$.
A3: $B(x, y, z) \Rightarrow \neg B(x, z, y)$.
A4: $B(x, y, z) \wedge B(y, z, u) \Rightarrow B(x, y, u) \wedge B(x, z, u)$.
A5: $B(x, y, z) \wedge B(x, u, y) \Rightarrow B(x, u, z) \wedge B(u, y, z)$.
A6: $B(x, y, z) \wedge B(x, u, z) \Rightarrow y = u \vee [B(x, u, y) \wedge B(u, y, z)]$
$$\vee [B(x, y, u) \wedge B(y, u, z)].$$

A7': $\neq (x, y, z) \Rightarrow A(x, y, z)$.

(b) The betweenness relation B of a tree T satisfies the properties A1–A6 for all x, y, z, u in N_T together with the following weakening of A7':

$$\text{A7: } \neq (x, y, z) \Rightarrow A(x, y, z) \vee \exists w.(B(x, w, y) \wedge B(y, w, z) \wedge B(x, w, z)).$$

Remark 6

(1) A7' says that if x, y, z are three elements in a linear order, then, one of them is between the two others. Property A7 says that, in a tree T, if x, y, z are three nodes not on a path, then there is some node w between any two of them. Actually :

$\{w\} = P_{x,y} \cap P_{y,z} \cap P_{x,z}$ where $P_{u,v}$ is the set of nodes on the path between u and v,

so that we have $B(x, w, y) \wedge B(y, w, z) \wedge B(x, w, z)$.

If T is a rooted tr ee, then w is the least common ancestor of x, y and z. In the tree T of Fig. 3(b) below, we have $w = 1$ if $x = a, y = d$ and $z = e$.

(2) Properties A1–A6 imply that the two cases of the conclusion of A7 are exclusive[6] and that, in the second one, there is a unique node w satisfying $B(x, w, y) \wedge B(y, w, z) \wedge B(x, w, z)$ (by Lemma 11 of [3]), that is denoted by $M_S(x, y, z)$.

(3) Properties A1–A5 belong to the axiomatization of betweenness in partial orders given in [7].

The letter B and its variants, B_T, B_1, etc. will denote ternary relations.

Definition 7: *More betweenness properties.*

We define the following properties of a structure (N, B) :

---

[6] The three cases of $A(x, y, z)$ are exclusive by A2 and A3.

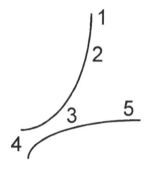

Fig. 1. Structure S of Example 8.

$A8 : \forall u, x, y, z.[\neq (u, x, y, z) \land B(x, y, z) \Rightarrow$
$\qquad B(u, x, y) \lor B(u, y, z) \lor B(x, y, u) \lor B(y, z, u)].$
$A8' : \forall u, x, y, z.[\neq (u, x, y, z) \land B(x, y, z) \land \neg A(y, z, u) \Rightarrow B(x, y, u)].$

If (N, B) satisfies A1–A6, the four cases of the conclusion of A8 are not exclusive : $B(u, x, y)$ implies $B(u, y, z)$ (because of $B(x, y, z)$ and A4).

Example 8: A1–A6 do not imply A8'.
Consider $S := ([5], B)$ where B satisfies (only) $B^+(1, 2, 3, 4) \land B^+(5, 3, 4)$. It is shown in Fig. 1. (There is no curve line going through 1,2,5 because $B(1, 2, 5)$ is not assumed to be valid).

Conditions A1–A6 hold but A8' does not, because we have $B(1, 2, 3) \land \neg A(2, 3, 5)$: A8' would imply $B(1, 2, 5)$ that is not assumed. By the next lemma, A1-A6 do not imply A8 either. □

In the following proofs and discussions about a structure (N, B), we will always assume (unless otherwise specified) that A1–A6 hold, and we will not make their use explicit. We say that (N, B) is trivial if $B = \emptyset$. In this case, Properties A1–A6, A8 and A8' hold trivially.

Lemma 9: Let (N, B) satisfy A1–A6.

(1) A8 is equivalent to A8'.
(2) A7 implies A8, and thus, A8'.
(3) If A8 holds, then the Gaifman graph of (N, B) is either edgeless (if $B = \emptyset$) or connected.

Definition 10: *Quasi-trees* [3].

(a) A *quasi-tree* is a structure $S = (N, B)$ such that B is a ternary relation on N, called the set of *nodes*, that satisfies conditions A1–A7. To avoid uninteresting special cases, we also require that N has at least 3 nodes. We say that S is *discrete* if $[x, y]_B := \{z \mid B(x, z, y)\}$ is finite for all x, y.
(b) From a join-tree $J = (N, \leq)$, we define a ternary relation B_J on N by :

$$B_J(x, y, z) :\Longleftrightarrow \neq (x, y, z) \wedge ([x < y \leq x \sqcup_J z] \vee [z < y \leq x \sqcup_J z]),$$

called its *betweenness relation*. Here, we take as a definition, the characterization of B_R for rooted trees given in Definition 4(b). Note that $x \sqcup_J z$ is always defined.

Theorem 11 [Proposition 5.6 of [4]]:

(1) The structure $qt(J) := (N, B_J)$ associated with a join-tree $J = (N, \leq)$ with at least 3 nodes is a quasi-tree. Every quasi-tree is $qt(J)$ for some join-tree J.
(2) A quasi-tree is discrete if and only if it is $qt(T)$ for some rooted tree T (that is a join-tree defined as the partial order $(N_T, \leq_T)$).

In this article, we will rather think of quasi-trees as betweenness relations of join-trees, axiomatized by A1–A7.

2.2   Other Betweenness Relations

If B is a ternary relation on V and $X \subseteq V$, then $B[X] := B \cap (X \times X \times X)$ is the *induced relation* of B on X.

Definition 12: *Induced betweenness in a quasi-tree*
If $Q = (N, B)$ is a quasi-tree, $X \subseteq N$, we say that $Q[X] := (X, B[X])$ is an *induced betweenness in Q*. It is *induced on X*. It need not be a quasi-tree because A7 does not hold for a triple (x, y, z) such that $M_Q(x, y, z)$ is not in X (cf. Proposition 5 and Remark 6).

We will prove that a ternary relation is an induced betweenness in a quasi-tree *if and only if* it satisfies Properties A1–A6 and A8. The proof uses O-trees.

Proposition 13: An induced betweenness in a quasi-tree satisfies properties A1–A6 and A8.

Proof: The sentences expressing A1–A6 and A8 are universal. The validity of such sentences is preserved under taking induced substructures (we are dealing with relational structures). The result follows from Theorem 11 and Lemma 9(2) showing that a quasi-tree satisfies A8. □

Definition 14: *Betweenness in O-forests.*

(a) From an O-forest $F = (N, \leq)$, we define a ternary relation B_F on N, called its *betweenness relation*, by:

$$B_F(x, y, z) :\Longleftrightarrow \neq (x, y, z) \wedge [(x < y \leq x \sqcup z) \vee (z < y \leq x \sqcup z)].$$
where the join $x \sqcup z$ must be defined.
(b) If $F = (N, \leq)$ is an O-forest and $X \subseteq N$, then $(X, B_F[X])$ is an *induced betweenness relation* in F.

Remark 15: The difference with Definition 10(b) is that if x and z have no least upper-bound, *i.e.*, if $x \sqcup z$ is undefined, then B_F contains no triple of the form (x, y, z). If F is a finite O-tree, it is a join-tree and thus, (N, B_F) is a quasi-tree. □

Thus we have *four classes of betweenness relations* $S = (N, B)$: quasi-trees, induced betweenness in quasi-trees, betweenness and induced betweenness in O-forests.

Here are some easy observations.

(1) The induced betweenness (X, B) on a set X of leaves of a tree is *trivial*, which means that $B = \emptyset$.
(2) The Gaifman graph of a betweenness structure S is connected in the following cases : S is a quasi-tree, or it is a nontrivial induced betweenness in a quasi-tree (by A8) or it is the betweenness relation of an O-tree with at least 3 nodes (easy proof). It may be not connected in the other cases.
(3) If S is an induced betweenness in an O-forest consisting of several disjoint O-trees, then two nodes in the different O-trees cannot belong to a same triple, and as a consequence, cannot be linked by a path in the Gaifman graph of S. Hence, a structure (N, B) is the betweenness of an O-forest, or an induced betweenness in an O-forest if and only if each of its connected components is so in an O-tree. We will only consider betweenness of O-trees (class **BO**) and induced betweenness in O-trees (class **IBO**).

We will denote by **QT** the class of quasi-trees and by **IBQT** the class of induced betweenness relations in quasi-trees. Figure 2 illustrates the following inclusions.

Proposition 16: We have the following strict inclusions :

$$\textbf{QT} \subset \textbf{IBQT}, \ \textbf{QT} \subset \textbf{BO} \subset \textbf{IBO} \text{ and } \textbf{QT} \subset \textbf{IBQT} \cap \textbf{BO}.$$

The classes **IBQT** and **BO** are incomparable. For finite structures, we have **QT = BO**.

All inclusions are clear from the definitions. Examples S_1, S_2, S_4 and S_5 given in [5] prove the strictness assertions.

3   Axiomatizations and Logically Defined Transformations

The letter B designates always ternary relations.

3.1   First-Order Axiomatizations

Induced Betweenness in Quasi-trees

Theorem 17 [5]**:** A structure (N, B) is an induced betweenness relation in a quasi-tree (is in **IBQT**) if and only if it satisfies Axioms A1–A6 and A8.

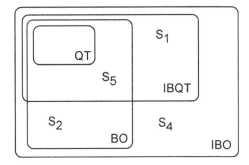

Fig. 2. Four classes and witnesses of proper inclusions.

We present a few notions for its proof. Let $S = (N, B)$ and $r \in N$. We define a binary relation on N :

$$x \leq_r y :\Longleftrightarrow x = y \lor y = r \lor B(x, y, r).$$

Lemma 18: If $S = (N, B)$ satisfies Axioms A1–A6 and $r \in N$, then $T(S, r) := (N, \leq_r)$ is an O-tree.

If S satisfies also A8, we will transform $T(S, r)$ into a witness that S is an induced betweenness. $\square$

Lemma 19: Let $S := (N, B)$ satisfy A1–A6 and A8, and $r \in N$. We have $B \subseteq B_{T(S,r)}$ if N is finite.$\square$

Remark and example 20

(a) In this lemma, we may have a strict inclusion, and the inclusion $B \subseteq B_{T(S,r)}$ may be false if S is infinite.
(b) The following example indicates how we can prove Theorem 17.
    Let $S := (N, B)$ such that $N := \{0, a, b, c, d, e, f, g, h\}$ and the following conditions (and no other one) hold:

$$B^+(0, a, b), B^+(0, c, d), B^+(0, e, f), B^+(0, g, h),$$
$$B^+(b, a, c, d), B^+(f, e, g, h),$$
$$B^+(b, a, 0, e, f), B^+(d, c, 0, e, f), B^+(b, a, 0, g, h), B^+(d, c, 0, g, h).$$

Figure 3(a) shows this structure without showing the last four conditions for the purpose of clarity. The curve line $bacd$ represents $B^+(b, a, c, d)$.

By adding new nodes 1 and 2 to $T(S, 0)$ such that $a < 1 < 0, c < 1 < 0, e < 2 < 0$ and $g < 2 < 0$, we get the rooted tree T of Fig. 3(b). Then $B = B[N]$, hence, is in **IBQT**. Because of the added node 1, we have $B^+(b, a, c, d)$ without having $B^+(b, a, 0, c, d)$.

The proof of Theorem 17 consists in adding new nodes to $T(S, r)$ for such cases.

(c) If $S = (N, B)$ satisfies A1–A7 (and thus A8 by Lemma 9(2)), then, for each $r \in N$, $T(S, r)$ is a join-tree and $B = B_{T(S,r)}$, cf. [4] . $\square$

We know from Definition 10 and Proposition 17 of [3] that a quasi-tree (N, B) is the betweenness relation of a tree if and only if B is *discrete*, *i.e.*, that each set $[x, y]_B := \{x, y\} \cup \{z \in N \mid B(x, z, y)\}$ is finite.

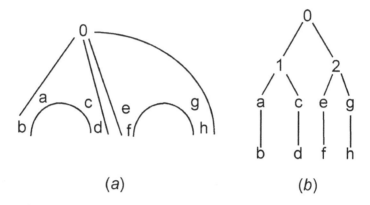

(a)   (b)

Fig. 3. (a) shows S and (b) shows T, Example 20.

Corollary 21: A nontrivial structure (N, B) is an induced betweenness relation in a tree if and only if it satisfies axioms A1–A6, A8 and is discrete. These conditions are monadic second-order expressible. $\square$

Axioms A1–A6, A8 are first-order. One cannot express by a first-order sentence that a linear order $(X, \leq)$ is finite. This is expressed by the conjunction of the following conditions :

(1) $(X, \leq)$ has a minimal element x_0 and a maximal one x_1.
(2) Each $x \in X - \{x_1\}$ has a successor.
(3) (x_0, x_1) belongs to the transitive closure of the successor relation, that exists by (2).

Monadic second-order logic is necessary to express Condition (3).

Remark 22: If $S = (N, B)$ is an induced betweenness in a quasi-tree, then any node r can be taken as root for defining an O-tree $T(S, r)$ and from it, a join-tree T such that $B = B_T[N]$. This fact generalizes the observation that the betweenness in a tree T does not dependent on any root.

Informally, quasi-trees and induced betweenness in quasi-trees are "undirected notions". This will not be the case for betweenness in O-trees.

Betweenness in O-Trees. We let $\mathbf{BO_{root}}$ be the class of betweenness relations of *rooted O-trees*. These relations satisfy A1–A6.

Proposition 23: The class $\mathbf{BO_{root}}$ is axiomatized by a first-order sentence.

Proof: Consider $S = (N, B)$. If B is the betweenness relation of an O-tree $(N, \leq)$ with root r, then, $\leq$ is nothing but $\leq_r$ defined before Lemma 18 from B and r. Let φ be the first-order (FO in short) sentence that expresses properties A1–A6 (relative to B) and the following one :

> A9 : there exists $r \in N$ such that the O-tree $T(S, r) = (N, \leq_r)$ whose partial order is defined by $x \leq_r y :\Longleftrightarrow x = y \vee y = r \vee B(x, y, r)$ has a betweenness relation $B_{T(S,r)}$ equal to B.

That S satisfies A1-A6 insures that $(N, \leq_r)$ is an O-tree with root r. The sentence φ holds if and only if S is in $\mathbf{BO_{root}}$. When it holds, the found node r defines, via $\leq_r$, the relevant O-tree. $\square$

An example detailed in [5] shows that $\mathbf{BO_{root}}$ *is strictly included in* $\mathbf{BO}$.

3.2   Monadic Second-Order Aximatisations

Our second main theorem (whose proof is not straightforward) is :

Theorem 24: The class $\mathbf{BO}$ is axiomatized by a monadic second-order sentence.

In the proof of Proposition 23, we have defined from $S = (N, B)$ satisfying A1–A6 and any node r a *candidate partial order* $\leq_r$ for $(N, \leq_r)$ to be an O-tree with root r whose betweenness relation would be B. The order $\leq_r$ being expressible by a first-order sentence, we finally obtained a first-order characterization of $\mathbf{BO_{root}}$. For $\mathbf{BO}$, a candidate order will be defined from a *line*, *i.e.*, an upwards closed and linearly ordered subset, and not from a single node. (Lemmas 25 and 26 show this definition). It follows that we need for our proof, a *set quantification*.

Lemma 25 [Proposition 5.3 of [4]]: Let (L, B) satisfy properties A1–A7' (for all $u, x, y, z \in L$, cf. Proposition 5). Let a, b be distinct elements of L. There exists a unique linear order $\leq$ on L such that $a < b$ and $B_{(L,\leq)} = B$. This order is quantifier-free definable in the logical structure (L, B) in terms of a and b.$\square$

We will denote this order by $\leq_{L,B,a,b}$. There is a quantifier-free formula λ, written with the ternary relation symbol B, such that, for all a, b, u, v in L, $(L, B) \models \lambda(a, b, u, v)$ if and only if $u \leq_{L,B,a,b} v$.

A *line* in a structure $S = (N, B)$ that satisfies A1–A6 is a set $L \subseteq N$ of at least 3 elements in which any 3 different elements are aligned (cf. Definition 4(c)) and that is convex, *i.e.*, $[x, y]_B \subseteq L$ for all x, y in L.

Lemma 26: Let $T = (N, \leq_T)$ be an O-tree, L a maximal line in T that has no largest node. Let $a, b \in L$, such that $a <_L b$, where $<_L$ is the restriction of $<_T$ to L.

(1) The partial order $\leq_T$ is first-order definable in a unique way in the structure (N, B_T) in terms of $L, \leq_L, a$ and b.
(2) It is first-order definable in (N, B_T) in terms of L, a and b.

Proof Sketch of Theorem 24: "Guess" a line L in the given $S = (N, B)$ and also $a, b \in L$. An associated order $\leq$ on N is FO definable from a, b, L by Lemma 26. Check then that it gives an O-tree U such that $B_U = B$. The only set quantification is for guessing the set L. $\square$

Next we examine in a similar perspective the class **IBO**. It is easy to see that **IBO** $=$ **IBO**$_{\mathrm{root}}$.

Proposition 27 [5]: Every structure in the class **IBO** satisfies Properties A1-A6 but these properties do not characterize this class.$\square$

The construction of Theorem 24 does not extend to **IBO** because a finite structure in **IBO** may not be an induced betweenness relation of any *finite* O-tree. No construction like the one used in the proof of Theorem 17 can produce an infinite structure from a finite one. Nevertheless:

Conjecture 28: The class **IBO** is axiomatized by a monadic second-order sentence.

3.3   Logically Defined Constructions

Each betweenness relation (considered in this article) is a structure $S = (N, B)$ defined from a structure $T = (N', \leq, N)$ where $(N', \leq)$ is an O-tree and $N \subseteq N'$, handled as a unary relation. The different cases are shown in Table 1. In each case a first-order sentence can check whether the structure $(N', \leq, N)$ is of the appropriate type, and the relation B is first-order definable in $(N', \leq, N)$.

Table 1. Transductions that build source structures from betweenness relations.

Structure (N, B)	Axiomatization	Source structure	Transduction
QT	FO: A1–A7, Theorem 11	join-tree $(N, \leq, N)$	FOT
IBQT	FO: A1–A6, A8, Theorem 17	join-tree $(N', \leq, N)$	MSOT
BO	MSO: Theorem 24	O-tree $(N, \leq, N)$	MSOT
IBO	MSO ?: Conjecture 28	O-tree $(N', \leq, N)$	not MSOT

The last column indicates which type of logically defined *transformation of structure* can construct from (N, B) a *source structure* $(N', \leq, N)$ witnessing its membership in the considered classes. We call *transductions*[7] such transformations of relational structures. They are *first-order transductions* (FOT in short) if they are specified by FO formulas. They are *monadic second-order transductions* (MSOT in short) if they are specified by MSO formulas.

For **QT**, this follows from the proof of Theorem 11: if $S = (N, B)$ satisfies A1–A7 and $r \in N$, then, the O-tree $T(S, r) = (N, \leq_r)$ is a join-tree and $B = B_{T(S,r)}$. For **BO**, the MSO sentence that axiomatizes the class constructs a relevant O-tree (it guesses one, *via* some line, and checks that the guess is correct). For **IBO**, we observed that the source tree may need to be infinite for defining a finite betweenness structure, which excludes the existence of an MSO transduction, because these transformations produce structures whose domain size is linear in that of the input structure. (cf. Definition 1.6, and Chapter 7 of [6]). It remains to prove the case of **IBQT**. This is our third main theorem.

Theorem 29: A join-tree $(N', \leq, N)$ witnessing that a given structure $S = (N, B)$ is in the class **IBQT** can be defined from S by MSO formulas.

The proof uses a notion of *structuring of O-trees*, adapted from the one defined in [4] for join-trees, that we will also use in Sect. 4. A structuring of T can be seen as a set of pairwise disjoint linearly ordered subsets whose union is $(N_T, \leq_T)$.

Informally, the construction used for Theorem 17 adds to a tree some "new" nodes so as to be upper-bounds of pairs of nodes (x, y). For having an MSO transduction, one can add "copies" of existing elements but not of pairs of elements. The notion of structuring makes it possible to specify a "hole" in the O-tree, *i.e.*, a missing least upper-bound, as a *copy of a single element*.

We can illustrate structurings in a simple case. If in a binary tree, each node is tagged "left son" or "right son", then, a structuring consists of the set of branches (paths) starting from the root or from a right son, and going down by always going to the left son. The least upper-bound of any two nodes is then the father of some right son (above one of them). This idea is extended to O-trees, that are not join-trees in [5].

4   Embeddings in the Plane

We give a geometric characterization of join-trees and of induced betweenness in quasi-trees, equivalently, in join-trees.

Definition 30: *Trees of lines in the plane.*

(a) In the Euclidian plane, let $\mathcal{L} = (L_i)_{i \in \mathbb{N}}$ be a family of *straight half-lines* (simply called *lines* below) with respective origins $o(L_i)$, that satisfies the following conditions:

---

[7] By reference to *Language Theory* where words, terms and trees are transformed by *transductions*. There are strong links between language theoretical and logically defined transductions, see [6].

(i) if $i > 0$, then $o(L_i) \in L_j$ for some $j < i$,

(ii) for all $i, j \in \mathbb{N}$, $L_i \cap L_j$ is $\{o(L_i)\}$ or $\{o(L_j)\}$ or is empty. (We may have $o(L_i) = o(L_j)$).

We call $\mathcal{L}$ a *tree of lines* : the union of the lines L_i is a connected set $\mathcal{L}^\#$ in the plane. A *path* (resp. a *cycle*) in $\mathcal{L}^\#$ is a homeomorphism h of the interval $[0, 1]$ of real numbers (respectively of the circle S^1) into $\mathcal{L}^\#$ such that $h(0) = x$ and $h(1) = y$ in the case of a path. For any two distinct $x, y \in \mathcal{L}^\#$, there is a unique path from x to y (it "follows the lines"), and consequently, there is no cycle. This path goes through lines L_k such that $k \leq \max\{i, j\}$ where $x \in L_i$ and $y \in L_j$, hence, through finitely many of them. This path uses a single interval of each line it goes through, otherwise, there is a cycle.

(b) We obtain a ternary *betweenness* relation :

$$B_{\mathcal{L}}(x, y, z) :\Longleftrightarrow \neq (x, y, z) \text{ and } y \text{ is on the path between } x \text{ and } z.$$

(c) On each line L_i, we define a linear order as follows :

$$x \preceq_i y \text{ if and only if } y = x \text{ or } y = o(L_i) \text{ or } y \text{ is between } x \text{ and } o(L_i).$$

On $\mathcal{L}^\#$, we define a partial order by :

$x \preceq y$ if and only if $x = y$ or

$x \prec_{i_k} o(L_{i_k}) \prec_{i_{k-1}} o(L_{i_{k-1}}) \prec_{i_{k-2}} \ldots \prec_{i_1} o(L_{i_1}) \prec_{i_0} y$

for some $i_0 < i_1 < \ldots < i_k$. If $k = 0$, then $x \prec_{i_0} y$.

It is clear that $(\mathcal{L}^\#, \preceq)$ is an uncountable rooted O-tree : for each x in $\mathcal{L}^\#$, the set $\{y \in \mathcal{L}^\# \mid x \preceq y\}$ is linearly ordered with greatest element $o(L_0)$.

Definition 31: *Embeddings of join-trees in trees of lines.*
Let $T = (N, \leq, \mathcal{U})$ be a structured (countable) join-tree where $\mathcal{U}$ is the set of lines. An *embedding* of T into a tree of lines $\mathcal{L}$ is an injective mapping $m : N \to \mathcal{L}^\#$ such that:

for each $U \in \mathcal{U}$, m is order preserving : $(U, \leq) \to (L_i, \preceq_i)$ for some $i \in \mathbb{N}$, and
if $i \neq 0$, then $m(lsub(U)) = o(L_i)$.

Here, $lsub(U)$ denotes the least element that is strictly above each element of U.

Lemma 32: If T is a structured join-tree embedded by m into a tree of lines $\mathcal{L}$, then, its betweenness satisfies:

$$B_T(x, y, z) \text{ if and only if } \neq (x, y, z) \wedge B_{\mathcal{L}}(m(x), m(y), m(z)). \square$$

Theorem 33: If $\mathcal{L}$ is a tree of lines and N is a countable subset of $\mathcal{L}^\#$, then $S := (N, B_{\mathcal{L}}[N])$ is an induced betweenness in a quasi-tree. Conversely, every induced betweenness in a quasi-tree is isomorphic to S as above for some tree of lines $\mathcal{L}$.

Proof: If $\mathcal{L}$ is a tree of lines and $N \subset \mathcal{L}^{\#}$ is countable, then $S := (N, B_{\mathcal{L}}[N])$ is in **IBQT**. A witnessing join-tree T is built as follows. Its set of nodes is $N \cup O$ where O is the set of origins of all lines in $\mathcal{L}$. Its order is the restriction to $N \cup O$ of the order $\preceq$ on $\mathcal{L}^{\#}$. Then $(N, B_{\mathcal{L}}[N]) = (N, B_T[N])$ hence belongs to **IBQT**.

Conversely, let $S = (N, B_T[N])$ such that T is a structured join-tree. It is isomorphic to $(N, B_{\mathcal{L}}[N])$ for some tree of lines.$\square$

The construction of this tree of lines uses the fact that between two straight half-lines with same origin A one can draw countably many straight half-lines with origin A by choosing angles between them of the form $\alpha/2^i$ for all i. The resulting tree of lines is clearly not printable!

5   Concluding Remarks

We exhibit in [5] an FO class of relational structures $\mathcal{C}$ such that $Ind(\mathcal{C})$, the class of induced substructures of those in $\mathcal{C}$, is not FO axiomatizable, and is even not MSO axiomatizable. This example shows that the FO characterization of **IBQT** does not follow by a standard logical argument from the FO characterization of the class **QT**, similar to the one used in Proposition 13.

Open Questions

(1) We conjecture that betweenness in O-trees is *not first-order axiomatizable*.
(2) We also conjecture that the class **IBO** of induced betweenness relations in O-trees has a monadic second-order axiomatization.
(3) In [2,4], we have defined quasi-trees and join-trees of different kinds from *regular infinite terms*, and proved that they are *equivalently* the unique models of monadic second-order sentences. Both types of characterizations yield finitary descriptions and decidability results, in particular for deciding isomorphism. In a future work, we will extend to O-trees and to their betweenness relations such descriptions by regular terms, in order to get equivalences between regularity and MSO-definability.

Acknowledgement. I thank the referee for comments helping me to clarify many points.

References

1. Chvatal, V.: Antimatroids, betweenness, convexity. In: Cook, W., Lovász, L., Vygen, J. (eds.) Research Trends in Combinatorial Optimization, pp. 57–64. Springer, Heidelberg (2008). https://doi.org/10.1007/978-3-540-76796-1_3
2. Courcelle, B.: Regularity equals monadic second-order definability for quasi-trees. In: Beklemishev, L., Blass, A., Dershowitz, N., Finkbeiner, B., Schulte, W. (eds.) Fields of Logic and Computation II 9300, 129–141. Lecture Notes in Computer Science. Springer, Cham (2015). https://doi.org/10.1007/978-3-319-23534-9_7
3. Courcelle, B.: Several notions of rank-width for countable graphs. J. Comb. Theory Ser. B **123**, 186–214 (2017)

4. Courcelle, B.: Algebraic and logical descriptions of generalized trees. Log. Methods Comput. Sci. **13**(3) (2017)
5. Courcelle, B.: Axiomatization of betweenness in order-theoretic trees, February 2019. https://hal.archives-ouvertes.fr/hal-02205829
6. Courcelle, B., Engelfriet, J.: Graph Structure and Monadic Second-order Logic: A Language Theoretic Approach. Cambridge University Press, Cambridge (2012)
7. Lihova, J.: Strict-order betweenness. Acta Univ. M. Belii Ser. Math. **8**, 27–33 (2000)
8. Oum, S.: Rank-width and vertex-minors. J. Comb. Theory Ser. B **95**, 79–100 (2005)

Relativization of Gurevich's Conjectures

Anatole Dahan[1]([✉]) and Anuj Dawar[2]

[1] ENS Paris, Paris, France
anatole.dahan@ens.fr
[2] University of Cambridge, Cambridge, UK

Abstract. Gurevich [6] conjectured that there is no logic for P or for
NP ∩ coNP. For the latter complexity class, he also showed that the
existence of a logic would imply that NP ∩ coNP has a complete problem
under polynomial time reductions. We show that there is an oracle with
respect to which P does have a logic and P ≠ NP. We also show that a
logic for NP ∩ coNP follows from the existence of a complete problem and
a further assumption about canonical labelling. For intersection classes
$\Sigma_n^p \cap \Pi_n^p$ higher in the polynomial hierarchy, the existence of a logic is
equivalent to the existence of complete problems.

1 Introduction

In a highly influential paper published in 1988 [6], Yuri Gurevich put forth the
conjecture that there is no logic that captures polynomial time computation. The
question of whether there is a logic for P has been a major driver of research in
finite model theory and descriptive complexity in the last thirty years. In this
line of work, the exact formulation of the question given by Gurevich has played
a central role. Roughly speaking (a precise definition is given later), the question
is whether there is a recursive set S of *polynomially-clocked* deterministic Turing
machines each of which decides an isomorphism-closed class of structures and
such that for every such class in P, there is a machine in S witnessing this fact.

Gurevich's conjecture that there is no logic for P implies that P is different from NP. This is not, as is often assumed, a simple consequence of Fagin's
result [5] that there is a logic for NP, i.e. existential second-order logic. Indeed,
knowing Fagin's theorem and assuming P = NP does not immediately yield a
computable translation from sentences of existential second-order logic to *deterministic* polynomially-clocked machines. The argument requires a little bit more
work. There is, however, another argument that takes us from P = NP to a
refutation of Gurevich's conjecture. This relies on the fact that P = NP would
imply the collapse of the polynomial hierarchy and, in particular, that there
is a polynomial-time algorithm for producing a canonical labelling of a graph
(see [1]). A polynomial-time algorithm for canonical labelling of graphs yields
a logic for P (see [2, Proposition 1.7]). Indeed, much of the research around
the existence of logics for P has been concerned with the existence of canonical
labelling algorithms on suitable classes of structures.

© Springer Nature Switzerland AG 2020
A. Blass et al. (Eds.): Gurevich Festschrift, LNCS 12180, pp. 95–104, 2020.
https://doi.org/10.1007/978-3-030-48006-6_7

Thus, while P = NP would imply the refutation of Gurevich's conjecture, the converse of this statement is not known. Indeed, it is often said that it is entirely consistent with our knowledge that P is different from NP but there is a logic for P. The second author of the present paper made this statement in a lecture in 2012 and was challenged from the audience to provide evidence for it. Theodore Slaman asked if there is a relativized world in which P is different from NP but there is a logic for P. In Sect. 4 we show that this is, indeed, the case. That is we give a construction of an oracle A such that there is a logic for P^A, but $P^A \neq NP^A$. This should be contrasted with the result shown in [3] that if P = NP (in the unrelativized sense), then there is a logic for P^A for all sets A.

Gurevich also conjectured in [6] that there is no logic for the complexity class NP ∩ coNP. Relativizations of this conjecture were considered in [3] (published on the occasion of Yuri's 70th birthday) where it was shown that this conjecture is subject to the relativization barrier, in the sense that there are relativized worlds in which it is true and also relativized worlds in which it is false. The construction of an oracle for which NP ∩ coNP does not have a logic is based on known constructions of oracles for which NP ∩ coNP does not admit complete problems under polynomial-time reductions (see [9]), and the fact that a logic for NP∩coNP would imply the existence of complete problems even under first-order reductions. This last statement is a theorem stated in [3, Theorem 4] though the proof was omitted as it is similar to the well-known proof of the corresponding statement for P [3]. In Sect. 3.1, we give a proof of this fact as a special case of a more general result about Δ-levels of the polynomial hierarchy. We are able to show, in Sect. 3.2, for all levels above the first that the existence of complete problems under polynomial-reductions is *equivalent* to the existence of complete problems under first-order reductions.

2   Preliminaries

We work with finite relational signatures. We write σ for an arbitrary such signature. All our structures are finite, so a σ-structure is a finite set A along with an interpretation on A of every relation symbol in σ. We write STRUC[σ] to denote the collection of all finite σ-structures. We do not consider any specific signatures except that of graphs, i.e. where σ consists of the single binary relation E. We refer to this signature as GRAPH. We assume a standard encoding of finite relational structures as strings, as given in [6]. We write $|S|$ for the size (i.e. number of elements) of a structure S, which is related by a polynomial factor to the length of the string encoding S. As these polynomial factors are unimportant for our discussion, we do not distinguish between S and the string encoding it. Note that, strictly speaking, an encoding of S depends on S *and* a choice of order on the universe of S. Where this is significant, we mention the order explicitly. For full background material on finite model theory, the reader is referred to [4].

We begin by stating the definition of a logic given by Gurevich [6]

Definition 2.1 (Logic). *A logic $\mathcal{L}$ is a pair* (SEN, SAT) *of functions, taking a signature σ as parameter, such that*

- SEN(σ) *is a recursive set. We call $\varphi \in$ SEN(σ) an $\mathcal{L}$-sentence on σ.*
- SAT(σ) *is a recursive subset of* $\{(S, \varphi) \mid \varphi \in$ SEN(σ)$, S \in$ STRUC$[\sigma]\}$, *such that for two isomorphic structures S and S'*

$$\forall \varphi \in \text{SEN}(\sigma), (S, \varphi) \in \text{SAT}(\sigma) \iff (S', \varphi) \in \text{SAT}(\sigma)$$

If φ is an $\mathcal{L}$-sentence on σ, we write MOD$[\varphi]$ *to mean* $\{S \mid (S, \varphi) \in \text{SAT}(\sigma)\}$.

Next, we reproduce Gurevich's definition of a logic capturing polynomial time.

Definition 2.2. *A logic $\mathcal{L}$ captures* P *if:*

- *there is a Turing machine $\mathcal{C}$ such that, on every input $\mathcal{L}$-sentence φ of signature σ, $\mathcal{C}$ outputs a pair (M, p), where M is a deterministic Turing machine and p is a polynomial, such that for all σ-structures S, $S \in$ MOD$[\varphi]$ if, and only if, M accepts S within time $p(|S|)$; and*
- *if $\mathcal{P} \subseteq$ STRUC$[\sigma]$ is an isomorphism-closed class of structures that belongs to* P, *then there exists an $\mathcal{L}$-sentence φ of signature σ such that* MOD$[\varphi] = \mathcal{P}$.

Definition 2.2 formalises the definition from the opening paragraph of Sect. 1. It does not give a general definition of capturing a logic for a complexity class, as it crucially depends on the idea of membership of a class of structures in P being *witnessed* by a pair (M, p). Different complexity classes have rather different notions of witness. In this spirit, the following is Gurevich's definition of a logic capturing NP ∩ coNP.

Definition 2.3. *A logic $\mathcal{L}$ captures* NP ∩ coNP *if:*

- *There is a Turing machine $\mathcal{C}$, such that, on every input $\mathcal{L}$-sentence φ of signature σ, $\mathcal{C}$ outputs a triple (M, N, p) where M and N are non-deterministic Turing machines and p is a polynomial such that:*
  - $\forall S \in$ STRUC$[\sigma], S \in$ MOD$[\varphi]$ *if, and only if, there is a computation of M of length at most $p(|S|)$ by which M accepts S.*
  - $\forall S \in$ STRUC$[\sigma], S \in$ MOD$[\varphi]$ *if, and only if, all computations of N on input S of length at most $p(|S|)$ lead to acceptance.*
- *If $\mathcal{P} \subseteq$ STRUC$[\sigma]$ is an isomorphism-closed class of structures that belongs to* NP ∩ coNP, *then there exists an $\mathcal{L}$-sentence φ of signature σ such that* MOD$[\varphi] = \mathcal{P}$.

Here the witness to membership in the class NP ∩ coNP is given by a triple (M, N, p). It should be noted that in the case of Definition 2.2, the collection of witnesses (M, p) is a recursive set where we put a *semantic*, undecidable condition that the class of structures accepted by (M, p) is isomorphism-closed. In contrast, in the case of Definition 2.3, we have *two* separate semantic conditions, namely that the two machines in the witness agree on the class of structures accepted *and* that this class is isomorphism-closed. As noted in [2], it is the first of these conditions that means that NP ∩ coNP is not even known to have complete problems under polynomial-time reductions and that Gurevich's conjecture with regard to NP ∩ coNP is subject to the relativization barrier.

It was proved in [3] that there is a logic for P in the sense of Definition 2.2 if, and only if, there is a problem in P that is complete under first-order reductions. A similar statement for a logic for NP ∩ coNP was stated in [3]. In the present paper, we prove this, and extend it to higher levels of the polynomial hierarchy. First, we introduce the relevant definitions and notations in connection with the polynomial hierarchy.

For any set A, P^A denotes the class of languages which are accepted by some deterministic Turing machine with an oracle for A in polynomial time. Similarly NP^A denotes the class of languages which are accepted by some nondeterministic Turing machine with an oracle for A in polynomial time. The classes of the polynomial hierarchy are defined as follows.

Definition 2.4. *For all $n \geq 1$,*

- *A language L is in Σ_1^p if, and only if, $L \in$ NP.*
- *A language L is in Σ_{n+1}^p if, and only if, there is some $A \in \Sigma_n^p$ such that $L \in \mathsf{NP}^A$.*
- *A language L is in Π_n^p if, and only if, $\bar{L} \in \Sigma_n^p$.*
- *A language L is in Δ_{n+1}^p if, and only if, there is some $A \in \Sigma_n^p$ such that $L \in \mathsf{P}^A$.*

It is clear that $\Delta_n^p \subseteq \Sigma_n^p \cap \Pi_n^p$ for all n, but equality is not known for any n. In terms of the existence of a logic, we know by Fagin's theorem [5] that there is a logic for NP, and this is extended by [10] to show that for each n, Σ_n^p is captured by the Σ_n-fragment of second-order logic. Similarly, Π_n^p is captured by the Π_n-fragment. We do not, however, obtain by these means a logic for $\Sigma_n^p \cap \Pi_n^p$. To make this precise, we introduce here a definition of what it would mean to capture these classes (in the spirit of Definition 2.3). Before doing so, it is useful to recall that we have, for each n, a problem that is complete for Σ_n^p under polynomial-time reductions. For our purposes, it suffices to take one such problem, Σ_n-QBF. This is the problem of deciding the truth of a quantified Boolean formula in prenex form with $n-1$ alternations of quantifiers, starting with an existential block. By the fact that this problem is Σ_n^p-complete, it follows that $\mathsf{NP}^{\Sigma_n\text{-QBF}} = \Sigma_{n+1}^p$ for all n.

Definition 2.5. *For any $n \geq 1$, a logic $\mathcal{L}$ captures $\Sigma_{n+1}^p \cap \Pi_{n+1}^p$ if:*

- *There is a Turing machine $\mathcal{C}$, such that, on every input $\mathcal{L}$-sentence φ of signature σ, $\mathcal{C}$ outputs a triple (M, N, p) where M and N are non-determinisitic oracle Turing machines and p is a polynomial such that:*
  - *$\forall S \in \mathrm{STRUC}[\sigma]$, $S \in \mathrm{MOD}[\varphi]$ if, and only if, there is a computation of M with oracle Σ_n-QBF of length at most $p(|S|)$ by which M accepts S.*
  - *$\forall S \in \mathrm{STRUC}[\sigma]$, $S \in \mathrm{MOD}[\varphi]$ if, and only if, all computations of N with oracle Σ_n-QBF on input S of length at most $p(|S|)$ lead to acceptance.*

– If $\mathcal{P} \subseteq \mathrm{STRUC}[\sigma]$ is an isomorphism-closed class of structures that belongs to $\Sigma^p_{n+1} \cap \Pi^p_{n+1}$, then there exists an $\mathcal{L}$-sentence φ of signature σ such that $\mathrm{MOD}[\varphi] = \mathcal{P}$.

3 Capturing Intersection Classes in the Polynomial Hierarchy

The relationship between the existence of a logic for a complexity class and the existence of complete problems can be somewhat subtle. In the case of *syntactic* complexity classes like P and NP, there are complete problems under what we might call *computational* reductions, even reductions in very weak computational classes such as AC^0. These classes have complete problems under *logical* reductions such as first-order reductions if, and only if, there is a logic capturing them. In the case of NP, we simply know this to be true, but for P it remains an open question. In the case of NP ∩ coNP, which is a *semantic* class, Gurevich already showed that the existence of a logic implies that the class has complete problems under polynomial-time reductions (again, we can take computational reductions in much weaker complexity classes). It was noted in [3] that this can be strengthened to the existence of logical reductions. In Sect. 3.1, we prove this and extend it to all intersection classes in the polynomial hierarchy.

This result has an interesting consequence in connection with the graph canonical labelling problem. It is well known that if there is a graph canonical labelling algorithm that runs in polynomial time, then there is a logic for P (see [2, Proposition 1.7]). In the case of NP ∩ coNP, we are able to show that if canonical labelling can be done in this class, a notion we make precise below, then the existence of a logic becomes equivalent to the question of whether the class has complete problems under polynomial-time reductions. For intersection classes higher up in the polynomial hierarchy, we know that canonical labelling can be done in the class and therefore the equivalence holds unconditionally. This is shown in Sect. 3.2.

3.1 Logics for Intersection Classes

The following strengthening of Gurevich's result showing that if NP ∩ coNP admits a logic capturing it, it has a complete problem under poly-time reductions was stated in [3, Theorem 4].

Theorem 3.1 ([3]). *NP ∩ coNP has a complete problem under FO reductions if, and only if, it admits a logic.*

We generalize this theorem to higher levels of the polynomial hierarchy as follows.

Theorem 3.2. *There is a $\Sigma^p_n \cap \Pi^p_n$-complete problem under first-order reductions if, and only if, there is a logic capturing $\Sigma^p_n \cap \Pi^p_n$.*

Proof. In order to prove this result, we need the following lemma:

Lemma 3.3. ([7], p. 228]). *Let σ be a finite relational vocabulary. Then, there exists first-order interpretations $I_\sigma : \text{STRUC}[\sigma] \rightarrow \text{STRUC}[\text{GRAPH}]$ and I_σ^{-1} such that*

$$\forall \mathcal{A} \in \text{STRUC}[\sigma], I_\sigma^{-1}(I_\sigma(\mathcal{A})) \cong \mathcal{A}$$

Moreover, $\forall \mathcal{A}, \mathcal{A}' \in \text{STRUC}[\sigma], \mathcal{A} \cong \mathcal{A}' \iff I_\sigma(\mathcal{A}) \cong I_\sigma(\mathcal{A}')$

We now use this to prove Theorem 3.2.

($\Rightarrow$) Let Q be a $\Sigma_n^p \cap \Pi_n^p$-complete problem under first-order reductions and let τ be the vocabulary of Q, and let I_τ^{-1} be the reduWe now use this to provection from Graphs to τ-structures given by Lemma 3.3. We define the following logic for any signature σ:
- $\text{SEN}(\sigma) = \{\Theta \mid \Theta$ is a first-order interpretation from σ to GRAPH$\}$
- $\text{SAT}(\sigma) = \{(S, \Theta) \mid I_\tau^{-1}(\Theta(S)) \in Q\}$

This logic obviously captures $\Sigma_n^p \cap \Pi_n^p$. This can be seen by taking a fixed (M, N, p) that witnesses the membership of Q in $\Sigma_n^p \cap \Pi_n^p$. Then, combining this with polynomial time machines that compute the interpretations Θ and I_τ^{-1} gives a computable map that takes $\Theta \in \text{SEN}(\sigma)$ to a witness $(M_\Theta, N_\Theta, p_\Theta)$ for $\text{MOD}(\Theta) \in \Sigma_n^p \cap \Pi_n^p$.

($\Leftarrow$) Let $\mathcal{L}$ be a logic for $\Sigma_n^p \cap \Pi_n^p$. Assume we have an encoding of sentences in $\text{SEN}(\text{GRAPH})$ as integers, and let $\mathcal{I}$ be the range of this encoding. Let $\mathcal{C}$ be a deterministic Turing Machine witnessing that $\mathcal{L}$ captures $\Sigma_n^p \cap \Pi_n^p$ (as in Definition 2.5).

We aim to define a class Q of structures complete for graph problems in $\Sigma_n^p \cap \Pi_n^p$ over $\tau = \langle V, E, \preceq, I \rangle$ where V and I are unary and E and $\preceq$ are binary relation symbols. A structure $\mathfrak{A} = \langle A, V, E, \preceq, I \rangle$ belongs to Q if:

1. $\preceq$ is a total, transitive, reflexive relation, i.e. a linear pre-order.
2. $\forall a, b, I(a) \wedge I(b) \implies a \preceq b \wedge b \preceq a$, and i is the greatest integer such that $\exists x_1, x_2 \ldots x_i, x_1 \not\gtrsim x_2 \not\gtrsim \cdots \not\gtrsim x_i \wedge I(x_i)$, where $x \not\gtrsim y \equiv (x \preceq y \wedge y \not\preceq x)$. In other words, I picks the i-th equivalence class in $\preceq$
3. $\mathcal{C}$ on input i runs in time $t \leq |A|$, and outputs (M, N, p)
4. $|A| \geq p(|V|)$
5. M accepts $\langle V, E \rangle$

Q is in $\Sigma_n^p \cap \Pi_n^p$: 1, 2, 3 and 4 are clearly computable deterministically in polynomial time. As for 5. it is both in Σ_n^p, by checking that there is a computation of M that accepts $\langle V, E \rangle$ in $p(|V|)$ steps, and in Π_n^p, by checking that all computations of N of length at most $p(|V|)$ accept $\langle V, E \rangle$. To show that Q is $\Sigma_n^p \cap \Pi_n^p$-hard, let $\mathcal{P}$ be a class of graphs in $\Sigma_n^p \cap \Pi_n^p$. Let $\varphi \in \text{SEN}(\text{GRAPH})$ be an $\mathcal{L}$-sentence such that $\text{MOD}[\varphi] = \mathcal{P}$. Let $i \in \mathcal{I}$ be the encoding of φ, t the length of the computation of $\mathcal{C}$ on input i and (M, N, p) the output of the computation. Let k and n_0 be integers such that $k \geq i$, $n^k \geq t$, $n^k \geq p(n)$ for all $n \geq n_0$. We describe a k-ary first-order interpretation $\Theta : \text{STRUC}[\text{GRAPH}] \rightarrow \text{STRUC}[\tau]$ which is a reduction from $\mathcal{P}$ to Q for all graphs with at least n_0 vertices. The finitely many cases of graphs with fewer than n_0 vertices can be dealt with by adding a disjunct to the formulas mapping them to some fixed structures inside or outside Q depending on whether or not they are in $\mathcal{P}$ in the standard way. Our reduction is given by the tuple of formulas $(\varphi_0, \varphi_V, \varphi_E, \varphi_\preceq, \varphi_I)$ as follows.

- $\varphi_0 \equiv \mathbf{true}$.
- $\varphi_V(x_1, \ldots, x_k) \equiv x_1 = x_2 = \cdots = x_k$.
- $\varphi_E(x_1, \ldots x_k, y_1, \ldots, y_k) \equiv \varphi_V(x_1, \ldots, x_k) \wedge \varphi_V(y_1, \ldots, y_k) \wedge E(x_1, y_1)$.
- $\varphi_\preceq$ defines an arbitrary ordering of basic equality types of k-tuples from V. Note that the condition $k \geq i$ guarantees, in particular, that there are at least i such types.
- φ_I defines the ith equality type.

$$\varphi_I(\overline{a}) \equiv \exists \overline{a_1}, \ldots, \overline{a_{i-1}}, \bigwedge_{1 \leq j < i-1} (\varphi_\preceq(\overline{a_j}, \overline{a_{j+1}}) \wedge \neg\varphi_\preceq(\overline{a_{j+1}}, \overline{a_j}))$$
$$\wedge\, \varphi_\preceq(\overline{a_{i-1}}, \overline{a}) \wedge \neg\varphi_\preceq(\overline{a}, \overline{a_{i-1}})$$
$$\wedge\, \forall \overline{b}, \varphi_\preceq(\overline{b}, \overline{a_i}) \implies \bigvee_{1 \leq j < i} (\varphi_\preceq(\overline{a_j}, \overline{b}) \wedge \varphi_\preceq(\overline{b}, \overline{a_j}))$$

For any graph G, $I(G) \in Q$ if and only if M accepts (V, E), if and only if $(V, E) \models \varphi$, as conditions 1, 2, 3 and 4 result from definition.

3.2   Logical and Computational Reductions

Theorem 3.2 has an interesting consequence. We know that if canonical labelling of graphs can be done in polynomial time, then there is a logic for P. In the case of NP ∩ coNP, if canonical labelling is in the class, we still need the additional condition that NP ∩ coNP is a syntactic class, i.e. it admits complete problems under *computational* (e.g. polynomial-time) reductions. Higher up in the polynomial hierarchy, for classes $\Sigma_n^p \cap \Pi_n^p$ where $n \geq 2$, we know that canonical labelling is, indeed, in the class. There the existence of a logic becomes equivalent to the question of whether there are complete problems under polynomial-time reductions. To make this precise, we first need to define what it means for canonical labelling to be in NP∩coNP, or $\Sigma_n^p \cap \Pi_n^p$, which are classes of decision problems.

   An *ordered graph* is a structure $(V, E, \leq)$ where (V, E) is a graph and $\leq$ is a linear order on V. A *canonical labelling function* is a function Can taking ordered graphs to ordered graphs such that

- if $\mathrm{Can}(V, E, \leq) = (V', E', \leq')$ then $(V, E) \cong (V', E')$; and
- if $(V, E) \cong (V', E')$ then for any linear orders $\leq$ and $\leq'$ on V and V' respectively, $\mathrm{Can}(V, E, \leq) \cong \mathrm{Can}(V', E', \leq')$.

   We say that a canonical labelling function is in FP (the class of function problems computable in polynomial time) if it can be computed by a deterministic Turing machine running in polynomial time. To define a corresponding notion for NP∩coNP, we use the class TFNP defined by Megiddo and Papadimitriou [8].

Definition 3.4. *We say that a canonical labelling function* Can *is in* TFNP *if the graph of the function, i.e.* $\{(X, Y) \mid \mathrm{Can}(X) = Y\}$ *is in* P.

As noted by Megiddo and Papadimitriou [8], TFNP (even though it is not a class of functions) can be understood as the function problems corresponding to NP ∩ coNP. This allows us to prove the following result.

Theorem 3.5. *If* NP∩coNP *admits a complete problem under polynomial reductions, and there is a canonical labelling function in* TFNP, *then* NP∩coNP *admits a complete problem under first-order reductions.*

Proof. If Can is in TFNP, there is a nondeterministic machine $\mathcal{G}$ which, given a string encoding an ordered graph G, runs in time polynomial in the size of G and each computation of $\mathcal{G}$ either ends in rejection or, produces on the output tape an encoding of $\mathrm{Can}(G)$. Indeed, the machine $\mathcal{G}$ can nondeterministically guess a string for $\mathrm{Can}(G)$, then verify that the guess is correct and write it on the output tape or reject if it is not.

Let $\mathcal{P}$ be an NP∩coNP-complete problem on graphs under polynomial reductions, and $(\mathcal{M}, \mathcal{N}, p)$ be a triple witnessing this membership.

Finally, let $(M_i, p_i)_{i \in \mathcal{I}}$ be an enumeration of pairs where M_i is a deterministic Turing machine with output tape and p_i is a polynomial. We write f_i for the function on strings computed by the machine M_i when clocked with the polynomial p_i.

We can now construct the following logic $\mathcal{L}$:

- $\mathrm{SEN}(\sigma) = \mathcal{I}$
- $\mathrm{SAT}(\sigma)$ is the set of all $(S, i), S \in \mathrm{STRUC}[\sigma], i \in \mathcal{I}$ such that $\mathcal{M}$ accepts $x = f_i(\mathrm{Can}(I_\sigma(S)))$ in $p(|x|)$ steps.

To see that this is a logic, i.e. that the satisfaction relation is well defined, let S and S' be two isomorphic σ-structures. By Lemma 3.3, $I_\sigma(S) \cong I_\sigma(S')$ and therefore $\mathrm{Can}(I_\sigma(S)) = \mathrm{Can}(I_\sigma(S'))$. Hence,

$$\forall \varphi \in \mathrm{SEN}(\sigma), S \models \varphi \iff S' \models \varphi.$$

To see that this logic captures NP ∩ coNP, let L be an NP ∩ coNP decidable class of structures of signature σ. Then, $I_\sigma(L)$ is an NP ∩ coNP problem (as $I_\sigma^{-1}(I_\sigma(L)) = L$), so there exists $i \in \mathcal{I}$ such that M_i computes a reduction from $I_\sigma(L)$ to $\mathcal{P}$ in time bounded by p_i. Therefore, for all $S \in \mathrm{STRUC}[\sigma]$, $S \in L \iff f_i(\mathrm{Can}(I_\sigma(S))) \in \mathcal{P}$. In other words, there is $i \in I$ such that $\mathrm{MOD}[i] = L$.

Finally, note that there is a computable translation that takes us from i to a witness (M, N, p) to the fact that $\mathrm{MOD}[i]$ is in NP ∩ coNP. Here M is the nondeterministic machine that takes as input a σ-structure S and first computes $I_\sigma(S)$. This can be done deterministically in polynomial time. It then runs the non-deterministic machine $\mathcal{G}$. Rejecting computations of this lead to M rejecting, but accepting computations produce $\mathrm{Can}(I_\sigma(S))$ on which we now run M_i for $p_i(|\mathrm{Can}(I_\sigma(S))|)$ steps. Finally we run $\mathcal{M}$ on the result. N is defined similarly except that in the last stage we run $\mathcal{N}$. It can now be checked that this satisfies all the conditions for a logic capturing $\mathsf{NP} \cap \mathsf{coNP}$. Hence by Theorem 3.1, there is an $\mathsf{NP} \cap \mathsf{coNP}$-complete problem under FO-reductions.

To lift the result to higher levels of the polynomial hierarchy, we first define what it means for graph canonical labelling to be in the functional variant of $\Sigma_n^p \cap \Pi_n^p$.

Definition 3.6. *We say that a canonical labelling function* Can *is in* $\mathsf{F}(\Sigma_n^p \cap \Pi_n^p)$ *if the graph of the function, i.e.* $\{(X,Y) \mid \mathrm{Can}(X) = Y\}$ *is in* Δ_n^p.

We can now state the following equivalence.

Theorem 3.7. *For* $n \geq 2$. $\Sigma_n^p \cap \Pi_n^p$ *admits a complete problem under polynomial-time reductions if, and only if, it admits a complete problem under first-order reductions.*

Proof. One implication is trivial. For the other one, the proof is exactly as for Theorem 3.5, except we know that there is a canonical labelling function in $\mathsf{F}(\Sigma_n^p \cap \Pi_n^p)$ (see [1]).

4   A Relativization of Gurevich's Conjecture

It is well-known that the conjecture of Gurevich that there is no logic for P implies the conjecture that P is different from NP. Here we show that there is a relativized world in which these two conjectures are different, i.e. the first fails while the second is true.

Theorem 4.1. *There is an oracle* A, *such that there is a logic for* P^A *and* $\mathsf{P}^A \neq \mathsf{NP}^A$.

Proof. As constructed in [11], let B be a set such that $\Delta_2^{P,B} \subsetneq \Sigma_2^{P,B}$. Then take A to be a $\Sigma_1^{P,B}$-complete set. Then, $\mathsf{P}^A = \Delta_2^{P,B} \subsetneq \Sigma_2^{P,B} = \mathsf{NP}^A$.

Moreover, since $\Delta_2^P \subset \mathsf{P}^A$, there is a graph canonical labelling function Can computable by a deterministic polynomial-time machine with an oracle for A. Let $(M_i, p_i)_{i \in \mathcal{I}}$ be an enumeration of polynomial time bounded oracle Turing Machines. We can now build a logic for P^A:

- $\mathrm{SEN}(\sigma) = \mathcal{I}$
- $\mathrm{SAT}(\sigma) = \{(S, i), \mathrm{Can}(I_\sigma(S)) \text{ is accepted by } M_i \text{ with oracle } A\}$.

5   Conclusion

A logic capturing a complexity class requires us to find an effective syntax for the machines that define the class *and* are isomorphism invariant. For complexity classes that are inherently syntactic, such as P and NP, this requirement can be met by finding a suitable canonical labelling algorithm. For other classes which are inherently semantic, such as $\mathsf{NP} \cap \mathsf{coNP}$, the requirement breaks down to finding a syntactic characterization (i.e. a complete problem) in addition to a canonical labelling algorithm. This allows us to explore these questions in relativized worlds. One interesting question to pursue would be whether the requirement for a canonical labelling algorithm can itself be done away with in a relativized world? Could one devise an oracle with respect to which canonical labelling is not in polynomial-time yet there is a logic for P?

References

1. Blass, A., Gurevich, Y.: Equivalence relations, invariants, and normal forms. SIAM J. Comput. **13**(4), 682–689 (1984)
2. Dawar, A.: Feasible computation through model theory. Ph.D. thesis, University of Pennsylvania (1993)
3. Dawar, A.: Generalized quantifiers and logical reducibilities. J. Logic Comput. **5**(2), 213–226 (1995)
4. Ebbinghaus, H.-D., Flum, J.: Finite Model Theory. SMM. Springer, Heidelberg (1995). https://doi.org/10.1007/3-540-28788-4
5. Fagin, R.: Generalized first-order spectra and polynomial-time recognizable sets. In: Karp, R.M. (ed.) Complexity of Computation, SIAM-AMS Proceedings, vol. 7, pp. 43–73 (1974)
6. Gurevich, Y.: Logic and the Challenge of Computer Science, pp. 1–57. Computer Science Press, Rockville (1988)
7. Hodges, W.: Model Theory. Encyclopedia of Mathematics and its Applications. Cambridge University Press, Cambridge (1993)
8. Megiddo, N., Papadimitriou, C.H.: A note on total functions, existence theorems, and computational complexity. Theor, Comput. Sci. **81**, 317–324 (1991)
9. Sipser, M.: On relativization and the existence of complete sets. In: Nielsen, M., Schmidt, E.M. (eds.) ICALP 1982. LNCS, vol. 140, pp. 523–531. Springer, Heidelberg (1982). https://doi.org/10.1007/BFb0012797
10. Stockmeyer, L.J.: The polynomial-time hierarchy. Theor. Comput. Sci. **3**(1), 1–22 (1976)
11. Torenvliet, L.: A second step toward the strong polynomial-time hierarchy. Math. Syst. Theory **21**, 99–123 (1988). https://doi.org/10.1007/BF02088009

Seventy Years of Computer Science

Martin Davis[✉]

Courant Institute, New York University, New York, USA
martin@eipye.com

Abstract. A quick tour through my long career with emphasis on how computer science has affected me and how I have affected computer science.

Keywords: Turing · Copeland · Neural net · Recursive functions · Computability · ORDVAC · Presburger arithmetic · ACE · Test data adequacy · **NP** · Hypercomputation · Universal · SAT · Linked conjunct · Obvious inferences

I delivered my typewritten doctoral dissertation to the Princeton University registrar in May 1950, just seventy years before May 2020. In this essay I will try to provide a very personal survey of my interactions with computer science, as participant and as observer, over this seventy year period.

The title of my dissertation was *On the Theory of Recursive Unsolvability*. In 1935 Alonzo Church[1] had declared that the *recursive functions*, defined on the natural numbers, are precisely those that are algorithmically computable. It was Gödel who had defined this class, and Church's student Kleene had found various alternative formulations of the class. Church and Kleene had also studied a class of functions, the λ–*definable* functions, defined in a very different manner, and it had been proved that the two classes were the same. Meanwhile in England, Alan Turing's[2] formulation, in terms of what came to be called Turing machines, was proved by Turing to be equivalent to these other two. E. L. Post[3] had a formulation very close to Turing's that he had developed independently. Post had also worked on a quite different formalism, his *canonical* and *normal* systems of productions, during the 1920s and proposed them as providing yet another formulation he expected to be equivalent to the other three.

In my dissertation I studied various aspects of the theory of recursive functions basing myself on Kleene's version of Gödel's formulation. I proved that Post's canonical systems were equivalent to the other formulations and, using Post's reduction of canonical to normal systems, obtained an unsolvable problem for normal systems. With this problem as a basis, I obtained my first unsolvable

---

[1] He was my adviser.

[2] Church was Turing's adviser as well. But Turing's computability paper was written before he became a Princeton student to work with Church.

[3] He was my teacher when I was an undergraduate at City College in New York.

© Springer Nature Switzerland AG 2020
A. Blass et al. (Eds.): Gurevich Festschrift, LNCS 12180, pp. 105–117, 2020.
https://doi.org/10.1007/978-3-030-48006-6_8

problem involving Diophantine equations. Was this computer science? A mile and a half away from the Princeton campus, von Neumann's computer at the Institute for Advanced Study was being built in 1950, not to be operational for another two years. But I was aware of this only dimly if at all. In any case, the thought that it had any relation to my dissertation would never have occurred to me. Still Gödel's advance to what Kleene called "general" recursion from the earlier "primitive" recursion corresponds to including *while* loops in programming languages in addition to simple looping constructs. A substantial part of my dissertation was to appear, couched in the language of Turing machines, in my book, *Computability and Unsolvability*, of 1958. In Computing Reviews this book was called "one of the few classics of computer science" when Dover reprinted it in 1982. Also, Chomsky's hierarchy of classes of formal languages was based explicitly on Post's production systems.

In the fall of 1950, amid considerable turmoil in my personal life, I found myself amid the corn fields of southern Illinois, where I had moved to take up a postdoc position at the University of Illinois at Champaign-Urbana. In the spring semester I was able to teach a graduate course on recursive functions. I liked the intuitive feeling of Turing machines and decided to base my presentation on them rather than on the general recursions in my dissertation. In showing that complicated algorithms could be coded for Turing machines, I was writing lots of specific Turing machine code on the blackboard. A freshly minted PhD in mathematics like me, Ed Moore, who had been auditing the course, came to the front of the room after one of the sessions and showed me how I could improve some of the code I had written. Then he said, "We have one of those across the street." He was referring to the ORDVAC, a computer built at the University of Illinois pretty much along the lines of von Neumann's machine in Princeton.

What brought me to the ORDVAC was the Korean War. When Truman decided to militarily oppose the invasion of South Korea from the north, a group of University of Illinois academics, mostly physicists, joined to try to use their scientific knowledge to aid the effort. I was recruited for this new organization, the Control Systems Laboratory, and I accepted the offer. To begin with, there was a heady brew of ideas in the air: Wiener's cybernetics, Shannon's theory of computation, and computers with their unknown potential. Eventually it was decided to build a prototype of a system in which the ORDVAC controlled physical devices. Specifically, it was to navigate 100 airplanes in real time. And the task of writing the program that would do this was given to me.

The ORDVAC was built around a William's memory in which data was stored as electric charge on the surface of cathode ray tubes (CRTs). There were 40 small CRTs each capable of storing 1024 bits in a 32×32 array. So the total memory was 5 KB. A memory access or an addition required 40 ms, and a multiplication or a division required a full millisecond. My program was to respond to "radar" information providing position information of the "planes" by computing a heading for each plane and transmitting it to the plane. The computation consisted of a sorting part, in which each radar input was matched with the corresponding plane, and a part in which the headings were computed.

I used a merge-sort algorithm for the first part. For the second part I had the help of a young physicist, Marius Cohen, who found an algorithm for computing the sine function to sufficient accuracy using just one division and no multiplications. All of this had to be interrupted regularly to intercept incoming radar data. I had to place these interruptions in the code based on a hand calculation using the published times required for the instructions to be carried out.

Programs for the ORDVAC were written in absolute binary machine language, with nothing like an assembly language available. The ORDVAC had no index register so control of loops required the code to operate on itself. Nevertheless I found programming lots of fun. Also it was clear to me that it was essentially the same activity that I had been engaged in in the classroom programming Turing machines. But it would be some time before I came to understand how intimate the connection is. It was fun, but it wasn't my own work. When I was able to obtain support for two years at the Institute for Advanced Study in Princeton, I eagerly seized the opportunity.

Back in Princeton with my pregnant wife Virginia, whom I had met and married in Champaign-Urbana, I was free to work out some of my ideas related to Gödel incompleteness. I also began working on the book that was to become *Computability and Unsolvability*. I wanted to show computability as a full-fledged subject in its own right with diverse applications. Basing it on Turing machines, I wanted the connections with computer practice to emerge. Before my two years at the Institute for Advanced Study were up, I was able to bring a complete handwritten manuscript to the typists. I knew that my handwriting had difficulties, but nevertheless I was dismayed by the poor job the typists had done. Every page needed many corrections, and when I brought the corrected typescript back to the typists, they refused to have anything to do with it. I suppose that after typing the work of such as Einstein, Gödel, and von Neumann, they felt entitled to ignore the needs of 26 year old mere visitor. The typescript languished in closets for over two years.

The terms of my support gave me the option of seeking summer employment, and we certainly needed the money. In the summer of 1953 I worked at Bell Labs, an easy commute from Princeton. My supervisor was Claude Shannon whose fundamental tract on information theory I had read in Champaign-Urbana. Ed Moore, who had first told me about the ORDVAC, was there as well. Shannon had designed a universal Turing machine with only two states. He raised the question: Can one provide a precise definition of universality? He pointed out that unless the input/output is carefully specified, a Turing machine might exhibit universal behavior only because of the way input data was coded. I liked the problem and wrote two papers about it.

For the following summer I had managed to receive funding for a project to program the decision procedure for Presburger arithmetic. I had permission to use the Institute for Advanced Study computer for the purpose. I completed the project, and we were off, driving across the country to Davis, California where I was going to be an assistant professor of mathematics at one of the campuses of the University of California. While there wasn't much intellectual activity in the

Davis mathematics department, in Berkeley, 80 miles away, the great logician Alfred Tarski led an outstanding group of young scholars. When I was invited to speak at the weekly colloquium of the Berkeley mathematics department, I took the opportunity to express my view of computability theory as an autonomous branch of mathematics. Tarski, who was in the audience, took strong exception during the discussion after my talk.

After Virginia and I were awakened by the onset of labor, our second son Nathan was born at home at 4AM. Other than us, the only person in the house was Nathan's two year old brother Harold. Virginia's obstetrician was far away in Berkeley, and we made do with an obstetric textbook. As I write, Harold and Nathan are men well into their sixties.

We remained in Davis for just one year and moved to Columbus, Ohio, where I was again an assistant professor of mathematics teaching elementary subjects. Again we left after a year. I eagerly accepted an offer from the Hartford Graduate Center that Rensselaer Polytechnic Institute had established in Eastern Connecticut. I remained there for three very fruitful years. With a faculty of perhaps a dozen, with only three of us teaching mathematics, it was quite an interesting place with mature students, quite different from those, not yet 20, that I had been teaching in Davis and Columbus.

The secretaries there were eager to be helpful and did an excellent job of turning my manuscript for *Computability and Unsolvability* into proper shape for being submitted to a publisher. McGraw-Hill offered me a contract and published it in their series on "Information Processing and Computers". In my preface I wrote:

> The existence of universal Turing machines ... confirms the belief ... that it is possible to construct a single "all-purpose" digital computer on which can be programmed ... for any conceivable deterministic digital computer.

A quarter of a century was to go by before I came to understand just how intimate was the relationship between Turing's abstract model of a universal computer and physical computers, that the former was the progenitor of the latter.

The book was written from the point of view of computability as an independent discipline. This view was reinforced by a section on applications with chapters on logic, algebra, and number theory. Tarski's equally valid view, expressed when he objected to what I had said in my Berkeley talk, was that computability is a branch of definability theory which is part of mathematical logic.

Of course at the time this book was written, the academic discipline of computer science didn't yet exist. Nevertheless computer science is indebted to computability theory in several ways. It supplied two models of computation, the Turing macine and the register machine that proved useful in quantifying the asymptotic complexity of specific algorithms. Also, the complexity classes poly-time, NP-completeness, and the levels of the poly-time hierarchy were all defined by analogy with categories from computability theory.

In the summer of 1957 (a year before *Computability and Unsolvability* was published) there was a remarkable five week "Institute for Logic" at Cornell

University in Ithaca, 220 miles northwest of New York City. 85 logicians attended, almost all from the U.S. The influence of the newly developing world of computers was already evident. Alonzo Church lectured on "Application of Recursive Arithmetic to the Problem of Circuit Synthesis". I spoke about my program for Presburger arithmetic. Abraham Robinson discussed "Proving a Theorem (As Done by Man, Logician, and Computer)". Rabin and Scott's fundamental work on finite automata was presented. IBM sent a contingent of 13 to the "Institute". Among other things they presented FORTRAN, initiating controversy on whether the loss of efficiency in programming in such a "high level" language compared to using assembly language was supportable. Altogether of the 82 talks presented, 19 had a definite computer science aspect.

I had become friendly with Hilary Putnam, a young philosopher at Princeton, and we decided to share a small house in Ithaca with our families for the duration of the Logic Institute. We were together nearly every day, and this led directly to our fruitful collaboration. I had studied what I had called Diophantine sets. A set S of natural numbers is *Diophantine* if there is a polynomial $p(a, x_1, x_2, \ldots, x_n)$ such that $a \in S$ if and only if there are natural numbers $x_1, x_2, \ldots, x_n$ for which $p(a, x_1, x_2, \ldots, x_n) = 0$. In my dissertation I had conjectured that every set of natural numbers which is *listable*[4], in the sense that there is an algorithm that generates a list of the members of the set, is also Diophantine. I had taken a first small step towards proving this conjecture. It was easy to see that the truth of the conjecture would yield a solution to the tenth of the 23 problems that Hilbert famously had proposed in 1900. Hilary and I began working on this conjecture; we found a new approach yielding a nice theorem that we were pleased to present at the Institute. I would not claim that this was computer science, but it would be impossible to omit it from any account of our collaboration.

We were so pleased by what we had accomplished that we decided to seek funding enabling us to work together during the summer months. Because the experts regarded my conjecture as very unlikely to be true, we thought it would be hopeless to seek funding for that. So we decided instead to write a proposal for work on computer generated proofs of theorems. Specifically we proposed to work on a proof procedure for first order logic. Our proposed procedure was to include an algorithm for what has come to be called SAT, the satisfiability problem. We wrote a proposal, but it was too late for submission to the funding agencies if we hoped to work together the following summer. A friend of Hilary suggested we send it to the National Security Agency (NSA). Neither of us had heard of this agency, but, nothing to lose, we submitted it to them. A phone call came inviting me to visit the NSA's headquarters in Maryland. When I told them that I had never heard of the agency, they laughed and said their publicity office was doing a good job. The NSA was not to remain so obscure for long. It became front-page news when two of their people defected to the Soviet Union.

When we talked about our proposal, they made it clear that they had no interest in proof procedures for first order logic, but they were interested in SAT.

---

[4] Other terms for this notion are *recursively enumerable set* and *computably enumerable set*.

They warned me that it is a difficult problem and doubted that we could make much headway in one summer. However if we were willing to work only on SAT, they were prepared to fund our proposal. I agreed at once. Our report[5] submitted to them at the end of the summer, made no mention of the funding agency, as they had requested. The report introduced the technique of initially transforming a Boolean formula being tested for satisfiability into conjunctive normal form. This amounted to a list of disjunctive clauses, a format that came into widespread use. Various techniques were offered for satisfiability testing with examples.

The following summer, we had funding from an agency whose mission was to support fundamental science. Not constrained, we set to work on my conjecture that every listable set is Diophantine. We managed to find a proof of the weaker result that every listable set is exponential Diophantine, meaning that variable exponents were permitted in the algebraic expression.[6] For the part of our report related to my conjecture, see [18] pp. 411–430. While we were writing our report, we recalled that our proposal to the agency called for work on machine theorem proving. So using a selection of the algorithms from our report of the previous summer together with an exhaustive search of the Herbrand universe (a term I later introduced in [2]), we had our proof procedure. We wrote it up for our report, and, on a whim, I submitted it to the Journal of the ACM. They published it [14] and it is easily the most cited of my publications, the source of the "Davis-Putnam procedure". Hard copies of our reports to the two agencies are in an archive maintained by Donald Knuth. Julia told me that when she brought a copy of our report for the Russian mathematicians, they were astonished that the US Air Force funded research on Diophantine sets, research that was very unlikely to lead to any practical applications.

In the spring of 1959, I was surprised to receive a letter offering me a year appointment at the Institute for Mathematics and Mechanics at New York University (NYU). I had flirted with them before, but their offer at that time had been unsatisfactory. This institute was totally the creation of Richard Courant. A Jew, he had been expelled from the mathematical institute at Göttingen of

---

[5] The report is available at [18] as Appendix A pp. 374–408.

[6] Our proof had a flaw. It used the fact that there are arbitrarily long arithmetic progressions consisting entirely of prime numbers. This fact was only proved in 2004 (by Ben Green and Terrence Tao); so we had to call it a hypothesis. We wrote our work up for our funding agency, the Office of Scientific Research of the US Air Force. We also submitted it for publication to a mathematical research journal. In addition we sent a copy to Julia Robinson whose methods had greatly influenced our approach. To our delight she succeeded in modifying the proof so it did not need this as yet unproved proposition. We withdrew our paper, and the theorem was published with the three of us as authors. It followed from the new result that my conjecture would follow if a single polynomial could be found that satisfied two simple conditions that Julia had proposed. After the three of us had been trying for a decade to find such a polynomial, we learned that Yuri Matiyasevich, at the age of 22, had actually done it. His proof that his equation satisfied Julia's conditions, though quite elementary, was intricate and beautiful.

which he had been a principal founder. There was no mathematical research activity of consequence at NYU when Courant arrived; he set out to remedy that, and he certainly succeeded. After his death, his institute was fittingly renamed: the Courant Institute of Mathematical Sciences. I was very happy to accept the offer. I was free to do my own research, I could teach a graduate course in mathematical logic, and I would have access to an IBM 704 computer. Convinced that we would be in New York for a long time, we cut our ties to Connecticut, and moved into an apartment overlooking the Hudson River, on the upper west side of New York.

My access to the IBM 704, tempted me to see how the proof procedure Hilary and I had developed, would do on a physical computer. I was provided with two excellent colleagues, both graduate students, Donald Loveland[7] and George Logemann, to do the actual programming. The deficiencies of the Davis-Putnam proof procedure for first order logic were soon made clear. On any but the simplest problems, the memory was overwhelmed. We decided to take advantage of the availability of external storage in the form of tape drives, by changing the algorithm to make use of them We replaced Rule III from [14] (which was what would later be called binary resolution) with Rule III*, we called "splitting", which led to the divide-and-conquer algorithm for SAT that came to be called DPLL. When a split into two cases occurs, the algorithm places one of them on a stack and attends to the other.[8] The Loveland-Logemann program incorporating the DPLL algorithm for SAT was a substantial improvement over the previous attempt, but still fell far short. The paper [17], with Loveland himself one of the authors, discusses this history in more detail, and brings it up to date in connection with contemporary SAT solvers.

Our experience made it clear that any serious progress would require taming the exponential growth of substitution instances of atomic formulas. A copy of Dag Prawitz's paper [19], that arrived by postal mail at this time, contained an important clue. Although the actual proof procedure in the paper was far too unwieldy to be the basis of a useful computer program, it did highlight the significance of substitutions that make pairs of literals negations of one another. This was emphasized in my article [2] written in connection with a talk I gave at a symposium sponsored by the American Mathematical Society. Alan Robinson's resolution principle [20] that pointed to a new compelling direction, took from our work the importance of complementary literals as well input in the form of a conjunction of clauses, each consisting of a disjunction of literals. I think that is why Siekmann and Wrightson awarded my [2] a star, signifying an important article, in their anthology [21]. I discuss the history more fully in [3].

As I had hoped and rather expected, I was offered a tenure-track position at NYU. However, a better offer came from an unexpected quarter. Yeshiva College in the Washington Height neighborhood of New York City had long been offering

---

[7] Don later was one of my first PhD students, and, still later, a colleague.

[8] Of course the terms "divide-and-conquer" and "stack" were not yet used in computer science at that time. It may be worth mentioning that both III and III* are already in the report [15] that Hilary and I had prepared for the NSA.

an undergraduate education that combined an American liberal arts curriculum with traditional orthodox Jewish rabbinical training. However, Yeshiva College had become Yeshiva University offering secular graduate education in a number of areas. As my year as a visitor at NYU was nearing its end, I received an offer from the newly founded Graduate School of Science at Yeshiva University. It was a much more attractive offer than the one I had received from NYU. The topics of the graduate courses I would be teaching would include my own specialty. I was happy to accept. The Courant Institute graciously continued to make the IBM 704 and the talents of Loveland and Logemann available, and we were able to complete our project.

In 1965, for a number of reasons, it was time to leave Yeshiva. I returned to NYU which was to be my academic home until I retired in 1996. I was Princcipal Investigator on a mechanical theorem-proving project, but it was Don Loveland, at that time a colleague at NYU, who seized the opportunity to see his model elimination procedure implemented. The paper [16] with a number of collaborators, was the result of this effort.

In the spring of 1969, I was living in London, on sabbatical leave, when a letter arrived from Jürgen Moser, Director of the Courant Institute. A new department of computer science was being formed at Courant with my old friend and colleague Jack Schwartz as chair. The letter asked me to join, and, after some soul searching, I accepted. I found myself involved in the efforts of the new department to find its place in the Courant Institute. This did not proceed without a certain amount of friction. The department not only hoped to achieve success with cutting edge fundamental research in the Courant tradition, but also offered an undergraduate major that quickly became very popular. The need for faculty to teach these students provided us with the opportunity to hire promising new faculty.

For the academic year 1976–77, I was again on sabbatical leave. I had spent two summers in Berkeley and was eager to try a whole year. To earn a little extra money, I approached John McCarthy (who had been a fellow student at Princeton) about a summer job. He suggested that I fly out and give a talk. I thought a question that Jack Schwartz had posed about extensibility of proof checkers would be an appropriate topic. I remember working out the easy details on the plane.[9] I had an enjoyable time working at for the month of July at John's Artificial Intelligence Laboratory at Stanford University. I loved the atmosphere of play that John had fostered. The terminals that were everywhere proclaimed "Take me, I'm yours", when not in use. I was encouraged to work with the FOL proof checker that had recently been developed by Richard Weyhrauch. Using this system, I developed a complete formal proof of the pigeon-hole principle from axioms for set theory. I found it neat to be able to sit at a keyboard and actually develop a complete formal proof, but I was irritated by the need to pass through many painstaking tiny steps to justify inferences that were quite obvious. FOL formalized a "natural deduction" version of **F**irst **O**rder **L**ogic. The standard

---

[9] Jack and I did publish a joint paper based on this which provided a path to my Erdös number 3. There was another path via Yuri Matiyasevich.

paradigm for carrying out inferences was to strip quantifiers, apply propositional calculus, and replace quantifiers. I realized that from the viewpoint of Herbrand proofs, each of these mini-deductions could be carried out using no more than one substitution instance of each clause. I decided that this very possibility provided a reasonable characterization of what it means for an inference to be *obvious*. Using the LISP source code for the linked-conjunct theorem prover that had been developed at Bell Labs, a Stanford undergraduate successfully implemented an "obvious" facility as an add-on to FOL. I found that having this facility available, cut the length of my proof of the pigeon-hole principle by a factor of 10. This work was described at the Seventh Joint International Congress on Artificial Intelligence held in Vancouver in 1981 [4].[10]

It became the Computer Science Department's policy to provide our new hires with a review as they were completing their third year with us, to help them and us with an initial indication of their prospects for achieving tenure after their sixth year. It must have been around 1980 that I was given the task of conducting such a review of the work of Elaine Weyuker. Her PhD from Rutgers had been in theoretical computer science. Reading her recent research papers, I was surprised that she was looking, with a theoretician's eye, at a very practical problem: software testing. Programmers will certainly try to eliminate the bugs from the programs they write. But it is very difficult to envision in advance all the various environments and other circumstances in which a given program will be used. Generally, before a program is released to the public, it is tested by assembling a set of input data, and then running the program on each of these inputs. It is well understood that for both theoretical and practical reasons, running a program with a finite set of inputs can not guarantee the correctness of a program. So, "quality assurance" professionals attempt to assemble test data that they regard as "adequate". Elaine was studying this notion of adequacy.

I was both impressed by her work and intrigued by the possibility of studying in an objective manner, a notion treated in practice subjectively based on intuition and experience. We soon began a collaboration. In addition to a textbook on theoretical computer science, we wrote three joint papers. [11] is concerned with the problem of testing a program whose expected input-output behavior is not known. In such a case one couldn't tell whether the output generated by a set of test data is correct. This paper is still cited. Our [12] and [13] suggested formal definitions of adequacy based on the intuition that an adequate set of test data should separate the program being tested from all other programs with the exception of those input-output equivalent to the given program.

An article entitled *The Other Turing Machine* that appeared in the Computer Journal in 1977 caught my attention. Up to that point, Turing's name had scarcely been mentioned in historical accounts of the origin of modern digital computers. Although I was convinced that Turing's exploration of the nature of computation with his construction of a universal machine had provided their theoretical underpinnings, I had no idea how concrete the connection was. From the article I learned that Turing's Ace Report of 1946 contained the complete

---

[10] Parts of this paragraph were copied verbatim from my [10].

design of a stored program computer, including the electronic circuits, and even estimated its total price. In 1986, the same authors, Brian Carpenter and Doran, published a collection of some of Turing's previously unpublished manuscripts including the ACE report itself as well as the text of a remarkable lecture that Turing had delivered to the London Mathematical Society in February 1947 [1]. In the lecture, Turing explicitly tied the idea of an all-purpose stored program computer to his concept of a universal machine. In addition he provided an expansive vision of the future capabilities of the computer.

By this time, it was clear to me that the debate over whether von Neumann should share the credit for the "stored program concept" was entirely misplaced. Von Neumann who had worked on Hilbert's foundational program and who was among the first to recognize the significance of Gödel undecidability, would surely have understood the practical relevance of Turing's theoretical investigations. Also, as a logician, I could not help being aware of the historical tradition in which Turing worked. I thought that it was important that the educated public become aware of some of this. I was determined to write a book that would tell this story. I applied for and received a Guggenheim award to fund the necessary research. My "Universal Computer" was published in 2000 [6,7]. In my Introduction I wrote

It was von Neumann's expertise as a logician and what he had learned from the English logician Alan Turing that enabled him to understand the fundamental fact that a computing machine is a logic machine. In its circuits are embodied the distilled insights of a remarkable collection of logicians, developed over centuries. Nowadays, when computer technology is advancing with such breathtaking rapidity, as we admire the truly remarkable accomplishments of the engineers, it is all too easy to overlook the logicians whose ideas made it all possible.

There was a second edition for Turing's centenary in 2012. A third edition of 2018 gave me the opportunity to write about the remarkable success of Go-playing computers using deep learning technology.

But I'm getting ahead of myself. The book was to be for the educated public. But first, I wanted to make the case for Turing's crucial role in the origin of the modern computer to fellow professionals. In my essay [5] I tried to do this, while including a brief initial section on Leibniz, so as not to neglect the historical underpinning of Turing's work.[11] Gradually Turing's role came to be recognized. By the time my book [6] appeared, I could quote Time magazine to that effect. The work of Carpenter and Doran played a crucial role in this change, as did Andrew Hodges's masterful biography of Turing. I would find it extremely gratifying to think that my essay might also have played a part.

I was surprised by an email message from Andrew Hodges, Turing's biographer, calling my attention to recent publications by the philosopher Jack

---

[11] In writing about Turing's work at Bletchley Park, I made the error of indicating that the Colossus was built to decrypt the Enigma traffic needed for the safety of Atlantic shipping. The Colossus was built to deal with an entirely different traffic.

Copeland that concerned Turing's introduction of the notion of an "oracle" in his Princeton dissertation. Copeland, was proposing that it was time to obtain such an oracle as a physical reality in order to be able to compute things that were uncomputable in the sense of the Church-Turing Thesis. In a popular article in the Scientific American 1999 (coauthored with Diane Proudfoot), he announced: "the search is on" for an oracle. He even proposed a capacitor storing a charge whose value was an infinite precision real number that could serve as the oracle. Anyone who read Turing's dissertation with a modicum of comprehension would have understood that Turing's oracle was a mathematical abstraction introduced for a specific mathematical purpose. And, as far as Copeland's capacitor is concerned, since the early years of the twentieth century, it has been understood that an electric charge consists of an *integer* number of electrons.

I had previously been astonished by an article by Hava Siegelmann in *Science* 1995 with the title *Computation Beyond the Turing Limit. Science* is the very prestigious journal of the American Association for the Advancement of Science, where one is used to seeing important research in the biological sciences. I was not impressed by Siegelmann's article. It was certainly true that given any language on a two-letter alphabet, she could produce one of her networks that would accept it. The secret was that the desired language was coded into an infinite precision real number which was then used as a weight in one of the "neurons" in her net. In effect the language was built into the net that accepted it. She reiterated her claim in her book, *Neural Networks and Analog Computation: Beyond the Turing Limit,* Birkhäuser, Boston 1999. I wrote about all of this in [8], and thought that was the end of the matter.

However, it seemed that there was a hypercomputation movement. There were various people who thought about computing the uncomputable, undeterred by the prospect of trying to do infinitely many things in a finite mount of time. There was quantum adiabatic cooling to solve Hilbert's tenth problem and some who were convinced that our brains are already hypercomputers. At a meeting of the American Mathematical Society in San Francisco, there was a special session on hypercomputation. I wrote two additional articles about this nonsense before saying farewell to it.

It seems to be an article of faith among theoretical computer scientists that $\mathbf{P} \neq \mathbf{NP}$. It has long seemed to me that this faith is misplaced. The heuristic arguments usually given depend on regarding $\mathbf{P}$ as the class of languages for which computationally feasible algorithms exist for deciding membership. But obviously an algorithm with cp^k as a time bound is utterly useless if c and/or k are large. In my lectures on this topic, I talk about linear programming as providing a useful lesson. Once thought to likely be $\mathbf{NP}$-hard, linear programming turned out to be in $\mathbf{P}$. Courtesy of Margaret Wright, I show an example of a large linear programming problem for which the old exponential time simplex method does better than the best "barrier" poly-time algorithm. I have no idea whether the proposition $\mathbf{P} = \mathbf{NP}$ is true. It may be that $\mathbf{P} \neq \mathbf{NP}$ is true, and that it hasn't been proved because of serious technical difficulties. But I think it is equally likely that it hasn't been proved because it is false. Perhaps there is a poly-time algorithm for SAT with a large exponent in the time bound. My experience with Hilbert's tenth problem and people's attitudes to what we were trying to do, has led me to believe that our intuitions about polynomials of high degree are not very reliable.

2012 was the year of Alan Turing's 100th birthday. So speakers who were able to give a lecture on a Turing-related subject were in considerable demand that year. I gave nine talks in places as far apart as Pisa in Italy and Arequipa in Peru. First in Ghent and then in Boston. my topic was *Universality is Ubiquitous* [9]. Turing's abstract model of computation had been able to achieve universality with just a few very rudimentary basic operations by providing his devices with unlimited memory. This suggested that the extent to which a physical device can approximate universality will depend critically on providing it with as large a memory as possible. Turing quite explicitly emphasized this in his address of 1947 [1], and it is evident in the expanding suite of things our devices can do as larger and larger memories are provided. Because so little is required of basic operations to achieve universality, it is pointless to retroactively confer universality on Babbage's analytic engine or the Colossus built in the Bletchley Park decryption effort, after imagining them provided with an infinite memory.

Do the non-coding parts of the DNA contain a computational capability? Perhaps playing a role in evolution? I shamelessly speculated along those lines.

My 90th birthday occurred in 2018. The special session on history and philosphy of computation at the meeting in Kiel of the *Computability in Europe* organization honored my birthday. I spoke on "Turing's Vision and Deep Learning". I recalled that Turing had imagined a time when a computer would have modified its original program to such an extent that the programmers would no longer understand what it was doing. Nevertheless, Turing suggested, it might be doing good work. The programmers of the neural nets that have achieved such remarkable success with the ancient game of Go find themselves in exactly this position. Likewise the programmers of self-driving cars. Thus, bringing together Turing's imaginings seventy years ago with some of the most advanced current technological achievements seems an excellent way to end this story.

References

1. Carpenter, B.E., Doran, R.W.: A. M. Turing's Ace Report of 1946 and Other Papers. MIT Press, Cambridge (1986)
2. Davis, M.: Eliminating the irrelevant from mechanical proofs. In: Proceedings of Symposia in Applied Mathematics, vol. 15, pp. 15–30 (1963). (reprinted in [21], pp. 315–330)
3. Davis, M.: The early history of automated deduction. In: Robinson, A., Voronkov, A. (eds.) Handbook of Automated Reasoning, vol. 1, pp. 5–15. Elsevier, North Holland (2001)
4. Davis, M.: Obvious logical inferences. In: Proceedings of the Seventh Joint International Congress on Artificial Intelligence, pp. 530–531 (1981)

5. Davis, M.: Mathematical logic and the origin of modern computers. In: Studies in the History of Mathematics, pp. 137–165. Mathematical Association of America (1987). (reprinted in Herken, R. (ed.) The Universal Turing Machine - A Half-Century Survey, pp. 149–174. Verlag Kemmerer & Unverzagt, Oxford University Press, Hamburg (1988))
6. Davis, M.: The Universal Computer: The Road from Leibniz to Turing. W.W. Norton (2000). (Turing Centenary Edition, CRC Press, Taylor & Francis (2012). Third Edition, CRC Press, Taylor & Francis (2018))
7. Davis, M.: Engines of Logic: Mathematicians and the Origin of the Computer. W.W. Norton (2001). (paperback edition of [6])
8. Davis, M.: The myth of hypercomputation. In: Teuscher, C. (ed.) Alan Turing: Life and Legacy of a Great Thinker, pp. 195–212. Springer, Heidelberg (2004). https://doi.org/10.1007/978-3-662-05642-4_8
9. Davis, M.: Universality is ubiquitous. In: Floyd, J., Bokulich, A. (eds.) Philosophical Explorations of the Legacy of Alan Turing. BSPHS, vol. 324, pp. 153–158. Springer, Cham (2017). https://doi.org/10.1007/978-3-319-53280-6_6
10. Davis, M.: My life as a logician. In: [18], pp. 1–33
11. Davis, M., Weyuker, E.J.: Pseudo-oracles for non-testable programs. In: ACM 1981 Conference Proceedings, pp. 254–257 (1981)
12. Davis, M., Weyuker, E.J.: A formal notion of program-based test data adequacy. Inf. Control **56**, 52–71 (1983)
13. Davis, M., Weyuker, E.J.: Metric space based test data adequacy criteria. Comput. J. **31**, 17–24 (1988)
14. Davis, M., Putnam, H.: A computing procedure for quantification theory. J. Assoc. Comput. Mach. **7**, 201–215 (1960). (reprinted in [21], pp. 125–139)
15. Davis, M., Putnam, H.: Feasible computational methods in the propositional calculus. In: [18], pp. 371–408
16. Fleisig, S., Loveland, D., Smiley, A.K., Yarmush, D.L.: An implementation of the model elimination proof procedure. J. Assoc. Comput. Mach. **21**, 124–139 (1974)
17. Loveland, D., Sabharwal, A., Selman, B.: DPLL: the core of modern satisfiability solvers. In: [18], pp. 315–335
18. Omodeo, E.G., Policriti, A. (eds.): Martin Davis on Computability, Computational Logic, and Mathematical Foundations. OCL, vol. 10. Springer, Cham (2016). https://doi.org/10.1007/978-3-319-41842-1
19. Prawitz, D.: An improved proof procedure. Theoria **26**, 102–139 (1960). (reprinted in [21], pp. 162–199)
20. Robinson, A.: A machine-oriented logic based on the resolution principle. J. Assoc. Comput. Mach. **12**, 23–41 (1965). (reprinted in [21])
21. Siekmann, J., Wrightson, G. (eds.): Automation of Reasoning, vol. 1. Springer, Heidelberg (1983). https://doi.org/10.1007/978-3-642-81955-1

Convergence and Nonconvergence Laws for Random Expansions of Product Structures

Anuj Dawar[1], Erich Grädel[2(✉)], and Matthias Hoelzel[2]

[1] University of Cambridge, Cambridge, UK
anuj.dawar@cl.cam.ac.uk
[2] RWTH Aachen University, Aachen, Germany
{graedel,hoelzel}@logic.rwth-aachen.de

*For Yuri Gurevich on the occasion of his
80th birthday*

Abstract. We prove (non)convergence laws for random expansions of product structures. More precisely, we ask which structures $\mathfrak{A}$ admit a limit law, saying that the probability that a randomly chosen expansion of $\mathfrak{A}^n$ satisfies a fixed first-order sentence always converges when n approaches infinity. For the groups $\mathbb{Z}_p$, where p is prime, we do indeed have such a limit law, even for the infinitary logic $L^\omega_{\infty\omega}$, and these probabilities always converge to dyadic rational numbers, whose denominator only depends on the expansion vocabulary. This can be used to prove that the Abelian group summation problem is not definable in $L^\omega_{\infty\omega}$. Further examples for structures with such a limit law are permutation structures and structures whose vocabulary only consists of monadic relations. As a negative example, we prove that the very simple structure $(\{0,1\}, \leq)$ does not have a limit law. Furthermore, we develop a method based on positive primitive interpretations that allows transferring (non)convergence results to other structures. Using this method, we are able to prove that structures with binary function symbols or unary functions that are not interpreted by permutations do not have a limit law in general.

1 Introduction

The study of convergence and nonconvergence laws for logical formulae on random finite structure has been an important topic of finite model theory since the discovery of the celebrated 0-1 law for first-order logic, discovered 50 years ago by Glebskiĭ et al. [6] and, independently, by Fagin [5]. Informally, this law says that any property of finite graphs or finite relational structures that is definable by a first-order sentence is either almost surely true or almost surely false on (sufficiently large) randomly chosen finite structures or graphs. More precisely, let ψ be a first-order sentence of vocabulary τ and, consider, for any positive natural number n, the probability $\mu_n(\psi)$, that a random τ-structure with universe

© Springer Nature Switzerland AG 2020
A. Blass et al. (Eds.): Gurevich Festschrift, LNCS 12180, pp. 118–132, 2020.
https://doi.org/10.1007/978-3-030-48006-6_9

$[n] := \{0, \ldots, n-1\}$ (chosen with uniform probability from all such structures) is a model of ψ. The 0-1 law says that, for each first-order sentence of any relational vocabulary, the sequence $\mu_n(\psi)$ converges exponentially fast to either 0 or 1, as n goes to infinity.

Since then, there has been an enormous amount of work on variations of such questions, related to many different logical systems as well as to more general probability distributions, focussing not just on 0-1 laws but on more general questions about convergence and nonconvergence of such sequences of probabilities $\mu_n(\psi)$. Yuri Gurevich has made significant contributions to this area. Together with Blass and Kozen, he proved the 0-1 law for the fixed-point logic LFP [2], a result that later motivated the generalization to the 0-1 law for $L^\omega_{\infty\omega}$, the infinitary logic with a bounded number of variables [10]. In [7] he presented a lucid survey on 0-1 laws. For further results we refer to [3].

Here we consider a further variation of questions about limit laws, which had originally been motivated by investigations concerning the logical definability of the Abelian group summation problem. Given a finite group or semigroup $(G, +, 0)$ and a subset $X \subseteq G$, we want to determine the sum over all elements of X. Algorithmically this is a very simple problem. If the elements of X come in some order, then we process them along that order and calculate the sum in a trivial way. However, the logical definability of this problem is much more delicate. If we consider G as an abstract structure and X as an abstract set, without a linear order and hence without a canonical way to process elements one by one, then it is unclear how to define the sum in any logic that does not have the power to quantify over a linear order. Indeed it had been conjectured that the Abelian summation problem would not even be expressible in Choiceless Polynomial Time with counting, one of the most powerful known candidates for a logic that might be capable of defining all polynomial-time computable properties of finite structures. Although it has eventually been proved in [1] that this conjecture is false and that, indeed, the summation problem for Abelian semigroups is even definable in fixed-point logic with counting (FPC), it turned out that even for the restricted case of groups $\mathbb{Z}^n_p$, the summation problem cannot be defined in fixed-point logic *without* counting, and in fact not even in the infinitary logic $L^\omega_{\infty\omega}$. This last result relied on a new limit kind of limit law for random expansions of $\mathbb{Z}^n_p$ that was also established in [1]. Here we investigate the question what kind of base structures, beyond the groups $\mathbb{Z}_p$, admit a limit law of this kind.

In the next section, we precisely define this problem. We shall then explain the proof from [1] for the groups $\mathbb{Z}_p$. In Sect. 4 we discuss some further cases where a similar limit law can be established, before we turn to nonconvergence results. The simplest base structure $\mathfrak{A}$ for which random expansions of $\mathfrak{A}^n$ do not admit a limit law for first-order logic is $\mathfrak{A} = (\{0, 1\}, <)$. We finally discuss a method based on positive primitive interpretations to transfer such convergence and nonconvergence results among different base structures, and establish a few more cases for nonconvergence laws of this kind.

2   The Problem

Let $\mathfrak{A}$ be a structure with a finite universe A of finite (not necessarily relational) vocabulary σ, and let τ be another finite relational vocabulary with $\sigma \cap \tau = \emptyset$. For each n, let $\mathfrak{A}^n$ be the n-fold product of $\mathfrak{A}$, defined in the usual way: The universe of $\mathfrak{A}^n$ is A^n, the set of n-tuples over A, written as functions $a \colon [n] \to A$ (sometimes also denoted as $a = (a(0), \ldots, a(n-1)))$; for each relation symbol $R \in \sigma$ of arity r and $a_1, \ldots a_r \in A^n$, we have that $\mathfrak{A}^n \models R(a_1, \ldots, a_r)$ if, and only if, $\mathfrak{A} \models R(a_1(i), \ldots, a_r(i))$ for all $i \in [n]$, and for each function symbol $f \in \sigma$ of arity r and $a_1, \ldots a_r, b \in A^n$, we have that $\mathfrak{A}^n \models f(a_1, \ldots a_r) = b$ if, and only if, $\mathfrak{A} \models f(a_1(i), \ldots, a_r(i)) = b(i)$ for all $i \in [n]$.

We consider the probability spaces $S_\tau^n(\mathfrak{A})$ consisting of all $(\sigma \cup \tau)$-expansions of $\mathfrak{A}^n$, with the uniform probability distribution. For every sentence $\psi \in \mathcal{L}(\sigma \cup \tau)$ (in whatever logic $\mathcal{L}$), let $\mu_n(\psi)$ denote the probability that a randomly chosen structure $\mathfrak{B} \in S_\tau^n(\mathfrak{A})$ is a model of ψ.

We are interested to know for which finite structures $\mathfrak{A}$ the following limit law holds: For every finite relational vocabulary τ and for every sentence $\psi \in \mathrm{FO}(\sigma \cup \tau)$ there exists a (dyadic rational) number q such that

$$\mu(\psi) := \lim_{n \to \infty} \mu_n(\psi) = q.$$

3   The Groups $\mathbb{Z}_p$

It has been shown in [1] that such a limit law holds for $\mathfrak{A} := (\mathbb{Z}_p, +, 0)$, for any prime p, not just for FO but also for $L_{\infty\omega}^\omega$. The proof generalizes the classical techniques, based on extension axioms, for proving the 0-1 law for FO and $L_{\infty\omega}^\omega$ on random graphs and random finite relational structures.

Consider the group $(\mathbb{Z}_p, +, 0)$, for some prime p, and an arbitrary finite relational vocabulary $\tau = \{X_1, \ldots, X_\ell\}$. For each $n \in \mathbb{N}$, we consider the probability spaces $S_n(\mathbb{Z}_p)$, consisting of all expansions of (the additive group of) the vector space $(\mathbb{Z}_p)^n$ by relations from τ, with the uniform probability distribution. We prove the following limit law.

Theorem 1. *For every relational vocabulary τ and for every sentence $\psi \in L_{\infty\omega}^\omega(\{+, 0\} \cup \tau)$,*

$$\lim_{n \to \infty} \mu_n(\psi) = \frac{r}{2^\ell}, \text{ for } \ell = |\tau| \text{ and some } r \leq 2^\ell.$$

Proof. Let $\delta_1, \ldots, \delta_m$ be the $m = 2^\ell$ atomic τ-types in the constant 0 (and without variables). For each j, δ_j is a conjunction over ℓ atoms or negated atoms of form $X_i(0, \ldots, 0)$, for $X_i \in \tau$. Obviously, for all $j \leq m$ and all n, $\mu_n(\delta_j) = 1/m$.

For any collection $a_1, \ldots, a_k$ of elements of $(\mathbb{Z}_p)^n$ let $\mathrm{span}(a_1, \ldots, a_k)$ be the subspace generated by $a_1, \ldots, a_k$. Clearly, the size of $\mathrm{span}(a_1, \ldots, a_k)$ in $(\mathbb{Z}_p)^n$ is bounded by p^k, for any n.

Recall that an atomic k-type $t(x_1, \ldots, x_k)$ of a vocabulary σ is a maximal consistent set of atoms and negated atoms in the variables $x_1, \ldots, x_k$. In our case, a k-type $t(x_1, \ldots, x_k)$ specifies the linear dependencies and independencies of $x_1, \ldots, x_k$ and the truth values of all atoms $X(y_1, \ldots, y_r)$ where $X \in \tau$, and each y_i is a $\mathbb{Z}_p$-linear combination of $x_1, \ldots, x_k$.

Definition 2. For each $j \leq m$, we define AT_j to be the set of all atomic types $t(x_1, \ldots, x_k)$ of vocabulary $\{+, 0\} \cup \tau$ such that

(1) t is consistent, i.e. realisable in some $\mathfrak{B} \in S_\tau^n(\mathfrak{A})$,
(2) $t \models \delta_j$,
(3) t implies, for each $i \leq k$, that $x_i \notin \mathrm{span}(x_1, \ldots, x_{i-1})$.

We then define T_j to be the theory of all extension axioms

$$\mathrm{ext}_{s,t} := \forall \bar{x}(s(\bar{x}) \rightarrow \exists x_{k+1} t(\bar{x}, x_{k+1}))$$

where s and t are, respectively, atomic k and $k+1$-types in AT_j with $t \models s$.

Please notice that condition (3) of Definition 2 is equivalent to: t entails the linear independence of $x_1, \ldots, x_k$.

Proposition 3. *Every extension axiom* $\mathrm{ext}_{s,t} \in T_j$ *has asymptotic probability one on the sequence of spaces* $S_\tau^n(\mathbb{Z}_p)$.

Proof. Let $(a_1, \ldots, a_k)$ be a realisation of the atomic type $s(\bar{x}) \in \mathrm{AT}_j$ in some randomly chosen expansion $\mathfrak{B}$ of $(\mathbb{Z}_p)^n$. The type $s(\bar{x})$ fixes the truth values of all τ-atoms in the variables $x_1, \ldots, x_k$ and the constant 0, and $t(\bar{x}, x_{k+1})$ additionally fixes truth-values for the τ-atoms that contain at least one term with the variable x_{k+1}. There is a bounded number q of such atoms. Therefore, if we fix some element $b \in (\mathbb{Z}_p)^n \setminus \mathrm{span}(a_1, \ldots, a_k)$, then the probability that $\mathfrak{B} \models t(\bar{a}, b)$ is 2^{-q}.

The elements b that we have to explore are those outside of $\mathrm{span}(a_1, \ldots, a_k)$. Each of them fixes $|\mathrm{span}(a_1, \ldots, a_k, b) \setminus \mathrm{span}(a_1, \ldots, a_k)| \leq (p-1)p^k$ new elements, so there are at least p^{n-k-1} independent choices for b. Since there are fewer than p^{nk} realisations of $s(\bar{x})$ in $\mathfrak{B}$, the probability that one of them cannot be extended to a realisation of $t(\bar{x}, x_{k+1})$ is at most

$$p^{nk}(1 - 2^{-q})^{p^{n-k-1}}$$

which tends to 0 exponentially fast as n goes to infinity.

Thus, the asymptotic probability of every extension axiom $\mathrm{ext}_{s,t} \in T_j$ is one on $S_\tau^n(\mathbb{Z}_p)$. □

For every $j \leq m$, $k < \omega$, let ϑ_j^k be the conjunction of all extension axioms in T_j with at most k variables. Further, let $E(k, j)$ be the class of all expansions $\mathfrak{B}$ of $\mathfrak{A}^n$ (for any finite $n \geq k$) such that $\mathfrak{B} \models \delta_j \wedge \vartheta_j^k$.

Lemma 4. $\mu(\delta_j \wedge \vartheta_j^k) = 1/m$ for all $j \leq m, k < \omega$.

Proposition 5. *For every $\psi \in L_{\infty\omega}^k$ and every $j \leq m$, either $\mathfrak{A} \models \psi$ for all $\mathfrak{A} \in E(k,j)$, or $\mathfrak{A} \models \neg\psi$ for all $\mathfrak{A} \in E(k,j)$.*

Proof. Take any two structures $\mathfrak{A}, \mathfrak{B} \in E(k,j)$. From the fact that both structures satisfy $\delta_j \wedge \vartheta_j^k$ we immediately get a winning strategy for the k-pebble game on $\mathfrak{A}$ and $\mathfrak{B}$ (for background on the model comparison games for k-variable logic, see [4]). Hence the two structures are $L_{\infty\omega}^k$-equivalent, so it cannot be the case that ψ is true in one and false in the other. □

Given any formula $\psi \in L_{\infty\omega}^k$, let $r(\psi) = |\{j \leq m : \psi$ is true in all $\mathfrak{A} \in E(k,j)\}|$. It follows that

$$\mu(\psi) = \lim_{n\to\infty} \mu_n(\psi) = \frac{r(\psi)}{m}.$$

Hence the limit law holds for $L_{\infty\omega}^\omega$. □

Theorem 6. *The Abelian group summation problem is not definable in $L_{\infty\omega}^\omega$.*

Proof. Suppose that the Abelian group summation problem is definable by a formula $\varphi(x) \in L_{\infty\omega}^k$ such that for every finite Abelian group $(H, +, 0)$, all $X \subseteq H$ and every $h \in H$,

$$(H, +, 0, X) \models \varphi(h) \iff \sum X = h.$$

Consider the sentence $\psi := \exists x(\varphi(x) \wedge X(x) \wedge X(0))$, which expresses that both 0 and the sum over all elements of X are contained in X. Let $G = (\mathbb{Z}_2, +, 0)$ and $H = \mathbb{Z}_2^n$. For a randomly chosen $X \subseteq H$ all elements of H have equal probability to be the sum of all elements of X. The probability that this sum is itself an element of X quickly converges to $1/2$. Thus the asymptotic probability of ψ on the spaces $S_\tau^n(\mathbb{Z}_2)$ converges to $1/4$.

However, since we use only one random relation, the denominator of the asymptotic probabilities in the limit law is 2, so $\mu_n(\psi)$ should converge to either 0,1, or $1/2$. Contradiction. □

Categoricity. A classical result about limit laws for finite random structures states that the theory of all extension axioms is ω-categorical, i.e. it has, up to isomorphism, precisely one countable model. We can prove an analogous categoricity result in our setting.

Let $\mathbb{Z}_p^*$ be the weak ω-product of $\mathbb{Z}_p$. Its elements are the functions $g : \omega \to \mathbb{Z}_p$ such that $g(n) = 0$ for all but finitely many n, addition is defined componentwise in the obvious way, and $\mathbf{0}$ is the constant function mapping all $n \in \omega$ to 0. The next observation says that the theories $\{\delta_j\} \cup T_j$ are categorical for expansions of $\mathbb{Z}_p^*$.

Proposition 7. *Let $\mathfrak{A}_\omega$ and $\mathfrak{B}_\omega$ be any two expansions of $\mathbb{Z}_p^*$ to $\{+, 0\} \cup \tau$-structures which are both models of $\{\delta_j\} \cup T_j$. Then $\mathfrak{A}_\omega$ and $\mathfrak{B}_\omega$ are isomorphic.*

Proof. The universes of both $\mathfrak{A}_\omega$ and $\mathfrak{B}_\omega$ are the same as for $\mathbb{Z}_p^*$. Fix an enumeration $\boldsymbol{g}_0, \boldsymbol{g}_1, \boldsymbol{g}_2, \ldots$ of this set, and define a sequence $(f_n)_{n \in \omega}$ of partial isomorphisms from $\mathfrak{A}_\omega$ to $\mathfrak{B}_\omega$ as follows. Let $f_0 = \{(\boldsymbol{0}, \boldsymbol{0})\}$. Since both $\mathfrak{A}_\omega$ and $\mathfrak{B}_\omega$ are models of δ_j, this is indeed a partial isomorphism. Suppose now that, for $k \geq 0$, f_k has already been defined, with domain $\mathrm{span}(\boldsymbol{a}_1, \ldots, \boldsymbol{a}_k)$, and image $\mathrm{span}(\boldsymbol{b}_1, \ldots, \boldsymbol{b}_k)$. Since f_k is a partial isomorphism $(\boldsymbol{a}_1, \ldots, \boldsymbol{a}_k)$ and $(\boldsymbol{b}_1, \ldots, \boldsymbol{b}_k)$ realise the same atomic type $s(\bar{x})$.

For even k, let $\boldsymbol{a}_{k+1}$ be the first element in the enumeration $\boldsymbol{g}_0, \boldsymbol{g}_1, \boldsymbol{g}_2, \ldots$ that does not appear in the domain of f_k, and let $t(\bar{x}, x_{k+1})$ be the atomic type realised by $(\boldsymbol{a}_1, \ldots, \boldsymbol{a}_k, \boldsymbol{a}_{k+1})$. Since $\mathfrak{B}_\omega \models \mathrm{ext}_{s,t}$ the tuple $(\boldsymbol{b}_1, \ldots, \boldsymbol{b}_k)$ can be extended by a suitable element $\boldsymbol{b}_{k+1}$ to a realisation of $t(\bar{x}, x_{k+1})$. This defines an extension of f_k to a partial isomorphism f_{k+1} from $\mathrm{span}(\boldsymbol{a}_1, \ldots, \boldsymbol{a}_{k+1})$ to $\mathrm{span}(\boldsymbol{b}_1, \ldots, \boldsymbol{b}_{k+1})$.

For odd k we proceed similarly, by choosing for $\boldsymbol{b}_{k+1}$ the first element in the enumeration of the universe that is not contained in the image of f_k. Since the appropriate extension axiom holds in $\mathfrak{A}_\omega$ the element $\boldsymbol{b}_{k+1}$ can then be matched by an element $\boldsymbol{a}_{k+1}$ to provide the extension f_{k+1}.

The union $f = \bigcup_{k \in \omega} f_k$ is then the desired isomorphism between $\mathfrak{A}_\omega$ and $\mathfrak{B}_\omega$.   □

4   Limit Laws for Other Structures

In this section, we show that the following structures also have a limit law:

- Structures only equipped with monadic relation symbols.
- Permutation structures, i.e. structures equipped with unary function symbols that are interpreted by bijective functions.

In Sect. 5, we see concrete examples of two structures that have a nonconvergence law instead. One of them has a binary relation symbol, while the another one has only unary function symbols that are interpreted by certain non-bijective functions.

4.1   Atomic Types and Extension Axioms in General Structures

We say that an element $a \in A$ is *uniformly* definable in some logic $\mathcal{L}$, if there exists an $\mathcal{L}$-formula $\varphi(x)$ such that

$$\mathfrak{A}^n \models \varphi(\bar{b}) \iff \bar{b} = (a, a, \ldots, a)$$

for every $n \in \mathbb{N}$ and $\bar{b} \in A^n$. For example, if $c \in \sigma$ is a constant symbol, then $\varphi(x) := x = c$ is such a uniform definition of $c^{\mathfrak{A}}$. Another example is the formula $\varphi_0(x) := \forall y (x + y = y)$ which uniformly defines the neutral element in a group $(G, +)$.

Now let $\bar{u} = (u_1, \ldots, u_p)$ be an enumeration of all uniformly FO-definable elements of $\mathfrak{A}$. Let $\sigma_{\mathfrak{A}} := \{c_1, \ldots, c_p\}$ be a vocabulary containing constant symbols for these uniformly definable elements and let $\mathfrak{A}'$ be the $(\sigma \cup \sigma_{\mathfrak{A}})$-expansion with $c_i^{\mathfrak{A}'} = u_i$. Furthermore, let $\delta_1, \ldots, \delta_m$ be the atomic $(\sigma_{\mathfrak{A}} \cup \tau)$-types (with no variables) of possible $(\sigma \cup \sigma_{\mathfrak{A}} \cup \tau)$-expansions of $\mathfrak{A}'$.

Similar to Definition 2, we define the sets AT_j (for each $j \leq m$) consisting of all atomic types $t(x_1, \ldots, x_k)$ over the vocabulary $\sigma \cup \sigma_{\mathfrak{A}} \cup \tau$ with the following properties:

(1) t is consistent, i.e. realisable in some $\mathfrak{B} \in S_\tau^n(\mathfrak{A}')$.
(2) $t \models \delta_j$
(3) $t \models x_i \neq h(x_1, \ldots, x_{i-1}, x_{i+1}, \ldots, x_n)$ where h is a $(\sigma \cup \sigma_{\mathfrak{A}})$-term.

Again, for every $j \in \{1, \ldots, m\}$, we let

$$T_j := \{\mathrm{ext}_{s,t} : s, t \in \mathrm{AT}_j, t \text{ is an extension type of } s\}$$

where $\mathrm{ext}_{s,t} := \forall \bar{x}(s(\bar{x}) \rightarrow \exists x_{k+1} t(\bar{x}, x_{k+1}))$.

4.2   Only Monadic Relations

Now we investigate the case that the vocabulary σ contains only monadic relation symbols. Thus, $\mathfrak{A}'$ has the form $(A, (P^{\mathfrak{A}})_{P \in \sigma}, (c_i^{\mathfrak{A}'})_{i=1,\ldots,p})$ where $P^{\mathfrak{A}} \subseteq A$ for every relation symbol $P \in \sigma$ and the $c_1, \ldots, c_p$ are interpreted by the uniformly FO-definable elements of $\mathfrak{A} := (A, (P^{\mathfrak{A}})_{P \in \sigma})$. If $|A| = 1$, then $\mathfrak{A}^n \cong \mathfrak{A}$ and the limit law holds due to trivial reasons. Therefore, we consider structures $\mathfrak{A}$ with $|A| \geq 2$.

Proposition 8. *Let $\mathcal{L}$ be a logic with $\mathrm{FO} \leq \mathcal{L}$. An element a of $\mathfrak{A}$ is uniformly definable in $\mathcal{L}$ if, and only if, there are some relation symbols $P_1, \ldots, P_k \in \sigma$ with $\bigcap_{i=1}^k P_i^{\mathfrak{A}} = \{a\}$.*

Proof. For the direction "$\Leftarrow$", we prove that $\bigcap_{i=1}^k P_i^{\mathfrak{A}} = \{a\}$ implies that the first-order formula $\varphi(x) := \bigwedge_{i=1}^k P_i x$ is in fact a uniform definition of a. Towards this end, let $\mathfrak{A}^n \models \varphi(\bar{b})$ for some $\bar{b} = (b_1, \ldots, b_n) \in A^n$. Then $b_j \in \bigcap_{i=1}^k P_i^{\mathfrak{A}} = \{a\}$ and, hence, $b_j = a$ for every j as desired.

"$\Rightarrow$": Now assume that some $\mathcal{L}$-formula $\varphi(x)$ is a uniform definition of a. Let $\sigma' := \{P \in \sigma : P \text{ monadic relation symbol and } a \in P^{\mathfrak{A}}\}$. Towards a contradiction, assume the existence of some $b \in \bigcap_{P \in \sigma'} P^{\mathfrak{A}} \setminus \{a\}$. Since $\varphi(x)$ is a uniform definition of a, we have $\mathfrak{A}^n \models \varphi((a, a, \ldots, a))$ but $\mathfrak{A}^n \not\models \varphi((b, a, \ldots, a))$. However, this is not possible, because the function $\pi : A^n \rightarrow A^n$ that swaps $(a, a, \ldots, a)$ with $(b, a, \ldots, a)$ (and maps every other element onto itself) is an isomorphism of $\mathfrak{A}^n$ for $n \geq 2$. Indeed, π is clearly bijective and for every relation symbol $P \in \sigma$, we can distinguish between the following two cases:

- $P \in \sigma'$: Then $(a, a, \ldots, a) \in P^{\mathfrak{A}^n}$ and $(b, a, \ldots, a) \in P^{\mathfrak{A}^n}$, because $a, b \in P^{\mathfrak{A}}$.
- $P \notin \sigma'$: Then $a \notin P^{\mathfrak{A}}$ and, hence, $(a, a, \ldots, a) \notin P^{\mathfrak{A}^n}$ and $(b, a, \ldots, a) \notin P^{\mathfrak{A}^n}$, because a occurs in both tuples at the second position. □

Proposition 9. *Let $\mathrm{ext}_{s,t} \in T_j$. Then $\mu(\mathrm{ext}_{s,t}) = 1$.*

Proof. Let $\text{ext}_{s,t} = \forall \bar{x}(s(\bar{x}) \to \exists y t(\bar{x}, y))$. Furthermore, let $\bar{a} = (a_1, \ldots, a_k)$ be a realisation of the atomic type $s(\bar{x}) \in \text{AT}_j$ in some randomly chosen expansion $\mathfrak{B}$ of $(\mathfrak{A}')^n$. Let σ^+ resp. σ^- be the set of all monadic relation symbols P such that Py resp. $\neg Py$ occurs in t. Because t is realisable, it cannot happen that $\bigcap_{P \in \sigma^+} P^{\mathfrak{A}} = \emptyset$. Furthermore, we must have $|\bigcap_{P \in \sigma^+} P^{\mathfrak{A}}| \geq 2$, because otherwise t could only be realised by a tuple consisting of some uniformly definable element, but then t violates (3). Choose $a, b \in \bigcap_{P \in \sigma^+} P^{\mathfrak{A}}$ with $a \neq b$. Let $\{P_1, \ldots, P_r\}$ be a complete enumeration of σ^- without repetitions. For every such $P_j \in \sigma^-$ there must be some $b_j \in \bigcap_{P \in \sigma^+} P^{\mathfrak{A}} \setminus P_j^{\mathfrak{A}}$, because of the same reason that t would not be realizable otherwise.

Now consider the tuples $\bar{d} := (b_1, \ldots, b_r, \bar{d}')$ where $\bar{d}' \in \{a, b\}^{n-r}$. Every such tuple that is different from $a_1, \ldots, a_k$ is a candidate for t, because the conditions (1)–(3) from the definition of AT_j are satisfied. Thus, there are at least $2^{n-r} - k$ many elements that might extend $\bar{a} = (a_1, \ldots, a_k)$ to a realisation of t. Each of them has a probability of 2^{-q} of being a realisation of t where q is the number of τ-literals in $t(\bar{x}, y)$ with y. Therefore, the probability that $\bar{a}$ cannot be extended to a realisation of t is at most $(1 - 2^{-q})^{2^{n-r} - k}$. There are at most $|A|^{nk}$ many realisations of s. The probability that one of them cannot be extended is at most

$$|A|^{nk} \cdot (1 - 2^{-q})^{2^{n-r} - k}$$

which tends to 0 exponentially fast as n goes to infinity. Thus $\mu(\text{ext}_{s,t}) = 1$. $\square$

By following the proof of Theorem 1, we obtain an analogous result for the case where the base structure $\mathfrak{A}$ exhibits only monadic relations.

Theorem 10. *Let σ be a vocabulary consisting only of monadic relation symbols, τ be some relational vocabulary and $\mathfrak{A}$ be some finite σ-structure. For every sentence $\psi \in L^\omega(\sigma \cup \tau)$,*

$$\lim_{n \to \infty} \mu_n(\psi) = \frac{r}{2^\ell}, \quad \text{for some } r \leq 2^\ell,$$

where $\mu_n(\psi)$ denotes the probability that a random τ-expansion of $\mathfrak{A}^n$ satisfies ψ. The number ℓ is the number of τ-structures with p elements where p is the number of uniformly definable elements of $\mathfrak{A}$.

In Sect. 5, we shall see a counterexample to the limit law for the case where $\mathfrak{A}$ is allowed to have binary relations.

4.3   Permutation Structures

Let σ be a vocabulary consisting only of unary function symbols and τ be any relational vocabulary. We say that $\mathfrak{A}$ is a permutation structure, if every $s^{\mathfrak{A}}$ (for $s \in \sigma$) is a permutation of A.

We shall prove that permutation structures admit a limit law. First of all, we observe that $\mathfrak{A}^n$ can be decomposed into disjoint copies of finitely many finite structures that only depend on $\mathfrak{A}$.

Theorem 11. *Let $\mathfrak{A}$ be a finite permutation structure. Then there are finitely many pairwise non-isomorphic finite structures $\mathfrak{B}_1, \ldots, \mathfrak{B}_q$ such that every $\mathfrak{A}^n$ is isomorphic to a disjoint union of copies from $\{\mathfrak{B}_1, \ldots, \mathfrak{B}_q\}$.*

Proof. Consider some element $a \in A^n$ of $\mathfrak{A}^n$ and let $\mathfrak{A}^n(a)$ be the substructure of $\mathfrak{A}^n$ that is generated by a. Let $\#(a) := |\{a(i) : i = 1, \ldots, n\}|$ be the number of pairwise different elements occurring in a. Clearly, we have $1 \leq \#(a) \leq \ell := |A|$. Choose some $b \in A^{\#(a)}$ such that $\{b(1), \ldots, b(\#(a))\} = \{a(1), \ldots, a(n)\}$ and for every $i \in \{1, \ldots, n\}$, let $\iota(i) \in \{1, \ldots, \#(a)\}$ be chosen such that $b(\iota(i)) = a(i)$. Notice that b must consist of pairwise different elements. Let $\mathfrak{A}^{\#(a)}(b)$ be the substructure of $\mathfrak{A}^{\#(a)}$ generated by b. We claim that $\mathfrak{A}^n(a)$ is isomorphic to the structure $\mathfrak{A}^{\#(a)}(b)$. Let $A^n(a)$ and $A^{\#(a)}(b)$ denote the universe of $\mathfrak{A}^n(a)$ resp. $\mathfrak{A}^{\#(a)}(b)$. $A^{\#(a)}(b)$ contains all elements of the form $[\![t(b)]\!]^{\mathfrak{A}^{\#(a)}}$, while $A^n(a)$ consists of all $[\![t(a)]\!]^{\mathfrak{A}^n}$ where $t(x)$ is some σ-term. By definition of $\mathfrak{A}^n$ resp. $\mathfrak{A}^{\#(a)}$, we have that $[\![t(b)]\!]^{\mathfrak{A}^{\#(a)}}(i) = [\![t(b(i))]\!]^{\mathfrak{A}}$ and $[\![t(a)]\!]^{\mathfrak{A}^n}(j) = [\![t(a(j))]\!]^{\mathfrak{A}}$. Since $\mathfrak{A}$ is a permutation structure, we can thus conclude that the equality type of a is the same of $[\![t(a)]\!]^{\mathfrak{A}^n}$ and that every $[\![t(b)]\!]^{\mathfrak{A}^{\#(a)}} \in B$ consists of pairwise different elements. Furthermore, we obtain in particular that $[\![t(a)]\!]^{\mathfrak{A}^n}(i) = [\![t(a(i))]\!]^{\mathfrak{A}} = [\![t(b(\iota(i)))]\!]^{\mathfrak{A}} = [\![t(b)]\!]^{\mathfrak{A}^{\#(a)}}(\iota(i))$. As a result, the mapping $\pi : A^{\#(a)}(b) \to A^n(a), (c_1, \ldots, c_{\#(a)}) \mapsto (c_{\iota(1)}, \ldots, c_{\iota(n)})$ is an isomorphism between $\mathfrak{A}^{\#(a)}(b)$ and $\mathfrak{A}^n(a)$. Thus, $\mathfrak{A}$ can be decomposed into disjoint copies of $\mathfrak{A}^k(c)$ where $c \in A^k$ consists of pairwise different elements and $1 \leq k \leq \ell = |A|$. So, there are (up to isomorphism) $q \leq \sum_{k=1}^{\ell} \binom{\ell}{k}$ many such (finite) structures $\mathfrak{B}_1, \ldots, \mathfrak{B}_q$ that allow the decomposition of any $\mathfrak{A}^n$. □

For every $i = 1, \ldots, q$ let $\#_i(n)$ be the number of disjoint copies of $\mathfrak{B}_i$ occurring in $\mathfrak{A}^n$. If $\#_i(r) \geq 2$ for some $r \in \mathbb{N}$, then there are two different tuples $\bar{a}_1, \bar{a}_2 \in A^r$ with $\mathfrak{B}_i \cong \mathfrak{A}^r(\bar{a}_1)$ and $\mathfrak{B}_i \cong \mathfrak{A}^r(\bar{a}_2)$. Now for $n = k \cdot r$, consider tuples of the form $(\bar{b}_1, \ldots, \bar{b}_k) \in A^n$ with $\bar{b}_i \in \{\bar{a}_1, \bar{a}_2\}$ for every $i \geq 1$. Clearly, we have $\mathfrak{B}_i \cong \mathfrak{A}^n(\bar{b}_1, \ldots, \bar{b}_k)$ for every such tuple, of which there are at least 2^k many. Thus, $\#_i(n) \geq 2^{\lfloor \frac{n}{2r} \rfloor}$ grows exponentially in n.

Now consider the case where $\#_i(r) \leq 1$ for every $r \in \mathbb{N}$. Clearly, there must be at least one $r \in \mathbb{N}$ with $\#_i(r) = 1$ (otherwise $\mathfrak{B}_i$ would not have been included in the list $\mathfrak{B}_1, \ldots, \mathfrak{B}_q$) and, consequently, there exists some tuple $\bar{a} \in A^r$ with $\mathfrak{B}_i \cong \mathfrak{A}^r(\bar{a})$. If $\bar{a}$ would consist of two different elements, then tuples with the same elements as $\bar{a}$ but with different equality type would induce more (even disjoint) copies $\mathfrak{B}_i$ as substructures. This implies that $\bar{a} = (a, \ldots, a)$ for some $a \in A$ and, thus, $\mathfrak{B}_i \cong \mathfrak{A}(a) \cong \mathfrak{A}^n(a, \ldots, a)$ for every $n \geq 1$. Therefore, we actually have that $\#_i(n) = 1$ for every $n \geq 1$. Furthermore, it must also be the case that $\pi(a) = a$ for every automorphism π of $\mathfrak{A}$, because otherwise we would again find more than one copy of $\mathfrak{B}_i$. Since $\mathfrak{B}_i$ occurs exactly once as a copy in every $\mathfrak{A}^n$ and since a is a fixed point of every automorphism of $\mathfrak{A}$, there is a first-order formula that locates the (unique) copy of $\mathfrak{B}_i$ and defines $(a, \ldots, a)$ in it, i.e. a must be uniformly definable.

Thus, for every $i = 1, \ldots, q$ we have

(i) either $\#_i(n)$ grows exponentially in n, or
(ii) $\#_i(n) = 1$ for every n and $\mathfrak{B}_i \cong \mathfrak{A}(a) \cong \mathfrak{A}^n(a, \ldots, a)$ for some uniformly FO-definable element $a \in A$.

Proposition 12. *Let $\mathfrak{A}$ be a finite permutation structure. Then $\mu(\mathrm{ext}_{s,t}) = 1$ for every $\mathrm{ext}_{s,t} \in T_j, j \leq m$.*

Proof. Let $\mathrm{ext}_{s,t} = \forall \bar{x}(s(\bar{x}) \rightarrow \exists y t(\bar{x}, y))$. Furthermore, let $\bar{a} = (a_1, \ldots, a_k)$ be a realisation of the atomic type $s(\bar{x}) \in \mathrm{AT}_j$ in some randomly chosen expansion $\mathfrak{B}$ of $(\mathfrak{A}')^n$. (Recall that $\mathfrak{A}'$ is the expansion of $\mathfrak{A}$ with names for the uniformly definable elements.) Let $b \in (\mathfrak{A}')^n$ be an element that satisfies the $(\sigma \cup \sigma_{\mathfrak{A}})$-part of t, i.e. we have $(\mathfrak{A}')^n \models t(\bar{a}, b) \cap \mathrm{FO}(\sigma \cup \sigma_{\mathfrak{A}})$. Such an element must exist (for n sufficiently large), because t is consistent (see also condition (1)). As in the proof of Theorem 11, there must be an index $i \in \{1, \ldots, q\}$ such that $\mathfrak{A}^n(b) \cong \mathfrak{B}_i$. It is not possible that $\#_i(n) = 1$ for every $n \in \mathbb{N}$, since otherwise b would have to be a tuple consisting only of some FO-definable element $a = c_j^{\mathfrak{A}'}$ for some $c_j \in \sigma_{\mathfrak{A}}$, but then we would have $y = c_j \in t$ in contradiction to condition (3) Therefore, $\#_i(n)$, the number of occurrences of $\mathfrak{B}_i$, grows exponentially in n. Let m_t be the number of τ-literals in $t(\bar{x}, y)$ with y. The probability that $\mathfrak{B} \models t(\bar{a}, b)$ is 2^{-m_t} and, therefore, the probability that $\bar{a}$ *cannot* be extended to a realisation of t is at most $(1 - 2^{-m_t})^{\#_i(n)-k}$. Since there are at most $|A|^{nk}$ realisations of s, the probability that one of them cannot be extended to a realisation of t is at most

$$|A|^{nk} \cdot (1 - 2^{-m_t})^{\#_i(n)-k}$$

which tends to 0 as n goes to infinity, because $\#_i(n)$ grows exponentially in n. Thus $\mu(\mathrm{ext}_{s,t}) = 1$. $\square$

Again, by following the proof of Theorem 1, we obtain a limit law for permutation structures.

Theorem 13. *Let $\mathfrak{A}$ be a finite permutation structure of vocabulary σ. Then there exists a number m such that for every sentence $\psi \in L^\omega(\sigma \cup \tau)$,[1]*

$$\lim_{n \to \infty} \mu_n(\psi) = \frac{r}{m}, \textit{ for some } r \leq m.$$

5   Nonconvergence for Linear Orders

The limit law for random expansions of products of the Abelian groups $\mathbb{Z}_p$ raised the question whether such a limit law could be proved for random expansions of products of *any* finite structure $\mathfrak{A}$.

However, this fails dramatically. Even in the very simple case where $\mathfrak{A} = (\{0, 1\}, \leq)$ we can establish a nonconvergence law, based on Kaufmann's proof of the nonconvergence law for monadic second-order logic on random finite structures [9]. The heart of Kaufmann's argument is the construction of a formula which almost surely defines a linear ordering.

---

[1] Please recall that m is still the number of atomic $(\tau \cup \sigma_{\mathfrak{A}})$-types that are realisable in $(\sigma \cup \sigma_{\mathfrak{A}} \cup \tau)$-expansions of $\mathfrak{A}'$. These types $\delta_1, \ldots, \delta_m$ have been defined in Sect. 4.1.

Proposition 14 (Kaufmann). *There exists a first-order formula $\varphi_<(x,y)$ of a vocabulary $\tau \cup \{Y_1, \ldots, Y_m\}$ (where τ consists of four binary predicates and the Y_i are monadic) such that on randomly chosen τ-structures with universe $[n]$, the probability that, for some interpretation of $Y_1, \ldots Y_m$, the formula $\varphi_<(x,y)$ defines a linear order, converges to 1 as n goes to infinity.*

To obtain an analogous first-order formula on random expansions of $\mathfrak{A}^n$, for $\mathfrak{A} = (\{0,1\}, \leq)$, we observe that $\mathfrak{A}^n$ is isomorphic to $(\mathcal{P}([n]), \subseteq)$. A random expansion of $\mathfrak{A}^n$ to a $(\{\leq\} \cup \tau)$-structure $\mathfrak{B}_n$ can thus be equivalently viewed as a random $(\tau \cup \{\subseteq\})$-structure $\mathfrak{C}_n$ with universe $\mathcal{P}([n])$. By restricting the τ-relations of $\mathfrak{C}_n$ to singleton sets we further get a random structure $\mathfrak{D}_n$ with universe $[n]$ where, for each $R \in \tau$ and $i_1, \ldots, i_k \in [n]$,

$$\mathfrak{D}_n \models R i_1 \ldots i_k \quad \Longleftrightarrow \quad \mathfrak{C}_n \models R\{i_1\} \ldots \{i_k\}.$$

Further, let

$$\mathrm{sing}(x) := \exists z (z \neq x \wedge \forall y (z \leq y \wedge (y \leq x \rightarrow (y = z \vee y = x)))).$$

Clearly, for $a = (a_1, \ldots, a_n) \in \{0,1\}^n$ we have that $\mathfrak{A}^n \models \mathrm{sing}(a)$ if, and only if, $a_i = 1$ for exactly one i, which means that a represents a singleton set of $\mathcal{P}([n])$.

We now translate arbitrary sentences $\varphi \in \mathrm{FO}(\tau \cup \{Y_1, \ldots, Y_m\})$ into formulae $\varphi^*(y_1, \ldots, y_m) \in \mathrm{FO}(\{\leq\} \cup \tau)$ by the following operations

- replace the set predicates Y_i by new element variables y_i;
- relativise every first-order quantifier Qz to $\mathrm{sing}(z)$, i.e. replace every subformula $\exists z \vartheta$ by $\exists z (\mathrm{sing}(z) \wedge \vartheta)$ and every subformula $\forall z \vartheta$ by $\forall z (\mathrm{sing}(z) \rightarrow \vartheta)$;
- replace atoms $Y_i z$ by $z \leq y_i$.

By induction on φ, one easily proves the following correspondence.

Lemma 15. *For any expansion of $\mathfrak{A}^n$ to a $(\{\leq\} \cup \tau)$-structure $\mathfrak{B}_n$ and the corresponding τ-structure $\mathfrak{D}_n$ over $[n]$, and for all sets $Y_1, \ldots Y_m \subseteq [n]$ we have that*

$$\mathfrak{D}_n \models \varphi(Y_1, \ldots, Y_m) \quad \Longleftrightarrow \quad \mathfrak{B}_n \models \varphi^*(f(Y_1), \ldots, f(Y_m))$$

where $f : \mathcal{P}([n]) \rightarrow \{0,1\}^n$ is the above mentioned bijection witnessing the isomorphism between $(\mathcal{P}([n]), \subseteq)$ and $\mathfrak{A}^n$.

By applying this translation to the $\mathrm{MSO}(\tau)$-sentence

$$\psi := \exists Y_1 \ldots \exists Y_m (\text{``}\varphi_<(x,y) \text{ defines a linear order''})$$

we get a first-order sentence $\psi^* \in \mathrm{FO}(\{\leq\} \cup \tau)$ (using first-order quantifiers $\exists y_1 \ldots \exists y_m$ to simulate $\exists Y_1 \ldots \exists Y_m$). Since ψ has asymptotic probability 1 on random τ-structures, it follows ψ^* has asymptotic probability 1 on random expansions of $\mathfrak{A}^n$. Notice that the linear order defined by $\varphi_<^*$ in ψ^* is not on the universe of $\mathfrak{A}^n$, but on those elements representing singleton sets in $\mathcal{P}([n])$. By standard constructions we now can get sentences that have no asymptotic probability. For instance, consider instead of ψ the MSO-sentence ψ_{odd}, with an additional existentially quantified set variable Z, saying that

- $\varphi_<(x,y)$ defines a linear order,
- Z contains precisely the even elements of this order,
- the minimal and the maximal element of the order belong to Z.

Translating ψ_{odd} as above results in a sentence $\psi^*_{\mathrm{odd}} \in \mathrm{FO}(\{\leq\}\cup\tau)$ such that $\mu_{2n}(\psi^*_{\mathrm{odd}}) = 0$ for all n, and $\lim_{n\to\infty} \mu_{2n+1}(\psi^*_{\mathrm{odd}}) = 1$. We thus have established the following nonconvergence law.

Theorem 16. *There exists a first-order sentence $\psi^* \in \mathrm{FO}(\{\leq\}\cup\tau)$ such that on random expansions of products of $\mathfrak{A} = (\{0,1\},\leq)$, the sequence of probabilities $\mu_n(\psi^*)$ does not converge.*

6   Transferring (Non-)Convergence to Other Structures

In this section we present a method that allows us to transfer (non)convergence laws for structures such as $(\{0,1\},\leq)$ to other structures. This method is based on special logical interpretations, only using *positive primitive* formulae. A formula $\varphi \in \mathrm{FO}(\sigma)$ is called *positive primitive*, if it consists only of $\exists, \wedge$ and σ-atoms. The following lemma is an immediate corollary of [8, Lemma 9.1.4].

Lemma 17. *Let $\mathfrak{A}$ be a σ-structure and $\varphi(x_1,\ldots,x_r) \in \mathrm{FO}(\sigma)$ a positive primitive formula. Then for every n and every $\bar{a}_1,\ldots,\bar{a}_r \in A^n$,*

$$\mathfrak{A}^n \models \varphi(\bar{a}_1,\ldots,\bar{a}_r) \iff \mathfrak{A} \models \varphi(\bar{a}_1(i),\ldots,\bar{a}_r(i)) \text{ for every } i \in [n].$$

Let σ_1, σ_2 be vocabularies where σ_2 is relational. A *positive primitive interpretation* from σ_1 to σ_2 (of arity k) is a first-order interpretation $\mathcal{I}$ consisting only of positive primitive formulae (and without congruence formula). More precisely, $\mathcal{I}$ is a sequence $(\delta, (\psi_S)_{S \in \sigma_2})$ of positive primitive $\mathrm{FO}(\sigma_1)$-formulae where

- $\delta = \delta(\bar{x})$ is the domain formula, and
- $\psi_S = \psi_S(\bar{x}_1,\ldots,\bar{x}_{\mathrm{ar}(S)})$ are the relation formulae for $S \in \sigma_2$.

Here, the tuples $\bar{x}, \bar{y}, \bar{x}_1, \ldots$ are of length k respectively. We also write $\mathrm{ar}(\mathcal{I})$ to denote the arity of $\mathcal{I}$, which is here the number k. For the sake of simplicity we always assume σ_2 to be relational, but it is not difficult to generalise these concepts to arbitrary vocabularies.

We say that $\mathcal{I}$ interprets a σ_2-structures $\mathfrak{B}$ in a σ_1-structure $\mathfrak{A}$ (and write $\mathcal{I}(\mathfrak{A}) \cong \mathfrak{B}$) if and only if there exists a bijection h, called the coordinate map, which maps $\delta^{\mathfrak{A}} = \{\bar{a} \in A^k : \mathfrak{A} \models \delta(\bar{a})\}$ to B such that for all $S \in \sigma_2$ and $\bar{a}_1,\ldots,\bar{a}_{\mathrm{ar}(S)} \in \delta^{\mathfrak{A}}$ holds

$$\mathfrak{A} \models \psi_S(\bar{a}_1,\ldots,\bar{a}_{\mathrm{ar}(S)}) \iff (h(\bar{a}_1),\ldots,h(\bar{a}_{\mathrm{ar}(S)})) \in S^{\mathfrak{B}}.$$

This coordinate map $h: \delta^{\mathfrak{A}} \to B$ induces coordinate maps $h_n: \delta^{\mathfrak{A}^n} \to B^n$ witnessing $\mathcal{I}(\mathfrak{A}^n) \cong \mathfrak{B}^n$. To see this, recall that $\delta^{\mathfrak{A}^n} = \{(\bar{a}_1,\ldots,\bar{a}_k) \in (A^n)^k : \mathfrak{A}^n \models \delta(\bar{a}_1,\ldots,\bar{a}_k)\}$. For every $(\bar{a}_1,\ldots,\bar{a}_k) \in \delta^{\mathfrak{A}^n}$ and every $i \in [n]$, let

$$(h_n(\bar{a}_1,\ldots,\bar{a}_k))(i) := h(\bar{a}_1(i),\ldots,\bar{a}_k(i)).$$

Using Lemma 17, it is straightforward (but technical) to verify that this is indeed the definition of a coordinate map for $\mathcal{I}(\mathfrak{A}^n) \cong \mathfrak{B}^n$.

Proposition 18. *Let $\mathcal{I}$ be a positive primitive interpretation with $\mathcal{I}(\mathfrak{A}) \cong \mathfrak{B}$. Then $\mathcal{I}(\mathfrak{A}^n) \cong \mathfrak{B}^n$ for every $n \geq 1$.*

A positive primitive interpretation $\mathcal{I} = (\delta, (\psi_S)_{S \in \sigma_2})$ not only defines copies of σ_2-structures inside σ_1-structures, but it also can be used to convert σ_2-formulae $\varphi(x_1, \ldots, x_\ell)$ into σ_1-formulae $\varphi^{\mathcal{I}}(\bar{x}_1, \ldots, \bar{x}_\ell)$ as follows:

- Replace every variable x by a new k-tuple of variables, denoted by $\bar{x}$.
- Equalities $x = y$ are turned into $\bigwedge_{1 \leq k} x_i = y_i$.
- Turn atoms like $Sx_1 \ldots x_{\mathrm{ar}(S)}$ for $S \in \sigma_2$ into $\psi_S(\bar{x}_1, \ldots, \bar{x}_{\mathrm{ar}(S)})$.
- Replace $\exists x \eta$ and $\forall x \eta$ by $\exists \bar{x}(\delta(\bar{x}) \wedge \eta^{\mathcal{I}})$ resp. $\forall \bar{x}(\delta(\bar{x}) \rightarrow \eta^{\mathcal{I}})$.

The connection between φ and $\varphi^{\mathcal{I}}$ is made precise in the following well-known interpretation lemma, which can be adapted for many different logics.

Lemma 19 (Interpretation Lemma for FO). *Let $\mathcal{I}(\mathfrak{A}) \cong \mathfrak{B}$ with coordinate map $h \colon \delta^{\mathfrak{A}} \rightarrow B$, $\varphi(x_1, \ldots, x_\ell) \in \mathrm{FO}(\sigma_2)$ and $\bar{a}_1, \ldots, \bar{a}_\ell \in \delta^{\mathfrak{A}}$. Then*

$$\mathfrak{A} \models \varphi^{\mathcal{I}}(\bar{a}_1, \ldots, \bar{a}_\ell) \Longleftrightarrow \mathfrak{B} \models \varphi(h(\bar{a}_1), \ldots, h(\bar{a}_\ell)).$$

Now let τ be another finite, relational vocabulary disjoint from $\sigma_1 \cup \sigma_2$. A positive primitive interpretation also serves as a bridge between random $(\sigma_2 \cup \tau)$-expansions of $\mathfrak{B}$ and of $(\sigma_1 \cup \tau^\star)$-expansions of $\mathfrak{A}^n$. Here, we use $\tau^\star := \{R^\star : R \in \tau\}$ where $R^\star$ is a new relation symbol of arity $\mathrm{ar}(\mathcal{I}) \cdot \mathrm{ar}(R) = k \cdot \mathrm{ar}(R)$ in order to account for the fact that $\mathcal{I}$ operates on k-tuples over $\mathfrak{A}$. Furthermore, let $\mathcal{I}_\tau$ be the result of adding the formulae $\psi_R(\bar{x}_1, \ldots, \bar{x}_{\mathrm{ar}(R)}) := R^\star(\bar{x}_1, \ldots, \bar{x}_{\mathrm{ar}(R)})$ for $R \in \tau$ to $\mathcal{I}$.

Using this new interpretation we can now translate a given $(\sigma_2 \cup \tau)$-sentence φ into a $(\sigma_1 \cup \tau^\star)$-sentence $\varphi^{\mathcal{I}_\tau}$. We write $\mu_n^{\mathfrak{B},\tau}(\varphi)$ to denote the probability that a random $(\tau \cup \sigma_2)$-expansion of $\mathfrak{B}^n$ satisfies φ, while $\mu_n^{\mathfrak{A},\tau^\star}(\varphi^{\mathcal{I}_\tau})$ is defined analogously. The connection between $\mu_n^{\mathfrak{B},\tau}(\varphi)$ and $\mu_n^{\mathfrak{A},\tau^\star}(\varphi^{\mathcal{I}_\tau})$ is clarified in the following theorem.

Theorem 20. *Let $\mathcal{I}(\mathfrak{A}) \cong \mathfrak{B}$ for a positive primitive interpretation $\mathcal{I}$ from σ_1 to σ_2. For every sentence $\varphi \in \mathrm{FO}(\sigma_2 \cup \tau)$ and every $n \geq 1$ it holds that $\mu_n^{\mathfrak{A},\tau^\star}(\varphi^{\mathcal{I}_\tau}) = \mu_n^{\mathfrak{B},\tau}(\varphi)$.*

Proof. As in Proposition 18, we have $\mathcal{I}(\mathfrak{A}^n) \cong \mathfrak{B}^n$ witnessed by a coordinate map $h_n \colon \delta^{\mathfrak{A}^n} \rightarrow B^n$ for every $n \geq 1$.

For a randomly chosen $(\sigma_1 \cup \tau^\star)$-expansion $\mathfrak{C}$ of $\mathfrak{A}^n$ we obtain a corresponding $(\sigma_2 \cup \tau)$-expansion $\mathfrak{D}$ of $\mathfrak{B}^n$ by setting

$$R^{\mathfrak{D}} := \{(h_n(\bar{a}_1), \ldots, h_n(\bar{a}_k)) : (\bar{a}_1, \ldots, \bar{a}_{\mathrm{ar}(R)}) \in (R^{\mathcal{I}})^{\mathfrak{C}} \cap (\delta^{\mathfrak{A}^n})^{\mathrm{ar}(R)}\}.$$

Then we have $\mathcal{I}_\tau(\mathfrak{C}) \cong \mathfrak{D}$ with coordinate map h_n and, by the interpretation lemma (Lemma 19), it follows that $\mathfrak{C} \models \varphi^{\mathcal{I}_\tau} \iff \mathfrak{D} \models \varphi$. Furthermore, this $(\sigma_2 \cup \tau)$-structure $\mathfrak{D}$ is already uniquely determined by $\mathfrak{C}$.

Conversely, for a randomly chosen $(\sigma_2 \cup \tau)$-expansion $\mathfrak{D}$ of $\mathfrak{B}^n$, we can define a corresponding $(\sigma_1 \cup \tau^\star)$-expansion $\mathfrak{C}$ of $\mathfrak{A}^n$ by setting $(R^\star)^{\mathfrak{C}} := h_n^{-1}(R^{\mathfrak{D}})$ where

$$h_n^{-1}(R^{\mathfrak{D}}) := \{(\bar{a}_1, \ldots, \bar{a}_{\mathrm{ar}(R)}) \in (\delta^{\mathfrak{A}^n})^{\mathrm{ar}(R)} : (h_n(\bar{a}_1), \ldots, h_n(\bar{a}_{\mathrm{ar}(R)})) \in R^{\mathfrak{D}}\}$$

for $R \in \tau$. Again, we have $\mathcal{I}_\tau(\mathfrak{C}) \cong \mathfrak{D}$ with coordinate map h_n and, because of the interpretation lemma, we again have $\mathfrak{C} \models \varphi^{\mathcal{I}_\tau} \iff \mathfrak{D} \models \varphi$. Please notice that we could also define $\mathfrak{C}$ differently in the case that $\delta^{\mathfrak{A}^n} \neq A^n$, because then $(R^\star)^{\mathfrak{C}}$ could theoretically contain tuples with elements from $A^n \backslash \delta^{\mathfrak{A}^n}$. However, for every $\mathfrak{D}$ we would have exactly the same number of possibilities. Thus, $\mu_n^{\mathfrak{A},\tau^\star}(\varphi^{\mathcal{I}_\tau}) = \mu_n^{\mathfrak{B},\tau}(\varphi)$ follows. $\qquad\square$

Please recall that a finite σ-structure $\mathfrak{A}$ has a *limit law*, if for every finite relational vocabulary τ and every sentence $\varphi \in \mathrm{FO}(\sigma \cup \tau)$, $\mu^{\mathfrak{A},\tau}(\varphi) := \lim_{n\to\infty} \mu_n^{\mathfrak{A},\tau}(\varphi)$ exists. Otherwise, we say that $\mathfrak{A}$ has no limit law.

Corollary 21. *Let σ_1, σ_2 be vocabularies where σ_2 is relational. Let $\mathfrak{A}, \mathfrak{B}$ be finite structures with $\mathcal{I}(\mathfrak{A}) \cong \mathfrak{B}$ for a positive primitive logical interpretation $\mathcal{I}$ from σ_1 to σ_2 without equality formula. Then:*

(i) If $\mathfrak{A}$ has a limit law, then $\mathfrak{B}$ has a limit law.
(ii) If $\mathfrak{B}$ has no limit law, then neither does $\mathfrak{A}$.

Proof. Since (ii) is just the contraposition of (i), it suffices to prove only one of these items. Towards proving (ii), assume that $\mathfrak{B}$ does not have a limit law. Thus, for some finite, relational vocabulary τ there exists a sentence $\psi \in \mathrm{FO}(\sigma_2 \cup \tau)$ such that $\mu^{\mathfrak{B},\tau}(\psi) = \lim_{n\to\infty} \mu_n^{\mathfrak{B},\tau}(\psi)$ does not exist. By Theorem 20, it follows that $\mu^{\mathfrak{A},\tau^\star}(\psi^{\mathcal{I}_\tau}) := \lim_{n\to\infty} \mu_n^{\mathfrak{A},\tau^\star}(\psi) = \lim_{n\to\infty} \mu_n^{\mathfrak{B},\tau}(\psi)$ does not exist as well. Therefore, $\mathfrak{A}$ has no limit law. $\qquad\square$

The following two examples demonstrate how Corollary 21 can be used to transfer nonconvergence laws to other structures.

Example 22. The structure $\mathfrak{A}_1 := (\{0,1\}, f_\leq^{\mathfrak{A}_1})$ with $f_\leq^{\mathfrak{A}_1}(a,b) = 1 \iff a \leq b$ inherits the nonconvergence law of $(\{0,1\}, \leq)$, because $\mathcal{I} := (\delta(x), \psi_\leq(x,y))$ where

$$\delta(x) := x = x$$
$$\psi_\leq(x,y) := f_\leq(x,y) = f_\leq(x,x)$$

is a positive primitive logical interpretation (without equality formula) with

$$\mathcal{I}(\mathfrak{A}_1) \cong (\{0,1\}, \leq).$$

By Corollary 21(ii), it follows that $\mathfrak{A}_1$ has no limit law.

The next example shows that even structures that are only equipped with unary functions may have a nonconvergence law.

Example 23. Consider $\mathfrak{A}_2 := (A_2, (s^{\mathfrak{A}_2}_{a \mapsto b})_{a,b \in A_2, a \neq b}, s^{\mathfrak{A}_2}_{\{0,1\}})$ where

- $A_2 := \{0, 1, 0'\}$,
- $s^{\mathfrak{A}_2}_{a \mapsto b}(a) := b$ and $s^{\mathfrak{A}_2}_{a \mapsto b}(c) := c$ for every $a, b, c \in A_2$ with $c \neq a$,
- $s^{\mathfrak{A}_2}_{\{0,1\}}(a) = 1$ for $a \in \{0, 1\}$ while $s^{\mathfrak{A}_2}_{\{0,1\}}(0') = 0$.

Here is a positive primitive logical interpretation $\mathcal{I} = (\delta(x), \psi_\leq)$ with $\mathcal{I}(\mathfrak{A}_2) \cong (\{0,1\}, \leq)$:

$$\delta(x) := s_{0' \mapsto 0}(x) = x$$
$$\psi_\leq(x, y) := \exists z(s_{0' \mapsto 0}(z) = x \wedge s_{0' \mapsto 0}(s_{0 \mapsto 1}(z)) = y).$$

Applying Corollary 21(ii) yields that $\mathfrak{A}_2$ has no limit law.

7   Future Work

While we have analysed some structures with respect to limit laws and introduced a new method to transfer (non)convergence laws between structures, the question of what structures have such a limit law is not fully settled. There are many structures for which we do not know whether or not they have a limit law and this paper is a first step towards a complete characterisation of structures with limit laws.

References

1. Abu Zaid, F., Dawar, A., Grädel, E., Pakusa, W.: Definability of summation problems for Abelian groups and semigroups. In: Proceedings of 32th Annual ACM/IEEE Symposium on Logic in Computer Science (LICS) (2017)
2. Blass, A., Gurevich, Y., Kozen, D.: A zero-one law for logic with a fixed point operator. Inf. Control **67**, 70–90 (1985)
3. Compton, K.: 0–1 laws in logic and combinatorics. In: Rival, I. (ed.) NATO Advanced Study Institute on Algorithms and Order, pp. 353–383. Kluwer, Alphen aan den Rijn (1989)
4. Ebbinghaus, H.-D., Flum, J.: Finite Model Theory. SMM. Springer, Heidelberg (1995). https://doi.org/10.1007/3-540-28788-4
5. Fagin, R.: Probabilities on finite models. J. Symb. Logic **41**, 50–58 (1976)
6. Glebskii, Y., Kogan, D., Liogon'kii, M., Talanov, V.: Range and degree of realizability of formulas in the restricted predicate calculus. Kibernetika **2**, 17–28 (1969)
7. Gurevich, Y.: Zero-one laws. Logic Comput. Sci. Column EATCS Bull. **46**, 90–106 (1992)
8. Hodges, W.: Model Theory. Cambridge University Press, Cambridge (1993)
9. Kaufmann, M.: A counterexample to the 0-1 law for existential monadic second-order logic. In: Internal Note. Computational Logic Inc. (1988)
10. Kolaitis, P., Vardi, M.: Infinitary logics and 0-1 laws. Inf. Comput. **98**, 258–294 (1992)

Medieval Arabic Notions of Algorithm: Some Further Raw Evidence

Wilfrid Hodges$^{(\boxtimes)}$

Herons Brook, Sticklepath, Okehampton, Devon EX20 2PY, England
wilfrid.hodges@btinternet.com
http://wilfridhodges.co.uk

Abstract. During YuriFest 2010 the discovery of a proof search algorithm devised in the 1020s by Ibn Sīnā (Avicenna) was announced. A Gurevich abstract state machine was given in evidence that Ibn Sīnā really did intend an algorithm; this was needed because Ibn Sīnā explained the algorithm by a long sequence of exercises, not by a rigorous definition. More recently a radically original logical decision algorithm has come to light in the work of the 12th century Baghdad scholar Abū al-Barakāt. Taking these algorithms alongside the already known algorithms of al-Khwārizmī for solving quadratic equations, and of al-Khalīl for listing finite sequences of letters, we can see that the medieval Arabic scholars uncovered a range of algorithms of various kinds. But it seems that they never brought these algorithms together under a single notion of 'algorithm'; in fact we know of no writer who drew a comparison between any two of these algorithms. A natural question for historical research is to uncover what kinds of entity the medieval Arabic scholars thought these algorithms were. The present paper assembles some raw material that should be relevant to this question, including a not very successful attempt by al-Fārābī to institute a theory of logical procedures.

Keywords: Algorithm · Medieval Arabic · al-Khalīl · Ibn Sīnā · Abū al-Barakāt

1 Introduction

'Further' in the title above refers to my paper [7] for YuriFest 2010, in which I gave an abstract state machine to describe the recursive proof search procedure that Ibn Sīnā (Avicenna) set out in his Arabic work *Qiyās* (Syllogism, [10]) in the 1020s. It turns out that there are a variety of other algorithms known to medieval Arabic writers. This is partly old news—it's well known that the name 'algorithm' comes from the early 9th century mathematician al-Khwārizmī who designed the formula for solving quadratic equations in the real numbers (or more strictly, to any required approximation in the rational numbers) [14]. But there are other kinds of example too.

I will discuss two examples in particular. One is the dictionary algorithm of al-Khalīl in the 8th century, which has been studied in the West for some

© Springer Nature Switzerland AG 2020
A. Blass et al. (Eds.): Gurevich Festschrift, LNCS 12180, pp. 133–146, 2020.
https://doi.org/10.1007/978-3-030-48006-6_10

decades (for example by Haywood in Chapter Four of his [6]). The other is the logical decision algorithm of Abū al-Barakāt in the mid 12th century; it seems that this algorithm was first correctly recovered from Barakāt's text only in 2017 [8]. Together with the algorithms of al-Khwārizmī and Ibn Sīnā, these are four different kinds of algorithm. As far as we know, nobody in the medieval Arabic world had a notion of 'algorithm' that covered all four. We know of no writer who even compared any two of them.

No doubt this is partly because the algorithms arose in three different disciplines: linguistics, mathematics, logic. But information spread freely in the early Islamic empire, and if there was a link to be noticed, somebody would have noticed it. More to the point, these four algorithms were algorithms in different senses.

Roshdi Rashed [13], in a study of a range of Arabic algorithms for solving numerical equations, opens by identifying three features of al-Khwārizmī's quadratic algorithm. (i) The procedure to be followed is described formally and without reference to any one example. (ii) The range of equations solvable by the algorithm is precisely defined. (iii) The algorithm is presented together with a proof that it gives a correct answer for each equation in the range. This looks a good preliminary set of criteria for a sound description of an algorithm. But when we try to apply the criteria to the other three algorithms (of al-Khalīl, Ibn Sīnā and Abū al-Barakāt), it is not even clear what they mean. For example a claimed solution of a numerical equation is correct if and only if the claimed solution is a number that satisfies the equation; but what counts as a correct outcome of a search? Is it the discovery of an item with some specified property, or is it a path that traverses the whole space to be searched?[1] Or for another example, Ibn Sīnā explains clearly enough what problems his proof search algorithm is intended to solve; but he sets it as an exercise to transfer the algorithm from predicative logic to hypothetical logic. The principles behind the algorithm do in fact transfer as he indicates, but then what is left of feature (ii)?

So there is work to be done in analysing the senses in which these four algorithms are algorithms, what commonalities between them could have been explained by the Arabic scholars with the notions that they had at their disposal, and how far these common features were recognised in each case. This is why the title of this paper speaks of 'raw evidence'. I had hoped to carry out some of this analysis in time for YuriFest 2020, but time was my enemy. The analysis is still worth attempting.

---

[1] In [7] I distinguished between listing algorithms and search algorithms, placing al-Khalīl's algorithm as a listing algorithm and Ibn Sīnā's as a search algorithm. I said that a search algorithm (unlike listing algorithms in general) finds a solution of a problem by running through a list of partial or total solutions of the problem. This was in the interests of identifying what was distinctive about Ibn Sīnā's algorithm. But I am not sure that was a sensible distinction. If the problem was to list the elements of a set, then in any listing of the set the initial segments of the list are partial solutions of the problem. So here I will treat search algorithms and listing algorithms as the same thing.

A third word in the title needs explaining too. These algorithms were all presented in the Arabic language, by writers who customarily wrote in Arabic. But colleagues from the Middle East often remind me that not everybody who writes in Arabic is an Arab. For the record, the more reliable sources suggest that al-Khalīl was an Arab originally from Yemen or Oman. Abū al-Barakāt was a Baghdad Jew. The ethnicity of Ibn Sīnā is unknown; his birthplace is now within Uzbekistan, but at that date his family could have been Persian or Sogdian.

For various kinds of information or enlightenment I thank Michael Carter, Saloua Chatti, Karine Chemla, Catherine Jami, Amirouche Moktefi, Seyed N. Mousavian, Roshdi Rashed and Robert Wisnovsky, none of whom should be blamed for any inadequacies below. Since the present paper is only preparatory, I may well have overlooked important material that should be taken into account.

2 Al-Khalīl, Searching Through a Language

Al-Khalīl bin Aḥmad (died c. 786) is a paradoxical character with one foot in history and the other in legend. On the side of legend, Talmon in his study of al-Khalīl [15] opens with a list of seventy-nine medieval sources of information about al-Khalīl, and he then proceeds to eliminate most of what these sources tell us, either as dubious inferences from al-Khalīl's own writings, or as attempts to bolster claims that his work should be credited to Arab or to Persian culture, or as ways of endorsing particular ideas by associating al-Khalīl's name with them. On the other side we have literally hundreds of reports by Sībawayhi, the founder of classical Arabic grammatical theory, of discussions that he had with al-Khalīl on details of Arabic grammar or usage. These discussions are full of subtle and sophisticated points that still provide insights for a modern grammarian, and allow us to feel that in reading al-Khalīl's contributions we are in direct contact with a first-class mind.

Somewhere between these two extremes lies the book *Kitāb al-ᶜayn* (Book of the letter *ᶜayn*) [12], al-Khalīl's contribution to lexicography. As it stands the book can hardly be the work of al-Khalīl, since it often refers to him in the third person and names other people who reported conversations with him. On the other hand the book contains an introduction setting out a highly original agenda for a science of lexicography, and describing in detail some research that al-Khalīl carried out in aid of this agenda. A common view among modern scholars is that al-Khalīl designed the book and wrote a substantial amount of it, but his friends and/or his students played some role in completing it after his death.

Part of al-Khalīl's agenda is to have a complete record of the entire vocabulary of a language. People interested in the history of lexicography have noted that this was the first time such an aim was articulated. All earlier dictionaries had been devoted to specific subject-matter, or to explanations of unusual or difficult words. One possible anticipation is the *Shuōwén Jiézì*, a Chinese dictionary compiled by Xu Shen in the first half of the second century AD. Dichy notes that this dictionary has entries for fewer than 10,000 ideographic characters, so that it 'could therefore not be deemed to be either a comprehensive lexicon, or even a dictionary aiming at comprehensiveness' ([3] p. 48).

Al-Khalīl's originality goes even further than Dichy argues. Making a dictionary involves arranging the entries in a linear order; both Xu Shen and al-Khalīl put careful thought into how the entries should be listed. But al-Khalīl was, as far as we know, the first person to propose a precise and non-trivial procedure for listing the entire contents of a pre-existing set, linguistic or otherwise. In this sense he was the first person to propose a search algorithm.

Al-Khalīl's search algorithm fails Rashed's test (i): it is not true that the procedure is described formally and without reference to any one example. The reason is that al-Khalīl is too concerned to find the best listing for an *Arabic* dictionary. Some of what he does could be put into an abstract form, but not all of it.

The procedure begins by identifying the separate consonants of the language, together with a canonical listing of these consonants. The consonants that he chooses are in one-to-one correspondence with the standard twenty-eight letters of the Arabic alphabet, except that he adds *hamza* (i.e. glottal stop) as a twenty-ninth consonant. But his criterion for choosing these letters is independent of the alphabet, and involves identifying the minimal phonetic segments of words. His ordering of the consonants is far from the usual alphabetic order, and rests on an analysis of the site of articulation, starting from the throat and moving to the lips. (The Indian Devanagari alphabet is organised on a similar principle, but there is no evidence that it influenced al-Khalīl.)

Now al-Khalīl lists the consonant bases of all Arabic words. He asserts that every Arabic word has a basis consisting of either two, three, four or five distinct consonants. He combines the ordering of letters with a scheme that puts groups of n letters before groups of $n + 1$ letters. Strikingly he brings together all the six permutations of a set of three distinct letters, and all the twenty-four permutations of a set of four distinct letters, and so on.

The *Kitāb al-ᶜayn* contains a number of calculations of permutations and combinations. These were taken up soon afterwards by Arabic mathematicians, and became the basis of the permutations and combinations that children now learn at school. The point is worth mentioning because it shows that the Arabic mathematical community was aware of al-Khalīl's work in the *Kitāb al-ᶜayn*. The fact (if it is a fact) that they never picked up the notion of a search algorithm from his work probably shows that the algorithmic aspect of his invention didn't connect with any notion in their mental armoury.

3   Ibn Sīnā, Proof Search

Avicenna (Ibn Sīnā, c. 980–1037) crafted the proof search algorithm that was the topic of my contribution to YuriFest 2010 [7]. Some technical details left open in [7] will be clarified in [9]. Below I start by sketching the background in Aristotle's categorical syllogisms—this will be background to the next section on Abū al-Barakāt too.

Aristotle's categorical syllogisms, at least as Ibn Sīnā understood them from the translations of and commentaries on Aristotle, used four kinds of sentence. We call sentences of these forms the categorical formal sentences, or for short the categorical sentences:

$(a)(B, A)$ Every B is an A
$(e)(B, A)$ No B is an A
$(i)(B, A)$ Some B is an A
$(o)(B, A)$ Some B is not an A.

The letters B, A are called the term letters; they can be replaced by any two other distinct letters. The symbolic abbreviations on the left are a modern convenience. Following al-Fārābī, Ibn Sīnā understood the four sentences as in the first-order formalisations

$(a)(B, A)$ $(\forall x(Bx \rightarrow Ax) \wedge \exists x Bx)$
$(e)(B, A)$ $\forall x(Bx \rightarrow \neg Ax)$
$(i)(B, A)$ $\exists x(Bx \wedge Ax)$ (1)
$(o)(B, A)$ $(\exists x(Bx \wedge \neg Ax) \vee \forall x \neg Bx)$

The set of four categorical sentences above is closed under negation, in the sense that the negation of each sentence ϕ is logically equivalent to one of the other forms, which we will write as $\overline{\phi}$. Thus $\overline{(a)(B, A)} = (o)(B, A)$ and $\overline{(e)(B, A)} = (i)(B, A)$.

Suppose Φ is a set of categorical sentences and θ is a categorical sentence. Then Ibn Sīnā explains what he means by saying that θ is a 'conclusion' of Φ. For our purposes his explanation is equivalent to saying that the sentences $\Phi \cup \{\overline{\theta}\}$ can be arranged around a circle:

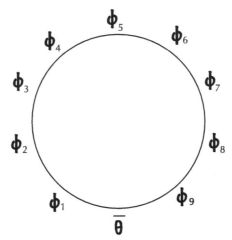

so that (a) any two adjacent sentences have one term letter in common, and this term letter occurs in no other sentences around the circle; (b) certain logical requirements are met which together have the consequence that the set of sentences around the circle is inconsistent (for example exactly one of the sentences around the circle is negative). We will express (b) as saying that the sentences are 'logically correct'.

Ibn Sīnā's proof search algorithm addresses the following problem. Suppose $\Phi \cup \{\bar{\theta}\}$ can be arranged around a circle as above, except that there is a gap somewhere in the part of the circle where the sentences of Φ are arranged—so that two adjacent sentences ϕ_i, ϕ_{i+1} have no letter in common. Suppose also that we have a supply Ψ of further categorical sentences. What is a sound procedure for searching for a completion of the circle using a set Ψ_0 of sentences from Ψ, in such a way that the resulting array of sentences proves that θ is a conclusion of $\Phi \cup \Psi_0$?

In a nutshell, Ibn Sīnā proceeds by trying to fill the gap starting at the lefthand side, using sentences taken from Ψ. The sentences of Ψ are delivered by an oracle. Suppose for example that the oracle proposes ϕ_{i1} and ϕ_{i2} as sentences with exactly one term letter in common with ϕ_i. Ibn Sīnā's algorithm checks for each of these sentences that logical correctness holds locally; otherwise he discards the sentences. If neither sentence joins up successfully with ϕ_{i+1} then we have two new examples of a circle with a gap. The algorithm is applied to each of these new examples, and further sentences are added to the side of the gap. This process continues until one of the chains of added sentences joins up at the righthand side with ϕ_{i+1} and logical correctness holds throughout the resulting circle.

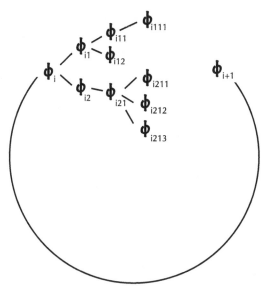

In this way the algorithm builds up a tree of attempts to fill the gap in the circle, continuing until one of these attempts succeeds.

Obviously any agent who tries to carry out the algorithm in real time is going to need a backtracking mechanism so that all undiscarded branches of the tree receive attention repeatedly. Ibn Sīnā never mentions this problem, still less solves it. But there is some hope that he was aware of it. He mentions the more complicated case of a circle with two gaps in it; in this case one would need to try to fill both gaps simultaneously, so one would have to backtrack between the two gaps. (At my talk at YuriFest 2010 Andreas Blass remarked that there is another ramification in this case: a segment of the circle between two gaps could be fitted into the circle in either of two directions.) Ibn Sīnā recognises that the two-gap case introduces a new complication, and he says he will address this complication in the Appendices to *Qiyās*. Unfortunately modern scholars working on Ibn Sīnā have given up hope of ever seeing these Appendices—probably he never got around to writing them.

The backtracking is a major element missing in Ibn Sīnā's account of his algorithm in *Qiyās* ix.6. Another missing item is Rashed's (iii): Ibn Sīnā says nothing to prove that the algorithm gives correct results. But these may be the only major elements missing. Part of the purpose of writing out the algorithm as a Gurevich abstract state machine was to test that Ibn Sīnā's text does resolve the other practical questions that have to be answered along the way. In some cases we have to read off the algorithm rules from Ibn Sīnā's examples rather than from any explicit statement of the rules; but given that, the algorithm survives the test remarkably well.

4   Abū al-Barakāt, Decision Methods

Abū al-Barakāt bin Malka al-Baghdādī (c. 1080–c. 1165) was a highly original and insightful scholar based in Baghdad. Until recently he was known chiefly for his encyclopedic book *Kitāb al-Muᶜtabar* (roughly 'Some conclusions that I came to') [1], which offers an integrated world view based on detailed study of issues ranging from mathematical physics to ontology. But Moshe Gil [5] has provided convincing evidence that he was in fact the same person as the respected Jewish scholar Rabbi Baruch ben Melekh, and this identification credits him with a body of Talmudic scholarship as well as some poetry.

Counting pages as in the printed text, Barakāt opens *Kitāb al-Muᶜtabar* [1] with 282 pages on knowledge and logic. The section on categorical syllogisms takes up pages 122 to 148. Let me describe what Barakāt does in these twenty-seven pages.

We must first go back to Aristotle. In his *Prior Analytics* Aristotle listed forty-eight premise-pairs, i.e. ordered pairs of formal categorical sentences with a single term letter in common. He grouped them into three 'figures'; the effect of this grouping was that each premise-pair has four associated categorical sentences that are available to be logical conclusions of the premise-pair. We will call these four sentences the 'candidate conclusions', or the 'candidates' for short. Next, Aristotle classified each of the forty-eight premise-pairs under one of two heads, which (following Ibn Sīnā) we will call 'productive' and 'sterile'. A premise-pair is sterile if it doesn't entail any of its four candidates. It is productive if it does entail at least one of its four candidates; its 'conclusion' is the logically strongest candidate that it entails.

For example the premise-pair 'Every C is a B. No A is a B.' is productive with conclusion 'No C is an A'. The premise-pair 'Some B is a C. Some B is not an A.' is sterile.

In Aristotle's eyes, entailment has to do with inferring and deducing. A conclusion is something that we can infer from the premises; except for four cases that he takes as axioms, he proves that something is a conclusion by giving a proof of it from the premises. Aristotle assumes that entailment preserves truth, in the sense that if an interpretation of the term letters makes the premises true, then it will make the conclusion true too. He points out how this fact can be used to prove sterility, by giving interpretations that make the premises true but between them falsify each one of the four candidates.

Barakāt's first innovation is that he takes this fact about interpretations as a *definition* (or at least a necessary and sufficient condition) of entailment. Thus if Φ is a premise-pair and θ a candidate,

$$\Phi \text{ entails } \theta$$
$$\text{if and only if} \tag{2}$$
$$\text{every interpretation making } \Phi \text{ true makes } \theta \text{ true.}$$

He shows that we can use this definition to give a decision method for productivity of premise-pairs. The idea is to list all interpretations that make the premises true, and see whether there is some candidate that is true in all these interpretations.

But how is this possible? For any premise-pair there are infinitely many different interpretations that make its premises both true. Here Barakāt notices (though without spelling it out) that we can draw diagrams that are pictures of interpretations, and any two interpretations that have the same diagram will make the same assignments of truth and falsehood. So it suffices to list the *diagrams* that verify both premises, and check whether there is a candidate conclusion verified by all of them. With two qualifications given below, there are exactly 109 diagrams of interpretations of the three letters A, B, C. So it is humanly quite feasible to run through them all, and it is trivial to check what sentences they verify.

The two qualifications will be easier to state after we have seen an example of a diagram. Thus:

C black
_____

A animal
_____

This is the diagram of a two-letter interpretation that assigns 'black' to C and 'animal' to A. Some animals are black, and this is shown by the overlap in the middle. Some black things are not animals; this is shown by the arm sticking out to the left. Some animals are not black; this is shown by the arm sticking out to the right.

Note that the diagram is *not* a diagram of a categorical sentence. We needed three categorical sentences to express three different parts of the diagram. The next appearance of line diagrams in logic after Barakāt is in notes of Leibniz five hundred years later, where we find for instance

As Leibniz makes clear, this diagram is intended to represent the sentence 'Some B is a C' (or equally 'Some C is a B'). In order to make the diagram represent this sentence and not the other two sentences mentioned above, Leibniz includes the vertical dashed lines as part of the diagram. The later diagrams of Euler and Venn were also primarily intended to represent sentences, with the effect of turning Aristotle's verbal proofs into pictorial proofs. This is *not* what Barakāt is doing.

The first qualification is that these diagrams can't represent an interpretation that assigns the empty set to some letter. At least before al-Fārābī in the tenth century, Aristotelian logicians were quite careless about whether a term can be read as empty. Al-Fārābī adopted a precise convention that allows empty terms (as in (1) above). One can show that if we rule out empty terms—as Barakāt does by implication—then this makes no difference to which premise-pairs are productive and which sentences they have as conclusions.

The second qualification is that not all interpretations of three letters allow diagrams in Barakāt's style. Here is an undiagrammable interpretation:

A : even nonnegative integer
B : prime nonnegative integer
C : integer $\geqslant 3$

But Barakāt is damn lucky. It turns out firstly that no undiagrammable interpretation verifies any productive premise-pair, and secondly that every sterile premise-pair can be shown to be sterile using only diagrammable interpretations. (Of course if he wanted to use undiagrammable interpretations he could invent some convention for drawing them.)

There are two major innovations in this work of Barakāt. The first is to use interpretations to prove entailment, rather than using them to prove failure of entailment. We don't find this idea stated clearly until Tarski [16] in 1936; though it could be argued that Gergonne in 1816/7 and Bolzano in 1837 together come close. (Barakāt's line diagrams are in fact equivalent to Gergonne's circle diagrams [4], but generalised from two to three letters.)

The second innovation is to use the same method to show both productivity and sterility. In fact Barakāt gives a decision procedure for productivity. As far as I know, no nontrivial logical decision procedure in this sense appears after Barakāt until the twentieth century, where it becomes visible in the work of Post, Behmann, Bernays and others in the 1920s.

Although Barakāt clearly intends his procedure to be used to classify premise-pairs as productive or sterile, it is not so clear that he thinks of it as a mechanical procedure. In his own remarks he tends to treat the diagrams as an aid to intuition,[2] and he is happy to allow intuition to take over some of the work. This is probably the main reason why his proofs of productivity never list more than four diagrams, although there are some cases that require sixteen diagrams for a full proof. Take for example the premise-pair

Not every C is a B. Every A is a B.

There are twelve diagrams that verify both these premises, but Barakāt gives just two:

C white	C white
B animal	B animal
A crow	A human

We can quickly explain why no further diagrams are needed. In both these diagrams the C line sticks out beyond the B line but the A line doesn't. Any further facts about the relationships between the lines, as in the remaining ten diagrams, are irrelevant to the conclusion. As Barakāt says: 'The example diagrams fully explain the conclusion without needing [any Aristotle-style proof]' ([1] 139.14f).

Here is one manuscript version of this passage:

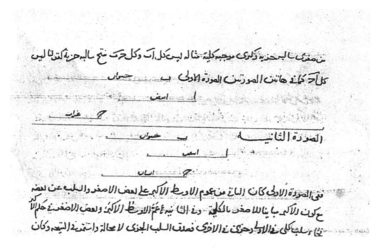

---

[2] 'Even if it is clear to anyone who forms the concepts that these four [premise-pairs] are productive, these diagrams—that list precisely the ways in which the terms can be related to each other as including or included—provide one with mental concepts that verify the productiveness and remove any doubts about it.' ([1] p. 131).

Inspection of this photo gives further information about both Barakāt and the copyist. First, comparing with the conventions he uses elsewhere, Barakāt has switched the letters A and C, and also transposed the first two lines of each diagram. This illustrates the fact that he is careless (perhaps deliberately) about points that don't affect the output of the algorithm.

Second, the copyist has drawn the lines wrong in the second diagram, so as to claim that every animal is human. This is in fact one of the more reliable manuscripts. The diagrams in the Hyderabad publication of the book [1] are almost all wrong. Evidently the copyists didn't have any idea what the diagrams were about. The explanation of Barakāt's diagrams in the great 13th century logical textbook *Asās al-iqtibās* of Naṣīr al-Dīn al-Ṭūsī makes similar mistakes to the copyists; Ṭūsī doesn't understand how line segments relate when one is higher in the page than the other. Also Ṭūsī seems to think the diagrams express sentences rather than interpretations.

There are some questions about where Barakāt was coming from in giving this decision algorithm. Other evidence [11] suggests that his main source in logic was a very early book by Ibn Sīnā, the *Ḥikmat al-ᶜArūḍīya*. Ibn Sīnā wrote this book when he was only about twenty-one years old, before he got into the details of designing his own logical system, and presumably before he came anywhere near putting together his recursive proof search algorithm. So Barakāt's algorithm was probably not influenced in any way by Ibn Sīnā's. Unfortunately the section of *Ḥikmat* dealing with categorical syllogisms is missing.

A fuller study of Barakāt will take on board some other relevant background. It's clear both that Barakāt took inspiration from Aristotle's method for proving sterility, and that he never read it carefully. He was probably unaware of the inconclusive discussions of the equivalence (2) by Alexander of Aphrodisias (c. AD 200), or of Paul the Persian's presentation of productiveness and sterility as parallels rather than opposites (6th century).

5   Formalising the Procedure

In the case of both Ibn Sīnā's proof search and Barakāt's decision procedure, it seems that nobody else had a concept of the problems that these procedures were intended to solve. Nobody asked 'How can we systematically fill in the gaps in a proof?' or 'How can we systematically discover whether a given set of premises has a conclusion?'. Even Ibn Sīnā and Barakāt themselves never explicitly stated the problems in terms like these. Al-Khalīl and al-Khwārizmī fared better: people understood what it is to write a dictionary where people know how to find the words they are looking for, and what it is to solve a quadratic equation.

More precisely, plenty of people did understand what counts as filling a gap in a proof, and what counts as determining that a premise-pair is or is not productive. Aristotle had already discussed these things. What apparently nobody except Ibn Sīnā and Barakāt understood was the added concept 'systematically', meaning that we operate according to a set of rules that cover all the relevant cases. The concept is close to Rashid's requirement (i): the procedure to be followed is described formally and without reference to any one example.

And again, even Ibn Sīnā and Barakāt gave their procedures through examples and not through a formal description without reference to particular examples. But at least in Ibn Sīnā's case we know that he considered he had given the rules in a form where a diligent reader would see how they applied to cases that go beyond his examples.

So it seems that the readers of Ibn Sīnā and Barakāt were missing some concepts that have to do with systematic procedures. Closer study should be able to pin down more precisely what was missing. We know that at least the mathematicians had good examples of procedures that raised the relevant questions. One was the construction of continued fraction representations of ratios between lengths. Already Plato knew that the ratio of the side of a square to its diagonal leads to a continued fraction that never halts. But I don't know whether the Arabic mathematicians ever thought explicitly in terms of procedures that do or do not halt, and if so, whether they or anybody else generalised these notions to non-numerical cases. Certainly neither Ibn Sīnā nor Barakāt says anything to suggest they had come across such generalisations.

But approaching the issues from a different direction, we do know of some discussion by Arabic logicians of the notion of a procedure. Saloua Chatti and I came across evidence of this in al-Fārābī's book *Qiyās* when we translated it for the series Ancient Commentators on Aristotle [2]. Al-Fārābī (c. 870–c. 950) can be quite scatterbrained and lacking in insight; it's hard to deny that he operates at a lower level than either Ibn Sīnā or Barakāt. But he raises good questions, sometimes by making interesting mistakes; Ibn Sīnā took him seriously and learned much by trying to improve on him. His failure to form a concept can be used as evidence that the concept was not common property at the time (i.e. in the early tenth century).

In the second half of his *Qiyās*, al-Fārābī studies and generalises two procedures discussed by Aristotle, namely induction and analogy. He sees these procedures as beginning with a stage that revolves around searching for concepts that fit certain conditions. In the case of induction the search is for a collection of particular cases $C_1, \ldots, C_n$ of the concept B that allow us to prove something about B by considering the particular cases separately. In the case of analogy we know that 'C is an A', and the search is for a single concept B such that C is a B, and C being a B is the *reason why* C is an A. When B has been found, we can use it to show that other things besides C are As 'by analogy with C'. Al-Fārābī refers to earlier authors who combined these two kinds of search.

Al-Fārābī says in several places that when the search has been completed and we have the sought-for concepts in hand, then all that remains is syllogistic logic. (This is not correct, as Ibn Sīnā pointed out; but the reason is irrelevant to us here.) He infers that this fact makes the search unhelpful. His point is not clear, since obviously the search did help if it found the required concepts. But he seems to want to devalue the search element of his procedures by comparison with the purely deductive element. This may reflect some bias in his Aristotelian background.

The idea of a search procedure that follows strict formal rules is absent from al-Fārābī's thinking. But he does have the idea of searches where we don't know in advance how many steps might be needed. An interesting example is in his book *Taḥlīl* ('Analysis'), where he describes a division procedure from Plato's dialogue *The Statesman* 262a–e. Plato is considering how to prove that every B is an A. He points out, using his notion of division, that it may be easier to prove that every B_1 is an A and every B_2 is an A, where the Bs consist of the B_1s and the B_2s. If we start by splitting B into B_1 and B_2, and find we still can't show that every B_2 is an A, we can try splitting B_2 into B_{21} and B_{22}, and checking whether we can show both that every B_{21} is an A and that every B_{22} is an A; and so on indefinitely until the process halts. Al-Fārābī's account of this procedure makes its recursive aspect very clear, and could have helped to steer Ibn Sīnā in the direction of his recursive proof search.

Another interesting point from al-Fārābī's treatment of procedures—though it could be just a figment of some careless copying in the manuscripts—is a passage in which he seems to distribute the steps of a procedure between 'us' and 'him' ([2] translation, 40, 5–42, 4). One way of reading the passage is that 'we' are trying to carry out a search procedure, and 'he' is our hired assistant (say Zayd) who does the actual searching according to our instructions. If this is right, then it could be an attempt by al-Fārābī to objectify the procedure in the form of the instructions that we give to Zayd. If so, the attempt works remarkably well, because any attentive reader can see that the instructions issued to Zayd overlook a point which is essential to ensure that Zayd finds things with the required properties. Al-Fārābī himself never notices the oversight. But the idea of objectifying a procedure by turning it into a set of instructions is insightful and some way ahead of its time.

References

1. Abū al-Barakāt, Kitāb al-muᶜtabar fī al-ḥikmat al-ilāhiyya, Byblion, Jbeil Lebanon (2007). (reprinted from Hyderabad 1938)
2. Chatti, S., Hodges, W.: Al-Fārābī, Syllogism: An Abridgement of Aristotle's Prior Analytics, Ancient Commentators on Aristotle. Bloomsbury Academic, London (2020, to appear)
3. Dichy, J.: Al-Ḥalīl's conjecture: how the first comprehensive dictionary in history was invented. In: Giolfo, M.E.B. (ed.) Arab and Arabic Linguistics: Traditional and New Theoretical Approaches, Journal of Semitic Studies Supplement 34, pp. 43–68. Oxford University Press, Oxford (2014)
4. Gergonne, J.D.: Variétés. Essai de dialectique rationnelle. Annales de Mathématiques Pures et Appliquées **7**, 189–228 (1816–1817)
5. Gil, M.: Jews in Islamic Countries in the Middle Ages, trans. David Strassler. Brill, Leiden (2004)
6. Haywood, J.A.: Arabic Lexicography. Brill, Leiden (1965)
7. Hodges, W.: Ibn Sīnā on analysis: 1. Proof search. Or: abstract state machines as a tool for history of logic. In: Blass, A., Dershowitz, N., Reisig, W. (eds.) Fields of Logic and Computation. LNCS, vol. 6300, pp. 354–404. Springer, Heidelberg (2010). https://doi.org/10.1007/978-3-642-15025-8_18

8. Hodges, W.: Two early Arabic applications of model-theoretic consequence. Logica Universalis **12**(1–2), 37–54 (2018)
9. Hodges, W.: Mathematical Background to the Logic of Ibn Sīnā, Perspectives in Logic, Association for Symbolic Logic (in preparation)
10. Sīnā, I.: In: Zayed, S. (ed.) Al-qiyās (Syllogism), Cairo (1964)
11. Janssens, J.: Ebü'l-Berekāt el-Baḡdādī'nin Kitābü'l-Muᶜteber'inin Mantık Kısmında İbn Sīnā'nın el-Hikmetü'l-Arūziyye'sini (veya onunla yakından ilişkili diğer bir eseri) Kullanımı. Nazariyat İslām Felsefe ve Bilim Tarihi Araştırmaları Dergisi **3/1** 1–22 (2016)
12. Al-Khalīl. In: al-Makhzūmī, M., al-Sāmarrā'ī, I. (ed.) Kitāb al-ᶜayn. Dār al-Rashīd lil-Nashr, Baghdad (1980–1985). 8 vols
13. Rashed, R.: Les méthodes algorithmiques. Enciclopedia Italiana (2002)
14. Rashed, R.: Al-Khwārizmī, Le Commencement de l'Algèbre. Blanchard, Paris (2007)
15. Talmon, R.: Arabic Grammar in its Formative Age. Brill, Leiden (1997)
16. Tarski, A.: On the concept of logical consequence. In: Corcoran, J. (ed.) Logic, Semantics, Metamathematics, pp. 409–420. Hackett, Indianapolis (1983)

On the Generalized Membership Problem
in Relatively Hyperbolic Groups

Olga Kharlampovich[1] and Pascal Weil[2,3(✉)]

[1] CUNY, Hunter College and Graduate Center, New York, USA
okharlampovich@gmail.com
[2] Univ. Bordeaux, CNRS, Bordeaux INP, LaBRI, UMR5800, Talence, France
pascal.weil@labri.fr
[3] CNRS, ReLaX, UMI2000, Siruseri, India

Abstract. The aim of this note is to provide a proof of the decidability of the generalized membership problem for relatively quasi-convex subgroups of finitely presented relatively hyperbolic groups, under some reasonably mild conditions on the peripheral structure of these groups. These hypotheses are satisfied, in particular, by toral relatively hyperbolic groups.

Keywords: Relatively hyperbolic groups · Generalized membership problem

The problem we consider here is the so-called *generalized membership problem*, in a group G generated by a finite set A: given a tuple $h_1, \ldots, h_k \in F(A)$ and letting H be the subgroup they generate in G (that is: H is the subgroup of G generated by the images of the h_i in G), given an additional element $g \in G$ (also in the form of a word in $F(A)$), decide whether $g \in H$.

Stated as above, this problem is known to be undecidable without strong assumptions on the group G. Even in the relatively simple case of the direct product of two rank 2 free groups, $F_2 \times F_2$, there are finitely generated subgroups with undecidable membership problem (see Mihailova's subgroup [28]).

Our main result deals with the case where $G = \langle A \mid R \rangle$ is finitely presented and relatively hyperbolic with respect to a peripheral structure subject to additional conditions—satisfied, in particular, by toral relatively hyperbolic groups, see Sect. 2. Note that in these groups, and even in hyperbolic groups, there are finitely generated subgroups with undecidable membership problem [30]. We offer a *partial algorithm* for the generalized membership problem in the following sense: an algorithm which may not stop on all instances but which will stop at least on those instances where H is relatively quasi-convex, and which decides whether $g \in H$ when it stops.

The first author was partially supported by the Simons Foundation, Award 422503, and the second author was partially supported by the DeLTA project (ANR-16-CE40-0007).

© Springer Nature Switzerland AG 2020
A. Blass et al. (Eds.): Gurevich Festschrift, LNCS 12180, pp. 147–155, 2020.
https://doi.org/10.1007/978-3-030-48006-6_11

We first survey some algorithmic results for groups, largely centered around this generalized membership problem, mainly focussing on those results that use graph-theoretic representations of subgroups, in particular the so-called Stallings graphs, as these are essential to our main result.

In the second section we use these results, and other results on the structure of relatively hyperbolic groups, to establish our main theorem.

1   Stallings Graphs and Algorithmic Problems

Stallings [36] formalized a method (now known as *Stallings foldings*) to associate with any finitely generated subgroup H of a free group $F(A)$ an effectively computable discrete structure, called the *Stallings graph* of H. This is a finite, oriented, labeled graph (the edges are labeled by elements of A) with a designated base vertex, in which the loops at the base vertex are labeled by reduced words representing the elements of H. Given a finite set of words in $F(A)$, we can compute the Stallings graph of the subgroup H they generate (in time almost linear [37]), compute the index, the rank and a basis for H, and solve the membership for H. In particular, this provides an elegant and computationally efficient solution of the generalized membership problem in $F(A)$: on input $(h_1, \ldots, h_n; g)$, one first computes the Stallings graph Γ of the subgroup generated by the h_i, and one then verifies whether the reduced word g can be read as a loop at the base vertex of Γ.

Given generators for another subgroup K, we can use the same tool of Stallings graphs to decide whether H and K are conjugates, compute their intersection and the finite collection (up to conjugacy) of intersections of their conjugates, and generally solve many other algorithmic problems, see *e.g.* [19,27,31]. Most of these problems are solved very efficiently (in polynomial time) by this method, see [5,19].

Several authors introduced similar constructions to study finitely generated subgroups of non-free groups. More specifically, we are talking here of having an effectively constructible labeled graph canonically associated with a subgroup, solving at least the membership problem and allowing the computation of intersections.

As mentioned in the introduction, one certainly needs to impose constraints on the group G. We also need to formulate assumptions on the subgroup $H \leq G$. Indeed, even in good situations (*e.g.* G is automatic, or even hyperbolic), not every finitely generated subgroup has decidable membership problem [30].

Pioneer work (published in 1996) came from two directions. Kapovich [18] used the Todd-Coxeter enumeration scheme to produce ever larger fragments of the Schreier (coset) graph $\mathsf{Schreier}(G, H)$, and showed that, if G is geodesically automatic and H is quasi-convex, one can decide when to stop this process and produce a Stallings-like graph to decide the membership problem for H. This yields a partial algorithm for the generalized membership problem, which halts exactly when the subgroup H is quasi-convex. At the same time, Arzhantseva and Ol'shanskii [4] studied a construction, starting with the Stallings graph of the subgroup $H_0 \leq F(A)$ generated by $h_1, \ldots, h_n$, and enriching it by a combination of Stallings foldings and surgical additions of fragments of relators of G (the so-called *AO-moves*). For each integer $k \geq 1$, they identified a small cancellation property which 'almost always' holds (it is exponentially generic among the presentations with r relators, r fixed) under which every k-generated subgroup is quasi-convex, and such that their construction halts after a finite number of moves, and solves the membership problem for H.

In [26], McCammond and Wise also start from the Stallings graph of the subgroup $H_0 \leq F(A)$, which they refine by so-called *2-cell attachments*. They then use a geometric assumption (the *perimeter reduction* hypothesis) on the complex representing the presentation $G = \langle A \mid R \rangle$, to show that their construction halts and produces a Stallings-like graph. They show that this geometric assumption holds in particular when R consists of large powers, or under certain combinatorial conditions.

Kapovich [18] used his result to show that one can compute the quasi-convexity index of a (quasi-convex) subgroup. Arzhantseva's and Ol'shanskii's method was used to prove that, generically, a finitely presented group satisfies the Howson property [2], see [3,20] for other applications. McCammond's and Wise's perimeter reduction hypothesis also leads to a number of algorithmic results, including the construction of Stallings-like graphs and the solution of the membership problem in large classes of presentations, many of which are locally quasi-convex (every finitely generated subgroup is quasi-convex) [26], see [32] for other applications.

A common feature of these papers above is that they identify a method to 'grow' a labeled graph, starting from the Stallings graph of a subgroup of the free group, and then exploit additional assumptions on both G and H to show that this growing process can be 'terminated' at some point.

It is natural, if we are going to rely on methods where words label paths in graphs (which one can view as automata), to consider, as Kapovich [18] does, finitely presented groups $G = \langle A \mid R \rangle$ equipped with an automatic structure, providing in particular a rational language[1] of representatives for the elements of G, that is, a rational language L over the alphabet $A \cup A^{-1}$, composed of reduced words, and such that $\mu(L) = G$ (where $\mu \colon F(A) \to G$ is the canonical onto morphism from the free group over A onto G). It is also natural in this context to consider only so-called *L-rational* subgroups H, that is, subgroups such that $L \cap \mu^{-1}(H)$ is a rational set as well. The notion of L-rationality, first considered by Gersten and Short [13], is equivalent to a geometric notion of L-quasi-convexity[2]. Classical quasi-convexity corresponds to the case where L is the set of geodesic representatives of the elements of G. See Short [33] for an example of the usage of automata-theoretic ideas to investigate quasi-convex subgroups.

---

[1] A language is *rational* (or *regular*) if it is accepted by a finite state automaton.

[2] Namely: there exists $\delta > 0$ such that every L-representative of an element of H stays within distance δ of H, in the Cayley graph of G.

An abundant literature considers the same set of problems for more specific classes of groups. Cai *et al.* [8] and later Gurevich and Schupp [15] investigate the complexity of the generalized membership problem in the modular group. Schupp [32] applies the results of [26] to large classes of Coxeter groups, which turn out to be locally quasi-convex. Kapovich, Miasnikov, Weidmann [21] solve the membership problem for subgroups of certain graphs of groups. Markus-Epstein [25] constructs a Stallings graph for the subgroups of amalgamated products of finite groups. Silva, Soler-Escriva, Ventura [34] do the same for subgroups of virtually free groups. Here again, the groups considered are locally quasi-convex, and the authors rely on a folding process, much like in the free group case, and a well-chosen set of representatives. Finally, we mention Delgado and Ventura's work [10], where they develop a strong generalization of Stallings graphs to represent, and to compute with, subgroups of direct products of free and free abelian groups.

In [22], Kharlampovich *et al.* proposed a general approach to generalize a number of the situations listed above while keeping the spirit of the construction of Stallings graphs. If G is an A-generated group and L is a set of (possibly not unique) representatives for the elements of G, we define the *Stallings graph of a subgroup H with respect to L* to be the fragment $\Gamma_L(H)$ of the Schreier graph Schreier(G, H) spanned by the loops at vertex H labeled by words of L (that is: by the L-representatives of the elements of H). It is easily verified that this graph is finite if and only if H is L-quasi-convex, or L-rational. We will use the following result in the next section.

Theorem 1 ([22]). *Let G be an A-generated group, equipped with an automatic structure with language of representatives L. There exists a partial algorithm which, given $g, h_1, \ldots, h_k \in F(A)$, halts exactly if the subgroup H generated by the h_i is L-quasi-convex, and in that case outputs the Stallings graph of H with respect to L.*

Note that hyperbolic groups admit an automatic structure with language of representatives the set of geodesics. In particular, the partial algorithm in Theorem 1 computes a Stallings graph for the quasi-convex subgroups of hyperbolic groups.

Theorem 1 yields a uniform method to solve algorithmic problems for L-quasi-convex subgroups in automatic groups, including the generalized word problem and the computation of intersections. It also allows deciding conjugacy and almost malnormality, provided the automatic structure on G satisfies a quantitative version of Hruska's and Wise's bounded packing property [17] (this condition is satisfied by the geodesic automatic structure of hyperbolic groups), see [22].

Theorem 1 was recently used by Kim in [23] where she, in particular, detects stability and Morseness in toral relatively hyperbolic groups.

Remark 1 ([18,22]). For the generalized membership problem in particular, the partial algorithm (halting exactly if H is L-quasi-convex) consists in computing the Stallings graph Γ as in Theorem 1, using the automatic structure to compute an L-representative w of g, and verifying whether w labels a loop at the base vertex of Γ.

2 The Generalized Membership Problem for Relatively Hyperbolic Groups

Let $G = \langle A \mid R \rangle$ be a finitely presented group and let $\mathcal{P}$ be a finite collection of finitely generated subgroups of G, called the *peripheral subgroups* of G. There are several definitions of G being *relatively hyperbolic with respect to the peripheral structure* $\mathcal{P}$, due to Gromov [14], Farb [12], Bowditch [6], Druțu and Sapir [11], Osin [29]. These definitions turn out to be equivalent (see Bumagin [7], Dahmani [9], Hruska [16, Theorem 5.1]), we refer to the literature for details [16,29].

If H is a subgroup of G, there are also several definitions of relative quasi-convexity for H, in terms of natural geometries on G. Again, these are equivalent (Hruska [16]) and we refer to the literature for precise definitions.

Properties of the *parabolic subgroups* of H, that is, the subgroups that are contained in a conjugate of a peripheral subgroup $P \in \mathcal{P}$, characterize certain subclasses of relatively quasi-convex subgroups, which will be useful in the sequel. We say that H is *peripherally finite* if every $H \cap P^x$ ($P \in \mathcal{P}$, $x \in G$) is finite[3]; more generally, we say that H has *peripherally finite index* if every infinite $H \cap P^x$ has finite index in P^x[4]. Such subgroups are always finitely generated (Osin [29, Thms 4.13 and 4.16] for the peripherally finite case, Kharlampovich *et al.* [22] for the peripherally finite index case).

To go forward, we introduce the following assumptions on the peripheral structure $\mathcal{P}$ of the relatively hyperbolic group G.

Assumptions (Hyp)

(H1) Each group $P \in \mathcal{P}$ satisfies the following: we are given a geodesically bi-automatic structure for P, on an alphabet X_P and with language of representatives L_P, and we can compute a geodesically bi-automatic structure on every finite generating set of P (given as a subset of $F(X_P)$).

(H2) The groups in $\mathcal{P}$ are *slender* (a.k.a. *noetherian*: every one of their subgroups is finitely generated) and LERF.

(H3) For each $P \in \mathcal{P}$, the set of tuples of words in L_P that generate a finite index subgroup of P is recursively enumerable.

(H4) We can solve the generalized membership problem in each $P \in \mathcal{P}$.

Remark 2. Hruska showed that every relatively quasi-convex subgroup of G is finitely generated, if and only if every group in $\mathcal{P}$ is slender [16, Cor. 9.2], so (H2) is a reasonable hypothesis to make in this algorithmic context.

---

[3] These subgroups are called *strongly quasi-convex* in [29], and differ from the strongly quasi-convex subgroups of Tran [38].

[4] These subgroups are called *fully quasi-convex* in [24].

Remark 3. (Hyp) is satisfied in particular if the peripheral structure $\mathcal{P}$ consists of finitely generated abelian groups, and notably, if G is *toral relatively hyperbolic* (that is: G is torsion free and $\mathcal{P}$ consists of non-cyclic free abelian groups).

We can now state the central result of this note.

Theorem 2. *Let $G = \langle A \mid R \rangle$ be a finitely presented group, relatively hyperbolic with respect to the peripheral structure $\mathcal{P}$, and satisfying (Hyp). There is a partial algorithm which, given $g, h_1, \ldots, h_k \in F(A)$,*

- *halts at least if $g \in H$ or if the subgroup H of G generated by the h_i is relatively quasi-convex and $g \notin H$;*
- *when it halts, decides whether $g \in H$.*

The algorithm in Theorem 2 is "impractical" in the following sense: there is no function bounding the time required for the algorithm to stop (if it will stop). It consists in two semi-algorithms, meant to be run concurrently, until one of them halts: one trying to witness the fact that $g \in H$ and the other trying to witness the opposite fact.

The rest of this paper consists in the description of these semi-algorithms.

Semi-algorithm to Verify that $g \in H$. It is a classical result that, given the presentation $\langle A \mid R \rangle$ for G and given a word $g \in F(A)$, there is a partial algorithm which halts exactly if $g = 1$ in G. Indeed, $g = 1$ in G if and only if a sequence of R-rewritings of g eventually leads to the empty word. A systematic exploration of the R-rewritings of g will eventually uncover this sequence if $g = 1$ in G.

This semi-algorithm is naturally extended to the problem at hand (does g belong to H?) as follows. One starts with the Stallings graph Γ of the subgroup of $F(A)$ generated by the h_i (see [36]), and iteratively:

- modify Γ by gluing at every vertex a loop labeled by r for every relator $r \in R$;
- fold Γ (this is the central step of the construction of Stallings graphs: it consists in identifying vertices p and q each time that there are edges labeled by a letter $a \in A$ from some vertex s to both p and q, or edges labeled by a letter a from both p and q to some vertex s);
- check whether g labels a loop at the base vertex of Γ. If that is the case, then $g \in H$ and we stop the algorithm. If not, repeat.

A detailed discussion of this semi-algorithm can be found in [22, Section 4.1].

Semi-algorithm to Verify that $g \notin H$. We call a subgroup of the form $H \cap P^x$ ($P \in \mathcal{P}$, $x \in G$) which is infinite, a *maximal infinite parabolic subgroup* of H. Our semi-algorithm relies on the following results.

[H] Hruska shows [16, Theorem 9.1] that, if H is relatively quasi-convex, then there exists a finite collection of maximal infinite parabolic subgroups $\{K_i\}_{1 \leq i \leq \ell}$ such that every infinite maximal parabolic subgroup of H is conjugated in H to one of the K_i.

[**MMP**] Manning and Martínez-Pedroza show the following, under Hypothesis (H2) [24, Theorem 1.7]. Suppose that $H \leq G$ is relatively quasi-convex, $\{K_i\}_{1 \leq i \leq \ell}$ is a collection of subgroups as in [**H**], say with $K_i = H \cap P_i^{x_i}$ $(1 \leq i \leq \ell, P_i \in \mathcal{P}, x_i \in G)$ and $g \notin H$. Then there exist subgroups $R_i \leq P_i^{x_i}$ such that R_i has finite index in $P_i^{x_i}$, $K_i \leq R_i$ and, if K is generated by H and the R_i, then $g \notin K$ and K has peripherally finite index. Note that [24, Theorem 1.7] is a little more concise than this statement, which is extracted from the proof in that paper [24, p. 319].

[**AC**] Antolin and Ciobanu [1, Cor. 1.9, Lemma 5.3, Thm 7.5] show that, under Hypothesis (H1), one can compute an automatic structure for G, with alphabet X containing A and the X_P ($P \in \mathcal{P}$), whose language L of representatives consists only of geodesics (on alphabet X) and contains the L_P ($P \in \mathcal{P}$), and satisfying additional properties.

[**KhMW**] Kharlampovich *et al.* [22, Sec. 7] build on [**AC**] to show that, if $H \leq G$ is relatively quasi-convex (with respect to alphabet A) and has peripherally finite index, then it is L-quasi-convex with respect to alphabet X [22, Thm 7.5]. The proof of that theorem uses Hypothesis (H4). As explained in Remark 1, this yields a solution of the membership problem in H.

We can now give our semi-algorithm. For clarity, we give it as a non-deterministic partial algorithm. Such a non-deterministic algorithm can be turned into a deterministic one by standard methods (see, *e.g.*, [35, Thm 3.16]).

(1) We first apply [**AC**] to compute an automatic structure for G on generator set X (using Hypothesis (H1)). Then we compute a finite presentation of G on X, say $\langle X \mid R_X \rangle$. For instance, R_X consists of R, the relators xu_x^{-1}, where $x \in X \setminus A$ and u_x is a fixed element of $F(A)$ such that $x = u_x$ in G, and all the cyclic permutations of these relators and their inverses.
    The words u_x can be computed as follows. Since the automatic structure for G allows us to solve the word problem, one systematically checks whether xu^{-1} is trivial, when u runs through $F(A)$. As G is A-generated, some $u \in F(A)$ is equal to x in G.
(2) Choose non-deterministically a tuple $\boldsymbol{x} = (x_1, \cdots, x_\ell)$ of elements of $F(A)$; for each $1 \leq i \leq \ell$, choose non-deterministically an element $P_i \in \mathcal{P}$ and a tuple $\boldsymbol{g}_i$ of elements of $F(X_{P_i})$ generating a finite index subgroup of P_i (this is possible under Hypothesis (H3)).
(3) For this choice of $\boldsymbol{x}$ and the $\boldsymbol{g}_i$ ($1 \leq i \leq \ell$), let $H_1 = \langle H \cup \bigcup_{i=1}^{\ell} \boldsymbol{g}_i^{x_i} \rangle$. Run the partial algorithm [**KhMW**] to decide whether $g \in H_1$ (using Hypothesis (H4)).

Result [**MMP**] (which assumes Hypothesis (H2)), shows that, if $g \notin H$ and H is relatively quasi-convex, then for an appropriate choice of $\boldsymbol{x}$ and the $\boldsymbol{g}_i$, H_1 is relatively quasi-convex and has peripherally finite index, and $g \notin H_1$. As H_1 has peripherally finite index, the partial algorithm in Step (3) will halt and certify that $g \notin H_1$, and hence that $g \notin H$ since $H \leq H_1$.

Summarizing: if $g \notin H$ and H is relatively quasi-convex, then one of the non-deterministic choices in Step (2) will be such that the partial algorithm halts and states that $g \notin H$. This completes the proof of Theorem 2.

References

1. Antolín, Y., Ciobanu, L.: Finite generating sets of relatively hyperbolic groups and applications to geodesic languages. Trans. Amer. Math. Soc. **368**(11), 7965–8010 (2016)
2. Arzhantseva, G.N.: Generic properties of finitely presented groups and Howson's theorem. Comm. Algebra **26**(11), 3783–3792 (1998)
3. Arzhantseva, G.N.: A property of subgroups of infinite index in a free group. Proc. Amer. Math. Soc. **128**(11), 3205–3210 (2000)
4. Arzhantseva, G.N., Ol'shanskiĭ, A.Y.: Generality of the class of groups in which subgroups with a lesser number of generators are free. Mat. Zametki **59**(4), 489–496, 638 (1996)
5. Birget, J.-C., Margolis, S., Meakin, J., Weil, P.: PSPACE-complete problems for subgroups of free groups and inverse finite automata. Theoret. Comput. Sci. **242**(1–2), 247–281 (2000)
6. Bowditch, B.H.: Relatively hyperbolic groups. Int. J. Algebra Comput. **22**(3), 1250016, 66 (2012)
7. Bumagin, I.: On definitions of relatively hyperbolic groups. In: Geometric Methods in Group Theory. Contemporary Mathematics, vol. 372, pp. 189–196. American Mathematical Society, Providence (2005)
8. Cai, J.-Y., Fuchs, W.H., Kozen, D., Liu, Z.: Efficient average-case algorithms for the modular group. In: 35th Annual Symposium on Foundations of Computer Science, Santa Fe, NM, pp. 143–152. IEEE Computer Society Press, Los Alamitos (1994)
9. Dahmani, F.: Les groupes relativement hyperboliques et leurs bords. Prépublication de l'Institut de Recherche Mathématique Avancée, 2003/13. Université Louis Pasteur, Strasbourg (2003)
10. Delgado, J., Ventura, E.: Algorithmic problems for free-abelian times free groups. J. Algebra **391**, 256–283 (2013)
11. Druţu, C., Sapir, M.: Tree-graded spaces and asymptotic cones of groups. Topology **44**(5), 959–1058 (2005). With an appendix by D. Osin and M. Sapir
12. Farb, B.: Relatively hyperbolic groups. Geom. Funct. Anal. **8**(5), 810–840 (1998)
13. Gersten, S.M., Short, H.B.: Rational subgroups of biautomatic groups. Ann. Math. (2) **134**(1), 125–158 (1991)
14. Gromov, M.: Hyperbolic groups. In: Gersten, S.M. (ed.) Essays in Group Theory. Mathematical Sciences Research Institute Publications, vol. 8, pp. 75–263. Springer, New York (1987). https://doi.org/10.1007/978-1-4613-9586-7_3
15. Gurevich, Y., Schupp, P.: Membership problem for the modular group. SIAM J. Comput. **37**(2), 425–459 (2007)
16. Hruska, G.C.: Relative hyperbolicity and relative quasiconvexity for countable groups. Algebr. Geom. Topol. **10**(3), 1807–1856 (2010)
17. Hruska, G.C., Wise, D.T.: Packing subgroups in relatively hyperbolic groups. Geom. Topol. **13**(4), 1945–1988 (2009)

18. Kapovich, I.: Detecting quasiconvexity: algorithmic aspects. In: Geometric and Computational Perspectives on Infinite Groups, Minneapolis, MN and New Brunswick, NJ, 1994. DIMACS: Series in Discrete Mathematics and Theoretical Computer Science, vol. 25, pp. 91–99. American Mathematical Society, Providence (1996)

19. Kapovich, I., Myasnikov, A.: Stallings foldings and subgroups of free groups. J. Algebra **248**(2), 608–668 (2002)

20. Kapovich, I., Schupp, P.: Genericity, the Arzhantseva-Ol'shanskii method and the isomorphism problem for one-relator groups. Math. Ann. **331**(1), 1–19 (2005). https://doi.org/10.1007/s00208-004-0570-x

21. Kapovich, I., Weidmann, R., Myasnikov, A.: Foldings, graphs of groups and the membership problem. Int. J. Algebra Comput. **15**(1), 95–128 (2005)

22. Kharlampovich, O., Miasnikov, A., Weil, P.: Stallings graphs for quasi-convex subgroups. J. Algebra **488**, 442–483 (2017)

23. Kim, H.: Algorithms detecting stability and Morseness for finitely generated groups. arXiv:1908.04460 (2019)

24. Manning, J.F., Martínez-Pedroza, E.: Separation of relatively quasiconvex subgroups. Pacific J. Math. **244**(2), 309–334 (2010)

25. Markus-Epstein, L.: Stallings foldings and subgroups of amalgams of finite groups. Int. J. Algebra Comput. **17**(8), 1493–1535 (2007)

26. McCammond, J.P., Wise, D.T.: Coherence, local quasiconvexity, and the perimeter of 2-complexes. Geom. Funct. Anal. **15**(4), 859–927 (2005). https://doi.org/10.1007/s00039-005-0525-8

27. Miasnikov, A., Ventura, E., Weil, P.: Algebraic extensions in free groups. In: Arzhantseva, G.N., Burillo, J., Bartholdi, L., Ventura, E. (eds.) Geometric Group Theory. TM, pp. 225–253. Birkhäuser, Basel (2007). https://doi.org/10.1007/978-3-7643-8412-8_12

28. Mihailova, K.A.: The occurrence problem for direct products of groups. Math. USSR Sbornik **70**, 241–251 (1966). English translation

29. Osin, D.V.: Relatively hyperbolic groups: intrinsic geometry, algebraic properties, and algorithmic problems. Mem. Amer. Math. Soc. **179**(843), vi+100 (2006)

30. Rips, E.: Subgroups of small cancellation groups. Bull. London Math. Soc. **14**(1), 45–47 (1982)

31. Roig, A., Ventura, E., Weil, P.: On the complexity of the Whitehead minimization problem. Int. J. Algebra Comput. **17**(8), 1611–1634 (2007)

32. Schupp, P.E.: Coxeter groups, 2-completion, perimeter reduction and subgroup separability. Geom. Dedicata. **96**, 179–198 (2003). https://doi.org/10.1023/A:1022155823425

33. Short, H.: Quasiconvexity and a theorem of Howson's. In: Group Theory from a Geometrical Viewpoint, Trieste, 1990, pp. 168–176. World Scientific Publishing, River Edge (1991)

34. Silva, P.V., Soler-Escrivà, X., Ventura, E.: Finite automata for Schreier graphs of virtually free groups. J. Group Theory **19**(1), 25–54 (2016)

35. Sipser, M.: Introduction to the Theory of Computation, 2nd edn. Thomson Course Technology, Boston (2006)

36. Stallings, J.R.: Topology of finite graphs. Invent. Math. **71**(3), 551–565 (1983)

37. Touikan, N.W.M.: A fast algorithm for Stallings' folding process. Int. J. Algebra Comput. **16**(6), 1031–1045 (2006)

38. Tran, H.: On strongly quasiconvex subgroups. Geom. Topol. **23**(3), 1173–1235 (2019)

Identities of the Kauffman Monoid $\mathcal{K}_4$ and of the Jones Monoid $\mathcal{J}_4$

Nikita V. Kitov and Mikhail V. Volkov$^{(\boxtimes)}$

Institute of Natural Sciences and Mathematics, Ural Federal University,
Lenina 51, 620000 Ekaterinburg, Russia
{n.v.kitov,m.v.volkov}@urfu.ru

Abstract. Kauffman monoids $\mathcal{K}_n$ and Jones monoids $\mathcal{J}_n$, $n = 2, 3, \ldots$, are two families of monoids relevant in knot theory. We prove a somewhat counterintuitive result that the Kauffman monoids $\mathcal{K}_3$ and $\mathcal{K}_4$ satisfy exactly the same identities. This leads to a polynomial time algorithm to check whether a given identity holds in $\mathcal{K}_4$. As a byproduct, we also find a polynomial time algorithm for checking identities in the Jones monoid $\mathcal{J}_4$.

1 Background I: Identities and Identity Checking

The present paper deals with the computational complexity of a combinatorial decision problem (identity checking problem) related to certain algebraic structures originated in knot theory (Kauffman and Jones monoids). Since our results and their proofs involve concepts from several different areas, the list of necessary prerequisites is relatively long. We assume the reader's familiarity with basic notions of computational complexity and semigroup theory; see, e.g., the early chapters of (Papadimitriou 1994) and (Clifford and Preston 1961), respectively. Modulo these basics, we tried to make the paper self-contained, to a reasonable extent. In particular, in this section we give a quick introduction into semigroup identities and their checking while the next section provides detailed geometric definitions of Kauffman and Jones monoids.

We fix a countably infinite set X which we call an *alphabet* and which elements we refer to as *letters*. The set X^+ of finite sequences of letters forms a semigroup under concatenation which is called the *free semigroup over X*. Elements of X^+ are called *words over X*. If $w = x_1 \cdots x_\ell$ with $x_1, \ldots, x_\ell \in X$ is a word over X, the set $\{x_1, \ldots, x_\ell\}$ is called the *content* of w and is denoted $\mathrm{alph}(w)$ while the number ℓ is referred to as the *length* of w and is denoted $|w|$. We say that a letter $x \in X$ *occurs* in a word $w \in X^+$ or, alternatively, w *involves* x whenever $x \in \mathrm{alph}(w)$.

An *identity* is an expression of the form $w \simeq w'$ with $w, w' \in X^+$. If $\mathcal{S}$ is a semigroup, we say that the identity $w \simeq w'$ *holds* in $\mathcal{S}$ or, alternatively, $\mathcal{S}$

M. V. Volkov—Supported by Ural Mathematical Center under agreement No. 075-02-2020-1537/1 with the Ministry of Science and Higher Education of the Russian Federation.

A. Blass et al. (Eds.): Gurevich Festschrift, LNCS 12180, pp. 156–178, 2020.
https://doi.org/10.1007/978-3-030-48006-6_12

satisfies $w \simeq w'$ if $w\varphi = w'\varphi$ for every homomorphism $\varphi \colon X^+ \to \mathcal{S}$. If $w \simeq w'$ does not hold in $\mathcal{S}$, we say that it *fails* in $\mathcal{S}$.

The following observations are immediate: if a semigroup $\mathcal{S}$ satisfies an identity $w \simeq w'$, so do each subsemigroup and each quotient of $\mathcal{S}$; if semigroups $\mathcal{S}_1$ and $\mathcal{S}_2$ satisfy $w \simeq w'$, so does their direct product $\mathcal{S}_1 \times \mathcal{S}_2$.

It is well known and easy to see that the free semigroup X^+ possesses the following universal property: for every semigroup $\mathcal{S}$, every mapping $X \to \mathcal{S}$ uniquely extends to a homomorphism $X^+ \to \mathcal{S}$. Thus, the homomorphisms $X^+ \to \mathcal{S}$ are in a 1-1 correspondence with the mappings $X \to \mathcal{S}$, which we call *substitutions*. Therefore we can restate the fact of $w \simeq w'$ holding in $\mathcal{S}$ also in the following terms: every substitution of elements in $\mathcal{S}$ for letters in X yields equal values to w and w'.

Given a semigroup $\mathcal{S}$, its *identity checking problem*[1] CHECK-ID($\mathcal{S}$) is the following decision problem. The instance of CHECK-ID($\mathcal{S}$) is an arbitrary identity $w \simeq w'$. The answer to the instance $w \simeq w'$ is 'YES' whenever the identity $w \simeq w'$ holds in $\mathcal{S}$; otherwise, the answer is 'NO'.

We stress that here $\mathcal{S}$ is fixed and it is the identity $w \simeq w'$ that serves as the input so that the time/space complexity of CHECK-ID($\mathcal{S}$) should be measured in terms of the size of the identity, that is, in $|ww'|$.

Studying computational complexity of identity checking in semigroups (and other 'classical' algebras such as groups and rings) was proposed by Sapir in the influential survey (Kharlampovich and Sapir 1995), see Problem 2.4 therein. For a **finite** semigroup $\mathcal{S}$, the problem CHECK-ID($\mathcal{S}$) is always decidable. Indeed, given an identity $w \simeq w'$, there are only finitely many substitutions of elements in $\mathcal{S}$ for letters in alph(ww'), and one can check whether or not each of these substitutions yields equal values to w and w'. Moreover, CHECK-ID($\mathcal{S}$) with $\mathcal{S}$ being finite belongs to the complexity class coNP: if for some words w, w' that involve m letters in total, the identity $w \simeq w'$ fails in the semigroup $\mathcal{S}$, then a nondeterministic algorithm can guess an m-tuple of elements in $\mathcal{S}$ witnessing the failure and then verify the guess by computing the values of the words w and w' under the substitution that sends the letters occurring in $w \simeq w'$ to the entries of the guessed m-tuple. With multiplication in $\mathcal{S}$ assumed to be performed in unit time, the algorithm takes linear in $|ww'|$ time.

In the literature, there exists many examples of finite semigroups whose identity checking problem is coNP-complete; see, e.g., (Almeida et al. 2008; Horváth et al. 2007; Jackson and McKenzie 2006; Kisielewicz 2004; Klíma 2009, 2012; Plescheva and Vértesi 2006; Seif 2005; Seif and Szabó 2006) and the references therein. However, the task of classifying finite semigroups according to the computational complexity of identity checking appears to be far from being feasible. In particular, it is not yet accomplished even in the case when the semigroup is a finite group. Just to give a hint of difficulties that one encounters when approaching this task, we mention the following result by Klíma (2009): a finite semigroup $\mathcal{S}$ with CHECK-ID($\mathcal{S}$) in P may have both a subsemigroup and a quotient whose identity checking problems are coNP-complete.

---

[1] Also called the '*term equivalence problem*' in the literature.

Studying the identity checking problem for **infinite** semigroups cannot rely on the 'finite' methods outlined above. Clearly, the brute-force approach of checking through all possible substitutions fails since the set of such substitutions becomes infinite if their range is an infinite semigroup. The nondeterministic guessing algorithm also fails in general because an infinite semigroup S may have undecidable word problem so that it might be impossible to decide whether or not the values of two words under a substitution are equal in S. Murskiĭ (1968) had constructed an infinite semigroup S such that the problem CHECK-ID(S) is undecidable. On the other hand, for many 'natural' infinite semigroups such as semigroups of transformations of an infinite set, or semigroups of relations on an infinite domain, or semigroups of matrices over an infinite ring, the identity checking problem trivializes since such 'big' semigroups satisfy only *trivial* identities, that is, identities of the form $w \eqcirc w$. Yet another class of 'natural' infinite semigroups with easy identity checking is formed by various commutative structures in arithmetics and algebra such as integer numbers or real polynomials, say, under addition or multiplication. It is folklore that these commutative semigroups satisfy exactly so-called balanced identities. (An identity $w \eqcirc w'$ is said to be *balanced* if every letter occurs in w and w' the same number of times. Clearly, this condition can be verified in linear in $|ww'|$ time.)

For a long time, there were no results on the computational complexity of identity checking for infinite semigroups, except for the two aforementioned extremes—undecidability and trivial or easy decidability in linear time. Only recently, the situation has started to change, and a few examples of infinite semigroups with identity checking decidable in a nontrivial way have appeared. An interesting instance here is the so-called bicyclic monoid $\mathcal{B}$ generated by two elements a and b subject to the relation $ba = 1$; this monoid is known to play a distinguished role in the structure theory of semigroups. The fact that $\mathcal{B}$ satisfies a nontrivial identity was first discovered by Adian (1962). After that, various combinatorial, computational, and geometric aspects of identities holding in $\mathcal{B}$ were examined in the literature, see, e.g., (Shneerson 1989; Shleifer 1990; Pastijn 2006), but only short while ago Daviaud et al. (2018) have shown that checking identities in $\mathcal{B}$ can be done in polynomial time via quite a tricky algorithm based on linear programming. Another example is the Kauffman monoid $\mathcal{K}_3$ generated by three elements h_1, h_2, and c subject to the relations $h_i h_{3-i} h_i = h_i$ and $h_i^2 = ch_i = h_i c$, $i = 1, 2$; a recent paper by Chen et al. (2020) provides an algorithm for checking identities in $\mathcal{K}_3$ in quasilinear time. The main result of the present paper extends this algorithm to the Kauffman monoid $\mathcal{K}_4$, which we define next.

2   Background II: Kauffman and Jones Monoids

Let n be an integer greater than 1. The *Kauffman monoid*[2] $\mathcal{K}_n$ can be defined as the monoid with n generators $c, h_1, \ldots, h_{n-1}$ subject to the following relations:

---

[2] The name comes from (Borisavljević et al. 2002); in the literature one also meets the name *Temperley–Lieb–Kauffman monoids* (see, e.g., Bokut' and Lee 2005).

$$h_i h_j = h_j h_i \qquad \text{if } |i - j| \geq 2, \ i, j = 1, \ldots, n - 1; \qquad (1)$$

$$h_i h_j h_i = h_i \qquad \text{if } |i - j| = 1, \ i, j = 1, \ldots, n - 1; \qquad (2)$$

$$h_i^2 = c h_i = h_i c \qquad \text{for each } i = 1, \ldots, n - 1. \qquad (3)$$

Kauffman monoids play an important role in knot theory, low-dimensional topology, topological quantum field theory, quantum groups, etc. As algebraic objects, these monoids belong to the family of so-called diagram or Brauer-type monoids that originally arose in representation theory (Brauer 1937) and have been intensively studied from various viewpoints over the last two decades; see, e.g., (Auinger 2012, 2014; Auinger et al. 2012, 2015; Dolinka and East 2017, 2018; Dolinka et al. 2015, 2017, 2019; East 2011a, 2011b, 2014a, 2014b, 2018, 2019a, 2019b; East and FitzGerald 2012; East and Gray 2017; East et al. 2018; FitzGerald and Lau 2011; Kudryavtseva et al. 2006; Kudryavtseva and Mazorchuk 2006, 2007; Lau and FitzGerald 2006; Maltcev and Mazorchuk 2007; Mazorchuk 1998, 2002) and references therein.

It is convenient to use, along with the above definition of the monoids $\mathcal{K}_n$ in terms of generators and relations, their more geometric definition due to Kauffman (1990). We present the latter definition, following (Auinger et al. 2015), where the monoids $\mathcal{K}_n$ arise as 'planar' submonoids in monoids from a more general (but easier to define) family.

Let $[n] := \{1, \ldots, n\}$, $[n]' := \{1', \ldots, n'\}$ be two disjoint copies of the set of the first n positive integers. Consider the set $\mathcal{W}_n$ of all pairs $(\pi; s)$ where π is a partition of the $2n$-element set $[n] \cup [n]'$ into 2-element blocks and s is a nonnegative integer referred to as the *number of circles*. Such a pair is represented by a *wire diagram* as shown in Fig. 1. We represent the elements of $[n]$ by points on the left hand side of the diagram (*left points*) while the elements of $[n]'$ are represented by points on the right hand side of the diagram (*right points*). We will omit the labels $1, 2, \ldots, 1', 2', \ldots$ in our further illustrations. Now, for $(\pi; s) \in \mathcal{W}_n$, we represent the number s by s closed curves ('circles') drawn

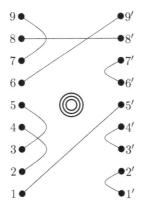

Fig. 1. Wire diagram representing an element of $\mathcal{W}_9$

somewhere within the diagram and each block of the partition π is represented by a line referred to as a *wire*. Thus, each wire connects two points; it is called an *ℓ-wire* if it connects two left points, an *r-wire* if it connects two right points, and a *t-wire* if it connects a left point with a right point. The wire diagram in Fig. 1 has three wires of each type and corresponds to the pair

$$\Big(\{\{1,5'\},\{2,4\},\{3,5\},\{6,9'\},\{7,9\},\{8,8'\},\{1',2'\},\{3',4'\},\{6',7'\}\};\, 3\Big).$$

Now we define a multiplication in $\mathcal{W}_n$. Pictorially, in order to multiply two diagrams, we glue their wires together by identifying each right point u' of the first diagram with the corresponding left point u of the second diagram. This way we obtain a new diagram whose left (respectively, right) points are the left (respectively, right) points of the first (respectively, second) diagram. Two points of this new diagram are connected in it if one can reach one of them from the other by walking along a sequence of consecutive wires of the factors, see Fig. 2. All circles of the factors are inherited by the product; in addition, some extra circles may arise from r-wires of the first diagram combined with ℓ-wires of the second diagram.

In more precise terms, if $\xi = (\pi_1; s_1)$, $\eta = (\pi_2; s_2)$, then a left point p and a right point q' of the product $\xi\eta$ are connected by a t-wire if and only if one of the following conditions holds:

- p — u' is a t-wire in ξ and u — q' is a t-wire in η for some $u \in [n]$;
- for some $s > 1$ and some $u_1, v_1, u_2, \ldots, v_{s-1}, u_s \in [n]$ (all pairwise distinct), p — u'_1 is a t-wire in ξ and u_s — q' is a t-wire in η, while u_i — v_i is an ℓ-wire in η and v'_i — u'_{i+1} is an r-wire in ξ for each $i = 1, \ldots, s-1$.

(The reader may trace an application of the second rule in Fig. 2, in which such a 'composite' t-wire connects 1 and $3'$ in the product diagram.)

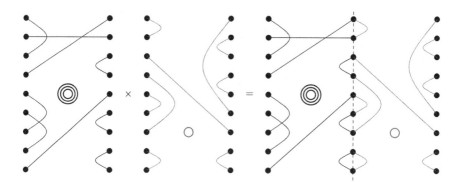

Fig. 2. Multiplication of wire diagrams

Analogous characterizations hold for the ℓ-wires and r-wires of $\xi\eta$. Here we include only the rules for forming ℓ-wires as the r-wires of the product are obtained in a perfectly symmetric way.

Two left points p and q of $\xi\eta$ are connected by an ℓ-wire if and only if one of the following conditions holds:

- $p \longrightarrow q$ is an ℓ-wire in ξ;
- for some $s \geq 1$ and some $u_1, v_1, u_2, \ldots, v_s \in [n]$ (all pairwise distinct), $p \longrightarrow u_1'$ and $q \longrightarrow v_s'$ are t-wires in ξ, while $u_i \longrightarrow v_i$ is an ℓ-wire in η for each $i = 1, \ldots, s$ and if $s > 1$, then $v_i' \longrightarrow u_{i+1}'$ is an r-wire in ξ for each $i = 1, \ldots, s - 1$.

(Again, Fig. 2 provides an instance of the second rule: look at the ℓ-wire that connects 6 and 8 in the product diagram.)

Finally, each circle of the product $\xi\eta$ corresponds to either a circle in ξ or η or a sequence $u_1, v_1, \ldots, u_s, v_s \in [n]$ with $s \geq 1$ and pairwise distinct $u_1, v_1, \ldots, u_s, v_s$ such that all $u_i \longrightarrow v_i$ are ℓ-wires in η, while all $v_i' \longrightarrow u_{i+1}'$ and $v_s' \longrightarrow u_1'$ are r-wires in ξ.

It easy to see that the above defined multiplication in $\mathcal{W}_n$ is associative and that the diagram with 0 circles and the n horizontal t-wires $1 \longrightarrow 1'$, $\ldots$, $n \longrightarrow n'$ is the identity element with respect to the multiplication. Thus, $\mathcal{W}_n$ is a monoid that we term the *wire monoid*.

Kauffman (1990) has defined the *connection monoid* $\mathcal{C}_n$ as the submonoid of $\mathcal{W}_n$ consisting of all elements of $\mathcal{W}_n$ that have a representation as a diagram whose wires do not cross. (Thus, the left factor and the product in the multiplication example in Fig. 2 are not elements of $\mathcal{C}_n$, while the right factor lies in $\mathcal{C}_n$.) Kauffman has shown that $\mathcal{C}_n$ is generated by the *hooks* $h_1, \ldots, h_{n-1}$, where

$$h_i := \Big(\{\{i, i+1\}, \{i', (i+1)'\}, \{j, j'\} \mid \text{for all } j \neq i, i+1\}; 0 \Big),$$

and the circle $c := \Big(\{\{j, j'\} \mid \text{for all } j = 1, \ldots, n\}; 1 \Big)$, see Fig. 3 for an illustration. It is easy to check that the generators $h_1, \ldots, h_{n-1}, c$ satisfy the relations (1)–(3), whence there exists a homomorphism from the Kauffman monoid $\mathcal{K}_n$ onto the connection monoid $\mathcal{C}_n$. In fact, this homomorphism is an isomorphism between $\mathcal{K}_n$ and $\mathcal{C}_n$; see (Kauffman 1990) for a proof outline and (Borisavljević et al. 2002) for a very detailed argument. Thus, we may (and will) identify $\mathcal{K}_n$ with $\mathcal{C}_n$ in what follows.

Denote by $\mathcal{J}_n$ the set of all diagrams in $\mathcal{K}_n$ without circles. Observe that this set is finite; in fact, it is known that the cardinality of $\mathcal{J}_n$ is the n-th Catalan number $\dfrac{1}{n+1}\dbinom{2n}{n}$. We define the multiplication of two diagrams in $\mathcal{J}_n$ as follows: we multiply the diagrams as elements of $\mathcal{K}_n$ and then reduce the product to a diagram in $\mathcal{J}_n$ by removing all circles. This multiplication makes $\mathcal{J}_n$ a monoid known as the *Jones monoid*[3]. Observe that $\mathcal{J}_n$ is **not** a submonoid of $\mathcal{K}_n$; at the same time, the 'erasing' map $\xi \mapsto \bar{\xi}$ that forgets the circles of each diagram $\xi \in \mathcal{K}_n$ is easily seen to be a surjective homomorphism of $\mathcal{K}_n$ onto $\mathcal{J}_n$.

---

[3] The name was suggested by Lau and FitzGerald (2006) to honor the contribution of V.F.R. Jones to the theory (see, e.g., Jones 1983 Section 4).

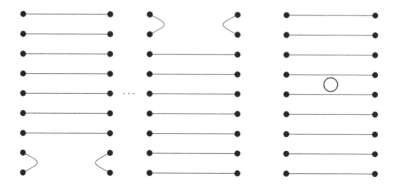

Fig. 3. The hooks $h_1, \ldots, h_8$ and the circle c in $\mathcal{C}_9$

The hooks $h_1, \ldots, h_{n-1}$ clearly satisfy $\bar{h}_i = h_i$ while $\bar{c}$ is the identity element of $\mathcal{J}_n$. This implies that the monoid $\mathcal{J}_n$ is generated by $\bar{h}_1, \ldots, \bar{h}_{n-1}$ and that $\bar{h}_i^2 = \bar{h}_i$ for each $i = 1, \ldots, n-1$. Moreover, if $\|\xi\|$ stands for the number of circles of the diagram $\xi \in \mathcal{K}_n$, then the map $\xi \mapsto (\bar{\xi}, \|\xi\|)$ is a bijection between $\mathcal{K}_n$ and the cartesian product of $\mathcal{J}_n$ with the set $\mathbb{N}_0$ of nonnegative integers. Here is a simple formula for multiplying diagrams from $\mathcal{K}_n$ in these 'coordinates':

$$(\bar{\xi}, \|\xi\|) \cdot (\bar{\eta}, \|\eta\|) = (\bar{\xi}\bar{\eta}, \|\xi\| + \|\eta\| + \langle \bar{\xi}, \bar{\eta} \rangle), \qquad (4)$$

where the term $\langle \bar{\xi}, \bar{\eta} \rangle$ denotes the number of circles removed when the product $\bar{\xi}\bar{\eta}$ in $\mathcal{J}_n$ is formed.

Now, following an idea by Auinger (personal communication), we embed the monoid $\mathcal{K}_n$ into a larger monoid $\widehat{\mathcal{K}}_n$ which is easier to deal with. In terms of generators and relations, the *extended Kauffman monoid* $\widehat{\mathcal{K}}_n$ can be defined as the monoid with $n+1$ generators $c, d, h_1, \ldots, h_{n-1}$ subject to the relations (1)–(3) and the additional relations

$$cd = dc = 1. \qquad (5)$$

Observe that the relations (3) and (5) imply that $dh_i = h_i d$ for each $i = 1, \ldots, n-1$. Indeed,

$$\begin{aligned}
dh_i &= d^2 c h_i && \text{since } dc = 1 \\
&= d^2 h_i c && \text{since } c h_i = h_i c \\
&= d^2 h_i c^2 d && \text{since } cd = 1 \\
&= d^2 c^2 h_i d && \text{since } c^2 h_i = h_i c^2 \\
&= h_i d && \text{since } d^2 c^2 = 1.
\end{aligned}$$

It is easy to see that the submonoid of $\widehat{\mathcal{K}}_n$ generated by $c, h_1, \ldots, h_{n-1}$ is isomorphic to $\mathcal{K}_n$.

The interpretation of the extended Kauffman monoid in terms of diagrams is a bit less natural as it requires introducing two sorts of circles: positive and negative. Each diagram may contain only circles of one sort. When two diagrams are multiplied, the following two rules are obeyed: all newly created circles (which arise when the diagrams are glued together) are positive; in addition, if the product diagram inherits some negative circles from its factors, then pairs of 'opposite' circles are consecutively removed until only circles of a single sort (or no circles at all) remain. The Kauffman monoid $\mathcal{K}_n$ is then nothing but the submonoid of all diagrams having only positive circles or no circles at all.

Clearly, the 'erasing' homomorphism of $\mathcal{K}_n$ onto $\mathcal{J}_n$ extends to the monoid $\widehat{\mathcal{K}}_n$. If we extend also the circle-counting map $\mathcal{K}_n \to \mathbb{N}_0$ to $\widehat{\mathcal{K}}_n$, letting $\|\xi\| = -n$ for each diagram ξ with n negative circles, we get that $\widehat{\mathcal{K}}_n$ can be identified with $\mathcal{J}_n \times \mathbb{Z}$, the cartesian product of the corresponding Jones monoid with the set of all integers, the multiplication on $\mathcal{J}_n \times \mathbb{Z}$ being defined by the formula (4).

3   Rees Matrix Semigroups and Their Identities

We briefly recall the Rees matrix construction; see (Clifford and Preston 1961 Chapter 3) for details and the explanation of the distinguished role played by this construction in the structure theory of semigroups. Let $\mathcal{G}$ be a group, 0 a symbol beyond $\mathcal{G}$, and I, Λ non-empty sets. Given a $\Lambda \times I$-matrix $P = (p_{\lambda i})$ over $\mathcal{G} \cup \{0\}$, we define a multiplication on the set $(I \times \mathcal{G} \times \Lambda) \cup \{0\}$ by the following rules:

$$a \cdot 0 = 0 \cdot a := 0 \quad \text{for all } a \in (I \times \mathcal{G} \times \Lambda) \cup \{0\},$$

$$(i, g, \lambda) \cdot (j, h, \mu) := \begin{cases} (i, g p_{\lambda j} h, \mu) & \text{if } p_{\lambda j} \neq 0, \\ 0 & \text{if } p_{\lambda j} = 0. \end{cases} \tag{6}$$

The multiplication is easily seen to be associative so that $(I \times \mathcal{G} \times \Lambda) \cup \{0\}$ becomes a semigroup. We denote it by $\mathcal{M}^0(I, \mathcal{G}, \Lambda; P)$ and call it the *Rees matrix semigroup over $\mathcal{G}$ with the sandwich matrix P*. If the matrix P has no zero entries, the set $I \times \mathcal{G} \times \Lambda$ forms a subsemigroup in $\mathcal{M}^0(I, \mathcal{G}, \Lambda; P)$. We denote this subsemigroup by $\mathcal{M}(I, \mathcal{G}, \Lambda; P)$ and apply the name 'Rees matrix semigroup' also to it.

We need a combinatorial characterization of identities holding in every Rees matrix semigroup over an abelian group. In order to formulate it, we recall a few definitions.

For a semigroup $\mathcal{S}$, the notation $\mathcal{S}^1$ stands for the least monoid containing $\mathcal{S}$, that is, $\mathcal{S}^1 := \mathcal{S}$ if $\mathcal{S}$ has an identity element and $\mathcal{S}^1 := \mathcal{S} \cup \{1\}$ if $\mathcal{S}$ has no identity element. In the latter case the multiplication in $\mathcal{S}$ is extended to $\mathcal{S}^1$ in a unique way such that the fresh symbol 1 becomes the identity element in $\mathcal{S}^1$. We adopt the following notational convention: for $s \in \mathcal{S}$, the expression s^0 stands for the identity element of $\mathcal{S}^1$.

Recall that we have fixed a countably infinite alphabet X. The monoid $X^* := (X^+)^1$ is called the *free monoid* over X. We say that a word $v \in X^+$ *occurs* in a word $w \in X^+$ if $w = u_1 v u_2$ for some $u_1, u_2 \in X^*$. Clearly, v may have several occurrences in w; we denote the number of occurrences of v in w by $\mathrm{occ}_v(w)$.

Proposition 1. *An identity $w \simeq w'$ holds in every Rees matrix semigroup over an abelian group if and only if the words w and w' satisfy the following three conditions:*

(a) *the first letter of w is the same as the first letter of w';*
(b) *the last letter of w is the same as the last letter of w';*
(c) *for each word v of length 2, $occ_v(w) = occ_v(w')$.*

Proof. The result is basically known. For the special case of Rees matrix semigroups of the form $\mathcal{M}(I, \mathcal{G}, \Lambda; P)$, it had been proven by Kim and Roush (1979); some other special cases were considered in a preprint by Mashevitzky (1980). For the reader's convenience, we provide a self-contained proof (which is not difficult at all).

For the 'only if' part, let $\mathbb{C}_\infty$ stand for the infinite cyclic group. We fix a generator c for $\mathbb{C}_\infty$ and consider the Rees matrix semigroup $\mathcal{S} := \mathcal{M}(\{1,2\}, \mathbb{C}_\infty, \{1,2\}; P)$ where $P := \begin{pmatrix} e & c \\ e & e \end{pmatrix}$, with $e := c^0$. Suppose the identity $w \simeq w'$ holds in $\mathcal{S}$. Define a substitution $\alpha \colon X \to \mathcal{S}$ by

$$x\alpha := \begin{cases} (1, e, 1) & \text{if } x \text{ is the first letter of } w, \\ (2, e, 2) & \text{otherwise.} \end{cases}$$

By (6), the first entry of the triple $w\alpha$ is 1, and since $w\alpha = w'\alpha$, so is the first entry of the triple $w'\alpha$. This is only possible provided that w' starts with x. We have thus shown that the condition (a) is satisfied. Similarly, by using the substitution $\omega \colon X \to \mathcal{S}$ such that

$$x\omega := \begin{cases} (1, e, 1) & \text{if } x \text{ is the last letter of } w, \\ (2, e, 2) & \text{otherwise,} \end{cases}$$

one verifies that (b) holds as well.

In order to verify (c), take a word v of length 2 that occurs in w. First consider the case of $v = yz$, with y and z being distinct letters. Here we invoke the substitution $\vartheta \colon X \to \mathcal{S}$ such that

$$x\vartheta := \begin{cases} (1, e, 1) & \text{if } x = y, \\ (2, e, 2) & \text{if } x = z, \\ (1, e, 2) & \text{otherwise.} \end{cases}$$

Using the rule (6) and the structure of the sandwich matrix P, we see that the middle entries of the triples $w\vartheta$ and $w'\vartheta$ are equal to $c^{occ_{yz}(w)}$ and respectively $c^{occ_{yz}(w')}$. Since $w\vartheta = w'\vartheta$, we get $occ_{yz}(w) = occ_{yz}(w')$.

It remains to analyze the case of $v = y^2$ for some letter y. In this case the substitution $\psi \colon X \to \mathcal{S}$ defined by

$$x\psi := \begin{cases} (2, e, 1) & \text{if } x = y, \\ (1, e, 2) & \text{otherwise} \end{cases}$$

has the property that the middle entries of the triples $w\psi$ and $w'\psi$ are equal to $c^{\mathrm{occ}_{y^2}(w)}$ and respectively $c^{\mathrm{occ}_{y^2}(w')}$. The equality $w\psi = w'\psi$ yields $\mathrm{occ}_{y^2}(w) = \mathrm{occ}_{y^2}(w')$. Thus, (c) holds for every word of length 2.

For the 'if' part, we isolate an observation that will be re-used later.

Lemma 1. *If two words w and w' satisfy the conditions* (a)–(c), *then each letter occurs in w and w' the same number of times.*

Proof. For each letter $x \in \mathrm{alph}(w)$, we have

$$\mathrm{occ}_x(w) = \sum_{y \in \mathrm{alph}(w)} \mathrm{occ}_{xy}(w) + \begin{cases} 1 & \text{if the last letter of } w \text{ is } x, \\ 0 & \text{otherwise.} \end{cases}$$

The same formula holds for w' and since, by (c), $\mathrm{occ}_{xy}(w) = \mathrm{occ}_{xy}(w')$ for every letter y and, by (b), w' ends with x if and only if so does w, we conclude that $\mathrm{occ}_x(w) = \mathrm{occ}_x(w')$. $\qquad\square$

Now consider an arbitrary abelian group $\mathcal{G}$ and an arbitrary Rees matrix semigroup $\mathcal{M}^0(I, \mathcal{G}, \Lambda; P)$ over $\mathcal{G}$. Take any substitution

$$\varphi \colon X \to \mathcal{M}^0(I, \mathcal{G}, \Lambda; P).$$

If $x\varphi = 0$ for some $x \in \mathrm{alph}(w)$, then clearly $w\varphi = 0$ and, by Lemma 1, $w'\varphi = 0$, too. Thus, assume that $x\varphi \in I \times \mathcal{G} \times \Lambda$ for every $x \in \mathrm{alph}(w)$. Let $x\varphi = (i(x), g(x), \lambda(x))$. The multiplication rule (6) then ensures that the equality $w\varphi = 0$ is only possible if $p_{\lambda(x)i(y)} = 0$ for some (not necessarily distinct) letters x, y such that the word xy occurs in w. By (c), xy occurs also in w' whence $w'\varphi = 0$. By symmetry, $w'\varphi = 0$ implies $w\varphi = 0$.

It remains to analyze the situation with both $w\varphi \neq 0$ and $w'\varphi \neq 0$, in which case $p_{\lambda(x)i(y)} \in \mathcal{G}$ whenever the word xy occurs in w. Let x_{first} and x_{last} be the first and respectively the last letter of w. Using the rule (6) and the fact that the group $\mathcal{G}$ is abelian, one readily computes that $w\varphi = (i(x_{\mathrm{first}}), g, \lambda(x_{\mathrm{last}}))$, with the middle entry g given by the following expression:

$$g = \prod_{x \in \mathrm{alph}(w)} g(x)^{\mathrm{occ}_x(w)} \quad \times \prod_{\substack{x,y \in \mathrm{alph}(w) \\ xy \text{ occurs in } w}} p_{\lambda(x)i(y)}^{\mathrm{occ}_{xy}(w)}.$$

In view of (a)–(c) and Lemma 1, we get $w'\varphi = (i(x_{\mathrm{first}}), g, \lambda(x_{\mathrm{last}}))$, with the same group entry g. Hence, the equality $w\varphi = w'\varphi$ holds. $\qquad\square$

4 Structure and Identities of $\mathcal{J}_4$

The main aim of the present paper is the identity checking problem for the Kauffman monoid $\mathcal{K}_4$. In view of the bijection between $\mathcal{K}_4$ and $\mathcal{J}_4 \times \mathbb{N}_0$, it is handy to have a closer look at the Jones monoid $\mathcal{J}_4$. The latter monoid consists of

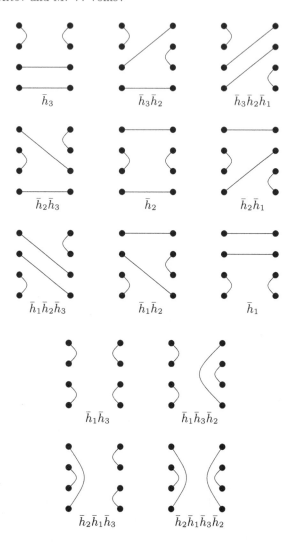

Fig. 4. The nonidentity diagrams in $\mathcal{J}_4$

$\dfrac{1}{5}\dbinom{8}{4} = 14$ diagrams: the identity diagram with four t-wires, nine diagrams with two t-wires, and four diagrams without t-wires. Figure 4 shows the nonidentity diagrams in $\mathcal{J}_4$.

As a warm-up for our core results, we prove here a structure property of the monoid $\mathcal{J}_4$. This property quickly leads to a polynomial time algorithm for CHECK-ID($\mathcal{J}_4$).

Let $\mathcal{J}_4^{\flat}$ be the ideal of $\mathcal{J}_4$ consisting of its nonidentity diagrams, that is, of the 13 diagrams shown in Fig. 4. We consider the following 'cutting' map $\mathfrak{c}\colon \mathcal{J}_4^{\flat} \to \mathcal{J}_4^{\flat}$: if a diagram has no t-wires, $\mathfrak{c}$ fixes it; if a diagram has two t-wires, $\mathfrak{c}$ cuts the

t-wires and then connects the loose ends, forming one new ℓ-wire and one new r-wire, see Fig. 5 for an illustration. More formally, the action of $\mathfrak{c}$ on a diagram with two t-wires amounts to:

- connecting the left points of the t-wires with an ℓ-wire;
- connecting the right points of the t-wires with an r-wire;
- removing the t-wires.

Observe that the above operations make sense for diagrams with two t-wires in the Jones monoid $\mathcal{J}_n$ for every even $n \geq 4$.

For the nine diagrams with two t-wires in the 3×3-matrix in the upper half of Fig. 4, the effect of the map $\mathfrak{c}$ can be described as follows:

- each of the four corner diagrams is sent to $\bar{h}_1 \bar{h}_3$;
- each of the two extreme diagrams in the middle row (column) is sent to $\bar{h}_2 \bar{h}_1 \bar{h}_3$ (respectively, $\bar{h}_1 \bar{h}_3 \bar{h}_2$);
- the central diagram is sent to $\bar{h}_2 \bar{h}_1 \bar{h}_3 \bar{h}_2$.

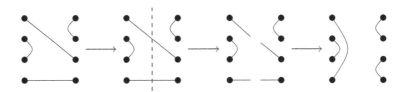

Fig. 5. The cutting map $\mathfrak{c}$ on $\mathcal{J}_4^\flat$

Lemma 2. *The map* $\mathfrak{c} \colon \mathcal{J}_4^\flat \to \mathcal{J}_4^\flat$ *is an endomorphism of* $\mathcal{J}_4^\flat$.

Proof. The lemma can be verified by a direct computation. We prefer a more geometric argument since it also works in a more general situation.

Let $\xi \in \mathcal{J}_4^\flat$ have two t-wires. Then the ℓ-wires of $\xi\mathfrak{c}$ are:

$$\text{the } \ell\text{-wire of } \xi, \text{ and} \tag{7}$$
$$\text{the } \ell\text{-wire that connects the left points of the } t\text{-wires of } \xi.$$

Now consider an arbitrary diagram $\eta \in \mathcal{J}_4^\flat$. The product $\xi\mathfrak{c} \cdot \eta\mathfrak{c}$ has the same ℓ-wires (7). The product $\xi\eta$ has either two or no t-wires. In the latter case its ℓ-wires coincide with those in (7). If $\xi\eta$ has two t-wires, their left points are the same as the left points of the t-wires of ξ whence the ℓ-wires of $(\xi\eta)\mathfrak{c}$ are those in (7) again.

We see that the ℓ-wires of $\xi\mathfrak{c} \cdot \eta\mathfrak{c}$ and $(\xi\eta)\mathfrak{c}$ are equal. By symmetry, $\xi\mathfrak{c} \cdot \eta\mathfrak{c}$ and $(\xi\eta)\mathfrak{c}$ have the same r-wires as well. Hence, $\xi\mathfrak{c} \cdot \eta\mathfrak{c} = (\xi\eta)\mathfrak{c}$. □

Remark 1. Let $n \geq 4$ be an even number. The set $\mathcal{J}_n^\flat$ of all diagrams with at most two t-wires forms a subsemigroup in the Jones monoid $\mathcal{J}_n$. The proof of Lemma 2 shows that the cutting map is an endomorphism of $\mathcal{J}_n^\flat$.

Remark 2. As the referee pointed out, the cutting map $\mathfrak{c}$ was first considered by East et al. (2018) in the course of their profound studies of congruences on Brauer monoids and also was used by Dolinka et al. (2019). The Brauer monoid $\mathcal{B}_n$ consists of all diagrams in $\mathcal{W}_n$ without circles. The multiplication in $\mathcal{B}_n$ is defined as follows: one multiplies diagrams as elements of $\mathcal{W}_n$ and then reduces the product to a diagram in $\mathcal{W}_n$ by removing all circles. Thus, the Brauer monoid $\mathcal{B}_n$ relates to the wire monoid $\mathcal{W}_n$ in the very same way as the Jones monoid $\mathcal{J}_n$ related to the Kauffman monoid $\mathcal{K}_n$. Clearly, the set $\mathcal{B}_n^\flat$ of all diagrams with at most two t-wires is a subsemigroup in $\mathcal{B}_n$ containing $\mathcal{J}_n^\flat$. Lemma 8.2 in (East et al. 2018) shows that the cutting map is an endomorphism of $\mathcal{B}_n^\flat$ for any even $n \geq 4$, and thus, it implies both Lemma 2 and Remark 1 of the present paper. The referee nevertheless recommended to retain the above proof of Lemma 2, as it is informative and keeps the paper self-contained, and we followed this recommendation.

An endomorphism that fixes each element in its image is called a *retraction*. We need the following folklore result of semigroup theory.

Lemma 3. *If φ is a retraction of a semigroup $\mathcal{S}$ such that $\mathcal{S}\varphi$ is an ideal of $\mathcal{S}$, then $\mathcal{S}$ is isomorphic to a subdirect product of the ideal $\mathcal{S}\varphi$ with the Rees quotient $\mathcal{S}/\mathcal{S}\varphi$.*   □

Proposition 2. *The semigroup $\mathcal{J}_4^\flat$ is isomorphic to a subdirect product of a 2×2 rectangular band with the Rees matrix semigroup $\mathcal{M}_3 :=$ $\mathcal{M}^0\left(\{1,2,3\}, \mathcal{E}, \{1,2,3\}; \left(\begin{smallmatrix} e & e & 0 \\ e & e & e \\ 0 & e & e \end{smallmatrix}\right)\right)$ over the one-element group $\mathcal{E} = \{e\}$.*

Proof. By the definition of the map $\mathfrak{c}\colon \mathcal{J}_4^\flat \to \mathcal{J}_4^\flat$, its image is the set $\mathcal{J}_4$ consisting of the four diagrams in $\mathcal{J}_4^\flat$ that have no t-wires. Since $\mathfrak{c}$ fixes each diagram in $\mathcal{J}_4$ and is an endomorphism by Lemma 2, $\mathfrak{c}$ is a retraction. Clearly, $\mathcal{J}_4$ is an ideal of $\mathcal{J}_4^\flat$. We are in a position to apply Lemma 3, which yields that $\mathcal{J}_4^\flat$ is isomorphic to a subdirect product of the ideal $\mathcal{J}_4$ with the Rees quotient $\mathcal{J}_4^\flat/\mathcal{J}_4$.

Obviously, $\mathcal{J}_4$ is a 2×2 rectangular band. As for the Rees quotient $\mathcal{J}_4^\flat/\mathcal{J}_4$, it can be mapped onto the Rees matrix semigroup $\mathcal{M}_3$ as follows: the zero of $\mathcal{J}_4^\flat/\mathcal{J}_4$ is sent to 0 and the diagram in the i-th row and j-th column of the 3×3-matrix in the upper half of Fig. 4 is sent to the triple (i, e, j). One can directly verify that the bijection defined this way is an isomorphism between $\mathcal{J}_4^\flat/\mathcal{J}_4$ and $\mathcal{M}_3$. □

Clearly, an identity holds in a subdirect product if and only if it holds in every factor of the product. Thus, Proposition 2 implies that an identity holds in the semigroup $\mathcal{J}_4^\flat$ if and only if it holds in both $\mathcal{J}_4$ and $\mathcal{M}_3$. Observe that the triples $(i, e, j) \in \mathcal{M}_3$ with $i, j \in \{1, 2\}$ form a 2×2 rectangular band. We see that $\mathcal{J}_4$ is isomorphic to a subsemigroup in $\mathcal{M}_3$, and thus, satisfies all identities of the latter semigroup. Hence, the semigroups $\mathcal{J}_4^\flat$ and $\mathcal{M}_3$ are *equationally equivalent*, that is, they satisfy the same identities.

A combinatorial characterization of the identities of $\mathcal{M}_3$ is known. Namely, it easily follows from a result by Trahtman (1981) that an identity $w \simeq w'$ holds in $\mathcal{M}_3$ if and only if the words w and w' satisfy the conditions (a) and (b) of Proposition 1 along with the following condition:

(c') each word of length 2 occurs in w if and only if it occurs in w'.

It is easy to characterize identities of a semigroup $\mathcal{S}$ that are inherited by the monoid $\mathcal{S}^1$. Namely, for a word $w \in X^+$ and a proper subset Y of $\mathrm{alph}(w)$, denote by w_Y the word obtained from w by removing all occurrences of the letters in Y. The following observation is another part of semigroup folklore.

Lemma 4. *Let $\mathcal{S}$ be a semigroup. The monoid $\mathcal{S}^1$ satisfies an identity $w \simeq w'$ with $\mathrm{alph}(w) = \mathrm{alph}(w')$ if and only if the identity $w_Y \simeq w'_Y$ holds in $\mathcal{S}$ for each $Y \subset \mathrm{alph}(w)$.* $\qquad\square$

The restriction $\mathrm{alph}(w) = \mathrm{alph}(w')$ in Lemma 4 is not essential for what follows because a monoid satisfying a semigroup identity $w \simeq w'$ with $\mathrm{alph}(w) \neq \mathrm{alph}(w')$ is easily seen to be a group while monoids we consider are very far from being groups.

Lemma 4 readily implies that if two semigroups $\mathcal{S}_1$ and $\mathcal{S}_2$ are equationally equivalent, so are the monoids $\mathcal{S}_1^1$ and $\mathcal{S}_2^1$. Hence, the Jones monoid $\mathcal{J}_4$ is equationally equivalent to the monoid $\mathcal{M}_3^1$. Summing up, we get the following characterization of the identities of the monoid $\mathcal{J}_4$.

Theorem 1. *An identity $w \simeq w'$ holds in the Jones monoid $\mathcal{J}_4$ if and only if $\mathrm{alph}(w) = \mathrm{alph}(w')$ and, for each $Y \subset \mathrm{alph}(w)$, the words $u := w_Y$ and $u' := w'_Y$ satisfy the following three conditions:*

(a) *the first letter of u is the same as the first letter of u';*
(b) *the last letter of u is the same as the last letter of u';*
(c') *each word of length 2 occurs in u if and only if it occurs in u'.* $\qquad\square$

Remark 3. It is not immediately clear whether Theorem 1 provides a polynomial time algorithm for CHECK-ID($\mathcal{J}_4$) since a brute force verification of the conditions (a)–(c') for every proper subset of the set $\mathrm{alph}(w)$ requires exponential in $|\mathrm{alph}(w)|$ time. In fact, there exist examples of finite semigroups $\mathcal{S}$ such that CHECK-ID($\mathcal{S}$) is in P while CHECK-ID($\mathcal{S}^1$) is coNP-complete, see, e.g., (Seif 2005; Klíma 2009). However, Seif and Szabó (2006) have proved that one can verify the conditions (a)–(c') in polynomial in $|ww'|$ time. Thus, CHECK-ID($\mathcal{J}_4$) lies in P. Moreover, using methods developed in (Chen et al. 2020), one can check whether or nor the monoid $\mathcal{J}_4$ satisfies an identity $w \simeq w'$ with $|\mathrm{alph}(w)| = k$ and $|ww'| = n$ in $O(kn \log(kn))$ time.

5   Structure of $\widehat{\mathcal{K}}_4$ and identities of $\mathcal{K}_4$

We are ready to attack the identity checking problem for the Kauffman monoid $\mathcal{K}_4$. We approach the problem via a structure property as we did in Sect. 4 for CHECK-ID($\mathcal{J}_4$). We start with lifting the cutting map $\mathfrak{c}$ from Jones to Kauffman monoids; technically, it is more convenient to lift the map to the extended Kauffman monoid $\widehat{\mathcal{K}}_4$.

Let $\widehat{\mathcal{K}}_4^\flat$ be the ideal of $\widehat{\mathcal{K}}_4$ consisting of all diagrams with at most two t-wires; in other words, $\widehat{\mathcal{K}}_4^\flat$ is nothing but the preimage of $\mathcal{J}_4^\flat$ under the erasing map $\xi \mapsto \bar{\xi}$. We define a map $\mathfrak{C}\colon \widehat{\mathcal{K}}_4^\flat \to \widehat{\mathcal{K}}_4^\flat$ as follows: $\mathfrak{C}$ fixes each diagram that has no t-wires; if a diagram has two t-wires, $\mathfrak{C}$ cuts out the middle of each t-wire and then connects the loose ends, forming one new ℓ-wire, one new r-wire, and a new **negative** circle, which then annihilates with a positive circle provided the initial diagram had positive circles. See Fig. 6 for an illustration.

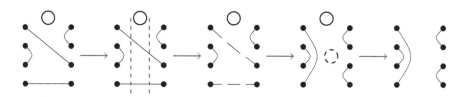

Fig. 6. The cutting map $\mathfrak{C}$ on $\widehat{\mathcal{K}}_4^\flat$; solid/dashed circles are positive/negative

Formally, if a diagram $\xi \in \widehat{\mathcal{K}}_4^\flat$ corresponds to the pair $\left(\bar{\xi}, \|\xi\|\right) \in \mathcal{J}_4^\flat \times \mathbb{Z}$, then $\xi\mathfrak{C}$ is the diagram corresponding to the pair $\left(\bar{\xi}\mathfrak{c}, \|\xi\| - 1\right)$ if ξ has two t-wires and $\xi\mathfrak{C} = \xi$ otherwise. Observe that $\overline{\xi\mathfrak{C}} = \bar{\xi}\mathfrak{c}$ for every $\xi \in \widehat{\mathcal{K}}_4^\flat$.

Lemma 5. *The map* $\mathfrak{C}\colon \widehat{\mathcal{K}}_4^\flat \to \widehat{\mathcal{K}}_4^\flat$ *is an endomorphism of* $\widehat{\mathcal{K}}_4^\flat$.

Proof. We have to show that $\xi\mathfrak{C} \cdot \eta\mathfrak{C} = (\xi\eta)\mathfrak{C}$ for arbitrary diagrams $\xi, \eta \in \widehat{\mathcal{K}}_4^\flat$. If both ξ and η have no t-wires, so does $\xi\eta$, and the required equality clearly holds. Thus, we may assume that at least one of the diagrams has two t-wires. Due to the symmetry, it is sufficient to analyze the situation when ξ has two t-wires.

In terms of the coordinatization of $\widehat{\mathcal{K}}_4$, the diagram $\xi\mathfrak{C} \cdot \eta\mathfrak{C}$ corresponds to the pair $\left(\overline{\xi\mathfrak{C} \cdot \eta\mathfrak{C}}, \|\xi\mathfrak{C} \cdot \eta\mathfrak{C}\|\right)$ while the pair corresponding to $(\xi\eta)\mathfrak{C}$ is $\left(\overline{(\xi\eta)\mathfrak{C}}, \|(\xi\eta)\mathfrak{C}\|\right)$. The equality of the first entries of these pairs easily follows from Lemma 2. Indeed,

$$
\begin{aligned}
\overline{\xi\mathfrak{C} \cdot \eta\mathfrak{C}} = \overline{\xi\mathfrak{C}} \cdot \overline{\eta\mathfrak{C}} = \bar{\xi}\mathfrak{c} \cdot \bar{\eta}\mathfrak{c} \qquad &\text{since } \xi \mapsto \bar{\xi} \text{ is a homomorphism} \\
= (\bar{\xi}\bar{\eta})\mathfrak{c} \qquad &\text{by Lemma 2} \\
= (\overline{\xi\eta})\mathfrak{c} = \overline{(\xi\eta)\mathfrak{C}} \qquad &\text{since } \xi \mapsto \bar{\xi} \text{ is a homomorphism.}
\end{aligned}
$$

Thus, it remains to compute the numbers of circles in $\xi\mathfrak{C} \cdot \eta\mathfrak{C}$ and in $(\xi\eta)\mathfrak{C}$ and to verify that these numbers are equal, that is, $\|\xi\mathfrak{C} \cdot \eta\mathfrak{C}\| = \|(\xi\eta)\mathfrak{C}\|$. The following aims to present the computation in a compact way.

From (4), we see that $\|\xi\mathfrak{C} \cdot \eta\mathfrak{C}\| = \|\xi\mathfrak{C}\| + \|\eta\mathfrak{C}\| + \langle \overline{\xi\mathfrak{C}}, \overline{\eta\mathfrak{C}} \rangle$. Since $\overline{\xi\mathfrak{C}} = \bar{\xi}\mathfrak{c}$ and $\overline{\eta\mathfrak{C}} = \bar{\eta}\mathfrak{c}$, the desired equality can be rewritten as

$$\|\xi\mathfrak{C}\| + \|\eta\mathfrak{C}\| + \langle \bar{\xi}\mathfrak{c}, \bar{\eta}\mathfrak{c} \rangle = \|(\xi\eta)\mathfrak{C}\|. \tag{8}$$

We say that a diagram $\gamma \in \mathcal{J}_4^\flat$ *matches* a diagram $\delta \in \mathcal{J}_4^\flat$ if for every r-wire $\{i', j'\}$ of γ, the set $\{i, j\}$ occurs as an ℓ-wire in δ. (Observe that we do not require the opposite: δ may have an ℓ-wire $\{s, t\}$, say, such that $\{s', t'\}$ is not an r-wire in γ.) Clearly, gluing $\{i', j'\}$ with $\{i, j\}$ creates a circle when the product $\gamma\delta$ is being formed.

We split the verification of (8) into three cases. Each of these cases covers a certain number of pairs $(\bar{\xi}, \bar{\eta})$ amongst $9 \times 13 = 117$ pairs that are subject to checking. (The assumption that ξ has two t-wires restricts the choice of $\bar{\xi}$ to the nine diagrams in the upper half of Fig. 4 while $\bar{\eta}$ can be any of the 13 diagrams from $\mathcal{J}_4^\flat$.) The reader may find it helpful to trace how the argument of each case works on a typical example; for this, we indicate such examples, after stating the conditions of the cases.

Case 1: $\bar{\xi}$ matches $\bar{\eta}$.

Here typical representatives are the pairs $(\bar{h}_1, \bar{h}_1\bar{h}_2)$ and $(\bar{h}_1, \bar{h}_1\bar{h}_3)$.

The condition that $\bar{\xi}$ matches $\bar{\eta}$ means that $\langle \bar{\xi}, \bar{\eta} \rangle = 1$. Further, it is easy to see that $\bar{\xi}\mathfrak{c}$ matches $\bar{\eta}\mathfrak{c}$ whence $\langle \bar{\xi}\mathfrak{c}, \bar{\eta}\mathfrak{c} \rangle = 2$. We have $\|\xi\mathfrak{C}\| = \|\xi\| - 1$ as ξ has two t-wires. If η also has two t-wires, then $\|\eta\mathfrak{C}\| = \|\eta\| - 1$. Thus, computing the left hand side of (8) yields

$$\|\xi\mathfrak{C}\| + \|\eta\mathfrak{C}\| + \langle \bar{\xi}\mathfrak{c}, \bar{\eta}\mathfrak{c} \rangle = (\|\xi\| - 1) + (\|\eta\| - 1) + 2 = \|\xi\| + \|\eta\|.$$

Besides that, the condition that $\bar{\xi}$ matches $\bar{\eta}$ implies that the t-wires of ξ and η combine and provide two t-wires in $\xi\eta$. Using this and (4), we get

$$\|(\xi\eta)\mathfrak{C}\| = \|\xi\eta\| - 1 = \|\xi\| + \|\eta\| + \langle \bar{\xi}, \bar{\eta} \rangle - 1 = \|\xi\| + \|\eta\| + 1 - 1 = \|\xi\| + \|\eta\|.$$

We conclude that the equality (8) holds.

Now assume that η has no t-wires. Then $\|\eta\mathfrak{C}\| = \|\eta\|$, whence the left hand side of (8) is equal to $\|\xi\| + \|\eta\| + 1$. However, in this subcase, the product $\xi\eta$ also omits t-wires and $\|(\xi\eta)\mathfrak{C}\| = \|\xi\eta\| = \|\xi\| + \|\eta\| + 1$, too. Thus, the equality (8) persists.

Case 2: $\bar{\xi}$ does not match $\bar{\eta}$ but $\bar{\xi}\mathfrak{c}$ matches $\bar{\eta}\mathfrak{c}$.

Here a typical representative is the pair $(\bar{h}_1, \bar{h}_3)$.

Case 2 is only possible if η has two t-wires whence $\|\eta\mathfrak{C}\| = \|\eta\| - 1$. We have $\langle \bar{\xi}, \bar{\eta} \rangle = 0$ but $\langle \bar{\xi}\mathfrak{c}, \bar{\eta}\mathfrak{c} \rangle = 2$. Thus, the left hand side of (8) is

$$\|\xi\mathfrak{C}\| + \|\eta\mathfrak{C}\| + \langle \bar{\xi}\mathfrak{c}, \bar{\eta}\mathfrak{c} \rangle = (\|\xi\| - 1) + (\|\eta\| - 1) + 2 = \|\xi\| + \|\eta\|.$$

Further, under the conditions of Case 2, $\xi\eta$ cannot possess t-wires. Therefore, $\|(\xi\eta)\mathfrak{C}\| = \|\xi\eta\| = \|\xi\| + \|\eta\|$, and the equality (8) holds.

Case 3: $\bar{\xi}\mathfrak{c}$ does not match $\bar{\eta}\mathfrak{c}$.

Here typical representatives are the pairs $(\bar{h}_1, \bar{h}_2)$ and $(\bar{h}_1, \bar{h}_2\bar{h}_1\bar{h}_3)$.

Since $\bar{\xi}\mathfrak{c}$ does not match $\bar{\eta}\mathfrak{c}$, we have $\langle\bar{\xi}\mathfrak{c}, \bar{\eta}\mathfrak{c}\rangle = 1$. In addition, $\bar{\xi}$ cannot match $\bar{\eta}$ whence $\langle\bar{\xi}, \bar{\eta}\rangle = 0$. If η has two t-wires, $\|\eta\mathfrak{C}\| = \|\eta\| - 1$ and the left hand side of (8) becomes

$$\|\xi\mathfrak{C}\| + \|\eta\mathfrak{C}\| + \langle\bar{\xi}\mathfrak{c}, \bar{\eta}\mathfrak{c}\rangle = (\|\xi\| - 1) + (\|\eta\| - 1) + 1 = \|\xi\| + \|\eta\| - 1.$$

If the r-wire of ξ is $\{i', j'\}$, the ℓ-wire of η must be $\{j, k\}$ for some $k \neq i$. The set $\{1, 2, 3, 4\} \setminus \{i, j, k\}$ consists of a unique number h, say. Then one of the t-wires of ξ has h' as its right point while one of the t-wires of η has h as its left point, and we see that $\xi\eta$ has got a t-wire. From this and (4), we compute

$$\|(\xi\eta)\mathfrak{C}\| = \|\xi\eta\| - 1 = \|\xi\| + \|\eta\| + \langle\bar{\xi}, \bar{\eta}\rangle - 1 = \|\xi\| + \|\eta\| - 1,$$

whence the equality (8) holds.

Finally, consider the subcase when η has no t-wires. Then $\|\eta\mathfrak{C}\| = \|\eta\|$ and the left hand side of (8) becomes $\|\xi\mathfrak{C}\| + \|\eta\mathfrak{C}\| + \langle\bar{\xi}\mathfrak{c}, \bar{\eta}\mathfrak{c}\rangle = (\|\xi\| - 1) + \|\eta\| + 1 = \|\xi\| + \|\eta\|$. Of course, if η omits t-wires, so does $\xi\eta$, whence $\|(\xi\eta)\mathfrak{C}\| = \|\xi\eta\| = \|\xi\| + \|\eta\|$, and the equality (8) holds again. $\qquad\square$

Remark 4. When we introduced the extended Kauffman monoids $\widehat{\mathcal{K}}_n$, we said that they are easier to deal with, compared with the 'standard' Kauffman monoids $\mathcal{K}_n$. Lemma 5 provides a supporting evidence for this claim. Indeed, it is not clear if the semigroup $\mathcal{K}_4^\flat$ consisting of diagrams with at most two t-wires from $\mathcal{K}_4$ admits any 'nice' endomorphism similar to the cutting map $\mathfrak{C}\colon \widehat{\mathcal{K}}_4^\flat \to \widehat{\mathcal{K}}_4^\flat$. We mention in passing that working with the monoid $\widehat{\mathcal{K}}_3$ rather than $\mathcal{K}_3$ would have somewhat simplified also the proofs of the main results in (Chen et al. 2020).

Remark 5. One can define the *extended wire monoid* $\widehat{\mathcal{W}}_n$ by allowing diagrams with negative circles and using the same multiplication as in $\widehat{\mathcal{K}}_n$. Let $\widehat{\mathcal{W}}_4^\flat$ be the ideal of $\widehat{\mathcal{W}}_4$ consisting of all diagrams with at most two t-wires. The referee observed that the cutting map $\mathfrak{C}\colon \widehat{\mathcal{K}}_4^\flat \to \widehat{\mathcal{K}}_4^\flat$ extends to an endomorphism of $\widehat{\mathcal{W}}_4^\flat$.

Recall that $\mathbb{C}_\infty$ stands for the infinite cyclic group. As above, we fix a generator c of $\mathbb{C}_\infty$ and denote by e the identity element of the group. Consider the Rees matrix semigroups $\mathcal{RC}_2 := \mathcal{M}\left(\{1,2\}, \mathbb{C}_\infty, \{1,2\}; \begin{pmatrix} c^2 & c \\ c & c^2 \end{pmatrix}\right)$ and $\mathcal{MC}_3 := \mathcal{M}^0\left(\{1,2,3\}, \mathbb{C}_\infty, \{1,2,3\}; \begin{pmatrix} c & e & 0 \\ e & c & e \\ 0 & e & c \end{pmatrix}\right)$.

Proposition 3. *The semigroup $\widehat{\mathcal{K}}_4^\flat$ is isomorphic to a subdirect product of the Rees matrix semigroups $\mathcal{RC}_2$ and $\mathcal{MC}_3$.*

Proof. By the definition of the map $\mathfrak{C}: \widehat{\mathcal{K}}_4^\flat \to \widehat{\mathcal{K}}_4^\flat$, its image is the set $\widehat{\mathcal{J}}_4$ of all diagrams in $\widehat{\mathcal{K}}_4^\flat$ that have no t-wires. By Lemma 5 $\mathfrak{C}$ is a retraction. Since $\widehat{\mathcal{J}}_4$ is an ideal of $\widehat{\mathcal{K}}_4^\flat$, Lemma 3 applies, providing a decomposition of $\widehat{\mathcal{K}}_4^\flat$ into a subdirect product of $\widehat{\mathcal{J}}_4$ with the Rees quotient $\widehat{\mathcal{K}}_4^\flat/\widehat{\mathcal{J}}_4$.

It remains to show that $\widehat{\mathcal{J}}_4$ is isomorphic to $\mathcal{RC}_2$ and $\widehat{\mathcal{K}}_4^\flat/\widehat{\mathcal{J}}_4$ is isomorphic to $\mathcal{MC}_3$. Both isomorphisms are easy to describe in terms of the coordinatization of diagrams from $\widehat{\mathcal{K}}_4$ by pairs from $\mathcal{J}_4 \times \mathbb{Z}$. If $\eta \in \widehat{\mathcal{J}}_4$ corresponds to the pair $(\bar\eta, m) \in \mathcal{J}_4 \times \mathbb{Z}$ and the diagram $\bar\eta$ occurs in the i-th row and j-th column of the 2×2-matrix in the lower half of Fig. 4, then η is sent to the triple $(i, c^m, j) \in \mathcal{RC}_2$. Similarly, if $\xi \in \widehat{\mathcal{K}}_4^\flat \setminus \widehat{\mathcal{J}}_4$ corresponds to the pair $(\bar\xi, n) \in \mathcal{J}_4 \times \mathbb{Z}$ and the diagram $\bar\xi$ occurs in the k-th row and ℓ-th column of the 3×3-matrix in the upper half of Fig. 4, then ξ is sent to the triple $(k, c^n, \ell) \in \mathcal{MC}_3$. Finally, the zero of the Rees quotient $\widehat{\mathcal{K}}_4^\flat/\widehat{\mathcal{J}}_4$ is sent to $0 \in \mathcal{MC}_3$. Thus, we have got a bijection between $\widehat{\mathcal{J}}_4$ and $\mathcal{RC}_2$, as well as a bijection between $\widehat{\mathcal{K}}_4^\flat/\widehat{\mathcal{J}}_4$ and $\mathcal{MC}_3$. The verification that these bijections constitute semigroup isomorphisms is immediate. □

Recall the description of the identities of $\mathcal{K}_3$ from (Chen et al. 2020).

Theorem 2. *An identity $w \simeq w'$ holds in the Kauffman monoid $\mathcal{K}_3$ if and only if $alph(w) = alph(w')$ and, for each $Y \subset alph(w)$, the words $u := w_Y$ and $u' := w'_Y$ satisfy the following three conditions:*

(a) *the first letter of u is the same as the first letter of u';*
(b) *the last letter of u is the same as the last letter of u';*
(c) *for each word of length 2, the number of its occurrences in u is the same as the number of its occurrences in u'.* □

Theorem 3. *The monoids $\mathcal{K}_3$ and $\mathcal{K}_4$ are equationally equivalent.*

Proof. The monoid $\mathcal{K}_3$ naturally embeds into $\mathcal{K}_4$: the submonoid of $\mathcal{K}_4$ generated by the hooks h_1, h_2 and the circle c is isomorphic to $\mathcal{K}_3$. Therefore, every identity that holds in $\mathcal{K}_4$ must hold in $\mathcal{K}_3$. In order to show the converse, we employ Theorem 2. Namely, we are going to verify that every identity $w \simeq w'$ that satisfies the conditions of Theorem 2 holds in the extended Kauffman monoid $\widehat{\mathcal{K}}_4$. Since $\mathcal{K}_4$ embeds into $\widehat{\mathcal{K}}_4$, this will prove the equational equivalence of $\mathcal{K}_3$ with $\mathcal{K}_4$, and moreover, with $\widehat{\mathcal{K}}_4$.

We have to check that $w\varphi = w'\varphi$ for an arbitrary homomorphism $\varphi: X^+ \to \widehat{\mathcal{K}}_4$. Clearly, $\widehat{\mathcal{K}}_4$ is the disjoint union of its group of units $\mathcal{H}$ generated (as a semigroup) by c and d and the ideal $\widehat{\mathcal{K}}_4^\flat$. Let $Y := \{y \in alph(w) \mid y\varphi \in \mathcal{H}\}$. Since $cd = dc = 1$, we write c^{-1} for d, and for each $y \in Y$, we let $k_y \in \mathbb{Z}$ be such that $y\varphi = c^{k_y}$. Denote the sum $\sum_{y \in Y} occ_y(w)k_y$ by N_Y. By Lemma 1 we have $occ_y(w) = occ_y(w')$, whence the sum $\sum_{y \in Y} occ_y(w')k_y$ is also equal to N_Y. If $Y = alph(w)$, we have $w\varphi = c^{N_Y} = w'\varphi$, and we are done.

Consider the situation where $Y \subset \mathrm{alph}(w)$. Using the fact that the generators c and d commute with the hooks h_1, h_2, h_3, we can represent $w\varphi$ and $w'\varphi$ as $c^{N_Y} w_Y \varphi$ and $c^{N_Y} w'_Y \varphi$ respectively. Therefore it remains to verify that $w_Y \varphi = w'_Y \varphi$, and for this, it suffices to show that the identity $u \simeq u'$ with $u := w_Y$ and $u' := w'_Y$ holds in the semigroup $\widehat{\mathcal{K}}^\flat_4$. Since the words u and u' satisfy the conditions (a)–(c), the identity $u \simeq u'$ holds in every Rees matrix semigroup over an abelian group by Proposition 1. In particular, $u \simeq u'$ holds in the semigroups $\mathcal{RC}_2$ and $\mathcal{MC}_3$, and by Proposition 3 it holds also in $\widehat{\mathcal{K}}^\flat_4$, as required. □

Remark 6. The result of Theorem 3 was unexpected for us since, informally speaking, the monoid $\mathcal{K}_4$ appeared to be much more complicated than its submonoid $\mathcal{K}_3$ and it was rather hard to believe that $\mathcal{K}_4$ could inherit all identities of the submonoid. Observe that the Jones monoids $\mathcal{J}_3$ and $\mathcal{J}_4$ are not equationally equivalent: $\mathcal{J}_3$ satisfies the identity $x^2 \simeq x$ that clearly fails in $\mathcal{J}_4$. Moreover, it follows from a result by Trahtman (1988) that the identities of $\mathcal{J}_3$ and $\mathcal{J}_4$ are very different in a sense: there are uncountably many pairwise equationally non-equivalent semigroups whose identity sets strictly contain the identity set of $\mathcal{J}_4$ and are strictly contained in that of $\mathcal{J}_3$. Further, the wire monoids $\mathcal{W}_3$ and $\mathcal{W}_4$ are not equationally equivalent: one can verify that $\mathcal{W}_3$ satisfies the identity $x^7 yx \simeq xyx^7$ that fails in $\mathcal{W}_4$. The same identity $x^7 yx \simeq xyx^7$ can be used to show that the Brauer monoids $\mathcal{B}_3$ and $\mathcal{B}_4$ are not equationally equivalent. Theorem 3 makes a strong contrast to these facts.

Using a suitable reformulation of Theorem 2, Chen et al. (2020 Section 2) have developed an algorithm that, given an identity $w \simeq w'$ with $|\mathrm{alph}(w)| = k$ and $|ww'| = n$, verifies whether or nor the identity holds in the monoid $\mathcal{K}_3$ in $O(kn \log(kn))$ time. Theorem 3 implies that this algorithm can be used to check identities in the monoid $\mathcal{K}_4$. In particular, we have the following fact.

Corollary 1. *The problem* CHECK-ID*($\mathcal{K}_4$) lies in* P. □

It has been shown in (Chen et al. 2020 Proposition 6) that the equational equivalence of $\mathcal{K}_3$ and $\mathcal{K}_4$ does not extend to the monoid $\mathcal{K}_5$. For instance, the identity $x^2 yx \simeq xyx^2$, which holds in $\mathcal{K}_3$ and $\mathcal{K}_4$ by Theorems 2 and 3, fails in $\mathcal{K}_5$ under the substitution $x \mapsto h_1 h_2 h_3$, $y \mapsto h_4$. The proof in (Chen et al. 2020) relies on a normal form for the elements of the monoid $\mathcal{K}_n$ suggested by Jones (1983). Figure 7 illustrates this example; in fact, Fig. 7 can be treated as an alternative argument showing that the identity $x^2 yx \simeq xyx^2$ fails in $\mathcal{K}_5$ in a way that complies with the geometric approach of the present paper.

At the moment, we possess no characterization of the identities of the monoid $\mathcal{K}_n$ for any $n > 4$. Neither do we know whether there are other pairs of equationally equivalent Kauffman monoids besides $\mathcal{K}_3$ and $\mathcal{K}_4$.

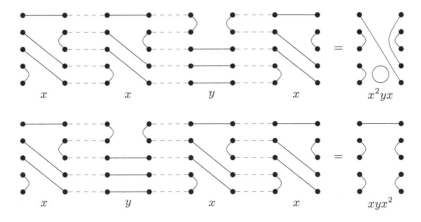

Fig. 7. The identity $x^2yx \doteq xyx^2$ fails in $\mathcal{K}_5$

Acknowledgements. The authors are grateful to the referee for his/her remarks and suggestions, especially, for the observations registered in Remarks 2 and 5.

References

Adian, S.: Identities in special semigroups. Doklady AN SSSR **143**(3), 499–502 (1962). (Russian; Engl. translation Soviet Math. Dokl. **3**, 401–404)

Almeida, J., Volkov, M.V., Goldberg, S.V.: Complexity of the identity checking problem for finite semigroups. Zap. Nauchn. Seminarov POMI **358**, 5–22 (2008). https://doi. org/10.1007/s10958-009-9397-z. (Russian; Engl. translation J. Math. Sci. **158**(5), 605–614 (2009))

Auinger, K.: Krohn-Rhodes complexity of Brauer type semigroups. Port. Math. **69**(4), 341–360 (2012). https://doi.org/10.4171/PM/1921

Auinger, K.: Pseudovarieties generated by Brauer-type monoids. Forum Math. **26**, 1–24 (2014). https://doi.org/10.1515/form.2011.146

Auinger, K., Chen, Y., Hu, X., Luo, Y., Volkov, M.V.: The finite basis problem for Kauffman monoids. Algebra Univers. **74**(3–4), 333–350 (2015). https://doi.org/10. 1007/s00012-015-0356-x

Auinger, K., Dolinka, I., Volkov, M.V.: Equational theories of semigroups with involution. J. Algebra **369**, 203–225 (2012). https://doi.org/10.1016/j.jalgebra.2012.06. 021

Bokut, L.A., Lee, D.V.: A Gröbner-Shirshov basis for the Temperley-Lieb-Kauffman monoid. Izvestija Ural. Gos. Univ. **36**, 47–66 (2005). (Russian)

Borisavljević, M., Došen, K., Petrić, Z.: Kauffman monoids. J. Knot Theory Ramifications **11**, 127–143 (2002). https://doi.org/10.1142/S0218216502001524

Brauer, R.: On algebras which are connected with the semisimple continuous groups. Ann. Math. **38**, 857–872 (1937). https://doi.org/10.2307/1968843

Clifford, A.H., Preston, G.B.: The Algebraic Theory of Semigroups, vol. I. American Mathematical Society, Providence (1961)

Chen, Y., Hu, X., Kitov, N.V., Luo, Y., Volkov, M.V.: Identities of the Kauffman monoid $\mathcal{K}_3$. Comm. Algebra **48**(5), 1956–1968 (2020). https://doi.org/10.1080/ 00927872.2019.1710164

Daviaud, L., Johnson, M., Kambites, M.: Identities in upper triangular tropical matrix semigroups and the bicyclic monoid. J. Algebra **501**, 503–525 (2018). https://doi.org/10.1016/j.jalgebra.2017.12.032

Dolinka, I., East, J.: The idempotent-generated subsemigroup of the Kauffman monoid. Glasgow Math. J. **59**(3), 673–683 (2017). https://doi.org/10.1017/S0017089516000471

Dolinka, I., East, J.: Twisted Brauer monoids. Proc. R. Soc. Edinb. Ser. A **148A**, 731–750 (2018). https://doi.org/10.1017/S0308210517000282

Dolinka, I., et al.: Enumeration of idempotents in diagram semigroups and algebras. J. Comb. Theory Ser. A **131**, 119–152 (2015). https://doi.org/10.1016/j.jcta.2014.11.008

Dolinka, I., et al.: Enumeration of idempotents in planar diagram monoids. J. Algebra **522**, 351–385 (2019). https://doi.org/10.1016/j.jalgebra.2018.11.014

Dolinka, I., East, J., Gray, R.: Motzkin monoids and partial Brauer monoids. J. Algebra **471**, 251–298 (2017). https://doi.org/10.1016/j.jalgebra.2016.09.018

East, J.: Generators and relations for partition monoids and algebras. J. Algebra **339**, 1–26 (2011a). https://doi.org/10.1016/j.jalgebra.2011.04.008

East, J.: On the singular part of the partition monoid. Int. J. Algebra Comput. **21**(1–2), 147–178 (2011b). https://doi.org/10.1142/S021819671100611X

East, J.: Partition monoids and embeddings in 2-generator regular *-semigroups. Periodica Math. Hung. **69**(2), 211–221 (2014a). https://doi.org/10.1007/s10998-014-0055-y

East, J.: Infinite partition monoids. Int. J. Algebra Comput. **24**(4), 429–460 (2014b). https://doi.org/10.1142/S0218196714500209

East, J.: Presentations for (singular) partition monoids: a new approach. Math. Proc. Camb. Philos. Soc. **165**(3), 549–562 (2018). https://doi.org/10.1017/S030500411700069X

East, J.: Idempotents and one-sided units in infinite partial Brauer monoids. J. Algebra **534**, 427–482 (2019a). https://doi.org/10.1016/j.jalgebra.2019.05.034

East, J.: Presentations for rook partition monoids and algebras and their singular ideals. J. Pure Appl. Algebra **223**(3), 1097–1122 (2019b). https://doi.org/10.1016/j.jpaa.2018.05.016

East, J., FitzGerald, D.G.: The semigroup generated by the idempotents of a partition monoid. J. Algebra **372**, 108–133 (2012). https://doi.org/10.1016/j.jalgebra.2012.09.014

East, J., Gray, R.: Diagram monoids and Graham-Houghton graphs: idempotents and generating sets of ideals. J. Comb. Theory Ser. A **146**, 63–128 (2017). https://doi.org/10.1016/j.jcta.2016.09.001

East, J., Mitchell, J.D., Ruškuc, N., Torpey, M.: Congruence lattices of finite diagram monoids. Adv. Math. **333**, 931–1003 (2018). https://doi.org/10.1016/j.aim.2018.05.016

FitzGerald, D.G., Lau, K.W.: On the partition monoid and some related semigroups. Bull. Aust. Math. Soc. **83**(2), 273–288 (2011). https://doi.org/10.1017/S0004972710001851

Horváth, G., Lawrence, J., Mérai, L., Szabó, C.: The complexity of the equivalence problem for nonsolvable groups. Bull. Lond. Math. Soc. **39**(3), 433–438 (2007). https://doi.org/10.1112/blms/bdm030

Jackson, M., McKenzie, R.: Interpreting graph colorability in finite semigroups. Int. J. Algebra Comput. **16**(1), 119–140 (2006). https://doi.org/10.1142/S0218196706002846

Jones, V.F.R.: Index for subfactors. Inventiones Math. **72**, 1–25 (1983). https://doi. org/10.1007/BF01389127

Kauffman, L.: An invariant of regular isotopy. Trans. Am. Math. Soc. **318**, 417–471 (1990). https://doi.org/10.1090/S0002-9947-1990-0958895-7

Kharlampovich, O.G., Sapir, M.V.: Algorithmic problems in varieties. Int. J. Algebra Comput. **5**(4–5), 379–602 (1995). https://doi.org/10.1142/S0218196795000227

Kim, K.H., Roush, F.: The semigroup of adjacency patterns of words. In: Algebraic Theory of Semigroups, pp. 281–297. North Holland, Amsterdam (1979). (Colloq. Math. Soc. János Bolyai **20**)

Kisielewicz, A.: Complexity of semigroup identity checking. Int. J. Algebra Comput. **14**(4), 455–464 (2004). https://doi.org/10.1142/S0218196704001840

Klíma, O.: Complexity issues of checking identities in finite monoids. Semigroup Forum **79**(3), 435–444 (2009). https://doi.org/10.1007/s00233-009-9180-y

Klíma, O.: Identity checking problem for transformation monoids. Semigroup Forum **84**(3), 487–498 (2012). https://doi.org/10.1007/s00233-012-9401-7

Kudryavtseva, G., Maltcev, V., Mazorchuk, V.: $\mathcal{L}$- and $\mathcal{R}$-cross-sections in the Brauer semigroup. Semigroup Forum **72**(2), 223–248 (2006). https://doi.org/10. 1007/s00233-005-0511-3

Kudryavtseva, G., Mazorchuk, V.: On presentations of Brauer-type monoids. Cent. Eur. J. Math. **4**(3), 413–434 (2006). https://doi.org/10.2478/s11533-006-0017-6

Kudryavtseva, G., Mazorchuk, V.: On conjugation in some transformation and Brauer-type semigroups. Publ. Math. Debrecen **70**(1–2), 19–43 (2007)

Lau, K.W., FitzGerald, D.G.: Ideal structure of the Kauffman and related monoids. Commun. Algebra **34**, 2617–2629 (2006). https://doi.org/10.1080/00927870600651414

Maltcev, V., Mazorchuk, V.: Presentation of the singular part of the Brauer monoid. Math. Bohem. **132**(3), 297–323 (2007)

Mashevitzky, G.I.: On identities holding in some classes of completely 0-simple semigroups, preprint (Deposited at VINITI, no. 3135-80 Dep.) (1980). (Russian)

Mazorchuk, V.: On the structure of Brauer semigroup and its partial analogue. Probl. Algebra **13**, 29–45 (1998)

Mazorchuk, V.: Endomorphisms of $\mathfrak{B}_n$, $P\mathfrak{B}_n$, and $\mathfrak{C}_n$. Commun. Algebra **30**(7), 3489–3513 (2002). https://doi.org/10.1081/AGB-120004500

Murskiĭ, V.L.: Several examples of varieties of semigroups. Mat. Zametki **3**(6), 663–670 (1968). https://doi.org/10.1007/BF01110600. (Russian; Engl. translation (entitled Examples of varieties of semigroups) Math. Notes **3**(6), 423–427)

Papadimitriou, C.H.: Computational Complexity. Addison-Wesley Publishing Company, Reading (1994)

Pastijn, F.: Polyhedral convex cones and the equational theory of the bicyclic semigroup. J. Aust. Math. Soc. **81**(1), 63–96 (2006). https://doi.org/10.1017/S1446788700014646

Plescheva, S.V., Vértesi, V.: Complexity of the identity checking problem in a 0-simple semigroup. Izvestija Ural. Gos. Univ. **43**, 72–102 (2006). (Russian)

Seif, S.: The Perkins semigroup has co-NP-complete term-equivalence problem. Int. J. Algebra Comput. **15**(2), 317–326 (2005). https://doi.org/10.1142/S0218196705002293

Seif, S., Szabó, C.: Computational complexity of checking identities in 0-simple semigroups and matrix semigroups over finite fields. Semigroup Forum **72**(2), 207–222 (2006). https://doi.org/10.1007/s00233-005-0510-4

Shleifer, F.G.: Looking for identities on a bicyclic semigroup with computer assistance. Semigroup Forum **41**(2), 173–179 (1990). https://doi.org/10.1007/BF02573388

Shneerson, L.M.: On the axiomatic rank of varieties generated by a semigroup or monoid with one defining relation. Semigroup Forum **39**(1), 17–38 (1989). https://doi.org/10.1007/BF02573281

Trahtman, A.N.: Graphs of identities of a completely 0-simple 5-element semigroup, preprint (Deposited at VINITI no. 5558-81 Dep.) (1981). https://doi.org/10.1007/BF02573687. (Russian; Engl. translation (entitled Identities of a five-element 0-simple semigroup) Semigroup Forum **48**, 385–387 (1994))

Trahtman, A.N.: A six-element semigroup generating a variety with uncountably many subvarieties. In: Algebraic Systems and Their Varieties, pp. 138–143. Ural State University, Sverdlovsk (1988) (Ural. Gos. Univ. Mat. Zap. **14**(3)). (Russian)

Relativistic Effects Can Be Used to Achieve a Universal Square-Root (Or Even Faster) Computation Speedup

Olga Kosheleva⑩ and Vladik Kreinovich$^{(\boxtimes)}$⑩

University of Texas at El Paso, El Paso, TX 79968, USA
{olgak,vladik}@utep.edu

Abstract. In this paper, we show that special relativity phenomenon can be used to reduce computation time of any algorithm from T to $\sqrt{T}$. For this purpose, we keep computers where they are, but the whole civilization starts moving around the computers – at an increasing speed, reaching speeds close to the speed of light. A similar square-root speedup can be achieved if we place ourselves near a growing black hole. Combining the two schemes can lead to an even faster speedup: from time T to the 4-th order root $\sqrt[4]{T}$.

1 Formulation of the Problem

Need for Fast Computations. At first glance, the situation with computing speed is very good. The number of computational operations per second has grown exponentially fast, and continues to grow. Faster and faster high performance computers are being designed and built all the time, and the only reason why they are not built even faster is the cost limitations.

However, while, because of this progress, it has indeed become possible to solve many computational problems which were difficult to solve in the past, there are still some challenging practical problems that cannot yet been solved now. An example of such a problem is predicting where a tornado will go in the next 15 min. At present, this tornado prediction problem can be solved in a few hours on a high performance computer, but by then, it will be too late. As a result, during the tornado season, broad warning are often so frequent that people often ignore them – and fall victims when the tornado hits their homes. There are many other problems like this.

What Can We Do – in Addition to What Is Being Done. Computer engineers and computer scientists are well aware of the need for faster computations, so computer engineers are working on new hardware that will enable faster computations, and computer scientists are developing new faster algorithms for solving different problems. Some of the hardware efforts are based on the same

This work was supported in part by the US National Science Foundation grant HRD-1242122 (Cyber-ShARE Center of Excellence).

A. Blass et al. (Eds.): Gurevich Festschrift, LNCS 12180, pp. 179–189, 2020.
https://doi.org/10.1007/978-3-030-48006-6_13

physical and engineering principles on which the current computers operate, some efforts aim to involve different physical phenomena – such as quantum computing (see, e.g., [5]).

Can we use other physical phenomena as well? We are talking about speeding up computations, i.e., about time, so a natural place to look for such physical phenomena is to look for physical effects that change the rate of different physical processes, i.e., make them run faster or slower.

What We Do in This Paper. This is what we will do in this paper: we will show how physical phenomena can be used to further speed up computations. Specifically, for this speed-up, in line with the general idea of relativistic computation (see, e.g., [1]), we will be using relativistic effects.

2   Physical Phenomena That Change the Rate of Physical Processes – and How to Use Them to Speed up Computations

Physical Phenomena That Change the Rate of Physical Processes: A Brief Reminder. Unfortunately for computations, there are no physical processes that *speed up* all physical phenomena, but there are two physical processes that *slow down* all physical phenomena; see, e.g., [2], Vol. I, Chapters 15–17, and Vol. II, Chapter 42, and [6], Chapters 2, 24, and 25.

First, according to Special Relativity Theory, if we travel with some speed v, then all the processes slow down. The proper time interval s – i.e., the time interval registered by the observer moving with the speed v – is related to the time interval t measured by the immobile observer by the formula

$$s = t \cdot \sqrt{1 - \frac{v^2}{c^2}}, \tag{1}$$

where c denotes the speed of light. The closer the observer's speed v to the speed of light c, the larger this slow-down.

Second, according to General Relativity Theory, in the gravitational field, time also slows down. For immobile observer in a gravitational field, the proper time interval s is equal to $s = \sqrt{g_{00}} \cdot t$, where t is the time as measured by a distant observer – who is so far away that this observer is not affected by the gravitational field – and g_{00} is the 00-component of the metric tensor g_{ij} that describes the geometry of space-time. In the spherically symmetric (Schwarzschild) solution, we have $g_{00} = 1 - \dfrac{r_s}{r}$, where r is the distance from the center of the gravitating body and $r_s \stackrel{\text{def}}{=} \dfrac{2G \cdot M}{c^2}$, where G is the gravitational constant and M is the mass of the central body.

Both slow-down effects have been experimentally confirmed with high accuracy.

How We Can Use These Phenomena to Speed Up Computations. If these phenomena would speed up all the processes, then it would be easy to speed up computations: we would simply place the computers in a body moving with a high speed and/or located in a strong gravitational field, and we would thus get computations faster.

In reality, these phenomena slow down all the processes, not speed them up. So, if we place computers in such a slowed-time environment, we will only slow down the computations. However, we *can* speed up computations if we do the opposite: namely, keep computers in a relatively immobile place with a reasonably low gravitational field, and place our whole civilization in a fast moving body and/or in a strong gravitational field. In this case, in terms of the computers themselves, computations will continue at the same speed as before, but since our time will be slowed down, we will observe much more computational steps in the same interval of proper time (i.e., time as measured by our slowed-down civilization).

In this paper, we analyze what speed up we can obtain in this way – by analyzing the above slowing-down physical phenomena one by one.

3   Possible Special-Relativity Speed-Up: Analysis of the Problem and Resulting Formulas

How to Use Special Relativistic Effects for a Computational Speed-Up: Reminder. To get a computational speed-up, we can place the computer at the center, and start moving around this computer at a speed close to the speed of light. Since we cannot immediately reach the speed of light or the desired trajectory radius, we need to gradually increase our speed and the radius. Let $v(t)$ denote our speed at time t, and let $R(t)$ denote the radius of our trajectory at moment t.

Preliminary Analysis of the Problem: Simplified Computations. According to the above formula (1), a change ds in proper time is related to the change dt in coordinate time (as measured by the computer clock) as

$$ds = dt \cdot S(t), \text{ where } S(t) \stackrel{\text{def}}{=} \sqrt{1 - \frac{v^2(t)}{c^2}}.$$

The possibility to travel is limited by the need to keep acceleration experienced by all moving persons below or at the usual Earth level g_0. The faster we go, the larger the slow-down effect – and thus, the larger the expected computational speed-up. Thus, to achieve the largest possible computational speed-up, we should accelerate as fast as possible. Since possible accelerations are limited by g_0, this means that, to achieve the largest possible speed-up, we should always accelerate with the maximum possible acceleration g_0.

When a body follows a circular orbit with velocity $v(t)$ and radius $R(t)$, it experiences coordinate acceleration $\dfrac{d^2x}{dt^2} = \dfrac{v^2(t)}{R(t)}$. As we accelerate, the velocity gets closer and closer to the speed of light. For large t, the velocity $v(t)$ becomes close to the speed of light $v(t) \approx c$, so we conclude that the following asymptotic equality holds: $\dfrac{d^2x}{dt^2} \approx \dfrac{c^2}{R(t)}$. Let us find out what is the value of the experienced acceleration $\dfrac{d^2x}{ds^2}$.

Here, $\dfrac{dx}{ds} = \dfrac{dx}{dt} \cdot \dfrac{dt}{ds} = \dfrac{dx}{dt} \cdot \dfrac{1}{S(t)}$, thus,

$$\frac{d^2x}{ds^2} = \frac{d}{ds}\left(\frac{dx}{dt} \cdot \frac{1}{S(t)}\right) = \frac{dt}{ds} \cdot \frac{d}{dt}\left(\frac{dx}{dt} \cdot \frac{1}{S(t)}\right) = \frac{1}{S(t)} \cdot \frac{d}{dt}\left(\frac{dx}{dt} \cdot \frac{1}{S(t)}\right).$$

When the body follows a circular orbit with a constant speed, the value $S(t)$ is a constant, so we have

$$\frac{d}{dt}\left(\frac{dx}{dt} \cdot \frac{1}{S(t)}\right) = \frac{1}{S(t)} \cdot \frac{d^2x}{dt^2}$$

and thus,

$$\frac{d^2x}{ds^2} = \frac{1}{S^2(t)} \cdot \frac{d^2x}{dt^2} \approx \frac{1}{S^2(t)} \cdot \frac{c^2}{R(t)}.$$

Here, the experienced acceleration $\dfrac{d^2x}{ds^2}$ should be equal to the usual Earth acceleration g_0, thus

$$g_0 \approx \frac{1}{S^2(t)} \cdot \frac{c^2}{R(t)}.$$

In this case, the relativistic slow-down has the form $S(t) = \dfrac{c}{\sqrt{g_0 \cdot R(t)}}$. The larger $R(t)$, the larger the slow-down effect and thus, the larger the expected computational speed up. All the speeds are limited by the speed of light, thus, we have $R(t) \leq v_0 \cdot t$, where $v_0 < c$ is the speed with which we increase the radius. To increase the computational speed-up effect, let us consider the case when $R(t) = v_0 \cdot t$. In this case, the relativistic slow-down effect has the form

$$S(t) \approx C^{-1} \cdot t^{-1/2},$$

where we denoted $C \stackrel{\text{def}}{=} \dfrac{\sqrt{g_0 \cdot v_0}}{c}$.

From $S(t) = \sqrt{1 - \dfrac{v^2(t)}{c^2}} = \dfrac{c}{\sqrt{g_0 \cdot v_0 \cdot t}}$, we conclude that $1 - \dfrac{v^2(t)}{c^2} = \dfrac{c^2}{g_0 \cdot v_0 \cdot t}$, and thus,

$$v(t) = c \cdot \sqrt{1 - \frac{c^2}{g_0 \cdot v_0 \cdot t}}.$$

At any moment of time t, we get the following relation between the increase dt in corresponding time and the increase ds in proper time (i.e., time experienced by us):

$$\frac{ds}{dt} = S(t) \approx C^{-1} \cdot t^{-1/2},$$

hence $ds \approx C^{-1} \cdot dt \cdot t^{-1/2}$. Integrating both sides of this asymptotic equality, we conclude that $s \approx 2C^{-1} \cdot \sqrt{t}$.

Once the computers finish their computations at time T, they need to send us the results. This can be done with the speed of light. So, at each moment $t \geq T$ of coordinate time, the signal reaches the distance $c \cdot (t - T)$ from the computers' location. We receive this signal when it reaches our location, i.e., at a moment t_r for which $c \cdot (t_r - T) = R(t_r) = v_0 \cdot t_r$. So, $(c - v_0) \cdot t_r = c \cdot T$ and $t_r = \dfrac{c}{c - v_0} \cdot T$. At this moment, our experienced time s_r is equal to

$$s_r \approx 2C^{-1} \cdot \sqrt{t_r} = 2C^{-1} \cdot \sqrt{\frac{c}{c - v_0}} \cdot \sqrt{T}.$$

Thus, in comparison with the usual (stationary) computations which would require time T, we indeed get a square-root computational speed-up.

This Is Probably All We Can Get. Please note that this square root speedup is probably all we can gain: indeed, we tried to extract as much slowing down as possible with the limitation that the acceleration does not exceed g_0. A further relativistic slow-down would probably require having accelerations much higher than our usual level g_0.

Detailed Analysis and the Resulting Computational Speed-Up Scheme. In the above simplified computations, we used the formulas which are valid for the case when the body is moving with a constant speed along the same circular orbit. In our scheme, both the speed and the radius $R(t)$ increase with time. Let us now perform a more accurate analysis, that takes these changes into account and leads to the same asymptotic speed-up. To be more precise, we will show that it is possible, for each $\varepsilon > 0$, to achieve a speed-up from T to $T^{1/2+\varepsilon}$. Since this value ε can be arbitrarily small, from the practical viewpoint, this means that, in effect, we get the square root speed-up.

To speed up computations, we place computers where they are now, and start moving the whole civilization. All the motion will be in a plane, with the civilization following – after some preparation time t_0 – a logarithmic spiral trajectory, i.e., a trajectory that in polar coordinates (R, φ) takes the form $R = R_0 \cdot \exp(k \cdot \varphi)$, i.e., equivalently, $\varphi = K \cdot \ln(R/R_0) = K \cdot \ln(R) - K \cdot \ln(R_0)$, where we denoted $K \stackrel{\text{def}}{=} k^{-1}$. To show that the corresponding speedup can be achieved, we will take $K = \dfrac{v_0/c}{\sqrt{1 - \dfrac{v_0^2}{c^2}}}$.

For the dependence of the distance $R(t)$ on time t, we consider the following formula

$$R(t) = \sqrt{c^2 - v_0^2} \cdot t - c_0 \cdot t^{2\varepsilon},$$

for an appropriate constant c_0 (that will be determined later). We will show that for an appropriately selected value c_0, the perceived acceleration $a \stackrel{\text{def}}{=} \left\| \dfrac{d^2 x_i}{ds^2} \right\|$

will not exceed the Earth's level g_0, and that this trajectory will indeed lead to the $T \to T^{1/2+\varepsilon}$ speedup. Since we are considering only moments after some time t_0, it is sufficient to prove that the asymptotic expression for the acceleration a does not exceed $g_0' \overset{\text{def}}{=} g_0 - \delta$ for some small $\delta > 0$; this will guarantee that the acceleration is smaller than g_0 for all moments t starting with some moment t_0.

Let us first estimate the relativistic slow-down. In the usual Cartesian coordinates, the trajectory has the form

$$x(t) = R(t) \cdot \cos(K \cdot \ln(R) - K \cdot \ln(R_0)), \quad y(t) = R(t) \cdot \sin(K \cdot \ln(R) - K \cdot \ln(R_0)).$$

Differentiating these formulas with respect to coordinate time t, we conclude that

$$\frac{dx}{dt} = R'(t) \cdot \cos(K \cdot \ln(R) - K \ln(R_0)) - R(t) \cdot \sin(K \cdot \ln(R) - K \cdot \ln(R_0)) \cdot \frac{K}{R(t)} \cdot R'(t)$$

$$= R'(t) \cdot (\cos(K \cdot \ln(R) - K \ln(R_0)) - K \cdot \sin(K \cdot \ln(R) - K \ln(R_0))),$$

where $R'(t)$ denotes the derivative of the function $R(t)$, and similarly

$$\frac{dy}{dt} = R'(t) \cdot (\sin(K \cdot \ln(R) - K \cdot \ln(R_0)) + K \cdot \cos(K \cdot \ln(R) - K \cdot \ln(R_0))).$$

Substituting these expressions into the formula

$$v^2 = \left(\frac{dx}{dt}\right)^2 + \left(\frac{dy}{dt}\right)^2,$$

taking into account that terms proportional to the product of sine and cosine cancel each other and that $\sin^2(z) + \cos^2(z) = 1$, we conclude that

$$v^2 = (R'(t))^2 \cdot (1 + K^2).$$

From the formula for $R(t)$, we get $R'(t) = \sqrt{c^2 - v_0^2} - c_0 \cdot 2\varepsilon \cdot t^{-(1-2\varepsilon)}$, thus

$$(R'(t))^2 = c^2 - v_0^2 - 2\sqrt{c^2 - v_0^2} \cdot c_0 \cdot 2\varepsilon \cdot t^{-(1-2\varepsilon)} + o,$$

where o denotes terms that are asymptotically smaller than all the terms present in this formula. So, $v^2 = (c^2 - v_0^2) \cdot (1 + K^2) - 2\sqrt{c^2 - v_0^2} \cdot c_0 \cdot 2\varepsilon \cdot (1 + K^2) \cdot t^{-(1-2\varepsilon)} + o$. By our selection of K, the first term in the formula for v^2 is equal to c^2, so $v^2 = c^2 - c_1 \cdot t^{-(1-2\varepsilon)} + o$, where we denoted $c_1 \overset{\text{def}}{=} 2\sqrt{c^2 - v_0^2} \cdot c_0 \cdot 2\varepsilon \cdot (1 + K^2)$. Thus, $1 - \frac{v^2}{c^2} = c_2 \cdot t^{-(1-2\varepsilon)} + o$, where $c_2 \overset{\text{def}}{=} \frac{c_1}{c^2}$ and hence, the relativistic slow-down is equal to $S(t) = c_3 \cdot t^{-(1/2-\varepsilon)} + o$, where $c_3 \overset{\text{def}}{=} \sqrt{c_2}$. So, asymptotically, $\frac{dt}{ds} = \frac{1}{S(t)} \sim t^{1/2-\varepsilon}$ and $\left(\frac{dt}{ds}\right)^2 \sim t^{1-2\varepsilon}$.

The perceived acceleration has the form $a = \|a_i\|$, where

$$a_i = \frac{d}{ds}\left(\frac{dx_i}{ds}\right) = \frac{d}{ds}\left(\frac{dx_i}{dt} \cdot \frac{dt}{ds}\right) = \frac{dt}{ds} \cdot \frac{d}{dt}\left(\frac{dx_i}{dt} \cdot \frac{dt}{ds}\right)$$

$$= \left(\frac{dt}{ds}\right)^2 \cdot \frac{d^2x_i}{dt^2} + \frac{dt}{ds} \cdot \frac{dx_i}{dt} \cdot \frac{d}{dt}\left(\frac{dt}{ds}\right).$$

In the second term in the expression for a_i, we have $\frac{dt}{ds} \sim t^{1/2-\varepsilon}$, $\frac{dx_i}{dt} \sim \text{const}$,

and $\frac{d}{dt}\left(\frac{dt}{ds}\right) \sim t^{-(1/2+\varepsilon)}$, so the product of these three factors is $\sim t^{-2\varepsilon}$ and thus, tends to 0 as t increases.

In the first term in the expression for a_i, from the above formula for $\frac{dx}{dt}$, we get

$$\frac{d^2x}{dt^2} = R'' \cdot (\cos(.) - K \cdot \sin(.)) - R' \cdot (\sin(.) + K \cdot \cos(.)) \cdot \frac{K}{R} \cdot R'.$$

For the first term in this expression, we have $R'' \sim t^{-(2-2\varepsilon)}$, so due to the above asymptotic for the factor $\left(\frac{dt}{ds}\right)^2$, the product of term proportional to R'' and this factor is $\sim t^{-1}$ – and thus, also tends to 0 as t increases.

For the remaining term, since $R' \sim t^{-(1-\varepsilon)}$ and $R \sim t$, the term proportional to $R' \cdot \frac{K}{R} \cdot R'$ is $\sim t^{-(1-2\varepsilon)}$ and thus, the product of this term and the factor $\left(\frac{dt}{ds}\right)^2 \sim t^{1-2\varepsilon}$ is asymptotically a constant – and a constant proportional to c_0.

A similar conclusion can be made about $\frac{d^2y}{dt^2}$. So, overall, a_i is bounded by a constant proportional to c_0. Hence, by appropriately selecting c_0, we can make this term – and thus, the whole expression a_i – as small as needed, in particular, smaller than the desired acceleration bound g'_0.

Let us now show that in this scheme, we indeed get the desired speed-up. Indeed, here, $\frac{ds}{dt} \sim t^{-(1/2-\varepsilon)}$, so for the proper time $s = \int \frac{ds}{dt}\,dt$ we get $s(t) \sim t^{1/2+\varepsilon}$.

Suppose that the centrally located computer finishes its computations at time T, and immediately sends the result to us. This result travels to us with the speed of light c. Let t_r denote the moment of (coordinate) time at which we receive this result. At this moment of time, we are at the distance $R(t_r)$, so it took the signal time $\frac{R(t_r)}{c}$ to reach us. Thus, $T + \frac{R(t_r)}{c} = t_r$. Asymptotically, $R(t) \sim \sqrt{c^2 - v_0^2} \cdot t$, so for large T, the above formula takes the following asymptotic form

$$T + \frac{\sqrt{c^2 - v_0^2}}{c} \cdot t_r = t_r, \text{ thus } T = t_r \cdot \left(1 - \sqrt{1 - \frac{v_0^2}{c^2}}\right) \text{ and } t_r = \frac{T}{1 - \sqrt{1 - \frac{v_0^2}{c^2}}} \sim T.$$

We have shown that our proper (perceived) time s depends on the coordinate time t as $s(t) \sim t^{1/2+\varepsilon}$. Thus, by our clocks, we get the result of the computation at the moment of time $s(t_r) \sim T^{1/2+\varepsilon}$. So, we indeed get a square root speed-up.

How Realistic Is This Scheme? How big a radius do we need to reach a reasonable speedup? As we will show, the corresponding radius is – by astronomical standards – quite reasonable. Indeed, for large t, when $v \approx c$, the above formulas relating $S(t)$ and $R(t)$ leads to

$$R(t) \approx \frac{c^2}{g_0} \approx \frac{(3 \cdot 10^8 \text{ m/sec})^2}{10 \text{ m/sec}^2} = 9 \cdot 10^{15} \text{ m}.$$

This radius can be compared with a light year – the distance that the light travels in 1 year – which is equal to

$$\approx (3 \cdot 10^8 \text{ m/sec}) \cdot (3 \cdot 10^7 \text{ sec/year}) \cdot (1 \text{ year}) = 9 \cdot 10^{15} \text{ m},$$

so for $v(t) \approx c$, the radius should be about 1 light year.

With time t, the radius is proportional to t, and the computational speed-up is proportional to $\sqrt{t}$. Thus, the radius grows as the square of the computational speed-up. So:

- to get an order of magnitude (10 times) speedup, we need an orbit of radius $10^2 = 100$ light years – reaching to the nearest stars;
- to get a two orders of magnitude (100 times) speedup, we need an orbit of radius $100^2 = 10^4$ light years – almost bringing us to the edge of our Milky Way Galaxy;
- to get a three orders of magnitude (1000 times) speedup, we need an orbit of radius $1000^2 = 10^6$ light years;
- with an orbit of the same radius as the radius of the Universe $R(t) \approx 20$ billion $= 2 \cdot 10^{10}$ light years, we can get $\sqrt{2 \cdot 10^{10}} \approx 1.5 \cdot 10^5$ speedup – more than hundred thousand times speedup.

This Is Similar to a Quantum Speedup. The above square root speedup is similar to the speedup of Grover's quantum algorithm for search in an unsorted array [3–5]; the difference is that:

- in quantum computing, the speedup is limited to search in an unsorted array, while
- in the above special-relativity scheme, we get the same speedup for *all* possible computations.

Comment. In Russia – where we are from – to ring the church bell, the bell-ringer moves the bell's "tongue" (clapper). In Western Europe, they move the bell itself. This example is often used in Russian papers on algorithm efficiency, with an emphasis on the fact that, in principle, it is possible to use a third way to ring the bell: by shaking the whole bell tower. In these papers, this third way is mentioned simply as a joke, but, as the above computations show, this is exactly what we are proposing here: since we cannot reach a speedup by making the computer move, we instead leave the computers intact and move the whole civilization.

Speculation. How can we check whether an advanced civilization is already using this scheme? In this scheme, a civilization rotates around a center, increasing its radius as it goes – i.e., follows a spiral trajectory. In this process, in order to remain accelerating, the civilization needs to gain more and more kinetic energy. The only way to get this energy is to burn all the burnable matter that it encounters along its trajectory. As a result, along the trajectory, where the matter has been burned, we have low-density areas.

Thus, as a trace of such a civilization, we are left with a shape in which there are spiral-shaped low-density areas starting from some central point. But this is exactly how our Galaxy – and many other spiral galaxies – look like. So maybe this is how spiral galaxies acquired their current shape?

4 Possible General-Relativity Speed-Up: Analysis of the Problem and Resulting Formulas

Idea. If we keep the computers where they are now, and place the whole civilization (but *not* the computers) in a strong gravitational field, by moving the civilization close to a far away massive body, then our proper time will slow down. Thus, the computations that take the same coordinate time t will require, in terms of our proper time s, much fewer seconds.

Analysis of the Problem. According to the Schwarzschild's formula for the gravitational field of a symmetric body of mass $M(t)$ at a distance $R(t)$ from the center, the change in the proper time ds (as experience by this body) is related to the change dt in time t as measured by the distant observer by the formula $ds = \varepsilon(t) \cdot dt$, where $\varepsilon(t) \overset{\text{def}}{=} \sqrt{1 - \dfrac{r_s}{R(t)}}$ and the parameter r_s (known as the *Schwarzschild radius*) is equal to

$$r_s \overset{\text{def}}{=} \frac{2G \cdot M(t)}{c^2};$$

see, e.g., [2], Vol. II, Chapter 42, and [6], Chapters 24 and 25.

We want to have as large computational speed-up as possible, so we need to make sure that the corresponding slow-down is as drastic as possible, i.e., that the slow-down factor $\varepsilon(t)$ is as small as possible. For a given r_s this means that we should take $R(t)$ to be as small as possible – i.e., we want to be able to get as close to the Schwarzschild radius as possible. For usual celestial bodies, the radius r_s is well within them: e.g., for our Sun, this radius is equal to 3 km, much smaller than the Sun's size of 1 million km. The only bodies for which their size is smaller than the Schwarzschild radius are black holes. Thus, in this scheme, the civilization should move close to a black hole.

Getting too close to the black hole is dangerous: if we get to the surface $R = r_s$ (known as the *event horizon*), we will never be able to get back to our world or even send a signal back to our world. Thus, it is desirable to always keep ourselves at a certain safe distance d_0 from the event horizon, a safe distance that enables us to move back if some unexpected fluctuation brings us too close to it. So, the closest we can get to the black hole is at the distance $R(t) = r_s + d_0$, for which $r_s = R(t) - d_0$. For these values, the slow-down factor takes the form

$$\varepsilon(t) = \sqrt{1 - \frac{R(t) - d_0}{R(t)}} = \sqrt{\frac{d_0}{R(t)}}.$$

Thus, to decrease this factor – and thus, to get larger and larger computational speed-up – we need to increase $R(t)$. Since we want to keep r_s to be equal to $R(t) - d_0$, this means that we need to also increase r_s – and since r_s is proportional to the mass $M(t)$ of the black hole, this means that we have to continuously increase its mass.

How fast can we increase the radius? Probably we cannot grow $R(t)$ faster than the speed of light – since otherwise, in the coordinates of the distant observer, we will have a physically impossible faster-than-light process. So, the fastest we can grow is at some speed v_0 not exceeding the speed of light. In this case, $R(t) = v_0 \cdot t$, so the speed-up is proportional to $\varepsilon(t) \sim t^{-1/2}$, and, similarly to the special relativity case, we get a square-root computational speed-up.

Resulting Speedup Scheme. To speed up computations, we place computers where they are now. Then we look for a faraway massive black hole, so far away that its gravitational effect on the computers is negligible.

Then we ourselves move close to this black hole, so that our distance from this black hole changes with time t as $R(t) = v_0 \cdot t$. While we are doing that, we are increasing the black hole's mass, so that its mass at time t becomes equal to $M(t) = \dfrac{c^2 \cdot (R(t) + d_0)}{2G}$, where G is the gravitational constant.

Once the computers finish their computations, they send the results to us by a direct light-speed signal.

In this scheme, we also get a square-root speedup.

This Is Probably All We Can Get. Please note that, similarly to the special relativity scheme, this square root speedup is probably all we can gain: indeed, we tried to extract as much slowing down as possible. A further speedup would probably bring too dangerously close to the event horizon.

5   Ideally, We Should Use both Speedups

Moving at a speed close to the speed of light decreases the proper time from the original value t to a much smaller amount $s \sim \sqrt{t}$. Similarly, a location near a black hole also decreases the observable computation time to a square root of its original value.

Thus, if we combine these two schemes – i.e., place ourselves near an ever-increasing black hole and move (together with this black hole) at a speed close to the speed of light, we will get both speedups, i.e., we will replace the perceived computation time from T to $\sqrt{\sqrt{T}} = \sqrt[4]{T}$.

Acknowledgments. The authors are greatly thankful to the anonymous referees for valuable suggestions.

References

1. Andréka, H., Madarász, J.X., Németi, I., Németi, P., Székely, G.: Relativistic computation. In: Cuffaro, M.E., Fletcher, S.C. (eds.) Physical Perspectives on Computation, Computational Perspectives on Physics, pp. 195–215. Cambridge University Press, Cambridge (2018)
2. Feynman, R., Leighton, R., Sands, M.: The Feynman Lectures on Physics. Addison Wesley, Boston (2005)
3. Grover, L.K.: A fast quantum mechanical algorithm for database search. In: Proceedings of the 28th ACM Symposium on Theory of Computing, pp. 212–219 (1996)
4. Grover, L.K.: Quantum mechanics helps in searching for a needle in a haystack. Phys. Rev. Lett. **79**(2), 325–328 (1997)
5. Nielsen, M., Chuang, I.: Quantum Computation and Quantum Information. Cambridge University Press, Cambridge (2000)
6. Thorne, K.S., Blandford, R.D.: Modern Classical Physics: Optics, Fluids, Plasmas, Elasticity, Relativity, and Statistical Physics. Princeton University Press, Princeton (2017)

Towards Verifying Logic Programs in the Input Language of CLINGO

Vladimir Lifschitz[1] , Patrick Lühne[2] , and Torsten Schaub[2] ([✉])

[1] University of Texas at Austin, Austin, USA
vl@cs.utexas.edu
[2] University of Potsdam, Potsdam, Germany
{patrick.luehne,torsten}@cs.uni-potsdam.de

Abstract. We would like to develop methods for verifying programs in the input language of the answer set solver CLINGO using software created for the automation of reasoning in first-order theories. As a step in this direction, we extend Clark's completion to a class of CLINGO programs that contain arithmetic operations as well as intervals and prove that every stable model is a model of generalized completion. The translator ANTHEM calculates the completion of a program and represents it in a format that can be processed by first-order theorem provers. Some properties of programs can be verified by ANTHEM and the theorem prover VAMPIRE, working together.

1 Introduction

Rules in a logic program and axioms in a first-order theory can serve, in many cases, as alternative mechanisms for expressing the same mathematical idea. For instance, the rule

$$q(X) \leftarrow p(X, Y) \tag{1}$$

defines a unary predicate q in terms of a binary predicate p in the language of logic programs. The same relationship between p and q can be expressed by the first-order formula

$$\forall X(q(X) \leftrightarrow \exists Y p(X, Y)). \tag{2}$$

Software used by practitioners of logic programming performs reasoning about predicates that are defined by rules. Consider, for instance, the file

$$
\begin{aligned}
&\texttt{q(X) :- p(X, Y).} \\
&\texttt{p(a, b). p(b, c).}
\end{aligned}
\tag{3}
$$

© Springer Nature Switzerland AG 2020
A. Blass et al. (Eds.): Gurevich Festschrift, LNCS 12180, pp. 190–209, 2020.
https://doi.org/10.1007/978-3-030-48006-6_14

Its first line represents rule (1); the second line expresses that p is the set $\{\langle a, b \rangle, \langle b, c \rangle\}$. If we feed this file into an answer set solver,[1] then the atoms

$$q(a) \quad q(b)$$

are generated: The solver tells us that q is the set $\{a, b\}$.

The efficiency of answer set solvers and the expressive possibilities of their input languages make them valuable tools for many applications [2, 6]. On the other hand, the class of reasoning tasks that they can perform is rather limited. For instance, it is clear that, under the assumption that q is defined by rule (1), one of the sets p, q is nonempty if and only if the other is nonempty. But there seems to be no way to instruct a logic programming system to verify this assertion. Its syntactic form is not suitable for the forms of automated reasoning implemented in these systems.

In the world of first-order theorem proving, the situation is different: The fact that the formula

$$\exists X q(X) \leftrightarrow \exists XY p(X, Y)$$

is entailed by (2) can be easily verified by a theorem prover.

We would like to develop methods for verifying properties of logic programs using software created for the automation of reasoning in first-order theories. In particular, we would like to verify the correctness of logic programs with respect to specifications expressed in traditional logical and mathematical notation. This paper describes initial steps towards that goal.

As an example, consider the CLINGO rule

$$q(X + Y) \ :- \ p(X), \ p(Y). \tag{4}$$

It describes an operation that transforms a set p of integers into another set q. The translator ANTHEM [11, 12], implemented as part of this project, turns this rule into a first-order formula describing the same transformation. The output of ANTHEM, along with a property of this transformation that we would like to verify, can be fed into a proof assistant or a theorem prover. In Sect. 5, we will see, for instance, that the theorem prover VAMPIRE [9] can use the output of ANTHEM to prove that, for every integer n, if all elements of p are less than or equal to n, then all elements of q are less than or equal to $2n$.

To take another example, the CLINGO program[2]

$$
\begin{aligned}
&\texttt{p(X) :- X = 0..n, X * X <= n.} \\
&\texttt{q(X) :- p(X), not p(X + 1).}
\end{aligned}
\tag{5}
$$

---

[1] Answer set solvers are logic programming systems that calculate stable models (answer sets) of logic programs. Some of the best-known systems of this kind are CLINGO (https://potassco.org/) and DLV (http://www.dlvsystem.com/).

[2] As discussed in Sect. 2.1, the "interval term" 0..n in the first rule of this program is an arithmetic expression that has multiple values—all integers from 0 to n. The equality between a variable and an interval term in the body of a rule expresses that the value of the variable is equal to one of the values of the term.

calculates the floor of $\sqrt{n}$, in the sense that the set q that it defines is the singleton $\{\lfloor\sqrt{n}\rfloor\}$. When CLINGO is called to find the stable model of this program, the value of the placeholder n is specified on the command line. In Sect. 5, we will see how the tandem of ANTHEM and VAMPIRE can be used to verify the claim about the relationship between n and q.

The translation performed by ANTHEM is a generalization of the well-known process of program completion [1,14]. When applied to rule (1), for instance, it gives a formula equivalent to (2). This generalization is applicable to programs containing arithmetic operations and intervals, such as (4) and (5). According to the theorem stated in Sect. 4.4 and proved in Sect. 6, this generalized completion formula is satisfied by all stable models of the program. It follows that any assertion that can be derived from it is a common property of all stable models. This fact is at the root of the verification method proposed in this paper.

2   Programs

2.1   Terms and Their Values

We assume that three countably infinite sets of symbols are selected: *numerals*, *symbolic constants*, and *program variables*.[3] We assume that a 1-to-1 correspondence between numerals and integers is chosen; the numeral corresponding to an integer n is denoted by $\bar{n}$. *Program terms* are defined recursively:

- Numerals, symbolic constants, program variables, and the symbols *inf* and *sup* are program terms;
- if t_1, t_2 are program terms and *op* is one of the *operation names*

$$+ \quad - \quad \times \quad / \quad \backslash \quad .. \tag{6}$$

    then $(t_1 \; op \; t_2)$ is a program term.

The expression $-t$ is shorthand for $\bar{0} - t$.

A program term, or another syntactic expression, is *ground* if it does not contain variables. A ground expression is *precomputed* if it does not contain operation names.

For every ground program term t, the set $[t]$ of its *values* is defined as follows:

- if t is a numeral, a symbolic constant, *inf*, or *sup*, then $[t]$ is $\{t\}$;
- if t is $(t_1 + t_2)$, then $[t]$ is the set of numerals $\overline{i+j}$ for all integers i, j such that $\bar{i} \in [t_1]$ and $\bar{j} \in [t_2]$; similarly when t is $(t_1 - t_2)$ or $(t_1 \times t_2)$;
- if t is (t_1/t_2), then $[t]$ is the set of numerals $\overline{\lfloor i/j \rfloor}$ for all integers i, j such that $\bar{i} \in [t_1]$, $\bar{j} \in [t_2]$, and $j \neq 0$;
- if t is $(t_1 \backslash t_2)$, then $[t]$ is the set of numerals $\overline{i - j \cdot \lfloor i/j \rfloor}$ for all integers i, j such that $\bar{i} \in [t_1]$, $\bar{j} \in [t_2]$, and $j \neq 0$;

---

[3] We talk about *program* variables and *program* terms to distinguish them from the variables and terms that are allowed in formulas (Sect. 3) and thus can be found in the output of ANTHEM.

- if t is $(t_1 .. t_2)$, then $[t]$ is the set of numerals $\overline{k}$ for all integers k such that, for some integers i, j,

$$\overline{i} \in [t_1], \quad \overline{j} \in [t_2], \quad \text{and } i \leq k \leq j.$$

It is clear that values of a ground program term are precomputed program terms and that the set of values of any term is finite. It can be empty; for instance, if c is a symbolic constant, then

$$[c + \overline{1}] = [\overline{1}/\overline{0}] = [\overline{1} .. \overline{0}] = \emptyset.$$

For any ground program terms $t_1, \ldots, t_n$, we denote by $[t_1, \ldots, t_n]$ the set of tuples $r_1, \ldots, r_n$ for all $r_1 \in [t_1], \ldots, r_n \in [t_n]$.

2.2 Rules and Programs

The programming language defined in this section is a subset of the input language of CLINGO. We write programs in abstract syntax [7] that disregards details related to representing rules by strings of ASCII characters. For example, expression (1) is the first rule of program (3) written in abstract syntax.

We assume a total order on precomputed program terms such that

- (i) *inf* is its least element and *sup* is its greatest element,
- (ii) for any integers m and n, $\overline{m} < \overline{n}$ iff $m < n$,
- (iii) for any integer n and any symbolic constant c, $\overline{n} < c$.

An *atom* is an expression of the form $p(\mathbf{t})$, where p is a symbolic constant and $\mathbf{t}$ is a tuple of program terms. The parentheses can be dropped if $\mathbf{t}$ is empty. A *literal* is an atom possibly preceded by one or two occurrences of *not*. A *comparison* is an expression of the form $(t_1 \prec t_2)$, where t_1, t_2 are program terms and $\prec$ is one of the *relation names*

$$= \quad \neq \quad < \quad > \quad \leq \quad \geq \tag{7}$$

A *rule* is an expression of the form

$$Head \leftarrow Body, \tag{8}$$

where

- *Body* is a conjunction (possibly empty) of literals and comparisons and
- *Head* is either an atom (then, we say that (8) is a *basic rule*), or an atom in braces (then, (8) is a *choice rule*), or empty (then, (8) is a *constraint*).

The arrow can be dropped if *Body* is empty.

A *program* is a finite set of rules.

An *interpretation* is a set of precomputed atoms. The semantics of programs [7], reviewed in Sect. 6.1, defines which interpretations are *stable models* of a program. We describe here a few features of the semantics that are related to the topic of this paper.

Terms with Multiple Values in the Head of a Rule. A rule of the form $p(t) \leftarrow Body$, where t is a ground term, has the same meaning as the collection of rules $p(r) \leftarrow Body$ over all values r of t. For instance, the one-rule program $p(\overline{1}..\overline{3})$ has the same meaning as the collection of facts $p(\overline{1})$, $p(\overline{2})$, $p(\overline{3})$. A rule of the form $p(\overline{1}/\overline{0}) \leftarrow Body$ has the same meaning as the empty program: The set of stable models of any program would not be affected by adding such a rule. Using the expression $\overline{1}/\overline{0}$ in a program is not considered an error.

Terms with Multiple Values in the Body of a Rule. Similarly, a rule of the form $Head \leftarrow p(t)$, where t is a ground term, has the same meaning as the set of rules $Head \leftarrow p(r)$ over all values r of t. A rule of the form $Head \leftarrow p(\overline{1}/\overline{0})$ has the same meaning as the empty program.

Instances of Rules. An *instance* of a rule R is a ground rule obtained from R by substituting precomputed program terms for program variables. The semantics of the language defines the stable models of a program in terms of the set of instances of its rules. In this sense, program variables are used as variables for arbitrary precomputed terms. For example, instances of the rule

$$q(X + \overline{1}) \leftarrow p(X) \tag{9}$$

are rules of the form

$$q(r + \overline{1}) \leftarrow p(r), \tag{10}$$

where r is an arbitrary precomputed term—a numeral, a symbolic constant, *inf*, or *sup*. But if r is not a numeral, then rule (10) is equivalent to the empty program, as discussed above. In this sense, the possibility of substituting terms other than numerals for r in the process of constructing instances of rule (9) is not essential. With the rule $q(X) \leftarrow p(X + \overline{1})$, the situation is similar.

2.3   Programs with Input

An input can be given to a CLINGO program in two ways: by specifying the predicates corresponding to some of the predicate symbols, as in programs (1) and (4), and by specifying the values of placeholders, as in program (5). The definition of a program with input [10, Section 3], reproduced below, makes this idea precise.

A *predicate symbol* is a pair p/n, where p is a symbolic constant and n is a nonnegative integer. About a program or another syntactic expression we say that a predicate symbol p/n *occurs* in it if it contains an atom of the form $p(t_1, \ldots, t_n)$.

A *program with input* is a pair (Π, P), where Π is a program and P is a finite set such that each of its elements is

– a symbolic constant or

– a predicate symbol that does not occur in the heads of the rules of Π.

The elements of P are the *input symbols* of (Π, P).

An *input* for (Π, P) is a function $\mathbf{i}$ defined on P such that

– for every symbolic constant c in P, $\mathbf{i}(c)$ is a precomputed term, and
– for every predicate symbol p/n in P, $\mathbf{i}(p/n)$ is a finite set of precomputed atoms containing p/n.

A *stable model* of (Π, P) for an input $\mathbf{i}$ is a stable model of the program consisting of

– all atoms in $\mathbf{i}(p/n)$ for all predicate symbols p/n in P and
– the rules obtained from the rules of Π by substituting simultaneously the precomputed terms $\mathbf{i}(c)$ for all occurrences of symbolic constants c in P.

We identify $(\Pi, \emptyset)$ with Π.

Example 1. The claim about rule (4) made in the introduction can be stated using this terminology as follows. Consider the program with input that consists of the rule

$$q(X + Y) \leftarrow p(X) \wedge p(Y) \tag{11}$$

(which is (4) written in abstract notation) and the input symbol $p/1$. We want to verify that

$$
\begin{gathered}
\text{for every integer } n, \\
\text{if } \mathcal{I} \text{ is a stable model of this program for an input } \mathbf{i} \\
\text{and every term } t \text{ such that } p(t) \in \mathbf{i}(p/1) \text{ is } \overline{m} \\
\text{for some integer } m \text{ such that } m \leq n, \\
\text{then every term } t \text{ such that } q(t) \in \mathcal{I} \text{ is } \overline{m} \\
\text{for some integer } m \text{ such that } m \leq 2n.
\end{gathered}
\tag{12}
$$

(The program in question has actually a unique stable model for every input $\mathbf{i}$. Verifying properties of this kind automatically goes beyond the scope of this paper.) Since $p/1$ does not occur in the head of (11), the condition $p(t) \in \mathbf{i}(p/1)$ in this statement can be replaced by $p(t) \in \mathcal{I}$.

Example 2. To reformulate the claim about program (5), consider the program with input that consists of the rules

$$
\begin{aligned}
p(X) &\leftarrow X = \overline{0} \mathinner{\ldotp\ldotp} n \wedge X \times X \leq n, \\
q(X) &\leftarrow p(X) \wedge not\, p(X + \overline{1})
\end{aligned}
\tag{13}
$$

(program (5) written in abstract notation) and the input symbol n. We want to verify that

$$
\begin{gathered}
\text{if } \mathcal{I} \text{ is a stable model of this program for an input } \mathbf{i} \\
\text{and } \mathbf{i}(n) \text{ is a nonnegative integer,} \\
\text{then the set } \{t : q(t) \in \mathcal{I}\} \text{ is the singleton } \{\lfloor \sqrt{\mathbf{i}(n)} \rfloor\}.
\end{gathered}
\tag{14}
$$

3   Formulas

In formula (2), the implication left-to-right tells us that X does not belong to q unless p contains a pair of the form $\langle X, Y \rangle$. In program (1), this property of q is not stated explicitly. Rather, we draw this conclusion from the fact that in the absence of rules other than (1), an element of p that has the form $\langle X, Y \rangle$ is the only possible evidence for the claim that X belongs to q. The completion process, which turns (1) into (2), encodes this form of reasoning, specific for logic programs, in the language of first-order logic.

The generalization of completion defined in this paper also takes into account another difference between CLINGO programs and first-order formulas. In CLINGO, a ground term may have several values or no values. In first-order logic, the value of every ground term is unique. Among the operation names (6) allowed in programs, not a single one represents a total function on the set of precomputed terms. Consequently, these operation names cannot be used as function symbols in a first-order language with variables for precomputed terms.

The formulas introduced in this section are first-order formulas with variables of two sorts: program variables (the same as in Sect. 2.1) that range over precomputed program terms and new *integer variables* that range over integers. In the semantics of the language, integers are identified with the corresponding numerals. The first three of symbols (6) correspond to total functions on integers, and they are allowed in terms with integer values. The last three are banned from formulas altogether.

The definitions below follow [12, Section 5]. *Arithmetic terms* are formed from numerals and integer variables using the operation symbols $+$, $-$, and $\times$. Arithmetic terms, symbolic constants, program variables, and the symbols *inf* and *sup* are collectively called *formula terms*. It is clear that precomputed formula terms are identical to precomputed program terms. For every ground formula term, its *value* is the precomputed term defined recursively in a natural way.

Atomic formulas are expressions of two forms: $p(\mathbf{t})$, where p is a symbolic constant and $\mathbf{t}$ is a tuple of formula terms, and $(t_1 \prec t_2)$, where t_1 and t_2 are formula terms and $\prec$ is one of relation names (7). *Formulas* are formed from atomic formulas using propositional connectives and quantifiers as usual in first-order logic.

An interpretation $\mathcal{I}$ *satisfies* a closed atomic formula $p(t_1, \ldots, t_n)$ if the formula $p(v_1, \ldots, v_n)$, where each v_i is the value of t_i, belongs to $\mathcal{I}$. This relation is extended to arbitrary closed formulas as usual in first-order logic.

A formula is *universally valid* if its universal closure is satisfied by all interpretations. For instance, if X is a program variable and I is an integer variable, then the formula $\exists X (X = I)$ is universally valid because so is its universal closure $\forall I \exists X (X = I)$. The formula $\exists I (X = I)$ expresses that X is an integer. We denote it by $is\_int(X)$.

Formulas F and G are *equivalent* to each other if $F \leftrightarrow G$ is universally valid. For instance, $p(I + J)$, where I and J are integer variables, is equivalent to $p(J + I)$.

4 Completion

4.1 Transforming Program Terms into Formulas

For any program term t, the formula $val_t(Z)$, where Z is a program variable that does not occur in t, expresses, informally speaking, that Z is one of the values of t [12, Section 6]. It is defined recursively:

- if t is a numeral, a symbolic constant, a program variable, *inf*, or *sup*, then $val_t(Z)$ is $Z = t$;
- if t is $(t_1 \, op \, t_2)$, where op is $+$, $-$, or $\times$, then $val_t(Z)$ is

$$\exists IJ(Z = I \, op \, J \land val_{t_1}(I) \land val_{t_2}(J))$$

where I, J are fresh integer variables;
- if t is (t_1/t_2), then $val_t(Z)$ is

$$\exists IJQR(I = J \times Q + R \land val_{t_1}(I) \land val_{t_2}(J)$$
$$\land J \neq \overline{0} \land R \geq \overline{0} \land R < Q \land Z = Q),$$

where I, J, Q, R are fresh integer variables;
- if t is $(t_1 \backslash t_2)$, then $val_t(Z)$ is

$$\exists IJQR(I = J \times Q + R \land val_{t_1}(I) \land val_{t_2}(J)$$
$$\land J \neq \overline{0} \land R \geq \overline{0} \land R < Q \land Z = R),$$

where I, J, Q, R are fresh integer variables;
- if t is $(t_1 .. t_2)$, then $val_t(Z)$ is

$$\exists IJK(val_{t_1}(I) \land val_{t_2}(J) \land I \leq K \land K \leq J \land Z = K),$$

where I, J, K are fresh integer variables.

For example, $val_{X+\overline{1}}(Z)$ is

$$\exists IJ(Z = I + J \land I = X \land J = \overline{1}),$$

which is equivalent to

$$\exists I(Z = I + \overline{1} \land I = X).$$

Another example: $val_{\overline{1}..X}(Z)$ is

$$\exists IJK(I = \overline{1} \land J = X \land I \leq K \land K \leq J \land Z = K),$$

which is equivalent to

$$is\_int(X) \land \overline{1} \leq Z \land Z \leq X.$$

4.2   Transforming Bodies of Rules into Formulas

The translation τ^b transforms bodies of rules into formulas.[4] For any atom $p(t_1, \ldots, t_n)$, each of $\tau^b(p(t_1, \ldots, t_n))$, $\tau^b(not\ not\ p(t_1, \ldots, t_n))$ is defined as

$$\exists Z_1 \ldots Z_n(val_{t_1}(Z_1) \wedge \cdots \wedge val_{t_n}(Z_n) \wedge p(Z_1, \ldots, Z_n))$$

(where each Z_i is a fresh program variable), and $\tau^b(not\ p(t_1, \ldots, t_n))$ is

$$\exists Z_1 \ldots Z_n(val_{t_1}(Z_1) \wedge \cdots \wedge val_{t_n}(Z_n) \wedge \neg p(Z_1, \ldots, Z_n)).$$

For any comparison $t_1 \prec t_2$, $\tau^b(t_1 \prec t_2)$ is

$$\exists Z_1 Z_2(val_{t_1}(Z_1) \wedge val_{t_2}(Z_2) \wedge Z_1 \prec Z_2).$$

If each of $E_1, \ldots, E_m$ is a literal or a comparison, then $\tau^b(E_1 \wedge \cdots \wedge E_m)$ stands for $\tau^b(E_1) \wedge \cdots \wedge \tau^b(E_m)$.

For instance, τ^b transforms $p(\bar{1}..X)$ into a formula equivalent to

$$is\_int(X) \wedge \exists Z(\bar{1} \leq Z \wedge Z \leq X \wedge p(Z)).$$

The expression $Y = \bar{1}..X$ is transformed into a formula equivalent to

$$\exists Z_1 Z_2(Z_1 = Y \wedge is\_int(X) \wedge \bar{1} \leq Z_2 \wedge Z_2 \leq X \wedge Z_1 = Z_2)$$

and consequently to

$$is\_int(X) \wedge \bar{1} \leq Y \wedge Y \leq X.$$

4.3   Completed Definitions

Given a program with input (Π, P) and a predicate symbol p/n that occurs in Π and does not belong to P, we describe a formula called the *completed definition* of p/n in (Π, P).

In completed definitions, the symbolic constants $c_1, \ldots, c_l$ from P are represented by program variables $C_1, \ldots, C_l$, which are assumed to be pairwise distinct and different from the variables occurring in Π.

The *definition* of a predicate symbol p/n in (Π, P) is the set of all rules of Π that have the forms

$$p(t_1, \ldots, t_n) \leftarrow Body \tag{15}$$

and

$$\{p(t_1, \ldots, t_n)\} \leftarrow Body. \tag{16}$$

If the definition of p/n in (Π, P) consists of the rules $R_1, \ldots, R_k$, then the *formula representations* $F_1, \ldots, F_k$ of these rules are constructed as follows. Take fresh program variables $V_1, \ldots, V_n$. If R_i is (15), then F_i is the formula

$$\tau^b(Body) \wedge val_{t_1}(V_1) \wedge \cdots \wedge val_{t_n}(V_n).$$

---

[4] It differs from the translation τ^B [12, Section 6] in that it disregards the combination *not not*. Double negations are essential in the formulas that characterize stable models but not in completion formulas.

If R_i is (16), then F_i is the formula

$$\tau^b(Body) \wedge p(V_1, \dots, V_n) \wedge val_{t_1}(V_1) \wedge \cdots \wedge val_{t_n}(V_n). \tag{17}$$

The *completed definition* of p/n in Π is obtained from the formula

$$\forall V_1 \cdots V_n \left(p(V_1, \dots, V_n) \leftrightarrow \bigvee_{i=1}^{k} \exists \mathbf{U}_i F_i \right),$$

where $\mathbf{U}_i$ is the list of all variables occurring in rule R_i, by substituting $C_1, \dots, C_l$ for $c_1, \dots, c_l$.

Example 1, continued. The completed definition of $q/1$ in this program is

$$\forall V(q(V) \leftrightarrow \exists XY(\tau^b(p(X)) \wedge \tau^b(p(Y)) \wedge val_{X+Y}(V))). \tag{18}$$

It is equivalent to

$$\forall V(q(V) \leftrightarrow \exists IJ(p(I) \wedge p(J) \wedge V = I + J)). \tag{19}$$

Example 2, continued. The completed definition of $p/1$ in this program is

$$\forall V(p(V) \leftrightarrow \exists X(\tau^b(X = \overline{0}..C) \wedge \tau^b(X \times X \leq C) \wedge V = X)).$$

It is equivalent to

$$\forall V(p(V) \leftrightarrow \exists I(I = V \wedge 0 \leq I \wedge I \leq C \wedge I \times I \leq C) \wedge is\_int(C)). \tag{20}$$

The completed definition of $q/1$ is

$$\forall V(q(V) \leftrightarrow \exists X(\tau^b(p(X)) \wedge \tau^b(not\, p(X + \overline{1})) \wedge V = X)).$$

It is equivalent to

$$\forall V(q(V) \leftrightarrow \exists I(I = V \wedge p(I) \wedge \neg p(I + \overline{1}))). \tag{21}$$

To clarify the role of substituting variables for input symbols in the process of forming a completed definition, consider the modification of the program from Example 2 in which n is not treated as an input symbol, so that the set of input symbols is empty. The completed definition of $p/1$ is equivalent, in this case, to

$$\forall V(p(V) \leftrightarrow \exists I(I = V \wedge 0 \leq I \wedge I \leq n \wedge I \times I \leq n) \wedge is\_int(n)). \tag{22}$$

The subformula $is\_int(n)$ is false because the symbolic constant n is not an integer. It follows that formula (22) is equivalent to $\forall V \neg p(V)$.

4.4 Soundness of Completion

The *completion* of a program with input (Π, P) is the conjunction of the following formulas:

- for every predicate symbol that occurs in Π and does not belong to P, its completed definition;
- for every constraint $\leftarrow$ *Body* in Π, the formula obtained from the universal closure of $\neg \tau^b(Body)$ by substituting the variables $C_1, \ldots, C_l$ for $c_1, \ldots, c_l$.

It is clear that the completion has no free variables other than $C_1, \ldots, C_l$.

In the statement of the theorem, (Π, P) is a program with input; the expression $Comp(C_1, \ldots, C_l)$ stands for its completion.

Theorem. *Every stable model of (Π, P) for an input $\mathbf{i}$ satisfies the sentence $Comp(\mathbf{i}(c_1), \ldots, \mathbf{i}(c_l))$.*

Corollary. *For any formula $F(C_1, \ldots, C_l)$ with all free variables explicitly shown, if the formula*

$$Comp(C_1, \ldots, C_l) \rightarrow F(C_1, \ldots, C_l) \tag{23}$$

is universally valid, then every stable model of (Π, P) for an input $\mathbf{i}$ satisfies $F(\mathbf{i}(c_1), \ldots, \mathbf{i}(c_l))$.

The corollary shows that properties of stable models of a program with input can be established by proving formulas of form (23) in a first-order theory with universally valid axioms.

Example 1, continued. Let $Comp$ be formula (19). To establish claim (12), it is sufficient to prove the universal validity of the formula

$$
\begin{aligned}
Comp &\rightarrow \forall N (\forall X (p(X) \rightarrow \exists I (I = X \wedge I \leq N)) \\
&\rightarrow \forall X (q(X) \rightarrow \exists I (I = X \wedge I \leq 2 \times N))),
\end{aligned}
\tag{24}
$$

where N and I are integer variables and X is a program variable.

Example 2, Continued. Let $Comp(C)$ be the conjunction of formulas (20) and (21). To establish claim (14), it is sufficient to prove the universal validity of the formula

$$
\begin{aligned}
Comp(C) &\rightarrow \forall N (N = C \wedge N \geq \bar{0} \\
&\rightarrow \exists M (\forall X (q(X) \leftrightarrow X = M) \wedge M \geq \bar{0} \\
&\wedge M \times M \leq N \wedge (M + \bar{1}) \times (M + \bar{1}) > N)),
\end{aligned}
\tag{25}
$$

where M and N are integer variables and X is a program variable.

```
forall X1
(
    q(X1)
    <-> exists X2, X3
    (
        exists X4 (X4 = X2 and p(X4))
        and exists X5 (X5 = X3 and p(X5))
        and exists N1, N2 (X1 = N1 + N2 and N1 = X2 and N2 = X3)
    )
)
```

Fig. 1. Completed definition (18) of $q/1$ from Example 1 generated by ANTHEM. The output of ANTHEM is reformatted to improve readability

5 Verifying Properties of Programs

5.1 Generating Completed Definitions

Recall that our goal is to use a reasoning system, such as VAMPIRE, for verifying properties of CLINGO programs, and that this can be accomplished by proving formulas of form (23). To prepare an input for such a system, we need to generate the completed definitions of predicate symbols that occur in the antecedent of (23). This calculation can be performed by version 0.3 of ANTHEM.[5] When instructed, for instance, to calculate the completed definition of $q/1$ in program (4), ANTHEM generates formula (18) as shown in Fig. 1. ANTHEM internally converts the output to the TFF ("typed first-order formula") format of the TPTP language [15] and passes it on to VAMPIRE as an axiom. Formulas in this format can be processed by many automated reasoners.

In the following experiments, we used VAMPIRE 4.4 with the options --mode casc and --cores 8.

5.2 Verification of Example 1

The set of axioms that were available to VAMPIRE in the experiment with Example 1 consists of two parts. One is the collection of properties of predicates and functions on integers that VAMPIRE treats as standard. The other includes several properties of the set of precomputed terms and of the correspondence between numerals and integers, such as those expressed by conditions (i)–(iii) in Sect. 2.2. All these axioms are universally valid in the sense of Sect. 3.

The claim about the relationship between $p/1$ and $q/1$ that we wanted to verify in this example is expressed as shown in Fig. 2. ANTHEM transformed this formula into the TFF format, and VAMPIRE derived it from the axioms and the completed definition generated by ANTHEM (Fig. 1) in a fraction of a second.

---

[5] https://github.com/potassco/anthem/releases.

```
forall N
(
    forall X (p(X) -> exists I (I = X and I <= N))
    -> forall X (q(X) -> exists I (I = X and I <= 2 * N))
)
```

Fig. 2. The claim from Example 1

```
p(0) and forall N (N >= 0 and p(N) -> p(N + 1))
-> forall N(N >= 0 -> p(N))
```

Fig. 3. The induction axiom for $p/1$ from Example 2

5.3   Verification of Example 2

Example 2 was more of a challenge to us as the users of VAMPIRE, in two ways. First, we were unable to prove its claim using only the axiom set described in Sect. 5.2. Two more axioms, both expressing properties of numbers, had to be added. One axiom says that an inequality can be multiplied by a positive integer. Surprisingly, VAMPIRE 4.4, the version we worked with, was not able to prove this fact. The other axiom expresses induction for the predicate $p/1$ (Fig. 3).

Second, VAMPIRE could not prove the conjecture that we are interested in "with one blow," at least in reasonable time. We used it as a proof assistant in a sense that we gave it a sequence of auxiliary conjectures, one by one. As soon as one of these "lemmas" was verified, we added it to the list of axioms.

Such interactive use of automated reasoners will be necessary, of course, when working on verifying more complex programs.

6   Proof of the Theorem

6.1   Review: Definition of a Stable Model

For any ground atom $p(\mathbf{t})$,

- $\tau(p(\mathbf{t}))$ stands for $\bigvee_{\mathbf{r}\in[\mathbf{t}]} p(\mathbf{r})$;
- $\tau(not\ p(\mathbf{t}))$ stands for $\bigvee_{\mathbf{r}\in[\mathbf{t}]} \neg p(\mathbf{r})$;
- $\tau(not\ not\ p(\mathbf{t}))$ stands for $\bigvee_{\mathbf{r}\in[\mathbf{t}]} \neg\neg p(\mathbf{r})$.

For any ground comparison $t_1 \prec t_2$, $\tau(t_1 \prec t_2)$ is

- $\top$ if the relation $\prec$ holds between some r_1 from $[t_1]$ and some r_2 from $[t_2]$;
- $\bot$ otherwise.

If each of $E_1, \ldots, E_m$ is a ground literal or a ground comparison, then $\tau(E_1 \wedge \cdots \wedge E_m)$ stands for $\tau E_1 \wedge \cdots \wedge \tau E_m$.

The *propositional image* of a ground rule R is the formula formed as follows. If R is a ground basic rule $p(\mathbf{t}) \leftarrow Body$, then its propositional image is

$$\tau(Body) \rightarrow \bigwedge_{\mathbf{r} \in [\mathbf{t}]} p(\mathbf{r}).$$

If R is a ground choice rule $\{p(\mathbf{t})\} \leftarrow Body$, then its propositional image is

$$\tau(Body) \rightarrow \bigwedge_{\mathbf{r} \in [\mathbf{t}]} (p(\mathbf{r}) \vee \neg p(\mathbf{r})).$$

If R is a ground constraint $\leftarrow Body$, then its propositional image is $\neg \tau(Body)$.

For any program Π, its *propositional image* is the set of the propositional images of all instances R of its rules. An interpretation is a *stable model* (or *answer set*) of a program Π if it is an answer set of the propositional image of Π [13].

6.2 Leading Special Case

It is sufficient to prove the theorem for the case when P is empty. To derive the general case, we can reason as follows. If $\mathcal{I}$ is a stable model of (Π, P), then $\mathcal{I}$ is a stable model of the program Π' obtained from Π as described in Sect. 2.3— by adding some rules of the form $p(\mathbf{t})$ for predicate symbols p/n from P and by substituting the terms $\mathbf{i}(c)$ for all symbolic constants c in P. By the special case of the theorem with the empty P, $\mathcal{I}$ satisfies the completion $Comp'$ of Π'. It remains to observe that every conjunctive term of $Comp(\mathbf{i}(c_1), \ldots, \mathbf{i}(c_l))$ is a conjunctive term of $Comp'$.

To prove the special case when P is empty, we need to justify three claims:

Claim 1. *If a program Π contains a constraint $\leftarrow Body$, then every stable model of Π satisfies the universal closure of $\neg \tau^b(Body)$.*

In the statements of Claim 2 and Claim 3, the symbols F_i, $\mathbf{U}_i$, and $V_1, \ldots, V_n$ are understood as in Sect. 4.3.

Claim 2. *For every predicate symbol p/n occurring in Π, every stable model of Π satisfies the universal closure of the formula*

$$\bigvee_{i=1}^{k} \exists \mathbf{U}_i F_i \rightarrow p(V_1, \ldots, V_n).$$

Claim 3. *For every predicate symbol p/n occurring in Π, every stable model of Π satisfies the universal closure of the formula*

$$p(V_1, \ldots, V_n) \rightarrow \bigvee_{i=1}^{k} \exists \mathbf{U}_i F_i.$$

6.3   Two Lemmas

The two lemmas below are similar to Propositions 1 and 2 from [12].

Lemma 1. *For any ground program term t and any precomputed term r, the formula $val_t(r)$ is equivalent to $\top$ if $r \in [t]$ and to $\bot$ otherwise.*

Proof. The proof is by induction on t. If t is a numeral, a symbolic constant, inf, or sup, then $r \in [t]$ iff r is t. On the other hand, $val_t(r)$ is $r = t$; this formula is equivalent to $\top$ if r is t and to $\bot$ otherwise.

Assume that the assertion of the lemma holds for t_1 and t_2.

If t is $(t_1 \, op \, t_2)$, where op is $+$, $-$, or $\times$, then $val_t(r)$ is

$$\exists IJ(r = I \, op \, J \wedge val_{t_1}(I) \wedge val_{t_2}(J)).$$

An arbitrary interpretation satisfies this formula iff there exist integers i, j such that

$$r \text{ is } \overline{i \, op \, j}, \quad \overline{i} \in [t_1], \quad \text{and } \overline{j} \in [t_2].$$

This condition holds iff $r \in [t]$.

If t is (t_1/t_2), then $val_t(r)$ is

$$\exists IJQR(I = J \times Q + R \wedge val_{t_1}(I) \wedge val_{t_2}(J)$$
$$\wedge J \neq \overline{0} \wedge R \geq \overline{0} \wedge R < Q \wedge r = Q).$$

An arbitrary interpretation satisfies this formula iff there exist integers i, j, q, rem such that

$$i = jq + rem, \quad \overline{i} \in [t_1], \quad \overline{j} \in [t_2], \quad j \neq 0, \quad 0 \leq rem < q, \quad \text{and } r \text{ is } \overline{q}.$$

Equivalently: Iff there exist integers i and j such that

$$\overline{i} \in [t_1], \quad \overline{j} \in [t_2], \quad j \neq 0, \quad \text{and } r \text{ is } \overline{\lfloor i/j \rfloor}.$$

This condition holds iff $r \in [t]$.

If t is $(t_1 \backslash t_2)$, then the proof is similar.

If t is $(t_1 .. t_2)$, then $val_t(r)$ is

$$\exists IJK(val_{t_1}(I) \wedge val_{t_2}(J) \wedge I \leq K \wedge K \leq J \wedge r = K).$$

An arbitrary interpretation satisfies this formula iff there exist integers i, j, k such that

$$\overline{i} \in [t_1], \quad \overline{j} \in [t_2], \quad i \leq k \leq j, \quad \text{and } r \text{ is } \overline{k}.$$

This condition holds iff $r \in [t]$.

Lemma 2. *If E is a ground literal or ground comparison, then $\tau^b(E)$ is equivalent to τE.*

Proof. This is immediate from Lemma 1.

6.4   Proof of Claim 1

Let $\mathcal{I}$ be a stable model of a program Π, let $\leftarrow E_1 \wedge \cdots \wedge E_m$ be a constraint from Π, let $\mathbf{x}$ be the list of variables occurring in this constraint, and let $\mathbf{r}$ be a list of precomputed terms of the same length as $\mathbf{x}$. Since the rule

$$\leftarrow (E_1)_{\mathbf{r}}^{\mathbf{x}} \wedge \cdots \wedge (E_m)_{\mathbf{r}}^{\mathbf{x}}$$

is an instance of a rule of Π, the propositional image of Π includes the formula

$$\neg(\tau((E_1)_{\mathbf{r}}^{\mathbf{x}}) \wedge \cdots \wedge \tau((E_m)_{\mathbf{r}}^{\mathbf{x}})). \tag{26}$$

Consequently, $\mathcal{I}$ satisfies (26). By Lemma 2, it follows that $\mathcal{I}$ satisfies the formula

$$\neg(\tau^b((E_1)_{\mathbf{r}}^{\mathbf{x}}) \wedge \cdots \wedge \tau^b((E_m)_{\mathbf{r}}^{\mathbf{x}})),$$

which can be also represented as

$$\neg(\tau^b(E_1)_{\mathbf{r}}^{\mathbf{x}} \wedge \cdots \wedge \tau^b(E_m)_{\mathbf{r}}^{\mathbf{x}})$$

and as

$$(\neg\tau^b(E_1 \wedge \cdots \wedge E_m))_{\mathbf{r}}^{\mathbf{x}}.$$

Since $\mathbf{r}$ here is an arbitrary tuple of precomputed terms, it follows that $\mathcal{I}$ satisfies the universal closure of $\neg\tau^b(E_1 \wedge \cdots \wedge E_m)$.

6.5   Proof of Claim 2

Let $\mathcal{I}$ be a stable model of a program Π, and let p/n be a predicate symbol occurring in Π. We need to show that $\mathcal{I}$ satisfies the universal closure of each of the formulas

$$F_i \to p(V_1, \ldots, V_n) \tag{27}$$

$(i = 1, \ldots, k)$. If F_i is a formula of form (17), corresponding to a choice rule, then $p(V_1, \ldots, V_n)$ is one of its conjunctive terms so that (27) is universally valid. Otherwise, F_i is the formula

$$\tau^b(E_1) \wedge \cdots \wedge \tau^b(E_m) \wedge val_{t_1}(V_1) \wedge \cdots \wedge val_{t_n}(V_n),$$

corresponding to a basic rule

$$p(t_1, \ldots, t_n) \leftarrow E_1 \wedge \cdots \wedge E_m. \tag{28}$$

The set of free variables of (27) consists of the variables $\mathbf{U}_i$ that occur in rule (28) and the variables $V_1, \ldots, V_n$. We need to prove that for every tuple $\mathbf{r}$ of precomputed terms of the same length as $\mathbf{U}_i$ and every tuple $s_1, \ldots, s_n$ of precomputed terms, the formula

$$(\tau^b(E_1))_{\mathbf{r}}^{\mathbf{U}_i} \wedge \cdots \wedge (\tau^b(E_m))_{\mathbf{r}}^{\mathbf{U}_i} \wedge val_{t_1'}(s_1) \wedge \cdots \wedge val_{t_n'}(s_n) \to p(s_1, \ldots, s_n), \tag{29}$$

where t'_j $(j = 1, \ldots, n)$ stands for $(t_j)^{\mathbf{U}_i}_{\mathbf{r}}$, is universally valid. By Lemma 1, the formula $val_{t'_j}(s_j)$ is equivalent to $\top$ if $s_j \in [t'_j]$ and to $\bot$ otherwise. Consequently, it is sufficient to consider the case when

$$s_1 \in [t'_1], \ldots, s_n \in [t'_n] \tag{30}$$

(otherwise, (29) is universally valid). It remains to show that, under condition (30), $\mathcal{I}$ satisfies the formula

$$(\tau^b(E_1))^{\mathbf{U}_i}_{\mathbf{r}} \wedge \cdots \wedge (\tau^b(E_m))^{\mathbf{U}_i}_{\mathbf{r}} \to p(s_1, \ldots, s_n).$$

This formula can be represented also as

$$\tau^b\left((E_1)^{\mathbf{U}_i}_{\mathbf{r}}\right) \wedge \cdots \wedge \tau^b\left((E_m)^{\mathbf{U}_i}_{\mathbf{r}}\right) \to p(s_1, \ldots, s_n).$$

By Lemma 2, it is equivalent to

$$\tau\left((E_1)^{\mathbf{U}_i}_{\mathbf{r}}\right) \wedge \cdots \wedge \tau\left((E_m)^{\mathbf{U}_i}_{\mathbf{r}}\right) \to p(s_1, \ldots, s_n). \tag{31}$$

To show that $\mathcal{I}$ satisfies (31), consider the instance

$$p(t'_1, \ldots, t'_n) \leftarrow (E_1)^{\mathbf{U}_i}_{\mathbf{r}} \wedge \cdots \wedge (E_m)^{\mathbf{U}_i}_{\mathbf{r}}$$

of rule (28). The propositional image of that instance has the form

$$\tau\left((E_1)^{\mathbf{U}_i}_{\mathbf{r}}\right) \wedge \cdots \wedge \tau\left((E_m)^{\mathbf{U}_i}_{\mathbf{r}}\right) \to C, \tag{32}$$

where C is a conjunction containing the conjunctive term $p(s_1, \ldots, s_n)$. Since the interpretation $\mathcal{I}$ is a stable model of Π, it satisfies (32) and, consequently, (31).

6.6 Proof of Claim 3

Consider the set Γ of formulas that includes

- for every instance $p(\mathbf{t}) \leftarrow Body$ of a basic rule of Π, the formulas

$$\tau(Body) \to p(\mathbf{r})$$

  for all $\mathbf{r}$ in $[\mathbf{t}]$, and
- for every instance $\{p(\mathbf{t})\} \leftarrow Body$ of a choice rule of Π, the formulas

$$\tau(Body) \wedge \neg\neg p(\mathbf{r}) \to p(\mathbf{r})$$

  for all $\mathbf{r}$ in $[\mathbf{t}]$.

This set is strongly equivalent [13] to the propositional image of the program obtained from Π by removing all constraints. It follows that every stable model $\mathcal{I}$

of Π is a stable model of Γ and, consequently, is supported by Γ [3, Proposition 2]. In other words, every element A of $\mathcal{I}$ is the consequent of an implication from Γ such that its antecedent is satisfied by $\mathcal{I}$.

To prove Claim 3, we need to show that for every predicate symbol p/n occurring in Π and every tuple $s_1, \ldots, s_n$ of precomputed terms, every stable model $\mathcal{I}$ of Π satisfies the formula

$$p(s_1, \ldots, s_n) \rightarrow \bigvee_{i=1}^{k} \exists \mathbf{U}_i (F_i)_{s_1, \ldots, s_n}^{V_1, \ldots, V_n}. \tag{33}$$

Assume that $p(s_1, \ldots, s_n)$ is an element of $\mathcal{I}$; we need to show that $\mathcal{I}$ satisfies the consequent of (33). Consider an implication from Γ with the consequent $p(s_1, \ldots, s_n)$ such that its antecedent is satisfied by $\mathcal{I}$.

Case 1. This implication is the formula

$$\tau\left((E_1)_{\mathbf{r}}^{\mathbf{U}_i}\right) \wedge \cdots \wedge \tau\left((E_m)_{\mathbf{r}}^{\mathbf{U}_i}\right) \rightarrow p(s_1, \ldots, s_n) \tag{34}$$

corresponding to an instance

$$p\left((t_1)_{\mathbf{r}}^{\mathbf{U}_i}, \ldots, (t_n)_{\mathbf{r}}^{\mathbf{U}_i}\right) \leftarrow (E_1)_{\mathbf{r}}^{\mathbf{U}_i} \wedge \cdots \wedge (E_m)_{\mathbf{r}}^{\mathbf{U}_i}$$

of a basic rule

$$p(t_1, \ldots, t_n) \leftarrow E_1 \wedge \cdots \wedge E_m$$

such that

$$s_1 \in \left[(t_1)_{\mathbf{r}}^{\mathbf{U}_i}\right], \ldots, s_n \in \left[(t_n)_{\mathbf{r}}^{\mathbf{U}_i}\right]. \tag{35}$$

By Lemma 2, the antecedent of (34) is equivalent to the formula

$$\tau^b\left((E_1)_{\mathbf{r}}^{\mathbf{U}_i}\right) \wedge \cdots \wedge \tau^b\left((E_m)_{\mathbf{r}}^{\mathbf{U}_i}\right),$$

which can be also represented as

$$(\tau^b(E_1))_{\mathbf{r}}^{\mathbf{U}_i} \wedge \cdots \wedge \tau^b((E_m))_{\mathbf{r}}^{\mathbf{U}_i}.$$

On the other hand, from conditions (35) and Lemma 1, we conclude that each of the formulas

$$val_{t_1}(s_1)_{\mathbf{r}}^{\mathbf{U}_i}, \ldots, val_{t_n}(s_n)_{\mathbf{r}}^{\mathbf{U}_i}$$

is equivalent to $\top$. It follows that $\mathcal{I}$ satisfies the conjunction

$$(\tau^b(E_1))_{\mathbf{r}}^{\mathbf{U}_i} \wedge \cdots \wedge \tau^b((E_m))_{\mathbf{r}}^{\mathbf{U}_i} \wedge val_{t_1}(s_1)_{\mathbf{r}}^{\mathbf{U}_i} \wedge \cdots \wedge val_{t_1}(s_1)_{\mathbf{r}}^{\mathbf{U}_i},$$

which can be written as

$$(F_i)_{s_1, \ldots, s_n, \mathbf{r}}^{V_1, \ldots, V_n, \mathbf{U}_i}.$$

It follows that I satisfies the consequent of (33).

Case 2. The implication from Γ with the consequent $p(s_1, \ldots, s_n)$ such that its antecedent is satisfied by $\mathcal{I}$ is the formula

$$\tau\left((E_1)_{\mathbf{r}}^{\mathbf{U}_i}\right) \wedge \cdots \wedge \tau\left((E_m)_{\mathbf{r}}^{\mathbf{U}_i}\right) \wedge \neg\neg p(s_1, \ldots, s_n) \rightarrow p(s_1, \ldots, s_n)$$

corresponding to an instance

$$\left\{p\left((t_1)_{\mathbf{r}}^{\mathbf{U}_i}, \ldots, (t_n)_{\mathbf{r}}^{\mathbf{U}_i}\right)\right\} \leftarrow (E_1)_{\mathbf{r}}^{\mathbf{U}_i} \wedge \cdots \wedge (E_m)_{\mathbf{r}}^{\mathbf{U}_i}$$

of a choice rule

$$\{p(t_1, \ldots, t_n)\} \leftarrow E_1 \wedge \cdots \wedge E_m$$

such that the terms $t_1, \ldots, t_n$ satisfy condition (35). The proof is similar.

7 Related Work

From early research on the relationship between stable models and completion for programs without arithmetic [5], we know that every stable model of such a program is a model of its completion and that the converse holds under a syntactic condition that is now called *tightness* [3,4]. That work has been extended to CLINGO programs with arithmetic [8], but completed definitions as defined in that paper are not expressed in a standard first-first order language and, consequently, cannot be processed by existing theorem provers.

The definition of a formula proposed in earlier work on ANTHEM [12] does not suffer from that defect. VAMPIRE is used there to verify the strong equivalence relation between logic programs.

Acknowledgements. We are grateful to Laura Kovács, Giles Reger, and Martin Suda for taking the time to answer our questions about the use of VAMPIRE. Also, we would like to thank the anonymous referee for giving us useful suggestions.

References

1. Clark, K.L.: Negation as failure. In: Gallaire, H., Minker, J. (eds.) Logic and Data Bases. Springer, Boston (1978). https://doi.org/10.1007/978-1-4684-3384-5_11
2. Erdem, E., Gelfond, M., Leone, N.: Applications of ASP. AI Mag. **37**(3), 53–68 (2016)
3. Erdem, E., Lifschitz, V.: Fages' theorem for programs with nested expressions. In: Codognet, P. (ed.) ICLP 2001. LNCS, vol. 2237, pp. 242–254. Springer, Heidelberg (2001). https://doi.org/10.1007/3-540-45635-X_24
4. Erdem, E., Lifschitz, V.: Tight logic programs. Theor. Pract. Logic Prog. **3**(4–5), 499–518 (2003)
5. Fages, F.: Consistency of Clark's completion and the existence of stable models. J. Methods Logic Comput. Sci. **1**, 51–60 (1994)
6. Falkner, A., Friedrich, G., Schekotihin, K., Taupe, R., Teppan, E.: Industrial applications of answer set programming. Künstliche Intelligenz **32**(2–3), 165–176 (2018)

7. Gebser, M., Harrison, A., Kaminski, R., Lifschitz, V., Schaub, T.: Abstract gringo. Theor. Pract. Logic Prog. **15**(4–5), 449–463 (2015). http://arxiv.org/abs/1507. 06576

8. Harrison, A., Lifschitz, V., Raju, D.: Program completion in the input language of GRINGO. Theor. Pract. Logic Prog. **17**(5–6), 855–871 (2017)

9. Kovács, L., Voronkov, A.: First-order theorem proving and VAMPIRE. In: Sharygina, N., Veith, H. (eds.) CAV 2013. LNCS, vol. 8044, pp. 1–35. Springer, Heidelberg (2013). https://doi.org/10.1007/978-3-642-39799-8_1

10. Lifschitz, V.: Achievements in answer set programming. Theor. Pract. Logic Prog. **17**(5–6), 961–973 (2017)

11. Lifschitz, V., Lühne, P., Schaub, T.: Anthem: transforming gringo programs into first-order theories (preliminary report). In: Fandinno, J., Fichte, J. (eds.) Proceedings of the Eleventh Workshop on Answer Set Programming and Other Computing Paradigms (ASPOCP 2018) (2018)

12. Lifschitz, V., Lühne, P., Schaub, T.: Verifying strong equivalence of programs in the input language of gringo. In: Balduccini, M., Lierler, Y., Woltran, S. (eds.) LPNMR 2019. LNCS, vol. 11481. Springer, Cham (2019). https://doi.org/10.1007/ 978-3-030-20528-7_20

13. Lifschitz, V., Pearce, D., Valverde, A.: Strongly equivalent logic programs. ACM Trans. Comput. Logic **2**(4), 526–541 (2001)

14. Lloyd, J., Topor, R.: Making Prolog more expressive. J. Logic Prog. **1**(3), 225–240 (1984)

15. Sutcliffe, G.: The TPTP problem library and associated infrastructure. J. Autom. Reason. **59**(4), 483–502 (2017)

Computing on Lattice-Ordered Abelian Groups

Daniele Mundici$^{(\boxtimes)}$ (ID)

Department of Mathematics and Computer Science, "Ulisse Dini" University
of Florence, Viale Morgagni 67/A, 50134 Florence, Italy
mundici@math.unifi.it

Abstract. Starting from a classical theorem of Gurevich and Kokorin we survey recent diverging developments of the theories of lattice-ordered abelian groups and their counterparts equipped with a distinguished order unit. We will focus on decision and recognition problems. As an application of Elliott's classification, we will touch on word problems of AF C*-algebras.

Keywords: Lattice-ordered abelian group · Unital ℓ-group · Word problem · Decision problem · Baker-Beynon duality · Markov unrecognizability theorem · Kroupa-Panti theorem · Marra-Spada duality · Regular complex · MV-algebra · Finitely generated projective ℓ-group · Cabrer characterization theorem · Elliott classification · AF C*-algebra

1 Developments of a Theorem of Gurevich and Kokorin

We refer to [6] for background on lattice-ordered abelian groups, *ℓ-groups* for short. A *unital* ℓ-group is an ℓ-group with a distinguished (strong) order unit. We let $\mathbb{R}$ denote the additive group of real numbers with its usual total order.

A key tool for Hájek's proof of the completeness of Basic Logic is provided by partial embeddings of totally ordered abelian groups into $\mathbb{R}$. As shown by Hájek himself in [35, pp. 25–26], the existence of such partial embeddings immediately follows from a theorem of Gurevich and Kokorin [34] stating that a universal formula in the first-order language of ordered abelian groups holds in all totally ordered abelian groups if it holds in $\mathbb{R}$. Actually, partial embeddings and ℓ-groups are intertwined in a symbiotic relationship: the construction in the following elementary proof finds several applications to the basic theory of unital and non-unital ℓ-groups.

Proposition 1. *Any totally ordered abelian group G is* partially embeddable *into $\mathbb{R}$. In other words, for each finite set $X \subseteq G$ there is a one-one map $f \colon X \to \mathbb{R}$ which is a* partial isomorphism, *in the sense that for all $x, y, z \in G$,*

(i) $z = x + y$ *iff* $f(z) = f(x) + f(y)$;
(ii) $x \leq y$ *iff* $f(x) \leq f(y)$.

Honoring Yuri Gurevich on his 80th birthday.

© Springer Nature Switzerland AG 2020
A. Blass et al. (Eds.): Gurevich Festschrift, LNCS 12180, pp. 210–225, 2020.
https://doi.org/10.1007/978-3-030-48006-6_15

Proof. Let $X = \{x_1, \ldots, x_n\} \subseteq G$ with $x_1 < \cdots < x_n$. For a uniquely determined integer $r \in \{1, \ldots, n\}$ the subgroup of G generated by X can (and will) be identified with the rank r free abelian group $\mathbb{Z}^r$. Accordingly, the set $C = \{x \in \mathbb{Z}^r \mid x \geq 0 \text{ in } G\}$ is a submonoid of $\mathbb{Z}^r$ such that

$$C \cap -C = \{0\} \quad \text{and} \quad C \cup -C = \mathbb{Z}^r.$$

For any two vectors $u, v \in \mathbb{Z}^r$ we write $u \leq_C v$ iff $v - u \in C$ (iff $u \leq v$ in G). Equipped with the binary relation $\leq_C$, $\mathbb{Z}^r$ becomes a totally ordered abelian group. We next set

$$d_l = x_{l+1} - x_l, \quad \text{whence} \quad 0 \neq d_l \in C, \quad (l = 1, \ldots, n-1). \tag{1}$$

Claim: If $0 \leq \mu_1, \ldots, \mu_{n-1} \in \mathbb{R}$ and $\sum_{l=1}^{n-1} \mu_l d_l = 0$ then $\mu_1 = \cdots = \mu_{n-1} = 0$.

Proof of Claim. For each $i = 1, \ldots, n$ we may write $x_i = (x_{i1}, \ldots, x_{ir})$ for suitable integers x_{ij}. For each $j = 1, \ldots, r$ and $l = 1, \ldots, n-1$, let $d_{lj} = x_{l+1j} - x_{lj}$. Arguing by way of contradiction, suppose the homogeneous linear system $\sum_{l=1}^{n-1} \mu_l d_{lj} = 0$ has a solution $\bar{\mu}_1, \ldots, \bar{\mu}_{n-1} \geq 0$ with $\bar{\mu}_e > 0$ for some $e \in \{1, \ldots, n-1\}$. We may safely assume that each one of $\bar{\mu}_1, \ldots, \bar{\mu}_{n-1}$ is *rational*. Multiplication by the least common denominator of $\bar{\mu}_1, \ldots, \bar{\mu}_{n-1}$ yields *integers* $\bar{m}_1, \ldots, \bar{m}_{n-1} \geq 0$ such that $\bar{m}_e \geq 1$ and $\sum_{l=1}^{n-1} \bar{m}_l d_l = 0$. Since by (1), $0 <_C d_l$ for each $l = 1, \ldots, n-1$, then $0 <_C d_e \leq_C \sum_{l=1}^{n-1} \bar{m}_l d_l = 0$, a contradiction that settles our claim.

For any vectors $u, v \in \mathbb{R}^r$ let $u \cdot v$ denote their scalar product. In view of our claim, Gordan's theorem[1] yields a vector $g = (\gamma_1, \ldots, \gamma_r) \in \mathbb{R}^r$ such that

$$d_l \cdot g > 0 \text{ for each } l = 1, \ldots, n-1. \tag{2}$$

Without loss of generality, the real numbers $\gamma_1, \ldots, \gamma_r$ can be assumed linearly independent over $\mathbb{Q}$. Stated otherwise, the map

$$\theta : y = (y_1, \ldots, y_r) \in \mathbb{Z}^r \mapsto y \cdot g = y_1 \gamma_1 + \cdots + y_r \gamma_r \in \mathbb{R} \tag{3}$$

is an isomorphism of $\mathbb{Z}^r$ onto the subgroup of $\mathbb{R}$ (freely) generated by $\gamma_1, \ldots, \gamma_r$. Therefore, the restriction f of θ to X satisfies condition (i), and the monoid $C' = \{h \in \mathbb{Z}^r \mid h \cdot g \geq 0\}$ satisfies

$$C' \cap -C' = \{0\} \quad \text{and} \quad C' \cup -C' = \mathbb{Z}^r, \tag{4}$$

and equips $\mathbb{Z}^r$ with a new total order $\leq_{C'}$. Since by (2), $0 <_{C'} d_l \in C'$, then by (1), $x_1 <_{C'} x_2 <_{C'} \cdots <_{C'} x_n$. By (i) and (3)–(4),

$$0 < \theta(d_l) = \theta(x_{l+1}) - \theta(x_l) = f(x_{l+1}) - f(x_l) \text{ for each } l = 1, \ldots, n-1,$$

whence $f(x_1) < f(x_2) < \cdots < f(x_n)$. Thus f also satisfies condition (ii). □

---

[1] Like its equivalent reformulation known as Farkas' lemma, this is one of the many "Theorems of the Alternative" in Linear Programming and Convex Analysis. See [8, Theorem 2.2.1, Lemma 2.2.7, Exercise 4, p. 25], [19, 16.10 (i), (ii)], [51, §7.3, and §7.8 (31)].

The foregoing proof abbreviates the original one in [21], and has a key role in the short proof [20, pp. 171–173] of the completeness theorem for Łukasiewicz infinite-valued logic, first proved by Rose and Rosser in [49] using a syntactical method, and then by Chang in [16] using model-theoretic techniques. Partial isomorphisms are also similarly applied to prove the following basic results in ℓ-group theory:

Proposition 2. *(a) If an equation fails in an ℓ-group then it fails in $\mathbb{R}$.*[2]

(b) If an equation fails in a unital ℓ-group then it fails in the additive group $\mathbb{R}$ of real numbers with the usual order and the element 1 as the distinguished order unit.

Using the continuity of the lattice operations in free ℓ-groups and in free unital ℓ-groups (see below for details), one can further replace $\mathbb{R}$ by $\mathbb{Z}$ in (a), and by $\mathbb{Q}$ in (b).

Gurevich devoted much energy to ℓ-groups, well beyond [34]. At the very beginning of his scientific career he obtained the following main results: Answering a question of Tarski, in [30,31] he proved that the first-order theory of totally ordered abelian groups is decidable. Answering a question of Malcev, in [32] he proved that the first-order theory of ℓ-groups is hereditarily undecidable. See [28] and [33, 1.2] for further information on his later work on the subject and its ramifications.

2 ℓ-groups and Unital ℓ-groups: Structural Differences

We will survey a selection of recent results in the theories of ℓ-groups and, especially, unital ℓ-groups and their underlying geometric structure, with particular reference to decision and recognition problems. In [36, §2] one can find a fairly updated account of the *similarities* between the classes of ℓ-groups and unital ℓ-groups. In the following sections we will instead single out a number of main structural *dissimilarities*. The equational definability of ℓ-groups vs. the first-order undefinability of unital ℓ-groups is not one of them, because there is a categorical equivalence Γ between unital ℓ-groups and the equational class of MV-algebras, [41, Theorem 3.9].

As a *first* example, maximal ideals need not exist in ℓ-groups, [6, 13.1.8], but they always exist in unital ℓ-groups, [6, 13.2.6]. As a consequence, for every unital ℓ-group, the Riesz representation theorem combined with the lattice version of the Stone-Weierstrass theorem yields the following result:

Proposition 3. (See [43, §10 and references therein].) *For every unital ℓ-group (G, u) the integral yields a one-one correspondence between the set of regular Borel probability measures on the maximal spectral space of G with the hull-kernel topology, and the set of normalized positive linear functionals on (G, u).*

---

[2] This result goes back to Weinberg [54] who proved that every free ℓ-group is a subdirect product of copies of the integers.

The MV-algebraic counterpart of Proposition 3, known as the *Kroupa-Panti theorem*, is easily obtainable as a corollary by a routine application of the Γ functor.

A *second* example is given by the following result. While this is a routine exercise for the working category theorist, a proof is given for the sake of completeness.

Proposition 4. *ℓ-groups and unital ℓ-groups do not form equivalent categories.*

Proof. The category of ℓ-groups has a zero (= both initial and terminal) object, namely the singleton ℓ-group $\{0\}$. The category of unital ℓ-groups has a terminal object $\{0\}$, an initial object $(\mathbb{Z}, 1)$, and these are not isomorphic. Since categorical equivalence preserves zero objects, these two categories are not equivalent.   □

The ℓ-isomorphism Problem for ℓ-groups

A *third* main dissimilarity between ℓ-groups and unital ℓ-groups stems from the different piecewise linear structures underlying their respective free objects.

As a Turing machine input, any combinatorial manifold may be coded by a finite union P of simplexes S_i in some euclidean space $\mathbb{R}^n$, where the coordinates of each vertex of S_i are rational. Any such P is said to be a *rational polyhedron*.[3] Homeomorphisms are correspondingly replaced by *rational PL-homeomorphisms*, i.e., invertible (affine) piecewise linear maps ϕ such that every linear piece of both ϕ and its inverse has rational coefficients.

The following celebrated result, known as *Markov unrecognizability theorem*, put an end to the time-honored program of equipping every combinatorial manifold P with a computable set of complete invariants:

Proposition 5. (A.A. Markov, 1958, see [18], [38, p.144], [52] and references therein.) *The problem whether two rational polyhedra P and Q are rationally PL-homeomorphic is undecidable.*

And yet, the recognition problem is recursively enumerable: some Turing machine effectively enumerates all pairs of rationally PL-homeomorphic rational polyhedra.

Let $\mathcal{F}_n$ denote the free n-generator ℓ-group. The Baker-Beynon duality theory [2], [5] yields a geometric representation of $\mathcal{F}_n$ as the ℓ-group of all real-valued piecewise *homogeneous linear* continuous functions over $\mathbb{R}^n$, each linear piece having integer coefficients. Every ℓ-group term $t(X_1, \ldots, X_n)$ is then interpreted in $\mathcal{F}_n$ as an element $\hat{t} \colon \mathbb{R}^n \to \mathbb{R}$ of $\mathcal{F}_n$. To this purpose, for each $i = 1, \ldots, n$ one sets $\widehat{X_i} =$ the ith coordinate function $\pi_i \colon \mathbb{R}^n \to \mathbb{R}$, and then inductively lets the operation symbols $\vee, \wedge, +, -$ act as the pointwise operations of max, min, sum and subtraction in $\mathbb{R}$. The zero symbol is interpreted as the constant zero function over $\mathbb{R}^n$.

The undecidability of the ℓ-isomorphism problem for finitely presented ℓ-groups follows by combining Markov's theorem with the Baker-Beynon duality:

---

[3] P need not be convex, nor connected. The simplexes S_i need not have the same dimension. This is the terminology of [53]. Polyhedra are called "compact polyhedra" in [50].

Proposition 6. [29, Theorem 1] *The following problem is undecidable:*
INSTANCE: *ℓ-group terms s and t in the same variables $X_1, \ldots, X_n$.*
QUESTION: *Is the quotient of the free n-generator ℓ-group $\mathcal{F}_n$ by the ideal generated by $\hat{s}$, isomorphic to the quotient of $\mathcal{F}_n$ by the ideal generated by $\hat{t}$?*

For the sake of completeness we record here further decidability and undecidability results concerning $\mathcal{F}_n$:

Proposition 7. [44, Theorem 1.1] *The following problem is decidable:*
INSTANCE: *ℓ-group terms $t_1, \ldots, t_n$ in the same variables $X_1, \ldots, X_m$.*
QUESTION: *Is the ℓ-subgroup of $\mathcal{F}_m$ generated by $\hat{t}_1, \ldots, \hat{t}_n$ isomorphic to $\mathcal{F}_n$?*

Proposition 8. [44, Theorem 1.2] *The following problem is undecidable:*
INSTANCE: *ℓ-group terms $t_1, \ldots, t_n$ in the same variables $X_1, \ldots, X_m$, and an integer $l > 0$.*
QUESTION: *Is the ℓ-subgroup of $\mathcal{F}_m$ generated by $\hat{t}_1, \ldots, \hat{t}_n$ isomorphic to $\mathcal{F}_l$?*

Proposition 9. [45, Theorem 1.3] *The following problem is decidable:*
INSTANCE: *ℓ-group terms $t_1, \ldots, t_n$ in the same variables $X_1, \ldots, X_n$.*
QUESTION: *Is $\{\hat{t}_1, \ldots, \hat{t}_n\}$ a free generating set of $\mathcal{F}_n$?*

The Unital ℓ-isomorphism Problem for Unital ℓ-groups
For $n = 1, 2, \ldots$, and nonempty compact set $Q \subseteq \mathbb{R}^n$ we denote by

$$\mathcal{M}_{\mathbb{R}}(Q) \tag{5}$$

the unital ℓ-group of all *integral* piecewise (affine) linear continuous functions $f: Q \to \mathbb{R}$. In other words, there are linear polynomials $p_1, \ldots, p_m$ with integer coefficients such that for all $x \in Q$ there is $i \in \{1, \ldots, m\}$ with $f(x) = p_i(x)$. $\mathcal{M}_{\mathbb{R}}(Q)$ is equipped with the pointwise operations $+, -, \max, \min$ of the totally ordered group $\mathbb{R}$, and with the constant function 1 on $[0,1]^n$ as the distinguished order unit.[4]

By McNaughton's representation theorem, [39], [22, Theorem 9.1.5], the equivalence Γ of [41, §3] sends $\mathcal{M}_{\mathbb{R}}([0,1]^n)$ into the free n-generator MV-algebra. The freeness properties of $\mathcal{M}_{\mathbb{R}}([0,1]^n)$ in the category of unital ℓ-groups are made explicit by Proposition 2(b), as well as by the following result together with Proposition 11 below:

Proposition 10. [41, Corollary 4.16] *The coordinate maps $\xi_i: [0,1]^n \to \mathbb{R}$ yield a generating set of $\mathcal{M}_{\mathbb{R}}([0,1]^n)$. For every unital ℓ-group (G, u) and elements $0 \le g_1, \ldots, g_n \le u$, if the set $\{g_1, \ldots, g_n, u\}$ generates G then there is a unique unital ℓ-homomorphism ψ of $\mathcal{M}_{\mathbb{R}}([0,1]^n)$ onto G such that $\psi(\xi_i) = g_i$ for each $i = 1, \ldots, n$.*

An *ideal* i of a unital ℓ-group (G, u) is the kernel of a unital ℓ-homomorphism of (G, u). We say that i is *principal* if it is finitely generated. Equivalently, i is generated by a single element of (G, u).

---
[4] $\mathcal{M}_{\mathbb{R}}(Q)$ is denoted $\mathcal{M}(Q)$ in [10].

A unital ℓ-group (G, u) is *finitely presented* if for some $n = 1, 2, \ldots$ and principal ideal $\mathfrak{j}$ of G there is a unital ℓ-isomorphism between (G, u) and the quotient $\mathcal{M}_{\mathbb{R}}([0, 1]^n)/\mathfrak{j}$.

In category theory there is a notion of "finitely presented object" that coincides with the algebraic one for equational classes (see [1] and [27]). However, this latter notion is inapplicable to unital ℓ-groups. More generally, let SET denote the category of sets with functions as arrows. Following Gabriel and Ulmer [27, 6.1] let us say that an object in a locally small category C is *finitely presentable in the categorical sense* if the hom-functor

$$\mathrm{Hom}_C(A, -) : C \to \mathsf{SET}$$

preserves filtered colimits.

Since unital ℓ-groups are equivalent to the equational class of MV-algebras via the Γ functor, from [1] or [27] we have:[5]

Proposition 11. *For every unital ℓ-group (G, u) the following conditions are equivalent:*

(i) (G, u) *is finitely presented, in symbols,* $(G, u) \cong \mathcal{M}_{\mathbb{R}}([0, 1]^n)/\mathfrak{j}$ *for some principal ideal $\mathfrak{j}$ of G.*

(ii) (G, u) *is finitely presentable in the categorical sense.*

Any unital ℓ-group terms s, t in the variables $X_1, \ldots, X_n$ determine elements $\hat{s}, \hat{t} \in \mathcal{M}_{\mathbb{R}}([0, 1]^n)$ in the usual way, once each variable X_i is interpreted as the ith coordinate function $\xi_i \colon [0, 1]^n \to \mathbb{R}$.

The counterpart of the decision problem in Proposition 6 for finitely presented unital ℓ-groups is as follows:

INSTANCE: Unital ℓ-group terms $s(X_1, \ldots, X_n)$ and $t(X_1, \ldots, X_n)$.
QUESTION: Is the quotient of the free n-generator unital ℓ-group $\mathcal{M}_{\mathbb{R}}([0, 1]^n)$ by the ideal generated by $\hat{s}$, unitally ℓ-isomorphic to the quotient of $\mathcal{M}_{\mathbb{R}}([0, 1]^n)$ by the ideal generated by $\hat{t}$?

It is not known whether this problem is undecidable.

The corresponding (via Proposition 13 below) geometric recognition problem is also open:

INSTANCE: Rational polyhedra P and Q in euclidean n-space.

QUESTION: Does there exist a $\mathbb{Z}$-*homeomorphism* of P onto Q, i.e., a PL homeomorphism η such that all linear pieces of η and η^{-1} have integer coefficients?

---

[5] See [10, Theorem 2.2] for details.

3   The Polyhedral Geometry of Unital ℓ-groups

Over past years, perhaps now more than ever before, the deep interplay between algebra, order, and geometry in the theory of unital ℓ-groups has found applications outside the realm of ordered groups. The next few lines are devoted to the relevant (altogether minimal) prerequisites in polyhedral geometry necessary to give an account of these applications.

Regular Triangulations and Rational Polyhedra

We refer to [50] and [53] for background on polyhedral topology. For any simplex T we denote by ∂T the set of its vertices. For any $F \subseteq \partial T$, the convex hull of F is called a *face* of T.

For every simplicial complex $\mathcal{K}$, its *support* $|\mathcal{K}|$ is the pointset union of all simplexes of $\mathcal{K}$, and $\partial \mathcal{K}$ denotes the set of its vertices, i.e., the set of the vertices of its simplexes. A simplicial complex $\mathcal{K}$ is said to be *rational* if each simplex T of $\mathcal{K}$ is *rational*, i.e., all vertices of T are rational. Given a rational polyhedron P, a *rational triangulation* of P is a rational simplicial complex $\mathcal{K}$ such that $P = |\mathcal{K}|$. It is well known that every rational polyhedron P can be equipped with a rational triangulation, (see, e.g., [4, Theorem 1]).

For any rational point $r = (r_1, \ldots, r_n) \in \mathbb{R}^n$ we let $\mathrm{den}(r)$ denote the least common denominator of the coordinates of r. The vector

$$(\mathrm{den}(r) \cdot r_1, \ldots, \mathrm{den}(r) \cdot r_n, \ \ \mathrm{den}(r)) \in \mathbb{Z}^{n+1}$$

is called the *homogeneous correspondent* of r.

A simplex $T \subseteq \mathbb{R}^n$ is said to be *regular*[6] if it is rational and the set of homogeneous correspondents of its vertices is part of a basis of the free abelian group $\mathbb{Z}^{n+1}$. A *regular triangulation* of a rational polyhedron P is a triangulation of P consisting of regular simplexes.

Proposition 12. *Every rational polyhedron has a regular triangulation.*

Proof. This is a consequence of the affine version of the desingularization procedure for rational fans, [26, p. 253], [48, Chapter 1]. See [42, Proposition 1] for details.   □

For any rational polyhedron $P \subseteq \mathbb{R}^n$ a map $\zeta \colon P \to \mathbb{R}^m$ is called a $\mathbb{Z}$-*map* if there is a rational triangulation $\mathcal{K}$ of P such that over every simplex T of $\mathcal{K}$, ζ coincides with some (affine) linear map η_T with integer coefficients. Thus in particular, a map $\iota \colon P \to Q$ is a $\mathbb{Z}$-homeomorphism iff it is a one-one $\mathbb{Z}$-map of P onto Q whose inverse is also a $\mathbb{Z}$-map.

A Duality

Let $\mathsf{P}_\mathbb{Z}$ denote the category whose objects are rational polyhedra in $\mathbb{R}^n$ ($n = 1, 2, \ldots$), and whose morphisms are $\mathbb{Z}$-maps. Let U_{fp} denote the category of finitely presented unital ℓ-groups with unital ℓ-homomorphisms.

---

[6] "Unimodular" in [22] and [42].

Proposition 13 (Duality). *Let the functor $\mathcal{M}_{\mathbb{R}} \colon \mathsf{P}_{\mathbb{Z}} \to \mathsf{U}_{\mathsf{fp}}$ be defined by[7]:*

Objetcs: *For $P \in \mathsf{P}_{\mathbb{Z}}$, $\mathcal{M}_{\mathbb{R}}(P)$ is the set of all $\mathbb{Z}$-maps from P into $\mathbb{R}$.*
Arrows: *For $\psi \colon P \to Q$ a $\mathbb{Z}$-map, $\mathcal{M}_{\mathbb{R}}(\psi)(f) = f \circ \psi$, for each $f \in \mathcal{M}_{\mathbb{R}}(Q)$,*

where $\circ$ denotes composition. Then $\mathcal{M}_{\mathbb{R}}$ yields a duality between the categories $\mathsf{P}_{\mathbb{Z}}$ and U_{fp}. Stated otherwise, $\mathcal{M}_{\mathbb{R}}$ is a categorical equivalence between $\mathsf{P}_{\mathbb{Z}}$ and the opposite category of U_{fp}.

Proof. Combine the *Marra-Spada duality theorem* [37, Theorem 3.4] with [41, §3], where the equivalence Γ between unital ℓ-groups and MV-algebras is constructed. By direct inspection, $\Gamma(\mathcal{M}_{\mathbb{R}}(P)) =$ the MV-algebra of $[0,1]$-valued functions of $\mathcal{M}_{\mathbb{R}}(P)$ equipped with the pointwise MV-algebraic operations of $[0,1]$. Recalling Proposition 11(i), finitely presented unital ℓ-groups correspond via Γ to finitely presented MV-algebras. $\square$

For later use we record here a nontrivial consequence of this duality:

Proposition 14. [10, Theorem 3.3] *Given rational polyhedra $P \subseteq \mathbb{R}^n$ and $Q \subseteq \mathbb{R}^m$, let us agree to say that a $\mathbb{Z}$-map $\eta \colon P \to Q$ is strict if it is a $\mathbb{Z}$-homeomorphism onto its range. Then the following conditions are equivalent:*

(i) η is a strict $\mathbb{Z}$-map.
(ii) $\operatorname{den}(\eta(x)) = \operatorname{den}(x)$ for each rational point $x \in P$.
(iii) For each regular simplex $T \subseteq P$, the image $\eta(T)$ is regular simplex, and $\operatorname{den}(\eta(x)) = \operatorname{den}(x)$ for each $x \in \partial T$.
(iv) For some (equivalently, for every) regular triangulation $\mathcal{K}$ of P such that η is (affine) linear on each simplex of $\mathcal{K}$, $\eta(\mathcal{K})$ is a regular triangulation of $\eta(P)$ and $\operatorname{den}(\eta(x)) = \operatorname{den}(x)$ for each $x \in \partial \mathcal{K}$.
(v) The map $\mathcal{M}_{\mathbb{R}}(\eta) \colon \mathcal{M}_{\mathbb{R}}(Q) \to \mathcal{M}_{\mathbb{R}}(P)$ is surjective.

4   Exact and Finitely Generated Projective Unital ℓ-groups

A unital ℓ-group (G, u) is said to be *exact* if it is finitely presented and there exists a one-one unital ℓ-homomorphism of (G, u) *into* some free unital ℓ-group $\mathcal{M}_{\mathbb{R}}([0,1]^n)$.

A simplex T is said to be *strongly regular* if it is regular and the greatest common divisor of the denominators of the vertices of T is equal to 1. A triangulation $\mathcal{K}$ of a polyhedron $P \subseteq [0,1]^n$ is *strongly regular* if each maximal simplex of $\mathcal{K}$ is strongly regular. When P has a strongly regular triangulation we say that P is *strongly regular*.

Proposition 15. *Let $\mathcal{K}$ and $\mathcal{H}$ be regular triangulations of a polyhedron $P \subseteq [0,1]^n$. Then $\mathcal{K}$ is strongly regular iff so is $\mathcal{H}$.*

---

[7] Note that our present $\mathcal{M}_{\mathbb{R}}(Q)$ agrees with (5) above.

Proof. [13, Lemma 4.2]. The proof relies on the positive solution of the weak Oda factorization conjecture, [26, p. 183] by Morelli, [40], and Włodarczyk, [56]. □

Example. To see that the cube $[0,1]^n$ is strongly regular let us equip the set $\{0,1\}^n$ of its vertices with the following partial order: $(v_1, \ldots, v_n) \sqsubseteq (w_1, \ldots, w_n)$ iff $v_i \leq w_i$ for each $i = 1, \ldots, n$. Let $\mathcal{K}$ be the triangulation of $[0,1]^n$ whose maximal simplexes are the convex closures of the $n!$ maximal chains in the poset $\langle \{0,1\}^n, \sqsubseteq \rangle$. Then $\mathcal{K}$ is strongly regular.

For all points $v, w \in \mathbb{R}^n$ we let $\mathrm{dist}(v, w)$ denote their euclidean distance. As usual, "gcd" denotes greatest common divisor.

Strong regularity has the following local characterization:

Proposition 16. *[10, Theorem 4.4] Let $P \subseteq \mathbb{R}^n$ be a rational polyhedron. Then the following conditions are equivalent:*

(i) *P is strongly regular.*
(ii) *For each $v \in P$ and $0 < \delta \in \mathbb{R}$ there exists $w \in P$ such that $\mathrm{dist}(v, w) < \delta$, and $\gcd(\mathrm{den}(v), \mathrm{den}(w)) = 1$.*

Proposition 17. *[10, Theorem 4.10] A unital ℓ-group is exact iff it is unitally ℓ-isomorphic to $\mathcal{M}_{\mathbb{R}}(P)$ for some strongly regular connected polyhedron $P \subseteq \mathbb{R}^n$ containing a vertex of the cube $[0,1]^n$.*

A $\mathbb{Z}$-map $\rho: P \to P$ is said to be a $\mathbb{Z}$-*retraction* of P if $\rho \circ \rho = \rho$. The rational polyhedron $R = \rho(P)$ is said to be a $\mathbb{Z}$-*retract of P.*

Proposition 18. *[14, Proposition 7.2] For R a rational polyhedron, presented as a union of rational simplexes in $[0,1]^n$, checking whether R is a $\mathbb{Z}$-retract of $[0,1]^n$ is an undecidable problem.*

Finitely Generated Projective Unital ℓ-Groups

As a particular case of a general definition, a unital ℓ-group (G, u) is said to be *projective* if whenever $\psi: (G_1, u_1) \to (G_2, u_2)$ is a unital ℓ-homomorphism onto (G_2, u_2) and $\phi: (G, u) \to (G_2, u_2)$ is a unital ℓ-homomorphism, there is a unital ℓ-homomorphism $\theta: (G, u) \to (G_1, u_1)$ such that $\phi = \psi \circ \theta$. Equivalently, there are unital ℓ-homomorphisms $\iota: (G, u) \to \mathcal{M}_{\mathbb{R}}([0,1]^n)$ and $\sigma: \mathcal{M}_{\mathbb{R}}([0,1]^n) \to (G, u)$ such that $\sigma \circ \iota$ is the identity map on G.

For unital ℓ-groups we have the following *proper* inclusions, [10, (4.1), Theorem 4.10]:

$$\text{Finitely generated projective} \subsetneq \text{Exact} \subsetneq \text{Finitely presented.}$$

Proposition 19. *A unital ℓ-group is finitely generated projective iff for some $n = 1, 2, \ldots$ it is unitally ℓ-isomorphic to $\mathcal{M}_{\mathbb{R}}(P)$ for some $\mathbb{Z}$-retract P of $[0,1]^n$.*

Proof. From Proposition 13. See [12, Theorem 1.2] for details.   □

A deeper characterization will be given in Proposition 21. To this purpose, let $\mathcal{K}$ be a simplicial complex, S an n-simplex of $\mathcal{K}$, and T an $(n-1)$-face of S which is not a face of any other n-simplex of $\mathcal{K}$. T is then called a *free face* S. If S has a free face, S is not a proper face of any simplex of $\mathcal{K}$, and hence $\mathcal{K} \setminus \{S, T\}$ is a subcomplex of $\mathcal{K}$. The transformation of $\mathcal{K} \mapsto \mathcal{K} \setminus \{S, T\}$ is known as an *elementary collapse*. If a simplicial complex Λ can be obtained from $\mathcal{K}$ by a sequence of elementary collapses we say that $\mathcal{K}$ *collapses to* Λ. A simplicial complex $\mathcal{K}$ is *collapsible* if it collapses to the simplicial complex consisting of one of its vertices (equivalently, of any of its vertices [55, p. 248]).

Proposition 20. [13, Theorem 6.1]   *Let $P \subseteq [0,1]^n$ be a polyhedron. Suppose P satisfies the following conditions:*
(i) P has a collapsible triangulation;
(ii) P contains a vertex of the cube $[0,1]^n$;
(iii) P is strongly regular.
Then P is a $\mathbb{Z}$-retract of $[0,1]^n$.

The last main dissimilarity between ℓ-groups and unital ℓ-groups considered in this paper concerns finitely generated projectives. Beynon [5, Theorem 3.1] proved that *an ℓ-group is finitely generated projective iff it is finitely presented.*[8] But for unital ℓ-groups being finitely generated projective is a much stricter condition than being finitely presented:

Proposition 21. *(a) Let (G, u) be a finitely generated projective unital ℓ-group. Arbitrarily pick elements $g_1, \ldots, g_n \in [0, u]$ that form a generating set of (G, u). Then (G, u) is unitally ℓ-isomorphic to the unital ℓ-group $\mathcal{M}_{\mathbb{R}}(P)$ obtained by restricting to P the functions of $\mathcal{M}_{\mathbb{R}}([0,1]^n)$, for some set P satisfying the following conditions:*
(i) P is a rational polyhedron in $[0,1]^n$ containing a vertex of the cube $[0,1]^n$;
(ii) P is contractible (i.e., homotopy equivalent to a point);
(iii) P is strongly regular.

(b) Conversely, if a unital ℓ-group (G, u) is unitally ℓ-isomorphic to $\mathcal{M}_{\mathbb{R}}(P)$ with P satisfying conditions (i)–(iii) for some n, then (G, u) is finitely generated and projective.

Proof. (a) [13, Theorem 5.2, Corollary 7.1(I)]. (b) This is Cabrer's characterization theorem [11, Theorem 4.8], a remarkable tour de force in algebraic topology. □

Computable Numerical Invariants

At the end of the day, ℓ-groups and unital ℓ-groups have very different geometric, topological, and algebraic properties. Further, every finitely presented unital ℓ-group $\mathcal{M}_{\mathbb{R}}(P)$ is blessed with the wealth of computable numerical invariants typically arising from the regular triangulations of its dual rational polyhedron P given by Proposition 13. These invariants include:

---

[8] Also see Baker's analysis of finitely generated projective vector lattices in [2, Theorem 5.1].

The number n_d of rational points of denominator d lying in P, $d = 1, 2, \ldots$.
(Proposition 14 shows that $\mathbb{Z}$-homeomorphisms preserve denominators of
rational points.)

The list L_P of cardinalities of all regular triangulations of P having the smallest possible number of vertices. (By Proposition 12, L_P is nonempty. Trivially,
L_P is finite.)

The smallest number $m = m_P$ such that there is a $\mathbb{Z}$-map η which embeds P
into $\mathbb{R}^m$ with preservation of denominators. (By Proposition 14, any such η
is necessarily a "strict" map.)

The d-dimensional rational volume $\lambda_d(P)$ of P, for each $d = 1, 2, \ldots, m_P$.
(See [42, Theorem 2.1].)

None of these invariants makes sense for finitely presented ℓ-groups and their
rational fans given by the Baker-Beynon duality. The abundance of these computable invariants may account for the impasse over the isomorphism problem
of finitely presented unital ℓ-groups, despite the time and effort devoted to it.

5   Unital ℓ-groups, MV-algebras, and Elliott's Classification

Finite and Infinite Quantum Systems

Any quantum system S with finitely many degrees of freedom has an irreducible
representation on a Hilbert space H_S which is uniquely determined up to unitary
equivalence (this is von Neumann's uniqueness theorem). Observables are self-
adjoint operators in H_S. Pure states are extremal positive linear normalized
functionals on the C*-algebra $B(H_S)$ of bounded linear operators on H_S. States
are weighted sums of pure states.

On the contrary, systems T in quantum statistical mechanics or in relativistic
quantum field theory have infinitely many degrees of freedom. T typically has
many inequivalent representations, corresponding to its macroscopically different
classes of states, and we can no longer speak of *the* Hilbert space of T. The
appropriate mathematization of T is given by a C*-algebra A_T. The observables
(resp., the states) of T are the self-adjoint elements of A_T, (resp., the normalized
positive linear functionals on A_T). In quantum statistical mechanics an essential
feature of a macroscopic assembly T of particles is that the state equations are
size independent. We are naturally led to an idealization of T as an infinite
volume limit of increasingly large finite systems $T_1 \subseteq T_2 \subseteq T_3 \subseteq \cdots$ with
constant density.[9] The observables of T are constructed from the self-adjoint
elements of what Bratteli [9] named an *AF C*-algebra* $\mathfrak{A} = \mathfrak{A}_T$, i.e., the norm
closure of an ascending sequence of finite-dimensional C*-algebras, all with the
same unit.

---

[9] In this way one can describe, for instance, phase transitions as singularities in the
thermodynamic potentials.

Projections and Their Murray-von Neumann Equivalence Classes

Propositions expressing the properties of a finite system S are interpreted by Birkhoff and von Neumann as projections of $B(H_S)$. The set of projections is equipped with a form of complementation and lattice operations that are reminiscent of the boolean connectives.

Projections in any AF C*-algebra $\mathfrak{A}$ have no lesser role than projections have in $B(H_S)$. Following [23], [24], for any two projections p, q of an AF C*-algebra $\mathfrak{A}$ we write $p \sim q$ if p is *Murray-von Neumann equivalent* to q. This means $p = x^*x$ and $q = xx^*$ for some $x \in \mathfrak{A}$. The equivalence class of p is denoted $[p]$. If p is equivalent to a subprojection of q we write $p \preceq q$. The reflexive and transitive $\preceq$-relation is preserved under equivalence. Further, by [23, Theorem IV.2.3], $p \preceq q \preceq p \Rightarrow p \sim q$. The partial order $\preceq$ on the set $L(\mathfrak{A})$ of equivalence classes of projections in $\mathfrak{A}$ is called the *Murray-von Neumann order*. *Elliott's partial addition* in $L(\mathfrak{A})$ is defined by setting $[p] + [q] = [p + q]$ whenever p and q are orthogonal. This yields a countable partially ordered "local" semigroup. Elliott's partial addition is monotone with respect to the $\preceq$-order.

By *Elliott's classification* [25], $L(\mathfrak{A}_1) \cong L(\mathfrak{A}_2)$ iff $\mathfrak{A}_1 \cong \mathfrak{A}_2$.

AFℓ-algebras, MV-algebras and Elliott's Classification

When the Murray-von Neumann order of projections of $\mathfrak{A}$ is a lattice we say that $\mathfrak{A}$ is an *AFℓ-algebra*. Many (if not most) classes of AF C*-algebras in the literature are in fact AFℓ-algebras, [46, Foreword].

Proposition 22. [47, Theorem 1] *For every AF C*-algebra $\mathfrak{A}$, Elliott's partial addition $+$ in $L(\mathfrak{A})$ has at most one extension to an associative, commutative, monotone operation $\oplus \colon L(\mathfrak{A})^2 \to L(\mathfrak{A})$ such that for each projection $p \in \mathfrak{A}$, $[1_{\mathfrak{A}} - p]$ is the $\preceq$-smallest equivalence class $[q] \in L(\mathfrak{A})$ satisfying $[p] \oplus [q] = [1_{\mathfrak{A}}]$.*

The semigroup $(S(\mathfrak{A}), \oplus)$ extending $L(\mathfrak{A})$ exists iff $\mathfrak{A}$ is an AFℓ-algebra. Let $\mathfrak{A}_1$ and $\mathfrak{A}_2$ be AFℓ-algebras. From Elliott's classification it follows that for each $j = 1, 2$, letting $\oplus_j$ be the extension of Elliott's addition, then

$$(S(\mathfrak{A}_1), \oplus_1) \cong (S(\mathfrak{A}_2), \oplus_2) \quad iff \quad \mathfrak{A}_1 \cong \mathfrak{A}_2.$$

By [47, Theorem 2, Proposition 2.2], for every AFℓ-algebra $\mathfrak{A}$, the operation $[p]^* = [1_{\mathfrak{A}} - p]$ transforms $(S(\mathfrak{A}), \oplus)$ into a countable involutive monoid $(\mathsf{E}(\mathfrak{A}), 0, ^*, \oplus)$. The Murray-von Neumann lattice order $\preceq$ of equivalence classes of projections $[p], [q] \in \mathsf{E}(\mathfrak{A})$ is definable from the involutive monoidal operations of $\mathsf{E}(\mathfrak{A})$, upon setting

$$[p] \vee [q] = ([p]^* \oplus [q])^* \oplus [q] \quad \text{and} \quad [p] \wedge [q] = ([p]^* \vee [q]^*)^*.$$

As a consequence:

Proposition 23. *Up to isomorphism, the map $\mathfrak{A} \mapsto (\mathsf{E}(\mathfrak{A}), 0, ^*, \oplus)$ is a one-one correspondence between AFℓ-algebras and countable MV-algebras.*

We say that $\mathsf{E}(\mathfrak{A})$ is the *Elliott (involutive) monoid* of $\mathfrak{A}$.

Word Problems in AF C*-algebras

Any commutative AF C*-algebra is isomorphic to the C*-algebra $C(X)$ of all continuous complex-valued functions defined over a separable *boolean* (i.e., totally disconnected, compact Hausdorff) space X. Thus AF C*-algebras may be thought of as a sort of *noncommutative boolean algebras* [7, §7.1]. For AFℓ-algebras this intuition is made more precise by Proposition 23, upon recalling that MV-algebras were introduced by Chang to give a proof of the completeness of the Łukasiewicz axioms. (See [15–17].) Chang himself noted in [15] that *boolean algebras coincide with MV-algebras satisfying the idempotency equation* $x \oplus x = x$.

In view of the categorical equivalence Γ between unital ℓ-groups and MV-algebras, one may naturally look for a characterization of the unital ℓ-group $G_{\mathfrak{A}}$ corresponding to the Elliott involutive monoid of an AFℓ-algebra $\mathfrak{A}$. By [41, Theorem 3.9],

$$G_{\mathfrak{A}} = \Gamma(K_0(\mathfrak{A}), \ K_0(\mathfrak{A})^+, \ [1_{\mathfrak{A}}]),$$

the latter being the unital ℓ-group associated to $\mathfrak{A}$ by the K_0-theoretic reformulation of Elliott's classification, [23], [24].

In [46] the computational theory of unital ℓ-groups and their equivalent reformulation in terms of MV-algebras is applied to investigate the complexity of the word problem of several classes of AFℓ-algebras. In view of Elliott's classification and Proposition 22, the problem asks whether two formulas in the language of MV-algebras (resp., in the language of unital ℓ-groups) denote the same Murray-von Neumann equivalence class of projections of a given AFℓ-algebra.

Polynomial time results are proved for the Behncke-Leptin C*-algebras $\mathcal{A}_{m,n}$, [3], as well as for a large set of Effros-Shen algebras $\mathfrak{F}_\theta$, [24], including the case when $\theta = 1/e$, or θ is a real algebraic number.

At the other extreme, Gödel incompleteness results for AFℓ-algebras are obtained in [41] and [46].

The natural deductive-algorithmic machinery of Łukasiewicz infinite-valued logic, combined with the arithmetic-geometric structure of the rational polyhedra dual to finitely presented unital ℓ-groups, thus provides a natural framework for the algorithmic theory of AFℓ-algebras.

Acknowledgement. The author is grateful to the reviewer for her/his valuable remarks and for providing a short proof of Proposition 4.

References

1. Adámek, J., Rosicky, J.: Locally Presentable and Accessible Categories. London Mathematical Society Lecture Note Series, vol. 189. Cambridge University Press, Cambridge (1994)
2. Baker, K.A.: Free vector lattices. Can. J. Math. **20**, 58–66 (1968)
3. Behncke, K.A., Leptin, H.: C*-algebras with a two-point dual. J. Funct. Anal. **10**, 330–335 (1972)
4. Beynon, W.M.: On rational subdivisions of polyhedra with rational vertices. Can. J. Math. **29**, 238–242 (1977)

5. Beynon, W.M.: Applications of duality in the theory of finitely generated lattice-ordered abelian groups. Can. J. Math. **29**, 243–254 (1977)
6. Bigard, A., Keimel, K., Wolfenstein, S.: Groupes etAnneaux Réticulés. Lecture Notes in Mathematics, vol. 608. Springer, Berlin (1971). https://doi.org/10.1007/BFb0067004
7. Blackadar, B.: K-Theory for Operator Algebras. Springer, New York (1986). https://doi.org/10.1007/978-1-4613-9572-0. Second revised edn., vol. 5. MSRI Publications, Cambridge University Press (1998)
8. Borwein, J.M., Lewis, A.S.: Convex Analysis and Nonlinear Optimization. Theory and Examples. Springer, New York (2006). https://doi.org/10.1007/978-0-387-31256-9
9. Bratteli, O.: Inductive limits of finite dimensional C*-algebras. Trans. Am. Math. Soc. **171**, 195–234 (1972)
10. Cabrer, L.: Simplicial geometry of unital lattice-ordered abelian groups. Forum Math. **27**(3), 1309–1344 (2015)
11. Cabrer, L.: Rational simplicial geometry and projective lattice-ordered abelian groups. arXiv:1405.7118v1
12. Cabrer, L., Mundici, D.: Projective MV-algebras and rational polyhedra. Algebra Univers. **62**, 63–74 (2009). Special issue in memoriam P. Conrad, (J.Martínez, Ed.)
13. Cabrer, L., Mundici, D.: Rational polyhedra and projective lattice-ordered abelian groups with order unit. Commun. Contemp. Math. **14**(3), 1250017 (2012). https://doi.org/10.1142/S0219199712500174. 20 pages
14. Cabrer, L., Mundici, D.: Idempotent endomorphisms of free MV-algebras and unital ℓ-groups. J. Pure Appl. Algebra **221**, 908–934 (2017)
15. Chang, C.C.: Algebraic analysis of many-valued logics. Trans. Am. Math. Soc. **88**, 467–490 (1958)
16. Chang, C.C.: A new proof of the completeness of the Łukasiewicz axioms. Trans. Am. Math. Soc. **93**, 74–90 (1959)
17. Chang, C.C.: The writing of the MV-algebras. Stud. Logica **61**, 3–6 (1998)
18. Chernavsky, A.V., Leksine, V.P.: Unrecognizability of manifolds. Ann. Pure Appl. Logic **141**, 325–335 (2006)
19. Chvatal, V.: Linear Programming. W.H. Freeman and Company, New York (1980)
20. Cignoli, R., Mundici, D.: An invitation to Chang's MV-algebras. In: Droste, M., Göbel, R. (eds.) Advances in Algebra and Model Theory. Algebra, Logic and Applications Series, vol. 9, pp. 171–197. Gordon and Breach Publishing Group, Readings (1997)
21. Cignoli, R., Mundici, D.: Partial isomorphisms on totally ordered abelian groups and Hájek's completeness theorem for basic logic. Multiple Valued Logic (Special issue dedicated to the memory of Grigore Moisil) **6**, 89–94 (2001)
22. Cignoli, R., D'Ottaviano, I.M.L., Mundici, D.: Algebraic Foundations of Many-valued Reasoning. Trends in Logic, vol. 7. Kluwer, Dordrecht (2000)
23. Davidson, K.R.: C*-Algebras by Example. Fields Institute Monographs, vol. 6. American Mathematical Society, Providence (1996)
24. Effros, E.G.: Dimensions and C*-Algebras. CBMS Regional Conference Series in Mathematics, vol. 46. American Mathematical Society, Providence (1981)
25. Elliott, G.A.: On the classification of inductive limits of sequences of semisimple finite-dimensional algebras. J. Algebra **38**, 29–44 (1976)
26. Ewald, G.: Combinatorial Convexity and Algebraic Geometry. Springer, New York (1996). https://doi.org/10.1007/978-1-4612-4044-0
27. Gabriel, P., Ulmer, F.: Lokal präsentierbare Kategorien. Lecture Notes in Mathematics, vol. 221. Springer, Heidelberg (1971). https://doi.org/10.1007/BFb0059396

28. Glass, A.M.W., Yuri Gurevich, Y.: The word problem for lattice-ordered groups. Trans. Am. Math. Soc. **280**, 127–138 (1983)
29. Glass, A.M.W., Madden, J.J.: The word problem versus the isomorphism problem. J. Lond. Math. Soc. **30**, 53–61 (1984)
30. Gurevich, Y.: Elementary properties of ordered abelian groups (Ph.D. Thesis, in Russian). Algebra and Logic **3**(1), 5–39 (1964)
31. Gurevich, Y.: Elementary properties of ordered abelian groups. AMS Transl. **46**, 165–192 (1965)
32. Gurevich, Y.: Hereditary undecidability of the theory of lattice-ordered abelian groups. Algebra Logic **6**(1), 45–62 (1967). (Russian)
33. Gurevich, Y.: Monadic second-order theories (Chap. XIII). In: Barwise, J., Feferman, S.(eds.) Model-Theoretic Logics. Springer, New York, (1985)
34. Gurevich, Y., Kokorin, A.I.: Universal equivalence of ordered abelian groups. Algebra i Logica **2**(1), 37–39 (1963). (Russian)
35. Hájek, P.: Metamathematics of Fuzzy Logic. Kluwer, Dordrecht (1998)
36. Marra, V., Mundici, D.: MV-algebras and abelian ℓ-groups: a fruitful interaction. In: Martínez, J. (ed.) Ordered Algebraic Structures. Honoring Paul Conrad on his 80th birthday, pp. 57–88. Kluwer, Dordrecht (2002)
37. Marra, V., Spada, L.: Duality, projectivity, and unification in Łukasiewicz logic and MV-algebras. Ann. Pure Appl. Logic **164**, 192–210 (2013)
38. Massey, W.S.: Algebraic Topology: An Introduction. Springer, New York (1977). Originally published by Harcourt, Brace & World Inc. (1967)
39. McNaughton, R.: A theorem about infinite-valued sentential logic. J. Symbolic Logic **16**(1), 1–13 (1951)
40. Morelli, R.: The birational geometry of toric varieties. J. Algebraic Geometry **5**, 751–782 (1996)
41. Mundici, D.: Interpretation of AF C*-algebras in Łukasiewicz sentential calculus. J. Funct. Anal. **65**, 15–63 (1986)
42. Mundici, D.: The Haar theorem for lattice-ordered abelian groups with order-unit. Discrete Contin. Dyn. Syst. **21**, 537–549 (2008)
43. Mundici, D.: Advanced Łukasiewicz Calculus and MV-Algebras. Trends in Logic, vol. 35. Springer, Berlin (2011). https://doi.org/10.1007/978-94-007-0840-2
44. Mundici, D.: Fans, decision problems and generators of free abelian ℓ-groups. Forum Math. **29**(6), 1429–1439 (2017)
45. Mundici, D.: Recognizing free generating sets of ℓ-groups. Algebra Universalis **79**, 24 (2018). https://doi.org/10.1007/s00012-018-0511-2
46. Mundici, D.: Word problems in Elliott monoids. Adv. Math. **335**, 343–371 (2018)
47. Mundici, D., Panti, G.: Extending addition in Elliott's local semigroup. J. Funct. Anal. **117**, 461–471 (1993)
48. Oda, T.: Convex Bodies and Algebraic Geometry. Springer, Berlin (1988)
49. Rose, A., Rosser, J.B.: Fragments of many-valued sentential calculus. Trans. Am. Math. Soc. **87**, 1–53 (1958)
50. Rourke, C.P., Sanderson, B.J.: Introduction to Piecewise-Linear Topology. Springer, New York (1972). https://doi.org/10.1007/978-3-642-81735-9
51. Schrijver, A.: Theory of Linear and Integer Programming. Wiley, Chichester (1986). Reprinted (1999)
52. Shtan'ko, M.A.: Markov's theorem and algorithmically non-recognizable combinatorial manifolds. Izvestiya RAN Ser. Math. **68**, 207–224 (2004)
53. Stallings, J.R.: Lectures on Polyhedral Topology. Tata Institute of Fundamental Research, Mumbay (1967)

54. Weinberg, E.C.: Free lattice-ordered abelian groups. II. Math. Ann. **159**, 217–222 (1965). https://doi.org/10.1007/BF01362439
55. Whitehead, J.H.C.: Simplicial spaces, nuclei and m-groups. Proc. Lond. Math. Soc. **45**, 243–327 (1939)
56. Włodarczyk, J.: Decompositions of birational toric maps in blow-ups and blow-downs. Trans. Am. Math. Soc. **349**, 373–411 (1997)

The Expressive Power of Temporal and First-Order Metric Logics

Alexander Rabinovich[(⊠)]

The Blavatnik School of Computer Science, Tel Aviv University, Tel Aviv-Yafo, Israel
rabinoa@tauex.tau.ac.il

Abstract. The First-Order Monadic Logic of Order ($FO[<]$) is a prominent logic for the specification of properties of systems evolving in time. The celebrated result of Kamp [14] states that a temporal logic with just two modalities Until and Since has the same expressive power as $FO[<]$ over the standard discrete time of naturals and continuous time of reals. An influential consequence of Kamp's theorem is that this temporal logic has emerged as the canonical Linear Time Temporal Logic (LTL). Neither LTL nor $FO[<]$ can express over the reals properties like P holds exactly after one unit of time. Such local metric properties are easily expressible in $FO[<, +1]$ - the extension of $FO[<]$ by $+1$ function. Hirshfeld and Rabinovich [10] proved that no temporal logic with a finite set of modalities has the same expressive power as $FO[<, +1]$.

$FO[<, +1]$ lacks expressive power to specify a natural global metric property "the current moment is an integer." Surprisingly, we show that the extension of $FO[<, +1]$ by a monadic predicate "x is an integer" is equivalent to a temporal logic with a finite set of modalities.

1 Introduction

1.1 Temporal Logics and Kamp's Theorem

Temporal Logics were introduced to Computer Science by Pnueli in [18]. They provide a convenient framework for reasoning about "reactive" systems. This made temporal logics a popular subject in the Computer Science community, enjoying extensive research in the past 30 years.

In a temporal logic we describe basic system properties by *atomic propositions* that hold at some points in time, but not at others. More complex properties are expressed by formulas built from the atoms using Boolean connectives and *Modalities* (temporal connectives): A k-place modality M transforms statements $\varphi_1, \ldots, \varphi_k$ possibly on 'past' or 'future' points to a statement $M(\varphi_1, \ldots, \varphi_k)$ on the 'present' point. The rule to determine the truth of a statement $M(\varphi_1, \ldots, \varphi_k)$ is called a *truth table*. The choice of particular modalities with their truth tables yields different temporal logics.

A basic modality is $\Diamond$ - eventually: $\Diamond P$ says: "P holds some time in the future." It is formalized by a formula $\varphi(z_0, P) := (\exists z > z_0)P(z)$ with one free variable z_0 (for the current moment). This is a formula of the First-Order

© Springer Nature Switzerland AG 2020
A. Blass et al. (Eds.): Gurevich Festschrift, LNCS 12180, pp. 226–246, 2020.
https://doi.org/10.1007/978-3-030-48006-6_16

Monadic Logic of Order ($FO[<]$) - a fundamental formalism in Mathematical Logic where formulas are built from atomic monadic formulas $P(z)$ and atomic order formulas $z_1 = z_2$, $z_1 < z_2$, by Boolean connectives and first-order quantifiers $\exists z$ and $\forall z$. Most modalities used in the literature are defined by such first-order truth tables, and, as a result, every temporal formula translates directly into an equivalent first-order formula. Thus, the different temporal logics may be considered a convenient way to present fragments of first-order logic. A first-order logic can also serve as a yardstick by which one can check the strength of temporal logics. A temporal logic is *expressively complete* for a fragment L of a predicate logic if every formula of L with a single free variable is equivalent to a temporal formula.

Actually, the notion of expressive completeness is with respect to the type of the underlying model since the question whether two formulas are equivalent depends on the domain over which they are evaluated. The standard linear time intended models are the Naturals $\langle \mathbb{N}, < \rangle$ for discrete time and the Reals $\langle \mathbb{R}, < \rangle$ for continuous time.

A major result concerning temporal logics is Kamp's theorem [5,14] which states that the temporal logic with two modalities "P Until Q" and "P Since Q" is expressively complete for $FO[<]$ over the above two linear time canonical models.

LTL (Linear Time Temporal Logic) is the temporal logic with two modalities Until and Since. An influential consequence of Kamp's result is that *LTL* has emerged as the canonical temporal logic.

1.2 Expressing Metrical Properties

The choice between $FO[<]$ and *LTL* is merely a matter of personal preference, as far as only the expressive power is concerned. For discrete time these logics suffice. Properties like "Every P will be followed promptly enough by a Q" can be explicitly written once a number k is chosen, and "promptly enough" is interpreted as: "within k steps."

LTL and $FO[<]$ are expressively equivalent whether the system evolves in discrete or in continuous time. However, for continuous time both logics lack the power to express properties of the kind just described, and we must strengthen their expressive power.

Some measure of length of time needs to be included, and the language must be adapted to it. This is done by assuming that there is a basic unit of length; let's call it "length 1." For predicate logic it is a standard procedure to extend the language by a name for the "$+1$" function, or for a corresponding relation. It will then be the question which fragment of the extended language $FO[<, +1]$ suits our needs.

Burgess and Gurevich [4] proved that $FO[<]$ is decidable over the reals. Unfortunately, $FO[<, +1]$ is undecidable over the reals. Much research was carried out to find decidable temporal logics which can specify some metric properties. Extending temporal logic, without relating it to a corresponding predicate logic, has led to a veritable babel of metric temporal logics over the reals [1–3,5,7–9,15,16,21]. The most popular among decidable temporal logics is *MITL* (Metric Interval Temporal Logic) introduced by Alur, Feder and Henzinger [1]. *MITL* uses infinitely many modalities. However, it has the same expressive power as *QTL* (Quantitative Temporal Logic [9]), which has besides the modalities *Until* and *Since* two metric modalities: $\Diamond_{(0,1)}P$ and $\Diamond_{(-1,0)}P$. The first one states that P will happen (at least once) within the next unit of time, and the second says that P happened within the last unit of time.

Adding the power to say "P will be true (at least once) within the next unit of time" is natural and necessary. There is, however, no reason to believe that this gives us the required expressive power. Is it enough, or do we need additional modalities? If we must add more modalities, which ones should we choose? A. Pnueli was the first to address these questions.

In previous work we have defined the *counting modalities* $C_n(P)$ and $\overleftarrow{C}_n(P)$ for $n \in Nat$. $C_n(P)$ says "P will hold at least at n points within the next unit of time" and its dual $\overleftarrow{C}_n(P)$ says "P was true at least at n points within the previous unit of time" [9,10].

TLC (Temporal Logic with Counting) is the extension of *LTL* by all counting modalities. For $n \in \mathbb{N}$, a fragment TLC_n of *TLC* has only finitely many modalities: Until, Since and C_k, $\overleftarrow{C}_k$ for $k \leq n$. In particular, TLC_1 is exactly *QTL* and has the same expressive power as *MITL*.

We proved in [9–11] the following:

1. *TLC* is decidable and equivalent to a natural fragment of $FO[<,+1]$.
2. TLC_n is strictly less expressive than TLC_{n+1}, so this is a strict hierarchy.
3. If the expressive power of a temporal logic $\mathcal{L}$ is between *TLC* and $FO[<,+1]$, then $\mathcal{L}$ has infinitely many modalities.

As a consequence of (3), and in contrast to Kamp's theorem, no temporal logic with a finite set of modalities is expressively equivalent to $FO[<,+1]$ over the reals.

1.3 Kamp's Theorem in Metric Setting

Over the reals, $FO[<,+1]$ still lacks expressive power to specify a natural global metric property "the current moment is an integer."

This paper is concerned with the expressive power of $FO[<,+1]$ over the expansion $\mathbb{R}_\mathbb{Z}$ of the reals by a monadic predicate interpreted as the set of integers. We prove that $FO[<,+1]$ has the same expressive power as a temporal logic with a finite set of modalities, hence an analog of Kamp's theorem holds.

More specifically, *MTL* (Metric Temporal Logic [15]) in addition to four modalities of *QTL* has two more modalities: $\Diamond_{=1}$ and $\Diamond_{=-1}$; $\Diamond_{=1}(P)$ says: "P is true exactly after one unit of time" its dual $\Diamond_{=-1}(P)$ says "P was true exactly before one unit of time."

Our main result states that $FO[<,+1]$ has the same expressive power as *MTL* over $\mathbb{R}_\mathbb{Z}$.

The paper is organized as follows. Section 2 provides definitions of the first-order monadic logics and of temporal logics. In Sect. 3, Kamp's theorem and our main result are stated. Section 4 outlines a proof of the main theorem. The structure of the proof of expressive completeness is similar to the simplified proof of Kamp's theorem [20]. We recall the relevant notions and propositions from [6,20] used in the proof of Kamp's theorem. Then, we generalize these propositions to the metric setting and prove expressive equivalence of MTL and $FO[<,+1]$ over $\mathbb{R}_{\mathbb{Z}}$. Sections 5–7 contain the proof of main technical lemmas, which uses some ideas from [17,19]. The last section presents conclusion and discusses related works.

2 Logics

In this section we recall definitions of the first-order monadic logics and of temporal logics.

Fix a set Σ of *atoms*. We use $P, R, S \ldots$ to denote members of Σ. The syntax and semantics of both logics are defined below with respect to such Σ.

2.1 First-Order Monadic Logics

In the context of first-order logics, the atoms of Σ are considered as *unary predicate symbols*.

The signature of $FO[<]$ (first-order monadic logic of order) in addition to Σ contains two binary relation symbols: $<$ and $=$. We use $x, y, z, \ldots$ for (first-order) variables. The formulas are defined by the following grammar:

$$atomic := x < y \mid x = y \mid P(x) \ \ (\text{where} \ P \in \Sigma)$$

$$\varphi := atomic \mid \neg\varphi \mid \varphi \vee \varphi \mid \varphi \wedge \varphi \mid \exists x\varphi \mid \forall x\varphi$$

We will also use the standard abbreviated notation for *bounded quantifiers*, e.g., $(\exists x)_{>z}(\ldots)$ denotes $\exists x((x > z) \wedge (\ldots))$, and $(\forall x)^{<z}(\ldots)$ denotes $\forall x((x < z) \to (\ldots))$, and $((\forall x)^{<z_2}_{>z_1}(\ldots)$ denotes $\forall x((z_1 < x < z_2) \to (\ldots))$, etc.

A Σ-structure (or just structure) $\mathcal{M}$ for $FO[<]$ is a tuple $\mathcal{M} = (\mathcal{T}, <, \mathcal{I})$ where $\mathcal{T}$ is a set - the *domain* of $\mathcal{M}$, $<$ is a linear order relation on $\mathcal{T}$, and $\mathcal{I} : \Sigma \to \mathcal{P}(\mathcal{T})$ is the *interpretation* of Σ (where $\mathcal{P}$ is the powerset notation).

$FO[<,+1]$ is the extension of $FO[<]$ by a unary $+1$ functional symbol. We mostly will be interested in the interpretations of $FO[<,+1]$ over the reals. Under such interpretations, the domain of $\mathcal{M}$ is the set $\mathbb{R}$ of reals, $<$ and $+1$ are interpreted in the standard way, and unary predicate symbols from Σ are interpreted as unary predicates on the reals. We call such structures $\mathbb{R}$-structures. If, in addition, Σ contains a predicate name Int, interpreted as the set $\mathbb{Z}$ of integers, a structure is called an $\mathbb{R}_{\mathbb{Z}}$ structure.

It will be convenient for us to use another first-order language which is equivalent to $FO[<,+1]$ over $\mathbb{R}_{\mathbb{Z}}$ structures. This is the extension of $FO[<]$ by a unary function symbol $\lfloor x \rfloor$ - interpreted as the integer part of x, and by the unary functions $+c$ for $c \in \mathbb{Z}$. Its terms are defined by the grammar $t := x \mid \lfloor t \rfloor \mid t + c$ for $c \in \mathbb{Z}$. A standard term is a term of the form $\lfloor x \rfloor + c$ or $x + c$. It is clear that every term is equivalent to a standard term. By abusing notations, this logic will be also denoted by $FO[<, +1]$.

We use the standard notation $\mathcal{M}, a_1, a_2, \ldots a_n \models \varphi(x_1, x_2, \ldots x_n)$ to indicate that the formula φ with free variables among $x_1, \ldots, x_n$ is satisfiable in $\mathcal{M}$ when x_i are interpreted as elements a_i of $\mathcal{M}$.

2.2   Temporal Logics

In the context of temporal logics the atoms of Σ are used as *atomic propositions* (also called *propositional atoms*). Formulas are built using these atoms, and a set (finite or infinite) B of *modality names*, where a non-negative integer *arity* is associated with each modality $\mathsf{M} \in B$.

LTL (Linear Time Temporal Logic) has two modalities *strict*-Until and *strict*-Since. *LTL* formulas are defined by the following grammar:

$$F := \quad P \mid \neg F \mid F \vee F \mid F \wedge F \mid F \text{ Until } F \mid F \text{ Since } F, \text{ where } P \in \Sigma.$$

MTL (Metric Temporal Logic) has four additional unary modalities: *MTL* syntax extends the syntax of *LTL* by the following rules: If F is a formula, then $\Diamond_{(0,1)}F$, $\Diamond_{(-1,0)}F$, $\Diamond_{=1}F$ and $\Diamond_{=-1}F$ are formulas.

QTL (Quantitative Temporal Logic) is the fragment of *MTL* which uses only the modalities Until, Since, $\Diamond_{(0,1)}$ and $\Diamond_{(-1,0)}$.

Semantics. The semantics defines when a temporal formula holds at a *time-point* (or *moment* or element of the domain) in a structure $\mathcal{M}$.

The semantics is defined inductively: given a structure $\mathcal{M}$ with a domain $\mathcal{T}$ and $a \in \mathcal{T}$, define when a formula F *holds* in $\mathcal{M}$ at a - notation: $\mathcal{M}, a \models F$ - as follows:

- $\mathcal{M}, a \models P$ iff $a \in \mathcal{I}(P)$ for any atom $P \in \Sigma$.
- $\mathcal{M}, a \models F \vee G$ iff $\mathcal{M}, a \models F$ or $\mathcal{M}, a \models G$; similarly ("pointwise") for $\wedge, \neg$.
- $\mathcal{M}, a \models F \text{ Until } G$ iff there is $a' > a$ such that $\mathcal{M}, a' \models G$ and $\mathcal{M}, b \models F$ for every b in an open interval (a, a').
- $\mathcal{M}, a \models F \text{ Since } G$ iff there is $a' < a$ such that $\mathcal{M}, a' \models G$ and $\mathcal{M}, b \models F$ for every b in an open interval (a', a).

MTL is interpreted over the reals with the standard interpretation of $+1$ and -1 functional symbols. It has four additional semantical clauses for modalities: $\Diamond_{(0,1)}$ - within the next unit of time, $\Diamond_{(-1,0)}$ - within the last unit of time, $\Diamond_{=1}$ - exactly after one unit of time, and $\Diamond_{=-1}$ - exactly before one unit of time.

- $\mathcal{M}, a \models \Diamond_{=1}F$ iff $\mathcal{M}, a + 1 \models F$.
- $\mathcal{M}, a \models \Diamond_{=-1}F$ iff $\mathcal{M}, a - 1 \models F$.
- $\mathcal{M}, a \models \Diamond_{(0,1)}F$ iff there is $a' \in (a, a + 1)$ such that $\mathcal{M}, a' \models F$.
- $\mathcal{M}, a \models \Diamond_{(-1,0)}F$ iff there is $a' \in (a - 1, a)$ such that $\mathcal{M}, a' \models F$.

In $\mathbb{R}_{\mathbb{Z}}$ structures Σ contains a symbol Int, interpreted as the set $\mathbb{Z}$ of integers, and

- $\mathcal{M}, a \models$ Int iff a is an integer.

We conclude this section by recalling a definition of a temporal logic TLC with an infinite sets of modalities. Thought TLC is not used directly in our technical results, it is useful to explain the role of $\mathbb{Z}$ in expressing the modality of TLC by MTL formulas.

TLC (Temporal Logic with Counting) is the extension of LTL by an infinite set of modalitues C_n and $\overleftarrow{C}_n$ for $n \in \mathbb{N}$ - counting modalities. The TLC syntax extends the syntax of LTL by the following rules: if F is a formula, then $C_n(F)$ and $\overleftarrow{C}_n(F)$ are formulas. The semantical clauses for modalities: $C_n(P)$ - "P will hold at least at n points within the next unit of time," and $\overleftarrow{C}_n(P)$ - "P was true at least at n points within the previous unit of time" are:

- $\mathcal{M}, a \models C_n(F)$ iff there are $a_1 < a_2 < \cdots < a_n \in (a, a+1)$ such that $\mathcal{M}, a_i \models F$ for $i \leq n$.
- $\mathcal{M}, a \models \overleftarrow{C}_n(F)$ iff there are $a_1 < a_2 < \cdots < a_n \in (a-1, a)$ such that $\mathcal{M}, a_i \models F$ for $i \leq n$.

Note that $C_1(P)$ (respectively, $\overleftarrow{C}_1(P)$) is equivalent to $\Diamond_{(-1,0)}(P)$ (respectively, $\Diamond_{=-1}(P)$).

In [19], we proved that all counting modalities are expressible in MTL over the expansion of the reals by two monadic predicate: integers and the even integers.

Let us illustrate the role of Int and show how to express all counting modalities $C_n(P)$ and $\overleftarrow{C}_n(P)$ (for $n \in Nat$) in MTL over $\mathbb{R}_{\mathbb{Z}}$. First, for every $k \in \mathbb{N}$, there is an LTL formula $Forward_k(P, Q)$ which expresses "from the current moment until the next occurrence of Q there are at least k points in P." Similarly, there is an LTL formula $Backward_k(P, Q)$ which expresses "between the current moment and the previous occurrence of Q (including the moment of this occurrence) there are at least k points in P." Finally, $C_n(P)$ - "P holds at least at n points within the next unit of time" - is equivalent to the conjunction of Int $\rightarrow Forward_n(P, \text{Int})$ and $\neg$Int $\rightarrow \vee_{k=0}^{n}(Forward_k(P, \text{Int}) \wedge \Diamond_{=1}Backward_{n-k}(P, \text{Int}))$. The dual modality $\overleftarrow{C}_n(P)$ is expressed similarly.

3   Expressive Equivalence

Equivalence between temporal and first-order formulas with a single free variable is naturally defined as: F is equivalent to $\varphi(x)$ over a class $\mathcal{C}$ of structures iff for any $\mathcal{M} \in \mathcal{C}$ and $a \in \mathcal{M}$: $\mathcal{M}, a \models F \Leftrightarrow \mathcal{M}, a \models \varphi(x)$.

Let $\mathcal{L}$ and $\mathcal{L}'$ be temporal logics. $\mathcal{L}$ is *expressively complete for* (or, at least as expressive as) $\mathcal{L}'$ over a class $\mathcal{C}$, if for every formula $F' \in \mathcal{L}'$ there is $F \in \mathcal{L}$ which is equivalent to F' over $\mathcal{C}$. In this case we write $\mathcal{L}' \preceq_{exp} \mathcal{L}$. Similarly, if $\mathcal{L}'$ is a first-order logic, $\mathcal{L}' \preceq_{exp} \mathcal{L}$ if for every formula $\varphi(x)$ in $\mathcal{L}$ with a single free variable, there is a formula $F \in \mathcal{L}$ equivalent to φ. $\mathcal{L}$ and $\mathcal{L}'$ are expressively equivalent (notation $\mathcal{L} =_{exp} \mathcal{L}'$) over $\mathcal{C}$ iff $\mathcal{L}' \preceq_{exp} \mathcal{L}$ and $\mathcal{L} \preceq_{exp} \mathcal{L}'$ over $\mathcal{C}$.

The fundamental result of Kamp [5,14] implies that a temporal logic with just two modalities Until and Since has the same expressive power as $FO[<]$ over the canonical linear time models $(\mathbb{N}, <)$, $(\mathbb{R}, <)$ and non-negative reals $(\mathbb{R}^{\geq 0}, <)$.

An influential consequence of Kamp's result is that LTL has emerged as the canonical temporal logic.

A technical notion that unifies the canonical linear time models is Dedekind completeness.

A linear order $(T, <)$ is *Dedekind complete* if every non-empty subset (of the domain) which has an upper bound has a least upper bound. The canonical linear time models $(\mathbb{N}, <)$, $(\mathbb{R}, <)$ and $(\mathbb{R}^{\geq 0}, <)$ are Dedekind complete, while the order of the rationals is not Dedekind complete.

Kamp's theorem states that LTL is expressively equivalent to $FO[<]$ over Dedekind complete orders.

Theorem 3.1 (Kamp [14]) *1. Given any LTL formula A there is an $FO[<]$ formula $\varphi_A(x)$ which is equivalent to A over all linear orders.*

2. Given any $FO[<]$ formula $\varphi(x)$ with one free variable, there is an LTL formula A_φ which is equivalent to φ over Dedekind complete orders.

Moreover, φ_A and A_φ are computable from A and φ.

The correspondence between predicate logics and temporal logics becomes considerably more complicated with the introduction of *metric* specifications.

All logics mentioned in Sect. 2.2 are less expressive than $FO[<, +1]$ over the reals. The translation from the formulas of these logics to equivalent formulas of $FO[<, +1]$ is straightforward.

Their expressive power can be summarized as follows: $QTL \prec_{exp} TLC$ [9, 10], and $QTL \prec_{exp} MTL$ [1]. Moreover, since TLC is decidable, while MTL is undecidable, it follows that TLC cannot express $\Diamond_{=1}P$. In [10] we proved that MTL cannot express $C_2(P)$ - "P occurs twice in the next unit interval." Hence, the expressive power of MTL and TLC is incomparable.

Actually, the main result of [10] is much stronger. In particular, it implies that if $\mathcal{L}$ is a temporal logic with a finite set of modalities and $\mathcal{L} \preceq_{exp} FO[<, +1]$, then there is n such that a counting modality $C_n(P)$ is not expressible in $\mathcal{L}$.

As a consequence, in contrast to Kamp's theorem, no temporal logic with a finite set of modalities is expressively equivalent to $FO[<, +1]$ over the reals.

Our main result is that over the expansions of $(\mathbb{R}, <, +1)$ by a monadic predicate "the current moment is an integer" $FO[<, +1]$ is expressively equivalent to a finite base temporal logic MTL.

Theorem 3.2 (Main) *1. Given any MTL formula A there is an $FO[<, +1]$ formula $\varphi_A(x)$ which is equivalent to A over $\mathbb{R}_{\mathbb{Z}}$.*

2. Given any $FO[<, +1]$ formula $\varphi(x)$ with one free variable, there is a MTL formula A_φ which is equivalent to φ over $\mathbb{R}_{\mathbb{Z}}$.

Moreover, φ_A and A_φ are computable from A and φ.

Theorem 3.2 (1) is easily proved by the structural induction. The main technical contribution of our paper is the proof of Theorem 3.2 (2). The proof is constructive. An algorithm which for every $FO[<,+1]$ formula $\varphi(x)$ constructs a MTL formula which is equivalent to φ is easily extracted from our proof.

It is a routine exercise to adapt the proof of Theorem 3.2 to the non-negative reals, and to show that MTL and $FO[<,+1]$ are expressively equivalent over the non-negative reals expanded by a predicate interpreted as the set of natural numbers.

4   Proof Outline

The structure of our proof is similar to the proof of Kamp's theorem in [20]. We first recall the relevant notions and propositions from [6,20]. Then, we state their generalization to metric setting and prove expressive equivalence of MTL and $FO[<,+1]$ over $\mathbb{R}_{\mathbb{Z}}$.

Definition 4.1 (Decomposition and $\overrightarrow{\exists}\forall$-formulas). *Let Σ be a set of monadic predicate names.*

- *A decomposition formula (D-formula) over Σ is a formula $\chi(z_0,\ldots,z_m)$ of the form:*

$$\exists x_n \ldots \exists x_1 \exists x_0 \, (x_n > x_{n-1} > \cdots > x_1 > x_0) \wedge$$

$$\bigwedge_{i=0}^{m} z_i = x_{k_i} \wedge \bigwedge_{j=0}^{n} \alpha_j(x_j) \wedge \bigwedge_{j=1}^{n} [(\forall y)^{<x_j}_{>x_{j-1}} \beta_j(y)] \tag{1}$$

$$\wedge \, (\forall y)_{>x_n} \beta_{n+1}(y) \wedge (\forall y)^{<x_0} \beta_0(y)$$

where $\overline{z} = \{z_0,\ldots,z_m\}$ and $\overline{x} = \{x_0,\ldots,x_n\}$ are disjoint lists of variables, $0 \le k_i < k_j \le n$ for $i < j$ and all α_j, β_j are quantifier free formulas with one variable over Σ. Observe that $\chi(z_0,\ldots,z_m)$ implies $\bigwedge_{i=0}^{m-1}(z_i < z_{i+1})$.
- *An $\overrightarrow{\exists}\forall$-formula over Σ is a conjunction of a D-formula as in (1) and $\bigwedge_{i=0}^{s}(u_i = z_{h(i)})$, where $u_0,\ldots,u_s$ are variables and $h : \{0,\ldots,s\} \to \{0,\ldots,m\}$.*

The next definition plays a major role in the proof of Kamp's theorem [6,20].

Definition 4.2. *Let $\mathcal{M}$ be a structure with the signature including unary predicate names Σ, and $\mathcal{L}$ be a temporal logic. We denote by $\mathcal{L}[\Sigma]$ the set of unary predicate names $\Sigma \cup \{A \mid A$ is an $\mathcal{L}$-formula over $\Sigma \}$. The canonical $\mathcal{L}$-expansion of $\mathcal{M}$ is an expansion of $\mathcal{M}$ to a structure with unary predicate names $\mathcal{L}[\Sigma]$, where each predicate name $A \in \mathcal{L}[\Sigma]$ is interpreted as $\{a \in \mathcal{M} \mid \mathcal{M}, a \models A\}$.*

Note that if A is an $\mathcal{L}$-formula over $\mathcal{L}[\Sigma]$ predicates, then it is equivalent to an $\mathcal{L}$-formula over Σ, and hence to an atomic formula in the canonical $\mathcal{L}$-expansions.

The $\overrightarrow{\exists}\forall$ formulas are defined as previously, but now they can use as atoms $\mathcal{L}$ definable predicates.

We say that first-order formulas in a signature which includes $\mathcal{L}[\Sigma]$ are equivalent over $\mathcal{M}$ (respectively, over a class $\mathcal{C}$ of structures) if they are equivalent in the canonical expansion of $\mathcal{M}$ (in the canonical expansion of every $\mathcal{M} \in \mathcal{C}$).

Propositions 4.4–4.5 were proved[1] in [20].

Proposition 4.3 (From $\overrightarrow{\exists}\forall$-formulas to temporal formulas). *Let $\mathcal{L}$ be a temporal logic such that $\mathcal{L} \succeq_{exp} LTL$. Then, every $\overrightarrow{\exists}\forall$-formula with one free variable is equivalent (over the canonical $\mathcal{L}$-expansions) to an $\mathcal{L}$ formula.*

Proposition 4.4 (From first-order formulas to $\overrightarrow{\exists}\forall$-formulas). *Let $\mathcal{L}$ be a temporal logic such that $\mathcal{L} \succeq_{exp} LTL$. Then every $FO[<]$ formula is equivalent (over the canonical $\mathcal{L}$ expansions of Dedekind complete orders) to a disjunction of $\overrightarrow{\exists}\forall$-formulas.*

Setting $\mathcal{L} := LTL$ in the next proposition we obtain Kamp's theorem.

Proposition 4.5. *Let $\mathcal{L} \succeq_{exp} LTL$ be a temporal logic. Then every $FO[<]$ formula with one free variable is equivalent (over the canonical $\mathcal{L}$-expansions) to an $\mathcal{L}$ formula.*

The structure of our proof is similar to that of Kamp's theorem. Recall that a substitution σ is a map from variables to terms. We use $\{t_0/z_0, \ldots, t_n/z_n\}$ for the substitution which maps z_i to t_i. For a formula ψ, the result of replacing free occurrences of z_i by t_i is denoted by $\psi\sigma$ (as usual, we have to avoid that the variables occurring in t_i are captured in $\psi\sigma$). Recall that the standard terms in $FO[<, +1]$ are variables or of the form $z + c$ or $\lfloor z \rfloor + c$, where $c \in \mathbb{Z}$. Every term of $FO[<, +1]$ is equivalent to a standard term. From now on we use the word "term" for "standard term."

Definition 4.6. *A simple (metric) formula is a formula of the form $\psi\sigma$, where ψ is an $\overrightarrow{\exists}\forall$-formula, and σ is a substitution.*

In a simple metric formula no bound variable is in the scope of function symbols $\lfloor \ \rfloor$ or $+c$ for $c \neq 0$, We will prove the next two Propositions which are adaptations of Propositions 4.4 and 4.3 to the metrical setting:

Proposition 4.7 (From simple formulas to *MTL* formulas). *Every simple metric formula with one free variable is equivalent (over the canonical MTL-expansions of $\mathbb{R}_\mathbb{Z}$) to an MTL formula.*

Proposition 4.8 (From first-order formulas to simple metric formulas). *Every $FO[<, +1]$ formula is equivalent (over the canonical MTL expansions of $\mathbb{R}_\mathbb{Z}$) to a disjunction of simple formulas.*

---

[1] For the sake of simplicity these propositions were stated for $\mathcal{L} := LTL$. However, their proofs are sound for any $\mathcal{L} \succeq_{exp} LTL$.

Propositions 4.8 and 4.7 immediately imply Theorem 3.2 (2) - our main result.

Proof. (of Theorem 3.2 (2).) Let $\varphi(x)$ be a $FO[<, +1]$ formula with one free variable. By Proposition 4.8, it is equivalent to a disjunction ψ_i of simple formulas. By Proposition 4.7, ψ_i is equivalent to a MTL formula A_i. Therefore, φ is equivalent to a MTL formula $\vee A_i$. □

Our proofs are organized as follows. The next section presents simple Lemmas. Proposition 4.7 is proved in Sect. 6 and Proposition 4.8 is proved in Sect. 7. The proofs of Propositions 4.7 and 4.8 often reuse Propositions 4.4 and 4.3.

5   Notations and Observations

Notations. As usual, $\Diamond_{=2}P$ abbreviates $\Diamond_{=1}\Diamond_{=1}P$, and $\Diamond_{=c}$ for $c \in Z$ is defined similarly. We denote by $\mathrm{FreeVar}(\varphi)$ the set of free variables of φ.

Let $\sigma := \{t_0/z_0, \ldots, t_i/z_n\}$ be a substitution. We use $\mathrm{dom}(\sigma)$ for $\{z_0, \ldots, z_n\}$ and $\mathrm{Term}(\sigma)$ for $\{\sigma(z) \mid z \in \mathrm{dom}(\sigma)\}$. Recall that the terms of $FO[<, +1]$ are of the form z, $\lfloor z \rfloor + c$ and $z + c$, where z is a variable; and in a simple metric formula no bound variable is in the scope of function symbols $\lfloor\ \rfloor$ or $+c$ for $c \neq 0$.

For a quantifier free formula φ we denote by $\mathrm{Term}(\varphi)$ the set of terms that appear in φ. For a simple formula $\varphi := \psi\sigma$ we use $\mathrm{Term}(\varphi)$ for $\{\sigma(z) \mid z \in \mathrm{FreeVar}(\psi)\}$. For a Boolean combination φ of simple and quantifier free formulas φ_i we denote by $\mathrm{Term}(\varphi)$ the union of $\mathrm{Term}(\varphi_i)$.

In this section we state simple lemmas which will be used in the proofs of Propositions 4.7 and 4.8. All these lemmas easily follow from the definitions.

Lemma 5.1. *Every atomic $FO[<, +1]$ formula is equivalent to a disjunction of simple formulas.*

Let T be a set of terms. An *order constraint Ord* over T is a conjunction of formulas of the form $t = t'$ and $t' < t$ for $t, t' \in T$. An order constraint *Ord* is *linear* if for every $t_1, t_2 \in \mathrm{Term}(Ord)$: either *Ord* implies $t_1 < t_2$, or *Ord* implies $t_2 < t_1$, or *Ord* implies $t_1 = t_2$.

Let φ be a simple formula $\psi\sigma$, where $\psi := \bigwedge_{i=0}^{s}(u_i = z_{h(i)}) \wedge \chi(z_0, \ldots, z_m)$ is an $\overrightarrow{\exists}\forall$-formula as in Definition 4.1. We denote by Ord_φ, the (linear) order constraint generated by φ over $\mathrm{Term}(\varphi)$, which is defined as $\bigwedge_{i=0}^{s} \sigma(u_i) = \sigma(z_{h(i)}) \wedge \bigwedge_{j=0}^{m-1} \sigma(z_j) < \sigma(z_{j+1})$.

Lemma 5.2. *1. Let Ord be an order constraint. Then Ord is equivalent to a disjunction of simple formulas, and $\neg Ord$ is equivalent to a disjunction of simple formulas.*

2. If φ is a simple formula, then $\neg\varphi$ is equivalent to a disjunction of simple formulas.

3. A Boolean combination of simple formulas is equivalent to a disjunction of simple formulas.

Proof. (1) is immediate.

(2) Let $\varphi := \psi\sigma$, where ψ is an $\overrightarrow{\exists}\forall$-formula. Then $\neg\varphi$ is equivalent to $\neg Ord_\varphi \vee (\neg\psi)\sigma$. Since, $\neg\psi$ is an $FO[<]$ formula, by Proposition 4.4, it is equivalent to a disjunction $\vee\psi_i$ of $\overrightarrow{\exists}\forall$-formulas. Therefore, $(\neg\psi)\sigma$ is equivalent to a disjunction of simple formulas, and $\neg\varphi$ is equivalent to a disjunction of simple formulas.

(3) immediately by (2).

$\square$

Lemma 5.3. *1. If Ord is an order constraint, then Ord is equivalent to a disjunction of linear order constraints Ord_i such that $Term(Ord_i) = Term(Ord)$ for every i.*

2. If φ is a simple formula and Ord is an order constraint, then $\varphi \wedge Ord$ is equivalent to a disjunction of simple formulas φ_i such that $Term(\varphi_i) = Term(\varphi) \cup Term(Ord)$ for every i.

Lemma 5.4. *Let $\chi(z_0, \ldots, z_m)$ be a D-formula as in (1) (hence, χ implies $\bigwedge_{i=0}^{m-1}(z_i < z_{i+1})$).*

1. χ is equivalent to a conjunction $\bigwedge_{i=0}^{m-1}\chi_i(z_i, z_{i+1})$ of D-formulas with two variables.

2. More generally, if $0 = l_0 < l_1 < l_2 < \cdots < l_s = m$, then χ is equivalent to a conjunction $\bigwedge_{i=0}^{s-1}\chi_i(z_{l_i}, \ldots, z_{l_{i+1}})$ of D-formulas with free variables as displayed.

3. Let z be a fresh variable. Then $\chi \wedge z < z_0$ is equivalent to a D-formula χ' with $Free\,Var(\chi') = \{z, z_0, \ldots, z_m\}$. Similarly, for $\varphi \wedge z_m < z$.

4. A conjunction of D-formulas with the same set of free variables is equivalent to a disjunction of (other) D-formulas with the same set of free variables.

Lemma 5.5 (Shifting monadic predicates by a constant). *Let $\varphi(z_0, \ldots, z_n)$ be an $FO[<, +1]$ formula, $c \in \mathbb{Z}$, and let φ^c be obtained from φ when every monadic predicate P in φ is replaced by (a monadic predicate definable by) $\Diamond_{=c}P$.*

1. Then $\mathcal{M}, a_0, \ldots, a_n \models \varphi^c$ iff $\mathcal{M}, a_0 + c, \ldots, a_n + c \models \varphi$.

2. If φ is a D (respectively, $\overrightarrow{\exists}\forall$ or simple) formula, then φ^c is a D (respectively, $\overrightarrow{\exists}\forall$ or simple) formula.

3. If ψ is an $\overrightarrow{\exists}\forall$-formula, then $\psi\sigma$ is equivalent to $\psi^c\sigma^{-c}$, where $\sigma^{-c}(z) := \sigma(z) - c$ for every $z \in Free\,Var(\psi)$.

6   From Simple Formulas to *MTL* Formulas - Proof of Proposition 4.7

In this section we prove Proposition 4.7 which states that every simple metric formula with one free variable is equivalent (over the canonical *MTL*-expansions of $\mathbb{R}_\mathbb{Z}$) to an *MTL* formula. Proposition 4.7 immediately follows from Claims 1 and 2 below.

Claim 1. A simple formula with one free variable z is equivalent to a disjunction of formulas of one of the following forms:

(A) $z = \lfloor z \rfloor \wedge \chi(z_0, z_1)\sigma_0$, where χ is a D-formula as in (1) and
$\sigma_0 := \{\lfloor z \rfloor + c/z_0, \lfloor z \rfloor + c + 1/z_1\}$.
(B) $\lfloor z \rfloor < z < \lfloor z \rfloor + 1 \wedge \chi(z_0, z_1, z_2)\sigma_0$, where χ is a D-formula as in (1) and
$\sigma_0 := \{\lfloor z \rfloor + c/z_0, z + c/z_1, \lfloor z \rfloor + c + 1/z_2\}$.

Claim 2. Any formula of the form (A) or (B) is equivalent to an *MTL* formula.

Proof of Claim 2. The only non-trivial metric constraint in formulas of these forms is that the distance between two integer points $\lfloor z \rfloor + c$ and $\lfloor z \rfloor + c + 1$ is one. This can be easily formalized in $FO[<]$ using the monadic predicate Int. Below are formal details.

We will translate formulas of the form (B) to equivalent *MTL* formulas (the translation of formulas of the form (A) is simpler).

If φ is of the form (B), then it is equivalent to the conjunction of $\neg\mathsf{Int}(z)$ and $(\exists z_0 z_2 (\mathsf{Int}(z_0) \wedge \mathsf{Int}(z_2) \wedge z_0 < z_1 < z_2 \wedge (\forall u)^{<z_2}_{>z_0}\neg\mathsf{Int}(y) \wedge \chi))\sigma$, where $\sigma := \{z + c/z_1\}$. Since $\exists z_0 z_2 (\mathsf{Int}(z_0) \wedge \mathsf{Int}(z_2) \wedge z_0 < z_1 < z_2 \wedge (\forall u)^{<z_2}_{>z_0}\neg\mathsf{Int}(y) \wedge \chi)$ is an $FO[<]$ formula, it is equivalent to an *MTL* formula A, by Proposition 4.5. Therefore, φ is equivalent to an *MTL* formula $\neg\mathsf{Int} \wedge \Diamond_{=c}A$. $\square$

Proof of Claim 1. We assume that a least term of φ w.r.t. Ord_φ is of the form $\lfloor z \rfloor + c$ (otherwise, by Lemma 5.3 we can rewrite φ as a disjunction of simple formulas with this property). There is $N \in \mathbb{N}$ such that Ord_φ implies that all terms in $\mathrm{Term}(\varphi)$ are less than $\lfloor z \rfloor + c + N$.

Let $T := \{\lfloor z \rfloor + c + j \mid j = 0, \ldots, N\} \cup \{z + c + j \mid j = 0, \ldots, N - 1\}$. Note that $\mathrm{Term}(\varphi) \subsetneq T$.

Let Ord_i (for $i < K \in \mathbb{N}$) be all satisfiable linear orders on T (there are finitely many such orders). Then φ is equivalent to $\vee_i(\varphi \wedge Ord_i)$. Hence, (by Lemma 5.3), φ is equivalent to a disjunction of simple formulas φ_i with $\mathrm{Term}(\varphi_i) = T$.

Since, $z + c, \lfloor z \rfloor + c \in T$, it follows that either $Ord_{\varphi_i} \rightarrow z = \lfloor z \rfloor$ or $Ord_{\varphi_i} \rightarrow z > \lfloor z \rfloor$. If Ord_{φ_i} implies $z = \lfloor z \rfloor$, we show that φ_i is equivalent to a disjunction of formulas of the form (A); if Ord_{φ_i} implies $z > \lfloor z \rfloor$, we show that φ_i is equivalent to a disjunction of formulas of the form (B).

We will show the second assertion (the first one is simpler). Assume $Ord_{\varphi_i} \rightarrow z > \lfloor z \rfloor$, then there is $\chi(z_0, \ldots, z_{2N})$ as in (1) such that φ_i is equivalent to $\lfloor z \rfloor < z \wedge \chi\sigma$ where $\sigma(z_{2j}) = \lfloor z \rfloor + c + j$ and $\sigma(z_{2j-1}) = z + c + j$ for $j = 0, \ldots, N$.

By Lemma 5.4(2), χ is equivalent to $\wedge_{j=0}^{N-1}\chi_j(z_{2j}, z_{2j+1}, z_{2j+2})$ where χ_j are D formulas with $\mathrm{FreeVar}(\chi_j) = \{z_{2j}, z_{2j+1}, z_{2j+2}\}$.

Replace in χ_j each monadic predicate P by a predicate definable by $\Diamond_{=c+j}P$, and rename its free variables $z_{2j}, z_{2j+1}, z_{2j+2}$ to z_0, z_1, z_2; the result is a D-formula $\psi_j(z_0, z_1, z_2)$. Then by Lemma 5.5, we obtain that $\chi\sigma$ is equivalent to $(\wedge_{j=0}^{N-1}\psi_j(z_0, z_1, z_2))\sigma_0$, where $\sigma_0 := \{\lfloor z \rfloor + c/z_0, z + c/z_1, \lfloor z \rfloor + c + 1/z_2\}$.

Finally, $\wedge_{j=0}^{N-1}\psi_j(z_0, z_1, z_2)$ is equivalent, by Lemma 5.4(4), to a disjunction of D formulas with free variables z_0, z_1, z_2. Therefore, φ_i is equivalent to a disjunction of formulas of the form (B). $\square$

7   From First-Order Formulas to Simple Formulas - Proof of Proposition 4.8

In this section we prove Proposition 4.8 which states that every $FO[<, +1]$ formula is equivalent (over the canonical MTL expansions of $\mathbb{R}_{\mathbb{Z}}$) to a disjunction of simple formulas.

The main technical result of this section is:

Proposition 7.1. *If φ is a simple formula, then $\exists z \varphi$ is equivalent to a Boolean combination of simple formulas.*

Proposition 4.8 follows (by a straightforward structural induction) from Proposition 7.1 and Lemmas 5.1 and 5.2(3).

In [17], we proved that for every $N \in \mathbb{N}$, every $FO[<, +1]$ sentence (no free variable) is equivalent to an MTL formula over the class of real intervals of length $< N$. The following locality properties of formulas with a single free variable play a key role in our proof of Proposition 4.7: if $\varphi(z)$ is a simple formula with one free variable, then there is $N \in \mathbb{N}$ such that Ord_φ implies that the distance between t_1 and t_2 is $< N$ for every $t_1, t_2 \in \text{Term}(\varphi)$. This locality property fails for formulas with several free variables. Yet, for every formula φ we can decompose Ord_φ into local components, as stated in Lemma 7.3.

Definition 7.2. *A linear order constraint Ord is local if there is $N \in \mathbb{N}$ such that Ord implies that for every $t_1, t_2 \in \text{Term}(Ord)$, the distance between t_1 and t_2 is less than N (i.e., $Ord \to (t_2 < t_1 + N \wedge t_1 < t_2 + N)$).*

A linear constraint can be decomposed into local constraints and a linear order between them.

Lemma 7.3. *Let Ord be a satisfiable linear constraint. Then, there are $Ord_0, \ldots, Ord_k$ such that:*

1. *Ord_i are local constraints.*
2. *$\text{Term}(Ord) = \cup_i \text{Term}(Ord_i)$.*
3. *$\text{FreeVar}(Ord_i) \cap \text{FreeVar}(Ord_j) = \emptyset$ for $i \neq j$.*
4. *Let t_i^{leat} be a leat and $t_i^{greatest}$ be a greatest term in Ord_i. Then, Ord is equivalent to $\bigwedge_{i=0}^{k} Ord_i \wedge \bigwedge_{i=0}^{k-1} (t_i^{greatest} < t_{i+1}^{least})$.*

Terminology. Ord_i and $\text{Term}(Ord_i)$, as above, are called *local components* of Ord. Whenever Ord is clear from the context and $z \in \text{FreeVar}(Ord_i)$, then Ord_i is also called the local component of z.

Proof. Define an equivalence relation $\sim$ on $\text{Term}(Ord)$ as: $t_1 \sim t_2$ if there is $N \in \mathbb{N}$ such that Ord implies that the distance between t_1 and t_2 is less than N. It is easy to see that $\sim$ is a convex equivalence relation, i.e., if $t_1 \sim t_2$, and $Ord \to (t_1 < t < t_2)$, then $t_1 \sim t \sim t_2$. Let T_i (for $i = 0, \ldots, k$) be the equivalence classes of $\sim$. It is clear that $\text{FreeVar}(T_i) \cap \text{FreeVar}(T_j) = \emptyset$ for $i \neq j$. Let Ord_i be the order *induced* by Ord on T_i, i.e., for $t_1, t_2 \in T_i$: (1) $t_1 < t_2 \in Ord_i$ iff $Ord \to t_1 < t_2$ and (2) $t_1 = t_2 \in Ord_i$ iff $Ord \to t_1 = t_2$.

It is easy to see that Ord_i are local orders which satisfy the conclusion of Lemma 7.3. □

Let us proceed with a proof of Proposition 7.1. Given a simple formula φ with $z \in$ FreeVar(φ). We show that $\exists z\varphi$ is equivalent to a Boolean combination of simple formulas, according to the following cases:

Case 1. Ord_φ has only one local component.

Case 2. The local component of z is the last or the first local component of Ord_φ.

Case 3. There are local components before and after the local component of z.

Let Ord_i be the local component of z. For each of the above cases we will consider two subcases: (A) z is the only variable in FreeVar(Ord_i), and (B) There are other variables in FreeVar(Ord_i).

The road map of the proof is as follows:

Subcase 1.A immediately follows from Proposition 4.7. The proof of subcase 1.B is very similar to the proof of Proposition 4.7; however, due to additional variables, the notations are heavier.

Subcases 2.A and 3.A easily follow from Proposition 4.7.

Subcases 2.B and 3.B are reducible to Case 1, using standard logical equivalences.

Though the proof is lengthy, it is simple.

7.1   Case 1

We consider two subcases:

Subcase A. FreeVar$(\varphi) = \{z\}$. In this subcase, by Proposition 4.7, there is an MTL formula A equivalent to φ. Hence, $\exists z\varphi$ is equivalent (in the canonical MTL expansion) to an $\overrightarrow{\exists}\forall$-sentence $\exists x A(x)$. It is also equivalent to an MTL formula $B := \Diamond A \vee A \vee \overline{\Diamond} A$, where $\Diamond A$ (respectively, $\overline{\Diamond} A$) abbreviates TrueUntil$A$ (respectively, TrueSince$A$).

Subcase B. There is $u \in$ FreeVar(φ) such that u is not z.

The proof for subcase B is similar to the proof of Proposition 4.7 (see Sect. 6).

First, we can assume that Ord_φ is satisfiable (otherwise, the formula is equivalent to False). Let $T :=$ Term(φ). We can assume that $\lfloor u \rfloor + c$ is a least term and $\lfloor u \rfloor + c + N$ is a greatest term in T, and if $t \in T$ and $Ord_\varphi \to (\lfloor u \rfloor + c \le t + d < \lfloor u \rfloor + c + N)$, then $t + d \in T$ (otherwise, use Lemma 5.3 to rewrite φ as a disjunction of formulas with these properties).

Next, we eliminate all terms of the form $\lfloor v \rfloor + d$ for each variable v which is different from u. Indeed, if such term t occurs in T, then $Ord_\varphi \to (\lfloor v \rfloor + d = \lfloor u \rfloor + c + i)$ for some $i < N$. Hence, we can replace t by $\lfloor u \rfloor + c + i$.

Therefore, we can assume that the set of terms $T :=$ Term(φ) of our formula φ has the following properties:

1. $\lfloor u \rfloor + c$ is the least and $\lfloor u \rfloor + c + N$ is the greatest element of T.
2. Let $V :=$ FreeVar(φ). Then, there are $c_v \in \mathbb{Z}$ for $v \in V$ such that $T = \{\lfloor u \rfloor + c + i \mid i \le N\} \cup \{v + c_v + i \mid i = 0, \ldots, N - 1\}$.

Define an equivalence relation $\approx$ on V as $v \approx v'$ if Ord_φ implies that v and v' have the same fractional part, i.e., if $Ord_\varphi \to (v + c_v = v' + c_{v'})$ for constants $c_v, c_{v'}$ defined in (2). Assume that $\approx$ has l equivalence classes $V_0, \ldots, V_l$. Define $v(i)$ to be a variable in V_i. Furthermore, we can assume that Ord_φ implies that $v(i) + c_{v(i)} < v(j) + c_{v(j)}$ for $i < j$.

Now, φ is equivalent to the conjunction of $E := \bigwedge_{i=1}^l (\bigwedge_{v \in V_i \setminus v(i)} v(i) + c_{v(i)} = v + c_v)$ and $\chi(z_0, \ldots, z_{N \times (l+1)}) \sigma$, where χ is a D formula and $\sigma(z_{j \times (l+1)}) := \lfloor u \rfloor + c + j$ for $j = 0, \ldots, N$ and $\sigma(z_{i+j \times (l+1)}) := v(i) + c_{v(i)} + j$ for $i = 1, \ldots, l$ and $j = 0, \ldots, N - 1$.

If the first conjunct E has an occurrence of z, i.e., $z + d = v + d'$ occurs there, then we can replace all occurrences of z in φ by $v + d' - d$. The resulting formula φ' does not have free occurrences of z and is equivalent to φ. Therefore, $\exists z \varphi$ is equivalent to φ'.

If E has no occurrence of z, then $\exists z \varphi$ is equivalent to $E \wedge \exists z(\chi \sigma)$.

Therefore, it remains to prove that $\exists z(\chi \sigma)$ is equivalent to a Boolean combination of simple formulas.

Our strategy is similar to the proof of Proposition 4.7 (see Sect. 6).

We are going to prove:

Claim 1. $\chi \sigma$ is equivalent to a disjunction of formulas of the form:

(C) $\psi(z_0, \ldots z_{l+1}) \sigma_0$, where
1. ψ is a D-formula, and Ord_ψ implies $z_0 < z_1 < \cdots < z_{l+1}$.
2. $\sigma_0(z_0) = \lfloor u \rfloor + c$, $\sigma_0(z_{l+1}) = \lfloor u \rfloor + c + 1$ and $\sigma_0(z_i) = v(i) + c_{v(i)}$ for $i = 1, \ldots, l$.
3. All variables $v(i)$ are different from each other.

Claim 2. If ψ and σ are as in (C), then $\exists z(\psi \sigma)$ is equivalent to a simple formula.

Claims 1 and 2 imply that $\exists z(\chi \sigma)$ is equivalent to a disjunction of simple formulas.

The proof of Claim 2 is easy. Indeed, $\exists x(\alpha\{x + c/x_i\})$ is equivalent to $\exists x_i \alpha$, whenever x is not free in α. Since z is $v(i)$ for some i, we obtain by the above equivalence that $\exists z(\psi \sigma_0)$ is equivalent to $(\exists z_i \psi) \sigma_0$. Observe that $\exists z_i \psi$ is an $\overrightarrow{\exists} \forall$-formula. Therefore, $\exists z(\psi \sigma_0)$ is equivalent to a simple formula $(\exists z_i \psi) \sigma_0$.

The proof of Claim 1 is similar to the proof of Claim 1 in Sect. 6.

Namely, we can rewrite $\chi(z_0, \ldots, z_{N \times (l+1)})$ as a conjunction of D-formulas $\chi_0(z_0, \ldots, z_{l+1}), \ldots, \chi_i(z_{i \times (l+1)}, \ldots, z_{(i+1) \times (l+1)}), \ldots, \chi_{N-1}(z_{(N-1) \times (l+1)}, \ldots, z_{N \times (l+1)})$, with free variables as displayed. Replace in χ_i each monadic predicate P by a predicate definable by $\Diamond_{=c+i} P$, and rename its free variables $z_{i \times (l+1)}, \ldots, z_{(i+1) \times (l+1)}$ to $z_0, \ldots z_l$; the result is a D formula $\psi_i(z_0, z_1, \ldots, z_{l+1})$.

By Lemma 5.5, $\chi \sigma$ is equivalent to $(\bigwedge_i \psi_i) \sigma_0$. Finally, since ψ_i are D-formulas and $\text{FreeVar}(\psi_i) = \{z_0, \ldots, z_{l+1}\}$, we obtain, by Lemma 5.4, that $\bigwedge_i \psi_i$ is equivalent to a disjunction of D-formulas, and $\chi \sigma$ is equivalent to a disjunction of formulas of the form (C).

This completes the proof of Claim 2.

7.2   Case 2

Let $Ord := Ord_\varphi$ and assume that Ord is decomposed as in Lemma 7.3, and $z \in \text{FreeVar}(Ord_k)$ (the case when z in the first local component is dual).

Let $Ord_{<k}$ be the order induced by Ord on $\cup_{i=0}^{k-1} T_i$ and Ord' be the order induced by Ord on $t_{k-1}^{greatest} \cup T_k$. Then, φ is equivalent to $\varphi_1 \wedge \varphi_2$, where φ_1 and φ_2 are simple formulas such that $\text{Term}(\varphi_1) = \cup_{i=0}^{k-1} T_i$, $\text{Term}(\varphi_2) = \{t_{k-1}^{greatest}\} \cup T_k$ and $Ord_{\varphi_2} = Ord'$. Since z is not free in φ_1, we obtain that $\exists z \varphi$ is equivalent to $\varphi_1 \wedge \exists z \varphi_2$. So, it remains to prove that $\exists z \varphi_2$ is equivalent to a Boolean combination of simple formulas.

φ_2 has two local components and the first one contains only one term.

We have reduced Case 2 to a slightly simpler version:

Ord_φ has two local components: $T_0 = \{t\}$ and T_1 such that $z \in \text{FreeVar}(T_1)$.

We consider two subcases:

Subcase A. z is the only free variable T_1.

Subcase B. There is $u \in \text{FreeVar}(\varphi)$ such that u is not z.

Subcase A. Let t_1 be a least term in T_1. We can assume that it is of the form $\lfloor z \rfloor + c$. Indeed, otherwise t_1 is $z + c$. From the following equivalence

$$(t < z + c \wedge z + c \neq \lfloor z \rfloor + c) \leftrightarrow (t < \lfloor z \rfloor + c \vee (\lfloor z \rfloor + c < t \wedge t < z + c))$$

We obtain that φ is equivalent to a disjunction of $(\varphi \wedge t < \lfloor z \rfloor + c)$ and of $\varphi \wedge z > t > \lfloor z \rfloor + c$. The second disjunct is equivalent to a formula with one local component. Hence, $\exists z (\varphi \wedge t > \lfloor z \rfloor + c)$ is equivalent to a Boolean combination of simple formulas by case 1. The first disjunct has the desirable property that the minimal term of T_1 is $\lfloor z \rfloor + c$.

Next, φ is equivalent to $\psi(z_0, z_1, \ldots, z_m)\sigma$ where ψ is an $\overrightarrow{\exists} \forall$-formula, $\sigma(z_0) = t$, $\sigma(z_1) = \lfloor z \rfloor + c$ and $\sigma(z_i) \in T_1$ for $i > 1$.

Hence, φ is equivalent to $\psi_1(z_0, z_1)\sigma \wedge \psi_2(z_1, \ldots z_m)\sigma$ for $\overrightarrow{\exists} \forall$-formulas ψ_1 and ψ_2.

Since $\psi_2\sigma$ contains only one free variable, it is equivalent to an MTL formula A, by Proposition 4.7.

Hence, $\exists z \varphi$ is equivalent to $(\exists z_1 \theta(z_0, z_1))\{t/z_0\}$, where $\theta(z_0, z_1)$ expresses the following:

1. $\psi_1(z_0, z_1) \wedge \text{Int}(z_1)$ and
2. A holds somewhere in the interval $[z_1 - c, z_1 - c + 1)$, i.e., $\Diamond_{=-c}(A \vee \Diamond_{(0,1)} A)(z_1)$.

Therefore, $\theta(z_0, z_1)$ is equivalent to an $FO[<]$ formula (in the canonical MTL-expansions). Hence, $\exists z_1 \theta(z_0, z_1)$ is equivalent to a disjunction of $\overrightarrow{\exists} \forall$-formulas and $\exists z \varphi$ is equivalent to a disjunction of simple formulas.

Subcase B. By standard logical equivalences this subcase is reducible to Case 1 considered in Sect. 7.1. Below are the details. T_1 is a local component (w.r.t. Ord_φ). Therefore, there is $N \in \mathbb{N}$ such that $\lfloor u \rfloor - N$ is less than all elements in T_1.

φ is equivalent to a disjunction of $\varphi_1 := t \geq \lfloor u \rfloor - N \wedge \varphi$ and $\varphi_2 := t < \lfloor u \rfloor - N \wedge \varphi$.

Hence, $\exists z \varphi$ is equivalent to $(\exists z \varphi_1) \vee (\exists z \varphi_2)$.

We are going to show that both disjuncts are equivalent to a Boolean combination of simple formulas; hence, so is $\exists z \varphi$.

Indeed, Ord_{φ_1} has only one local component (since $t < t'$ for every $t' \in T_1$ and $u \in \mathrm{FreeVar}(T_1)$). Therefore, by Case 1, $\exists z \varphi_1$ is equivalent to a Boolean combination of simple formulas.

φ_2 is equivalent to $\psi(z_0, z_1, \ldots, z_m)\sigma$ where (1) ψ is an $\overrightarrow{\exists}\forall$-formula such that $Ord_\psi \to z_0 < z_1 \wedge \bigwedge_{i=2}^m (z_1 < z_i)$ and (2) $\sigma(z_0) = t$, $\sigma(z_1) = \lfloor u \rfloor - N$ and $\sigma(z_i) \in T_1$ for $i > 1$.

Therefore, ψ is equivalent to $\psi_1(z_0, z_1) \wedge \psi_2(z_1, \ldots z_m)$, where ψ_i are $\overrightarrow{\exists}\forall$-formulas. Now, $\psi\sigma$ is equivalent to $\psi_1\sigma \wedge \psi_2\sigma$ and (a) $z \notin \mathrm{FreeVar}(\psi_1\sigma)$ and (b) $\psi_2\sigma$ has only one local component. Hence, $\exists z \varphi_2$ is equivalent to a conjunction of simple formulas $\psi_1\sigma$ and of $\exists z(\psi_2\sigma)$ which is equivalent, by case 1, to a Boolean combination of simple formulas.

This completes the proof of subcase B of case 2.

7.3   Case 3

First, similarly to Case 2, we can reduce this case to a version with three local components, where the minimal and the maximal components have one term.

Next, let the local components of Ord_φ be T_0, T_1 and T_2, where $T_0 = \{t_0\}$ and $T_2 = \{t_2\}$ and $z \in \mathrm{FreeVar}(T_1)$. Consider two subcases:

Subcase A. z is the only free variable in T_1.

Subcase B. There is $u \in \mathrm{FreeVar}(\varphi)$ such that u is not z.

In subcase A, we can further assume that the least term of T_1 is $\lfloor z \rfloor + c$ and the greatest is $\lfloor z \rfloor + d$ for some $c, d \in \mathbb{N}$.

Then, φ is equivalent to $\psi(z_0, z_1, \ldots z_m, z_{m+1})\sigma$, where ψ is an $\overrightarrow{\exists}\forall$-formula and

- $Ord_\psi \to (z_0 < z_1 < z_m < z_{m+1} \wedge \bigwedge_{i=2}^{m-1} (z_1 < z_i < z_m)$ and
- $\sigma(z_0) = t_0$, $\sigma(z_{m+1}) = t_2$, and $\sigma(z_1) = \lfloor z \rfloor + c$, $\sigma(z_m) = \lfloor z \rfloor + d$ are integers, and $\sigma(z_i) \in T_1$ for $i = 2, \ldots, m - 1$.

Hence, ψ is equivalent to a conjunction $\psi_1(z_0, z_1) \wedge \psi_2(z_1, \ldots z_m) \wedge \psi_3(z_m, z_{m+1})$ of $\overrightarrow{\exists}\forall$ formulas.

The only free variable in $\psi_2\sigma$ is z, and therefore, by Proposition 4.7, $\psi_2\sigma$ is equivalent to $A(z)$, where A is an atomic predicate (in the canonical *MTL*-expansion).

Therefore, $\exists z \varphi$ is equivalent to $(\exists z_1 z_m \theta(z_0, z_1, z_m, z_{m+1}))\{t_0/z_0, t_2/z_{m+1}\}$, where $\theta(z_0, z_1, z_2, z_3)$ expresses the following:

1. $\psi_1(z_0, z_1) \wedge \mathsf{Int}(z_1) \wedge \mathsf{Int}(z_m) \wedge \psi_3(z_m, z_{m+1})$ and
2. $\mathsf{Int}(z_1) \wedge \mathsf{Int}(z_m) \wedge z_m = z_1 + d - c$ and
3. A holds somewhere in the interval $[z_1 - c, z_1 - c + 1)$, i.e., $\Diamond_{=-c}(A \vee \Diamond_{(0,1)} A)(z_1)$.

The second item states: "there are $d - c - 1$ integer points in (z_1, z_2) and $\mathsf{Int}(z_1) \wedge \mathsf{Int}(z_2)$," and it is expressible by a $FO[<]$ formula over $\mathbb{R}_{\mathbb{Z}}$. Therefore, $\theta(z_0, z_1, z_m, z_{m+1})$ is equivalent to a $FO[<]$.

Hence, $\exists z_1 z_m \theta$ is equivalent to a disjunction of $\overrightarrow{\exists} \forall$-formulas and $\exists z \varphi$ is equivalent to a disjunction of simple formulas.

By standard logical equivalences, subcase B is reducible to case 1 or case 2. We skip the details.

8   Conclusion and Related Works

A major result concerning temporal logics is Kamp's theorem [5,14] which implies that the temporal logic with two modalities "P Until Q" and "P Since Q" is expressively equivalent to First-Order Monadic Logic of Order ($FO[<]$) over the standard linear time intended models - the Naturals $\langle \mathbb{N}, < \rangle$ for discrete time and the Reals $\langle \mathbb{R}, < \rangle$ for continuous time.

$FO[<]$ is a fundamental formalism; however, $FO[<]$ cannot express over the reals properties like "P holds exactly after one unit of time." Such local metric properties are easily expressible in $FO[<, +1]$ - the extension of $FO[<]$ by $+1$ function. In contrast to the Kamp theorem, no temporal logic with a finite set of modalities is expressively equivalent over the reals to $FO[<, +1]$ [10].

Actually, in [10] a much stronger result is proved. Recall that counting modalities $C_n(P)$ - "P will hold at least at n points within the next unit of time" are defined by $FO[<, +1]$ formulas. In [10], we proved that no temporal logic with a finite *or infinite* family of modalities which are defined by $FO[<, +1]$ formulas with bounded quantifier depth can express over $\mathbb{R}$ all the modalities $C_n(P)$.

$FO[<, +1]$ lacks expressive power to specify the natural global metric property "the current moment is an integer."

Surprisingly, our main result states that $FO[<, +1]$ has the same expressive power as the temporal logic MTL (with only six modalities) over the expansion of the reals by a monadic predicate "x is an integer." We could use alternative notations. Let $FO[<, +1, Int]$ be the expansion of the monadic first-order logic by a unary function symbol $+1$ and a unary relation symbol Int interpreted over the reals as the plus one function and as the set of integers. Let $MTL[Int]$ be obtained from MTL by adding modality Int defined by $\mathcal{M}, a \models Int$ iff a is an integer. Our main result - Theorem 3.2 - can be rephrased as $FO[<, +1, Int]$ is expressively equivalent over $\mathbb{R}$ to $MTL[Int]$. (Technically, it is slightly more convenient in our proof to treat Int as a monadic predicate and not as a modality.)

Our proof uses some techniques from [17], where we proved a result that can be viewed as an extension of Kamp's theorem to metric logics over bounded real time domains: for every $N \in \mathbb{N}$, $FO[<, +1]$ and MTL are expressively equivalent over the class of real intervals of length $< N$. Note that for every MTL formula A there is $FO[<, +1]$ formula ψ_A which is equivalent to A over all real time intervals[2]. For every $FO[<, +1]$ formula ψ with one free variable, we constructed

---

[2] Formally, $FO[<, +1]$ over bounded intervals uses a binary relation "x at distance one from y" instead of $+1$ function.

in [17] an MTL formula A_ψ^N which is equivalent to ψ over the real intervals of length $< N$; MTL formulas $A_\psi^{N_1}$ and $A_\psi^{N_2}$ are different for $N_1 \neq N_2$. It can be proved that there is no uniform (independent from N) translation from $FO[<,+1]$ to an equivalent (over $[0,N)$ interval) MTL formula. Finally, note that for every $N \in \mathbb{N}$, there is a $FO[<,+1]$ formula $int_N(t)$ which defines the set of integers in the interval $[0,N)$. Indeed, let $\alpha_0(t)$ be $\forall t'(t' \leq t)$ and $\alpha_{i+1}(t) := \exists t'(\alpha_i(t') \wedge t = t' + 1)$ for $i < N - 1$. The unique element which satisfies $\alpha_i(t)$ in $[0,N)$ is i; hence, $int_N(t)$ can be defined as $\vee_{i=0}^{N-1}\alpha_i(t)$. Therefore, the expansion of interval $[0,N)$ by a monadic predicate "x is an integer" does not increase the expressive power of $FO[<,+1]$.

Our results were obtained in 2012, independently of the result of Paul Hunter [12] which states that the temporal logic $MTLC$ which in addition to MTL modalities has all counting modalities is expressively equivalent to $FO[<,+1]$ (without the need for the additional unary predicate for the integers). Though $MTLC$ has infinitely many modalities, Hunter's result implies the main result of this paper, since one can express the counting modalities in MTL, using the monadic predicate for the integers, as shown in the last paragraph of Sect. 2. On the other hand, Hunter's result can be proved by a minor modification of our proof. In particular, Propositions 4.7 and 4.8 hold when MTL is replaced by $MTLC$ and $\mathbb{R}_\mathbb{Z}$ is replaced by $\mathbb{R}$.

The proof techniques of this paper and of [12] - though possessing common elements - are quite different.

In [13], the logic $FO[<,+\mathbb{Q}]$ was introduced. This logic adds to $FO[<,+1]$ an infinite family of unary function symbols: $+q$ for each rational q. Every fragment of $FO[<,+\mathbb{Q}]$ which uses only finitely many $+q$ functions is strictly less expressive than $FO[<,+\mathbb{Q}]$. Therefore, no temporal logic with finitely many modalities is expressively equivalent to $FO[<,+\mathbb{Q}]$. The main result of [13] states that $FO[<,+\mathbb{Q}]$ is expressively equivalent to $MTL_\mathbb{Q}$, where $MTL_\mathbb{Q}$ is a temporal logic obtained from MTL by adding modality $\diamond_{=q}$, for every rational q, and modalities $\diamond_{(0,q)}$ and $\diamond_{(-q,0)}$ for every positive rational q. Recall that a counting modality $C_2(P)$ - "P will hold at least twice within the next unit of time" is definable by an $FO[<,+1]$ formula $\psi(z_0) := \exists x_1 \exists x_2 (z_0 < x_1 < x_2 < z_0 + 1) \wedge P(x_1) \wedge P(x_2)$, and $C_2(P)$ is not expressible in MTL over the reals [10]. Let us illustrate how $C_2(P)$ was expressed in $MTL_\mathbb{Q}$ using fractional constants [13]. The idea is to consider three cases according to whether P is true twice in the interval $(z_0, z_0 + \frac{1}{2}]$, twice in the interval $[z_0 + \frac{1}{2}, z_0 + 1)$ or once in $(z_0, z_0 + \frac{1}{2})$ and $(z_0 + \frac{1}{2}), z_0 + 1)$. The last case is equivalent to an $MTL_\mathbb{Q}$ formula $\diamond_{(0,\frac{1}{2})}P \wedge \diamond_{=1}(\diamond_{(-\frac{1}{2},0)}P)$; an $MTL_\mathbb{Q}$ formula $\diamond_{(0,\frac{1}{2})}(P \wedge \diamond_{(0,\frac{1}{2})}P)$ holds in the first case and implies $C_2(P)$; an $MTL_\mathbb{Q}$ formula $\diamond_{=1}(\diamond_{(-\frac{1}{2},0)}(P \wedge \diamond_{(-\frac{1}{2},0)}P)$ holds in the second case and also implies $C_2(P)$. Therefore, $C_2(P)$ is equivalent to a disjunction of these three formulas.

Note that every predicate logic is expressively equivalent to a modal logic with an infinite set of modalities. For every predicate formula $\psi(t)$ with one free first-order variable, one can consider the modality with a truth table defined by ψ. The modal logic with all these modalities and the predicate logic are expressively equivalent. Hence, if a predicate logic is expressively equivalent to no temporal logic with a finite set of modalities, one can try to find an equivalent temporal logic with an infinitely many modalities which are "natural" or "simple" in some sense.

Table 1 lists predicate logics and corresponding expressively equivalent temporal logics and summarizes our comparison. Note, thought both $MTLC$ and $MTL_\mathbb{Q}$ use infinitely many modalities, all modalities in $MTL_\mathbb{Q}$ are defined by $FO[<,+\mathbb{Q}]$ formulas of quantifier depth at most two, while the $MTLC$ modalities cannot be defined in a fragment of $FO[<,+1]$ of bounded quantifier depth.

Table 1. Predicate logics and corresponding expressively equivalent temporal logics

Predicate logic	Temporal logic	Models	Cardinality of the set of modalities	Reference
$FO[<]$	LTL	All Dedekind complete linear orders	Finite	[14]
$FO[<,+1]$	MTL	Intervals $[0,N)$	Finite	[17]
$FO[<,+1]$	MTL	$\mathbb{R}_\mathbb{Z}$	Finite	This paper
$FO[<,+1,Int]$	$MTL[Int]$	$\mathbb{R}$	Finite	This paper
$FO[<,+1]$	$MTLC$	$\mathbb{R}$	Infinite	[12]
$FO[<,+\mathbb{Q}]$	$MTL_\mathbb{Q}$	$\mathbb{R}$	Infinite	[13]

Acknowledgment. I would like to thank an anonymous referee for the insightful comments about related works.

References

1. Alur, R., Feder, T., Henzinger, T.A.: The benefits of relaxing punctuality. JACM **43**(1), 116–146 (1996)
2. Alur, R., Henzinger, T.A.: Logics and models of real time: a survey. In: de Bakker, J.W., Huizing, C., de Roever, W.P., Rozenberg, G. (eds.) REX 1991. LNCS, vol. 600, pp. 74–106. Springer, Heidelberg (1992). https://doi.org/10.1007/BFb0031988
3. Barringer, H., Kuiper, R., Pnueli, A.: A really abstract concurrent model and its temporal logic. In: Proceedings of the 13th Annual Symposium on Principles of Programing Languages, pp. 173–183 (1986)
4. Burgess, J.P., Gurevich, Y.: The decision problem for linear temporal logic. Notre Dame J. Formal logic **26**(2), 115–128 (1985)
5. Gabbay, D., Hodkinson, I., Reynolds, M.: Temporal Logic: Mathematical Foundations and Computational Aspects. Oxford University Press, Oxford (1994)
6. Gabbay, D., Pnueli, A., Shelah, S., Stavi, J.: On the temporal analysis of fairness. In: POPL 1980, pp. 163–173 (1980)
7. Henzinger, T.A.: It's about time: real-time logics reviewed. In: Sangiorgi, D., de Simone, R. (eds.) CONCUR 1998. LNCS, vol. 1466, pp. 439–454. Springer, Heidelberg (1998). https://doi.org/10.1007/BFb0055640

8. Henzinger, T.A., Raskin, J.-F., Schobbens, P.-Y.: The regular real-time languages. In: Larsen, K.G., Skyum, S., Winskel, G. (eds.) ICALP 1998. LNCS, vol. 1443, pp. 580–591. Springer, Heidelberg (1998). https://doi.org/10.1007/BFb0055086

9. Hirshfeld, Y., Rabinovich, A.: Logics for real time: decidability and complexity. Fundam. Inform. **62**(1), 1–28 (2004)

10. Hirshfeld, Y., Rabinovich, A.: Expressiveness of metric modalities for continuous time. Logical Methods Comput. Sci. **3**(1) (2007)

11. Hirshfeld, Y., Rabinovich, A.: Decidable metric logics. Inf. Comput. **206**(12), 1425–1442 (2008)

12. Hunter, P.: When is metric temporal logic expressively complete? In: CSL 2013, pp. 380–394 (2013)

13. Hunter, P., Ouaknine, J., Worrell, J.: Expressive completeness for metric temporal logic. In: LICS 2013, pp. 349–357 (2013)

14. Kamp, H.: Tense logic and the theory of linear order. Ph.D. thesis, University of California, Los Angeles (1968)

15. Koymans, R.: Specifying real-time properties with metric temporal logic. Real-Time Syst. **2**(4), 255–299 (1990)

16. Manna, Z., Pnueli, A.: Models for reactivity. Acta informatica **30**, 609–678 (1993)

17. Ouaknine, J., Rabinovich, A., Worrell, J.: Time-bounded verification. In: Bravetti, M., Zavattaro, G. (eds.) CONCUR 2009. LNCS, vol. 5710, pp. 496–510. Springer, Heidelberg (2009). https://doi.org/10.1007/978-3-642-04081-8_33

18. Pnueli, A.: The temporal logic of programs. In: Proceedings of IEEE 18th Annual Symposium on Foundations of Computer Science, New York, pp. 46–57 (1977)

19. Rabinovich, A.: Complexity of metric temporal logics with counting and the Pnueli modalities. Theor. Comput. Sci. **411**(22–24), 2331–2342 (2010)

20. Rabinovich, A.: A proof of Kamp's theorem. Logical Methods Comput. Sci. **10**(1) (2014)

21. Wilke, T.: Specifying timed state sequences in powerful decidable logics and timed automata. In: Langmaack, H., de Roever, W.-P., Vytopil, J. (eds.) FTRTFT 1994. LNCS, vol. 863, pp. 694–715. Springer, Heidelberg (1994). https://doi.org/10.1007/3-540-58468-4_191

Two First-Order Theories of Ordinals

Peter H. Schmitt$^{(\boxtimes)}$

Department of Informatics, Karlsruhe Institute of Technology (KIT),
Am Fasanengarten 5, 76131 Karlsruhe, Germany
pschmitt@ira.uka.de

Abstract. This paper compares a first-order theory of ordinals proposed by the author to the theory published 1965 by Gaisi Takeuti. A clarification of the relative deductive strength of the two theories is obtained.

1 Introduction and Main Results

In [3] the author proposed the theory Th_{Ord} of ordinals. This paper also mentions the theory Th_{Tak} of ordinals published by Gaisi Takeuti in [6] already in 1965. The aim of Th_{Ord} was to provide a set of axioms amenable for implementation in a theorem prover and strong enough for possible applications in program verification. The theory Th_{Ord} was indeed implemented in the KeY program verification system, [1], and used to automatically prove termination of the Goodstein sequences. A closer description of this verification effort is contained in [3]. Takeuti's aim with Th_{Tak}, on the other hand, was to find a first-order theory that gets as close as possible to prove all properties of the ordinals that can be proved in full ZF set theory. The present paper provides a comparison of the two theories Th_{Ord} and Th_{Tak} which was missing until now.

Contents. After settling the terminology in Sect. 2 the axioms systems for Th_{Ord} and Th_{Tak} are presented with explanatory comments in Sect. 3. The main effort in the comparison of the two theories is to show that the well-ordering of pairs of ordinals and the resulting coding of pairs of ordinals that is part of the axioms of Th_{Tak} can also be derived in Th_{Ord}. This is done in Sects. 4 and 5. Section 6 exposes the limitation of Th_{Ord} that the existence of epsilon numbers cannot be derived. Section 7 gives a short review of the results from the paper [6].

2 Preliminaries

The two theories we want to compare use different vocabularies. Thus enriching a vocabulary becomes a frequent necessity. To avoid ambiguities in terminology we collect here the relevant definitions and facts.

Definition 1. *Let T_1, T_2 be theories with languages $L_1 \subseteq L_2$.*
T_2 is called a conservative *extension of T_1 if for every sentence ϕ in the smaller language L_1*

$$T_1 \vdash \phi \Leftrightarrow T_2 \vdash \phi$$

© Springer Nature Switzerland AG 2020
A. Blass et al. (Eds.): Gurevich Festschrift, LNCS 12180, pp. 247–257, 2020.
https://doi.org/10.1007/978-3-030-48006-6_17

Definition 2. *Let a theory T_1 with language L_1 be given, $r(\bar{x})$ a new relation, $f(\bar{x})$ a new function symbol and $\phi(\bar{x})$, $\psi(\bar{x}, y)$ formulas in L_1. The theory T_2 obtained from T_1 by adding the axiom*

$$\forall \bar{x}(r(\bar{x}) \leftrightarrow \phi(\bar{x}))$$

or

$$\forall \bar{x} \forall y(f(\bar{x}) = y \leftrightarrow \psi(\bar{x}, y))$$

is called a relational, resp. functional extension by explicit definition.

Every relational extension by explicit definition is a conservative extension. A functional extension by explicit definition is a conservative extension only if $T_1 \vdash \forall \bar{x} \exists y(\psi(\bar{x}, y))$.

We will also use below recursive definitions, as usual, and implicit definitions of the functions *decode*1 and *decode*2 in Fig. 6 on page 8 below. All extensions of this type lead to conservative extensions.

Definition 3. *Let T_1, T_2 be theories with languages $L_1 \subseteq L_2$.*

T_2 is called a reducible extension of T_1 if for every sentence ϕ_2 in the language L_2 there is a sentence ϕ_1 in the language L_1 satisfying

$$T_2 \vdash \phi_1 \leftrightarrow \phi_2$$

Here *reducible* is my nomenclature, I did not find another name in the literature.

Extensions by explicit or implicit definitions are reducible. Extension by recursive definitions are reducible only in very special cases, e.g.; in classical Peano arithmetic where a coding of finite sequences of natural numbers of arbitrary length is available. I found no analog coding for finite sequences of ordinals.

The following criterion is sometimes useful to establish conservative extensions.

Lemma 1. *Let T_1, T_2 be theories with languages $L_1 \subseteq L_2$ such that*

1. *For every model $\mathcal{M}_2$ of T_2 the restriction of $\mathcal{M}_2$ to the language L_1 is a model of T_1*
2. *For every model $\mathcal{M}_1$ of T_1 there is an expansion of $\mathcal{M}_1$ to the language L_2 that is a model of T_2*

Then T_2 is a conservative extension of T_1.

3   Comparing Th_{Ord} and Th_{Tak}

The first-order language L_{Ord} of Th_{Ord} is built on the vocabulary with the binary predicate symbols $<$, $\leq$, the unary predicate symbol lim, the unary function $+1$, and the constants 0 and ω. The axioms are listed in Fig. 1. Items 1 to 6 are axioms for Peano arithmetic. To get beyond Peano arithmetic a new counting principle besides the successor is needed. This role is in our case taken by the supremum

1. $\forall x, y, z(x < y \land y < z \rightarrow x < z)$ transitivity
2. $\forall x(\neg x < x)$ strict order
3. $\forall x, y(x < y \lor x \doteq y \lor y < x)$ total order
4. $\forall x(0 \leq x)$ 0 is smallest element
5. $\forall x(x < x + 1) \land \forall x, y(x < y \rightarrow x + 1 \leq y)$ successor function
6. $\forall x(\forall y(y < x \rightarrow \phi(y/x)) \rightarrow \phi) \rightarrow \forall x \phi$ transfinite induction scheme
7. $\forall z(z < n \rightarrow m[z/x] \leq sup_{x<n}m)$ def of supremum, part 1
8. $\forall u(\forall z(z < n \rightarrow m[z/x] \leq u) \rightarrow sup_{x<n}m \leq u)$ def of supremum, part 2
9. $0 < \omega \land \neg \exists x(\omega \doteq x + 1)$ ω is a limit ordinal
10. $\forall y(0 < y \land \forall x(x < \omega \rightarrow x + 1 < y) - > \omega \leq y)$ ω is the least limit ordinal

11. $\forall x, y(x \leq y \leftrightarrow x < y \lor x = y)$ Def. of $\leq$
12. $\forall x(lim(x) \leftrightarrow x \neq 0 \land \neg \exists y(x = y + 1))$ Def. of limit ordinal

Fig. 1. The axioms of Th_{Ord}

operator, axioms 7 and 8. The standard natural numbers are still a model of the axioms from 1 to 8. The existence of a limit number is needed to get the ball rolling, axioms 9 and 10. The definitions of $\leq$ and lim are already included in the core set of axioms for Th_{Ord} since they are utterly convenient in the formulation of the axioms.

The *sup* operator is a variable-binding term constructor, thus not listed in the vocabulary. If t and b are terms and x a variable not occurring in b then $sup_{x<b}t$ is a term. It is well known that these constructors can be equivalently replaced by ordinary function symbols. A proof of a quite general case may be found in [7, Sect. 2.3.3].

Let L_{Ord}^+ be the language extending L_{Ord} by increasing the vocabulary by the constant 1 and the binary function max, $+$ (ordinal addition), $*$ (ordinal multiplication), ^ (ordinal exponentiation). The theory Th_{Ord}^+ extends Th_{Ord} by the usual definitions of the new symbols. Th_{Ord}^+ is a conservative extension of Th_{Ord}.

Figure 2 lists the axioms of Takeuti's theory of ordinals in the order as they occur in the paper [6]. We changed the original notation a bit and use $x + 1$ instead of x', $encode(x, y)$ for $j(x, y)$, $decode1(x)$ for $g^1(x)$ and $decode2(x)$ for $g^2(x)$.

We notice immediately that Th_{Tak} is at least as strong as Th_{Ord}, axioms 1 to 3 and axiom 5 in Fig. 2 guarantee that $<$ is a strict total ordering with least element 0, axioms 4, 8, and 9 characterize ω as the least limit ordinal, axioms 6 and 7 stipulate the $x + 1$ is the immediate successor of x. Since the term constructor *sup* from Th_{Ord} is not a symbol in Th_{Tak} the phrase *at least as strong* has to be taken with a little grain of salt: There is a definitional extension of Th_{Tak} that implies all axioms of Th_{Ord}. Indeed the replacement axiom, 21, guarantees that adding the bounded supremum constructor is a conservative definitional extension. Finally the axiom scheme for transfinite induction is literally the same in both theories.

1. $x < y \lor x \doteq y \lor y < x$
2. $\neg x < x$
3. $x < y \land y < z \to x < z$
4. $0 < \omega$
5. $0 \le x$
6. $x < y \to x + 1 \le y$
7. $x < x + 1$
8. $x < \omega \to x + 1 < \omega$
9. $0 < y \land \forall x(x < y \to x + 1 < y)- > \omega \le y)$
10. $x \le y \leftrightarrow max(x,y) \doteq y$
11. $max(x,y) \doteq max(y,x)$
12. $x < y \leftrightarrow less(x,y) \doteq 0$
13. $less(x,y) \le 1$
14. $encode(decode1(x), decode2(x)) = x$
15. $decode1(encode(x,y)) = x$
16. $decode2(encode(x,y)) = x$
17. $encode(v,w) < encode(x,y) \leftrightarrow max(v,w) < max(x,y)\lor$
$$(max(v,w) \doteq max(x,y) \land w < y)\lor$$
$$(max(v,w) \doteq max(x,y) \land w \doteq y \land v < x)$$
18. $(t(c) \doteq 0 \land c < b) \to t(\mu_{x<b}t(x)) \doteq 0 \land t(\mu_{x<b}t(x)) < c$
19. $\mu_{x<b}t(x) \doteq 0 \lor (t(\mu_{x<b}t(x)) \doteq 0 \land \mu_{x<b}t(x) < b)$
20. $\forall x(\forall y(y < x \to \phi(y)) \to \phi) \to \forall x\phi$ transfinite induction scheme
21. $\forall x, y, z(\phi(x,y) \land \phi(x,z) \to y = z) \to$ replacement axiom scheme
$\forall a \exists b \forall y(\exists x(\phi(x,y) \land x < a) \to y < b)$
22. $\exists u(\forall v, x, y, z(\phi(y,x,v) \land \phi(z,x,v) \to y = z)$ cardinality axiom scheme
$\to \forall v \exists x(x < u \land \forall y(y < a \to \neg\phi(x,y,v))))$

Fig. 2. Takeuti's Theory of Ordinals Th_{Tak}

Next we turn to investigate the reverse implication: is Th_{Ord} as strong as Th_{Tak}? It is easily seen that the axioms and schemes 1 to 9, and 20 if they are not literally axioms are derivable in Th_{Ord}. Axioms 12 and 13 in Fig. 2 define a *Boolean* binary predicate *less* that codes the order relation $<$, while axioms 18 and 19 define a bounded μ-operator. We can equally well add these definitions to Th_{Ord} and nothing needs to be checked since the axioms of Th_{Tak} do not claim any properties of the thus defined new vocabulary. Adding the μ-operator leads to a conservative extension since the existence of a minimal instance follows from the least number principle, which is an easy consequence of transfinite induction. A tiny bit different is the situation with the maximum operator. It is defined in axiom 14 and axiom 17 requires this operator to be symmetric. But, symmetry also follows effortlessly from the definition.

This leaves us with the axioms 14 to 17. These state that *encode* is an injective and surjective coding function for pairs of ordinals with *decode1* and *decode2* being the decoding functions for the first and second coordinate. Furthermore, *encode* should satisfy a certain monotonicity property. No definition of these functions is offered. In the next section we will present a definitional extension of Th_{Ord} and demonstrate that axioms 14 to 17 can be derived from it.

Finally, we note that the axiom schemes 22 and 21 in Fig. 2 apparently cannot be derived in Th_{Ord}. Takeuti gives the cardinality axiom special status and marks every theorem of Th_{Tak} that depends on it with an asterisk *. In the proof that the inner model constructed in [6] is indeed a model of ZF axiom scheme 22 is only needed to prove that the power set axiom holds true.

4   A Well-Ordering of Pairs of Ordinals

The results of this and the next section are well-known. Proofs using an automated reasoning tool, however, have, to the best of my knowledge, not been reported before. The theory Th_{Ord} and its extensions have been implemented in the KeY verification system, [1], and more than 200 theorems, among them all the results listed in this paper, have been interactively proved with KeY. Further details may be found in the technical report [4]. Proof files are available at https://www.key-project.org/flocs2018. Thus, we do not give any proofs in the following two sections. The more accessible results are just stated while for the more demanding verifications lists of intermediate stepping-stone-lemmas are provided.

The goal of the next section, Sect. 5, is to extend Th_{Ord} with definitions for the functions *encode*, *decode1*, and *decode2*, plus some auxiliary functions and predicates, such that in this definitional extension axioms 14 to 17 in Fig. 2 are provable.

In the present section we take a preparatory step towards this goal. We add a predicate for the left-hand side of the formula in line 17 in Fig. 2.

$$(v, w) \ll (x, y) \leftrightarrow max(v, w) < max(x, y) \vee \qquad (1)$$
$$(max(v, w) \doteq max(x, y) \wedge w < y) \vee$$
$$(max(v, w) \doteq max(x, y) \wedge w \doteq y \wedge v < x)$$

The relation $\ll$ is an ordering of pairs of ordinals. If the maximum of x and y is greater than the maximum of v and w then $(v, w) \ll (x, y)$. If the maxima are equal the pairs are sorted lexicographically the second coordinate being the most significant. The relation $\ll$ is a strict total ordering and turns out to be even a well-ordering on pairs of ordinals. Since the well-ordering property cannot be expressed in first-order logic we verify that the following implication is true for every formula ϕ.

$$\forall v_1, v_2 \, (\forall v_3, v_4((v_3, v_4) \ll (v_1, v_2) \rightarrow \phi(v_3, v_4)) \rightarrow \phi(v_1, v_2)) \qquad (2)$$
$$\rightarrow \forall v_1 \forall v_2 \phi(v_1, v_2)$$

Now, that we know that $\ll$ is a well-ordering it makes sense to introduce the predicates for successor and limit elements

$$succp((v, w, x, y) \Leftrightarrow (x, y) \text{ is the immediate successor of } (v, w) \text{ w.r.t } \ll$$
$$limp(x, y) \qquad \Leftrightarrow \text{there is no } (v, w) \text{ with } succp((v, w, x, y)$$
$$\qquad \qquad i.e.; (x, y) \text{ is a limit pair in the ordering } \ll$$

1. $\forall v_1, v_2, v_3(succp(v_1, v_1, v_1 + 1, 0))$
2. $\forall v_1, v_2(v_2 + 1 < v_1 \rightarrow succp(v_1, v_2, v_1, v_2 + 1)$
3. $\forall v_1, v_2; (v_2 + 1 = v_1 \rightarrow succp(v_1, v_2, 0, v_2 + 1))$
4. $\forall v_1, v_2(v_1 < v_2 \rightarrow succp(v_1, v_2, v_1 + 1, v_2))$
5. $succp(v1, v1, w1, w2) \rightarrow w1 \doteq v1 + 1 \wedge w2 \doteq 0$
6. $(v2 + 1 < v1 \wedge succp(v1, v2, w1, w2) \rightarrow w1 \doteq v1 \wedge w2 \doteq v2 + 1$
7. $succp(v2 + 1, v2, w1, w2) \rightarrow w1 \doteq 0 \wedge w2 \doteq v2 + 1$
8. $(v1 < v2 \wedge succp(v1, v2, w1, w2)) \rightarrow w1 \doteq v1 + 1 \wedge w2 \doteq v2$
9. $\forall v_1, v_2 \exists w_1, w_2(succp(v_1, v_2, w_1, w_2))$
10. $succp(v_1, v_2, w_1, w_2) \rightarrow max(w_1, w_2) \leq max(v_1, v_2) + 1$

Fig. 3. Successor pairs in the well-ordering $\ll$

For successor pairs the properties in Fig. 3 can be derived. This properties are broken down into small parts that can more easily be applied during, preferably automatic, proof search. Taken together they give necessary and sufficient conditions for (x, y) to be the successor pair of (v, w) which may be summarized as

$$
\begin{aligned}
succp(v, w, x, y) \leftrightarrow\ & v = w & \wedge\ x = v + 1 \wedge y = 0 && (3)\\
& \vee\\
& v < w & \wedge\ x = v + 1 \wedge y = w\\
& \vee\\
& v > w + 1 \wedge x = v & \wedge\ y = w + 1\\
& \vee\\
& v = w + 1 \wedge x = 0 & \wedge\ y = w + 1
\end{aligned}
$$

1. $limp(0, 0)$
2. $\forall v_1, v_2(lim(v_2) \wedge v_2 \leq v_1 \rightarrow limp(v_1, v_2))$
3. $\forall v_1, v_2(lim(v_1) \wedge v_1 \leq v_2 \rightarrow limp(v_1, v_2 + 1))$
4. $\forall v(lim(v) \rightarrow limp(0, v))$
5. $\forall v(lim(v) \rightarrow limp(v, 0))$
6. $\forall v_1, v_2(lim(v_1) \wedge lim(v_2) \rightarrow limp(v_1, v_2))$
7. $\forall v_1, v_2(limp(v_1, v_2) \rightarrow (v_1 = 0 \wedge v_2 = 0) \vee (v_1 = 0 \wedge lim(v_2)) \vee$
$\qquad\qquad (lim(v_1) \wedge v_2 = 0) \vee (lim(v_1) \wedge lim(v_2)) \vee$
$\qquad\qquad (v_2 \leq v_1 \wedge lim(v_2)) \vee (lim(v_1) \wedge \exists v_3(v_2 = v_3 + 1 \wedge v_1 < v_2))$

Fig. 4. Limit pairs in the well-ordering $\ll$

Figure 4 provides an analog analysis of limit pairs in the ordering $\ll$ which may be summarized as follow:

$$limp(x, y) \leftrightarrow x = 0 \wedge y = 0 \qquad (4)$$
$$\vee$$
$$x = 0 \wedge lim(y)$$
$$\vee$$
$$lim(x) \wedge y = 0$$
$$\vee$$
$$lim(x) \wedge lim(y)$$
$$\vee$$
$$y \leq x \wedge lim(y)$$
$$\vee$$
$$y > x \wedge lim(x) \wedge \exists z(y = z + 1)$$

The distinction between successor pairs and limit pairs makes it possible to formulate and prove a second form of the transfinite induction principle whose help in proving complex statements can hardly be overrated.

$$\forall v_1, v_2(\ \phi(v_1, v_2) \rightarrow (\forall w_1, w_2(succp(v_1, v_2, w_1, w_2) \rightarrow \phi(w_1, w_2))) \qquad (5)$$
$$\wedge$$
$$limp(v_1, v_2) \wedge$$
$$\forall w_1, w_2((w_1, w_2) \ll (v_1, v_2) \rightarrow \phi(w_1, w_2)) \rightarrow \phi(v_1, v_2))$$
$$\rightarrow \quad \forall v_1, v_2 \phi(v_1, v_2)$$

5   Coding Pairs of Ordinals

The idea for the coding function *encode* is quite simple: $encode(v_1, v_2)$ is the position of the pair (v_1, v_2) in the well-ordering $\ll$. This leads to

$$
\begin{aligned}
encode(0, 0) \quad &= 0 \\
encode(w_1, w_2) &= encode(v_1, v_2) + 1 \quad \text{if } succp(v_1, v_2, w_1, w_2) \\
encode(w_1, w_2) &= \text{the least ordinal greater than } encode(v_1, v_2) \\
&\quad \text{for all } (v_1, v_2) \ll (w_1, w_2) \quad \text{if } limp(w_1, w_2)
\end{aligned}
\qquad (6)
$$

These definitions correspond to Lines 1 to 3 in Fig. 5. As first consequences we list $encode(v_1, v_2) = n$ for $1 \leq n \leq 4$ in Line 4 of Fig. 5.

As a proper coding function *encode* should be injective. As a stepping stone we first prove (strict) monotony as formulated in Line 5 of Fig. 5 while injectivity follows in Line 6. It is a special, and very convenient, feature of the encoding function *encode* that it is surjective, i.e. every ordinal is the code of a pair of ordinals, Line 10 of Fig. 5. In the course of the proof of surjectivity the weak increasing property from Line 7 is used.

Let us now turn to decoding. The definition of the two decoding functions is given in the one axiom in Line 1 of Fig. 6. On the face of it this axiom looks just a some property that we want the decoding functions to satisfy. But, by what

1. $encode(0,0)) \doteq 0$
2. $succp(v_1, v_2, w_1, w_2) \rightarrow encode(w_1, w_2) \doteq encode(v_1, v_2) + 1$
3. $limp(v_1, v_2) \rightarrow (\forall w_1, w_2((w_1, w_2) \ll (v_1, v_2) \rightarrow encode(w_1, w_2) < encode(v_1, v_2))$
$$\wedge$$
$$\forall x(\forall w_1, w_2((w_1, w_2) \ll (v_1, v_2) \rightarrow encode(w_1, w_2) < x)$$
$$\rightarrow encode(v_1, v_2) \leq x)$$
4. $encode(1,0) = 1 \wedge encode(0,1) = 2 \ \wedge$
$encode(1,1) = 3 \wedge encode(2,0) = 4$
5. $(v_1, v_2) \ll (w_1, w_2) \rightarrow encode(v_1, v_2) < encode(w_1, w_2)$
6. $encode(v_1, v_2) = encode(w_1, w_2) \rightarrow (v_1, v_2) = (w_1, w_2)$
7. $\forall v_1, v_2(max(v_1, v_2) \leq encode(v_1, v_2))$
8. $\forall x, y(a + x \leq encode(a, x))$
9. $\forall v_1, v_2, w_1, w_2; (encode(v_1, v_2) < encode(w_1, w_2) \rightarrow (v_1, v_2) \ll (w_1, w_2))$
10. $\forall w \exists v_1, v_2(encode(v_1, v_2) = w)$

Fig. 5. Encoding pairs of ordinals

1. $\forall w(encode(decode1(w), decode2(w)) = w)$
2. $\forall v_1, v_2(decode1(encode(v_1, v_2)) = v_1)$
3. $\forall v_1, v_2(decode2(encode(v_1, v_2)) = v_2)$

Fig. 6. Decoding for pairs of ordinals

we have proved about the encoding function there is exactly one way to define *decode1* and exactly one way to define *decode2* such that the axiom holds true. Lines 2, 3 in Fig. 6 present two lemmas derivable from the defining axiom.

6   Limitations of Th_{Ord}

Definition 4 (Epsilon naught).
$\omega_0 \quad = \omega$
$\omega_{n+1} = \omega^{\omega_n}$
$\epsilon_0 \quad = sup_{n<\omega}(\omega_n)$
It is convenient to stipulate $\omega_{-1} = 1$.

This is a semantic definition. There is no term denoting ϵ_0 in Th_{Ord}.

Lemma 2.

1. *For $n < m < \omega$ we have $\omega_n < \omega_m$.*
2. *For all $n, m < \omega$*
   (a) $\omega_n + \omega_m < \omega_{max\{n,m\}+1}$
   (b) $\omega_n * \omega_m < \omega_{max\{n,m\}+1}$,
   (c) $\omega_n^{\omega_m} < \omega_{max\{n,m\}+2}$
3. $\omega^\alpha = \alpha$ *implies $\omega_m < \alpha$ for all m.*

4. $\alpha, \beta < \omega_n$ implies $\alpha + \beta < \omega_n$.
5. $\alpha, \beta < \omega_n$ implies $\alpha * \beta < \omega_n$.

Proof. The proofs are routine. We provide a sketch for the last two items. In both proofs it suffices to consider the case $\alpha = \beta$

(4) The claim is trivial for $n = 0$. We consider $\alpha < \omega^{\omega_{n-1}}$. Let $\alpha = \omega^{\alpha_0} * a_0 + \omega^{\alpha_1} * a_1 + \ldots + a_{r-1}$ be the Cantor normal form of α. We have $\alpha_0 < \omega_{n-1}$. By [2, page 60ff] the CNF of $\alpha + \alpha = \omega^{\alpha_0} * (a_0 + a_0) + \omega^{\alpha_1} + a_1 * \ldots a_{r-1}$. This implies $\alpha + \alpha < \omega^{\alpha_0+1}$. Since $\alpha_0 + 1$ is still less than ω_{n-1} we get $\alpha + \alpha < \omega^{\omega_{n-1}} = \omega_n$

(5) The claim is trivial for $n = 0$. Let $\alpha = \omega^{\alpha_0} * a_0 + \omega^{\alpha_1} * a_1 + \ldots + a_{r-1}$ be the Cantor normal form of α, as above. The normal form of $\alpha + \alpha$ is $\omega^{\alpha_0+\alpha_0} + a_0 + R$ where R is a sum of $\omega^{\gamma} * c$ with $\alpha_0 + \alpha_0 > \gamma$. From $\alpha_0 < \omega_{n-1}$ we get from (4) $\alpha_0 + \alpha_0 < \omega_{n-1}$ and thus in total $\alpha * \alpha < \omega^{\omega_{n-1}}$. $\square$

Lemma 3. *For a term t in the language L^+_{Ord} of Th^+_{Ord} with the free variables $x_1, \ldots, x_n$ we denote by f_t the n-place function that associates argument tuples $\alpha_1, \ldots, \alpha_n$ with the value $f_t(\alpha_1, \ldots, \alpha_n)$ that is obtained by evaluating term t under the variable assignment $x_i \rightsquigarrow \alpha_i$.*

For every term t there is natural number $b_t < \omega$ such that

$$\alpha_i < \omega_{m_i} \text{ for } 1 \leq i \leq n \quad \text{implies} \quad f_t(\alpha_1, \ldots, \alpha_n) < \omega_{k+b_t}$$
$$\text{with } k = max\{m_i \mid 1 \leq i \leq n\}$$

Proof. The proof proceeds by structural induction on t. The claim is trivial if t is just a variable or a constant or $t \equiv max(t_1, t_2)$

If $t = t_1 + t_2$ there are by induction hypothesis bounds b_{t_1}, b_{t_2} such that for all tuples $\alpha_1, \ldots, \alpha_n$ with $\alpha_i < \omega_{m_i}$ for all $1 \leq i \leq n$ and $k = max\{m_i \mid 1 \leq i \leq n\}$. we have $f_{t_1}(\alpha_1, \ldots, \alpha_n) < \omega_{k+b_{t_1}}$ and $f_{t_2}(\alpha_1, \ldots, \alpha_n) < \omega_{k+b_{t_2}}$. By (2.a) of Lemma 2 we get $f_t(\alpha_1, \ldots, \alpha_n) < \omega_{k+b+1}$ with $b = max\{b_{t_1}, b_{t_2}\}$.

The cases $t = t_1 * t_2$ and $t = t_1^{t_2}$ are handled analogously.

It remains to consider $t = sup_{x_0 < t_1}(t_2)$.

By induction hypothesis there are bounds b_{t_1}, b_{t_2} such that for all arguments $\alpha_0, \alpha_1, \ldots, \alpha_n$ with $\alpha_i < \omega_{m_i}$ we know $f_{t_1}(\alpha_1, \ldots, \alpha_n) < \omega_{max\{m_1, \ldots, m_n\}+b_{t_1}}$ and $f_{t_2}(\alpha_0, \alpha_1, \ldots, \alpha_n) < \omega_{max\{m_0, m_1, \ldots, m_n\}+b_{t_2}}$. Observe, that the variable x_0, to which α_0 is assigned, is not allowed to occur in t_1. For fixed $\alpha_1, \ldots, \alpha_n$ with $\alpha_i < \omega_{m_i}$ $\omega_{max\{m_1, \ldots, m_n\}+b_{t_1}}$ is an upper bound for the assignments to x_0. We thus get for all instantiations α_0 for x_0 that $f_{t_2}(\alpha_0, \alpha_1, \ldots, \alpha_n) < \omega_{max\{m_1, \ldots, m_n\}+b_{t_1}+b_{t_2}}$. Thus the left hand side is also an upper bound for the supremum, i.e. $f_t(\alpha_1, \ldots, \alpha_n) < \omega_{max\{m_1, \ldots, m_n\}+b_{t_1}+b_{t_2}}$. $\square$

Definition 5 (ϵ-Standard Model).
The ϵ standard model

$$\mathcal{S} = (U, <, 0, 1, \omega, max, +, *, exp)$$

has as universe U the set of all ordinals strictly less than ϵ_0: $U = \{\alpha \mid \alpha < \epsilon_0\}$. The constants, the ordering, the maximum function, ordinal addition, multiplication, exponentiation and the supremum operator sup are determined by the usual set theoretic definitions.

Lemma 3 guarantees that the evaluations of all function symbols from the vocabulary L_{Ord}^+ and the sup operator never exceed ϵ_0 on arguments from U.

Theorem 1. $\mathcal{S}$ *is a model for Th_{Ord}.*

Proof. Obvious.

Note, that as a consequence of Theorem 1 the existence of ϵ_0 cannot be proved in Th_{Ord}.

7   Properties of Th_{Tak}

For the convenience of the reader we provide a short review of the results in [6]. In the main body of this paper Gaisi Takeuti construct, mimicking Gödel's technique used in his proof of the consistency of the continuum hypothesis, for an arbitrary model $\mathcal{M}$ of Th_{Tak} a model $\mathfrak{S}_\mathcal{M}$ of ZF set theory. The construction also yields a Δ_0 formula $f_\epsilon(x, y)$ in the language of Th_{Tak} such that for any closed formula ϕ in the language of set theory (i.e. ϵ is the only predicate occurring in ϕ)

$$\mathcal{M} \models \phi^o \Leftrightarrow \mathfrak{S}_\mathcal{M} \models \phi \tag{7}$$

is true where formula ϕ^o is obtained from ϕ by replacing every subformula $t_1 \epsilon t_2$ by $f_\epsilon(t_1, t_2)$.

The last page of [6], that is §8, is very cryptic. The opening quote

> If we assume the set theory, then we can construct our theory of ordinal numbers in the set theory (cf. [5]). In this section it is understood that our theory of ordinal numbers is a subtheory of the set theory in this sense and . . .

leaves much room for interpretation.

If $\mathcal{M}$ is a model of Th_{Tak} of this kind in a model $\mathcal{T}$ of set theory then it is assumed that for formulas ϕ in the language L_{Tak} there are translations ϕ^* into the language of set theory such that

$$\mathcal{M} \models \phi \Leftrightarrow \mathcal{T} \models \phi^* \tag{8}$$

In this special case the universe $S_\mathcal{M}$ of $\mathfrak{S}_\mathcal{M}$ can be described as $S_\mathcal{M} = \{F(\alpha) \mid \alpha \in M\}$, where F is Gödel's fundamental function. Furthermore we have the following

Lemma 4. *For any formula $\phi(x)$ in the language of set theory and all parameters $\bar{\alpha}$ form the universe of $\mathcal{M}$*

$$\mathcal{M} \models \phi^o[\bar{\alpha}] \Leftrightarrow \mathcal{T} \models \phi[F(\bar{\alpha})]$$

Proof. This is proved by induction on the structural complexity of ϕ. For the only base case, the atomic formula $\alpha_1 \in \alpha_2$, [6] offers the hint to prove this by transfinite induction. This is possible since truth in $\mathcal{M}$ is expressible in $\mathcal{T}$.

This does however shed no light on the expressive strength of Th_{Tak}.

8   Concluding Remarks

Takeuti advertises in the introduction to his paper [6] his theory Th_{Tak} as a natural extension of Peano arithmetic. In my opinion the main achievement of the paper is an analysis of minimal requirements to carry through Gödel's construction of an inner model of ZF. It is not surprising that these requirements can be formulated as properties of the ordinals rather than properties of arbitrary sets.

The theory Th_{Ord} was intended as a basis for an implementation in an automated theorem prover and has so far met expectations. That the existence of epsilon numbers cannot be proved in Th_{Ord} does not seem to diminish its usefulness in all practical matters. It might be worthwhile considering the addition of the replacement axiom scheme. This was already deliberated as a possible variant of Th_{Ord} in [3]. Of course, one would not expect that an end user would apply instances of the scheme or that the system would use it automatically. Rather, the replacement scheme would be used to prove within the system the correctness of the pragmatic proof rules. As an aesthetic benefit one could drop the *sup* term constructor in the initial language and add it in a conservative definitional extension. I could not settle the question whether the ϵ-standard model from Definition 5 is a model of the replacement scheme or not. I guess it is.

References

1. Ahrendt, W., Beckert, B., Bubel, R., Hähnle, R., Schmitt, P.H., Ulbrich, M. (eds.): Deductive Software Verification - The KeY Book - From Theory to Practice. LNCS, 10001st edn. Springer, Cham (2016). https://doi.org/10.1007/978-3-319-49812-6
2. Bachmann, H.: Transfinite Zahlen. Ergebnisse der Mathematik und ihrer Grenzgebiete, vol. 1, 2nd edn. Springer, Berlin (1967). https://doi.org/10.1007/978-3-642-88514-3
3. Schmitt, P.H.: A mechanizable first-order theory of ordinals. In: Schmidt, R.A., Nalon, C. (eds.) TABLEAUX 2017. LNCS (LNAI), vol. 10501, pp. 331–346. Springer, Cham (2017). https://doi.org/10.1007/978-3-319-66902-1_20
4. Schmitt, P.H.: Takeuti's first-order theory of ordinals revisited. Technical report 2, Department of Informatics, Karlsruhe Institute of Technology (2018)
5. Takeuti, G.: On the theory of ordinal number, s ii. J. Math. Soc. Japan **10**, 106–120 (1958)
6. Takeuti, G.: A formalization of the theory of ordinal numbers. J. Symb. Logic **30**, 295–317 (1965)
7. Ulbrich, M.: Dynamic Logic for an intermediate language: verification, interaction and refinement. Ph.D. thesis, Karlsruhe Institute of Technology, June 2013. http://nbn-resolving.org/urn:nbn:de:swb:90-411691

Randomness Tests: Theory and Practice

Alexander Shen$^{(\boxtimes)}$ (iD)

LIRMM, University of Montpellier, CNRS, Montpellier, France
alexander.shen@lirmm.fr

*To Yury Gurevich, with whom we have had
a lot of interesting and sometimes heated
discussions on many topics, including
randomness.*

Abstract. The mathematical theory of probabilities does not refer to
the notion of an *individual* random object. For example, when we toss a
fair coin n times, all 2^n bit strings of length n are equiprobable outcomes
and none of them is more "random" than others. However, when testing
a statistical model, e.g., the fair coin hypothesis, we necessarily have to
distinguish between outcomes that contradict this model, i.e., the outcomes that convince us to reject this model with some level of certainty,
and all other outcomes. The same question arises when we apply randomness tests to some hardware random bits generator.

A similar distinction between random and non-random objects
appears in algorithmic information theory. Algorithmic information theory defines the notion of an individual random sequence and therefore
splits all infinite bit sequences into random and non-random ones. For
finite sequences there is no sharp boundary. Instead, the notion of *randomness deficiency* can be defined, and sequences with greater deficiency
are considered as "less random" ones. This definition can be given in
terms of randomness tests that are similar to the practical tests used for
checking (pseudo)random bits generators. However, these two kinds of
randomness tests are rarely compared and discussed together.

In this survey we try to discuss current methods of producing and
testing random bits, having in mind algorithmic information theory as
a reference point. We also suggest some approach to construct robust
practical tests for random bits.

1 Testing a Statistical Hypothesis

Probability theory is nowadays considered as a special case of measure theory:
a random variable is a measurable function defined on some probability space
that consists of a set Ω, some σ-algebra of the subsets of Ω, and some σ-additive
measure defined on this σ-algebra. A random variable determines a probability
distribution on the set of possible values.

Supported by ANR-15-CE40-0016-0 RaCAF project.

A. Blass et al. (Eds.): Gurevich Festschrift, LNCS 12180, pp. 258–290, 2020.
https://doi.org/10.1007/978-3-030-48006-6_18

When probability theory is applied to some "real world" case, it provides a statistical hypothesis that is a mathematical model of the process. For example, for n trials and the fair coin the corresponding model is the uniform distribution on the set $\mathbb{B}^n$ of all possible outcomes, i.e., on all n-bit binary strings. Each string has probability 2^{-n}. The set $\mathbb{B}^n$ can be considered as a probability space, and ith coin tossing is represented by a random variable ξ_i defined on this space: $\xi_i(x_1 x_2 \ldots x_n) = x_i$.

Having a mathematical model for a real-life process, we need some way to check whether this model is adequate or not. Imagine that somebody gives us a coin, or a more advanced random bits generator. This coin can be asymmetric, and the bit generator can be faulty. To check whether this is the case, we need to perform some experiment and look at its results. Assume, for example, that we toss a coin and get 85 heads in a row, as it happened to Rosencrantz and Guildenstern in Stoppard's play [34, Act 1]. Should we reject the fair coin hypothesis? Probably we should—but how can we justify this answer? One can argue that for a fair coin such an outcome is hardly possible, since its probability is negligible, namely, equals 2^{-85}. However, any other sequence of 85 heads and tails has the same negligible probability—so why this reasoning cannot be applied to any other outcome?

To discuss this problem in a more general case, let us introduce suitable terminology. Consider some set X of possible outcomes. We assume that X is finite. Fix some *statistical model* P, i.e., a hypothetical probability distribution on X. A *randomness test* is an event $T \subset X$ that has small probability according to P. If an experiment produces an outcome that belongs to T, the test is not passed, and we may reject P. This approach has two main problems. The first problem, mentioned earlier, is that in most cases every individual outcome $x \in X$ has negligible probability, so the singleton $\{x\}$ is a test that can be used to reject P. We discuss this problem later. Now let us comment on the other problem: how to choose the threshold value for the probability, i.e., how small should be the probability of T to consider T as a valid randomness test.

In practice, the statistical model is often called the *null hypothesis*. Usually we have some experimental data that, as we hope, exhibit some effect. For example, we may hope that a new drug increases the survival rate, and indeed we see some improvement in the experimental group. However, this improvement could be just a random fluctuation while in fact the survival probability remains unchanged. We formulate the null hypothesis based on the old value of the survival probability and then apply some test. The rejection of the null hypothesis means that we do not consider the data as a random fluctuation, and claim that the new drug has at least some effect.[1]

In this approach, the choice of the threshold value obviously should depend on the importance of the question we consider. Any decision based on statistical considerations is inherently unreliable, but an acceptable level of this unreliability depends on the possible consequences of a wrong decision. The more important the consequences are, the smaller threshold for statistical tests is

---

[1] Of course, in practice we want also to be convinced that this effect is beneficial.

needed. The choice of the threshold value is often debated. For example, there is a paper [2] signed by 72 authors that proposes "to change the $\langle \ldots \rangle$ threshold for statistical significance from 0.05 to 0.005 for claims of new discoveries". It may look ridiculous—obviously both the old threshold and the new one are chosen arbitrarily—but it reflects the existing situation in natural sciences. Other people point out that fixing a threshold, whatever it is, is a bad practice [1].

2   Randomness Tests

Now let us address the other problem mentioned above. After the experiment is made, we can find a set T of very small measure that contains the actual outcome of the experiment, and declare it to be a randomness test. For example, Rosencrantz could toss a coin 85 times, write down the sequence x of heads and tails obtained, and then try to convince Guildenstern that the fair coin hypothesis should be rejected, because the set $T = \{x\}$ is a test that has probability 2^{-85} according to the hypothesis and still the actual outcome is in T.

This argument is obviously wrong, but it is not that easy to say what exactly is wrong here. The simplest—and rather convincing—answer is that the *test should be fixed before the experiment*. Indeed, if Rosencrantz showed some sequence of heads and tails to Guildenstern and *after that* the coin tossing gave exactly the same sequence, this would be a very convincing reason to reject the null hypothesis of a fair coin.

Still this answer is not universal. Imagine that we buy a book called "A Million Random Digits"[2]. We open it and find that it is filled with zeros. Do we have reasons to complain? If we have said "Look, this book is suspicious; may be it contains only zeros" *before opening the book*, then we definitely do—but what if not? Or what if we find out that the digits form the decimal expansion of 8.5π? Note that this hypothesis hardly can come to our mind before we study the book carefully.

Sometimes the experiment is already in the past, so we look at the data already produced, like Kepler did when analyzing the planet observations. Probably, in this case we should require that the test is chosen without knowing the data, but it is (a) more subjective and (b) rarely happens in practice, usually people do look at the data before discussing them.

On the other hand, even the test formulated before the experiment could be dubious. Imagine that there are many people waiting for an outcome of the coin tossing, and each of them declares her own statistical test, i.e., a set of outcomes that has probability at most ε. Here ε is some small number; it is the same for all tests. After the experiment it is found that the outcome fails one of the tests, i.e., belongs to the small set declared by one of the observers. We are ready to declare that the null hypothesis is rejected. Should we take into account that there were many tests? One can argue that the probability to fail at least one of the N tests is bounded by $N\varepsilon$, not ε, so the result is less convincing than the

---

[2] By the way, one can still buy such a book [27] now (August 2019) for 50.04 euro, or 903.42 euro, if you prefer the first edition, but agree to get a second-hand copy.

same result with only one observer. This correction factor N is often called the *Bonferroni correction* and is quite natural. On the other hand, the observer who declared the failed test could complain that she did not know anything about other observers and it is a completely unacceptable practice if actions of other people beyond her control and knowledge are considered as compromising her findings. And it is difficult to answer in a really convincing way to this complaint.

In fact, this is not only a philosophical question, but also an important practical one. If a big laboratory with thousand researchers uses threshold value 0.05 for statistical significance, then we could expect dozens of papers coming from this lab where this threshold is crossed—even if in fact the null hypothesis is true all the time.

There are no universally accepted or completely convincing answers to these questions. However, there is an important idea that is a philosophical motivation for algorithmic information theory. We discuss it in the next section.

3   "Remarkable" Events as Tests

Recall the example with zeros in the table of random numbers and the corresponding singleton test that consists of the zero sequence. Even if we have not explicitly formulated this test before reading the table, one can say that this test is so simple that it *could* be formulated before the experiment. The fact that all outcomes are heads/zeros is remarkable, and this makes this test convincing.

This question is discussed by Borel [5]. He quotes Bertrand who asked whether we should look for a hidden cause if three stars form an equilateral triange. Borel notes that nobody will find something strange if the angle between two stars is exactly $13°42'51.7''$, since nobody would ask whether this happens or not before the measurement ("car on ne se serait jamais posé cette question précise avant d'avoir mesuré l'angle"). Borel continues:

> La question est de savoir si l'on doit faire ces mêmes réserves dans le cas où l'on constate qu'un des angles du triangle formé par trois étoiles a une valeur *remarquable* et est, par exemple, égal à l'angle du triangle équilatéral ⟨...⟩ Voici ce que l'on peut dire à ce sujet : on doit se défier beaucoup de la tendance que l'on a à regarder comme *remarquable* une circonstance que l'on n'avait pas précisée *avant l'expérience*, car le nombre des circonstances qui peuvent apparaître comme remarquables, à divers points de vue, est très considérable [5, p. 112–113][3]

This quotation illustrates a trade-off between the probability of the event specified by some randomness test and its "remarkability": if there are N events

---

[3] The question is whether we should have the same doubts in the case where one of the angles of a triangle formed by tree stars has some *remarkable* value, for example, is equal to the angle of an equilateral triangle. ⟨...⟩ Here we could say the following: one should resist strongly to the tendency to consider some observation that was not specified *before the experiment* as remarkable, since the number of circumstances that may look remarkable from different viewpoints is quite significant.

of probability at most ε that are "as remarkable as the test event" (or "more remarkable"), then the probability of the combined test event is at most $N\varepsilon$. In other words, we should consider not an individual test, but the union of all tests that have the same probability and the same (or greater) "remarkability".

The problem with this approach is that we need to quantify somehow the "remarkability". The algorithmic information theory suggests to take into account the Kolmogorov complexity of the test, i.e., to count the number of bits needed to specify the test. More remarkable tests have shorter descriptions and smaller complexity. The natural way to take the complexity into account is to multiply the probability by $O(2^n)$ if the complexity of the test is n, since there is at most $O(2^n)$ different descriptions of size at most n bits and therefore at most $O(2^n)$ tests of complexity at most n.

However, the word "description" is too vague. One should fix a "description language" that determines which test corresponds to a given description, i.e., to a given sequence of bits. Algorithmic information theory does not fix a specific description language; instead, it defines a class of description languages and proves that there are *optimal* description languages in this class. Optimality is understood "up to $O(1)$ additive term": a language L is optimal if for any other language L' in the class there exist a constant c (depending on L') with the following property: if a test T has description of length k via L', it has a description of length at most $k+c$ via L. This implies that two different optimal languages lead to complexity measures that differ at most by $O(1)$ additive term.

Probably this $O(1)$ precision is the best thing a mathematical theory could give us. However, if one would like to define "the gold standard" for valid use of statistical tests, this is obviously not enough, and one should fix some specific description language. It looks like a difficult task and there are no serious attempts of this type. Still one could expect that this language should be domain-specific and take into account the relations and constants that are "naturally defined" for the objects in question. This is discussed in details by Gurevich and Passmore [9]. The authors note that questions about statistical tests and their validity do arise in courts when some statistical argument is suggested as evidence, but there are no established procedures to evaluate statistical arguments.[4] One could also mention a similar (and quite important) case: statistical "fingerprints" for falsified elections. There are many examples of this type (see the survey [31] and references within). Let us mention two examples that illustrate the problem of "remarkable post factum observations". Figure 1 (provided by Kupriyanov [15]) presents the official results of the "presidential elections" in Russia in 2018 and is constructed as follows: for every polling station where both the reported participation rate and the fraction of votes for de facto president of

---

[4] In this paper some thought experiments and one real story are considered as examples. One of the thought experiments is as follows: the wife of a president of a state lottery turns out to be its winner. Recently I learned that this example is not so far from the real life as one could think: in 2000 BBC reported that "Zimbabwean President Robert Mugabe has won the top prize [about \$2600] in a lottery organised by a partly state-owned bank" (http://news.bbc.co.uk/2/hi/africa/621895.stm).

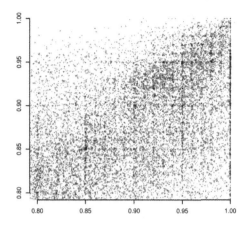

Fig. 1. "Putin's grid" in 2018 [15]. Note that vertical and horizontal lines are formed by data points, they are not the added grid lines.

Russia (Putin) exceed 80%, a corresponding grey point is shown. If several points coincide, a darker/bigger point appears. Looking at the "grid lines" formed by these points (for integer percentages; more visible lines appear for the percentages that are multiples of 5), one probably agrees that such a remarkable grid has negligible probability to appear naturally for any kind of elections. However, it is far from obvious which statistical test should be considered here and how can we quantitatively estimate its complexity and its probability.

Related example is provided by "referendum results" in Crimea (Ukraine). As noted by Alexander Kireev [13], the "official results" in Sevastopol (Crimea) include the following data: total numbers of registered voters (306258), total number of ballots (274101) and the number of "yes for the annexation" votes (262041). The two main ratios (the participation rate and "yes" rate) are suspiciously round: $274101/306258 = 0.895\mathbf{000}294$ and $262041/274101=0.956\mathbf{00}162$. Indeed, in both cases the numerator can be obtained by multiplying the denominator by the integer number of promilles and rounding to the closest integer. Probably most statisticians would agree that this coincidence is remarkable and has very small probability, but it is difficult to agree on a specific quantitative estimate of the corresponding probability after a suitable Bonferroni correction.[5]

---

[5] A rough estimate is attempted in the survey mentioned above [31, p. 49–50]. It takes into account other information about the case. Both anomalies, the integer grid and round percentages, appeared in earlier "elections", so it is not really fair to call them "post factum observations". For the Crimea's "referendum results" the upper bound for the probability after the correction is estimated as 0.1%.

4 Randomness as Incompressibility

Algorithmic information theory (also called Kolmogorov complexity theory) is outside the scope of this survey[6], but let us mention a few results that have philosophical importance and should be kept in mind when discussing randomness at any level.

Roughly speaking, algorithmic information theory says that *randomness is incompressibility*. More precisely, a binary string looks plausible as an outcome of a fair coin (does not convince us to reject the fair coin hypothesis) if it is incompressible, i.e., if there is no program that produces this string and is much shorter than the string itself. In other words, we

- define Kolmogorov complexity of a string as the minimal length of a program that produces it; in this definition we use some optimal programming language that makes complexity minimal up to an $O(1)$ additive term;
- note that all n-bit strings have complexity at most $n + O(1)$, since a trivial program "print x" has almost the same size as x;
- note that at most 2^{-c} fraction of n-bit strings have complexity less than $n - c$, so this is a very small minority for non-negligible values of c; we treat members of this minority as non-random strings.

This approach is consistent with what we said above about valid tests for randomness as simple sets of small probability. Namely, we consider a test that consists of highly compressible strings, and note that this test is universal in some sense, i.e., it is as sensitive as any other test, up to an $O(1)$-constant.

Technically speaking, there is a result that relates complexity to the randomness deficiency in terms of tests. We state this result for a simple case (uniform distribution on the set of strings of given length; see the textbook [33, Sect. 14.1] for a more general statement). It uses the notion of *conditional complexity* $C(x|u)$ of a string x given some u (an integer) defined as the minimal length of a program that produces x given u as an input.

Consider some integer function $d(x)$ defined on bit strings. Call it a *deficiency function* if it satisfies two requirements:

- $d(x)$ is *lower semicomputable*, i.e., $d(x)$ can be presented as a limit of a non-decreasing computable sequence of integers (uniformly in x), and
- for every k, the fraction of n-bit strings such that $d(x) > k$, is $O(2^{-k})$.

Such a deficiency function determines, for every n, a series of tests for uniformly distributed n-bit strings, where the kth test set for n-bit strings consists of strings of length n such that $d(x) > k$. In terms of the next section, $2^{d(x)}$ is a probability bounded test up to a constant factor. The second requirement guarantees that the test sets have small probability according to the uniform

---

[6] The short introduction can be found in the lecture notes [30] or in the introductory part of the textbook [33]. The algorithmic statistics, the part of algorithmic information theory that deals specifically with the statistical hypotheses and their testing, is discussed in two surveys [36,37].

distribution. The first one means, informally speaking, that the test is "semi-effective": if x has some peculiar property that makes it non-random, then we will ultimately discover this property and $d(x)$ will become large, but we never can be sure that x does *not* have properties that make it non-random, since $d(\cdot)$ is not required to be computable.

Proposition 1. *Among the deficiency functions there is a maximal one up to $O(1)$, i.e., a deficiency function d such that for every other deficiency function d' we have $d(x) \geqslant d'(x) - c$ for some c and all x. This maximal function is equal to $n - C(x|n) + O(1)$ for n-bit strings x.*

This result shows that the difference between length and complexity is the "universal measure of non-randomness" that takes into account all regularities that make a string x non-random. It is easy to prove also that if a string x belongs to a simple small set, then its deficiency is large, thus confirming the informal idea that a small set exhibits non-randomness of its elements.

There are many results about randomness deficiencies in this sense, but we cannot go into the details here and return instead to some other topics that are important for practical randomness tests.

5   Families of Tests and Continuous Tests

The law of large numbers says that for independent Bernoulli trials, e.g., for fair coin tossing, the number of successful trials is with high probability close to its expectation, i.e., to $n/2$ for n coin tossings. Therefore, large deviation is a rare event and can be used as a randomness test: as the deviation threshold increases, the probability of the event "the deviation exceeds this threshold" decreases, usually rather fast.

Instead of fixing some significance level and the corresponding threshold one could consider a family of tests: for every significance level ε we consider a set T_ε of measure at most ε. It consists of the outcomes where deviation exceeds some threshold that depends on ε. As ε decreases, the threshold increases, and the set T_ε and its measure decrease.

Such a family of tests can be combined into one non-negative function $t(x)$ defined on the set of possible outcomes, if we agree that T_ε is the set of outcomes where $t(x) \geqslant 1/\varepsilon$. Here we use $c = 1/\varepsilon$ as the threshold instead of ε to simplify the comparison with expectation-bounded tests discussed below. In this language the bound for the probability of T_ε can be reformulated as

$$\Pr[t(x) \geqslant c] \leqslant 1/c \quad \text{for every } c > 0 \qquad (*)$$

Informally speaking, $t(x)$ measures the "rarity", or "randomness deficiency" of an outcome x: the greater $t(x)$ is, the less plausible is x as an outcome of a random experiment.

Functions t that satisfy the condition $(*)$ are called *probability-bounded randomness tests* [3]. Sometimes it is convenient to use the logarithmic scale and replace t by $\log t$. Then the condition $(*)$ should be replaced by the inequality $\Pr[t(x) \geqslant d] \leqslant 2^{-d}$. Note that a similar condition was used for deficiency functions in Sect. 4.

The condition $(*)$ is a consequence of a stronger condition $\int t(x)\,dP(x) \leqslant 1$ where P is the probability distribution on the space of outcomes. In other terms, this stronger requirement means that the expected value of t (over the distribution P) is at most 1, and the condition $(*)$ is its consequence, guaranteed by Markov's inequality. The functions t that satisfy this stronger condition are called *expectation-bounded randomness tests* [3].

In fact these two notions of test are rather close to each other: if t is a probability-bounded test, then $t/\log^2 t$ is an expectation-bounded test up to $O(1)$-factor. Moreover, the following general result is true:

Proposition 2. *For every monotone continuous function* $u\colon [1, +\infty] \to [0, \infty]$ *such that* $\int_1^\infty u(z)/z^2\,dz \leqslant 1$ *and for every probability-bounded test* $t(\cdot)$ *the composition* $u(t(\cdot))$ *is an expectation-bounded test.*

The statement above [7] is obtained by applying Proposition 2 to $u(z) = z/\log^2 z$.

6 Where Do We Get Randomness Tests?

As we have mentioned, different classical results of probability theory can be used as randomness tests. Take for example the law of large numbers. It says that some event, namely, a large deviation from the expected value, has small probability. This event can be considered as a test set. Mathematical statistics provides a whole bunch of tests of this type for different distributions, including χ^2-test, Kolmogorov–Smirnov test, and others.

Another source of statistical tests, though less used in practice, is provided by the probabilistic existence proofs. Sometimes we can prove that there exists an object with a given combinatorial property, say, a graph with good expansion properties, and the proof goes as follows. We consider a probabilistic process that constructs a random object. In our example this object is a graph. We prove that with high probability this random object satisfies the combinatorial property. Now we use the bit source that we want to test as a source of random bits for the algorithm. If we find out that the object constructed by the algorithm does *not* have the combinatorial property in question, we conclude that a rare event happened, and our source of random bits failed the test.

One should also mention tests inspired by algorithmic information theory (see, e.g., a 1992 paper by Maurer [20]) Each file compressor (like `zip`, `bzip`, etc.) can be considered as a random test. Assume that we have a sequence of bits, considered as a file, i.e., a sequence of bytes. If this file can be compressed by n bytes for some non-negligible n, say, by a dozen of bytes, then this bit sequence fails the test and can be considered as non-random one. Indeed, the probability of this event is at most 256^{-n}, up to a factor close to 1. The Bonferroni correction here says that we should multiply this probability by the number of popular compressors, but even if we assume that there are thousands of them in use, it usually still keeps the probability astronomically small.

There is also a general way to construct probability-bounded tests. It is called "p-values", and the two previous examples of randomness tests can be considered as its special cases. Consider an arbitrary real-valued[7] function D defined on the space of outcomes. The value $D(x)$ is treated as some kind of "deviation" from what we expect, so we use the letter D. Then consider the function

$$p_D(x) = \Pr[\{y\colon D(y) \geqslant D(x)\}].$$

(defined on the same set of outcomes). In other words, for every threshold d we consider the set

$$T_d = \{y\colon D(y) \geqslant d\}$$

of all outcomes where the deviation is at least d, and measure the probability of this event, thus "recalibrating" the deviation function. In this language, $p_D(x)$ is the probability of the event $T_{D(x)}$, the chance to have in a random experiment of the given type the same deviation as it happened now, or a larger one.

Proposition 3.
   (a) *For every $c \geqslant 0$, the probability of the event $p_D(x) \leqslant c$ is at most c.*
   (b) *If each value of function D has probability at most ε, then the probability of the event $p_D(x) \leqslant c$ is between $c - \varepsilon$ and c.*

Proof. The probability $p_d = \Pr[T_d]$ decreases (more precisely, does not increase) as d increases. The function $d \mapsto p_d$ is left-continuous since the inequalities $D \geqslant d'$ for all $d' < d$ imply $D \geqslant d$. However, it may not be right-continuous, and a similar argument shows that the gap between the value of p_d and the right limit $\lim_{d' \to d+0} p_{d'}$ is the probability of the event $\{x\colon D(x) = d\}$. Now we add to this picture some threshold c, see Fig. 2. It may happen (case 1) that c is among the values p_d. This case is shown on the left and right pictures (Fig. 2). On the right picture the function p_d is constant on an interval where there are no values

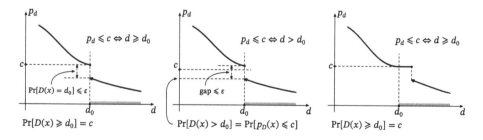

Fig. 2. Proof of Proposition 3

---

[7] This trick in a more general situation where the values of D are elements of some linearly ordered set, is considered in a paper by Gurevich and Vovk [10].

of D or these values have probability 0. Case 2: the threshold c may fall in a gap
between some value of p_d and the right limit in the same point (denoted by d_0),
as shown in the middle picture. The size of the gap is the probability of the event
$D(x) = d_0$ and is at most ε according to our assumption. For the left and right
pictures the inequality $p_D(x) \leqslant c$ means that $D(x) \geqslant d_0$, and the probability of
the event $p_D(x) \leqslant c$ is exactly $p_{d_0} = c$, so both statements (a) and (b) are true.
In this case the value of ε does not matter. For the middle picture $p_D(x) \leqslant c$
when $d > d_0$, and the probability of this event is not the value of p_d when $d = d_0$
but the right limit of p_d as $d \to d_0 + 0$. Still the difference does not exceed ε
according to the assumption in (b), and again both statements are true.

Remark 1. This proof is given for the general case (X may be infinite); in the
finite case the function p_d has only finitely many values, and the graph is a finite
family of horizonal lines.

Remark 2. Proposition 3 obviously implies that the function $1/p_D(x)$ is a probability-bounded test. This observation allows us to construct many probability-
bounded tests, starting from almost any random variable D. For example, we get
a test from a probabilistic existence proof if we let D be the function that appears
in the combinatorial statement, e.g., the second eigenvalue for the probabilistic
proof that expander graphs exists. The only caveat is that we need to compute
the function $d \mapsto p_d$, and this is usually not so easy. This function is often
replaced by some its approximation, and this may lead to problems; see the
discussion below.

Remark 3. If we apply this procedure to a function D that is already a probability-bounded test, then by definition we get some new test $t = 1/p_D$ such that
$t(x) \geqslant D(x)$ for all x. In general, the function t could exceed D if the inequality
in the condition $(*)$, Sect. 5, is strict.

7   Secondary Tests

There is an important type of randomness tests that can be called "secondary
tests". Tests of this type appeared already in the classical book of Knuth [14,
Sect. 3.3.1, B] and are extensively used in practical test suites [17]. Recall Proposition 3 and assume for a while that every individual value of D has very small
probability, so we may assume that there are (almost) no gaps in the graph of p_d.
Then Proposition 3 says that the random variable p_D is uniformly distributed
on $[0, 1]$. Repeat the test N times, using fresh random bits (from the generator
we are testing) for each repetition. Assuming that the null hypothesis is true,
we get N independent reals that are uniformly distributed in $[0, 1]$. Then we
may apply any test for the independent uniformly distributed variables, e.g., the
Kolmogorov–Smirnov test for this distribution.

This procedude converts any p-value test for a random bits generator that has
negligible probabilities of individual values into a "secondary test" that could
be much more sensitive. Knuth describes a similar trick, but he does not use

the recalibration using p-values and applies the Kolmogorov–Smirnov (KS) test directly to the values of D and the distribution that should appear if the null hypothesis is true:[8]

> ...We should observe that the KS test may be used in conjunction with the χ^2 test... Suppose we have made, say, 10 independent χ^2 tests of different parts of a random sequence, so that values $V_1, V_2, \ldots, V_{10}$ have been obtained. It is not a good policy simply to count how many of the V's are suspiciously large or small. This procedure will work in extreme cases, and very large or very small values may mean that the sequence has too much local nonrandomness; but a better general method would be to plot the empirical distribution of these 10 values and to compare it to the correct distribution... This would give a clearer picture of the results of the χ^2 tests, and in fact the statistics K_{10}^+ and K_{10}^- [from KS test] could be determined as an indication of the success or failure... [Speaking about an example discussed earlier:] Notice that *all 20 observations in Fig. 4 (c)* [a figure from Knuth's book that we do not reproduce] *fall between the 5 and 95% levels*, so we would not have regarded *any* of them as suspicious, individually; yet collectively the empirical distribution shows that these observations are not at all right [14, Sect. 3.3.1, p. 50–51].

We return to the use of secondary tests in practical test suites in the next section.

8   Testing (Pseudo)randomness in Practice

There are several suits of randomness tests that are often used. The early history of randomness tests (as well as pseudorandom number generators) is described by Knuth [14, Sect. 3.3]. He starts with χ^2 and Kolmogorov–Smirnov tests, explains secondary testing (see the quote in the previous section) and also describes several *ad hoc* tests.

8.1   Diehard

Later George Marsaglia developed a `diehard` series of tests that were included (as C and Fortran sources) in a CD that he prepared [17]. That CD also included a collection of files with "random" bits, constructed by combining the output of hardware random bits generators with some deterministic pseudorandom sequences, see below Sect. 10. The description of the tests could be found in Marsaglia's papers [16,19]; see also the file `tests.txt` in the source code of the tests [17].

However, there are some problems with these tests. They heavily use the secondary test approach but not always in a correct way. First, one of the tests computes p-values for data that are not independent, as the following description, copied verbatim from the source code, shows:

---

[8] This is an equivalent approach since KS-test gives the same result after any monotone recalibration of the empirical values and theoretical distribution.

This is the BIRTHDAY SPACINGS TEST
Choose m birthdays in a year of n days. List the spacings
between the birthdays. If j is the number of values that
occur more than once in that list, then j is asymptotically
Poisson distributed with mean m^3/(4n). Experience shows n
must be quite large, say n>=2^18, for comparing the results
to the Poisson distribution with that mean. This test uses
n=2^24 and m=2^9, so that the underlying distribution for j
is taken to be Poisson with lambda=2^27/(2^26)=2. A sample
of 500 j's is taken, and a chi-square goodness of fit test
provides a p value. The first test uses bits 1-24 (counting
from the left) from integers in the specified file.
      Then the file is closed and reopened. Next, bits 2-25 are
used to provide birthdays, then 3-26 and so on to bits 9-32.
Each set of bits provides a p-value, and the nine p-values
provide a sample for a KSTEST.

As we see from this description, the different p-values use overlapping bits (2–
25, 3–26, etc.) of the same numbers. There is no reason to expect that they
are independent, contrary to the requirements of the Kolmogorov–Smirnov test.
This description also exhibits another problem that appears in many tests from
diehard suite. We use some asymptotic approximation, in this case the Poisson distribution, instead of the true distribution, ignoring the approximation
error for which we have no upper bounds. Moreover, even if the error can be
upper-bounded for the primary test, this upper bound does not translate easily
into a bound for an error in the secondary test where we use the approximate
distribution for recalibrating the deviations. Sometimes even the parameters of
approximate distribution are only guessed. For example, in the description of one
of the tests (named OQSO) Marsaglia writes about the distribution: "The mean
is based on theory; sigma comes from extensive simulation". For the other one
(called "parking lot test") even the mean is based on simulation: "Simulation
shows that k should average 3523 with sigma 21.9 and is very close to normally
distributed. Thus $(k - 3523)/21.9$ should be a standard normal variable, which,
converted to a uniform variable, provides input to a KSTEST based on a sample
of 10". Here KSTEST is the Kolmogorov–Smirnov test for uniform distribution.
The arising problem is described by Marsaglia as follows:

NOTE: Most of the tests in DIEHARD return a p-value, which should
be uniform on $[0, 1)$ if the input file contains truly independent random
bits. Those p-values are obtained by $p = F(X)$, where F is the assumed
distribution of the sample random variable X—often normal. But that
assumed F is just an asymptotic approximation, for which the fit will be
worst in the tails. Thus you should not be surprised with occasional p-
values near 0 or 1, such as .0012 or .9983. When a bit stream really FAILS
BIG, you will get p's of 0 or 1 to six or more places. By all means, do
not, as a Statistician might, think that a $p < .025$ or $p > .975$ means that

the RNG has "failed the test at the .05 level". Such p's happen among the hundreds that DIEHARD produces, even with good RNG's. So keep in mind that "p happens".

This note combines two warnings. One is quite general and is related to the question of many tests applied to one sequence, see the discussion of the Bonferroni correction above, Sect. 2. The other one that should be separated from the first (but is not) is that `diehard` tests are not really tests in statistical sense, since they use the approximate distribution for recalibration and therefore small p-values could appear more often than they should.

Some other tests (not included in `diehard`) were later suggested by Marsaglia and Tsang [18].

8.2 Dieharder

A decade later Robert Brown [6] produced an extended version of the `diehard` test suite, called `dieharder`. The code was rewritten and published under GNU public license, integrated with GNU statistical library and parametrized, so now one can vary the sample size and the number of p-values easily. New tests were added and other improvements made. The resulting package is supported by mainstream Linux distributions. The package involves an extensive documentation. In particular, the `man` page says:

> A failure of the distribution of p-values at any level of aggregation signals trouble. ⟨...⟩ The question is, trouble with what? Random number tests are themselves complex computational objects, and there is a probability that their code is incorrectly framed or that roundoff or other numerical— not methodical—errors are contributing to a distortion of the distribution of some of the p-values obtained.

In this quote two problems are noted: the coding errors in the tests, and the problems related to the mathematical flaws in the approximate data used to construct the tests. The suggested solution for both problems is the same: testing these tests on "reference" random number generators. The `man` page says:

> There are a number of generators that we have theoretical reasons to expect to be extraordinarily good and to lack correlations out to some known underlying dimensionality, and that also test out extremely well quite consistently. By using several such generators and not just one, one can hope that those generators have (at the very least) different correlations and should not all uniformly fail a test in the same way and with the same number of p-values. When all of these generators consistently fail a test at a given level, I tend to suspect that the problem is in the test code, not the generators, although it is very difficult to be certain...
> Tests (such as the diehard `operm5` and `sums` test) that consistently fail at these high resolutions are flagged as being "suspect" ⟨...⟩ and they are strongly deprecated! Their results should not be used to test random

number generators pending agreement in the statistics and random number community that those tests are in fact valid and correct so that observed failures can indeed safely be attributed to a failure of the intended null hypothesis.

Unfortunately, `dieharder-3.31.1`, the last version available as of September 2019, also has some problems. One of them, affecting almost all tests, is the incorrect code that computes the Kolmogorov – Smirnov statistic. This code produces incorrect values, sometimes even impossibly small values, and in this case the computation of p-value gives 1. Indeed, in this case with probability 1 the deviation will be bigger than this impossibly small value. This is (correctly) interpreted as the test failure. Fortunately, it seems that for larger sample sizes the error in the statistics computation becomes less important.

8.3   NIST Test Suite

In 2000 the National Institute of Standards published a description of a test suite for randomness, including the source code. Now there exists an updated version [21].[9]

The description starts with some general words about randomness: "For example, a physical source such as electronic noise may contain a superposition of regular structures, such as waves or other periodic phenomena, which may appear to be random, yet are determined to be non-random using statistical tests" (p. 1–2). Then the authors speak about two types of possible errors: Type I (rejecting a good generator) and Type II (accepting a bad one) and about probabilities of these errors. However, their comments are misleading. Authors explain that a Type I error probability is a probability for a random sequence to get into the rejection set under a null hypothesis H_0—and this is correct. But then they say something confusing about the Type II errors: "Type II error probability is $\langle \ldots \rangle$ $P(\text{accept} H_0 | H_0 \text{is false})$" [21, p. 1–4]. While H_0 is a statistical hypothesis (model), namely, the assumption that the bits are independent and uniformly distributed, the words "H_0 is false" do not define any distribution, so one cannot speak about this conditional probability. The authors acknowledge this by saying "The probability of a Type II error is denoted as β. $\langle \ldots \rangle$ Unlike α [the probability of a Type I error], β is not a fixed value. $\langle \ldots \rangle$ The calculation of Type II error β is more difficult than the calculation of α because of the many possible types of non-randomness"—but still one could conclude from what the authors say that Type II error probability is well defined and is some number, though difficult to compute. This is a gross misunderstanding.

Then the authors explain the meaning of p-values, but again their explanations sound confusing, to say the least: "If a *P-value* for a test is determined to be equal to 1, then the sequence appears to have perfect randomness" (page

---

[9] The original version contained 16 randomness tests. In 2004 some errors in two tests were pointed out [12]. Correcting these errors, the revised version (2010) deleted one of the tests (the Lempel – Ziv test) and corrected the other one (the Fourier spectral test).

1–4). In reality the value 1 is not much better than the value 0, since the correctly computed p-values have uniform distribution. Even more strange is the following remark: "For a *P-value* ≥ 0.001, a sequence would be considered to be random with a confidence of 99.9%. For a *P-value* < 0.001, a sequence would be considered to be non-random with a confidence of 99.9% [21, p. 1–4, line 6 from below]. The second part could be interpreted in a reasonable way, though one should be cautious here, especially in the case of many tests. But the first part is completely misleading. Of course, one test that did not fail convincingly does not mean that the sequence is random with high confidence!

General remarks about tests constitute Part I of [21]. Parts II and III consist of the description and commentary for 15 tests. Some are similar to the tests in diehard while some other are different. The final Part IV, "Testing strategy and the Result Interpretation", recommends two ways to analyze the results of the tests. When several runs of a test produce a sequence of p-values, two forms of analysis of this sequence are recommended: "Proportion of Sequences Passing a Test" (4.2.1) and "Uniform Distribution of *P-values*" (4.2.2). Both are some variants of secondary tests: assuming that the distribution of p-values is uniform in $[0, 1]$, authors recommend to look at the proportion of values exceeding some threshold and to compare it with the Bernoulli distribution (4.2.1), or divide the interval $[0, 1]$ into some number of bins and apply χ^2-test (4.2.2). This approach replaces the Kolmogorov–Smirnov test used by Marsaglia in diehard, and in dieharder.

As for the case of dieharder, many tests from the NIST collection use approximations for computing p-values. The only warning about the consequences of this approach appears in the last section (p. 4-3):

In practice, many reasons can be given to explain why a data set has failed a statistical test. The following is a list of possible explanations. The list was compiled based upon NIST statistical testing efforts.

(a) An incorrectly programmed statistical test. $\langle\ldots\rangle$

(b) An underdeveloped (immature) statistical test.
There are occasions when either probability or complexity theory isn't sufficiently developed or understood to facilitate a rigorous analysis of a statistical test. Over time, statistical tests are revamped in light of new results. Since many statistical tests are based upon asymptotic approximations, careful work needs to be done to determine how good an approximation is.

(c) An improper implementation of a random number generator. $\langle\ldots\rangle$

(d) Improperly written codes to harness test input data. $\langle\ldots\rangle$

(e) Poor mathematical routines for computing *P-values*. $\langle\ldots\rangle$

(f) Incorrect choices for input parameters.

It is hardly surprising that with such a relaxed approach to statistical testing ("over time, statistical tests are revamped") the authors have included two bad tests in the original version of the document, see the paper [12] where the errors are noted. It is instructive to look at the errors in these tests. The first error, in the Fourier spectral test, happened because the expectation and variance of the approximating normal distribution were computed incorrectly. The second is more interesting, since two different (and quite predictable) problems with the p-values approach appeared at the same time. First, the distribution of the test statistics based on the Lempel–Ziv compression algorithm was not computed exactly but was approximated using some presumably good pseudorandom number generator as reference. The experiments with other generators made in the paper [12] showed that this approximation is dubious. The other problem could be related to the non-negligible probability of individual values. As we have mentioned, in this case the distribution of the p-values differs from the uniform one. The results of numerical experiments described in the paper suggest that this could be the reason for the rejection of truly random sequences. In the current version of the NIST document[10] this test is excluded (it contains 15 tests instead of 16).

9   How to Make a Robust Test

There are different ways to deal with errors in statistical tests. Finding and correcting the coding errors is a general problem for all software, and tests are no exceptions here. One may argue that, since errors are anyway possible for many reasons (see the list above), we should not insist on the mathematical correctness of tests, just deleting the tests when they are discovered to be incorrect. Still the other approach is to do whatever we can to avoid errors that could be avoided. In this section we explain, following the technical report [32], how one could avoid problems related (a) to the approximation errors while computing p-values, and (b) to the non-negligible probabilities of individual outcomes. This will be done in two steps.

Step 1. Let us still assume that a reference generator that is truly random is available. But instead of using the reference generator to find the approximate distributions or to look for suspicious tests, as suggested by the authors of dieharder and NIST tests, we use it directly. Recall that the we used the Kolmogorov–Smirnov test to check that the distribution of p-values is consistent with the uniform distribution, and our problem was that due to approximation errors and non-zero probabilities of individual deviation values the distribution of p-values is not exactly uniform under the null hypothesis. However, there is a version of the Kolmogorov–Smirnov test that deals with *two* samples. Here the null hypothesis is that the two samples are formed by independent random variables with the same distribution, but nothing is assumed about this distribution.

---

[10] Unfortunately, the current version of the NIST report [21] was not checked carefully either. For example, the description of the serial test (Sect. 2.11.4, (5)) contains conflicting instructions for computing p-values: the example includes division by 2 that is missing in the general formula. The C code follows the example, not the general formula. Also the values of igamc function in this section are incorrect, while the correct values do appear few lines later, in Sect. 2.11.6.

Therefore, we may proceed as follows. The first sample of p-values is constructed using the random numbers generator that we test, as before. The second sample is constructed exactly in the same way but using the reference generator. Then we apply the Kolmogorov–Smirnov test for two samples. This procedure remains valid even if the formulas used to convert the deviations into p-values are only approximately true, or even completely wrong, since even completely wrong formulas would be the same for both generators, the one we test and the reference one. So we can omit the recalibration step completely and just consider the samples of deviations.

Remark 4. In fact, only the ordering is important, so the Kolmogorov–Smirnov test for two samples can be presented as follows. We have two arrays of reals, $x_1, \ldots, x_n$ (one sample) and $y_1, \ldots, y_m$ (another sample). Then we combine them into one array of length $n + m$ and sort this array, keeping track of the origin: elements that came from the first and second samples are marked by letters X and Y respectively. In this way we get a sequence of $n + m$ letters X and Y that contains n letters X and m letters Y, and consider some test statistic for the following null hypothesis: *all $\binom{n + m}{m}$ sequences of this type are equiprobable.* The Kolmogorov–Smirnov test uses some specific statistic, namely, the maximal difference between the frequencies of X's and Y's in all prefixes, but the same approach can be used with any other test for this distribution.

Remark 5. In this way we get a test that does not depend on the approximations to the distributions that we do not know how to compute. However, there is some price for it. Since now the reference generator is an additional source of random variations, we need more samples to get the same sensitivity of the test. This increase, however, is rather modest.

Step 2. We constructed a randomness test that does not rely on unproven assumptions about distributions that we cannot compute exactly. However, it uses a reference generator that is assumed to be truly random, and this is crucial. Obviously, if we use a faulty reference generator to test a truly random one, the test will fail (the procedure is symmetric, so we get exactly the same result when testing a faulty random generator against a truly random reference). In some sense, we constructed only a "randomized test of randomness". This is unsatisfactory, but can be easily avoided using the following trick.

Let us consider n deviation values $d_1, \ldots, d_n$ obtained by using bits from the generator we are testing. Then construct the other sample, $d'_1, \ldots, d'_m$, but this time let us use not the reference generator but the bitwise `xor` of the bits from the reference generator and fresh bits from the generator we are testing. Then we apply the Kolmogorov–Smirnov test to these two samples. If

1. the generator that we are testing is truly random, and
2. the reference generator and the test generator are independent,

then the probability to fail the test is guaranteed to be small due to Kolmogorov–Smirnov's result.

Remark 6. Of course, if the reference generator is not independent with the one that we want to test, the correctness claim is no more true. For example, if during the second part the reference generator produces the same bits as the generator we are testing, the xor bits will be all zeros. However, the independence condition looks much easier to achieve. For example, the reference bits could be produced in different place, or in advance, or can even be an output of a fixed deterministic pseudorandom generator.

Remark 7. If the reference generator produces truly random bits that are independent from the output of the generator we are testing, then xor-bits are also truly random. So our new test is as sensitive as the previous one (the comparison with the reference generator) if the reference generator is truly random, but the correctness of the new test does not depend on the assumption of true randomness for the reference generator.

Remark 8. There is one small problem that we have not mentioned yet: while sorting the array of deviations, we may have ties. If some value from the first sample coincides with some value from the second sample, then the letter (X or Y in our notation, see above) is not well defined. However, we can break the ties randomly, using the bits of the generator we are testing. In this way we may assume that these bits are truly random when bounding the probability of Type I error.

Remark 9. The same idea can be used even for "informal" tests. For example, imagine that we construct some image based on the bits we test, and then people look at this image and decide whether it looks similar to the pictures of the same type that use reference generator or there are some visible differences[11]. Recalling the interactive non-isomorphism proof and using the same trick as before, we can make a robust test. Take $2n$ disjoint bit blocks from the generator under testing. Use n of them to create images, and do the same for other n blocks but use the bitwise xor of these blocks and n blocks of the same size from some other origin. As a source of these auxiliary blocks one may use a reference generator, or the binary representation of π, or any other source. The only requirement is that the auxiliary blocks should be fixed before sampling our generator. If a human expert (or a machine-learning algorithm), looking at the resulting $2n$ images, can correctly classify them into two groups according to their origin, then the generator fails the test, and the probability of this for a true random bits generator is 2^{-2n}, up to a poly(n)-factor.

One can also consider a more advanced version of this test. Several experts say how "random" the images are. Then the images are ordered according to their approval ratings and Kolmogorov–Smirnov test for two samples is used.

---

[11] This is not a purely theoretic possibility: the documentation for some hardware random bit generators contains pictures of this type.

10   Hardware Random Generators

Randomness is ubiquitous—from the coin tossing and cosmic rays to the thermal noise in audio and video recordings, Brownian motion, quantum measurements and radioactive decay. So one may think that constructing a good randomness generator is an easy task. However, if we require that the output distribution is guaranteed with high precision, the problem becomes much more difficult. Coins may be biased, the independence between the two consecutive coin tosses may be not absolute, the circuit with the noise is affected also by some undesirable signals that may not be random, etc. In addition, some technical errors could happen.

For an illustration one may look at the sequences of bits that are included in the CD prepared by Marsaglia [17]. Among them there are two bit sequences that he got from two devices he bought (one from Germany, one from Canada) and a third bit sequence produced (as Marsaglia says) by some hardware random generator in California. The names are `canada.bit`, `germany.bit` and `calif.bit`. The device makers claimed that the bits produced by their devices are perfectly random. However, applying `diehard` tests to these sequences, Marsaglia found that they are far from being random. In fact, looking at two of them (Canada and Germany), one could guess one of the reasons for their non-randomness [8]. Namely, splitting the bit sequences into bytes (integers in $0 \ldots 255$ range) and searching for the two-byte substring 10 10, we find that this substring does not appear at all (at least among the first 10^6 bytes I tested), while the expected number of occurrences is several dozens. To get an idea why this happens, one may also count the substrings of the form 13 x and find out that one of them appears much more often than the others: the substring 13 10 occurs more than four thousand times (instead of expected few dozens).

If the reader worked a lot with Unix and MSDOS computers in 1990s, she would immediately see a plausible explanation: the file was converted as a text file from Unix to MSDOS encoding. In Unix the lines of a text file were separated just by byte 10, while in MSDOS they were separated by 13 10. Converting 10 to 13 10, we make substrings 10 10 impossible and drastically increase the number of substrings 13 10.

The third file `calif.bit` probably had some other history that did not involve Unix to MSDOS conversion, but still fails the tests for the other reasons.[12]

Marsaglia solved this problem by combining (`xoring`) the output of the hardware random generators with pseudorandom sequences obtained by some deterministic generators [17, file `cdmake.ps`]

> The sixty 10-megabyte files of random numbers are produced by combining two or more of the most promising deterministic generators with sources of random noise from three physical devices (white noise), for those who feel that physical sources of randomness are better than deterministic sources.

---

[12] We also tested the corrected files, replacing groups 13 10 by 10 in `canada.bit` and `germany.bit`. They still fail many tests in the `dieharder` suite.

Some of the files have white noise combined with black noise, the latter from digital recordings of rap music. And a few of the files even had naked ladies thrown into the mix, from pixel files on the network. The last two, digitized music and pictures, are thrown in to illustrate the principle that a satisfactory stream of random bits remains so after combination [xor-ing] with the bits of any file.

2   TABLE OF RANDOM DIGITS

00050	09188 20097	32825 39527	04220 86304	83389 87374	64278 58044
00051	90045 85497	51981 50654	94938 81997	91870 76150	68476 64659
00052	73189 50207	47677 26269	62290 64464	27124 67018	41361 82760
00053	75768 76490	20971 87749	90429 12272	95375 05871	93823 43178
00054	54016 44056	66281 31003	00682 27398	20714 53295	07706 17813

Fig. 3. A fragment of table of random digits from [27]

A similar combination of the hardware source of somehow random bits and post-processing was used for the table of random digits published in 1955 [27] (see Fig. 3 for a small fragment of it):

The random digits in this book were produced by rerandomization of a basic table generated by an electronic roulette wheel. Briefly, a random frequency pulse source, providing an average about 100,000 pulses per second, was gated about once per second by a constant frequency pulse. Pulse standardization circuits passed the pulses through a 5-place binary counter. In principle the machine was a 32-place roulette wheel which made, on the average, about 3000 revolutions per trial and produced one number per second. A binary-to-decimal converter was used which converted 20 of the 32 numbers (the other twelve were discarded) and retained only the final digit of two-digit numbers; this final digit was fed into an IBM punch to produce finally a punched card table of random digits.

Production from the original machine showed statistically significant biases, and the engineers had to make several modifications and refinements of the circuits before production of apparently satisfactory numbers was achieved. The basic table of a million digits was then produced during May and June of 1947. This table was subjected to fairly extensive tests and it was found that it still contained small but statistically significant biases. ⟨...⟩

[Comparing the results of tests before and after one month of continuous operations:] Apparently the machine had been running down despite the fact that periodic electronic checks indicated that it had remained in good order.

The table was regarded as reasonably satisfactory because the deviations from expectations in the various tests were all very small—the largest being less than 2%—and no further effort was made to generate better numbers with the machine. However, the table was transformed by adding pairs of digits modulo 10 in order to improve the distribution of the digits. There were 20,000 punched cards with 50 digits per card; each digit on a given card was added modulo 10 to the corresponding digit of the preceding card to yield a rerandomized digit. It is this transformed table which is published here ⟨...⟩

These tables were reproduced by photo-offset of pages printed by the IBM model 856 Cardatype. Because of the very nature of the table, it did not seem necessary to proofread every page of the final manuscript to catch random errors of the Cardatype. All pages were scanned for systematic errors, every twentieth page was proofread ⟨...⟩

We see that the same scheme was used here. However, the post-processing algorithms used in both cases are far from perfect. The sum modulo 10 used by RAND is almost reversible (if we know the resulting table and the first card, then we can reconstruct all the cards), so it cannot significantly change the entropy or the Kolmogorov complexity of the data string. This entropy is probably insufficient if simple tests fail on the string. The same can be said about xor-ing with a (deterministic) pseudorandom sequence used by Marsaglia. In the latter case, the rap music and naked ladies could save the day, assuming that these strings have enough complexity (generating processes have enough entropy) and are independent from the data from the electronic devices. But obviously one would like to have less frivolous and more regular procedure.

11   Random Source and Post-processing

Noise sources are cheap and easy to find. A classical example is a Zener diode which costs few cents; the noise generated by it is strong enough to be captured by an inexpensive audio card that has microphone inputs, and one can then try to convert this noise to a high-quality random bits ("white noise") using some processing called "conditioning" or "whitening". Many commercial devices uses this scheme (usually with a higher frequency and a lower precision than used in typical audio cards); here is the description of one of devices of this type:

The TrueRNG Hardware Random Number Generator uses the avalanche effect in a semiconductor junction to generate true random numbers. The avalanche effect has long been used for generation of random number/noise and is a time-tested and proven random noise source. The semiconductor junction is biased to 12 volts using a boost voltage regulator (since USB only supplies 5V), amplified, then digitized at high-speed. The digitized data is selected and whitened internal to the TrueRNG and sent over the USB port with more than 400 kilobits/second of throughput. ⟨...⟩

The new entropy mixing algorithm takes in 20 bits of entropy and outputs 8 bit to ensure that maximum entropy is maintained. The algorithm uses multiplication in a Galois field similar to a cyclic redundancy check to mix the ADC inputs thoroughly while spreading the entropy evenly across all bits [35].

On the other hand, one should be careful here, since the properties of Zener diodes are not guaranteed[13], as a simple experiment shows (Fig. 4). It is quite possible that noise properties may change over time and depend on the environment (exact voltage and current, temperature etc.) The post-processing should somehow be robust enough to convert these varying types of noise into random bits with the same uniform distribution.

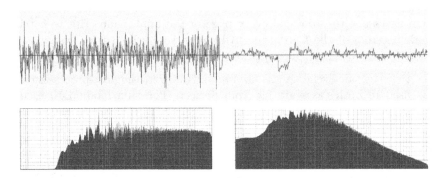

Fig. 4. The noise signal and its spectrum for two Zener diodes from the same roll, digitized by the same sound card (Behringer 1204usb) and analyzed by the same program (`audacity`).

The scheme of such a hardware random number generator is shown in a picture from NIST publication [23] (Fig. 5). In addition to the analog source and the conditioning block this scheme also provides a "health tests" block, with the obvious goal to raise an alarm when, for example, the analog noise source becomes broken for some reason, or drastically changed its parameters. The circuit is called an "entropy source", not a random bits generator, and the conditioning block is optional, since in [23] a more complicated scheme is considered: the output of this block is subjected to the next layer of conditioning before being sent to the customer. See below Sect. 13.

12   What We Would Like to Have

The ideal situation can be described as follows. There exist

- some mathematical property (E) of the output distribution of the (digital) noise source; its informal meaning is that "there is enough randomness in the output of the noise source";
- some hardware device for which the physicists guarantee (E) unless the device is visibly broken;

---

[13] The manufacturers of Zener diodes do not care much about the noise since the primary purpose of Zenèr diodes is different (and somehow opposite): to produce a stable voltage.

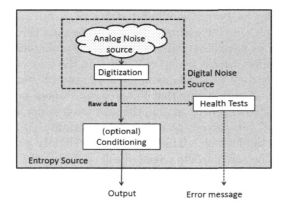

Fig. 5. A general scheme of a hardware entropy sources [23, p. 5]

– a deterministic transformation ("conditioning") and a mathematical theorem that guarantees that the output of this transformation is distributed almost uniformly if its input has the property (E).

Unfortunately, the current practice is rather far from this ideal. The NIST publication mentioned above suggests the property "min-entropy is large" as (E). This means that each individual outcome has small probability (by definition, the min-entropy of a distribution is at least k if every outcome has probability at most 2^{-k}). Here is what they say:

> The central mathematical concept underlying this Recommendation is entropy. Entropy is defined relative to one's knowledge of an experiment's output prior to observation, and reflects the uncertainty associated with predicting its value—the larger the amount of entropy, the greater the uncertainty in predicting the value of an observation. There are many possible measures for entropy; this Recommendation uses a very conservative measure known as min-entropy, which measures the effectiveness of the strategy of guessing the most likely output of the entropy source [23, p. 4].

However, min-entropy, being a very important notion, is still not enough to guarantee the good distribution after any (deterministic) conditioning transformation. Namely, for any transformation $T \colon \mathbb{B}^n \to \mathbb{B}$ that maps n-bit strings into bits, there is a random variable ξ with values in $\mathbb{B}^n$ that has min-entropy at least $n - 1$ (almost maximal) such that $T(\xi)$ is a constant. Indeed, one of the preimages $T^{-1}(0)$ and $T^{-1}(1)$ has size at least 2^{n-1}, and we may let ξ be uniformly distributed in this preimage.

Moreover, even a stronger requirement than high min-entropy, introduced long ago by M. Santha and U. Vazirani [29], is not enough. This requirement, for a sequence of random Boolean variables $\xi_1, \xi_2, \ldots, \xi_n$, says that

$$\Pr[\xi_m = 1 \mid \xi_1 = x_1, \ldots, \xi_{m-1} = x_{m-1}] \in \left(\frac{1}{2} - \delta, \frac{1}{2} + \delta \right)$$

for every $m \leqslant n$ and for every $(m-1)$-bit string $x_1 \ldots x_{m-1}$. Here $\delta \in (0, 1/2)$ is some constant. Assume for example that $\delta = 1/6$; then the requirement says that whatever bits we have observed, the conditional probabilities to have 0 and 1 as the next bit differ at most by factor 2, being in the interval $(1/3, 2/3)$. This implies that min-entropy (and Shannon entropy) grows linearly with n, but is a much stronger condition, saying that in no circumstances we may predict the next bit reliably. Still, as proven in [29], this condition is not enough to extract even one "whitened" bit: there is no whitening algorithm that is better than the trivial one (taking the first bit). This claim can be slightly generalized: no way to extract k bits is better than the trivial one (just taking the first k bits). Here is the exact statement that implies this result.

Proposition 4. *Let $A \subset \mathbb{B}^n$ be a subset that has uniform probability p and let $\delta \in (0, 1/2)$. Then there exists a sequence of n random Boolean variables $\xi_1, \ldots, \xi_n$ that satisfies the Santha–Vazirani condition for this δ, such that*

$$\Pr[\xi_1 \ldots \xi_n \in A] \geqslant p^\alpha,$$

where α is a number such that $(1/2)^\alpha = \left(\dfrac{1}{2} + \delta \right)$.

Therefore, if the uniform probability of A is $(1/2)^k$ for some k, then the probability of the event $\xi_1 \ldots \xi_n \in A$ guaranteed by Proposition 4 (for some Santha–Vazirani source) is at least $(1/2 + \delta)^k$. This means that no transformation $T \colon \mathbb{B}^n \to \mathbb{B}^k$ can be better (in terms of extracting min-entropy from Santha–Vazirani source) than taking the first k bits. Indeed, one of the points in $\mathbb{B}^k$ has T-preimage in $\mathbb{B}^n$ of uniform probability at least $(1/2)^k$, and applying Proposition 4 to this preimage we conclude that for some Santha–Vazirani source $\xi_1, \ldots, \xi_n$ the min-entropy of $T(\xi_1 \ldots \xi_n)$ is not better than just for $\xi_1 \ldots \xi_k$: probability of some point in the image distribution is at least $(1/2 + \delta)^k$.

Proof. We need to construct a distribution on $\mathbb{B}^n$ that satisfies Santha–Vazirani condition and assigns large probability to A. We do it inductively, following the suggestion by Ruslan Ishkuvatov. The case $n = 1$ is obvious. For $n > 1$, we split A into two parts $0A_0$ and $1A_1$ according to the first bit, where A_0 and A_1 are subsets of $\mathbb{B}^{n-1}$ that can be considered as two faces of the Boolean cube. Let p_0 and p_1 be the probabilities of A_0 and A_1 according to the uniform distribution in $\mathbb{B}^{n-1}$, so their average is p. Assume that $p_0 \leqslant p_1$, so $p_0 = p - x$ and $p_1 = p + x$ for some $x \in [0, p]$. The induction assumption gives two Santha–Vazirani distributions on $\mathbb{B}^{n-1}$ that give large probabilities to A_0 and A_1, namely, at least p_0^α and p_1^α. They can be combined into one distribution on $\mathbb{B}^n$, we only need to chose the probability (between $1/2 - \delta$ and $1/2 + \delta$) for the first bit, and then use the two Santha–Vazirani distributions provided by the induction assumption as conditional distributions. To maximize the resulting probability, we should put maximal allowed weight on the face where the probability is greater. It remains to prove then that

$$\left(\frac{1}{2} - \delta \right) p_0^\alpha + \left(\frac{1}{2} + \delta \right) p_1^\alpha = \left(\frac{1}{2} - \delta \right) (p - x)^\alpha + \left(\frac{1}{2} + \delta \right) (p + x)^\alpha \geqslant p^\alpha.$$

For $\alpha \leqslant 1$, the function $t \mapsto t^\alpha$ is concave, therefore the left hand side is a concave function of x, and it is enough to check this inequality for endpoints $x = 0$ (where it is obvious), and $x = p$. In the latter case we need to prove that $(1/2 + \delta)(2p)^\alpha \geqslant p^\alpha$, and this follows directly from the definition of α.

Remark 10. A very simple proof for the case of 1-bit output [28] goes as follows. If $p \geqslant 1/2$, then for some Santha–Vazirani distribution with parameter δ one can achieve probability at least $1/2 + \delta$. Why? It is enough to spread the probability $1/2 + \delta$ uniformly on a subset $A' \subset A$ with uniform probability $1/2$, and spread the remaining probability $1/2 - \delta$ uniformly on the complement of A'.

So the situation is far from ideal: large min-entropy and even stronger Santha–Vazirani condition are not enough to guarantee the correct distribution after whitening, for any fixed whitening function. Still some practical solutions, i.e., some common sense recommendations that help us to avoid obviously faulty generators, are needed, even if no theoretical guarantees are provided. In the next section we look at the NIST approach to this problem.

13   What We Have

There are three documents produced by NIST that cover different aspects of random bits generation. The first, SP 800-90A [22], deals with algorithmic pseudorandom bits (or numbers) generators, called there *deterministic random bits generators*[14]. Here the relevant mathematical theory is not the algorithmic information theory but the complexity theory where the notion of (cryptographically strong) pseudorandom number generator was introduced by Manuel Blum, Silvio Micali and Andrew Yao [4,38]. This theory goes far beyond the scope of our survey.

Roughly speaking, such a generator is a polynomial-time algorithm that maps a truly random seed into a (much longer) sequence of bits that is "indistinguishable" from a random one by polynomial-size circuits. The indistinguishability means that no polynomial-size circuit can have significantly different probabilities of (a) accepting the output of the generator for a truly random seed, and (b) accepting a sequence of truly random bits. An equivalent definition says that there is no way to predict by a polynomial-size circuit the next bit of the output sequence (for a random seed) significantly better than by guessing.

The existence of generators with these properties is equivalent to the existence of one-way functions [11], and this existence is an unproven assumption. This assumption implies $P \neq NP$, while the reverse implication is not known. For this reason we do not know any cryptographically strong pseudorandom number generator for which this property can be proven. Moreover, since the constructions from [11] are quite complicated, practical pseudorandom generators may use stronger assumptions, like hardness of factoring, or just have no theoretical justification at all. In fact, NIST [22] not only recommends but also insists

---

[14] Note an oxymoron.

on using "allowed" methods to generate random bits from the seed, and these methods are far from being justified mathematically, even in a very weak sense. For example, one of the methods uses hash values for consecutive bit strings (see Fig. 6). As explained in [22, page 37], "mechanisms specified in this Recommendation have been designed to use any **approved** hash function and may be used by consuming applications requiring various security strengths, providing that the appropriate hash function is used and sufficient entropy is obtained for the seed". On the next page a list of these "approved" hash functions is provided that includes SHA-1, SHA-224, SHA-512/224, SHA-256, SHA512/256, SHA-384, SHA-512. According to NIST [25]:

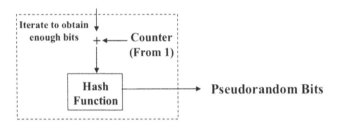

Fig. 6. Part of Fig. 8 on p. 39 in [22] related to the random bit generation using a hash function (the initialization part is omitted).

An approved hash function is expected to have the following three properties:

1. Collision resistance: It is computationally infeasible to find two different inputs to the hash function that have the same hash value. That is, if *hash* is a hash function, it is computationally infeasible to find two different inputs x and x' for which $hash(x) = hash(x')$. Collision resistance is measured by the amount of work that would be needed to find a collision for a hash function with high probability. If the amount of work is 2^N, then the collision resistance is N bits ⟨...⟩
2. Preimage resistance ⟨...⟩
3. Second preimage resistance ⟨...⟩

Obviously, for a specific function like SHA-1 or any other mentioned in the list above, the collision resistance requirement makes no sense if understood literally: computation infeasibility means high complexity of some function, and here we have no function. If somebody comes with a collision pair x, x', the collision resistance in the naïve sense disappears starting from this moment, so it is not a mathematical property of a hash function (a mathematical property cannot suddenly become false), but some property of the current state of art (still measured in bits!). Moreover, the hash functions mentioned above are obtained by a complicated *ad hoc* construction and there are no reasons to believe that something similar to collision resistance can be proven. Finally, as it is mentioned [22, p. 89],

Hash_DRBG's [the random generator based on hash functions] security depends on the underlying hash function's behavior when processing a series of sequential input blocks. If the hash function is replaced by a random oracle, Hash_DRBG is secure. It is difficult to relate the properties of the hash function required by Hash_DRBG with common properties, such as collision resistance, pre-image resistance, or pseudorandomness.

Indeed, it is impossible to relate the "required" properties with "common" properties, since a function with no known collisions and high preimage resistance still may have much more 1s than 0s in most of its outputs, or have the last bit always equal to 1, therefore being completely unsuitable for Hash_DRBG.[15] So the reference to the security properties of the allowed hash functions can only create a false feeling of security.

The second NIST publication, SP 800-90B [23], describes the allowed constructions of the "entropy source" (see Fig. 5 above) while the third one [24] "addresses the construction of RBGs from the mechanisms in SP 800-90A and the entropy sources in SP 800-90B" [23, p. 1]. The idea here is that the whitening (conditioning) process is splitted into two stages. The first stage, described in SP 800-90B, does only some "rough" conditioning and may not produce a distribution that is very close to the uniform one. We hope only that the entropy of its output is close to the output length or at least is a significant fraction of the length. Then the second stage that may involve deterministic random bits generators or not is used for "fine-tuning".[16]

But what is meant by "entropy" in this description? As we have said, the NIST recommendations claim to use min-entropy. Still there are some problems with this approach.

- There is no way to get a reliable lower bound for the min-entropy of a physical source. If there is some isolated value that appears with probability 2^{-k}, the min-entropy is at most k, but one needs to make $\Theta(2^k)$ trials to have a reasonable chance to see this value at least once.[17]

---

[15] And the claim about the random oracle model is obviously true and obviously irrelevant.

[16] The final stage may also use pseudorandom bit generators to provide additional "backup" layer if the physical source stops working. For example, one may follow Marsaglia and produce xor of the bit sequences from physical and deterministic sources. Note that this operation, hiding the problems with physical source, makes the testing of the output sequence almost useless; testing should be done before this last step.

[17] Things are much better for independent identically distributed (i.i.d.) variables [23, p. 11]; there are also some physical sources where i.i.d. assumptions are reasonable, and some tests that can detect some violations of i.i.d. property.

- Quite often the NIST recommendations treat the notion of entropy informally, as some mystical substance that can be present in a binary string (and not in a random variable) and even can be accumulated and/or condensed[18]. For example, it is written [23, p. 11] that "in all cases, the DRBG [deterministic random bits generator] mechanism expects that when entropy input is requested, the returned bitstring will contain at least the requested amount of entropy." The closest approximation to this interpretation is Kolmogorov complexity, but it is (a) non-computable and (b) defined up to a constant, and different reasonable optimal programming languages easily can give the values that differ by several thousands, so it does not make sense to ask whether the complexity exceeds (say) 512 or not.
- Moreover, in some cases even more enigmatic explanations are given: "For the purposes of this Recommendation, an n-bit string is said to have full entropy if the string is the result of an approved process whereby the entropy in the input to that process has at least $2n$ bits of entropy (see [ILL89] and Sect. 4.2)" [24, p. 11]. Here [ILL89] is the preliminary version of [11] and neither says anything about approved processes nor justifies the requirement about $2n$ bits of entropy.
- As mentioned above for a similar situation, the properties of the functions used for conditioning, in particular the standard requirements for the security of a hash function, do not guarantee, even informally, that the output distribution for the hash function applied to an input source of high min-entropy, is close to the uniform distribution. However, this is implicitly assumed in the recommendations when an approved process of obtaining a string of full entropy is described.
- The recommendations encourage the designer to use different combinations of "approved" constructions (see, e.g., Fig. 7); even if some good properties of one-stage construction are plausible, the claim that the composition of several stages will still have good properties, is much less founded.

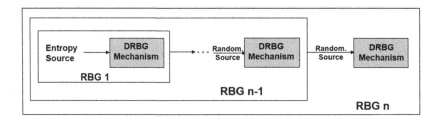

Fig. 7. The construction of a random bits generator with several layers [24, p. 19].

---

[18] "When the entropy [string?] produced by the entropy source(s) is very long (e.g., because the entropy rate of the entropy source(s) is very low), and the entropy bits may need to be condensed into a shorter bitstring, the **Get_Entropy** function in Sect. 10.3.1.1 or Sect. 10.3.1.2 shall be used to condense the entropy bits without losing the available entropy in the bit string." [23, Sect. 10.3.1, p. 44].

All these critical remarks do not mean that NIST recommendations are unnecessary: they reflect the current state of technology, the existing practice and prevent the appearance of completely bogus generators, therefore playing a very important role. However, one should keep in mind that they are not based on any "hard science"; they sometimes use mathematical notions and results but only as hints and sources of inspiration.

Could we have better recommendations? This is a difficult question. One can hope for the *security through obscurity*: if a long sequence of different mathematical operations is performed, this could make an attack much more difficult. However, the idea that *random actions give random results* does not look as a good plan for designing random bits generators. It could be that the careful choice of a noise source plus one-layer conditioning procedure that is based on something more suitable than just hash functions, would give a better result than a complicated multi-layer approach using cryptographic primitives.

14   Final Remarks

The space limitations do not allow us to discuss other interesting questions related to theory and practice of random bit generators.

On the theory side, there is a lot of knowledge about randomness extractors—from a complexity-theoretic viewpoint, they are much closely related to the practical task of conditioning raw randomness than hash functions. It is not completely clear to what extent we can achieve the goal: to have a clear and reasonable assumption about raw distribution that provably guarantees that the output distribution is close to the uniform one. Still we may hope that some constructions inspired by this theory could be practically useful. In particular, there are results about extractors with many sources that could be easier to use (literally or as a source of inspiration), since independence appears more often in the "real world" than uniform distributions.

From the viewpoint of physics there is a difference between a "random noise" that comes from statistical mechanics, say, the thermal noise in a resistor, or the Brownian motion, or some chaotic dynamical systems with external noise, and more "refined" randomness that comes out of quantum mechanical systems where the events related to individual microscopic objects can be observed, for example, experiments with individual photons. However, one can argue that

- there is no clear distinction between two categories: how do we classify Geiger counter events for a macroscopic piece of slightly radioactive material? how do we classify the noise in a PN junction (definitely related to some quantum effects but in multi-particle systems)?
- from the practical viewpoint, it is not clear if one can construct an experimental device that is "clean" enough to avoid the conditioning step. And if we use conditioning, do we really have an advantage using a delicate quantum-mechanical experiment instead of cheaper alternatives? One can argue that it is better to have "true randomness" instead of "mere chaos", or something like this. It definitely sounds good for philosophers or for a sales brochure, but are there more essential advantages?

Last but not least, the notions that appear in this discussion (randomness tests, individual random objects) can be studied from the viewpoint of algorithmic information theory. There are many interesting questions and results of this type [3, 26] that are starting points for the "quantitative" theory of randomness. In this approach, roughly speaking, a result of the form "if α is algorithmically random, then β is algorithmically random" is made more precise by proving the upper bound for the randomness deficiency of β in terms of the random deficiency of α. Interesting questions also appear when we try to translate the results about some combinatorial constructions (say, randomness extractors or secret sharing) into the language of algorithmic information theory. But this is a topic for another long survey.

Acknowledgments. The author is grateful to all the people in the RaCAF project and the ESCAPE team (LIRMM, Montpellier), Kolmogorov Seminar (Moscow), Theoretical Computer Science Lab (Moscow, HSE), and all others from whom I learned about randomness including my (late) teacher Vladimir Uspensky, Leonid Levin, Alexander Zvonkin, Nikolay Vereshchagin, Vladimir Vovk, Vladimir Vyugin, Andrei Romashchenko, Bruno Durand, Gregory Lafitte, Laurent Bienvenu, Péter Gács, Wolfgang Merkle, Paul Vitányi, Daniil Musatov, Andrei Rumyantsev, Mikhail Andreev, Gleb Novikov, Bruno Bauwens, Konstantin Makarychev, Yury Makarychev, Ilya Razensteyn, Gleb Posobin, Alexey Vinogradov, Ruslan Ishkuvatov. The work was supported by ANR RaCAF grant ANR-15-CE40-0016-0.

References

1. Wasserstein, R.L., Lazar, N.A.: Editorial: the ASA's statement on p-values: context, process, and purpose. Am. Stat. **70**(2), 129–133 (2016). https://doi.org/10.1080/00031305.2016.1154108
2. Benjamin, D.J., et al.: Redefine statistical significance. Nat. Hum. Behav. **2**, 6–10 (2018)
3. Bienvenu, L., Gáacs, P., Hoyrup, M., Rojas, C., Shen, A.: Algorithmic tests and randomness with respect to a class of measures. Proc. Steklov Inst. Math. **274**, 34–89 (2011). http://arxiv.org/abs/1103.1529
4. Blum, M., Micali, S.: How to generate cryptographically strong sequences of random bits. SIAM J. Comput. **13**(4), 850–864 (1984). https://doi.org/10.1137/0213053. (preliminary version was presented at FOCS 1982 conference)
5. Borel, É.: Le Hasard. Librarire Félix Alcan (1920)
6. Brown, R.G.: Dieharder: a GNU public random generator, version 3.31.1. Technical report, Duke University Physics Department (2006–2018). http://www.phy.duke.edu/~rgb/General/dieharder.php
7. David, A.P., de Rooij, S., Shafer, G., Shen, A., Vereshchagin, N., Vovk, V.: Insuring against loss of evidence in game-theoretic probability. Stat. Probab. Lett. **81**, 157–162 (2011). https://doi.org/10.1016/j.spl.2010.10.013
8. Davies, R.: Hardware random number generators. Technical report, Statistics Research Associates Limited (2000). http://robertnz.net/hwrng.htm. Presented at 15th Australian Statistics Conference, July 2000, and 51st Conference of New Zealand Statistical Association, September 2000

9. Gurevich, Y., Passmore, G.O.: Impugning randomness, convincingly. Studia Logica **100**(1–2), 193–222 (2012). https://link.springer.com/article/10.1007/s11225-012-9375-1. See also https://arxiv.org/pdf/1601.00665.pdf, https://www.cl.cam.ac.uk/~gp351/Gurevich-Passmore-IRC.pdf

10. Gurevich, Y., Vovk, V.: Test statistics and p-values. Technical report, arXiv (2017). Working paper #16, On-line compression modelling project (new series). http://www.alrw.net/articles/16.pdf. See also https://arxiv.org/pdf/1702.02590.pdf

11. Håstad, J., Impagliazzo, R., Levin, L.A., Luby, M.: A pseudorandom generator from any one-way function. SIAM J. Comput. **28**(4), 1364–1396 (1999). https://doi.org/10.1137/S0097539793244708

12. Kim, S.Y., Umeno, K., Hasegava, A.: Corrections of the NIST statistical test suite for randomness. Technical report (2004). https://eprint.iacr.org/2004/018.pdf

13. Kireev, A.: On the falsified results of the "referendum" in Sevastopol (in Russian). Technical report, LiveJournal, November 2014. https://kireev.livejournal.com/1095568.html

14. Knuth, D.: The Art of Computer Programming. Seminumerical Algorithms, vol. 2, 2nd edn. Addison-Wesley, Boston (1981). ISBN 0-201-03822-6

15. Kupriyanov, A.: Gauss against Churov: preliminary conclusions. Technical report, Troitsky variant (Russian newspaper), May 2018. https://trv-science.ru/2018/05/08/gauss-protiv-churova-promezhutochnyj-itog

16. Marsaglia, G.: A current view of random number generators. In: Computer Science and Statistics, Sixteenth Symposium on the Interface, pp. 3–10. Elsevier, North-Holland (1985)

17. Marsaglia, G.: Random numbers CDROM including the Diehard battery of tests of randomness. Technical report, University of Florida (1995). http://stat.fsu.edu/pub/diehard/, was available at http://stat.fsu.edu/pub/diehard/; now (2019) still available as snapshots from https://web.archive.org. Contains the preprint version of [16, 19]

18. Marsaglia, G., Tsang, W.W.: Some difficult-to-pass tests of randomness. J. Stat. Softw. **7**(3) (2002). https://www.jstatsoft.org/article/view/v007i03

19. Marsaglia, G., Zaman, A.: Monkey tests for random number generators. Comput. Math. Appl. **26**(9), 1–10 (1993)

20. Maurer, U.M.: A universal statistical test for random bit generators. J. Cryptol. **5**(2), 89–105 (1992). https://link.springer.com/article/10.1007/BF00193563

21. Rukhin, A., et al.: A statistical test suite for random and pseudorandom number generators for cryptographic applications, revision 1 by Lawrence E. Bassham III. Special Publication 800-22-1a, National Institute of Standards and Technology, Technology Administration, U.S. Department of Commerce (NIST), April 2010. https://www.nist.gov/publications/statistical-test-suite-random-and-pseudorandom-number-generators-cryptographic. Previous version seems to be unavailable at this site, but the review of Elaine B. Barker, ITL Bulletin (December 2000, 3 pp.), is available at https://tsapps.nist.gov/publication/get_pdf.cfm?pub_id=151231. The Lempel–Ziv test, criticised in [12], was there (#10) according to the review; it is missing in the updated version

22. Barker, E., Kelsey, J.: Recommendation for random number generation using deterministic random bit generators. Special Publication 800-90A, National Institute of Standards and Technology, Technology Administration, U.S. Department of Commerce (NIST), June 2015. https://csrc.nist.gov/publications/detail/sp/800-90a/rev-1/final. Previous Version: January 2012

23. Turan, M.S., Barker, E., Kelsey, J., McKay, K., Baish, M., Boyle, M.: Recommendation for the entropy sources used for random bit generation. Special Publication 800-90B, National Institute of Standards and Technology, Technology Administration, U.S. Department of Commerce (NIST), January 2018. https://csrc.nist.gov/publications/detail/sp/800-90b/final
24. Barker, E., Kelsey, J.: Recommendation for random bit generator (RBG) constructions (second draft). Special Publication 800-90C, National Institute of Standards and Technology, Technology Administration, U.S. Department of Commerce (NIST), April 2016. https://csrc.nist.gov/CSRC/media/Publications/sp/800-90c/draft/documents/sp800_90c_second_draft.pdf
25. Dang, Q.: Recommendation for applications using approved hash algorithms, revision 1. Special Publication 800-107r1, National Institute of Standards and Technology, Technology Administration, U.S. Department of Commerce (NIST), August 2012. https://nvlpubs.nist.gov/nistpubs/Legacy/SP/nistspecialpublication800-107r1.pdf
26. Novikov, G.: Randomness deficiencies. In: Kari, J., Manea, F., Petre, I. (eds.) CiE 2017. LNCS, vol. 10307, pp. 338–350. Springer, Cham (2017). https://doi.org/10.1007/978-3-319-58741-7_32
27. RAND Corporation: A Million Random Digits with 100,000 Normal Deviates. Free Press (1955). Reissued in 2001 as ISBN 0-8330-3047-7
28. Reingold, O., Vadhan, S., Wigderson, A.: A note on extracting randomness from Santha–Vazirani sources. Technical report, available from Reingold (2014). https://omereingold.files.wordpress.com/2014/10/svsources.pdf
29. Santha, M., Vazirani, U.V.: Generating quasi-random sequences from semi-random sources. J. Comput. Syst. Sci. **33**, 75–87 (1986). https://doi.org/10.1016/0022-0000(86)90044-9
30. Shen, A.: Around Kolmogorov complexity: basic notions and results. In: Vovk, V., Papadopoulos, H., Gammerman, A. (eds.) Measures of Complexity, pp. 75–115. Springer, Cham (2015). https://doi.org/10.1007/978-3-319-21852-6_7
31. Shen, A.: Election and statistics: the case of "United Russia", 2009–2018 (in Russian), preprint (2018). https://arxiv.org/abs/1204.0307
32. Shen, A.: Making randomness tests more robust. Technical report, HAL, February 2018. https://hal.archives-ouvertes.fr/hal-01707610
33. Shen, A., Uspensky, V.A., Vereshchagin, N.K.: Kolmogorov Complexity and Algorithmic Randomness. American Mathematical Society (2017). http://www.lirmm.fr/~ashen/kolmbook-eng-scan.pdf
34. Stoppard, T.: Rosencrantz and Guildenstern Are Dead, a Play (1966). Grove Press (1971). ISBN 978-0-8021-3275-8
35. TrueRNG: TrueRNG documentation. Technical report, Ubld.it (2019). http://ubld.it/truerng_v3
36. Vereshchagin, N., Shen, A.: Algorithmic statistics revisited. In: Vovk, V., Papadopoulos, H., Gammerman, A. (eds.) Measures of Complexity, pp. 235–252. Springer, Cham (2015). https://doi.org/10.1007/978-3-319-21852-6_17. https://arxiv.org/abs/1504.04950v2
37. Vereshchagin, N., Shen, A.: Algorithmic statistics: forty years later. In: Day, A., Fellows, M., Greenberg, N., Khoussainov, B., Melnikov, A., Rosamond, F. (eds.) Computability and Complexity. LNCS, vol. 10010, pp. 669–737. Springer, Cham (2017). https://doi.org/10.1007/978-3-319-50062-1_41. https://arxiv.org/abs/1607.08077
38. Yao, A.C.: Theory and application of trapdoor functions. In: 23rd Annual Symposium on Foundations of Computer Science (FOCS), pp. 80–91 (1982). http://ieeexplore.ieee.org/document/4568378/

On Entropic Convergence of Algorithms

Anatol Slissenko[(⊠)]

University Paris-East Créteil, Créteil, France
`slissenko@u-pec.fr`

Abstract. The paper describes an approach to measuring convergence of an algorithm to its result in terms of an entropy-like function of partitions of its inputs of a given length. It is a way to relate the set-theoretic definition of a function to the program that computes it. The approach, though very preliminary, may show how to improve a given algorithm.

Keywords: Algorithm as sequences of literals · Entropic weight · Entropic convergence

1 Introduction

We understand intuitively that an algorithm extracts information from its inputs while processing them. Unfortunately, as it was noticed by philosophers many years ago (e.g., see [1]), there is no mathematical theory of information that reflects our intuition. However, mathematical notion of entropy, that is a measure of uncertainty is, in a way, related to the quantity of information. More general way to treat the question of information extraction is by introducing a geometry in computations but how to do it productively remains an open question. So I try to approach the subject by means of an entropy-like function.

I introduce one such function that is called *entropic weight*. This function is defined for events (i.e., executions of individual commands) of finite sets of traces of algorithm represented as sequences of literals. So, formally speaking, no notion of algorithm is needed here. However, I rely it to algorithms that, for simplicity, are 'low level' abstract programs. An algorithm considered in this general framework is denoted $\mathfrak{A}$, and the function that it computes, is denoted $\boldsymbol{F}$. This function is total and of bounded computational complexity (think not higher than $\boldsymbol{NP} \cup \boldsymbol{coNP}$ though formally it is not needed). All its inputs of size $\boldsymbol{n}$ (the size is polynomially related to the bit size) constitute the set $\boldsymbol{dm}$, and the codomain is denoted $\boldsymbol{rn} =_{df} \boldsymbol{F}(\boldsymbol{dm})$. For better intuition think that $\boldsymbol{dm}$ is of exponential size.

For simplicity I consider only one-component functions, i.e., functions whose output can be put in one register within our model of computation. Convolution or sorting are examples of multi-component functions.

Partially supported by French "Agence Nationale de la Recherche" under the project EQINOCS (ANR-11-BS02-004) and by Government of the Russian Federation, Grant 074-U01.

A. Blass et al. (Eds.): Gurevich Festschrift, LNCS 12180, pp. 291–304, 2020.
https://doi.org/10.1007/978-3-030-48006-6_19

In Sect. 2 a model of computation is defined, and its runs are reduced to sequences of literals, i.e., to logic. To illustrate the whole approach I use one simple function, namely, maximal prefix-suffix **maxPS** that for a given input word gives the length of maximal nontrivial prefix that is also its suffix. This function is denoted φ. For **maxPS** two algorithms are compared, one straightforward of quadratic complexity, denoted $\mathfrak{A}_0(\varphi)$, and the other one of linear complexity, denoted $\mathfrak{A}_1(\varphi)$.

A probabilistic measure and entropic weight are defined in Sect. 3. The algorithms under consideration are deterministic, however in order to get something like entropy one needs a probabilistic measure. Such a measure on $\boldsymbol{dm}$ is introduced on the basis of Principle of Maximal Uncertainty that says that all outputs of $\mathfrak{A}$ are equiprobable at the beginning of its work, i.e., for all $v \in \boldsymbol{rn}$ the measure of its pre-image is $\frac{1}{|\boldsymbol{rn}|}$, here and below $|U|$ is the cardinality of a set U. In this paper the measure is stationary, i.e., it does not change during the work of $\mathfrak{A}$. The entropic weight of events is defined in terms of partitions of $\boldsymbol{dm}$.

Exact or even 'sufficiently good' approximate evaluation of entropic weight, even for $\mathfrak{A}_k(\varphi)$, is hard, it brings us to open combinatorial problems (see [5]). But one can estimate the behavior of entropic weight qualitatively and get useful information about the quality of algorithms. We discuss this at the end of Sect. 3.

The goal of this paper is conceptual: to show that there is a possibility to define quantitative measures that permit to evaluate some kind of 'information' convergence of algorithms.

2   Traces of Algorithms and Event Partitions

In description of algorithms we use logical terminology (not programming one) similar to that was used by Yu. Gurevich [2] for his abstract state machines, though our model is a traditional sequential algorithm. What are variables in programming are dynamic functions in our context. We name different objects in our examples as 'update', 'guard', 'event', 'input' etc. before giving general explanations afterwards.

In particular, the inputs are external functions that may have different values (i.e., they are dynamic) and cannot be changed by the algorithm. But the algorithm can change its internal functions. Without loss of generality, the output function is supposed to be updated only once to produce the result. The symbol % introduces comments in algorithm descriptions.

2.1   Example : Two Algorithms for maxPS

The **maxPS** problem: given a word over alphabet $\mathbb{A}$, $\alpha =_{df} |\mathbb{A}| \geq 2$, find the length of the maximal (longest) prefix, different from the entire word, that is also a suffix of the word.

Input: A word w over an alphabet $\mathbb{A}$ of length $n \geq 1$ (so $\boldsymbol{n} = n$).

Output: $\boldsymbol{\varphi}(n,w) = \boldsymbol{\varphi}(w) = \max\{k : 0 \leq k \leq (n-1) \wedge w(1..k) = w(n-k+1..n)\}$

($w(i..j)$ denotes $w(i)w(i+1)\ldots w(j)$ for $i \leq j$ and the empty word for $i > j$, and $w(i)$ is the ith character of w).

We consider two algorithms for **maxPS**: a straightforward one $\mathfrak{A}_0(\boldsymbol{\varphi})$ with complexity $\mathcal{O}\left(n^2\right)$, and another one $\mathfrak{A}_1(\boldsymbol{\varphi})$ with complexity $\mathcal{O}(n)$. The first one is trivial, the second one is simple and well known. (In the descriptions of algorithms below we aline **else** with **if**, not with **then**, in order to economize the space.)

Algorithm $\mathfrak{A}_0(\boldsymbol{\varphi})$ straightforwardly tries all possible values of $\boldsymbol{\varphi}$ starting with the biggest one, i.e., $(n-1)$. In the case of failure it takes the next smaller value if any. The output is denoted by letter φ (not boldface), no initial value is needed.

Algorithm $\mathfrak{A}_0(\boldsymbol{\varphi})$

```
1:     h := 0;                                  %initialization of the external loop
2:     if h ≥ (n−1) then φ := 0; halt;          %here φ is a nullary output function
3:     else                                     % case h < (n − 1)
4:        begin
5:          h := h + 1; i := 1;
6:          if w(i) = w(i + h) then
7:            (if i < n − h then i := i + 1; goto 6;
8:              else φ := n − h; halt;)          %case i ≥ (n − h), i.e., i = (n − h)
9:            else goto 2                        %case w(i) ≠ w(i + h)
          end
```

The second algorithm that we consider is $\mathfrak{A}_1(\boldsymbol{\varphi})$. It recursively calculates $\boldsymbol{\varphi}(m,w)$ for all m starting from $m = 1$. Denote by letter φ (not boldface) an internal function of $\mathfrak{A}_1(\boldsymbol{\varphi})$ of type $[0..n] \rightarrow [0..n-1]$, i.e., an array, that represents $\boldsymbol{\varphi}(w,m)$ as $\varphi(m)$. Its initial value is $\varphi(0) = 0$. This function outputs the result.

Denote by $\varphi^k(m)$ the kth iteration of $\varphi(m)$, $k \geq 1$: $\varphi^1(m) = \varphi(m)$ and $\varphi^{k+1}(m) = \varphi(\varphi^k(m))$, and assume that $\varphi^0(m) = -1$ for all m, $\varphi(0,w) = 0$ and $\min \emptyset = 0$.

Suppose that $\varphi(m)$ is defined for $m < n$. Algorithm $\mathfrak{A}_1(\boldsymbol{\varphi})$ computes $\varphi(m+1)$ as $\varphi^s(m) + 1$, where $s = \min\{k : w(\varphi^k(m) + 1) = w(m+1)\}$. Clearly, this computing of $\varphi^s(m)$ takes $\mathcal{O}(s)$ steps. The whole complexity of $\mathfrak{A}_1(\boldsymbol{\varphi})$ is linear.

Algorithm $\mathfrak{A}_1(\boldsymbol{\varphi})$

```
1:     i := 1; φ(1) := 0; ψ := 0;                    %initialisation;
2:     if i ≥ n then (φ(n) = r := ψ; halt);          %by r we denote our
                                                      %standard output;
3:        else (i := i + 1;                          %case i < n
4:          if w(ψ + 1) = w(i) then ( φ(i) := ψ + 1; ψ := ψ + 1; goto 2)
5:          else                                     % case w(ψ + 1) ≠ w(i)
6:            if ψ > 0 then ψ := φ(ψ); goto 4
7:            else goto 2 )                          %case ψ = 0
```

The both algorithms $\mathfrak{A}_k(\varphi)$ start their work by verifying $w(i) = w(i + 1)$ for $i = 1, 2, ...$, and while the equality holds they augment i (lines 6, 7 of $\mathfrak{A}_0(\varphi)$ and lines 3, 4 of $\mathfrak{A}_1(\varphi)$). Suppose that event $w(n - 1) \neq w(n)$ happens. Then $w(i) = w(i+1)$ for all $i \leq (n-2)$, hence the input has the form $w_1 = a^{n-1}b, a \neq b$. And inversely, for such an input any $\mathfrak{A}_k(\varphi)$ arrives at the event $w(n - 1) \neq w(n)$ (the traces for input w_1 are given in the next Sect. 2). So the information in the datum $w(n - 1) \neq w(n)$ suffices to conclude that $\varphi = 0$. So any $\mathfrak{A}_k(\varphi)$ has enough information to output the result. However, none of these algorithms does it, they continue to work. The question is what information they are processing, and how they converge to the result.

2.2   Traces of an Algorithm

In our general framework we consider sets of traces, that can be viewed as sets of sequences of commands. One can take traces abstractly, so we do not need too detailed notion of algorithm. However, in order to relate the general setting to the examples more clearly, we make precisions on the representation of algorithms.

An algorithm $\mathfrak{A}$ is defined as a program over a vocabulary $\mathbb{V}$.

This vocabulary consists of sets and functions (logical purism demands to distinguish symbols and interpretations but do not do it). The sets are always pre-interpreted, i.e., each has a fixed interpretation: natural numbers $\mathbb{N}$, integers $\mathbb{Z}$, rational numbers $\mathbb{Q}$, elements of finite ring $\mathbb{F}_m$, alphabet $\mathbb{B} = \{0, 1\}$, alphabet $\mathbb{A}$, Boolean values *Bool*, words over one of these alphabets of a fixed length. Elements of these sets are *constants* (from the viewpoint of logic their symbols are nullary static functions). We assume that the values of functions we consider are constants. We also assume that the length of these values is bounded by $\log n + \mathcal{O}(1)$, where n is the input length, mentioned in Sect. 1 and that is explained just below. This permits to avoid some pathological situations that are irrelevant to realistic computations, though this constraint is not essential for our examples.

The functions are classified as *pre-interpreted* or *abstract*. Pre-interpreted functions are: addition and multiplication by constants over $\mathbb{N}$, $\mathbb{Z}$ and $\mathbb{Q}$, operations over $\mathbb{F}_m$, Boolean operations over *Bool*, basic operations over words if necessary. Notice that symbols of constants are also pre-interpreted functions. The vocabulary used in our examples is more modest, we take a richer vocabulary that can cover other examples (e.g., like in [5]).

Abstract functions are *inputs*, that are external, i.e., cannot be changed by $\mathfrak{A}$, and *internal* ones. We assume that in each run of $\mathfrak{A}$ the output is assigned only once to the output function, and just at the end, before the command **halt**. Notice that what is called variable in programming is a *nullary* function in our terminology, a 1-dimensional array is a function of arity 1 etc. The arguments of an internal function serve as index (like, e.g., the index of a 1-dimensional array).

Terms and formulas are defined as usual. In particular, *atomic formula* is a formula of the form $P(\Theta)$, where P is a predicate symbol and Θ is a list of terms whose length is equal to the arity of P. *Literal* is an atomic formula or its negation. In the examples below the predicates are equalities of characters or order relations between very basic arithmetic terms. The algorithms of the examples are simple, for more involved algorithms more 'powerful' predicates may be useful. However, even in our general definitions the formulas are literals, no more general ones.

Inputs, as well as outputs of $\mathfrak{A}$ are sets of substructures over $\mathbb{V}$ without proper internal functions. For inputs and output there is defined *size* that is polynomially related to their bitwise size (e.g., the length of a word, the number of vertices in graph etc.). We fix the size and denote it n. For technical simplicity and without loss of generality we consider the inputs of size exactly n.

As it was mentioned above, the function computed by $\mathfrak{A}$ is denoted F. Notations dm and rn were introduced in Sect. 1. Variables for inputs are X, Y maybe with indices.

The worst case computational complexity of $\mathfrak{A}$ is denoted t, and the complexity for a given input X is denoted by $t(X)$. We write $t \to \infty$ instead of $t \to t$ or $t \to t(X)$.

Two basic commands of $\mathfrak{A}$ are guard verification and update; the command **halt** is not taken into consideration in traces. A *guard* is a literal (this does not diminish the generality), and an *update* (assignment) is an expression of the form $g(\Theta) := \eta$, where g is an internal function, Θ is a list of terms matching the arity of g, and η is a term.

A program of $\mathfrak{A}$ is constructed by sequential composition from updates, branchings of the form **if** *guard* **then** Op **else** Op', where Op and Op' are programs, **goto** *label* or **halt**.

Given an input X, a *trace* of $\mathfrak{A}$ for X denoted $tr(X)$, is a sequence of updates and guards that correspond to the sequence of commands executed by $\mathfrak{A}$ while processing X. More precisely, the updates are the updates executed by $\mathfrak{A}$, and the guards are the guards that are true in the branching commands. So such a guard is either the guard that is written in **if**-part or its negation. These elements of traces are called *events*. The commands **halt** and **goto** are not included in traces. The last event of a trace is an update of the output function. The event at an instant t is denoted $tr(X,t)$.

We assume that the values of internal functions are assigned by $\mathfrak{A}$, and are defined when used in updates. In other words, there are no initial values at instant 0 (or we can say that all these functions have a special value $\natural$, meaning *undefined*, that is never assigned later), all internal functions are initialized by $\mathfrak{A}$. This means, in particular, that the first update is necessarily by an 'absolute' constant or by an input value.

Everywhere below, the letter Θ in expressions like $f(\Theta)$, is a list $\tau_1, \ldots, \tau_m$ of terms whose number of elements is the arity of f.

Definition 1. *The value of a term θ in a trace $tr(X)$ at instant t, denoted $\theta[X,t]$, is defined straightforwardly as follows:*

- *if γ is an external function then its value for any value Θ of its argument Θ is already defined for a given input X, independently of time instant, and is denoted $\gamma(\Theta)[X]$ or $\gamma(\Theta)[X,t]$ to have homogenous notations.*

- *if $\theta = \gamma(\Theta)$, where γ is an external function then*

$$\theta[X,t] = \gamma(\Theta[X,t])[X] = \gamma(\tau_1[X,t],\ldots,\tau_m[X,t])[X];$$

- *if $\theta = g(\Theta)$, where g is an internal function, and if θ is not updated at t then*

$$\theta[X,t] = \theta[X,t-1] = g(\tau_1[X,t-1],\ldots,\tau_m[X,t-1])[X,t-1],$$

and if $\mathbf{tr}(X,t)$ is an update $g(\Theta) := \eta$ then $g(\Theta)[X,t] = g(\Theta[X,t-1])[X,t] = \eta[X,t-1]$ (an update defines g for some concrete arguments that should be evaluated before the update).

2.3   Trace Literals

Definition 2. *Input image of a term θ at t in $\mathbf{tr}(X)$, denoted $\theta\langle X,t\rangle$, is defined by recursion over time t and term construction:*

- *for a term $\gamma(\Theta)$, where γ is an external function, we set $\gamma(\Theta)\langle X,t\rangle = \gamma(\Theta\langle X,t\rangle)$ for all X and t;*
- *for $g(\Theta)$, where g is a internal function and $\mathbf{tr}(X,t)$ is not an update $g(\Theta[X,t-1]) := \eta$, we set $g(\Theta[X,t-1])\langle X,t\rangle = g(\Theta[X,t-1])\langle X,t-1\rangle$;*
- *for $g(\Theta)$, where g is a internal function and $\mathbf{tr}(X,t)$ is an update $g(\Theta[X,t-1]) := \eta$, we set $g(\Theta[X,t-1])\langle X,t\rangle = \eta\langle X,t-1\rangle$.*

One can see that the input image of $g(\Theta)$, where g is a internal function, is a term related to g with a concrete argument, i.e., to some kind of nullary function. We can treat the only output in some special way, and we do it later, in order not to loose its trace.

Logical purism demands that for constants we distinguish the symbol and the value. So for a loop counter i with updates $i := 0$, $i := i+1$, $i := i+1$ we get as input images of i the terms $\mathbf{0}$, $\mathbf{0}+\mathbf{1}$ and $(\mathbf{0}+\mathbf{1})+\mathbf{1}$, where boldface refers to symbols.

Lemma 1. *Input image of a term does not contain internal functions (i.e., is constructed from pre-interpreted functions and inputs).*

Proof. By straightforward induction on the construction of input image.

Definition 3. *(Trace) literal of an event $E = \mathbf{tr}(X,t)$ is denoted $E\langle X,t\rangle$ or $tl(X,t)$ and is defined as follows:*

- *if E is an update $g(\Theta) := \eta$ and g is not output then $E\langle X,t\rangle$ is the literal*

$$g(\Theta[X,t-1])\langle X,t\rangle = \eta[X,t];$$

- *if E is an update $g(\Theta) := \eta$ and g is an output function then as $E\langle X,t\rangle$ we take the literal $g(\Theta[X,t-1]) = \eta[X,t]$;*
- *if E is a guard $P(\Theta)$ then $E\langle X,t\rangle$ is the literal $P(\Theta\langle X,t\rangle)$;*

For the example of loop counters $i := 0$, $i := i + 1$, $i := i + 1$ we get as trace literals $\mathbf{0} = 0$, $\mathbf{0 + 1} = 1$ and $(\mathbf{0 + 1}) + 1 = 2$. These literals are often not instructive for the convergence of $\mathfrak{A}$ to its result.

Trace literals not containing input functions are *constant trace literals* (parameter $\mathbf{n}$ is treated as a constant that does not depend on other inputs).

In further constructions, as we illustrate in the examples just below, we do not distinguish symbols and values of constants, and write, e.g., $0 + 1 + 1 = 2$ instead of $(\mathbf{0 + 1}) + 1 = 2$. Moreover, instead of a sum of 1's taken, say m times, we write simply m or $(m - 1) + 1$ according to the context (that always permits to understand what is meant by this notation).

2.4 Traces for MaxPS Algorithms

The trace of algorithm $\mathfrak{A}_0(\varphi)$ from subsection 2.1 for input $w_1 =_{df} a^{n-1}b$ with $a \neq b$ has the form (in order to facilitate the reading we put the current or acquired value v of a term θ behind it as $\theta[v]$):

$h := 0$, $h < (n - 1)$, $h[1] := h + 1$, $i := 1$, $w(1) = w(2)$, $i[1] < (n - 1)$, $i[2] := i + 1$,
$w(2) = w(3), \ldots, w(n - 2) = w(n - 1)$, $i[n - 2] < (n - 1)$, $i[n - 1] := i + 1$,
$w(n - 1) \neq w(n)$, $h[1] < (n - 1)$, $h[2] := h + 1, \ldots, w(1) \neq w(n)$,
$h[n - 1] \geq (n - 1)$, $\varphi := 0$

The respective trace literals are (denote this sequence $tl_0(w_1)$):

$0 = 0$, $0 < (n - 1)$, $1 = 1$, $1 = 1$, $w(1) = w(2)$, $0 + 1 < (n - 1)$, $1 + 1 = 2$,
$w(2) = w(3), \ldots, w(n - 2) = w(n - 1)$, $(n - 3) + 1 < (n - 1)$,
$(n - 2) - 1 = n - 1$, $w(n - 1) \neq w(n)$, $1 < (n - 1)$, $2 = 2, \ldots, w(1) \neq w(n)$,
$n - 1 \geq (n - 1)$, $\varphi = 0$

The trace of $\mathfrak{A}_1(\varphi)$ from subsection 2.1 for input $a^{n-1}b$ with $a \neq b$ has the form:

$i := 1$, $\varphi(1) := 0$, $\psi := 0$, $i < n$, $i := i + 1[2]$, $w(1) = w(2)$, $\varphi(2) := \psi + 1[1]$,
$\psi := \psi + 1[1]$, $i < n$, $i := i + 1[3]$, $w(2) = w(3)$, $\varphi(3) := \psi + 1[2]$,
$\psi := \psi + 1[2], \ldots, i[n - 2] < n$, $i[n - 2] := i + 1[n - 1]$, $w(n - 2) = w(n - 1)$,
$\varphi(n - 1) := \psi + 1[n - 2]$, $\psi := \psi + 1[n - 2]$, $i[n - 1] < n$, $i := i + 1[n]$,
$w(n - 1) \neq w(n)$, $\psi[n - 2] > 0$, $\psi := \varphi(n - 2)[n - 3]$, $w(n - 2) \neq w(n)$,

$\psi[n - 3] > 0$, $\psi := \varphi(n - 3)[n - 4]$, $w(n - 3) \neq w(n), \ldots, \psi[1] > 0$, $\psi := \varphi(1)[0]$,
$w(1) \neq w(n)$, $\psi \leq 0$, $i[n] \geq n$, $\varphi(n) := 0$, $r := 0$
The sequence of trace literals of this trace (denote it $tl_2(w_1)$) is:

$1 = 1$, $0 = 0$, $0 = 0$, $0 < n$, $1 + 1 = 2$, $w(1) = w(2)$, $0 + 1 = 1$, $0 + 1 = 1$,
$1 + 1 < n$, $2 + 1 = 3$, $w(2) = w(3)$, $1 + 1 = 2$, $1 + 1 = 2, \ldots, (n - 3) + 1 < n$,
$(n-2)+1 = n-1$, $w(n-2) = w(n-1)$, $(n-3)+1 = n-2$, $(n-3)+1 = n-2$,
$(n - 1) < n$, $(n - 1) + 1 = n$, $w(n - 1) \neq w(n)$, $(n - 2) > 0$, $(n - 3) = n - 3$, $w(n - 2) \neq w(n)$,

$(n-3) > 0$, $(n-4) = n-4$, $w(n-3) \neq w(n), \ldots, 1 > 0$, $0 = 0$, $w(1) \neq w(n)$, $0 \leq 0$, $n \geq n$, $0 = 0$, $r = 0$

Replace constants by their values and delete trivially valid literals from the trace literal sequences above. We get
for the trace of $\mathfrak{A}_0(\varphi)$:

$$w(1) = w(2),\ w(2) = w(3),\ \ldots, w(n-2) = w(n-1),\ w(n-1) \neq w(n),$$
$$\ldots, w(1) \neq w(n),\ \varphi = 0 \quad (1)$$

for the trace of $\mathfrak{A}_1(\varphi)$:

$$w(1) = w(2),\ w(2) = w(3),\ \ldots, w(n-2) = w(n-1),\ w(n-1) \neq w(n),$$
$$w(n-2) \neq w(n),\ w(n-3) \neq w(n), \ldots, w(1) \neq w(n),\ r = 0 \quad (2)$$

Definition 4. *A weeded trace of input X, denoted $\boldsymbol{wtr}(X)$, is a subsequence of the sequence $(\boldsymbol{tl}(X,t))_t$ of trace literals obtained from $(\boldsymbol{tl}(X,t))_t$ by deleting all constant literals.*

Denote by $\boldsymbol{wtr}(X,k)$ the kth element of $\boldsymbol{wtr}(X)$, and by $\boldsymbol{tm}(X,\Lambda)$, where Λ is an occurrence of a literal in $\boldsymbol{wtr}(X)$, the time instant t such that $\Lambda = \boldsymbol{tl}(X,t)$, i.e., such that Λ is the trace literal of $\boldsymbol{tr}(X,t)$.

In a weeded trace, a trace literal that contains a symbol of an input function may be true or not depending on the value of the input, though we consider occurrences of this symbol in the trace for a particular input X. In $\boldsymbol{wtr}(X)$ we leave only such non-trivial, non-constant literals.

These 'weeded' trace literal sequences simplify the estimation of entropic convergence below. The literals in these weeded traces represent events that are directly involved in processing inputs. In the general case one can insert in a 'good' algorithm events of this kind that are useless, just to hide what is really necessary to do in order to compute the result. So in the general case weeded traces cannot help much, however for concrete practical algorithms they are useful.

3   Inputs Partitions and Entropic Weight

In this section the main notions are defined.

3.1   Partitions of Inputs and Measure

A partition of $\boldsymbol{dm}$ is defined by a chosen similarity relation between events that is denoted $\sim$. We assume that $\sim$ is an equivalence relation. The choice of the probabilistic measure is based on informal *Principle of Maximal Uncertainty*. In examples we use as $\sim$ the equality of trace literals of events, i.e., two events are similar if their trace literals are equal.

Let $M = |rn|$. Fix an order of elements of $rn = (\omega_1, \ldots, \omega_M)$, and denote $\widehat{F}_k = F^{-1}(\omega_k)$. Now the sets $\widehat{F}_k$ are ordered according to k.

To an event $E = tr(X, t)$ we relate a set of inputs $\widehat{E} = \widehat{E}[X, t]$:

$$\widehat{E}[X, t] = \{X' \in dm : \exists t'. \ E \sim tr(X', t')\}$$

(notice, there is no order relation between t and t'), and an ordered partition

$$\pi(E) = \pi(\widehat{E}) =_{df} (\widehat{E} \cap \widehat{F}_1, \ \widehat{E} \cap \widehat{F}_2, \ \ldots, \widehat{E} \cap \widehat{F}_M).$$

In particular,

$$\Pi =_{df} \pi(dm) = (\widehat{F}_1, \ \widehat{F}_2, \ \ldots, \ \widehat{F}_M)$$

$$\Pi_k = \Pi_{F_k} =_{df} \pi(\widehat{F}_k) = (\emptyset, \ \ldots, \emptyset, \ \widehat{F}_k, \ \emptyset, \ldots, \emptyset)$$

The latter partitions Π_k represent the graph of F in our context, we denote it $gr(F) =_{df} \{\Pi_k\}_k$.

We define a measure on dm according to the *Principle of Maximal Uncertainty*. Imagine that $\mathfrak{A}$ plays against an adversary that chooses any input to ensure the maximal uncertainty for $\mathfrak{A}$. In this case all outputs of $rn(f)$ are equiprobable. We consider a static measure, i.e., that one does not change during the execution of $\mathfrak{A}$.

We set $P(\widehat{F}_v) = \dfrac{1}{M}$ for any $v \in rn(F)$, and define P as uniform on each $\widehat{F}_v$.

Practical calculation of $P(S)$ for a set S is combinatorial: $P(S) = \sum_k \dfrac{|S \cap \widehat{F}_k|}{M \cdot |\widehat{F}_k|}$, where where $|U|$ is the cardinality of a set U. The the measure of one point of $\widehat{F}_k$ is $\dfrac{1}{M \cdot |\widehat{F}_k|}$.

Remark that we can define a metric between ordered partitions $(A_1, \ldots, A_M)$ and $(B_1, \ldots, B_M)$:

$$d((A_1, \ldots, A_M), (B_1, \ldots, B_M)) = \sum_{1 \leq i \leq M} P(A_i \triangle B_i),$$

where $\triangle$ is symmetric difference of sets, though it remains unclear whether this kind of metric may help to deepen the understanding of algorithmic processes.

3.2   Entropic Weight

We would like to evaluate the uncertainty of events in a way that says how the algorithm approaches the result. As a measure of uncertainty we introduce a function $\mathcal{D}$ over partitions $\pi(E)$ (that can be also seen as a function over events E or sets $\widehat{E}$) that has the following properties:

(D1) $\mathcal{D}(dm) = \mathcal{D}(\Pi) = \log M$ (maximal uncertainty),

(D2) $\mathcal{D}(\widehat{E}) = 0$ for $\widehat{E} \subseteq \widehat{F}_k$ for all k, in particular $\mathcal{D}(\widehat{F}_k) = 0$
   (the event $E = \boldsymbol{tr}(X, t)$ determines the result $\boldsymbol{F}(X)$ with certainty),
(D3) $\mathcal{D}$ is monotone: it is non-increasing when $\widehat{E}$ diminishes.

Look at conditional probability $\frac{P(\widehat{E} \cap \widehat{F}_k)}{P(\widehat{E})}$. Intuitively, it measures a contribution of event E (via its set $\widehat{E}$) to determining what is the probability to have ω_k as the value of $\boldsymbol{F}$ in trace $\boldsymbol{tr}(X)$ and in other traces that contain an event similar to E. If $\widehat{E} \subseteq \widehat{F}_k$ then $\frac{P(\widehat{E} \cap \widehat{F}_k)}{P(\widehat{E})} = 1$, i.e., according to E the result is ω_k. So we can take as an entropy-like measure this or that average of the conditional information function $-\log \frac{P(\widehat{E} \cap \widehat{F}_k)}{P(\widehat{E})}$. As we are interested only in the relation of E with $\boldsymbol{F}$, we take some kind of average over $\widehat{E}$—we take it using the measure over $\widehat{E}$ induced by $\boldsymbol{P}$ (then the measure of the whole $\widehat{E}$ may be smaller than 1).

Definition 5. Entropic weight of event E *(in fact, that of $\pi(E)$) is*

$$\mathcal{D}(E) = \mathcal{D}(\widehat{E}) = \mathcal{D}(\pi(E)) = -\sum_k \boldsymbol{P}(\widehat{E} \cap \widehat{F}_k) \log \frac{\boldsymbol{P}(\widehat{E} \cap \widehat{F}_k)}{\boldsymbol{P}(\widehat{E})}. \tag{3}$$

This function has the properties (D1)–(D3), the properties (D1)–(D2) are evident, and (D3) is proven in Theorem 1 below.
   We use in this proof the formula (4) below that is equivalent to (3) as $\sum_k \boldsymbol{P}(\widehat{E} \cap \widehat{F}_k) = \boldsymbol{P}(\widehat{E})$:

$$\mathcal{D}(E) = -\sum_k \boldsymbol{P}(\widehat{E} \cap \widehat{F}_k) \log \boldsymbol{P}(\widehat{E} \cap \widehat{F}_k) + \boldsymbol{P}(\widehat{E}) \log \boldsymbol{P}(\widehat{E}) \tag{4}$$

Theorem 1. *For any sets $S_0, S_1 \subseteq \boldsymbol{dm}$ if $S_0 \subseteq S_1$ then $\mathcal{D}(S_0) \leq \mathcal{D}(S_1)$*

Proof. Take any interval of time $[0, T]$, $T > 0$. Set $T_i = \frac{iT}{|\boldsymbol{dm}|}$, and let S be a function from $[0, T]$ to subsets of $\boldsymbol{dm}$ such that

- $S(0) = \boldsymbol{dm}$, $S(T) = \emptyset$,
- $S(T_i)$ is constant on $[T_i, T_{i+1})$ $(0 \leq i < |\boldsymbol{dm}| - 1)$
- $|S(T_i) \setminus S(T_{i+1})| = 1$.

In other words, S is a decreasing function having subsets of $\boldsymbol{dm}$ as values $(t_0 \leq t_1$ implies $S(t_1) \subseteq S(t_0))$ that looses one element at each point T_i and remains constant between these points.
   Let $z_k = z_k(t) = \boldsymbol{P}(S(t) \cap \widehat{F}_k)$. It is a decreasing step-function. Replace it by a decreasing differentiable function x_k that coincides with z_k at points T_i. We have $0 \leq x_k \leq z_k \leq \frac{1}{M}$ for all t, and $0 \leq \sum_k x_k \leq 1$.
   Define a function $D = -\sum_k x_k \log x_k + (\sum_k x_k) \log(\sum_k x_k)$. Notice that $\boldsymbol{P}(S(t)) = \sum_k z_k$. From this equality and (4) we have

$$D(T_i) = \left(-\sum_k z_k \log z_k + (\sum_k z_k) \log(\sum_k z_k)\right)(T_i) = \mathcal{D}(S(T_i)). \tag{5}$$

As z_k is decreasing then if $(\sum_k z_k)(t) = 0$ for some t, it remains 0 for all bigger t. We consider $D(t)$ for t for which $(\sum_k z_k)(t) > 0$, these t constitute an initial interval of $[0, T]$. Take derivative of D (recall that $\log x = \frac{\ln x}{\ln 2}$):

$$D'(t) = -\sum_k \left(x'_k \log x_k + x_k \frac{x'_k}{x_k \cdot \ln 2} \right)$$

$$+ \left(\sum_k x'_k \right) \log \left(\sum_k x_k \right) + \left(\sum_k x_k \right) \frac{\left(\sum_k x'_k \right)}{\left(\sum_k x_k \right) \ln 2}$$

$$= -\sum_k \left(x'_k \log x_k + \frac{x'_k}{\ln 2} \right) + \left(\sum_k x'_k \log \left(\sum_k x_k \right) + \frac{x'_k}{\ln 2} \right) \tag{6}$$

In formula (6) the terms $x'_k \log x_k$ with $x_k = 0$ are zeros as can be seen by applying L'Hôpital's rule. Leaving only $x_k > 0$ (for a given t) we infer from (6) formula (where k are only for $x_k > 0$)

$$D'(t) = \sum_k x'_k \cdot \log \frac{\left(\sum_k x_k \right)}{x_k} \tag{7}$$

The functions x_k are decreasing, thus $x'_k \leq 0$. As $\sum_k x_k \geq x_k$, the value of (7) is non-positive, hence $D(t)$ is decreasing when $S(t)$ decreases. Coming back to (5) we get the conclusion of the theorem.

We mention two inequalities that are sometimes useful for the analysis of the behavior of entropic weight.

Lemma 2. *For any $\mathcal{J} \subseteq [1..M]$, $M \geq 3$, and $S \subseteq dm$*

$$\Delta(S, \mathcal{J}) =_{df} -\sum_{k \in \mathcal{J}} P(S \cap \widehat{F}_k) \log \frac{P(S \cap \widehat{F}_k)}{P(S)} \leq \frac{|\mathcal{J}|}{M} \log M \tag{8}$$

Proof. We have

$$\Delta(S, \mathcal{J}) =_{df} -\sum_{k \in \mathcal{J}} P(S \cap \widehat{F}_k) \log \frac{P(S \cap \widehat{F}_k)}{P(S)} \leq$$

$$-\sum_{k \in \mathcal{J}} P(S \cap \widehat{F}_k) \log \frac{P(S \cap \widehat{F}_k)}{P(dm)} = -\sum_{k \in \mathcal{J}} P(S \cap \widehat{F}_k) \log P(S \cap \widehat{F}_k) \tag{9}$$

Function $x \log x$ is increasing for $0 \leq x \leq 0.36 < \frac{1}{e}$, where e is the base of natural logarithm.

Indeed, take derivative of $-x \log x = -\frac{1}{\ln 2} x \ln x$. We get $-\frac{1}{\ln 2} (\ln x + 1)$; this expression is zero when $\ln x = -1$, i.e., $x = \frac{1}{e}$. And the derivative is positive for $0 \leq x < \frac{1}{e}$.

Thus, for $M \geq 3$ the right-hand side of (8) is a sum of functions increasing for $0 \leq P(S \cap \widehat{F}_k) \leq \frac{1}{3}$ when S grows. Hence,

$$\Delta(S, \mathcal{J}) \leq - \sum_{k \in \mathcal{J}} P(\widehat{F}_k) \log P(\widehat{F}_k) = - \sum_{k \in \mathcal{J}} \frac{1}{M} \log \frac{1}{M} = \frac{|\mathcal{J}|}{M} \log M, \quad (10)$$

that gives (8).

Lemma 3. *For any $\mathcal{J} \subseteq [1..M]$ and $S \subseteq \boldsymbol{dm}$ such that $S \cap \widehat{F}_k = \emptyset$ for all $k \notin \mathcal{J}$, there holds*

$$\Delta(S, \mathcal{J}) \leq P(S) \log |\mathcal{J}| \leq \log |\mathcal{J}| \quad (11)$$

where we use notation from (8).

Proof. Clearly,

$$P(S) = \sum_{1 \leq k \leq M} P(S \cap \widehat{F}_k) = \sum_{k \in \mathcal{J}} P(S \cap \widehat{F}_k), \sum_{k \in \mathcal{J}} \frac{P(S \cap \widehat{F}_k)}{P(S)} = 1.$$

Hence, $\frac{P(S \cap \widehat{F}_k)}{P(S)}$ is a probability distribution, and the maximal value of its entropy is

$$- \sum_{k \in \mathcal{J}} \frac{P(S \cap \widehat{F}_k)}{P(S)} \log \frac{P(S \cap \widehat{F}_k)}{P(S)} \leq \log |\mathcal{J}| \Leftrightarrow \Delta(S, \mathcal{J}) \leq P(S) \log |\mathcal{J}|. \quad (12)$$

As $P(S) \leq 1$ from (12) we get (11).

The bound of Lemma 2, when applicable, is better than the last inequality of Lemma 3 except one small value of $|\mathcal{J}|$. Some applications of these inequalities can be found in [5].

3.3   On the Behavior of Entropic Weight of Examples

Some information about the quality of $\mathfrak{A}$ is in the behavior of local minima of entropic weight in traces. However, local minima in a whole trace are technically difficult to describe rigorously though often they are intuitively clear. But one can look at local minima in prefixes of traces that may be also informative and that are often much easier to detect and describe. A local minimum in a prefix of a trace may be the last event of the prefix whose entropic weight is smaller than that its predecessor. So by taking the last local minima in consecutive prefixes of a trace we extract sequences of decreasing entropic weights that give an interesting information about the behavior of $\mathfrak{A}$.

To illustrate this, take the same 'worst-case' input as above, i.e., $w_1 = a^{n-1}b$ and look at local minima of entropic weight in traces of $\mathfrak{A}_0(\varphi)$ and of $\mathfrak{A}_0(\varphi)$ for this input. For simplicity we take weeded traces.

Look at the trace of $\mathfrak{A}_0(\varphi)$ for w_1. We rewrite (1) introducing notations ξ_i for pieces of $\boldsymbol{wtr}(w_1)$:

$$\left. \begin{array}{l} \xi_{n-1}: \ w(1) = w(2), \ w(2) = w(3), \ \ldots, \ w(n-1) \neq w(n) \\ \xi_{n-2}: \ w(1) = w(3), \ w(2) = w(4), \ \ldots, \ w(n-2) \neq w(n) \\ \quad \cdots\cdots\cdots\cdots\cdots\cdots\cdots\cdots\cdots \\ \xi_2: \ w(1) = w(n-1), \ w(2) \neq w(n) \\ \xi_1: \ w(1) \neq w(n) \end{array} \right\} \quad (13)$$

Notations for more detailed vision:

$$\xi_{k,i} =_{df} (w(i) = w(i+(n-k))) \quad \text{for } 1 \le i \le (k-1), \quad \xi_{k,k} =_{df} (w(k) \ne w(n)).$$

Entropic weight of an event $\xi_{k,i}$ is $\mathcal{D}(\xi_{k,i}) = \mathcal{D}(\widehat{\xi}_{k,i}) = \mathcal{D}(\{w : \bigwedge_{j \le i} \xi_{k,j} \wedge \varphi(w) \le k\})$ for $i < k$. And it decreases when i goes from 1 to k. Thus the events $\xi_{k,i}$, $1 < i < k$, give local minima of prefixes of $\boldsymbol{wtr}(w_1)$. The number of these local minima is of order n^2.

It is much harder to prove that events $\xi_{k,k}$, at least for $\frac{n}{2} \le k \le (n-1)$, are local minima of the whole trace $\boldsymbol{wtr}(w_1)$, and their number is of order n.

Consider the trace $\boldsymbol{wtr}(w_1)$ for $\mathfrak{A}_1(\varphi)$, see (2). The events $\xi_{n-1,i}$ are the same as in the previous case and give of order n local minima for prefixes, and one global minimum $\mathcal{D}(\xi_{n-1,n-1}) = 0$ as in the previous case. Whatever be the remaining behavior, we see that the number of local minima of prefixes is of order n. One can prove that the number of local minima in the whole trace is a constant.

So we see that the behavior of $\mathfrak{A}_0(\varphi)$ is much less efficient from the point of view of extraction of information than that of $\mathfrak{A}_1(\varphi)$. And the behavior of the entropic weight of $\mathfrak{A}_0(\varphi)$ may give some hints how to improve the algorithm and its convergence.

Notice that it is interesting to analyze the behavior of entropic weight of algorithm whose complexity is unknown, not like $\mathfrak{A}_1(\varphi)$ or standard wave algorithm for the shortest path in graphs. For example, algorithms for SAT are of interest. For such problems the basic operations that constitute traces should be more 'coarse', more powerful in order not to be submerged by secondary details. For example, evaluating of a propositional formula for a given distribution of values of variables can be one operation.

3.4   Concluding Remarks

The same measure, namely entropic weight, can be applied to describe the convergence of Boolean circuits. For the latter it is easier to define such a measure of convergence. For a circuit $\mathcal{C}$ take all vertices f at a distance h from the output. For an input X denote by $f(X)$ the value of f for X. Our events are of the form $f(X) = a$, $a \in \{0,1\}$. For each f define $\mathcal{D}(f,X)$ as in (3), where $\widehat{E} = \{X : f(X) = a\}$ and in $\widehat{F}_k$ the index k is from $\{0,1\}$. As a measure of convergence take the minimum of all $\mathcal{D}(f,X)$, it depends on d. On may introduce also some kind of integral measure. This gives some setting for the analysis.

As mentioned in the introduction, the goal of this paper is mainly conceptual, just to show that one can find a way to quantitatively evaluate the convergence of an algorithm to its results in terms related to the quantity of information. The described framework is technically hard to apply because of combinatorial difficulties arising in the evaluation of the entropic weight. Besides that it would be more interesting and useful to be able to apply such an approach to the analysis of problems, not only algorithms. There is hope that the framework can be developed or can inspire a more geometric approach (recall the relation between measure, entropy and metric [3,4]) and with more relaxed notion of algorithm.

Acknowledgements. I am thankful to Eugène Asarine and Vladimir Lifschitz for discussions and comments that were stimulating, and to anonymous referee for very useful remarks.

References

1. Floridi, L.: Semantic conceptions of information. In: Zalta, E.N. (ed.) The Stanford Encyclopedia of Philosophy, Spring 2013 edn. (2013)
2. Gurevich, Y.: Evolving algebra 1993: lipari guide. In: Börger, E. (ed.) Specification and Validation Methods, pp. 9–93. Oxford University Press, Oxford (1995)
3. Kolmogorov, A.N., Tikhomirov, V.M.: ε-entropy and ε-capacity of sets in function spaces. Uspekhi Mat. Nauk **14**(8(2(86))), 3–86 (1959). (in Russian) In: Selected Works of A.N. Kolmogorov: Volume III: Information Theory and the Theory of Algorithms (Mathematics and its Applications). Kluwer Academic Publishers (1992)
4. Martin, N.F.G., England, J.W.: Mathematical Theory of Entropy. Encyclopedia of Mathematics and its Applications, vol. 12. Addison-Wesley, Boston (1981)
5. Slissenko, A.: On entropic convergence of algorithms in terms of domain partitions. Technical report, University Paris-East Créteil, Laboratory for Algorithmics, Complexity and Logic (LACL) (2016). http://arxiv.org/abs/1605.01519

The Power of Spreadsheet Computations

Jerzy Tyszkiewicz$^{(\boxtimes)}$ (iD)

Institute of Informatics, University of Warsaw, Warsaw, Poland
`jty@mimuw.edu.pl`

Abstract. We investigate the expressive power of spreadsheets. We consider spreadsheets which contain only formulas, and assume that they are small templates, which can be filled to a larger area of the grid to process input data of variable size. Therefore we can compare them to well-known machine models of computation. We consider a number of classes of spreadsheets defined by restrictions on their reference structure. Two of the classes correspond closely to parallel complexity classes: we prove a direct correspondence between the dimensions of the spreadsheet and amount of hardware and time used by a parallel computer to compute the same function. As a tool, we describe spreadsheets which are universal in these classes, i.e. can emulate any other spreadsheet from them. In other cases we provide spreadsheet implementations of a solver for a polynomial-time complete problem, which indicates that the such spreadsheets are unlikely to have efficient parallel evaluation algorithms. Thus we get a picture how the computational power of spreadsheets depends on their dimensions and structure of references.

Keywords: Spreadsheets · Expressive power · Lower bounds · Upper bounds · Parallel Random Access Machines · Circuit Value Problem · PTIME · NC

1 Introduction

1.1 Why Spreadsheets?

Spreadsheets are an extremely popular type of software systems. They have conquered very diverse areas of present day politics, business, research, and, last but not least, our private lives. However, this prevalence is not so evident, because spreadsheets are typically used in the back office and are not presented to the public. They make to the news only when something goes really wrong: for instance a spreadsheet used to justify a widely implemented public policy, as in the case of the extremely influential report [17] concerning a purported causal relationship between high national debt and low economic growth, turns out to contain an error in a formula, affecting the outcome of the calculations [11].

Electronic supplementary material The online version of this chapter (https://doi.org/10.1007/978-3-030-48006-6_20) contains supplementary material, which is available to authorized users.

© Springer Nature Switzerland AG 2020
A. Blass et al. (Eds.): Gurevich Festschrift, LNCS 12180, pp. 305–322, 2020.
https://doi.org/10.1007/978-3-030-48006-6_20

An *Excel* spreadsheet model was used to manage the investments of JPMorgan Chase & Co. bank, which led to trade losses estimated in billions of dollars [6]. Research is not an exception, and a careful reader of *Science* magazine can read [7,10], in which a scientific controversy finally turns out to be related to a spreadsheet mistake. Those notable failures indicate the widespread use and critical role of spreadsheets in business and research.

Indeed, spreadsheets are among the most frequently used software tools of any kind. More than 30 years ago after *VisiCalc*, the first spreadsheet and the first killer app in the history of personal computers, still relatively little is known about their computational power.

In recent years there was a significant amount of interest in parallelizing spreadsheet computations, witnessed both by research papers and patent applications [2–4,12,14,19]. In this paper, we analyze the computations expressible in spreadsheets and their relation to parallel complexity classes. Our findings shed light both on parallelization potential of certain structures in spreadsheets, and on the fundamental limitations of this approach.

1.2   Measuring the Expressiveness of Spreadsheets

The aim of this paper is to analyze the power of spreadsheets considered as a tool for specifying general-purpose computations. Our analysis is intended to concern the spreadsheet model of computation rather than real-life spreadsheet software. Each spreadsheet is indeed a fully functional program, consisting of many equations (a.k.a. formulas) located in cells, which are computed in data-dependent order, with no side-effects. For mathematical convenience, we assume that the spreadsheet grid is actually infinite and there is no bound on the number of cells with formulas. Next, we assume that the only data type represented in spreadsheets are true, unbounded integers. These two assumptions allow us to apply the methods of computational complexity, which are asymptotic in nature, to the study of spreadsheets. No macros and user-defined functions written in a general programming language are permitted. We also reduce the set of functions permitted in spreadsheets, to keep our analysis manageable. Still, these modifications do not affect the underlying general idea of this model of computation.

Spreadsheets belong to the nonuniform computation models, where for each input size there is a separate computing device. Uniformity can be introduced to such a model by imposing that there is a common, low complexity procedure to create those devices, given the input size. In this respect, spreadsheets come with a natural, built-in tool to do just that: *filling*. It is performed by selecting a rectangular range of cells, clicking a small handle in the lower right corner of it and extending its boundaries either horizontally or vertically, which results in copying the formulas present in the initial range to the new, larger area of the worksheet, with suitable reference adjustments. Filling is the usual way to produce a spreadsheet processing a large amount of data from a few formulas prepared manually, or to extend an already existing one to accommodate a new supply of data.

1.3   Technicalities of Spreadsheets

Each cell in the spreadsheet is identified by its column letter and row number, e.g. C2 is located in the third column and second row. A cell may contain a constant value or a formula, which calculates a value of that cell. An example formula A\$1+SUM(\$A\$2:\$A5) *references* a single cell A1 and a (vertical) range A2:A5, consisting of 4 cells in the rectangular spanned by A2 and A5 and its meaning is self-explanatory. The \$ signs indicate how to *copy* this formula to another cell and do not affect its evaluation. Upon copying, column and row identifiers with \$ in front remain unchanged, while those without are modified to remain in the same relative position to the cell holding the formula as in the original one. If the above formula is copied to another cell two rows down and one column to the right, the copy is B\$1+SUM(\$A\$2:\$A7), i.e., it now references cell B1 and a range A2:A7 consisting of 6 cells.

Finally, the key feature we want to use is *filling*. It is indeed systematic copying of formulas. If, e.g., a range A1:B2 consisting of four cells with formulas is marked and filled down, then the formulas in A3, A5, ... are created by copying (according to the method explained above) the formula from A1; those in B3, B5, ... are copies of the one from B1 etc. In effect, the filled region is covered by 2×2 tiles of copies of cells from the original range. Filling can be repeated.

The spreadsheet software automatically chooses an evaluation order of the formulas which follows the references (we do not consider cyclic references).

It is generally quite difficult to describe an algorithm behind a spreadsheet program in plain words. In our case, a small spreadsheet is expanded by filling to an interconnected network of modified copies of itself, resulting in the code to be eventually executed. Its operation involves complex interactions between formulas, their locations which serve as their identifiers, and the mechanism of filling, which produces adjusted references in the newly created cells. Therefore we have decided to provide algorithms in the form of commented spreadsheets in the Electronic Supplementary Material (ESM) of this paper, available from the Publisher. Apart form *Microsoft Excel*, they work also under *LibreOffice*, *Microsoft Excel Online* and *Google sheets*.

1.4   Main Results

The structural properties of spreadsheets which we prove to determine their computational properties are defined by restrictions on the pattern of references in formulas, in the sense described above.

Definition 1. A spreadsheet S is *row-organized* iff all its formulas refer to single cells and fragments of rows, only.

Dually, S is *column-organized* iff all its formulas refer to single cells and fragments of columns, only.

S is *un-organized* iff it is neither row-organized nor column-organized. In each case, references to the inputs of S are exempt from those limitations.

Definition 2. A spreadsheet S is *row-directed* iff every formula in it refers only to cells and ranges located above itself. Such an S can be evaluated in any top-down order.

Dually, S is *column-directed* iff every formula refers only to cells and ranges located to the left of itself. Such an S can be evaluated in any left-right order.

S is *un-directed* iff it is neither row- nor column-directed. S is *bi-directed* iff it is both row- and column-directed. Again, references to the input part of S are exempt from those limitations.

The above properties are preserved by filling.

We describe the computational power of spreadsheets by relating them to Parallel Random Access Machines (PRAM for short), both CRCW priority write and CREW ones.

On several occasions we proceed by implementing instances of the P-complete *Circuit Value Problem* (abbreviated CVP) in spreadsheets, in order to demonstrate that they are unlikely to have efficient parallel evaluation algorithms.

Our first main result is that any given initial row-organized row-directed spreadsheet can be converted into a program π for an CREW PRAM such that the function computed by that spreadsheet filled to the dimensions of c columns and r rows is always the same as that computed by π evaluated on a PRAM with c processors, $O(c)$ cells of memory and running for $O(r \log c)$ time. Thus, if a spreadsheet is row-organized row-directed, its evaluation can be efficiently parallelized: the number of columns contributes only a logarithmic factor to the total computation time. This sets an upper bound on the computational power of row-organized row-directed spreadsheets. An analogous result holds for column-organized column-directed spreadsheets.

In order to get a lower bound, and thus determine the class of functions computable by those spreadsheets, we prove our second main result: there is a row-organized row-directed spreadsheet with 19 formulas which is a universal CRCW PRAM evaluator, i.e., one which given a (suitably encoded) program π together with its input, and filled to the dimensions of p columns and $10t$ rows, computes in its last row the description of PRAM after executing t steps of π on p processors and with p cells of shared memory. This demonstrates that spreadsheets can implement a natural and broad class of general-purpose computations.

The same spreadsheet is also a universal row-organized row-directed spreadsheet: any other spreadsheet from this class can be equivalently expressed as a program for a PRAM, which in turn can be executed on that spreadsheet. This above results demonstrate that row-organized row-directed spreadsheets and PRAMs are almost equivalent in computing power, with clear relations between the resources in both models. Indeed, translating a spreadsheet into an equivalent program for PRAM, and then back to spreadsheet, incurs only a logarithmic overhead, a common effect of translations between different parallel computation models.

At the same time PRAMs and spreadsheets are extremely different: the former have only programming primitives and no data analysis ones, while the latter

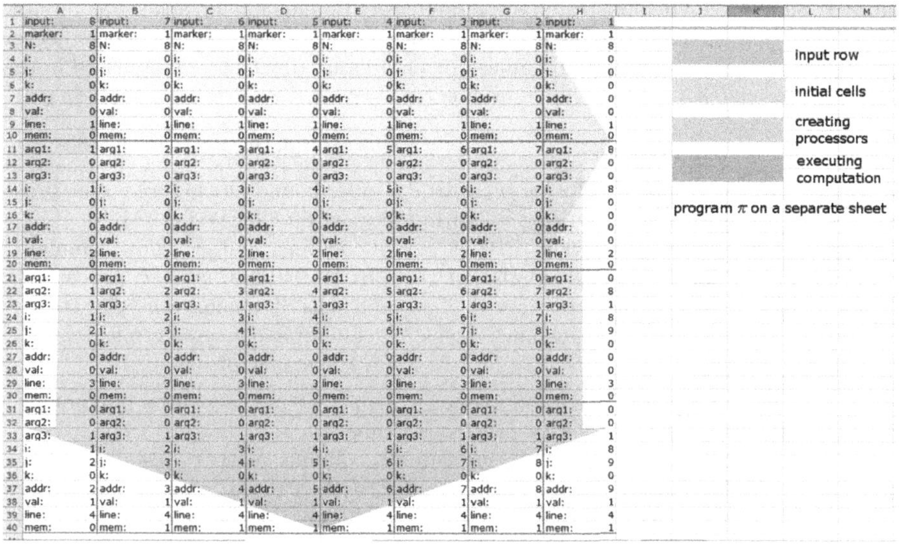

Fig. 1. PRAM evaluator in a row-organized row-directed spreadsheet S1: structure and mode of operation. Processors are located in columns, and computation time advances downward. A vertical group of 10 cells constitutes a snapshot of a processor at a given time, so that extending computation time by one unit requires filling 10 rows. The filling process is shown in ESM video V1. S1 is provided in ESM.

have only data analysis functions and do not support any form of programming on the level of the spreadsheet itself.

Further, we demonstrate a row-organized but not row-oriented PRAM simulator (ESM spreadsheet S2), significantly more powerful than the one previously described. If it is extended to c columns and r rows, computes the description of PRAM after executing $cr/10p$ steps of π on p processors and with p cells of shared memory, where $p \leq c$ is a part of the input. Thus this PRAM simulator can perform either a parallel or a sequential computation, as instructed in the input, trading off the number of processors and cells of memory for more computation time.

To get the results for other classes of spreadsheets, we implement instances of CVP in them. Each time we do so, we get hypothetical lower bounds on the parallel complexity of evaluating spreadsheets in this class, following from the anticipated but thus far unproven $NC \subsetneq P$. The larger instance we implement, the higher the lower bound is.

We summarize our results in Table 1. The highlights are the following:

First, row-oriented but not row-organized spreadsheets have parallel evaluation algorithms with c processors and of time complexity $O(r \log cr)$, similar to those for row-organized row-oriented ones discussed above, except that they need much more memory: $O(cr)$ instead of $O(c)$ cells.

Table 1. Summary of demonstrated upper and lower bounds for spreadsheet computations, depending on their structure. We disregard small changes depending on whether spreadsheets are row- or column-organized or un-organized, which are discussed in the main text.

	Column directed	Column un-directed
Row directed	Upper bounds $O(r \log cr)$ with c processors and $O(c \log cr)$ with r processors on CREW PRAM No known PRAM simulation $2n$ columns and $4n$ rows implement CVP instance of size n	Upper bound $O(r \log cr)$ with c processors on CREW PRAM c columns and r rows simulate CRCW PRAM with c processors and cells of memory for $r/10$ steps 1 column and n rows implement CVP instance of size n
Row un-directed	Upper bound $O(c \log cr)$ time on CREW PRAM with r processors c columns and r rows simulate PRAM with r processors and cells of memory for $c/10$ steps n columns and 1 row implement CVP instance of size n	Upper bound sequential polynomial time c columns and r rows simulate CRCW PRAM with p processors and cells of memory for $cr/10p$ steps, p is a part of the input c columns and r rows implement CVP instance of size $cr/8$

Second, for spreadsheets which are row-oriented but not column-oriented, and its dual class, one of the dimensions contributes a logarithmic factor to the computation time, while a CVP instance can be encoded in the other dimension, which causes its size to appear as a linear factor in the computation time.

Third, for spreadsheets which are simultaneously row-oriented and column-oriented, one has choice which of the dimensions will contribute a logarithmic factor and which a linear one to the computation time. However, it is unlikely that there is an algorithm polylogarithmic with respect to both dimensions, because if both are large, a large CVP instance can be still encoded.

All the above results taken together give a comprehensive picture of the computing power of spreadsheets without macros. It turns out that this power is strongly influenced by the pattern of references within the spreadsheet, in addition to its size.

2   Spreadsheets

As we have already indicated, we assume that the spreadsheet grid is actually infinite and any number of rows and columns can be filled with copies of the initial cells. We never consider spreadsheets of unbounded size: all ranges used have cells as corners, and the size of the spreadsheet is for us the total number of cells which contain formulas or are referenced in formulas. The only data type are true, unbounded integers.

The mechanisms of copying formulas and filling have already been described in Sect. 1.3. Syntactically the present paper is based on *Microsoft Excel* and the reference to syntax and meaning of formulas is the on-line help of *Microsoft Excel* [13]. The ESM software accompanying this paper has been also prepared with *Excel*.

We frequently use names in the ESM spreadsheets. This is a method to assign a name to a frequently used range of cells, and later on use that name in formulas to denote that range. We use it for the sole purpose of making formulas shorter and easier to understand. This method does not increase the computational abilities of spreadsheets.

2.1 Functions in Spreadsheets

We use standard arithmetical functions: $+$, $\cdot$, $-$ and $/$.

The syntax of comparison functions is `value1`*rel*`value2`, where *rel* is any of =, <, >, <=, >=, <>. `value1` and `value2` can be numbers, formulas or cell references to numbers. The result is `TRUE` if the arguments are in the specified relation, and `FALSE` otherwise.

Logical functions `AND(value1,value2,...)` and `OR(value1,value2,...)` compute the logical conjunction and disjunction of their arguments, respectively.

The flow control functions are the following.

`IF(test,value1,value2)`. If `test` is, refers or evaluates to `TRUE`, the function returns `value1`, if `test` is, refers or evaluates to `FALSE` it returns `value2`. In all other cases the result is a `#VALUE!` error.

`IFERROR(value1,value2)`. This function returns `value2` if `value1` is, refers to or evaluates to any error value, and `value1` otherwise.

`CHOOSE(index-num,value1,value2,...)` is a kind of generalization of `IF`, because in one formula it allows the choice among up to 29 possible values to be returned. `index-num` specifies which value argument is selected. `index-num` must be a number between 1 and 29, or a formula or reference to a cell containing a number between 1 and 29. If `index-num` is i, `CHOOSE` returns `value`i.

We use two address functions: `ROW()` and `COLUMN()`, which return the number of row (column, resp.) of the cell in which they are located. In case they are given an argument, a reference to a single cell, they return the row (column, resp.) in which that reference is located.

We also use aggregating functions. We use only their one-dimensional variants: all range arguments must be contiguous fragments of either single rows or single columns.

In `MATCH(lookup-value,lookup-range,match-type)`, `lookup-value` is the value to be found in a range specified by `lookup-range`. `lookup-value` can be a number, a formula or a cell reference to a number. `match-type` in the spreadsheets we create is typically 0 and causes `MATCH` to find the first value that is exactly equal to `lookup-value` and return its relative position in the `lookup-range`.

If `match-type` is 1, then values in `lookup-range` are assumed to be sorted into an increasing order, and `MATCH` finds the first value that is larger or equal to `lookup-value` and returns its relative position in the `lookup-range`. If match-type is -1, then values in `lookup-range` are assumed to be sorted into a decreasing order, and `MATCH` finds the first value that is smaller or equal to `lookup-value` and returns its relative position in the `lookup-range`.

In all three cases, if no value is found which satisfies the criteria, the result is an error `#N/A!`. In case of `match-type` equal ± 1 `lookup-value` is larger (smaller, resp.) than all values in the sorted `lookup-range`, the result is the number of the last non-empty cell in `lookup-range`.

In `INDEX(array,num)`, `array` is a range of cells, `num` can be a number, a formula yielding number or a cell reference to a number. The result of the function is a value whose relative position in `array` is given by `num`.

The last function is `SUMIF(criteria-range,criteria,sum-range)`, which computes the sum of all values present in `sum-range`, in the rows/columns, in which `criteria-range` contains a value satisfying `criteria`. The latter argument has the form *rel*`value`, where *rel* is any of =, <, >, <=, >=, <> and `value` is a number, formula yielding a number or reference to a single cell. `sum-range` and `criteria-range` must be both horizontal or bot vertical. E.g., `SUMIF(A1:A5,<>B1,C1:C5)` sums those values from range `A1:A5` for which the corresponding element in `C1:C5` is not equal to the value in `B1`. This function is treated as a representative of a broad class of spreadsheet functions, which can be treated by methods similar to what we employ below.

2.2 Locality

Assume that a small initial spreadsheet S has been filled (perhaps in several steps) to create a large spreadsheet T.

If k is the height (width, resp.) of S, and a formula in cell c of T references a range R, then each corner of R is vertically (horizontally, resp.) at most k rows (columns, resp.) away from either the top row (leftmost column, resp.) due to an absolute reference, or from c (due to a relative reference).

In particular, in row-organized spreadsheets this very much restricts which rows can be indeed referenced: only those close to the origin and those close to the referencing cell. An analogous property holds for column-organized spreadsheets. We use these *locality properties* several times below.

3 PRAM Model

A PRAM machine A consists of the following components:

- Unbounded number of cells of global read-and-write shared memory, numbered from 1 on, capable of storing one integer.

- Unbounded number of cells of global read-only input memory, analogous to shared memory.
- Unbounded number of processors, numbered from 1 on. Each of them has three private read and write registers i, j, k for storing integers. Each of them can access the following read-only registers: s with its own serial number, N equal to the total number of active processors and M equal to the number of active cells of shared memory.
  The number of private registers can be chosen arbitrarily. We needed some fixed limit, so we have decided to use 3 of them.
- Program π, which is a list of consecutively numbered instructions of the following forms, and where x is ranging over i, j, k and u, v over i, j, k, s, N, M, $M[i], M[j], M[k], M[s], I[i], I[j], I[k], I[s]$ and integer constants, ℓ ranges over integer constants:
  1. $x := u$
  2. $x := u \circ v$, where $\circ$ is among $\{+, -, *, /\}$
  3. $M[x] := u$
  4. $M[x] := u \circ v$, where $\circ$ is among $\{+, -, *, /\}$
  5. **if** $u < v$ **then goto** ℓ

$M[x]$ stands for the shared memory cell whose address is x, and $I[x]$ stands for the input memory cell whose address is x.

The input sequence v of integers is located in the input memory cells, and $I[1]$ contains the length of the input sequence, including itself (so that the empty input sequence is passed to the machine as 1 in $I[1]$).

Then a fixed number of its processors (say p) is initialized, and a fixed number of shared memory cells (say m) is initialized.

During the computation each of the processors follows π, updating its private instruction counter. The state of A at each time t of its computation on input v is defined to be the sequence of p 4-tuples of integers and a sequence of m integers: the n-th tuple is the state of the n-th processor, consisting of: the values of its local variables i, j and k, the value of its instruction counter, while the sequence of integers represents the content of the shared memory.

Initially (i.e., at time $t = 0$) the values of local registers are 0, the instruction counter is 1, and the shared memory values are 0.

A single step of computation of A corresponds to a parallel, simultaneous change of all p 4-tuples and m integers describing the processors and shared memory of A.

An attempt to read from a nonexistent input or shared memory cell (i.e., of address higher than $I[1]$ or than p, resp.) or to read from cells of numbers smaller than 1 is an error and the result of this operation is unpredictable: it may cause the machine to break and stop operating, or to retrieve some value and continue computation.

An attempt to write to a shared memory cell of zero or negative number is permitted, but has no effect, and similarly if that number is higher than p. If more than one processor attempts to read from the same shared or input memory cell, all of them succeed and get the same value. If more than one processor attempts to write to the same shared memory cell, all the requests are executed, and the new value of that memory cell is the one written by the processor with the lowest serial number; the values written by the remaining processors get lost. Reading is performed before writing, so the processors which read from a shared memory cell to which other processors wish to write, get the "old" value.

The way of executing its program by A is obvious, with the provision that if the value of the instruction counter becomes higher than the number of lines in the program, the processor halts. Thus, given a PRAM A as above and its input vector v, the computation of M on v is represented by a finite or infinite sequence of states of A, which may but need not be constant from some moment on. The result of computation of A after n steps is the content of the shared memory after completing that step.

Another, substantially weaker model of PRAM is CREW, which results from CRCW by forbidding concurrent writes altogether.

The programming language of our PRAM machines is extremely simple, but, as it is well-known, equivalent in computing power to even very rich ones, so indeed each processor separately has a universal computing power, equivalent to that of a Turing machine. PRAM is a machine which can easily implement referential data structures, such as lists, trees, etc., as well as arrays. Therefore we use them without any further explanation.

4   Complexity Theory

In this paper we use the P-complete problem *Circuit Value Problem* (abbreviated CVP). An instance of CVP is a sequence of n Boolean substitutions (the reason for starting numbering from 2 is purely technical and explained below):

$$p_2 := conn_2(inputs_2); \ p_3 := conn_3(inputs_3); \ \ldots \ p_n := conn_n(inputs_n).$$

The connectives $conn_i$ can be binary **and** and **or** and unary **not**. Each of the inputs in $inputs_k$ can be either *true*, or *false*, or a variable p_i with $i < k$, indicating that the value of that variable should be used.

The CVP problem is that, given an instance of CVP, to decide if the last variable is *true*. This problem is known to be P-complete. We encode CVP in various spreadsheets in order to demonstrate that they are unlikely to be efficiently parallelizable. For convenience, when we do so we use 0 in place of *false*, 1 in place of *true*, for variables we use their numbers as names (we have started numbering from 2, so this does not lead to confusing truth values with variables), and we drop all conventional symbols like :=, parentheses and commas, so that an example instance of CVP

$$p_2 := \mathbf{and}(true, false); \ p_3 := \mathbf{or}(p_2, false); \ p_4 := \mathbf{not}(p_3); \ p_5 := \mathbf{or}(p_4, p_3)$$

is encoded by

and 1 0; **or** 2 0; **not** 3; **or** 4, 3

In this paper we estimate the size of CVP instances, which are computable in the spreadsheets in question. Each time it is easy to translate the size of CVP instances we produce into the potential lower bounds.

5   Un-directed Spreadsheets I: Complexity

It is obvious, that if the cells of a small initial spreadsheet S are filled to create c columns and r rows of formulas, then the resulting spreadsheet can be computed in time polynomial in cr, given the initial S, the dimensions c, r and the input data of S. The following theorem is neither surprising nor difficult to demonstrate. It implies that evaluating spreadsheets is P-complete.

Theorem 1. *There exists an un-directed, un-organized spreadsheet S4, such that when it is extended to dimensions of either n rows and 6 columns or 6 rows and n columns, it computes the solution to the CVP problem of size n, given its description as input.*

Proof. A fully commented spreadsheet S4 is provided in ESM. It consists of two functionally separate fragments, which can be independently converted into row-oriented and column-oriented structure.   ☐

6   Directed Spreadsheets I: Simulating Spreadsheet by PRAM

In this section, we are going to formulate and prove a theorem about evaluating spreadsheets by PRAM machines. In our model spreadsheets can be of unbounded size, so we can use asymptotic notation to describe the resources needed by a PRAM to execute a spreadsheet of a given size. The theorem below is formulated for row-organized row-directed spreadsheets. Its dual form for column-organized column-directed spreadsheets holds, too.

Theorem 2. *For any row-directed spreadsheet S with input data, there exists a program π for CREW PRAM, such that if that spreadsheet is filled to make c columns and r rows, the values of all its cells can be computed by π run for $O(r \log cr)$ time on c processors and cr cells of memory, given the initial S, c, r and the input data of S.*

If S is additionally row-organized, then the values of the cells in the last row can be computed by π run for $O(r \log c)$ steps on a PRAM with c processors and c cells of memory.

Proof. For each column of the spreadsheet we designate one processor, which will be responsible for it. Let the serial number of that processor be equal to the number of the column. The computation of PRAM will be organized into in rounds, where each round corresponds to computing the next row. The codes for evaluating particular formulas are hard-coded into the program π.

For each round we assume that certain auxiliary data structures are available, which enable evaluating aggregating functions efficiently. During each round, first the new values are computed, and then these structures are updated, so that they include the cells in the newly created row, as well. Separately, we must explain how the auxiliary data structures are initialized before the first round.

Auxiliary Data Structures. We assume that during each round all the previously created columns and rows are stored in two copies. Each row is stored in several copies:

1. for INDEX: in the original form,
2. for MATCH: as a sorted array, where we sort and store two-element records consisting of the value from the original row and its original address,
3. for SUMIF: for every subset of already existing rows, which potentially may play hold sum-range and criteria-range in each call of SUMIF, the records formed from the corresponding elements in these two ranges are sorted according to the keys in the criteria-range, and then prefix sums are computed from the sum-range values.

Each column is stored in similar copies:

1. for INDEX: in the original form,
2. for MATCH: as a balanced binary search tree, in which we store two-element records consisting of the value from the original row (which is the key) and its original address.
3. for SUMIF: for every subset of already existing columns, which potentially may hold sum-range and criteria-range in a call of SUMIF, the records formed from the corresponding elements in these two ranges are formed. They are stored in a balanced binary search tree, with keys taken from the criteria-range, and each node additionally stores the sum of the values from sum-range in the subtree rooted at this node.

The key observation is that by locality properties described in Sect. 2.2, there is a bounded number of possible pairs of columns (rows, resp.) that must be indexed using prefix sums and binary search trees.

Initialization of Auxiliary Data Structures. The size of the initial spreadsheet with input data is fixed, so this initialization takes constant time and requires constant amount of memory.

Execution of a Round. Computing Formulas. Henceforth, PRAM must first evaluate formulas. Due to the row-oriented structure of the spreadsheet, the formulas to be computed refer only to data above themselves, so all of them can be evaluated independently in parallel. For each of the cells, it is done by a single processor, responsible for the column of that cell. The values of all functions except MATCH, INDEX and SUM can be obviously evaluated in constant number of steps. Note that COLUMN function can be evaluated, because each processor knows its serial number, equal to the column number. ROW on the other hand is evaluated by clocking the advancing computation time.

If MATCH looks up a row, a sorted version of that row is in the auxiliary data structures. The processor can find there the suitable value (and its accompanying address to be returned) using binary search in time $O(\log c)$.

If MATCH looks up a column, a binary search tree version of that column is in the auxiliary data structures, in which the processor can find the suitable value (and its accompanying address, which should be returned) in time $O(\log r)$.

INDEX calls require retrieving a value of a known location from a horizontal or vertical range, so after recomputing the address to be relative to the complete row (column, resp.), the values are retrieved from the auxiliary data structures.

Each SUMIF call requires summing values from a horizontal or vertical range in the auxiliary data structure, as specified by a constraint regarding the values in criteria-range. Identifying its boundaries is done by binary search using the key fields, and then the sum can be found using two accesses to the fields with prefix sums.

In total, computing the new values takes $O(\log c + \log r) = O(\log cr)$ time.

Execution of a Round. Updating Auxiliary Data Structures. Updating auxiliary data structures requires sorting several rows of values (including the newly created row) combined with creating their accompanying prefix sums, and inserting new records into the binary search trees holding data about columns. The former can be performed in $O(\log c)$ time using logarithmic time linear memory sorting employing all c processors, like the one described in [9, Section 5.2], and the prefix sums can be then computed by the algorithm described in [8, Section 30.1.2].

Then all processors in parallel insert the new values from their columns into the corresponding trees and update sums, in time $O(\log r)$.

In total, updating the necessary data structures takes $O(\log c + \log r) = O(\log cr)$ time.

Cost of the Algorithm. First, initialization of auxiliary data structures takes constant time. Then the PRAM computation performs r rounds, each of them takes $O(\log cr)$ time, so the total time is $O(r \log cr)$. The memory used is constant times cr.

For the second claim, in a row-organized spreadsheet there is no need to access columns, so we do not need to maintain their auxiliary data structures. Thus in this modified version each round can be completed in $O(\log c)$ time and the total running time is $O(r \log c)$. By locality properties described in Sect. 2.2, we need to store constantly many rows simultaneously, and therefore the total amount of necessary memory is $O(c)$.   □

7   Directed Spreadsheets II: Simulating PRAM by Spreadsheet

At this point, we have demonstrated that directed spreadsheets can be evaluated by quite efficient parallel algorithms, establishing thereby an upper bound on their expressive power. The question of lower bounds arises naturally.

In order to provide an answer, we are going to demonstrate now that there exists a spreadsheet program, with the following property: any given CRCW PRAM A can be simulated by a row-organized row-oriented spreadsheet, if suitably encoded in the form of spreadsheet data.

Theorem 3. *There exists a row-organized row-directed spreadsheet, which is able to simulate any PRAM A for which $p = m$, so that columns correspond to processors of A and rows correspond to computation time.*

Precisely speaking, there exists a single spreadsheet S1 consisting of 19 cells (A2 to A20) with formulas, one row for input and a separate input area for representation of a program, such that for every CRCW PRAM A with program π, p processors and p cells of shared memory, and for every input vector v for A, if one

1. *pastes the encoding of π into the program area of S1*
2. *marks and fills the initial range A2:A20 to the right creating p columns (corresponding to the processors and shared memory cells of A)*
3. *selects the rows from 11 to 20 of these p columns and fills downward so that the bottom row of the new range is $10t + 10$,*
4. *pastes into S1 the input vector v of A in the first row,*

then the cells of the bottom 10 rows compute the state of A after t steps of computation on v.

This means, that the spreadsheet created from S1 in steps 1, 2 and 3 performs the first t steps of the computation of A on every input, i.e., it simulates A.

Proof. ESM spreadsheet S1 is the implementation of PRAM in a spreadsheet with explanation of the formulas used for that purpose, and is depicted in Fig. 1. Below we highlight the main elements of the construction of S1.

Conceptually, the idea is to make a spreadsheet which computes the sequence of configurations of the run of A on its input. Time is advancing downward and configurations are horizontal blocks of 10 rows each. Each column corresponds to one processor and one cell of shared memory, and formulas located there take care of advancing the computation and handling read and write operations. We may conveniently assume that the processor has been made responsible for operating its associated shared memory cell.

PRAM is a machine with random access. To the contrary, in a spreadsheet cells (which can be thought of as simple processors) can do random read, but are allowed to write only to the memory cell they are associated with. Therefore we have to simulate random writes by other means.

The idea is that any processor willing to write its contents to some shared memory cell, has to announce this in a globally visible location, indicating the address to which it attempts to write and the value to be written. Then all processors use function MATCH to search among the announcements for writes to their shared memory cells, and if there is one, fetch the value to be written from the leftmost one using INDEX. This conforms to the priority write CRCW conflict resolution policy. □

Apart from ESM spreadsheet S1, we also provide its minor variant S5, permitting structural programming with **while-endwhile** and **if-endif** rather than **goto** jump instructions.

The construction in S1 provides answer for our questions:

1. There is not much room for improvement over Theorem 2. Indeed, it offers $O(r \log cr)$ and $O(r \log c)$ algorithm for PRAM with c processors and $O(c)$ cells of memory, when the spreadsheet is row-directed and row-organized. On the other hand, every PRAM computation taking time t, using c processors and c cells of memory can be simulated in a row-directed and row-organized spreadsheet with c columns and about $10t$ rows.
2. The class of computations expressible in row-directed and row-organized spreadsheets is indeed very rich, and it includes a natural parallel complexity class.

It is worth noting, that according to the results already proven, we have the following.

Corollary 1. *S1 is a universal row-oriented row-organized spreadsheet.*

Proof. Given a row-oriented row-organized spreadsheet S, one can derive an CREW PRAM program π, computing the same function as S. This π can be encoded and provided as (a part of) input to S1, which can execute it.

If the initial S has c columns and r rows, then π should be run on a PRAM with $O(c)$ processors and memory cells and $O(r \log c)$ time. Then, in order to simulate it, S1 needs $O(c)$ columns and $O(r \log c)$ rows.

Thus the overhead of simulating a spreadsheet by the universal one is logarithmic, typical for other universal devices.   □

The interest in the corollary is that S1 uses very few functions, in particular does not use SUMIF. Therefore this result indicates that the function set with MATCH and INDEX as the only aggregating functions might form a kind of core of the spreadsheet language of formulas, at least for the row-oriented row-organized ones. Thus, in an attempt to create a theoretical model of spreadsheets, this restricted function set appears as a candidate to be the set of basic operations, from which the remaining ones can be defined. It would be very much like the relational algebra and its role in the theoretical formalization of relational databases. Of course, it concerns only row-oriented row-organized spreadsheets created by filling.

8   Bi-directed Spreadsheets: Complexity

A bi-directed, column organized spreadsheet extended to dimensions r and c can be, according to Theorem 2, evaluated on a PRAM using $O(cr)$ cells of memory and

1. $O(r)$ processors in time $O(c \log r)$, if treated as column-organized column-directed.
2. $O(c)$ processors and in time $O(r \log cr)$, if treated as row-directed.

One might be tempted to believe that it is possible to combine somehow those two methods together to yield a parallel evaluation algorithm of even better time complexity. However, we prove below that there is no evaluation algorithm of $O(\log^{O(1)} cr)$ time complexity unless $P = NC$.

Theorem 4. *There exists a bi-directed, column-organized spreadsheet S3, such that when it is extended to dimensions of $3n$ rows and $8n$ columns, it computes the solution to any CVP instance of size n, given its description as input.*

Proof. The main idea is to implement CVP "diagonally", and a fully commented implementation is provided as ESM spreadsheet S3.   □

Bi-directed spreadsheets are clearly more restrictive than those which are directed in one dimension only. Author's personal experience from the development of S3 is that the bi-directed structure is quite unnatural, especially in the column-organized version. Otherwise very simple computation of CVP required a significant effort to be programmed. At the same time this structure does not seem to offer any noticeable advantage in terms of complexity of evaluation.

9   Un-directed Spreadsheets II: What Can They Compute?

After a successful implementation of a PRAM in a row-directed spreadsheet and demonstrating that a large class of PRAM computations can be expressed in spreadsheets, it seems natural to attempt a similar goal for un-directed ones, too.

We demonstrate below, that one can create an un-directed row-organized spreadsheet which implements PRAM in a much more flexible way than the row-directed row-organized one.

Theorem 5. *There exists a row-organized (but not row-directed) spreadsheet S2 consisting of 21 cells (A2 to A22) with formulas, one row for input and a separate input area for representation of a program (including a value of p), such that for every CRCW PRAM A with program π for every input vector v, if one*

1. *pastes the encoding of π into the program area of S2*
2. *marks and fills the initial range A2:A22 to the right for q columns,*
3. *selects rows from 13 to 22 of these q columns and fills downward so that the bottom row of the new range is $10t + 12$,*
4. *pastes into S2 the input vector v of A in the first row;*
5. *inserts a number into the input cell p*

then the cells at the intersection of the bottom 10 rows with p columns of numbers from $q - p - q \pmod{p}$ to $q - q \pmod{p}$ compute the state of A after $t*(q/p-1)$ steps of computation on v.

Informally, the spreadsheet S2 above is able to simulate any PRAM A, for which $p = m$ in such a way, that filled to $10t$ rows and $q \geq p$ columns, it can utilize this computation area to encode a PRAM with p processors and p cells of shared memory, running for tq/p time. Moreover, the parameter p is a part of the input, so only the whole input specifies, how many processors will be used in the computation. In particular, for $p = 1$, this results in a fully sequential computation of length tq.

Proof. The commented spreadsheet is provided as ESM spreadsheet S2. It is recommended that the reader first analyzes S1, on which S2 is based.   □

It is instructive to compare spreadsheet S4 mentioned in Sect. 5 with the present S2. It seems at the first glance that the former is a special case of the latter. However, it is not the case. During the whole computation expressed in S4 it is always possible to refer to the values computed in the past, no matter how distant. In S2 the simulated PRAM can only refer to the values computed in the previous step of simulation. This indicates the difficulty of describing the computations of a spreadsheet by a machine model. In a spreadsheet, every cell is immutable, but its value remains accessible forever. In typical machine models of computation, memory locations are mutable and write operations delete their previous contents.

10   Summary and Related Research

We have investigated spreadsheets as a class of algorithms, by assuming that they are small templates, which are filled to a larger area of the grid to process data of variable size.

Under this scenario we have identified simple structural properties of spreadsheets, defined in the terms of the pattern of references between cells, which determine the complexity of the expressible computations.

In this paper, we analyze the computations expressible in spreadsheets and their relation to parallel complexity classes. Our findings shed light both on parallelization potential of certain structures in spreadsheets, and on the fundamental limitations of this approach. We have already mentioned research on parallelizing spreadsheet computations [2–4,12,14,19]. There was very little previous research on lower bounds of the computational power of spreadsheets, although already [5] observed that they have universal computing power. The papers [1], [15] and [16] demonstrate simulations of various algorithms and models o computation using spreadsheets, but without any intent to estimate the full power of this computation paradigm. Paper [20] demonstrates how to implement relational algebra queries and several other general algorithms in spreadsheets (which turn out to be column-organized, but not necessarily column-oriented). [18] presents an implementation of a subset of Java in a spreadsheet, but without considering parallelism, which is the core topic of the present paper.

Acknowledgments. Research funded by Polish National Science Centre (Narodowe Centrum Nauki). The author wishes to thank Jacek Sroka and Aleksy Schubert for many valuable discussions on the topic.

References

1. Bernstein, M.: Using spreadsheet languages to understand sequence analysis algorithms. Comput. Appl. Biosci. **3**, 217–221 (1987)

2. Biermann, F.: Data-Parallel Spreadsheet Programming, Ph.D. thesis. IT University of Copenhagen, Computer Science (2018)
3. Bock, A.A.: Static partitioning of spreadsheets for parallel execution. In: Alferes, J.J., Johansson, M. (eds.) PADL 2019. LNCS, vol. 11372, pp. 221–237. Springer, Cham (2019). https://doi.org/10.1007/978-3-030-05998-9_14
4. Bock, A.A., Biermann, F.: Puncalc: task-based parallelism and speculative reevaluation in spreadsheets. J. Supercomput. 1–21 (2019). https://doi.org/10.1007/s11227-019-02823-8
5. Casimir, R.J.: Real programmers don't use spreadsheets. SIGPLAN Not. **27**(6), 10–16 (1992)
6. Cavanagh, M.: JPMorgan Chase & Co: Report of JPMorgan Chase & Co., Management Task Force Regarding 2012 CIO Losses (2012)
7. Chesler, E.J., et al.: In silico mapping of mouse quantitative trait loci. Science **294**(5551), 2423 (2001). In Technical Comments
8. Cormen, T.H., Leiserson, C.E., Rivest, R.L., Stein, C.: Introduction to Algorithms, 2nd edn. MIT Press, Cambridge (2001)
9. Gibbons, A., Rytter, W.: Efficient Parallel Algorithms. Cambridge University Press, Cambridge (1988)
10. Grupe, A., et al.: In silico mapping of complex disease-related traits in mice. Science **292**(5523), 1915–1918 (2001)
11. Herndon, T., Ash, M., Pollin, R.: Does high public debt consistently stifle economic growth? A critique of Reinhart and Rogoff. Camb. J. Econ. **38**(2), 257–279 (2014)
12. Kulkarni, S.G., Wierer, J.J., Xu, M.: Calculation of spreadsheet data. US Patent 8,006,175, August 2011
13. Microsoft Corp.: Excel help. http://office.microsoft.com/en-us/excel-help/
14. Olkin, T.M.: Threading spreadsheet calculations. US Patent 10289672, May 2019
15. Premachandra, I.M.: Modeling a turing machine on a spreadsheet: a learning tool. Int. J. Inf. Manag. Sci. **4**(2), 81–92 (1993)
16. Rautama, E., Sutinen, E., Tarhio, J.: Excel as an algorithm animation environment. In: Proceedings of the 2nd Conference on Integrating Technology into Computer Science Education, ITiCSE 1997, pp. 24–26. ACM, New York (1997)
17. Reinhart, C.M., Rogoff, K.S.: Growth in a time of debt. Am. Econ. Rev. **100**(2), 573–578 (2010)
18. Schubert, A., Sroka, J., Tyszkiewicz, J.: Systematic programming in a spreadsheet. In: IS-EUD 2017 6th International Symposium on End-User Development, pp. 10–17. Eindhoven University of Technology (2017)
19. Sroka, J., Leśniewski, A., Kowaluk, M., Stencel, K., Tyszkiewicz, J.: Towards minimal algorithms for big data analytics with spreadsheets. In: Proceedings of the 4th ACM SIGMOD Workshop on Algorithms and Systems for MapReduce and Beyond, p. 1. ACM (2017)
20. Sroka, J., Panasiuk, A., Stencel, K., Tyszkiewicz, J.: Translating relational queries into spreadsheets. IEEE Trans. Knowl. Data Eng. **27**(8), 2291–2303 (2015)

Non-Algorithmic Theory of Randomness

Vladimir Vovk$^{(\boxtimes)}$ ⓘ

Department of Computer Science, Royal Holloway, University of London, London, UK
v.vovk@rhul.ac.uk

Abstract. This paper proposes an alternative language for expressing results of the algorithmic theory of randomness. The language is more precise in that it does not involve unspecified additive or multiplicative constants, making mathematical results, in principle, applicable in practice. Our main testing ground for the proposed language is the problem of defining Bernoulli sequences, which was of great interest to Andrei Kolmogorov and his students.

Keywords: Algorithmic randomness · Betting score · E-value · Exchangeability · P-value · Statistical hypothesis testing · Statistical randomness

1 Introduction

Yuri's research interests are extremely diverse, and one of them is the mathematical foundations of statistics (a subject that the vast majority of professional statisticians tend to ignore). The standard approach to testing statistical hypotheses is based on the notion of p-values. Yuri was the driving force behind the paper [6], which pointed out difficulties, and suggested ways of overcoming them, in the standard concept of p-values.

There has been a great deal of criticism of the notion of p-value lately, and in particular, Glenn Shafer [20] defended the use of betting scores instead. This paper refers to betting scores as e-values and demonstrates their advantages by establishing results that become much more precise when they are stated in terms of e-values instead of p-values.

Both p-values and e-values have been used, albeit somewhat implicitly, in the algorithmic theory of randomness: Martin-Löf's tests of algorithmic randomness [16] are an algorithmic version of p-functions (this is Yuri's and my [6] term for functions producing p-values) while Levin's tests of algorithmic randomness [2,13] are an algorithmic version of e-functions (this is the term we will use in this paper for functions producing e-values). Levin's tests are a natural modification of Martin-Löf's tests leading to simpler mathematical results; similarly, many mathematical results stated in terms of p-values become simpler when stated in terms of e-values.

Supported by Astra Zeneca and Stena Line.

A. Blass et al. (Eds.): Gurevich Festschrift, LNCS 12180, pp. 323–340, 2020.
https://doi.org/10.1007/978-3-030-48006-6_21

The algorithmic theory of randomness is a powerful source of intuition, but strictly speaking, its results are not applicable in practice since they always involve unspecified additive or multiplicative constants. The goal of this paper is to explore ways of obtaining results that are more precise; in particular, results that may be applicable in practice. The price to pay is that our results may involve more quantifiers (usually hidden in our notation) and, therefore, their statements may at first appear less intuitive.

In Sect. 2 we define p-functions and e-functions in the context of testing simple statistical hypotheses, explore relations between them, and explain the intuition behind them. In Sect. 3 we generalize these definitions, results, and explanations to testing composite statistical hypotheses.

Section 4 is devoted to testing in Bayesian statistics and gives non-algorithmic results that are particularly clean and intuitive. They will be used as technical tools later in the paper. In Sect. 5 these results are slightly extended and then applied to clarifying the difference between statistical randomness and exchangeability. (In this paper we use "statistical randomness" to refer to being produced by an IID probability measure; there will always be either "algorithmic" or "statistical" standing next to "randomness" in order to distinguish between the two meanings).

Section 7 explores the question of defining Bernoulli sequences, which was of great interest to Kolmogorov [8], Martin-Löf [16], and Kolmogorov's other students. Kolmogorov defined Bernoulli sequences as exchangeable sequences, but we will see that another natural definition is narrower than exchangeability. A precise relation between the two definitions is deduced from a general result in Sect. 6, which can be regarded as another finitary analogue of de Finetti's theorem.

Kolmogorov paid particular attention to algorithmic randomness with respect to uniform probability measures on finite sets. On one hand, he believed that his notion of algorithmic randomness in this context "can be regarded as definitive" [10], and on the other hand, he never seriously suggested any generalizations of this notion (and never endorsed generalizations proposed by his students). In Sect. 7 we state a simple result in this direction that characterizes the difference between Bernoulliness and exchangeability.

In Sects. 4 and 7 we state our results first in terms of e-functions and then p-functions. Results in terms of e-functions are always simpler and cleaner, supporting Glenn Shafer's recommendation in [20] to use betting scores more widely.

Remark 1. There is no standard terminology for what we call e-values and e-functions. In addition to Shafer's use of "betting scores" for our e-values,

- Grünwald et al. [5] refer to e-values as "s-values" ("s" for "safe"; the expression "s-values" has been used [4] in a completely different sense, as the minus binary log of p-values),
- and Gammerman and Vovk [3] refer to the reciprocals of e-values as "i-values" ("i" for "integral"; this term and its variations were used widely in discussions in the Department of Computer Science at Royal Holloway, University of London, around 2000: cf., e.g., "i-test" [18] and "i-randomness" [28]).

Our "e-value" is motivated by expectation playing a role similar to that of probability in "p-value" [21, Section 3.8].

No formal knowledge of the algorithmic theory of randomness will be assumed in this paper; the reader can safely ignore all comparisons between our results and results of the algorithmic theory of randomness.

Notation
Our notation will be mostly standard or defined at the point where it is first used. If $\mathcal{F}$ is a class of $[0, \infty]$-valued functions on some set Ω and $g : [0, \infty] \to [0, \infty]$ is a function, we let $g(\mathcal{F})$ stand for the set of all compositions $g(f) = g \circ f$, $f \in \mathcal{F}$ (i.e, g is applied to $\mathcal{F}$ element-wise). We will also use obvious modifications of this definition: e.g., $0.5\mathcal{F}^{-0.5}$ would be interpreted as $g(\mathcal{F})$, where $g(u) := 0.5u^{-0.5}$ for $u \in [0, \infty]$.

2 Testing Simple Statistical Hypotheses

Let P be a probability measure on a measurable space Ω. A *p-function* [6] is a measurable function $f : \Omega \to [0, \infty]$ such that, for any $\epsilon > 0$, $P\{f \leq \epsilon\} \leq \epsilon$. (Since P is a probability measure, we can assume, without loss of generality, that f takes values in $[0, 1]$.) An *e-function* is a measurable function $f : \Omega \to [0, \infty]$ such that $\int f \, dP \leq 1$. (As already mentioned, e-functions have been promoted in [20] and [5], and also in [22, Section 11.5], using different terminology.)

Let $\mathcal{P}_P$ be the class of all p-functions and $\mathcal{E}_P$ be the class of all e-functions, where the underlying measure P is shown as subscript. We can define p-values and e-values as values taken by p-functions and e-functions, respectively. The intuition behind p-values and e-values will be discussed later in this section.

The following is an algorithm-free version of the standard relation (see, e.g., [15, Lemma 4.3.5] or [23, Theorem 43]) between Martin-Löf's and Levin's algorithmic notions of randomness deficiency.

Proposition 1. *For any probability measure P and $\kappa \in (0, 1)$,*

$$\kappa \mathcal{P}_P^{\kappa-1} \subseteq \mathcal{E}_P \subseteq \mathcal{P}_P^{-1}. \tag{1}$$

Proof. The right inclusion in (1) follows from the Markov inequality: if f is an e-function,

$$P\{f^{-1} \leq \epsilon\} = P\{f \geq 1/\epsilon\} \leq \epsilon. \tag{2}$$

The left inclusion in (1) follows from [22, Section 11.5]. The value of the constant in front of the $\mathcal{P}_P^{\kappa-1}$ on the left-hand side of (1) follows from $\int_0^1 p^{\kappa-1} \, dp = 1/\kappa$. □

Both p-functions and e-functions can be used for testing statistical hypotheses. In this section we only discuss *simple statistical hypotheses*, i.e., probability measures. Observing a large e-value or a small p-value with respect to a simple statistical hypothesis P entitles us to rejecting P as the source of the observed data, provided the e-function or p-function were chosen in advance. The e-value can be interpreted as the amount of evidence against P found by our chosen e-function. Similarly, the p-value reflects the amount of evidence against P on a different scale; small p-values reflect a large amount of evidence against P.

Remark 2. Proposition 1 tells us that using p-values and using e-values are equivalent, on a rather crude scale. Roughly, a p-value of p corresponds to an e-value of $1/p$. The right inclusion in (1) says that any way of producing e-values e can be translated into a way of producing p-values $1/e$. On the other hand, the left inclusion in (1) says that any way of producing p-values p can be translated into a way of producing e-values $\kappa p^{\kappa-1} \approx 1/p$, where the "$\approx$" assumes that we are interested in the asymptotics as $p \to 0$, $\kappa > 0$ is small, and we ignore positive constant factors (as customary in the algorithmic theory of randomness).

Remark 3. Proposition 1 can be greatly strengthened, under the assumptions of Remark 2. For example, we can replace (1) by

$$H_\kappa(\mathcal{P}_P) \subseteq \mathcal{E}_P \subseteq \mathcal{P}_P^{-1},$$

where

$$H_\kappa(v) := \begin{cases} \infty & \text{if } v = 0 \\ \kappa(1+\kappa)^\kappa v^{-1}(-\ln v)^{-1-\kappa} & \text{if } v \in (0, e^{-1-\kappa}] \\ 0 & \text{if } v \in (e^{-1-\kappa}, 1] \end{cases} \qquad (3)$$

and $\kappa \in (0, \infty)$ (see [22, Section 11.1]). The value of the coefficient $\kappa(1+\kappa)^\kappa$ in (3) follows from

$$\int_0^{e^{-1-\kappa}} v^{-1}(-\ln v)^{-1-\kappa}\, dv = \frac{1}{\kappa(1+\kappa)^\kappa}.$$

We can rewrite (1) in Proposition 1 as

$$\kappa^{-1}\mathcal{P}_P^{1-\kappa} \subseteq \mathcal{E}_P^{-1} \subseteq \mathcal{P}_P, \qquad (4)$$

as

$$\mathcal{E}_P^{-1} \subseteq \mathcal{P}_P \subseteq \kappa^{\frac{1}{1-\kappa}} \mathcal{E}_P^{\frac{1}{\kappa-1}}, \qquad (5)$$

and as

$$\mathcal{E}_P \subseteq \mathcal{P}_P^{-1} \subseteq \kappa^{\frac{1}{\kappa-1}} \mathcal{E}_P^{\frac{1}{1-\kappa}}. \qquad (6)$$

3   Testing Composite Statistical Hypotheses

Let Ω be a measurable space, which we will refer to as our *sample space*, and Θ be another measurable space (our *parameter space*). We say that $P = (P_\theta \mid \theta \in \Theta)$ is a *statistical model* on Ω if P is a Markov kernel with source Θ and target Ω: each P_θ is a probability measure on Ω, and for each measurable $A \subseteq \Omega$, the function $P_\theta(A)$ of $\theta \in \Theta$ is measurable.

The notions of an e-function and a p-function each split in two. We are usually really interested only in the outcome ω, while the parameter θ is an auxiliary modelling tool. This motivates the following pair of simpler definitions. A measurable function $f : \Omega \to [0, \infty]$ is an *e-function* with respect to the statistical model P (which is our *composite statistical hypothesis* in this context) if

$$\forall \theta \in \Theta : \int_\Omega f(\omega) P_\theta(\mathrm{d}\omega) \leq 1.$$

In other words, if $P^*(f) \leq 1$, where P^* is the upper envelope

$$P^*(f) := \sup_{\theta \in \Theta} \int f(\omega) P_\theta(\mathrm{d}\omega) \tag{7}$$

(in Bourbaki's [1, IX.1.1] terminology, P^* is an encumbrance provided the integral in (7) is understood as the upper integral). Similarly, a measurable function $f : \Omega \to [0, 1]$ is a *p-function* with respect to the statistical model P if, for any $\epsilon > 0$,

$$\forall \theta \in \Theta : P_\theta\{\omega \in \Omega \mid f(\omega) \leq \epsilon\} \leq \epsilon.$$

In other words, if, for any $\epsilon > 0$, $P^*(1_{\{f \leq \epsilon\}}) \leq \epsilon$.

Let $\mathcal{E}_P$ be the class of all e-functions with respect to the statistical model P, and $\mathcal{P}_P$ be the class of all p-functions with respect to P. We can easily generalize Proposition 1 (the proof stays the same).

Proposition 2. *For any statistical model P and $\kappa \in (0, 1)$,*

$$\kappa \mathcal{P}_P^{\kappa - 1} \subseteq \mathcal{E}_P \subseteq \mathcal{P}_P^{-1}.$$

For $f \in \mathcal{E}_P$, we regard the e-value $f(\omega)$ as the amount of evidence against the statistical model P found by f (which must be chosen in advance) when the outcome is ω. The interpretation of p-values is similar.

In some case we would like to take the parameter θ into account more seriously. A measurable function $f : \Omega \times \Theta \to [0, \infty]$ is a *conditional e-function* with respect to the statistical model P if

$$\forall \theta \in \Theta : \int_\Omega f(\omega; \theta) P_\theta(\mathrm{d}\omega) \leq 1.$$

Let $\bar{\mathcal{E}}_P$ be the class of all such functions. And a measurable function $f : \Omega \times \Theta \to [0, 1]$ is a *conditional p-function* with respect to P if

$$\forall \epsilon > 0 \, \forall \theta \in \Theta : P_\theta \{\omega \in \Omega \mid f(\omega; \theta) \leq \epsilon\} \leq \epsilon.$$

Let $\bar{\mathcal{P}}_P$ be the class of all such functions.

We can embed $\mathcal{E}_P$ (resp. $\mathcal{P}_P$) into $\bar{\mathcal{E}}_P$ (resp. $\bar{\mathcal{P}}_P$) by identifying a function f on domain Ω with the function f' on domain $\Omega \times \Theta$ that does not depend on $\theta \in \Theta$, $f'(\omega; \theta) := f(\omega)$.

For $f \in \bar{\mathcal{E}}_P$, we can regard $f(\omega; \theta)$ as the amount of evidence against the specific probability measure P_θ in the statistical model P found by f when the outcome is ω.

We can generalize Proposition 2 further as follows.

Proposition 3. *For any statistical model* P *and* $\kappa \in (0, 1)$,

$$\kappa \bar{\mathcal{P}}_P^{\kappa-1} \subseteq \bar{\mathcal{E}}_P \subseteq \bar{\mathcal{P}}_P^{-1}. \tag{8}$$

Remarks 2 and 3 are also applicable in the context of Propositions 2 and 3.

4   The Validity of Bayesian Statistics

In this section we establish the validity of Bayesian statistics in our framework, mainly as a sanity check. We will translate the results in [31], which are stated in terms of the algorithmic theory of randomness, to our algorithm-free setting. It is interesting that the proofs simplify radically, and become almost obvious. (And remarkably, one statement also simplifies).

Let $P = (P_\theta \mid \theta \in \Theta)$ be a statistical model, as in the previous section, and Q be a probability measure on the parameter space Θ. Together, P and Q form a *Bayesian model*, and Q is known as the *prior measure* in this context.

The joint probability measure T on the measurable space $\Omega \times \Theta$ is defined by

$$T(A \times B) := \int_B P_\theta(A) Q(\mathrm{d}\theta),$$

for all measurable $A \subseteq \Omega$ and $B \subseteq \Theta$. Let Y be the marginal distribution of T on Ω: for any measurable $A \subseteq \Omega$, $Y(A) := T(A \times \Theta)$.

The *product* $\bar{\mathcal{E}}_P \mathcal{E}_Q$ of $\bar{\mathcal{E}}_P$ and $\mathcal{E}_Q$ is defined as the class of all measurable functions $f : \Omega \times \Theta \to [0, \infty]$ such that, for some $g \in \bar{\mathcal{E}}_P$ and $h \in \mathcal{E}_Q$,

$$f(\omega, \theta) = g(\omega; \theta) h(\theta) \quad T\text{-a.s.} \tag{9}$$

Such f can be regarded as ways of finding evidence against (ω, θ) being produced by the Bayesian model (P, Q): to have evidence against (ω, θ) being produced by (P, Q) we need to have evidence against θ being produced by the prior measure Q or evidence against ω being produced by P_θ; we combine the last two amounts of evidence by multiplying them. The following proposition tells us that this product is precisely the amount of evidence against T found by a suitable e-function.

Proposition 4. *If* $(P_\theta \mid \theta \in \Theta)$ *is a statistical model with a prior probability measure* Q *on* Θ, *and* T *is the joint probability measure on* $\Omega \times \Theta$, *then*

$$\mathcal{E}_T = \bar{\mathcal{E}}_P \mathcal{E}_Q. \tag{10}$$

Proposition 4 will be deduced from Theorem 1 in Sect. 5. It is the analogue of Theorem 1 in [31], which says, in the terminology of that paper, that the level of impossibility of a pair (θ, ω) with respect to the joint probability measure T is the product of the level of impossibility of θ with respect to the prior measure Q and the level of impossibility of ω with respect to the probability measure P_θ. In an important respect, however, Proposition 4 is simpler than Theorem 1 in

[31]: in the latter, the level of impossibility of ω with respect to P_θ has to be conditional on the level of impossibility of θ with respect to Q, whereas in the former there is no such conditioning. Besides, Proposition 4 is more precise: it does not involve any constant factors (specified or otherwise).

Remark 4. The non-algorithmic formula (10) being simpler than its counterpart in the algorithmic theory of randomness is analogous to the non-algorithmic formula $H(x,y) = H(x) + H(y \mid x)$ being simpler than its counterpart $K(x,y) = K(x) + K(y \mid x, K(x))$ in the algorithmic theory of complexity, H being entropy and K being prefix complexity. The fact that $K(x,y)$ does not coincide with $K(x) + K(y \mid x)$ to within an additive constant, K being Kolmogorov complexity, was surprising to Kolmogorov and wasn't noticed for several years [7,8].

The *inf-projection* onto Ω of an e-function $f \in \mathcal{E}_T$ with respect to T is the function $(\mathrm{proj}_\Omega^{\mathrm{inf}} f) : \Omega \to [0, \infty]$ defined by

$$\left(\mathrm{proj}_\Omega^{\mathrm{inf}} f\right)(\omega) := \inf_{\theta \in \Theta} f(\omega, \theta).$$

Intuitively, $\mathrm{proj}_\Omega^{\mathrm{inf}} f$ regards ω as typical under the model if it can be extended to a typical (ω, θ) for at least one θ. Let $\mathrm{proj}_\Omega^{\mathrm{inf}} \mathcal{E}_T$ be the set of all such inf-projections.

The results in the rest of this section become simpler if the definitions of classes $\mathcal{E}$ and $\mathcal{P}$ are modified slightly: we drop the condition of measurability on their elements and replace all integrals by upper integrals and all measures by outer measures. We will use the modified definitions only in the rest of this section (we could have used them in the whole of this paper, but they become particularly useful here since projections of measurable functions do not have to be measurable [24]).

Proposition 5. *If T is a probability measure on $\Omega \times \Theta$ and Y is its marginal distribution on Ω,*

$$\mathcal{E}_Y = \mathrm{proj}_\Omega^{\mathrm{inf}} \mathcal{E}_T. \tag{11}$$

Proof. To check the inclusion "$\subseteq$" in (11), let $g \in \mathcal{E}_Y$, i.e., $\int g(\omega) Y(\mathrm{d}\omega) \leq 1$. Setting $f(\omega, \theta) := g(\omega)$, we have $\int f(\omega, \theta) T(\mathrm{d}\omega, \mathrm{d}\theta) \leq 1$ (i.e., $f \in \mathcal{E}_T$) and g is the inf-projection of f onto Ω.

To check the inclusion "$\supseteq$" in (11), let $f \in \mathcal{E}_T$ and $g := \mathrm{proj}_\Omega^{\mathrm{inf}} f$. We then have

$$\int g(\omega) Y(\mathrm{d}\omega) = \int g(\omega) T(\mathrm{d}\omega, \mathrm{d}\theta) \leq \int f(\omega, \theta) T(\mathrm{d}\omega, \mathrm{d}\theta) \leq 1. \qquad \square$$

Proposition 5 says that we can acquire evidence against an outcome ω being produced by the Bayesian model (P, Q) if and only if we can acquire evidence against (ω, θ) being produced by the model for all $\theta \in \Theta$.

We can combine Propositions 4 and 5 obtaining

$$\mathcal{E}_Y = \mathrm{proj}_\Omega^{\mathrm{inf}} \left(\bar{\mathcal{E}}_P \mathcal{E}_Q\right).$$

The rough interpretation is that we can acquire evidence against ω being produced by Y if and only if we can, for each $\theta \in \Theta$, acquire evidence against θ being produced by Q or acquire evidence against ω being produced by P_θ.

The following statements in terms of p-values are cruder, but their interpretation is similar.

Corollary 1. *If $\kappa \in (0,1)$ and (P,Q) is a Bayesian model,*

$$\kappa^{-1} \mathcal{P}_T^{1-\kappa} \subseteq \bar{\mathcal{P}}_P \mathcal{P}_Q \subseteq \kappa^{\frac{2}{1-\kappa}} \mathcal{P}_T^{\frac{1}{1-\kappa}}.$$

Proof. We will use the restatements (4) and (5) of Proposition 1 and similar restatements of Propositions 3 and 2. Therefore, by (10) in Proposition 4,

$$\kappa^{-1} \mathcal{P}_T^{1-\kappa} \subseteq \mathcal{E}_T^{-1} = (\bar{\mathcal{E}}_P \mathcal{E}_Q)^{-1} = \bar{\mathcal{E}}_P^{-1} \mathcal{E}_Q^{-1} \subseteq \bar{\mathcal{P}}_P \mathcal{P}_Q$$

and

$$\bar{\mathcal{P}}_P \mathcal{P}_Q \subseteq \kappa^{\frac{2}{1-\kappa}} (\bar{\mathcal{E}}_P \mathcal{E}_Q)^{\frac{1}{\kappa-1}} = \kappa^{\frac{2}{1-\kappa}} \mathcal{E}_T^{\frac{1}{\kappa-1}} \subseteq \kappa^{\frac{2}{1-\kappa}} \mathcal{P}_T^{\frac{1}{1-\kappa}}. \qquad \square$$

Corollary 2. *If $\kappa \in (0,1)$, T is a probability measure on $\Omega \times \Theta$, and Y is its marginal distribution on Ω,*

$$\kappa^{-1} \operatorname{proj}_\Omega^{\sup} \mathcal{P}_T^{1-\kappa} \subseteq \mathcal{P}_Y \subseteq \kappa^{\frac{1}{1-\kappa}} \operatorname{proj}_\Omega^{\sup} \mathcal{P}_T^{\frac{1}{1-\kappa}},$$

where $\operatorname{proj}_\Omega^{\sup}$ is defined similarly to $\operatorname{proj}_\Omega^{\inf}$ (with sup in place of inf).

Proof. As in the proof of Corollary 1, we have

$$\kappa^{-1} \operatorname{proj}_\Omega^{\sup} \mathcal{P}_T^{1-\kappa} \subseteq \operatorname{proj}_\Omega^{\sup} \mathcal{E}_T^{-1} = \mathcal{E}_Y^{-1} \subseteq \mathcal{P}_Y$$

and

$$\mathcal{P}_Y \subseteq \kappa^{\frac{1}{1-\kappa}} \mathcal{E}_Y^{\frac{1}{\kappa-1}} = \kappa^{\frac{1}{1-\kappa}} \operatorname{proj}_\Omega^{\sup} \mathcal{E}_T^{\frac{1}{\kappa-1}} \subseteq \kappa^{\frac{1}{1-\kappa}} \operatorname{proj}_\Omega^{\sup} \mathcal{P}_T^{\frac{1}{1-\kappa}}. \qquad \square$$

5   Parametric Bayesian Models

Now we generalize the notion of a Bayesian model to that of a parametric Bayesian (or *para-Bayesian*) model. This is a pair consisting of a statistical model $(P_\theta \mid \theta \in \Theta)$ on a sample space Ω and a statistical model $(Q_\pi \mid \pi \in \Pi)$ on the sample space Θ (so that the sample space of the second statistical model is the parameter space of the first statistical model). Intuitively, a para-Bayesian model is the counterpart of a Bayesian model in the situation of uncertainty about the prior: now the prior is a parametric family of probability measures rather than one probability measure.

The following definitions are straightforward generalizations of the definitions for the Bayesian case. The joint statistical model $T = (T_\pi \mid \pi \in \Pi)$ on the measurable space $\Omega \times \Theta$ is defined by

$$T_\pi(A \times B) := \int_B P_\theta(A) Q_\pi(\mathrm{d}\theta), \tag{12}$$

for all measurable $A \subseteq \Omega$ and $B \subseteq \Theta$. For each $\pi \in \Pi$, Y_π is the marginal distribution of T_π on Ω: for any measurable $A \subseteq \Omega$, $Y_\pi(A) := T_\pi(A \times \Theta)$. The product $\bar{\mathcal{E}}_P \mathcal{E}_Q$ of $\bar{\mathcal{E}}_P$ and $\mathcal{E}_Q$ is still defined as the class of all measurable functions $f : \Omega \times \Theta \to [0, \infty]$ such that, for some $g \in \bar{\mathcal{E}}_P$ and $h \in \mathcal{E}_Q$, we have the equality in (9) T_π-a.s., for all $\pi \in \Pi$.

Remark 5. Another representation of para-Bayesian models is as a sufficient statistic, as elaborated in [12]:

- For the para-Bayesian model (P, Q), the statistic $(\theta, \omega) \in (\Theta \times \Omega) \mapsto \theta$ is a sufficient statistic in the statistical model (T_π) on the product space $\Theta \times \Omega$.
- If θ is a sufficient statistic for a statistical model (T_π) on a sample space Ω, then (P, Q) is a para-Bayesian model, where Q is the distribution of θ, and P_θ are (fixed versions of) the conditional distributions given θ.

Remark 6. Yet another way to represent a para-Bayesian model (P, Q) is a Markov family with time horizon 3:

- the initial state space is Π, the middle one is Θ, and the final one is Ω;
- there is no initial probability measure on Π, the statistical model (Q_π) is the first Markov kernel, and the statistical model (P_θ) is the second Markov kernel.

Theorem 1. *If (P, Q) is a para-Bayesian model with the joint statistical model T (as defined by (12)), we have (10).*

Proof. The inclusion "$\supseteq$" in (10) follows from the definition of T: if $g \in \bar{\mathcal{E}}_P$ and $h \in \mathcal{E}_Q$, we have, for all $\pi \in \Pi$,

$$\int_{\Omega \times \Theta} g(\omega; \theta) h(\theta) T_\pi(\mathrm{d}\omega, \mathrm{d}\theta) = \int_\Theta \int_\Omega g(\omega; \theta) P_\theta(\mathrm{d}\omega) h(\theta) Q_\pi(\mathrm{d}\theta)$$

$$\leq \int_\Theta h(\theta) Q_\pi(\mathrm{d}\theta) \leq 1.$$

To check the inclusion "$\subseteq$" in (10), let $f \in \mathcal{E}_T$. Define $h : \Theta \to [0, \infty]$ and $g : \Omega \times \Theta \to [0, \infty]$ by

$$h(\theta) := \int f(\omega, \theta) P_\theta(\mathrm{d}\omega)$$

$$g(\omega; \theta) := f(\omega, \theta) / h(\theta)$$

(setting, e.g., $0/0 := 0$ in the last fraction). Since by definition, $f(\omega, \theta) = g(\omega; \theta)h(\theta)$ T_π-a.s., it suffices to check that $h \in \mathcal{E}_Q$ and $g \in \bar{\mathcal{E}}_P$. The inclusion $h \in \mathcal{E}_Q$ follows from the fact that, for any $\pi \in \Pi$,

$$\int_\Theta h(\theta)Q_\pi(d\theta) = \int_\Theta \int_\Omega f(\omega, \theta)P_\theta(d\omega)Q_\pi(d\theta) = \int_{\Omega \times \Theta} f(\omega, \theta)T_\pi(d\omega, d\theta) \leq 1.$$

And the inclusion $g \in \bar{\mathcal{E}}_P$ follows from the fact that, for any $\theta \in \Theta$,

$$\int g(\omega; \theta)P_\theta(d\omega) = \int \frac{f(\omega, \theta)}{h(\theta)}P_\theta(d\omega) = \frac{\int f(\omega, \theta)P_\theta(d\omega)}{h(\theta)} = \frac{h(\theta)}{h(\theta)} \leq 1$$

(we have ≤ 1 rather than $= 1$ because of the possibility $h(\theta) = 0$).   □

6   IID vs Exchangeability: General Case

De Finetti's theorem (see, e.g., [19, Theorem 1.49]) establishes a close connection between IID and exchangeability for infinite sequences in $\mathbf{Z}^\infty$, where $\mathbf{Z}$ is a Borel measurable space: namely, the exchangeable probability measures are the convex mixtures of the IID probability measures (in particular, their upper envelopes, and therefore, e- and p-functions, coincide). This section discusses a somewhat less close connection in the case of sequences of a fixed finite length.

Fix $N \in \{1, 2, \dots\}$ (time horizon), and let $\Omega := \mathbf{Z}^N$ be the set of all sequences of elements of $\mathbf{Z}$ (a measurable space, not necessarily Borel) of length N. An *IID probability measure* on Ω is a measure of the type Q^N, where Q is a probability measure on $\mathbf{Z}$. The *configuration* $\mathrm{conf}(\omega)$ of a sequence $\omega \in \Omega$ is the multiset of all elements of ω, and a *configuration measure* is the pushforward of an IID probability measure on Ω under the mapping conf. Therefore, a configuration measure is a measure on the set of all multisets in $\mathbf{Z}$ of size N (with the natural quotient σ-algebra).

Let $\mathcal{E}_{\mathrm{iid}}$ be the class of all e-functions with respect to the family of all IID probability measures on Ω and $\mathcal{E}_{\mathrm{conf}}$ be the class of all e-functions with respect to the family of all configuration probability measures. Let $\mathcal{E}_{\mathrm{exch}}$ be the class of all e-functions with respect to the family of all exchangeable probability measures on Ω; remember that a probability measure P on Ω is *exchangeable* if, for any permutation $\pi : \{1, \dots, N\} \to \{1, \dots, N\}$ and any measurable set $E \subseteq \mathbf{Z}^N$,

$$P\{(z_1, \dots, z_N) \mid (z_{\pi(1)}, \dots, z_{\pi(N)}) \in E\} = P(E).$$

The *product* $\mathcal{E}_{\mathrm{exch}}\mathcal{E}_{\mathrm{conf}}$ of $\mathcal{E}_{\mathrm{exch}}$ and $\mathcal{E}_{\mathrm{conf}}$ is the set of all measurable functions $f : \Omega \to [0, \infty]$ such that, for some $g \in \mathcal{E}_{\mathrm{exch}}$ and $h \in \mathcal{E}_{\mathrm{conf}}$,

$$f(\omega) = g(\omega)h(\mathrm{conf}(\omega))$$

holds for almost all $\omega \in \Omega$ (under any IID probability measure).

Corollary 3. *It is true that*

$$\mathcal{E}_{\mathrm{iid}} = \mathcal{E}_{\mathrm{exch}}\mathcal{E}_{\mathrm{conf}}. \tag{13}$$

Proof. It suffices to apply Theorem 1 in the situation where Θ is the set of all configurations, P_θ is the probability measure on $\mathbf{Z}^N$ concentrated on the set of all sequences with the configuration θ and uniform on that set (we can order θ arbitrarily, and then P_θ assigns weight $1/N!$ to each permutation of that ordering), Π is the set of all IID probability measures on Ω, and Q_π is the pushforward of $\pi \in \Pi$ with respect to the mapping conf. $\qquad\square$

Corollary 3 is the non-algorithmic analogue of Theorem 3 of [29], given without a proof.

The next theorem gives the ranges of $\mathcal{E}_{\mathrm{iid}}$, $\mathcal{E}_{\mathrm{exch}}$, and $\mathcal{E}_{\mathrm{conf}}$. For any set of functions $\mathcal{F}$ we set

$$\sup \mathcal{F} := \sup_{f \in \mathcal{F}} \sup f;$$

i.e., $\sup \mathcal{F}$ is the supremum of the values attained by the functions in $\mathcal{F}$. Remember that the length N of the sequences considered in this section is fixed.

Theorem 2. *Suppose* $|\mathbf{Z}| \geq N$. *Then*

$$\sup \mathcal{E}_{\mathrm{iid}} = N^N, \tag{14}$$

$$\sup \mathcal{E}_{\mathrm{exch}} = N! \sim (2\pi N)^{1/2} (N/e)^N, \tag{15}$$

$$\sup \mathcal{E}_{\mathrm{conf}} = N^N/N! \sim (2\pi N)^{-1/2} e^N, \tag{16}$$

where the two "$\sim$" refer to the asymptotics as $N \to \infty$.

Theorem 2 shows that (13) remain true when we put sup in from of each of the three function classes. The counterpart of (16) in the algorithmic theory of randomness is Theorem 4 in [29].

A crude interpretation of Corollary 3 and Theorem 2 is that the condition of being an IID sequence can be split into two components: exchangeability and having an iid configuration; the first component is more important.

Proof (Proof of Theorem 2). For any $\omega \in \Omega$, $\sup_{f \in \mathcal{E}_{\mathrm{iid}}} f(\omega)$ is attained at f that takes a non-zero value only at ω. Therefore,

$$\sup \mathcal{E}_{\mathrm{iid}} = \sup_{\omega \in \Omega} \frac{1}{\sup_P P(\{\omega\})},$$

P ranging over the IID probability measures. The supremum will not change if P ranges over the probability measures on $\mathbf{Z}$ concentrated on the elements of the sequence ω, which we will assume. Consider an ω consisting of n distinct elements of $\mathbf{Z}$. Order these distinct elements, and let m_i, $i = 1, \ldots, n$, be the number of times the ith of these elements occurs in ω. Using the maximum likelihood estimate for the multinomial model, we can see that

$$\frac{1}{\sup_P P(\{\omega\})} = (N/m_1)^{m_1} \ldots (N/m_n)^{m_n} = \frac{N^N}{m_1^{m_1} \ldots m_n^{m_n}}.$$

The supremum of the last expression is attained when $n = N$ and $m_1 = \cdots = m_n = 1$, and it is equal to N^N. This completes the proof of (14).

A similar argument also works for (16). We have

$$\sup \mathcal{E}_{\text{conf}} = \sup_{m_1,\ldots,m_n} \frac{(N/m_1)^{m_1} \ldots (N/m_n)^{m_n}}{\binom{N}{m_1,\ldots,m_n}} = \frac{N^N/N!}{(m_1^{m_1}/m_1!)\ldots(m_n^{m_n}/m_n!)}.$$

$$(17)$$

Since $(m^m)/m! \geq 1$ for all $m \in \{1,2,\ldots\}$ and $(m^m)/m! > 1$ for all $m \in \{2,3,\ldots\}$, the second supremum in (17) is also attained when $n = N$ and $m_1 = \cdots = m_n = 1$, which completes the proof of (16).

As for (15), it suffices to notice that

$$\sup_{m_1,\ldots,m_n} \binom{N}{m_1,\ldots,m_n} = \sup_{m_1,\ldots,m_n} \frac{N!}{m_1!\ldots m_n!}$$

is attained at $n = N$ and $m_1 = \cdots = m_n = 1$.

The asymptotic equivalences in (15) and (16) follow from Stirling's formula. □

Since the suprema in Theorem 2 are attained at functions that zero everywhere except one point, we have the following corollary.

Corollary 4. *If* $|\mathbf{Z}| \geq N$,

$$\inf \mathcal{P}_{\text{iid}} = N^{-N},$$

$$\inf \mathcal{P}_{\text{exch}} = 1/N! \sim (2\pi N)^{-1/2}(e/N)^N,$$

$$\inf \mathcal{P}_{\text{conf}} = N!/N^N \sim (2\pi N)^{1/2}e^{-N}.$$

7   IID vs Exchangeability: Bernoulli Sequences

In this section we apply the definitions and results of the previous sections to the problem of defining Bernoulli sequences. Kolmogorov's main publications on this topic are [8] and [9]. The results of this section will be algorithm-free versions of the results in [25] (also described in V'yugin's review [32], Sections 11–13).

The definitions of the previous section simplify as follows. Now $\Omega := \{0,1\}^N$ is the set of all binary sequences of length N. Let $\mathcal{E}_{\text{Bern}}$ be the class of all e-functions with respect to the family of all Bernoulli IID probability measures on Ω (this is a special case of $\mathcal{E}_{\text{iid}}$) and $\mathcal{E}_{\text{bin}}$ be the class of all e-functions with respect to the family of all binomial probability measures on $\{0,\ldots,N\}$ (this is a special case of $\mathcal{E}_{\text{conf}}$); remember that the Bernoulli measure B_p with parameter $p \in [0,1]$ is defined by $B_p(\{\omega\}) := p^k(1-p)^{N-k}$, where $k := +\omega$ is the number of 1s in ω, and the binomial measure bin_p with parameter $p \in [0,1]$ is defined by $\text{bin}_p(\{k\}) := \binom{N}{k}p^k(1-p)^{N-k}$. (The notation $+\omega$ for the number k of 1s in ω is motivated by k being the sum of the elements of ω.)

We continue to use the notation $\mathcal{E}_{\text{exch}}$ for the class of all e-functions with respect to the family of all exchangeable probability measures on Ω; a probability measure P on Ω is exchangeable if and only if $P(\{\omega\})$ depends on ω only via

$+\omega$. It is clear that a function $f : \Omega \to [0, \infty]$ is in $\mathcal{E}_{\mathrm{exch}}$ if and only if, for each $k \in \{0, \dots, N\}$,

$$\binom{N}{k}^{-1} \sum_{\omega \in \Omega : +\omega = k} f(\omega) \leq 1.$$

The product $\mathcal{E}_{\mathrm{exch}}\mathcal{E}_{\mathrm{bin}}$ of $\mathcal{E}_{\mathrm{exch}}$ and $\mathcal{E}_{\mathrm{bin}}$ is the set of all functions $\omega \in \Omega \mapsto g(\omega)h(+\omega)$ for $g \in \mathcal{E}_{\mathrm{exch}}$ and $h \in \mathcal{E}_{\mathrm{bin}}$. The following is a special case of Corollary 3.

Corollary 5. *It is true that*

$$\mathcal{E}_{\mathrm{Bern}} = \mathcal{E}_{\mathrm{exch}}\mathcal{E}_{\mathrm{bin}}.$$

The intuition behind Corollary 5 is that a sequence $\omega \in \Omega$ is Bernoulli if and only if it is exchangeable and the number of 1s in it is binomial. The analogue of Corollary 5 in the algorithmic theory of randomness is Theorem 1 in [25], which says, using the terminology of that paper, that the Bernoulliness deficiency of ω equals the binomiality deficiency of $+\omega$ plus the conditional randomness deficiency of ω in the set of all sequences in $\{0, 1\}^N$ with $+\omega$ 1s given the binomiality deficiency of $+\omega$. Corollary 5 is simpler since it does not involve any analogue of the condition "given the binomiality deficiency of $+\omega$".

Remark 7. Kolmogorov's definition of Bernoulli sequences is via exchangeability. We can regard this definition as an approximation to definitions taking into account the binomiality of the number of 1s. In the paper [8] Kolmogorov uses the word "approximately" when introducing his notion of Bernoulliness (p. 663, lines 5–6 after the 4th displayed equation). However, it would be wrong to assume that here he acknowledges disregarding the requirement that the number of 1s should be binomial; this is not what he meant when he used the word "approximately" [11].

The reason for Kolmogorov's definition of Bernoulliness being different from the definitions based on e-values and p-values is that $+\omega$ carries too much information about ω; intuitively [26], $+\omega$ contains not only useful information about the probability p of 1 but also noise. To reduce the amount of noise, we will use an imperfect estimator of p. Set

$$p(a) := \sin^2\left(aN^{-1/2}\right), \quad a = 1, \dots, N^* - 1, \quad N^* := \left\lfloor \frac{\pi}{2} N^{1/2} \right\rfloor, \tag{18}$$

where $\lfloor \cdot \rfloor$ stands for integer part. Let $E : \{0, \dots, N\} \to [0, 1]$ be the estimator of p defined by $E(k) := p(a)$, where $p(a)$ is the element of the set (18) that is nearest to k/N among those satisfying $p(a) \leq k/N$; if such elements do not exist, set $E(k) := p(1)$.

Denote by $\mathfrak{A}$ the partition of the set $\{0, \dots, N\}$ into the subsets $E^{-1}(E(k))$, where $k \in \{0, \dots, N\}$. For any $k \in \{0, \dots, N\}$, $\mathfrak{A}(k) := E^{-1}(E(k))$ denotes the element of the partition $\mathfrak{A}$ containing k. Let $\mathcal{E}_{\mathrm{sin}}$ be the class of all e-functions with respect to the statistical model $\{U_k \mid k \in \{0, \dots, N\}\}$, U_k being the uniform probability measure on $\mathfrak{A}(k)$. (This is a Kolmogorov-type statistical model, consisting of uniform probability measures on finite sets; see, e.g., [30, Section 4].)

Theorem 3. *For some universal constant* $c > 0$,

$$c^{-1}\mathcal{E}_{\mathrm{sin}} \subseteq \mathcal{E}_{\mathrm{bin}} \subseteq c\mathcal{E}_{\mathrm{sin}}.$$

The analogue of Theorem 3 in the algorithmic theory of randomness is Theorem 2 in [25], and the proof of Theorem 3 can be extracted from that of Theorem 2 in [25] (details omitted).

Remark 8. Paper [25] uses a net slightly different from (18); (18) was introduced in [26] and also used in [32].

To state corollaries in terms of p-values of Corollary 5 and Theorem 3, we will use the obvious notation $\mathcal{P}_{\mathrm{Bern}}$, $\mathcal{P}_{\mathrm{exch}}$, and $\mathcal{P}_{\mathrm{bin}}$.

Corollary 6. *For each* $\kappa \in (0, 1)$,

$$\kappa^{-1}\mathcal{P}_{\mathrm{Bern}}^{1-\kappa} \subseteq \mathcal{P}_{\mathrm{exch}}\mathcal{P}_{\mathrm{bin}} \subseteq \kappa^{\frac{2}{1-\kappa}}\mathcal{P}_{\mathrm{Bern}}^{\frac{1}{1-\kappa}}. \qquad (19)$$

Proof. Similarly to Corollary 1, the left inclusion of (19) follows from

$$\kappa^{-1}\mathcal{P}_{\mathrm{Bern}}^{1-\kappa} \subseteq \mathcal{E}_{\mathrm{Bern}}^{-1} = \mathcal{E}_{\mathrm{exch}}^{-1}\mathcal{E}_{\mathrm{bin}}^{-1} \subseteq \mathcal{P}_{\mathrm{exch}}\mathcal{P}_{\mathrm{bin}},$$

and the right inclusion of (19) follows from

$$\mathcal{P}_{\mathrm{exch}}\mathcal{P}_{\mathrm{bin}} \subseteq \kappa^{\frac{2}{1-\kappa}}\left(\mathcal{E}_{\mathrm{exch}}\mathcal{E}_{\mathrm{bin}}\right)^{\frac{1}{\kappa-1}} = \kappa^{\frac{2}{1-\kappa}}\mathcal{E}_{\mathrm{Bern}}^{\frac{1}{\kappa-1}} \subseteq \kappa^{\frac{2}{1-\kappa}}\mathcal{P}_{\mathrm{Bern}}^{\frac{1}{1-\kappa}}.$$

$\square$

Corollary 7. *There is a universal constant* $c > 0$ *such that, for each* $\kappa \in (0, 0.9)$,

$$c\kappa^{-1}\mathcal{P}_{\mathrm{sin}}^{1-\kappa} \subseteq \mathcal{P}_{\mathrm{bin}} \subseteq c^{-1}\kappa^{\frac{1}{1-\kappa}}\mathcal{P}_{\mathrm{sin}}^{\frac{1}{1-\kappa}}. \qquad (20)$$

Proof. As in the previous proof, the left inclusion of (20) follows from

$$\kappa^{-1}\mathcal{P}_{\mathrm{sin}}^{1-\kappa} \subseteq \mathcal{E}_{\mathrm{sin}}^{-1} \subseteq c^{-1}\mathcal{E}_{\mathrm{bin}}^{-1} \subseteq c^{-1}\mathcal{P}_{\mathrm{bin}},$$

and the right inclusion from

$$\mathcal{P}_{\mathrm{bin}} \subseteq \kappa^{\frac{1}{1-\kappa}}\mathcal{E}_{\mathrm{bin}}^{\frac{1}{\kappa-1}} \subseteq c^{-1}\kappa^{\frac{1}{1-\kappa}}\mathcal{E}_{\mathrm{sin}}^{\frac{1}{\kappa-1}} \subseteq c^{-1}\kappa^{\frac{1}{1-\kappa}}\mathcal{P}_{\mathrm{sin}}^{\frac{1}{1-\kappa}},$$

where c stands for a positive universal constant. $\square$

In conclusion of this section, let us state the binary version of Theorem 2 and its corollary.

Theorem 4. *Suppose* $N \in \{2, 4, \dots\}$ *is an even number. Then*

$$\sup \mathcal{E}_{\mathrm{Bern}} = 2^N, \qquad (21)$$

$$\sup \mathcal{E}_{\mathrm{exch}} = \binom{N}{N/2} \sim (\pi N/2)^{-1/2} 2^N, \qquad (22)$$

$$\sup \mathcal{E}_{\mathrm{bin}} = 2^N / \binom{N}{N/2} \sim (\pi N/2)^{1/2}, \qquad (23)$$

where the two "$\sim$" again refer to the asymptotics as $N \to \infty$.

Proof. The argument is similar to that in the proof of Theorem 2. The supremum in (21) is attained at the function that takes value 2^N at the sequence $0 \ldots 01 \ldots 1$ ($N/2$ 0s followed by $N/2$ 1s) and is zero everywhere else. Replacing 2^N by $\binom{N}{N/2}$, we obtain a function attaining the supremum in (22). The supremum in (23) is attained at the function on $\{0, \ldots, N\}$ that takes value $2^N / \binom{N}{N/2}$ at $N/2$ and is zero everywhere else. Finally, the asymptotic equivalences follow from Stirling's formula. $\qquad\square$

We can see that $\sup \mathcal{E}_{\text{bin}}$ (given by (23)) is much smaller than $\sup \mathcal{E}_{\text{Bern}}$ and $\sup \mathcal{E}_{\text{exch}}$ (given by (21) and (22), respectively). This might be interpreted as exchangeability being the main component of Bernoulliness.

Corollary 8. *If N is an even number,*

$$\inf \mathcal{P}_{\text{Bern}} = 2^{-N},$$

$$\inf \mathcal{P}_{\text{exch}} = 1 / \binom{N}{N/2} \sim (\pi N/2)^{1/2} 2^{-N},$$

$$\inf \mathcal{P}_{\text{bin}} = \binom{N}{N/2} 2^{-N} \sim (\pi N/2)^{-1/2}.$$

8   Conclusion

In this section we discuss some directions of further research. A major advantage of the non-algorithmic approach to randomness proposed in this paper is the absence of unspecified constants; in principle, all constants can be computed. The most obvious open problem is to find the best constant c in Theorem 3.

In Sect. 7 we discussed a possible implementation of Kolmogorov's idea of defining Bernoulli sequences. However, Kolmogorov's idea was part of a wider programme; e.g., in [9, Section 5] he sketches a way of applying a similar approach to Markov sequences. For other possible applications, see [30, Section 4] (most of these applications were mentioned by Kolmogorov in his papers and talks). Analogues of Corollary 5 in Sect. 7 can be established for these other applications (cf. [12] and Remark 5), but it is not obvious whether Theorem 3 can be extended in a similar way.

Acknowledgments. Thanks to Wouter Koolen, Vladimir V'yugin, Alex Gammerman, and Ilia Nouretdinov for useful discussions.

Appendix: Non-algorithmic Theory of Complexity

The definitions of p-functions and e-functions given at the beginning of Sect. 2 can be applied, without changing a word, to any measure P on Ω, without the restriction $P(\Omega) = 1$. It is interesting that, for some P, such generalizations also have useful applications. In particular, the following generalization of Proposition 1 includes an algorithm-free version of standard relations (see, e.g., [14, Theorem 4]) between plain and prefix Kolmogorov complexities.

Proposition 6. *Let $h : [0, \infty] \to [0, \infty]$ be a continuous function that is strictly decreasing over $\{h > 0\}$ and satisfies $\int h \leq 1$, where $\int$ stands for the integration with respect to the Lebesgue measure. For any measure P,*

$$h(\mathcal{P}_P) \subseteq \mathcal{E}_P \subseteq \mathcal{P}_P^{-1}. \tag{24}$$

Proof. The right inclusion in (24) still follows from the Markov inequality (2). As for the left inclusion, we have, for any $f \in \mathcal{P}_P$ and any h satisfying the conditions of the proposition,

$$\int h(f) \, dP = \int_0^\infty P(h(f) \geq c) \, dc = \int_0^\infty P(f \leq h^{-1}(c)) \, dc$$
$$\leq \int_0^\infty h^{-1}(c) \, dc = \int h^{-1} = \int h \leq 1,$$

where the last equality follows from Fubini's theorem. □

An example of a function h satisfying Proposition 6 is

$$h(c) := \begin{cases} \frac{\kappa}{2} c^{\kappa-1} & \text{if } c \leq 1 \\ \frac{\kappa}{2} c^{-\kappa-1} & \text{if } c \geq 1, \end{cases} \tag{25}$$

where $\kappa \in (0, 1)$ is a constant.

Let P be the counting measure on $\mathbb{N}$. An example of $f \in \mathcal{P}_P$ is $f := 2^{C+1}$, where C is plain Kolmogorov complexity; this function f is the smallest, to within a constant factor, upper semicomputable element of $\mathcal{P}_P$ (see [23, Theorem 8]). An example of $m \in \mathcal{E}_P$ is the largest, to within a constant factor, lower semicomputable measure on $\mathbb{N}$ (see [23, Section 4.2]). Proposition 6 applied to the function (25) gives

$$\frac{\kappa}{2}(2^{C+1})^{-\kappa-1} \leq^\times m \leq^\times (2^{C+1})^{-1},$$

where $\leq^\times$ stands for inequality to within a constant factor. The last equation can be rewritten as

$$C \leq^+ K \leq^+ (1 + \kappa)C,$$

where K is prefix complexity and $\leq^+$ stands for inequality to within an additive constant. (Better inequalities can be obtained if we use h of a form similar to (3).)

Remark 9. The main reason [17] for using "i-values" instead of "e-values" in the late 1990s and early 2000s (see Remark 1) was the desire to cover the case of measures P that are not necessarily probability measures, such as counting measures, which makes "integral" more appropriate than "expectation".

References

1. Bourbaki, N.: Elements of Mathematics. Integration. Springer, Heidelberg (2004). https://doi.org/10.1007/978-3-642-59312-3, https://doi.org/10.1007/978-3-662-07931-7. In two volumes. The French originals published in 1952–1969
2. Gács, P.: Uniform test of algorithmic randomness over a general space. Theoret. Comput. Sci. **341**, 91–137 (2005)
3. Gammerman, A., Vovk, V.: Data labelling apparatus and method thereof (2003). US Patent Application 0236578 A1. Available on the Internet. Accessed Feb 2020
4. Greenland, S.: Valid P-values behave exactly as they should: some misleading criticisms of P-values and their resolution with S-values. Am. Stat. **73**(S1), 106–114 (2019)
5. Grünwald, P., de Heide, R., Koolen, W.M.: Safe testing. Technical report. arXiv:1906.07801 [math.ST], arXiv.org e-Print archive, June 2019
6. Gurevich, Y., Vovk, V.: Test statistics and p-values. Proc. Mach. Learn. Res. **105**, 89–104 (2019). COPA 2019
7. Kolmogorov, A.N.: Несколько теорем об алгоритмической энтропии и алгоритмическом количестве информации. Успехи математических наук **23**(2), 201 (1968). Abstract of a talk before the Moscow Mathematical Society. Meeting of 31 October 1967
8. Kolmogorov, A.N.: Logical basis for information theory and probability theory. IEEE Trans. Inf. Theor. IT **14**, 662–664 (1968). Russian original: К логическим основам теории информации и теории вероятностей, published in Проблемы передачи информации
9. Kolmogorov, A.N.: Combinatorial foundations of information theory and the calculus of probabilities. Russ. Math. Surv. **38**, 29–40 (1983). Russian original: Комбинаторные основания теории информации и исчисления вероятностей
10. Kolmogorov, A.N.: On logical foundations of probability theory. In: Prokhorov, Y.V., Itô, K. (eds.) Probability Theory and Mathematical Statistics. Lecture Notes in Mathematics, vol. 1021, pp. 1–5. Springer, Heidelberg (1983). https://doi.org/10.1007/BFb0072897. Talk at the Fourth USSR-Japan Symposium on Probability Theory and Mathematical Statistics (Tbilisi, August 1982) recorded by Alexander A. Novikov, Alexander K. Zvonkin, and Alexander Shen. Our quote follows Selected Works of A. N. Kolmogorov, volume II, Probability Theory and Mathematical Statistics, edited by A. N. Shiryayev, Kluwer, Dordrecht, p. 518
11. Kolmogorov, A.N.: Personal communication (1983)
12. Lauritzen, S.L.: Extremal Families and Systems of Sufficient Statistics. Lecture Notes in Statistics, vol. 49. Springer, New York (1988). https://doi.org/10.1007/978-1-4612-1023-8
13. Levin, L.A.: Uniform tests of randomness. Sov. Math. Dokl. **17**, 337–340 (1976). Russian original: Равномерные тесты случайности
14. Levin, L.A.: Various measures of complexity for finite objects (axiomatic description). Soviet Mathematics Doklady **17**, 522–526 (1976). Russian original: О различных мерах сложности конечных объектов: аксиоматическое описание
15. Li, M., Vitányi, P.: An Introduction to Kolmogorov Complexity and Its Applications. Texts in Computer Science. Springer, New York (2008). https://doi.org/10.1007/978-0-387-49820-1
16. Martin-Löf, P.: The definition of random sequences. Inf. Control **9**, 602–619 (1966)
17. Nouretdinov, I.: Personal communication, February 2020

18. Nouretdinov, I., V'yugin, V., Gammerman, A.: Transductive confidence machine is universal. In: Gavaldá, R., Jantke, K.P., Takimoto, E. (eds.) ALT 2003. LNCS (LNAI), vol. 2842, pp. 283–297. Springer, Heidelberg (2003). https://doi.org/10.1007/978-3-540-39624-6_23

19. Schervish, M.J.: Sequential analysis. Theory of Statistics. SSS, pp. 536–569. Springer, New York (1995). https://doi.org/10.1007/978-1-4612-4250-5_9

20. Shafer, G.: The language of betting as a strategy for statistical and scientific communication. Technical report. arXiv:1903.06991 [math.ST], arXiv.org e-Print archive, March 2019

21. Shafer, G.: On the nineteenth-century origins of significance testing and p-hacking. The Game-Theoretic Probability and Finance project. Working Paper 55, September 2019, first posted July 2019. http://probabilityandfinance.com

22. Shafer, G., Vovk, V.: Game-Theoretic Foundations for Probability and Finance. Wiley, Hoboken (2019)

23. Shen, A., Uspensky, V.A., Vereshchagin, N.: Kolmogorov Complexity and Algorithmic Randomness. American Mathematical Society, Providence (2017)

24. Souslin, M.Y.: Sur une définition des ensembles mesurables B sans nombres transfinis. Comptes rendus hebdomadaires des séances de l'Académie des sciences **164**, 88–91 (1917)

25. Vovk, V.: On the concept of the Bernoulli property. Russ. Math. Surv. **41**, 247–248 (1986). Russian original: О понятии бернуллиевости. Another English translation with proofs: [27]

26. Vovk, V.: Learning about the parameter of the Bernoulli model. J. Comput. Syst. Sci. **55**, 96–104 (1997)

27. Vovk, V.: On the concept of Bernoulliness. Technical report. arXiv:1612.08859 [math.ST], arXiv.org e-Print archive, December 2016

28. Vovk, V., Gammerman, A.: Statistical applications of algorithmic randomness. In: Bulletin of the International Statistical Institute. The 52nd Session, Contributed Papers, vol. LVIII, Book 3, pp. 469–470 (1999)

29. Vovk, V., Gammerman, A., Saunders, C.: Machine-learning applications of algorithmic randomness. In: Proceedings of the Sixteenth International Conference on Machine Learning, pp. 444–453. Morgan Kaufmann, San Francisco (1999)

30. Vovk, V., Shafer, G.: Kolmogorov's contributions to the foundations of probability. Probl. Inf. Transm. **39**, 21–31 (2003)

31. Vovk, V., V'yugin, V.V.: On the empirical validity of the Bayesian method. J. Roy. Stat. Soc. B **55**, 253–266 (1993)

32. V'yugin, V.V.: Algorithmic complexity and stochastic properties of finite binary sequences. Comput. J. **42**, 294–317 (1999)

Author Index

Printed in the United States
By Bookmasters